W9-CMC-901

The **Rough Guide** to

The Philippines

written and researched by

David Dalton and Stephen Keeling

with additional contributions from
Simon Foster and John Oates

ROUGH
GUIDES

www.roughguides.com

Contents

Filipino food colour section following p.176

Diving in the Philippines colour section following p.336

◄◄ Waterfall near Dumaguete, Negros ◄ White Beach, Boracay

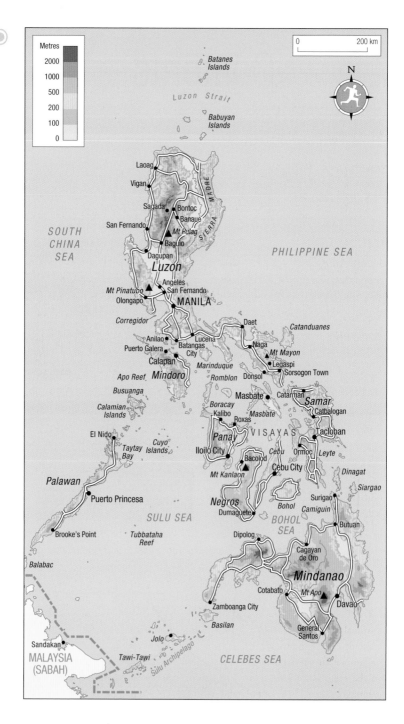

Introduction to

The Philippines

Graced by dazzling beaches, year-round sun and numerous opportunities for diving, island-hopping and surfing, the Philippines has long attracted a steady stream of foreign visitors. Yet there's far more to these islands than sand and snorkelling. Beyond the coastline are mystical tribal villages, ancient rice terraces, jungle-smothered peaks and crumbling Spanish churches. Look closer and you'll see the influence of the island's rich stew of cultures – Islamic, Malay, Spanish and American – in an exuberant array of festivals, tantalizing food and elegant colonial towns that has more in common with Latin America than the rest of Asia.

Indeed, cut off from the main Southeast Asian overland route by the South China Sea, the Philippines is often misunderstood by travellers and its Asian neighbours, casually dismissed as a supplier of maids, tribute bands, mail-order brides and corrupt politicians, epitomized by the gaudy excesses of Imelda Marcos. Don't be put off; while poverty and corruption remain serious problems, the Philippines is far more complex – and culturally rich – than the stereotypes suggest.

The Filipino people, who speak more than 150 languages and dialects, are variously descended from early Malay settlers, Muslim Sufis from the Middle East, Spanish conquistadors and friars, and later Chinese traders. It's an old cliché, but largely true: Filipinos take pride in making visitors welcome, even in the most rustic barrio home. Equally important is the culture of entertaining, evident in the hundreds of colourful fiestas that are held throughout

5

Jeepneys

Millions of Filipinos depend on jeepneys – a kind of informal minibus service – to get to school and the office, or to transport livestock to market. Jeepneys are able to operate where roads are too narrow for regular buses, and as a result most travellers end up using them at least once – despite the discomfort, for many it's one of the highlights of their trip, a genuine slice of Filipino life.

The original jeepneys, cannibalized from vehicles left behind by departing Americans at the end of World War II, have evolved over the past five decades into the mass-produced versions that you see on the streets today, decorated with chrome trinkets, blinking fairy lights and images of celebrities. Others sport religious mottos, crucifixes and images of saints, perhaps understandable given the high accident rates they rack up.

the country, many tied to the Roman Catholic calendar. Never far behind partying is eating and Filipino food is heavily influenced by Spanish and native traditions – expect plenty of fresh fish, roasted meats (pork and chicken) and unlike the rest of Asia, a plethora of addictive desserts, many utilizing the vast array of tropical fruits on offer.

Even the politics in Asia's first democracy is rich in showmanship and pizzazz. From Ferdinand Marcos to the "housewife President" Cory Aquino to current paparazzi favourite Ninoy Aquino, the country's leaders have never been short on charisma. But despite impressive economic gains in the last twenty years, all have conspicuously failed to rid the country of its grinding poverty, visible everywhere you go in shanty towns and rickety barrios. Ordinary people somehow remain stoical in the face of these problems, infectiously optimistic and upbeat. This determination to enjoy life is a national characteristic, encapsulated in the common Tagalog phrase *bahala na* – "what will be will be".

Where to go

Most flights to the Philippines arrive in **Manila**, the crazy, chaotic capital which, despite first impressions, is worth at least a day or two of your time. The city's major historical attraction is the old Spanish walled city of **Intramuros**, while the best museums in the

country can be found in nearby Rizal Park and skyscraper-smothered Makati. There are also some worthwhile day-trips from the city; top of the list is the island of **Corregidor** in Manila Bay, which was fought over bitterly during World War II and, with its now-silent guns and ruins, is a poignant place to soak up the history of the conflict.

Within easy striking distance of Manila – about two hours south by road – the province of **Batangas** features Tagaytay with its mesmerizing views over **Lake Taal**, the picture-perfect crater lake with **Taal Volcano** in the middle. Around the small coastal town of **Anilao** you'll find the best scuba diving near Manila, while the adjacent agricultural province of **Laguna** is known for its therapeutic hot springs and luscious *buko* (coconut) pies.

To the north of Manila the theme parks, beaches and wreck dives of Subic Bay make a tempting break before the long bus ride to the extraordinary attractions and spell-binding mountain scenery of **northern Luzon**. From the mountain city of **Baguio**, it's a rough but memorable trip north along winding roads to tribal communities such as **Sagada**, known for its hanging coffins, and **Banaue**, where you can trek through awe-inspiring rice-terrace countryside. Off Luzon's northern tip are the alluring islands of **Batanes**, one of the country's greatest secrets, while along Luzon's west coast you can surf around San Fernando or explore the ravishing colonial town of **Vigan**, a UNESCO World Heritage site.

Head south from Manila through the **Bicol** region and you'll reach perhaps the best-known of Philippine volcanoes, **Mayon**, an almost perfect cone that towers over the city of Legaspi and is a strenuous four- or five-day climb. Around **Donsol** you can swim with whale sharks, and in **Bulusan Volcano**

Festive spirits

Filipinos love their fiestas, with almost every town, barrio and village celebrating national holidays, saints' days and numerous other dates throughout the year. Here are the five most memorable:

Ati-Atihan (Second week of Jan) Kalibo, Panay. Aklan province. Honours the Santo Niño (Infant Jesus), with exuberant street dancing and wild costumes. See p.315.

Flores de Mayo (Throughout May) Countrywide. Vibrant flower festival held in honour of the Virgin Mary and to celebrate the coming of the rains. See p.37.

Masskara (Third week of Oct) Bacolod, Negros. Modern, Rio-style mardis gras which fills the streets of Bacolod with elaborately dressed masked dancers. See p.37.

Lanzones Festival (Third week of Oct) Lambajao, Camiguin. This celebration of the island's crop of *lanzones* (a tropical fruit) involves street dancing, parades and parties. See p.400.

Sinulog (Third Sun in Jan) Cebu City. Another huge festival honouring the Santo Niño (Infant Jesus), with boisterous street parades and live music. See p.269.

National Park trek through lush rainforest to waterfalls, hot springs and volcanic craters. Even further off the tourist trail, **Catanduanes** offers excellent surfing while **Marinduque** is a pastoral island backwater that only gets touristy for the annual Moriones festival, held at Easter.

For most visitors, the myriad islands and islets of the **Visayas**, right at the heart of the archipelago, are top of the agenda. The captivating little island of **Boracay**, with its pristine beach, is on almost everyone's itinerary. If Boracay's a little too touristy for you, try **Panglao Island** off Bohol, the tantalizing beaches and waters of **Malapascua** off the northern top of Cebu Island or tiny **Apo Island** near Negros, a marine reserve where the only accommodation is in rustic cottages. For trekking and climbing make for **Mount Kanlaon National Park** on Negros, one of the country's finest wilderness areas. The largest city in the Visayas, **Cebu City**, is the arrival point for a limited number of international flights – as well as a major hub for domestic flights – making it a good alternative base to Manila. It's friendly, affordable and has a buzzing nightlife scene, with great restaurants and live music.

If you're looking for some serious diving (see also *Diving in the Philippines* colour section), head for **Puerto Galera** on the northern coast of **Mindoro Island**. It also boasts some excellent beaches, and trekking through the jungled interior to tribal communities. There's more world-class diving off the west coast of Mindoro at **Apo Reef**, although you'll have to join a liveaboard boat to get here.

To the west of the archipelago, out in the northern Sulu Sea, is the bewitching island of **Palawan**, most of it still wild and unspoiled. Many visitors come for the superb scuba diving, especially on the sunken World War II wrecks around **Coron Town** in the **Calamian Islands** to the north of Palawan proper. Palawan itself is home to the seaside town of **El Nido** and the **Bacuit archipelago**, hundreds of gem-like limestone islands with sugar-white beaches and lagoons. From **Puerto Princesa**, Palawan's likeable capital, strike out for the laidback beach town of **Port Barton** or the **Underground River**, a entrancing cavern system only accessible by boat.

In the far south, the large island of **Mindanao** has long been the Muslim heartland of the Philippines, with enticing destinations ranging from the surf beaches and secret lagoons of **Siargao Island**, to the pristine waters of the Enchanted River and tribal homelands of the T'boli people around **Lake Sebu** in the south. Off the island's northern coast, one of the area's major attractions is the wonderfully friendly and scenic island of **Camiguin**. Mindanao's biggest city is durian-capital **Davao**, from where you can head inland to **Mount Apo**, the tallest mountain in the archipelago and a tough ascent even for experienced climbers. Note that much of western Mindanao, including the Sulu archi-pelago, is dangerous to visit because of continuing Muslim separatist unrest.

When to go

The Philippines has a hot and humid tropical climate with a wet season (southwest monsoon, or *habagat*) from May to October and a dry season (northeast monsoon, or *amihan*) from November to April. The best time to visit is during the dry season, although even during the wet season it doesn't

Catholic nation

Catholicism was introduced to the Philippines in 1521 with the arrival of Magellan, and today around 80 percent of the population is Roman Catholic; just 10 percent is Protestant, 5 to 10 percent Muslim and the remainder Buddhist, animist and other religions. Every barangay, town and city has its patron saint, for whom grand fiestas are held annually, and churches, many beautifully weathered colonial relics, are well attended. Daily life, too, is shot through with Catholic imagery, whether it's government announcements in the press urging people to pray the rosary, or television footage of god-fearing presidential candidates appealing to the heavens for guidance.

always rain torrentially and days can be hot and sunny, with short, intense downpours at dusk. January and February are the coolest months and good for travelling, while March, April and May are very hot: expect sunshine all day and temperatures to peak at a broiling 36°C. As well as higher humidity, the wet season also brings typhoons, with flights sometimes cancelled and roads impassable. The first typhoon can hit as early as May, although typically it is June or July before the rains really start, with July and August the wettest months. The southern Visayas and Palawan are less prone to this danger, and Mindanao sees less rain during the wet season and no typhoons.

Average temperatures and rainfall

	Jan	Feb	Mar	Apr	May	Jun	Jul	Aug	Sep	Oct	Nov	Dec
Manila												
°C	25	27	28.5	31.5	31	29	28.5	27.6	28	28.5	28	26.9
°F	77	80.6	83.3	88.7	87.8	84.2	83.2	81.7	82.4	83.3	82.4	80.4
Rainfall (mm)	0.74	0.46	0.58	1.1	4.2	8.5	13.9	13.6	11.8	6.2	4.8	2.1
Baguio												
°C	17	19	20.5	23.5	23	21	20.5	19.5	20	20.5	20	18.5
°F	62.6	66.2	68.9	74.3	73.4	69.8	68.9	67.1	68	68.9	68	65.3
Rainfall (mm)	0.74	1.2	1.1	1.4	4.8	10.2	14.8	14.2	12.6	8.4	6.6	3.2
Siargao												
°C	25.5	26	26	27	27	27	27	27	27	27	26	26.5
°F	77.9	78.8	78.8	80.6	80.6	80.6	80.6	80.6	80.6	80.6	78.8	79.7
Rainfall (mm)	17.5	13.4	16.3	8.4	5	4.2	5.7	4.1	5.6	8.8	14.2	20

18 things not to miss

It's not possible to see everything the Philippines has to offer in one trip – and we don't suggest you try. What follows is a selective taste of the country's highlights: idyllic beaches, spectacular hikes, historic churches and fascinating wildlife. They're arranged in five colour-coded categories, in no particular order, which you can browse through to find the very best things to see and experience. All entries have a page reference to take you straight into the Guide, where you can find out more.

01 Boracay Beach Page **324** • Enchanting White Beach on picture-postcard Boracay Island is one of the country's major tourist draws.

02 **Ati-Atihan Festival** Page **322** • At this lively festival in Kalibo, on Panay Island, held annually in honour of the Santo Niño (Infant Jesus), everyone wears indigenous dress and learns tribal dances.

04 **Rice terraces** Page **182** • The mind-boggling rice terraces around Banaue stand as one of Asia's greatest sights, and offer superb trekking.

03 **El Nido** Page **371** • The strikingly beautiful limestone islands around El Nido in Palawan offer exceptional exploring and adventure.

06 **Vigan** Page **144** • Wonderfully preserved slice of colonial Spain, with cobblestone streets, gorgeous Baroque architecture and horse-drawn carriages.

05 **Halo-halo** See *Filipino food* **colour section** • Nothing beats a tall glass of this icy Filipino treat on a hot day, a concoction of syrups, beans, fruits and ice cream.

07 **Swimming with whale sharks** Page **221** • Swimming alongside a giant but gentle whale shark off the coast of Sorsogon, in southern Luzon, is an unforgettable experience.

08 **Coron Island by bangka** Page **382** • Tour the jagged, gasp-inducing coast of Coron Island by bangka, taking in hidden coves, secret beaches and two pristine mountain lakes fed by springs.

09 **Chocolate Hills** Page **289** • Soak up the bizarre landscape of Bohol's iconic Chocolate Hills, conical brown-green mounds said to be the calcified tears of a broken-hearted giant.

10 **San Agustin Church** Page **94** • This elegantly weathered Spanish pile in the heart of old Manila is the oldest stone church in the archipelago and the resting place of Miguel Lopez de Legazpi.

11 **Surfing at Siargau** Page **407** • Avid surfers will find several locations where they can catch some decent waves, but Siargau, off the tip of Mindanao is one of the best.

12 **Apo Reef Marine Natural Park** Page **254** • The gin-clear waters Apo Reef, off the west coast of Mindoro, are a scuba diver's dream.

14 **Underground River** Page **367** • Accessible only by boat, one of the longest subterranean rivers in the world has eerie stalactites, vast caverns and hidden chambers.

13 **Puerto Galera** Page **237** • Only a few hours from the bustle of Manila, scenic Puerto Galera is a great place to relax, be pampered, as well as learn to dive.

15 **Mount Mayon** Page **215** • The almost perfectly symmetrical cone of volcanic Mount Mayon, near Legaspi, makes for a challenging but thrilling climb.

17 Mount Pinatubo Page **124** • The lower slopes of Mount Pinatubo feature canyons formed after the massive 1991 eruption, while the crater is filled by a pristine mountain lake.

16 Tarsiers Page **288** • Admire these tiny primates with the enormous, sorrowful eyes at their protected sanctuary in Bohol.

18 Corregidor Page **109** • During World War II this tiny island in Manila Bay was the scene of bitter fighting between the Allies and the Japanese.

Basics

Basics

Getting there

There are some nonstop flights to the Philippines from the west coast of North America and from Australia; from Europe, the only nonstop flights are from Amsterdam. Otherwise, reaching the Philippines from outside Asia usually involves a stopover in Hong Kong, Singapore or Dubai; most major airlines in the region have regular flights to Manila, with a few also flying to Cebu.

High season for Philippines travel is November to April, though **airfares** vary relatively little with the season. This is because the low season for the Philippines (May–Oct) is the peak season in Europe and the US, so flights heading out of these regions to various hub airports are often full.

If the Philippines is only one stop on a longer journey, you might want to consider buying a **Round-the-World (RTW)** ticket. In addition, some agents also offer **Circle Pacific** tickets, which cover Australia, New Zealand, the west coast of North America and destinations in the Pacific. You can include Manila and/or Cebu on some of the itineraries.

From the UK and Ireland

While there are no nonstop flights to Manila from the UK or the Republic of Ireland, there are routes involving only one stop on the way – in **East Asia**, in **Europe** or at a **Middle Eastern hub** such as Dubai or Doha. **From London**, the quickest journey is to fly to Hong Kong, from where there are numerous onward flights daily to Manila (total flying time is around 15hr, including the stopover), and Cebu. From Ireland, the cheapest option is to take a budget airline to London and change there.

As for **fares**, flying in August, low season in the Philippines, London–Manila costs around £500 return, rising to around £650–700 in January. From the Republic of Ireland, the best fares are around €900 via the UK and the Middle East.

From the US and Canada

Philippine Airlines operates **nonstop** flights to Manila from Los Angeles, San Francisco, Las Vegas and Vancouver, charging around US$1500 or Can$1500 for the round trip in high season. However, you can save around twenty percent on this fare if you travel on another airline such as Delta via, say, South Korea, Taiwan or Japan.

From Los Angeles or San Francisco, the **flying time** to Manila is around eleven hours. From the east coast of North America, flying via the Pacific, the journey will take around twenty hours excluding any layover (allow at least 2hr extra) along the way. If you choose to fly from New York via Paris, say, expect the journey to take around 24 hours altogether.

From Australia, New Zealand and South Africa

Philippine Airlines flies nonstop to Manila from Brisbane twice a week, Melbourne five times a week and Sydney five times a week; fares online can be as low as Aus$1000. Qantas flies Sydney to Manila nonstop just three times a week, and from Brisbane just once a week, but fares are always much higher (from Aus$1800 in high season). If you want to get to Cebu City, you can fly via Hong Kong or Kuala Lumpur, although it's probably easiest simply to change in Manila.

From **New Zealand** there are no nonstop flights to the Philippines, so you'll have to go via Australia or a Southeast Asian hub such as Singapore or Hong Kong. A typical fare is NZ$3000 Auckland–Manila via Kuala Lumpur, the journey taking 25 to 30 hours.

From **South Africa** you'll always make at least one stop en route to Manila, and often two. Depending on the length of the stop, the trip will take from 16 to 26 hours. Qatar Airways has flights from around ZAR7000 return in high season from Johannesburg that stop in Doha. South African Airways and Cathay Pacific both have daily nonstop flights to Hong Kong from Johannesburg where you can connect with Cathay Pacific on to Manila; return fares are much higher in high season, costing around ZAR20,000.

From Asia

You can fly direct to the Philippines from almost every major city in Asia, with several budget airlines offering cheap fares. Numerous flights make the two-hour trip from **Hong Kong** to Manila via Cathay Pacific, Philippine Airlines, Dragonair, Hong Kong Express Airways and Cebu Pacific, with the latter offering rates as low as HK$390 (US$50).

The **Singapore**–Manila route (3hr 30min) is very competitive, served by Philippine Airlines, Singapore Airlines, Airphil Express, Jetstar Asia Airways, Tiger Airways and Cebu Pacific from S$90 (US$70). Cebu Pacific also offers cheap flights from Bangkok, Jakarta, Kota Kinabalu, Kuala Lumpur, Shanghai, Seoul and Taipei to Manila, and several routes direct to Cebu City.

Handy regional flights include the Silk Air service linking Singapore with Davao (Mindanao), and the Mandarin Airlines flight between Kaohsiung (Taiwan) and Laoag (northern Luzon).

By boat

Many unlicensed **boats** ply back and forth between the Malaysian state of Sabah and the southern Philippines, but these are considered unsafe for tourists. The primary licensed (and safer) ferry route links **Zamboanga City** from Sandakan, Sabah. The M/V *Danica Joy* (Mon & Thurs 1pm; P3000; 20hr) belonging to Aleson Shipping (☎062/991-2687) serves this route, offering cheap bunk-bed accommodation on deck, as well as a limited number of cabins. SRN Fast Seacraft (☎062/992-3756) has small, but modern ferries that operate twice a week from Sandakan to Zamboanga (from P3000; 13hr), with stops in Jolo and Bongao, Tawi-Tawi.

Six steps to a better kind of travel

At Rough Guides we are passionately committed to travel. We feel strongly that only through travelling do we truly come to understand the world we live in and the people we share it with – plus tourism has brought a great deal of **benefit** to developing economies around the world over the last few decades. But the extraordinary growth in tourism has also damaged some places irreparably, and of course **climate change** is exacerbated by most forms of transport, especially flying. This means that now more than ever it's important to **travel thoughtfully** and **responsibly**, with respect for the cultures you're visiting – not only to derive the most benefit from your trip but also to preserve the best bits of the planet for everyone to enjoy. At Rough Guides we feel there are six main areas in which you can make a difference:

• Consider what you're contributing to the **local economy**, and how much the services you use do the same, whether it's through employing local workers and guides or sourcing locally grown produce and local services.

• Consider the **environment** on holiday as well as at home. Water is scarce in many developing destinations, and the biodiversity of local flora and fauna can be adversely affected by tourism. Try to patronize businesses that take account of this.

• Travel with a purpose, not just to tick off experiences. Consider **spending longer** in a place, and getting to know it and its people.

• Give thought to how often you **fly**. Try to avoid short hops by air and more harmful night flights.

• Consider **alternatives to flying**, travelling instead by bus, train, boat and even by bike or on foot where possible.

• Make your trips **"climate neutral"** via a reputable carbon offset scheme. All Rough Guide flights are offset, and every year we donate money to a variety of charities devoted to combating the effects of climate change.

There are no regular ferry services to northern Sulawesi, Indonesia, from the Philippines. Illegal, small boats often make the trip from General Santos; it's far safer and faster to fly via Manila and Kuala Lumpur.

Airlines, agents and operators

Many discount travel websites offer you the opportunity to book flight tickets and holiday packages online, cutting out the costs of agents and middlemen; these are worth going for, as long as you don't mind the inflexibility of non-refundable, non-changeable deals. There are some bargains to be had on auction sites too, if you're prepared to bid keenly. Almost all airlines have their own websites, offering flight tickets that can sometimes be just as cheap, and are often more flexible.

The Philippines is not a major destination for **package tours**, most tour operators to the region preferring to stick to the Southeast Asian mainland. Those that do offer Philippines tours tend to focus on Manila, Cebu, Boracay and Banaue, which means you don't have much flexibility in choosing where to go. You'll need to weigh the convenience of having accommodation, transport and excursions arranged for you against the fact that you'll pay significantly more than if you travel independently.

Airlines

Airphil Express Philippines ☎02/855-9000, ⓦwww.airphilexpress.com.
Asiana Airlines US ☎1-800/227-4262, ⓦwww.flyasiana.com.
Cathay Pacific UK ☎020/8834 8888, Australia ☎13 17 47, New Zealand ☎09/379 0861, South Africa ☎2711/700 8900; ⓦwww.cathaypacific.com.
Cebu Pacific Philippines ☎02/702-0888, ⓦwww.cebupacificair.com.
China Airlines US ☎917/368-2003, ⓦwww.china-airlines.com.
Continental Airlines US & Canada ☎1-800/523-3273, ⓦwww.continental.com.
Delta US ☎404/773-0305, ⓦwww.delta.com.
Dragonair HK ☎852/3193-3888, ⓦwww.dragonair.com.
Emirates UK ☎0870/243 2222, South Africa ☎12711/303 1951; ⓦwww.emirates.com.

Etihad Airways UK ☎0870/241 7121, ⓦwww.etihadairways.com.
EVA Airways US & Canada ☎1-800/695-1188, ⓦwww.evaair.com.
Gulf Air UK ☎0870/777 1717, Ireland ☎0818/272 818; ⓦwww.gulfairco.com.
Hong Kong Express Airways HK ☎852/3151-1888, ⓦwww.hkairlines.com.
JAL Japan Airlines US & Canada ☎1-800/525-3663, ⓦwww.jal.com.
Jetstar Australia ☎03/9092 6500, Singapore ☎800/616-1977; ⓦwww.jetstar.com.
KLM UK ☎0870/507 4074, ⓦwww.klm.com.
Korean Air US & Canada ☎1-800/438-5000, ⓦwww.koreanair.com.
Malaysia Airlines UK ☎0870/607 9090, Republic of Ireland ☎01/676 2131, US & Canada ☎1-800/552-9264, Australia ☎13 26 37, New Zealand ☎0800/777 747, South Africa ☎2711/880 9614; ⓦwww.malaysiaairlines.com.
Mandarin Airlines Taiwan ☎02/2717-1230, ⓦwww.mandarin-airlines.com.
Philippine Airlines (PAL) Philippines ☎632 855-888, UK ☎01293/596 680, US ☎1-800/4359-725, Australia ☎1-300/888-PAL, New Zealand ☎09/308-5206; ⓦwww.philippineairlines.com.
Qantas Australia ☎13 13 13, New Zealand ☎0800/808 767 or 09/357 8900; ⓦwww.qantas.com.
Qatar Airways UK ☎020/7896 3636, ⓦwww.qatarairways.com.
Royal Brunei UK ☎020/7584 6660, Australia ☎07/3017 5000, New Zealand ☎09/977 2240; ⓦwww.bruneiair.com.
Silk Air Singapore ☎65/6223-8888, ⓦwww.silkair.com.
Singapore Airlines UK ☎0844/800 2380, Republic of Ireland ☎01/671 0722, US ☎1-800/742-3333, Canada ☎1-800/ 663-3046, Australia ☎13 10 11, New Zealand ☎0800/808-909, South Africa ☎2721/674 0601; ⓦwww.singaporeair.com.
South African Airways South Africa ☎0861/359722, International ☎2711/978 5313; ⓦwww.flysaa.com.
Thai Airways UK ☎0870/606 0911, US ☎212/949-8424, Canada ☎416/971-5181, Australia ☎1300 651 960, New Zealand ☎09/377 3886; ⓦwww.thaiair.com.
Tiger Airways Singapore ☎65/6808-4437, ⓦwww.tigerairways.com.

Agents and operators

Absolute Asia US ☎1-800/736-8187, ⓦwww.absoluteasia.com. Luxury tours to the Philippines that can be combined with other destinations in Southeast Asia. The fourteen-day Highlights of the Philippines tour includes Manila, Banaue, Sagada, Baguio, Bohol and Cebu City, for US$4630, excluding international flights.

Allways Dive Expeditions Australia ☏1800/338 239 or 03/9885 8863, ⓦwww.allwaysdive.com .au. All-inclusive dive packages to prime locations in Southeast Asia and elsewhere from Aus$2240 for six nights (including flights). Destinations in the Philippines include Coron and El Nido in Palawan, and Sangat Island Resort and Puerto Galera in Mindoro.

Dive Worldwide UK ☏0845/130 6980, ⓦwww .diveworldwide.com. Specialist dive operator offering trips to a number of destinations in the Philippines, including Palawan, Bohol, Dumaguete and Puerto Galera. A typical 11-day trip to Donsol to see the whale sharks including flights, domestic transfers and accommodation starts at £1699.

Grasshopper Adventures UK ☏020/8123 8144, US ☏818/921-7101; ⓦwww.grasshopper adventures.com. Bicycle and guided tour specialists, with a variety of bike tours all over Asia and a 13-day guided tour of the Philippines (Manila to Bohol via Baguio and Banaue), for US$2950.

North South Travel UK ☏01245/608291, ⓦwww .northsouthtravel.co.uk. Friendly, competitive travel agency, offering discounted fares worldwide. Profits are used to support projects in the developing world, especially the promotion of sustainable tourism.

Philippine Island Connections UK ☏020/7404 8877, ⓦwww.pic-uk.com. Philippines specialist offering flights to the Philippines, plus hotel bookings, holiday packages and tours. They also offer domestic flight reservations, though it's often cheaper to book once you're in the Philippines.

STA Travel UK ☏0871/2300 040, US ☏1-800/781-4040, Australia ☏13 47 82, New Zealand ☏0800/474 400, South Africa ☏0861/781 781; ⓦwww.statravel.co.uk. Worldwide specialists in independent travel; also student IDs, travel insurance, car rental, rail passes, and more. Good discounts for students and under-26s.

Swagman Travel Australia ☏0401/337401, Philippines ☏02/523-8541; ⓦwww.swaggy .com. Australian company with offices throughout the Philippines, offering everything from flights, cheap accommodation, diving, sailing, golf tours and domestic transport.

Trailfinders UK ☏0845/058 5858, Ireland ☏01/677 7888, Australia ☏1300/780 212; ⓦwww.trailfinders.com. One of the best-informed and most efficient agents for independent travellers.

Travel CUTS Canada ☏1-866/246-9762, US ☏1-800/592-2887; ⓦwww.travelcuts.com. Canadian youth and student travel firm.

USIT Ireland ☏01/602 1906, Northern Ireland ☏028/9032 7111; ⓦwww.usit.ie. Ireland's main student and youth travel specialists.

Getting around

The large number of budget flights and ferry services between major destinations makes it easy to cover the Philippine archipelago, even on a tight budget, though the main drawback is that everything routes through Manila and Cebu. Long-distance road transport largely comprises buses and jeepneys – the utilitarian passenger vehicles modelled on American World War II jeeps. Throughout the provinces, and in some areas of cities, tricycles – motorbikes with steel sidecars – are commonly used for short journeys.

Airlines and major bus and ferry companies operate to timetables and have published **fares**, but for smaller ferries, jeepneys and tricycles, it's often a question of asking other passengers how much to pay in order to avoid being surcharged as a tourist.

Note that **holiday weekends** are bad times to travel, with buses full and roads

jammed – cities start to empty on Friday afternoon and the exodus continues into the night, with a mass return on Sunday evening and Monday morning. Travelling is a particular hassle at Christmas, New Year and Easter with buses and ferries full (sometimes illegally overloaded), airports chaotic and resorts charging more than usual. Almost everyone seems to be on the move at these times of year, particularly heading out of big cities to the provinces, and the transport system can become strained. If you have to travel at these times, book tickets in advance or turn up at bus stations and ferry piers early and be prepared to wait.

By air

Air travel is a godsend for island-hoppers in the Philippines, with a number of airlines linking Manila with most of the country's major destinations; you will usually, however, have to backtrack to a major hub when jumping from one region to another. **Philippine Airlines** (PAL; ⓦwww.philippineairlines.com) has a comprehensive domestic schedule, while two of the newer airlines, **Airphil Express** (ⓦwww.airphils.com) and **Cebu Pacific** (ⓦwww.cebupacificair.com), offer even more routes and very cheap fares, particularly if you book some way in advance. There are two good smaller airlines – **Zest Air** (ⓦwww.zestair.com.ph) and **Seair** (ⓦwww.flyseair.com) – serving a number of popular routes. Zest Air's network includes Cebu City, Masbate, Virac, Busuanga and Tacloban. Seair flies from Manila to, among other places, Clark, Caticlan (for Boracay), Batanes and Tablas. Cebu Pacific runs numerous flights out of its hub in Cebu City, saving you the effort of backtracking to Manila – you can, for instance, fly straight from Cebu City to Caticlan (for Boracay) and Siargao. Davao is a lesser developed third hub, with connections to Cebu City, Cagayan de Oro, Iloilo and Zamboanga, but even here you'll have to transfer in Manila and Cebu for other destinations.

Airfares

There's not a great deal of variation in domestic **airfares** offered by the four budget carriers, and PAL is usually the most expensive, being the only one offering traditional cabin service (snacks, drinks etc). Cebu Pacific has been known to sell seats for P1, and regularly offers fares of P499 one-way Manila to Coron (Busuanga) and P999 Manila to Zamboanga. But note that the low prices you see quoted on budget airline websites usually don't include taxes

and unlike most PAL flights, you can't change bookings once you've paid; there are also charges for bags and seat reservations (P100).

By ferry

Ferries and **bangkas** – wooden outrigger boats – were once the bread and butter of Philippine travel. Though still important, especially in the Visayas (where there's hardly a coastal barrio that doesn't have some sort of ferry service), most of the longer routes have been made redundant by the growth of budget air travel. Not only are flights faster and as cheap (or cheaper) than cabins on longer ferry routes (Manila to Mindanao for example), they are invariably **safer**. Indeed, despite some improvements in recent years, **ferry accidents** remain common in the Philippines and even in the dry season the open ocean can get surprisingly rough. The smaller bangkas are often poorly equipped, with little shelter from the elements, while even many of the larger vessels have been bought secondhand from Japan or Europe and are well past their prime. Ferries of all sizes are frequently crowded.

Having said that, for many shorter inter-island trips ferries remain the only form of transport available, and especially in the Visayas, island-hopping by boat can be an enjoyable and rewarding part of your trip.

Ferry companies

There's a hierarchy of vessels, with proper ferries at the top; so-called **big bangkas**, taking around fifty passengers, in the middle; and ordinary bangkas at the bottom. A number of large ferry lines operate large ships between major ports in the Philippines. They are: **SuperFerry** (ⓦwww.superferry.com.ph), **Negros Navigation** (ⓦwww.negrosnavigation.ph), **Cebu Ferries** (ⓦwww.cebuferries.com), **Supercat** (part of Super-Ferry; ⓦwww.supercat.com.ph), **Montenegro Lines** (ⓦwww.montenegrolines.com.ph), **Cokaliong** (ⓦwww.cokaliongshipping.com) and **TransAsia** (ⓦwww.transasiashipping.com). These companies have regular sailings on routes between Manila and major cities throughout the Visayas and Mindanao, or on secondary routes within the Visayas. Most post schedules and fares on their websites. On less popular routes you might have to take your chances with smaller companies, which rarely operate to published timetables. In rural areas you may have to ask around at the harbour or wharf as to what boats are leaving, for where and when.

Ferry fares and accommodation

Ferry **fares** are very low by Western standards, especially if booked in advance, for example Manila–Cebu from P750, Manila–Mindanao for P1150; add on around P1000 for a private cabin. **Tickets** can be bought at the pier up until departure, though it's often more convenient to avoid the long queues and buy in advance: travel agents sell ferry tickets, and the larger ferry companies have ticket offices in cities and towns. SuperFerry also offers online ticketing.

The cheapest **accommodation** is in bunk beds in cavernous dorms either below deck or on a semi-open deck, with shared toilets and showers. Older ships might have just a handful of cramped cabins sharing a tiny shower and toilet. The major operators generally have newer ships with a range of accommodation that includes dorms, straw mats in an air-conditioned area, shared cabins (usually for four) with bathroom. These ferries usually also have a bar, karaoke lounge and a canteen serving basic meals.

By bus

Bus travel can be relatively uncomfortable and slow, but you'll get a real glimpse of rural Philippine life from the window, and meet Filipinos from all walks of life. Buses are also incredibly convenient: hundreds of routes spread out like a web from major cities and even the most isolated barrio will have a service of some sort. You won't go hungry either. At most stops local vendors will jump on and offer you various snacks and drinks, while on the longer hauls, buses stop every three or four hours to give passengers a chance to stretch their legs and buy some food.

There are some downsides. Though the largest bus companies have fleets of reasonably new air-conditioned buses for longer routes, most rarely have toilets. On shorter

routes buses can be dilapidated contraptions with no air conditioning and, in some cases, no glass in the windows. You'll also need to have a high tolerance to loud music or Tagalog movies played at full blast throughout the trip.

Bus fares and timetables

Fares are low; around P435 from Manila to Baguio and P500 to Naga. Roads can be poor, and even when the distances involved aren't great, the buses will make numerous stops along the way. Some bus companies advertise **express** services, but in reality a bus that goes from A to B without stopping is unheard of. Buses that have a "derecho" sign (meaning "straight" or "direct") in the window usually make the fewest stops.

Published **timetables** for most bus companies are nonexistent, but departures on popular routes such as Manila to Baguio or Manila to Vigan usually happen every hour or half-hour. The **larger operators** – Victory Liner (ⓦwww.victoryliner.com), Philtranco (ⓦwww.philtranco.com) and Philippine Rabbit – allow you to **book seats** in advance, either by telephone (be warned, the lines are often engaged) or at the terminal. For a list of bus companies with offices in Manila, see box on p.66.

By jeepney, FX taxi and tricycle

The **jeepney** is the ultimate Philippine icon (see Introduction, p.6), and in Manila, Cebu City, Davao and Baguio, jeepneys are important for **city transport**, with frequent services between important locations in each city. In the provinces jeepneys connect isolated barrios to nearby towns and towns to cities, but they might run only two or three times a day, depending on demand, the weather and the mood of the driver. There are absolutely no timetables.

Routes are painted on the side or on a signboard in the window. Even so, using jeepneys takes a little local knowledge because they make numerous stops and deviations to drop off and pick up passengers. There's no such thing as a designated jeepney stop, so people wait in the shade at the side of the road and flag one down. The vehicles are **cramped** and incredibly uncomfortable, usually holding about twenty passengers inside and any number of extras clinging to the back or sitting precariously on top. It can be a hassle to get **luggage** on and off – small items might end up on the floor, but larger items will go on the roof. At least jeepneys are a great social equalizer; you'll soon find yourself involved in jolly conversations with the rest of the passengers about your nationality, destination and marital status.

Fares are low: in the provinces they start at P7 for a trip of a few kilometres, rising to P50 for two- or three-hour drives. In the cities, a trip of a few hundred metres costs around P7, rising to P25 on longer routes. To pay, hand your money to the passenger next to you and say *bayad po* (pay please). If you're not sitting close to the driver, the fare will be passed down the line of passengers until it reaches him; he will then pass back any change.

FX taxis

Not unlike jeepneys in the way they operate, **FX taxis** are air-conditioned Toyota minivans, with signs in the window indicating their destination. They made their debut in Manila in the late 1990s, and now operate in other cities and on some popular inter-city routes. However, routes are often not set, so it takes a little local knowledge to know where to catch the right vehicle. The vans can be a little claustrophobic – the driver won't even think about moving until he's got ten people on board, three more than the vehicle is designed for. In Manila most of these vehicles are often labelled "GT Express" and usually charge P2 per kilometre.

Tricycles

The cheapest form of shared transport, **tricycles** (*habel-habel*) are ubiquitous in the provinces. In Manila and Cebu City they are prohibited from using certain roads, but almost everywhere else they go where they like, when they like and at speeds as high as their small engines are capable of. The sidecars are designed for four passengers – two facing forwards and two backwards – but it's not uncommon to see extras clinging on wherever they can, the only limiting factor being whether or not the machine can actually move under the weight of the extra bodies. Tricycles never follow fixed routes, so it's usually a question of flagging one down and telling the driver your destination.

Fares typically start at P7 per person for a short trip of a few hundred metres. Many tricycles charge a set rate per person for trips within town or city boundaries, usually around P7–25. If you want to use the tricycle as a private taxi you'll have to negotiate a price – P25 is reasonable for a trip of up to 2km in the provinces. Anything further than that and the driver will ask for at least P50, though you can always try to bargain him down.

Addresses in the Philippines

For buildings, it is common to give the **address** as, for example, 122 Legaspi corner Velasco Streets, meaning the junction of Legaspi Street and Velasco Street. G/F denotes street level, after which comes 2/F, 3/F and so on; "first floor" or 1/F isn't used. Some addresses include the name of a **barangay**, which is officially an electoral division for local elections, but is generally used to mean a village or, when mentioned in connection with a town, a neighbourhood or suburb. The word barangay isn't always written out in the address, although it's sometimes included in official correspondence and signposts, often abbreviated to "Brgy" or "Bgy". The term "National Highway" in an address doesn't necessarily refer to a vast motorway – on the smaller islands or in provincial areas, it could mean the coastal road or the main street in town. When it comes to discussing islands, Filipinos generally talk loosely in terms of the main island in the vicinity – so, for example, they would talk about visiting Panay when they actually mean offshore Pan de Azucar. We've adopted a similar approach in parts of the Guide, implicitly including small islands in coverage of the nearest large island.

By car

It's possible to **rent a self-drive car** in the Philippines – a standard saloon car costs about P2000 per day. The question is whether you'd want to. Not only is traffic in Manila and other cities often gridlocked, but most Filipino drivers have a very relaxed attitude towards the rules of the road. Swerving is common, as is changing lanes suddenly and driving with one hand permanently on the horn, particularly with bus and jeepney drivers. On the other hand, if you're used to driving in London, LA or New York this might not phase you too much, and in any case, once you reach more rural areas – northern Luzon for example – travelling by car can be incredibly convenient and open up a whole range of otherwise hard-to-reach destinations. Many travellers also rent motorbikes, but this is only recommended for experienced riders – the chances of having an accident are statistically fairly high. It's best to avoid driving at night altogether.

If you do drive you'll require your **driving licence** and be prepared to show it if you get stopped (rentals are allowed for up to 90 days – longer stays will require a Philippine licence). Vehicles in the Philippines drive on the right side of the road and distances and car speeds are in kilometres (one mile equals about 1.6 km). The freeways usually have a nominal **speed limit** of 100kph, but anywhere else you'll rarely be going faster than 30kph thanks to congestion.

Always **drive defensively** – cars, animals and pedestrians will pull out in front of you without warning (in many rural areas people are still not used to traffic), and always give way to jeepneys, which will happily drive you off the road. When passing anything, sound your horn twice as a warning (horns are rarely used in anger).

Note that police and "traffic enforcers" – uniformed men and women employed by local authorities to supplement the police – might try to elicit a bribe from you. If this happens it's best to play the dumb foreigner

and hand over the "on-the-spot fine" of a few hundred pesos (make sure you have cash with you). If you take the moral high ground and refuse to play along, you'll probably end up having your licence confiscated or, in the worst case, your car towed away and impounded until you pay a fine to get it back.

Car and motorcycle rental agencies

AAA Budget Motorcycle And Car Rental Ⓦ www.aaabudget.com.ph.
Avalon Transport Services Ⓦ www.avalonrentacar.com.
Avis Ⓦ www.avis.com.ph.
Budget Ⓦ www.budget.com.ph.
Enterprise Ⓦ www.enterprise.com.
Europcar Ⓦ www.europcar.com.ph.
Hertz Ⓦ www.hertz.com.
JB Rent A Car Ⓦ www.jbrentacar.com.
National Ⓦ www.nationalcar.com.
Nissan Rent-A-Car Ⓦ www.nissanrentacar.com.
Pitstop Bike Adventure Ⓦ www.pitstopbikeadventure.com
Rent A Car Manila Ⓦ www.rentacarmanila.com.
Viajero Rent A Car Ⓦ www.viajerorentacar.com.
VIP Rent-A-Car Ⓦ www.viprentacar.com.ph.

Hiring a driver

For about P1600 (plus fuel, driver's food, parking/toll fees) you can hire a small **car and driver** from some car rental agencies for up to eight hours, the extra expense more than justified by the peace of mind a local driver brings.

It can be much cheaper to strike a private deal with a car or van owner looking for extra work. A typical rate for their services is P1500 a day (plus fuel and tolls), although you'll need to negotiate. A good way to find someone with a vehicle is to ask at your accommodation; alternatively, locals with cars wait at many airports and ferry ports in the hope of making a bit of money driving arriving passengers into town. You can ask these drivers if they're available to be hired by the day.

Accommodation

The Philippines has accommodation to suit everyone, from international five-star hotels and swanky beach resorts to simple rooms – sometimes no more than a bamboo hut on a beach – and budget hotels that vary wildly in price and comfort.

It's generally not necessary to book in advance unless you are visiting at peak times – Easter, Christmas, New Year, or during a major local festival (see pp.36–37). As always you'll find the cheapest rates online, but if you do want to book by phone, note that some hotels in out-of-the-way areas won't have a landline telephone on site, in which case they may have a mobile number and/or a booking office in a city (often Manila); details are given in the text as appropriate.

Hotels and beach resorts

The terms **hotel** and **beach resort** cover a multitude of options in the Philippines. A **hotel** can mean anything from the most luxurious five-star establishment to dingy budget pensions or guesthouses with bars on the windows. **Beach resorts** in turn range from sybaritic affairs on private atolls,

with butlers and health spas, to dirt-cheap, rickety one-room cottages on a deserted island. "Resort hotels" are a mid-range or top-range hybrid of the two, sometimes with their own area of private beach.

Many hotels and beach resorts accept **credit cards**, although there are exceptions, such as in rural areas where electricity supply is not dependable and also in the cheapest budget accommodation, where you must pay cash.

It can be worth checking that the air conditioner, where available, isn't noisy. Rooms on lower floors overlooking main roads are best avoided as they can be hellishly noisy; always go for something high up or at the back (or both).

Budget

Budget hotels offer little more than a bed, four walls and a fan or small air-conditioning unit, although if you're by the beach, with a

Accommodation price codes

All accommodation in the guide has been categorized according to the following **price codes**, which represent the cost of the cheapest double or twin room – or beach hut sleeping two – in **peak season**, namely November to April. Prices during the May–October rainy season are usually about twenty percent lower. Conversely, during Christmas, New Year and Easter, rates in the popular beach resorts such as Boracay can spike by around 20 percent. In some cases hotels will include breakfast in the price but it's worth asking about this when you book. You'll also find that as a "walk-in" guest you'll usually be able to get a cheaper rate than the rack rate listed on hotel websites, especially in the off-season or in less touristy areas.

Government tax of 12 percent and a service charge of 10 percent is sometimes included in the published rates, but not always. If you see a room advertised at P1000++ ("plus plus") it means you'll pay P1000 plus VAT plus service charge – a total of P1220. These additional charges have been factored into all our rates. Where dormitory accommodation is available, we've given the price of a dorm bed in pesos.

❶ P499 and under	❹ P1500–1999	❼ P3000–4999
❷ P500–999	❺ P2000–2499	❽ P5000–6999
❸ P1000–1499	❻ P2500–2999	❾ P7000 and over

pleasant sea breeze blowing and the windows open, air conditioning isn't really necessary. If you do get a private bathroom it will only have cold water, and the "shower" is sometimes little more than a tap sticking out of the wall producing a mere trickle of water. Breakfast is unlikely to be included in the rate, though there may be a canteen or coffee shop on the premises where you can buy food. At the higher end of the budget range, rooms are usually simple but can be reasonably spacious, perhaps – if they are on or near a beach – with a small balcony.

Mid-range

There are plenty of **mid-range hotels**, mostly in towns and cities. The rooms typically have air conditioning and a private bathroom with hot water, but they may not boast a TV or other frills. Beach cottages in this bracket are usually quite spacious and will often have a decent-sized veranda too. Most mid-range accommodation will feature a small coffee shop or restaurant with a choice of Filipino and Western **breakfasts** that may be included in the rate; If it's not expect to pay around P100–150.

Top-end

In Manila and Cebu as well as the most popular beach destinations such as Boracay you can splash out on **five-star** comfort at hotels and beach resorts owned and operated by international chains. The cottages at the most expensive resorts are more like chic apartments, often with a separate living area. Many of these establishments include a buffet breakfast in the rate, and sports facilities and outdoor activities are on offer, though you'll have to pay extra to partake.

Campsites, hostels and homestays

Campsites are almost unknown in the Philippines. A small number of resorts allow you to pitch tents in their grounds for a negligible charge, but otherwise the only camping you're likely to do is if you go trekking or climbing and need to camp overnight in the wilderness – in which case note that rental outlets for equipment are few and far between, so you might need to bring your own gear from home.

There are very few **youth hostels** in the country, most of them in university cities where they may be booked up by students throughout term time. A Hostelling International (HI) card can in theory give you a tiny saving of around P25 a night at the handful of YMCAs and YWCAs in the big cities. The problem is that few staff have any idea what an HI card is.

There's no official **homestay** programme in the Philippines, but in rural areas where there may be no formal accommodation, you'll often find people willing to put you up in their **home** for a small charge, usually no more than P200 a night, including some food. If you enjoy the stay, it's best to offer some sort of tip when you leave, or a gift of soft drinks and sweets for the children. You can ask around at town halls if you're interested.

Food and drink

The high esteem in which Filipinos hold their food is encapsulated by the common greeting "Let's eat!" Though Filipino food has a reputation for being one of Asia's less adventurous cuisines, there is a lot more to it than adobo (the richly marinated pork or chicken national dish), and young, entrepreneurial restaurateurs and chefs have started to give native dishes an increasingly sophisticated touch.

In the Philippines snacks – **merienda** – are eaten in between the three main meals, and not to partake when offered can be considered rude. It's not unusual for breakfast to be eaten early, followed by merienda at 10am, lunch as early as 11am (especially in the provinces where many people are up at sunrise), more merienda at 2pm and 4pm, and dinner at 7pm. Meals are substantial, and even busy office workers prefer to sit down at a table and make the meal last. Never be afraid to ask for a doggy bag – everyone does.

Don't be confused by the absence of a knife from most table settings. It's normal to use just a **fork and spoon**, cutting any meat with the edge of the fork and using the spoon to put it in your mouth. This isn't as eccentric as it first seems. Most meat is served in small chunks, not steak-like slabs, so you usually don't have to cut it at all. Fish can be skewered with your fork and cut with the side of your spoon. And a spoon is so much easier for the local **staple**, steamed rice, than a knife and fork. That said, in some "native-style" restaurants food is served on banana leaves and you're expected to eat with your hands, combining the rice and food into mouthful-sized balls with your fingers – if you don't feel up to this it's fine to ask for cutlery.

Filipino cuisine

Filipino food (see also *Filipino food* colour section and pp.455–459 for a food and drink **glossary**) is an intriguing mixture of the familiar, such as pork and rice, and the exotic – tamarind, screwpine and purple yam, for instance. The two main "national" dishes **adobo** and **lechon** (see *Filipino food* colour section) are based around chicken and pork respectively. Pork is also the basis of **Bicol Express** (the best known of very few spicy local dishes), consisting of pork ribs cooked in coconut milk, soy and vinegar, with chillies (a vegetable version also exists).

In the world's second largest archipelago, there's obviously a lot of **seafood** to enjoy, much of it fresher and tastier in the provinces than Manila. The king of Filipino fish is the *lapu-lapu*, a grouper that is cooked in dozens of different ways, but is best grilled over a fire and flavoured with *calamansi* (native limes). *Bangus* (milkfish, which is about the size of a trout and has soft brown flesh) is one of the staples of the diet and can be eaten for breakfast, lunch or dinner. It's usually slit down the middle, de-boned and fried, then served with a tangy dipping sauce of vinegar and garlic. While swordfish, tuna, blue marlin, crab and lobster are all on seafood-restaurant menus, Filipinos also love smaller, humbler fish such as *galunggong* (round scad), which is part of the everyday diet in the provinces.

Vegetables are not considered an integral part of the meal, but may well be mixed in with the meat or offered as a side dish. In restaurants serving Filipino food, some of the most common vegetable dishes include *pinakbet*, an Ilocano dish, and a version of Bicol Express with leafy vegetables such as *pechay* (aka pak choy) and *camote* tops (sweet potato leaves) in place of pork. Also popping up on many menus is a version of chop suey, here a vegetable stir-fry, often containing shrimp or small bits of pork.

Noodles (*pancit*) are frequently used in Filipino cooking and come in various forms. Pancit *canton* is ribbon-like, stir-fried rice noodles, while *sotanghon* refers to thin, vermicelli-like rice noodles.

Breakfast

At many hotels and resorts you'll be offered a Filipino **breakfast**, which typically consists of *longganisa* (garlic sausage), *tocino* (cured pork), fried *bangus* fish, corned beef or beef *tapa* (beef marinated in vinegar), with a fried egg and garlic rice. If this sounds too much for you, there's usually fresh fruit and toast, though note that local **bread**, either of the sliced variety or in rolls known as *pan de sal*, is often slightly sweet (wholegrain or rye breads are unusual in all but a few big hotels). Another option is to ask for a couple of hot *pan de sal* with corned-beef filling, the beef taking away some of the bread's sweetness. Coffee is usually instant, served in "three-in-one" packets, and dominated by Nescafé, though local, Malaysian and Indonesian brands are also available. Where brewed coffee is served, it's often local and very good.

Desserts and snacks

The only difference between lunch and dinner is that the latter is more likely to be followed by a **dessert**. Traditionally this would be a sweet cake containing coconut, though these days dessert could mean fresh fruit, caramel custard, *halo-halo, buko pie* (see *Filipino food* colour section) or *brazos*, a cream-filled meringue log cake. Filipinos also eat a huge amount of **ice cream** in a unorthodox range of flavours, including *ube* (purple yam), jackfruit, corn, avocado and even cheese.

For a snack in a packet, try salted dried fish like *dilis*, which can be bought in supermarkets and convenience stores. *Dilis* are a little like anchovies and are eaten whole, sometimes with a vinegar and garlic dip; they're often served along with other savouries (under the collective name *pulutan*) during drinking sessions. Salted dried *pusit* (squid) is also common.

Filipino fruits

The Philippines is justly celebrated for its variety and quality of **fresh fruit**, especially its **mangoes**, which are ubiquitous throughout the islands and always juicy and delicious. The below list is just a selection.

Atis (custard apple or sugar-apple) Pine-cone shaped, and about 10cm long with green scaly skin, the ripe flesh of the *atis* is gloriously sweet and soft; it might look a bit like custard but it tastes like a combination of banana, papaya and strawberry, or more prosaically, bubble gum. With black pips scattered throughout it can be messy to eat. The main season is late summer to October.

Bananas (*saging*) Bananas are a staple crop in the Philippines, with a remarkable range of size and types grown in Mindanao and the western Visayas throughout the year; the country is one of the largest exporters of bananas in the world.

Calamansi Little green lime that is squeezed into juices, hot tea, over noodles, fish, *kinilaw*, and into numerous dipping sauces.

Coconut (*buko*) Another Philippine staple grown throughout the archipelago year-round, harvested casually by villagers as much as by commercial plantations for its refreshing juice and nutty white flesh. Used to make *buko* pie and a variety of desserts.

Durian The "king" of tropical fruit is spiky, heavy and smells like a drain blocked with garbage – but its creamy inner flesh tastes like heaven. Rich in protein, minerals and fat, the durian is one of the more expensive fruit in the Philippines, though in Davao, the centre of production, you can buy whole ones for P50.

Jackfruit (*langka*) The largest tree-borne fruit in the world (it can reach 40 kilos) is also one of the most delicious, with an interior of large, yellow bulbs of sweet banana and flowery-flavoured flesh.

Lanzones Small round fruit grown mostly on southern Luzon, especially in Laguna, and available October to December. It's also grown in northern Mindanao and especially Camiguin, where there is a festival in its honour (p.400). It tastes a bit like a combination of grape and sweet grapefruit.

Mangoes (*mangga*) Eat as much mango as you can in the Philippines – you won't taste any better. Most grown on the islands turn from green to yellow as they ripen and are always very sweet. The main season runs June through August.

Mangosteen Nothing like a mango, this sumptuous fruit the size of a tangerine has a thick, purplish skin and creamy white flesh; the season also runs June through August.

Marang If you travel in Mindanao look out for this special fruit (a bit like a breadfruit), a cross between jackfruit and *atis*, but with a taste all its own.

Papaya You'll see papaya plants growing in gardens and along roadsides all over the Philippines and it's one of the cheapest fruits. Some 98 percent of the annual crop is consumed locally and it's extremely nutritious.

Pineapple (*piña*) The Spanish introduced the pineapple to the Philippines and thanks to the huge plantations run by Del Monte and Dole (both in Mindanao), it's one of the nation's biggest export earners.

Santol The *santol* is an apple-sized fruit, with a white juicy pulp often eaten sour with some salt. It's also popular as a jam or a bitter marmalade.

Where to eat

The choice of **places to eat** ranges from bewildering in Manila to extremely limited in the provinces. In the latter it will almost always consist of straightforward Filipino dishes such as grilled fish or chicken and rice followed by mango. If you're staying in a small resort the staff will often ask you in advance what you want for dinner and then buy it from the market or straight from a returning fisherman. As long as you don't mind simple food, this can beat the big city for taste hands down. The **final bill** you get in a restaurant usually includes VAT of twelve percent and a service charge of ten percent, adding 22 percent to the price shown on the menu.

Fast food

You'll find *McDonald's* in almost every big town, but the Philippines has its own successful chains fashioned after the US giant, with hundreds of branches of *Jollibee*, *Chowking*, *Mang Inasal* (with unlimited rice) and *Max's* (for fried chicken) throughout the country – indeed, the corpulent "jolly bee" mascot is more ubiquitous than Ronald McDonald. Western-style sandwich bars are starting to appear too.

Most shopping malls also have **food courts**, indoor marketplaces that bring together dozens of small stalls serving Filipino, Japanese, Chinese, Thai and Korean food. Here you can get a decent lunch for under P250 including a soft drink.

In many provincial cities, look out also for **ihaw-ihaw** (grill) restaurants, usually native-style bamboo structures where meat and fish are cooked over charcoal and served with hot rice and soup.

Street food

Though not as common as it is in Thailand or India, **street food** still has a special place in the hearts (and stomachs) of Filipinos as much for its plain weirdness as for its culinary virtues. Hawkers with portable stoves tend to appear towards the end of the working day from 5–8pm and at lunch in bigger cities. Much of the food is grilled over charcoal and served on sticks kebab-style, or deep fried in a wok with oil that is poured into an old jam jar and re-used day after day. Highlights include deep-fried fishballs and squidballs (mashed fish or squid blended with wheat flour), grilled pig intestines and *adidas* – chicken's feet, named after the sports-shoe manufacturer. Prices start from a few pesos a stick.

Street vendors also supply the king of Filipino aphrodisiacs, **balut**, a half-formed duck embryo eaten with beak, feathers and all; sellers advertise their proximity with a distinctive baying cry.

Carinderias and seafood buffets

Carinderias allow you to choose from a number of dishes placed on a counter in big aluminium pots. Carinderia fare includes *adobo*, pancit and **tapsilog**, a contraction formed from *tapa* (fried beef), *sinangag* (garlic fried rice) and *itlog* (egg) – which is exactly what you get, a bowl of rice with *tapa* and a fried egg on top. Other "combo" dishes include *tosilog* (with *tocino*, which is marinated fried pork) and *longsilog* (with longganisa). The only problem with carinderias is that the food has usually been standing around a while and is often served lukewarm.

In urban areas you'll also find **seafood restaurants** displaying a range of seafood on ice; order by pointing at what you want and telling the waiter how you would like it cooked.

European, Chinese and Japanese

There are some excellent French, Spanish and Italian restaurants in Manila and Cebu City, and dozens of European restaurants in Boracay. Prices depend on where you are. In areas of Manila, you can spend P2500 or more for a good three-course meal for two;

in Boracay you could have a similar meal for half that. However, European cuisine on the coast tends to be a little less sophisticated, simply because it's hard to guarantee supplies of the necessary ingredients.

There are **Chinese** restaurants in every city and in many provincial towns. Don't expect modish Oriental cuisine though; most Chinese restaurants are inexpensive places offering straightforward, tasty food designed to be ordered in large portions and shared by a group. A good Chinese meal for two often costs no more than P500. Another of the Philippines' favourite cuisines is Japanese – there are Japanese restaurants in every city, ranging from fast-food noodle parlours to expensive restaurants serving sushi and tempura.

Drinking

Bottled water is cheap; good local brands such as Nestlé Pure Life, Viva and Hidden Spring cost P20–30 in convenience stores. **Fizzy soft drinks** such as Coca-Cola and Pepsi are available everywhere.

At resorts and hotels, the "juice" which usually comes with breakfast is – irritatingly in a country rich in fresh fruit – often made from powder or concentrate. Good fresh **juices**, usually available only in the more expensive restaurants, include watermelon, ripe mango, sour mango and papaya. Fresh *buko* (coconut) juice is a refreshing choice, especially on a hot day. In general, **sugar** is added to fresh juices and shakes unless you specify otherwise. You might well want sugar

with the delightful soda made from *calamansi*, a small native lime.

Filipinos aren't big **tea** drinkers and except in the best hotels, the only tea on offer is usually made from Lipton's tea bags. **Coffee** is popular and can be ordered anywhere, but the quality varies widely. Fresh milk is rare outside the cities so you'll often find yourself being offered tinned or powdered milk with coffee or tea. Latte-addicts may be tempted by *Starbucks* which has scores of branches across Manila and is popping up in provincial towns such as Bacolod.

Alcohol

The **beer** of choice in the Philippines is San Miguel, the local pilsner established in 1890 and still dominating 90 percent of the domestic market (San Miguel also produces Red Horse Extra Strong lager). The only competition comes from Asia Brewery, which produces the uninspiring Beer na Beer and Colt 45 brands. Only a few foreign beers are available in bars and super-markets, notably Heineken, Budweiser and Japanese brands. For something stronger there are plenty of Philippine-made **spirits** such as Tanduay rum, San Miguel Ginebra (gin) and Fundador brandy. **Wine** can be found in liquor stores in the larger cities though the range is usually limited to Australian or New Zealand mass-market brands.

All restaurants, fast-food places excepted, serve alcohol, but wine is rarely drunk; a cold

---

Special diets

Committed **vegetarians and vegans** face a difficult mission to find suitable food in the Philippines. It's a poor country and many Filipinos have grown up on a diet of what's available locally, usually chicken and pork. If you ask for a plate of stir-fried vegetables it might come with slices of pork in it, or be served in a meat gravy. Fried rice always contains egg and meat.

Chinese and Japanese restaurants offer the best range of vegetable-based dishes, though you'll have to emphasize that you want absolutely no bits of meat added. In Manila, and to some extent in other cities, and in Boracay, pizzas are an option, or you could head to an upmarket restaurant and ask the chef to prepare something special. At least breakfast is straightforward – even in the most rural resorts, you can ask for a toast or pancakes and, if you're not vegan, an omelette or scrambled eggs.

It's much the same story for anyone looking for halal or kosher fare, except in Muslim areas of Mindanao where almost every carinderia and restaurant serves halal food. There are also one or two halal food outlets in the Ermita area of Manila.

beer or fresh fruit juice is much preferred. European restaurants usually have a limited wine list. For an average bottle of Australian Chardonnay or Merlot expect to pay at least P750. For something authentically native, try the strong and pungent *tapuy* (rice wine) or a speciality called *lambanog*, made from almost anything that can be fermented, including fruit. In the provinces both can be difficult to find because they're usually brewed privately for local consumption, though *lambanog* is now being bottled and branded, and can be found on some super-market shelves in Manila and other cities.

Health

As long as you're careful about what you eat and drink and how long you spend in the sun, you shouldn't have any major health problems in the Philippines. Hospitals in cities and even in small towns are generally of a good standard, although health care is rudimentary in the remotest barrios. Anything potentially serious is best dealt with in Manila. Doctors and nurses almost always speak English, and doctors in major cities are likely to have received some training in the US or the UK, where many attend medical school.

We've listed hospitals in the accounts of cities and major towns in the Guide; for a full list of hospitals in the country and a searchable database of doctors by location and speciality, check Ⓦwww.rxpinoy.com. There are **pharmacies** on almost every street corner where you can buy local and international brand medicines. Branches of Mercury Drug, the country's biggest chain of pharmacies, are listed on Ⓦwww.mercurydrug.com.

If you are hospitalized, you'll have to pay a deposit on your way in and settle the bill – either in person or through your insurance company (see p.50 for advice on insurance).

Stomach upsets

Food- and waterborne diseases are the most likely cause of illness in the Philippines. Travellers' diarrhoea can be caused by viruses, bacteria or parasites, which can contaminate food or water. There's also a risk of typhoid or cholera – occasional cases are reported in the Philippines, mostly in poor areas without adequate sanitation. Another potential threat is that of hepatitis A. The authorities in Manila claim **tap water** in many areas is safe for drinking, but it's not worth taking the chance – stick to bottled water.

Mosquito-borne diseases

Dengue fever, a debilitating and occasionally fatal viral disease, is on the increase across tropical Asia. Many cases are reported in the Philippines each year, mostly during or just after the wet season when the day-biting mosquito that carries the disease is most active. There is no vaccine against dengue. Initial symptoms – which develop five to eight days after being bitten – include a fever that subsides after a few days, often leaving the patient with a bad rash all over their body, headaches and fierce joint pain. The only treatment is rest, liquids and paracetamol or any other acetaminophen painkiller (not aspirin). Dengue can result in death, usually among the very young or very old, and serious cases call for hospitalization.

In the Philippines **malaria** is found only in isolated areas of southern Palawan and the Sulu archipelago, and few travellers bother with anti-malarials if they are sticking to the tourist trail. If you are unsure of your itinerary it's best to err on the safe side and consult your doctor about malaria medication. Anti-malarials must be taken before you enter a malarial zone, and note that resistance to chloroquine, one of the common drugs, is a significant problem in Mindanao and Palawan.

To avoid mosquito bites, wear long-sleeved shirts, long trousers and a hat. Use an insect repellent that contains DEET (diethylmethyltoluamide) and – unless you are staying in air-conditioned or well-screened accommodation – buy a mosquito net impregnated with the insecticide permethrin or deltamethrin. In the Philippines mosquito nets are hard to find, so buy one before you go. If you are unable to find a pretreated mosquito net you can buy one and spray it yourself.

Leeches and rabies

If you're trekking through rainforest, especially in the rainy season, there's a good chance you'll encounter **leeches**, blood-sucking freshwater worms that attach themselves to your skin and can be tricky to remove. If you find a leech on your skin it's important not to pull it off because the mouth parts could be left behind and cause infection. Use an irritant like salt or heat from a cigarette or match to make the leech let go, then treat the wound with antiseptic. You can guard against leeches in the first place by securing cuffs and trouser bottoms. Climbers in the Philippines say rubbing ordinary soap with a little water on your skin and clothes helps keep leeches at bay.

Stray and badly cared for dogs are everywhere in the Philippines, and **rabies** claims about eight hundred lives a year. The stereotype of rabid animals being deranged and foaming at the mouth is just that; some infected animals become lethargic and sleepy, so don't presume a docile dog is a safe one. If you are scratched or bitten by a stray dog, wash the wound immediately with soap and water, then get yourself to a hospital.

Medical resources for travellers

Canadian Society for International Health
Ⓦ www.csih.org. Extensive list of travel health centres.
CDC ☎1-877/394-8747, Ⓦ www.cdc.gov/travel. Official US government travel health site.
Hospital for Tropical Diseases Travel Clinic
☎0845/155-5000 or 020/7387-4411, Ⓦ www.thehtd.org.
International Society for Travel Medicine
☎1-770/736-7060, Ⓦ www.istm.org. Has a full list of travel health clinics worldwide.
MASTA (Medical Advisory Service for Travellers Abroad) ☎0870/606-2782, Ⓦ www.masta-travel-health.com or for the nearest clinic in the UK.
Travellers' medical and Vaccination Centre
☎1300/658844, Ⓦ www.tmvc.com.au. Lists travel clinics in Australia, New Zealand and South Africa.
Tropical Medical Bureau Republic of Ireland
☎1850/487 674, Ⓦ www.tmb.ie.

The media

Filipinos are inordinately proud of their nation's status as the first democracy in Asia, a fact reflected in their love of a free press. Once Marcos was gone and martial law with him, the shackles truly came off and the Philippine media became one of the most vociferous and freewheeling in the world. There is a dark side to this, however – the Philippines is also one of the most dangerous places in the world to be a journalist, with many killed every year. If you're looking for news from home, most cities and tourist areas now have cable TV with CNN and possibly the BBC. Foreign news publications are harder to find. The best bet is to visit a five-star hotel, where lobby gift shops sometimes stock the International Herald Tribune, Time, Newsweek and The Economist.

Newspapers and magazines

Major English-language daily **broadsheet** newspapers include the *Philippine Daily Inquirer* (Ⓦwww.inquirer.net), the *Philippine Star* (Ⓦwww.philstar.com) and *the Manila Times* (Ⓦwww.manilatimes.net). There are dozens of tabloids on the market, all of them lurid and often gruesome. Most of these are in Tagalog, though *People's Tonight* (Ⓦwww.journal.com.ph) is largely in English with Filipino thrown in where the vernacular better expresses the drama, such as in quotations from victims of crime and from the police.

Some of the most trusted reporting on the Philippines comes from the **Philippine Centre for Investigative Journalism** (Ⓦwww.pcij.org), founded in 1989 by nine Filipino journalists who wanted to go beyond the day-to-day razzmatazz and inanities of the mainstream press. Journalists working for the PCIJ were responsible for the exposé of former President Joseph Estrada's unexplained wealth, which led eventually to his downfall.

Television and radio

Terrestrial **television networks** include **GMA** (Ⓦwww.gmanetwork.com) and **ABS-CBN** (Ⓦwww.abs-cbn.com), offering a diet of histrionic soaps, chat shows and daytime game shows with sexy dancers. **Cable television** is now widely available in the Philippines, with the exception of some of the most undeveloped rural areas. Most providers carry BBC World, CNN and Australian ABC. At weekends during the season there's American football, baseball and English Premier League football on Star Sports or ESPN. Movie channels include HBO, Cinemax and Star Movies.

There are over 350 **radio** stations in the Philippines, and between them they present a mind-boggling mix of news, sport, music and chitchat. Radio news channels such as DZBB and RMN News AM tend to broadcast in Filipino, but there are dozens of FM pop stations that use English with a smattering of Filipino. The music they play isn't anything special, mostly mellow jazz and pop ballads by mainstream artists. Among the most popular FM stations are Wow FM (103.5MHz) and Crossover (105.1 MHz). A shortwave radio also gives access to the **BBC World Service** (Ⓦwww.bbc.co.uk/worldservice), **Radio Canada** (Ⓦwww.rcinet.ca), **Voice of America** (Ⓦwww.voa.gov) and **Radio Australia** (Ⓦwww.abc.net.au/ra), among other international broadcasters.

Festivals

Every community in the Philippines – from small barrio to busy metropolis – has at least a couple of festivals a year in honour of a patron saint, to give thanks for a good harvest, or to pay respects to a biblical character. It's well worth timing your visit to see one of the major events; the main fiesta months are from January to May, but exact dates often vary. Everyone is in a hospitable mood at these events. The beer flows, pigs are roasted, and there's dancing in the streets for days on end.

Major mardi-gras-style festivals include the **Ati-Atihan** in January in Kalibo (see p.315), and the **Sinulog** in January in Cebu (see p.269). One of the biggest nationwide festivals is the **Flores de Mayo**, a religious parade held across the country throughout May in honour of the Virgin Mary.

A festivals calendar

Listing all Filipino festivals below is impossible. Those included here are larger ones that you might consider making a special trip for, at least if you happen to be in the area.

January and February

Feast of the Black Nazarene (Jan 9) Quiapo, Manila. Devotees gather in the plaza outside Quiapo Church to touch a miraculous image of Christ. See p.86 for more.

Sinulog (Third Sun in Jan) Cebu City ⓦwww.sinulog.ph. The second city's biggest annual event, in honour of the Santo Niño (an image of Jesus as a child). Huge street parade, live music, plenty of food and drink. See p.269 for more.

Ati-Atihan (Variable, usually second week of Jan) Kalibo, Aklan province. Street dancing and wild costumes at arguably the biggest festival in the country, held to celebrate an ancient land pact between settlers and indigenous Atis. See p.315 for more.

Dinagyang (Fourth week of Jan) Iloilo ⓦwww.dinagyangsailoilo.com. Relatively modern festival based on the Ati-Atihan and including a parade on the Iloilo River.

Philippine Hot Air Balloon Fiesta (Feb) Clark, Pampanga ⓦwww.philballoonfest.net. Balloon rides, microlight flying, skydiving and aerobatics displays.

Pamulinawen (First two weeks in Feb) Laoag City. City-wide fiesta in honour of St William the Hermit. Events include street parties, beauty pageants, concerts and religious parades.

Panagbenga (Baguio Flower festival) (Third week in Feb) Baguio City. The summer capital's largest annual event includes parades of floats beautifully decorated with flowers from the Cordillera region. There are also flower-related lectures and exhibitions.

Suman festival (Third week in Feb) Baler, Aurora. Another mardi-gras-style extravaganza featuring street parades, dancing and floats decorated with the native delicacy suman, sticky rice cake rolled in banana leaves.

March and April

Moriones (Easter weekend) Marinduque. A celebration of the life of the Roman centurion Longinus, who was blind in one eye. Legend says that when he pierced Christ's side with his spear, blood spurted into his eye and cured him. See p.201 for more.

Arya! Abra (First or second week of March) Bangued, Abra. Highlights include hair-raising bamboo-raft races along the frisky Abra River and gatherings of northern tribes.

Bangkero festival (First or second week of March) Pagsanjan, Laguna. Parade along the Pagsanjan River.

Kaamulan festival (First week of March) Malaybalay City, Bukidnon, Mindanao. Showcase of tribal culture and arts.

Pasayaw festival (Third week of March) Canlaon City, Negros Oriental. Thanksgiving festival to God and St Joseph, with twelve barangays competing for honours in an outdoor dancing competition. The final "dance-off" is held in the city gym.

Boracay International Dragon Boat Festival (April) Boracay, ⓦwww.boracaydragonboat.ph. A local version of Hong Kong's dragon-boat races, featuring domestic and international teams competing in long wooden canoes on a course off White Beach.

Allaw Ta Apo Sandawa (Second week of April) Kidapawan City, North Cotabato. Gathering of highland tribes to pay respects to the sacred Mount Apo.

All Saints' Day

It's the day for Catholic Filipinos to honour their dead, but **All Saints' Day** on November 1 is nothing to get maudlin about. Sometimes called All Souls' Day, it's when clans reunite at family graves and memorials, turning cemeteries throughout the country into fairgrounds. You don't pay your respects in the Philippines by being miserable, so All Saints' Day is a chance to show those who have gone before how much those who have been left behind are prospering. Filipinos approach All Saints' Day with the same gusto as Christmas, running from shop to shop at the last minute looking for candles to burn, food and offerings. The grave is painted, flowers are arranged and rosaries fervently prayed over, but once the ceremonial preliminaries are over, the fun begins. Guitars appear, capacious picnic hampers are opened and liquor flows freely. Many families gather the night before and sleep in the cemetery. With many family graves in the provinces, Manila empties fast the day before All Saints' Day, people leaving the city by anything on wheels. Needless to say, it's a bad time to travel.

Turumba festival (April & May) Pakil, Laguna. Religious festival commemorating the seven sorrows of the Virgin Mary. The festival consists of seven *novenas*, one for each sorrow, held at weekends.

May

Flores de Mayo (Throughout May) Countrywide. Religious procession celebrating the coming of the rains, with girls dressed as the various "Accolades of our Lady", including Faith, Hope and Charity. Processions are sometimes held after dark and lit by candles, a lovely sight.

Carabao Carroza (May 3–4) Iloilo, Panay Island. Races held to celebrate the humble *carabao* (water buffalo), beast of burden for many a provincial farmer.

Pahiyas (May 15) Lucban, Quezon; also celebrated in the nearby towns of Candelaria, Tayabas, Sariaya, Tiaong and Lucena. Colourful harvest festival which sees houses gaily decorated with fruits and vegetables. It's held in honour of San Isidro Labrador, the patron saint of farmers. See p.197 for more.

Obando Fertility Rites (May 17–19) Obando, Bulacan. On the feast day of San Pascual, women gather in the churchyard to chant prayers asking for children. See p.109 for more.

June to September

Kadayawan sa Davao (Third week of Aug) Davao City ⓦ www.kadayawan.com. Week-long harvest festival with civic parades, military parades, street dances and horsefighting.

Peñafrancia Fluvial festival (Third Sat in Sept) Naga, Camarines Sur. A sacred statue of Our Lady of Peñafrancia, the patron saint of Bicol, is paraded through the streets, then sailed down the Bicol River back to its shrine.

October to December

Kansilay (Oct 19 or closest weekend) Silay, Negros Occidental. Modern festival commemorating Silay's charter day. Eating and drinking contests, beauty pageants and an elaborate street parade.

Ibalong (Third week of Oct) Legaspi and throughout Bicol. Epic dances and street presentations portraying Bicol's mythical superheroes and gods.

Lanzones festival (Third week of Oct) Lambajao, Camiguin. Vibrant and good-natured outdoor party giving thanks for the island's crop of *lanzones* (a tropical fruit). See p.400 for more.

MassKara (Third week of Oct) Bacolod, Negros Occidental. Festivities kick off with food fairs, mask-making contests, brass-band competitions and beauty pageants, followed by the climax – a mardi-gras parade where revellers don elaborate mask and costumes and dance to Latin rhythms Rio de Janeiro-style. See p.296 for more.

Outdoor activities and sports

There are some superb wilderness areas in the Philippines and dozens of volcanoes and mountains to be climbed, from the tallest in the country, Mount Apo (2954m), to more manageable peaks close to Manila in Batangas and Rizal provinces, some of which can be tackled in a day-trip. The country also offers opportunities for caving, whitewater rafting, surfing and sailing. When it comes to sport, basketball and boxing are among the biggest passions in the Philippines.

But for a sizeable proportion of the tourists who visit the Philippines every year, the main attraction is the **scuba diving**. The abundance of exceptional dive sites and the high standard of diving instruction available have made the archipelago one of the world's foremost diving destinations.

Scuba diving

Diving is one of the most popular activities in the Philippines and one of the best dive sites in the world. It's possible year-round here, with surface water temperatures in the 25–28°C range, the warmest conditions being from February to June. On deeper dives temperatures can drop to 22°C due to the upwelling of deeper, cooler water, so a wet suit is essential. During the typhoon season from June to November, be prepared for your plans to be disrupted if a major storm hits and dive boats are unable to venture out. Visibility depends on water temperature, the strength of the current and wind direction, but generally lies in 10–30m range, as good as anywhere in the world. Popular locations include the coast around Palawan, the wrecks around Coron Town, Puerto Galera, Padre Burgos, Anilao and the more remote but scintillating reefs at Tubbataha and Apo.

Most dives **cost** around P1800 to P2000, including rental of the boat and equipment such as mask, booties, wet suit, fins, weight belt and air tanks. For night dives and more demanding technical dives, expect to pay around P500 extra. If you've booked a package, two dives a day will normally be included in the cost.

See the *Diving in the Philippines* colour section for more.

Courses

All PADI-accredited resorts offer a range of courses run by qualified professional instructors. If you haven't been diving before and aren't sure if you'll take to it, try a gentle twenty-minute "discovery dive", guided by an instructor for around P1500, or the longer PADI Discover Scuba Diving course for around P3000. The main course for beginners is the PADI **Open Water Diver Course** (from P18,000) which will allow you to dive at depths up to 18m. You might want to consider doing the pool sessions and written tests before you travel, then doing the checkout dives at a PADI resort in the Philippines. It saves time and means you don't have to slave over homework in the tropical heat. If you choose this option, make sure you bring your PADI referral documents with you.

Once you've passed the course and been given your certification card, you are free to dive not just anywhere in the Philippines, but anywhere in the world. You might also want to take another step up the diving ladder by enrolling in a more **advanced** course. There are many to choose from, including Advanced Open Water Diver (from P14,000), Emergency First Response (from P6000), which is also suitable for non-divers and Rescue Diver (from P18,000).

Liveaboards

There are two great advantages to diving from a **liveaboard** (a boat that acts as a mobile hotel) – you can get to places that are inaccessible by bangka and once you're there you can linger for a night or two. Liveaboards allow you to explore terrific destinations such as Apo Reef off the coast of Mindoro and Tubbataha in the Sulu Sea, arguably the best dive spot in the country. Packages include all meals and dives, but vary significantly according to destination; Tubbataha costs at least US$1200–1600 per week, while trips around Coron start at around US$130 per day. Most of the boats used have air-conditioned en-suite cabins for two. Packages often include unlimited diving and are always full board.

ABC Dive Coron ✪ www.abcdive.com. Operated out of Coron Town, Palawan, the *Maribeth* accommodates only eight people, making it ideal for small groups. Destinations include Apo Reef and Tubbataha (around US$1000 for eight nights), or you can simply pay by the day to potter around the dive sites of Busuanga. The daily rate is €100 per person (around US$130), including meals, hot drinks, unlimited diving, tanks and weights.

Atlantis Dive Resorts ✪ atlantishotel.com. Operates the thirty-two-metres-long *Atlantis Azores* with eight luxurious cabins with private bathrooms. Trips to Apo Reef, Tubbataha, Bohol and Padre Burgos (most trips US$2000–3000 for 7 nights, 6 days).

Diving World ✪ www.divingworld.co.uk. Operates the *Stella Maris Explorer* with ten twin a/c cabins each with en-suite toilet and shower. Ten-day packages from the UK to Apo Reef and the Coron wrecks, including flights and three dives a day from £1650.

Expedition Fleet ✪ expeditionfleet.com. Trips to Apo Reef (US$970; 5 days, 4 nights), Tubbataha (from US$1550; 6 days, 5 nights), the Visayas (from US$900; 5 days, 4 nights) and around the Puerto Galera area (US$1950; 8 days, 7 nights). There are five boats to choose from (see website).

Seadive Resort ✪ www.seadiveresort.com. Trips to Apo Reef and the Coron wrecks from US$1100 (6 nights/7 days), including 13 dives and all meals/ entry fees. Eight twin cabins with fans share two bathrooms with hot water.

Victory Divers ✪ www.victorydivers.com. Overnight trips from Boracay to Maniguin Island, Apo Reef and Panagatan Keys, where there are whale sharks, sharks, rays and turtles. P7500/day (minimum of four people).

Recompression chambers

There are six recompression chambers (aka hyperbaric chambers) in the Philippines to treat recompression sickness. All offer a 24-hour emergency service. You might also want to check that your dive operator is aware of the nearest facility. If he's not, go somewhere else.

Batangas City St Patrick's Hospital, Lopez Jaena St ☎ 043/723-8388.
Cavite City Sangley Recompression Chamber, NSWG, Philippine Fleet Naval Base ☎ 046/524-2061.
Cebu City Viscom Station Hospital, Military Camp Lapu-Lapu, Lahug ☎ 032/232-2464-8.
Manila AFP Medical Center, V. Luna Rd, Quezon City ☎ 02/920-7183; DAN (Divers Alert Network), Suite 123, Makati Medical Center, 2 Amorsolo St, Makati City ☎ 02/817-5601.
Subic Bay Subic Bay Freeport Zone ☎ 047/252-2566.

Diving resources

Asian Diver ✪ www.asiandiver.com. Online edition of the diving magazine with lots of general Asia information as well as some articles about the Philippines.
Asia Divers ✪ www.asiadivers.com. Thoroughly professional dive outfit with an office in Manila and a dive centre and accommodation in Puerto Galera. Good people to learn with.
Divephil ✪ www.divephil.com. Useful guide to scuba diving in the Philippines, plus information about destinations and accommodation.
Scuba Globe Asia Pacific ✪ www.scubaglobe .com. Comprehensive overview of diving around the region, but with links to some Philippines sites.
Seaquest ✪ www.seaquestdivecenter.net. Long- established operator with centres in Bohol and Cebu, offering general diving advice, safaris, courses and accommodation.

Diving dos and don'ts

Divers can cause damage to reefs, sometimes inadvertently. Be aware of your fins because they can break off coral heads that take years to re-grow. Don't grab coral to steady yourself and always maintain good buoyancy control – colliding with a reef can be destructive. Don't kick up sediment, which can choke and kill corals. For more informa- tion about reef conservation efforts in the Philippines, check out ✪ www.oceanheritage .com.ph, the website of the Ocean Heritage Foundation, a local environmentalist group. Below is a list of additional dos and don'ts:
Collecting aquatic life Resist the temptation to take home corals or shells, and never take souvenirs from wreck dives or remove anything dead or alive – except rubbish – from the ocean.
Riding aquatic life Hard to credit, but some divers still think it's a great lark to hang onto the

back of a turtle or manta ray. Simply put, there are no circumstances in which this is right.

Spear-fishing This has been outlawed in the Philippines, and environmental groups are increasingly reporting spear-fishers to the authorities for prosecution.

Touching and handling aquatic life For many organisms this is a terrifying and injurious experience. Handling marine life is best left to people who have experience with the creatures concerned.

Trekking and climbing

The Philippines offer plenty of opportunities to explore pristine wilderness areas. **Luzon**, for example, has the Sierra Madre and the Balbalasang-Balbalan National Park in Kalinga, both rarely visited by tourists and offering exhilarating trekking through dense rainforest and across dizzying peaks. In **Bicol** there are some terrific **volcano** climbs (Mount Mayon and Mount Isarog, for instance), while Mindoro, Palawan and the Visayas between them have dozens of national parks, heritage areas, wildlife sanctuaries and volcanoes. **Mount Kanlaon**, an active volcano in **Negros**, is one of the country's more risky climbs, while the nearby **Northern Negros Forest Reserve** is a raw, mesmerizing landscape of peaks, waterfalls and fumaroles, typical of wilderness areas throughout the archipelago.

The country actually has more than sixty national parks and protected areas, but because funds for their management are scarce, you won't find the kind of **infra-structure** that exists in national parks in the West. While the most popular climbs – **Mount Apo** in Mindanao and **Mount Pulag** in Mountain province, for example – have **trails** that are relatively easy to find and follow, it's important to realize that trails are generally poorly maintained and hardly marked, if they're marked at all. There are seldom more than a few badly paid wardens or rangers responsible for huge tracts of land. Where **accommodation** exists, it will be extremely basic. Some national parks have administrative buildings where you might be able to get a bed in a dorm for the night, or where you can roll out a mattress or sleeping bag on the floor. They may also have basic cooking facilities, but the closest

you'll get to a shower is filling a bucket and washing outside. Deep within park territory, the best you can hope for is a wooden shack to shelter in for the night.

This lack of facilities means you'll need to **hire a reliable guide**. Often, the place to make contact with guides is the municipal hall in the barangay or town closest to the trailhead. Fees range from P800–1500 per day depending where you are, plus food and water, which you'll have to bring with you as it's unlikely you'll come across anywhere to buy anything once you're on the trail.

There are some outdoor shops in big cities – mainly Manila – where you can buy a basic frame-tent for P3000 and a sleeping bag for P1500. Other essentials such as cooking equipment, lanterns and backpacks are also available, and you may be able to rent some items, though the range of gear on offer is limited even in the best shops.

Trekking and climbing resources

Metropolitan Mountaineering Society ⓦ www.metropolitanms.org. Sociable trekking group running expeditions throughout the year. On the easier treks they may well be willing to take you along at short notice, though you might need to take a basic survival course to be allowed on the more challenging expeditions.

Mountaineering Federation of the Philippines ⓦ fedphil.blogspot.com. An umbrella group that can offer general information about routes and practicalities.

Pinoy Mountaineer ⓦ www.pinoymountaineer.com. This detailed and well-maintained site is a good place to read up about trekking and climbing, and has sample itineraries for major climbs and a long list of climbing clubs in the country.

Caving

It's hardly surprising that **caving** – spelunking – is a growth industry, as there are huge caves to explore throughout the country. The largest cave systems are in northern Luzon – in Sagada (see p.175) and in Cagayan province near Tuguegarao, where the Peñablanca Protected Area (see p.158) has three hundred caves, many deep, dangerous and not yet fully explored. The other exciting caving area is the Sohoton Natural Bridge National Park in Samar (see p.341).

Whitewater rafting

Whitewater rafting is becoming more popular in the Philippines, notably along the Cagayan River and Chico River in northern Luzon (p.177) and Cagayan de Oro River in Mindanao (p.394). **Zip lines** have mushroomed all over the islands, but some are much tamer than others – some of the best are near Cagayan de Oro (p.394) and Davao (p.420). You can also take a thrilling ride in a **microlight** near Cagayan de Oro (p.394).

Surfing

Surfing is also becoming popular, with good waves in eastern Bicol, Catanduanes, eastern Mindanao (especially Siargao Island and Tandag), and around San Fernando in La Union. There are also any number of hard-to-reach areas in the archipelago that are visited only by a handful of die-hard surfers, such as Baler in northern Luzon (see p.160), or around Borongan (see p.342) in eastern Samar.

Basketball

The Filipinos embraced basketball as they did everything else American, from pizza to popcorn. Every barrio and town has a basketball court, even if all it consists of are a couple of makeshift baskets nailed to wooden poles in the church plaza. The major league – the equivalent of the NBA – is the **Philippine Basketball Association** (PBA; Ⓦwww.pba.com.ph), founded in 1975. Ten teams compete for honours, all of them sponsored by a major corporation and taking their sponsors' name. You might find yourself watching Meralco Bolts play Powerade Tigers, or San Miguel Beermen take on Talk 'N Text Tropang Texters. PBA games are all played in Manila; see the box on p.102 for details.

The San Miguel Beermen is the most successful team, while the Barangay Ginebra Kings is the most popular. The players are household names to most Filipinos; James Yap (with the Derby Ace Llamados), Jayjay Helterbrand (Barangay Ginebra Kings), Kelly Williams (Talk 'N Text), Willie Miller (Barangay Ginebra Kings) and Dondon Hontiveros (San Miguel Beermen) command huge attention.

Boxing

Boxing has been big business in the Philippines since the Americans introduced the sport in the early twentieth century. In recent years, one name stands out in particular: **Manny "the Pacman" Pacquiao**, the poor boy from Mindanao who became world **champion** (see p.434). Though you are unlikely to see the great man himself, fights are held almost every week, with major venues in Caloocan (Manila), Cebu City, Mandaluyong (Manila), Tagaytay City, Victoria (Negros) and Taytay in the Luzon province of Rizal. **Tickets** are cheap and often sell out; whenever there's a bout of any significance Filipinos gather around every available television set. You can check schedules for fights at Ⓦwww.philboxing.com.

In addition to Manny Pacquiao, at the time of writing the Philippines could boast another four world champions: Nonito "The Filipino Flash" Donaire, Gerry Peñalosa, Donnie "Ahas" Nietes and Brian "Hawaiian Punch" Viloria.

Pool

Every town and city in the country has some sort of **billiards hall**, even if it's just a few old tables on the pavement, where games are played by kerosene lamps, between locals, for the price of a few San Miguels. The sport has always been popular – it's cheap and reasonably accessible – but has boomed over the past decade because of the success of **Efren Reyes** and **Francisco Bustamante**. Reyes, sometimes called "The Magician", is one of the pool world's great characters; a diminutive fellow with a toothy grin, he picked up the nickname "Bata" ("The Kid") while helping out in his uncle's pool halls in Manila as a child. He was born in Pampanga province, to the north of Manila, and can still occasionally be found on a Friday or Saturday night shooting pool in his hometown bars around Clark, good-naturedly scalping unsuspecting tourists' drinks. In 2006, Reyes and Francisco "Django" Bustamante represented their country as Team Philippines and won the inaugural **World Cup of Pool** by defeating Team USA – a victory of major significance for a country with few global sporting heroes. They repeated the feat in 2009.

Cockfighting and the Filipino

Cockfighting has a long history in the Philippines. National hero José Rizal, martyred by the Spanish in 1896, once pointed out that the average Filipino loves his rooster more than he does his children.

Contrary to received wisdom, cockfighting was not introduced to the country by the Spanish. When conquistadors landed in Palawan shortly after the death of Magellan, they discovered native men already breeding domestic roosters to fight, putting them in shared cages and letting them scrap over small amounts of food.

Social scientists say cockfighting is popular in the Philippines because it reflects the national passion for brevity or a quick payoff, the trait of **ningas cogon** (*cogon* being a wild grass that burns ferociously and quickly). Part of the appeal is the **prize money**. For a P200 entrance fee, a struggling farmer from the backwoods could finish the day with P300,000 in his pocket, all thanks to a trusty rooster he has groomed and trained assiduously for months.

Cockfighting

Cockfighting is the Filipino passion few Westerners get to see or understand, for obvious reasons. It's a brutal blood sport where fighting cocks literally peck and jab each other to death as onlookers make bets on the outcome. The fight begins when the two roosters are presented to each other in the pit. Both have a razor-sharp curved blade three inches long strapped to their leg. The fight is over in a burst of feathers in no more than a few minutes, when one rooster is too bloodied and wounded, or simply too dead, to peck back at its opponent when provoked. To make the evening last, most major cockfights feature seven contests. Anyone who likes animals should definitely stay well away.

If you do attend a cockfight (*sabong* in Tagalog), you'll be experiencing Filipino culture at its rawest – at the very least it might make you think again about how much "American influence" dominates the culture. It's best to start at one of the major cockpits in Manila (see p.102), or ask your hotel for the nearest place to see one. Entrance fees are minimal, but you'll rarely see women attending – the **cockpit** is the exclusive preserve of men, who see it as an egalitarian refuge from the world's woes, a place where class differences are temporarily put to one side and everyone wears flip-flops and vests. In Manila foreign females should be OK at the main venues, but in the provinces you'll probably feel more comfortable with a male companion.

Culture and etiquette

For many travellers the Philippines seems less immediately "exotic" than other countries in Asia. English is spoken almost everywhere, people wear Western clothes and visit malls and the main religion is Catholicism. Combined with the approachability and sunny disposition of your average Filipino, and this appears to make for a trouble-free assimilation into the ways and values of the Philippines.

However, this can lead to a false sense of security, which over time – as differences begin to surface – gives way to bewilderment and confusion. There are complex rules of engagement that govern behaviour among Filipinos, and failure to be sensitive to them can cast you unwittingly in the role of the ugly foreigner, ranting and raving with frustration at everyone from the bellhop to the bank teller.

Filipino etiquette

One of the major controlling elements in Filipino society – undetected by most visitors – is **hiya**, a difficult word to define, though essentially it means a sense of shame. *Hiya* is a factor in almost all social situations. It is a sense of *hiya* that prevents someone asking a question, for fear he may look foolish. It is *hiya* that sees many Filipinos refuse to disagree openly, for fear they may cause offence. To not have *hiya* is a grave social sin. To be accused of being *walang-hiya* (to be shameless) is the ultimate insult. *Hiya* goes hand in hand with the preservation of **amor-propio** (the term literally means "love of self"), ie to avoid losing face. If you ever wonder why a Filipino fails to broach awkward subjects with you, or to point out that your flies are undone, it is because *hiya* and *amor-propio* are at work.

If you are ever in doubt about how to behave in the Philippines, bring to mind the value of **pakikisama**, which in rough translation means "to get along". Don't flaunt your gauche liberal values and don't confront the waiter or bark insults if he gets your order wrong. This offends his sense of *amor-propio* and marks you out as being an obnoxious *walang-hiya* foreigner. Talk to him quietly and ask that the order be changed. The same rules apply with government officials, police, ticket agents, hotel receptionists and cashiers. If there's a problem, sort it out quietly and patiently. A sense of **delicadeza** is also important to Filipinos. This might be translated as "propriety", a simple sense of good behaviour, particularly in the presence of elders or ladies.

BASICS | Culture and etiquette

Yes, no, maybe…

One of the root causes of frustration during social intercourse is the use of the word **yes**. In their desire to please, many Filipinos find it difficult to say no. So they say yes instead. Yes (actually *oo* in Tagalog, pronounced oh-oh, though most Filipinos would use the English word when talking to foreigners) can mean one of a multitude of things, from a plain and simple "yes" to "I'm not sure", "perhaps", "if you say so", or "sorry, I don't understand". A casual yes is never taken as binding. The concepts of *hiya* and *amor-propio* also filter through to the language in the form of a multitude of euphemisms for the word **no** (*hindi* in Tagalog). Instead of replying in the negative, in order not to upset you a Filipino will typically say "maybe" (*siguro nga*), "whatever" (*bahala na*) or "if you say so" (*kung sinabi mo ba e*). These subtleties of language are symptomatic of the unseen ebbs and flows of the tides that govern all social behaviour in the Philippines, few foreigners ever fully coming to terms with the eddies and whirls underneath.

Questions and greetings

Filipinos are **outgoing** people who don't consider it rude to ask personal questions. Prepare to be pleasantly interrogated by everyone you meet. Filipinos will want to know where you are from, why you are in the

Street kids

Despite the very real economic progress made in the last twenty years, millions of Filipinos still live in poverty. **Street children** (many orphaned) are one of the saddest consequences of this – some reports estimate some 1.5 million kids are living rough. In Manila and other large cities you'll see very small children begging for money in the street or dancing in front of cars at dangerous interchanges for tips. You'll also come across kids aggressively begging for change; sometimes they are known as "rugby boys" – nothing to do with the sport but a famous brand of glue that they sniff. Many locals refuse to give them money for fear of encouraging dangerous behaviour – others give a few pesos out of pity. If you want to help a good place to start is Street Kids International (⊛ www.streetkids.org), or the Cavite-based Life Child (⊛ www.lifechild.org).

Videoke crazy

Videoke - "video karaoke" - is a major fad in the Philippines, with cheap videoke bars in almost every town and neighbourhood. While it can be fun to participate in a Filipino singing session, being regaled by drunken wailings wafting through your hotel window in the early hours isn't so amusing. Adding to the mix, most Filipino families own one (or more) karaoke machines that are used throughout the week, but especially on special occasions, birthdays and weddings. Incidentally, a Filipino inventor (Roberto del Rosario) actually holds the patent for the karaoke machine.

Philippines, how old you are, whether you are married, if not why not, and so on and so forth. They pride themselves on their hospitality and are always ready to share a meal or a few drinks. Don't offend them by refusing outright.

It's still common for foreign men to be greeted by passers-by with calls of "Hey Joe!" This harks back to the GI Joes of World War II and American occupation.

Filipino time

Why do you never ask a Filipino to do something by the end of the week? He might think you're being pushy. That's an exaggeration of course, but beyond the cities, the old joke still resonates for longtime residents of the Philippines.

In recent years, perhaps due to the number of young Filipinos returning home after an overseas education, the attitude towards punctuality has begun to change. For medical or work-related appointments you'll need to be on time, but for social gatherings turn up half an hour late: it is considered impolite to be on time for a party, for instance, simply because it makes you look like a glutton who wants to grab the food. The speed of service in restaurants in the Philippines has also improved, but you should still expect your patience to occasionally be tested.

Gay and lesbian travellers

Few Filipinos, even the most pious, pay much heed to the Catholic Church regarding homosexuality, and the prevailing attitude is that people can carry on doing what's right for them. **Gay culture** in the Philippines is strong and largely unimpeded by narrow-mindedness, with the possible exceptions of politics and the military, where heterosexuality is still considered correct. Gays are respected as arbiters of fashion and art, and beauty parlours are often staffed by transsexuals.

The word **bakla** is used generically by many Filipinos and visitors to the Philippines to refer to gays, but that would be inaccurate. A *bakla* considers himself a male with a female heart – a *pusong babae*. Most are not interested in a sex-change operation and consider themselves a "third sex", cross-dressing and becoming more "female" than many women. Another category of male homosexual is known as **tunay ne lalake**, men who identify themselves publicly as heterosexual but have sex with other men. Homosexuals who aren't out permeate every stratum of Philippine society; rumours circulate almost daily of this-or-that tycoon or politician who is *tunay ne lalake*.

Lesbians are much more reticent about outing themselves than gay men, no doubt because there is still societal pressure for young women to become the quintessential Filipina lady – gracious, alluring and fulfilled by motherhood and the home (see above). Indeed, some Filipina lesbians complain that the more outspoken **tomboys** – lesbians are often referred to as tomboys – make the fight for women's rights even harder.

The **gay scene** is centred on the bars and clubs of Malate in Manila (see p.98), though there are also smaller scenes in other major cities such as Cebu, Davao and Cagayan de Oro. The websites ⓦ www.utopia-asia.com and www.fridae.com are useful sources of info on local gay life.

Women travellers

Women travellers rarely experience problems in the Philippines, either travelling alone or as part of a group. The culture, however, is a

Prostitution and sex tourism

The Philippines, like some other Southeast Asian countries, has an unfortunate reputation for **prostitution** and **sex tourism**. It's a huge industry domestically with an estimated 800,000 men, women and, sadly, children working in the trade. The country's international image as a sex destination was largely a result of the US military presence here during and after World War II when "go go" or "girlie" bars flourished around the bases at Clark and Subic Bay.

While it's **illegal** to sell or procure sex, the trade still operates under the guise of entertainment: sex workers are employed as singers, dancers, waitresses or "guest relations officers" in clubs and bars where they are expected to leave with any client who pays a fee. Then there's what are euphemistically dubbed "freelancers", prostitutes that independently cruise bars looking for paying customers.

According to the Coalition Against Trafficking in Women (Ⓦwww.catw-ap.org), some fifteen thousand Australian men a year visit Angeles, north of Manila, on **sex tours**; plenty of Americans, Brits and Europeans join them, while Koreans, Taiwanese and Chinese have developed their own networks, usually based on karaoke bars and restaurants. Manila, Cebu City, Subic Bay and Pasay City are also major sex destinations.

Child prostitution

Child Protection in the Philippines (Ⓦwww.childprotection.org.ph) estimates that almost half the prostitutes in the Philippines are **underage**, many of them street children lured from the provinces by the promise of work or simply food and water. If you suspect someone of being a paedophile or engaging in any abusive behaviour towards minors, call **hotline** ☏1-6-3 or check Ⓦwww.bantaybata163.com.

"Mail-order brides"

Though you will often see older Western men accompanied by young, attractive Filipina women, don't assume all of these are prostitutes; the situation is confused further by the legal and equally popular phenomenon of **mail-order brides** (most now arranged by online dating sites) – plenty of the men you'll see have been matched with their Filipina "girlfriend" and intend to marry them, however dubious this might seem.

macho one and, especially in the provinces, foreign women may experience being stared at or the occasional catcall or lewd comment in Tagalog. In the barrios, Filipino men hold dear the oft-regurgitated image of themselves in local movies as gifted romancers, able to reduce any lady to jelly with a few choice words and the wink of an eye.

Reacting to this attention is the worst thing you can do. If you smile and remain good-natured but distant, your potential suitors will get the message and leave you alone. To shout back or to poke fun, particularly if Romeo is with his friends, will cause him serious loss of face and lead to resentment and the possibility that they will try to get back at you.

Modesty is essential to the behaviour of young Filipinas, especially in the provinces, and this should also be the case with visitors. Shorts and T-shirts are fine for women anywhere, but bikinis are only for the beach, and even then, it's considered bad form to wander through a resort's restaurant or souvenir shop without covering up first (a sarong is perfect for this). Topless sunbathing is unheard of among Filipinos, and tourists in popular resorts such as Boracay who remove their clothes are likely to attract an amazed, gossiping crowd of locals. For some Filipino men this reinforces the stereotype that foreign women on holiday are game for anything.

Shopping

The Philippines is a great place to buy indigenous art, woodwork, masks and religious artefacts, mostly at rock-bottom prices. Manila also contains a number of shiny malls with stores offering much the same designer gear you can find in London or New York. The country's two main department-store chains are Rustan's and SM. Both are good for clothes and shoes, at slightly lower prices than in the West; children's clothes are especially inexpensive.

CDs are a bargain in the Philippines, at around P500 apiece for legitimately produced items, though the choice is limited to mainstream Western artists and **OPM** ("original Pilipino music") from local stars. **DVDs** are also cheaper than in the West (P500–950 for legitimate releases), the range limited to Hollywood blockbusters and local movies. Note that **pirated** products are sold in many malls and on the street for a fraction of the price. The best places to buy legitimate releases are in Manila (see p.104); elsewhere it's a case of scouting around in the malls to find local retailers.

Souvenirs

Typical souvenirs include models of jeepneys, wooden salad bowls, cotton linen and small items such as fridge magnets made of coconut shell or carabao horn. In department stores you can find cutlery sets made from carabao horn and bamboo and costing less than P2000. Woven placemats and coasters are inexpensive and easy to pack to take home. Filipino picture frames are eye-catching and affordable. Made from raw materials such as carabao horn and Manila hemp, they are available in most department stores. All towns have **markets** that sell cheap local goods such as sleeping mats (*banig*) that make colourful wall hangings, and earthernware water jars or cooking pots that make attractive additions to a kitchen.

For serious souvenir-hunting, you'll have to rummage around in small **antique shops**. There aren't many of these, and they're often tucked away in low-rent areas. The better shops in big cities are listed in the Guide; elsewhere, ask around at your hotel or look in the local *Yellow Pages* under "Antique dealers". Many of the items in these shops are religious artefacts, although you'll also find furniture, decorative vases, lamps, old paintings, mirrors and brassware.

Some souvenir stores and antique shops will **ship** goods home for you for an extra charge. Otherwise you could send bulky items home by regular post (see p.51). Note that the trade in **coral** and **seashells** as souvenirs in beach areas is decidedly unsound environmentally, as is the manufacture of decorative objects and jewellery from seashells.

Bargaining

Prices are fixed in department stores and most retail outlets in malls, but in many antique shops and in markets, you're expected to haggle. Bargaining is always amicable and relaxed, never confrontational. Filipinos see it as something of a polite game, interjecting their offers and counter offers with friendly chitchat about the weather, the state of the nation or, if you're a foreigner, where you come from and what you're doing in the Philippines.

Never play hardball and make a brusque "take it or leave it" offer because that's likely to cause embarrassment and offence. Start by offering fifty to sixty percent of the initial asking price and work your way up from there. Foreigners tend to get less of a discount than Filipinos, so if you're travelling with Filipino friends, ask them to do the haggling for you and hover in the background as if you're not interested.

Tribal and religious artefacts

Not all tribal and religious artefacts are genuine, but even the imitations make good gifts. **Woven baskets and trays** of the kind used by Cordillera tribes are a bargain, starting from only a few hundred pesos. They come in a range of sizes and shapes, including circular trays woven from grass that are still used to sift rice, and baskets worn like a backpack for carrying provisions. The best are the original tribal baskets, which cost a little more than the reproductions, but have an appealing nut-brown timbre as a result of the many times they have been oiled. You can find them in antique shops around the country and also in markets in Banaue and Sagada.

Some exceptional home accessories and ornaments are produced by tribes in Mindanao, particularly in less touristy areas such as Marawi City and around Lake Sebu. Beautiful **brass jars**, some of them more than a metre tall, cost around P2000, while exquisite **wooden chests** inlaid with mother-of-pearl cost around P3000, inlaid serving trays P500.

Rice gods (*bulol*; see p.104), carved wooden deities sometimes with nightmarish facial expressions, are available largely in Manila and the Cordilleras. In Manila, they cost anything from a few hundred pesos for a small reproduction to P20,000 for a genuine figurine of modest size; they're much

cheaper if you haggle for them in Banaue or Sagada. At markets in the Cordilleras, look out also for wooden bowls, various wooden wall carvings and fabric wall hangings.

The best place to look for **Catholic religious art** is in Manila (see p.104), though antique shops in other towns also have a selection. Wooden Catholic statues called **santos** and large wooden crucifixes are common. Cheaper religious souvenirs such as rosaries and icons of saints are sold by street vendors outside many of the more high-profile pilgrimage cathedrals and churches such as Quiapo in Manila and Santo Niño in Cebu.

Textiles

In market areas such as Divisoria in Manila, Colon in Cebu and the Palitan barter centre in Marawi, Mindanao, you can find colourful raw cloth and finished **batik** products. Don't leave Mindanao without investing a couple of hundred pesos in a **malong**, a versatile tube-like garment of *piña* (pineapple fibre) that can be used as a skirt, housedress, blanket or bedsheet. Ceremonial *malong* are more ornate and expensive, from P4000 to P10,000. Another native textile is **Manila hemp**, which comes from the trunk of a particular type of banana tree. Both *piña* and Manila hemp are used to make attractive home accessories sold in department stores, such as laundry baskets, lampshades and

Sari-sari stores

A Philippine institution, the humble sari-sari store – **sari-sari** means "various" or "a variety" – is often no more than a barrio shack or a hole in the wall selling an eclectic but practical range of goods. If you're short of shampoo, body lotion, cigarettes, rum, beer or you've got a headache and need a painkiller, the local sari-sari store is the answer, especially in areas without supermarkets. All items are sold in the smallest quantities possible: shampoo comes in packets half the size of a credit card, medicine can be bought by the pill and cigarettes are sold individually. Buy a soft drink or beer and you may be perplexed to see the store holder pour it into a plastic bag, from which you're expected to drink it through a straw. This is so they can keep the bottle and return it for the deposit of a few centavos. Most sari-sari stores are fiercely **familial**, their names – the Three Sisters, the Four Brothers or Emily and Jon-Jon's – reflecting their ownership.

The sari-sari store is also held dear by Filipinos as an **unofficial community centre**. Many sari-sari stores, especially in the provinces, have crude sitting areas outside, encouraging folk to linger in the shade and gossip or talk basketball and cockfighting.

vases. The versatile and pliable native grass, **sikat**, is woven into everything from placemats to rugs.

Department stores everywhere have a good selection of Philippine **linen** products with delicate embroidery and lace flourishes. Some of these are handmade in Taal (see p.118); a good set of pillowcases and bedsheets will cost about P2000 in Taal's market, half the price in Rustan's or SM. In beach areas you'll find a good range of cotton **sarongs**, cheap (from P200), colourful and versatile – they can be used as tablecloths or throws.

Jewellery

The malls are full of stalls selling cheap jewellery, but you'll also find silver-plated earrings, replica tribal-style jewellery made with tin or brass, and attractive necklaces made from bone or polished coconut shell. In Mindanao – as well as in some malls in Manila, Cebu City and at souvenir stalls in Boracay – **pearl** jewellery is a bargain. Most of the pearls are cultivated on pearl farms in Mindanao and Palawan. White pearls are the most common, but you can also find pink and dove grey. They are made into earrings, necklaces and bracelets; simple earrings cost around P450 while a necklace can range from P1000 for a single string up to P10,000 for something more elaborate.

Musical instruments

In **Cebu**, and increasingly on the streets of Manila and Davao, you can pick up a locally made handcrafted guitar, *bandurria* (mandolin) or ukelele. Though the acoustic quality is nothing special, the finish may include mother-of-pearl inlays, and prices are low – a steel-string acoustic guitar will set you back P2000. Mindanao's markets – such as Aldevinco in Davao – are a good place to rummage for decorative drums and Muslim gongs.

Travel essentials

Costs

While upmarket resorts in the Philippines can be as expensive as anywhere else in the world, for anyone with modest spending habits and tastes, the country is inexpensive. You can get by on a frugal budget of around **P800** per person (£13/US$20/€15) a day, but you might need to avoid the most popular tourist destinations such as Boracay (or visit during the off-season), and you'll be limited to bare-bones cottages and pokey rooms in basic hotels, usually without air conditioning or hot water. On this budget you'd also have to confine your eating to local restaurants and carinderias, with little leeway for slap-up meals in nice restaurants. You'd also have to plan any flights carefully, only buying the very cheapest tickets online or limiting yourself to buses and ferries. A budget of P1600 (£26/US$40/€30) a day will take your standard of living up a few notches, allowing you to find reasonable beach cottage and hotel rooms and have enough left for modest eating out, drinking and budget flights.

On P3200 (£52/US$80/€60) a day, you can afford to stay in solid, reasonably spacious cottages on the beach, usually with a veranda and air conditioning, and have plenty for domestic flights and good meals in local restaurants.

Crime and personal safety

The Philippines has a reputation as a somewhat dangerous place to travel (at least in the US and UK), but if you exercise discretion and common sense this really isn't the case. Politically the Philippines is a volatile place, with secessionist movements present in Mindanao (see box, p.389) and communist guerrillas active in a number of areas. Insurgency rarely has an impact on tourists, but you should avoid troublespots. Updated travel advisories are available on foreign office or state department websites including Ⓦwww.state.gov in the US and www.fco.gov.uk in the UK.

There are occasional reports of thieves holding up vehicles at traffic lights and removing mobiles and cash from passengers. If you're in a taxi, keep the windows closed and the doors locked, just to be safe. In the Malate area of Manila, the so-called Ativan Gang has used the drug lorazepam (Ativan is one of its proprietary names) to make their victims drowsy or put them to sleep. Several members of the gang were arrested in 2010, but similar cases have been reported in Baguio and Banaue, and it's best to be on your guard if you're approached by people who seem unusually keen to offer you assistance.

Drug laws in the Philippines are stringent and the police are enthusiastic about catching offenders. No one, foreigner or otherwise, caught in possession of hard or recreational drugs is likely to get much sympathy from the authorities. Carrying 500 grams or more of marijuana is deemed to be trafficking and carries the death penalty, while a lesser amount will usually result in a prison sentence. The 24-hour **emergency number** throughout the Philippines is ☏117.

Electricity

Usually 220 volts (similar to Australia, Europe and most of Asia), although you may come across 110 volts in some rural areas – it's best to ask before plugging in appliances. Most cell-phones, cameras, MP3 players and laptops are dual voltage (hair-dryers are the biggest problem for North American travellers). Plugs have two flat, rectangular pins (same as the US and Canada). Power cuts (known locally as "brownouts") are common, especially in the provinces. If you are worried about using valuable electrical equipment in the Philippines – a laptop computer, for instance – you should plug it into an automatic voltage regulator (AVR), a small appliance that ensures the voltage remains constant even if there is a sudden fluctuation or surge in the mains.

Entry requirements

Most tourists do not need a visa to enter the Philippines for up to 21 days, though a passport valid for at least six months and an onward plane or ship ticket to another country are required.

You can apply for a 59-day **visa** from a Philippine embassy or consulate before you travel. A single-entry visa, valid for three months from the date of issue, costs around US$40, and a multiple-entry visa, valid for one year from the date of issue, around US$90. Apart from a valid passport and a completed application form (downloadable from some Philippine embassy websites) you will have to present proof that you have enough money for the duration of your stay in the Philippines.

Your 21-day visa can be **extended** by 38 days (giving a total stay of 59 days) at immigration offices (see relevant chapters). The charge for this is around P2000, and you may be asked if you want to pay a P500 Express fee that is supposed to guarantee the application is dealt with within 24 hours. If you don't pay the fee, the process can take at least a week. Note that it pays to be presentably dressed at immigration offices, as staff might refuse to serve you if you turn up wearing a vest, shorts or flip-flops.

Many travel agents in tourist areas such as Malate in Manila and Boracay offer a **visa extension service**, saving you the hassle of visiting immigration centres. Whatever you do, don't be tempted to use one of the fixers that hang around immigration offices, particularly in Manila. The "visa" they get you is often a dud and you run the risk of being detained and fined when you try to leave the country.

Customs

Visitors are allowed to bring in four hundred cigarettes, two tins of tobacco and two bottles of wine and spirits not exceeding one litre. If you arrive with more than US$10,000 (unlikely) in **cash** you are meant to declare it, and you won't be allowed to take out more than this sum in foreign currency on leaving. Note that not more than P10,000 in local currency may be taken out of the country, though this is rarely, if ever, enforced.

Philippine embassies and consulates

For a full list of the Philippines' embassies and consulates, check the government's Department of Foreign Affairs website at Ⓦ www.dfa.gov.ph.

Australia 1 Moonah Placa, Yarralumla, Canberra ACT ☏ 612/6273 2535, Ⓦ www.philembassy.org.au.
Canada Suite 606, 130 Albert St, Ottawa ☏ 613/233-1121, Ⓦ philippineembassy.ca; 161 Eglinton Ave East, Suite 800, Toronto, Ontario ☏ 416/922-7181, Ⓦ www.philcongen-toronto.com.
New Zealand 50 Hobdon St, Thorndon, Wellington ☏ 644/472 9848, Ⓦ www.philembassy.org.nz.
UK 6–8 Suffolk St, London W8 4QE ☏ 020/7451 1800, Ⓦ www.philembassy-uk.org.
US 1600 Massachusetts Ave, NW, Washington DC ☏ 202/467-9300, Ⓦ www.philippineembassy-usa .org.

Insurance

A typical travel insurance policy usually provides cover for the loss of baggage, tickets and cash or cheques, as well as cancellation or curtailment of your journey. When securing baggage cover, make sure that the per-article limit will cover your most valuable possession. Most policies exclude so-called dangerous sports unless an extra premium is paid: in the Philippines this can mean scuba diving, whitewater rafting, windsurfing, trekking and kayaking.

If you need to make a **claim**, you should keep receipts for medicines and medical treatment, and in the event you have anything stolen, you must obtain an official statement from the police. In the Philippines this is sometimes a slow process that involves the police officer copying, by hand, the details of your loss into what is known as the police "blotter", or file. Once this has been signed by a superior officer you'll get an authorized copy.

Internet

Major cities have dozens of **internet cafés** and even in small towns and isolated resort areas you can usually find somewhere to log on and send email; wi-fi is becoming more common in cafés and hotels throughout the country. The cost of getting online at an internet café starts at around P40–60 per hour in the cities, while in the provinces it can be as cheap as P15–20 per hour.

Laundry

There are no coin-operated launderettes in the Philippines, but there are laundries all over the place offering serviced washes for about P150 for an average load. Most of these places will iron clothes for you for an extra charge. It's also possible to get clothes washed at pretty much any guesthouse, resort or hotel.

Living and working in the Philippines

Opportunities to work in the Philippines are limited. Most jobs require specialist qualifications or experience and, unlike other parts of Asia, there's no market for teaching English as a foreign language. One possibility is to work for a diving outfit as a dive master or instructor. Rates of pay are low, but board and lodging may be provided if you work for a good operator or resort in a busy area (Boracay or Puerto Galera, for instance). For more on learning to dive, see p.38. Some international organizations also offer

Rough Guides travel insurance

Rough Guides has teamed up with WorldNomads.com to offer great **travel insurance** deals. Policies are available to residents of over 150 countries, with cover for a wide range of **adventure sports**, 24hr emergency assistance, high levels of medical and evacuation cover and a stream of **travel safety information**. Roughguides.com users can take advantage of their policies online 24/7, from anywhere in the world – even if you're already travelling. And since plans often change when you're on the road, you can extend your policy and even claim online. Roughguides.com users who buy travel insurance with WorldNomads.com can also leave a positive footprint and donate to a community development project. For more information go to Ⓦ **www.roughguides.com/shop**.

voluntary placements in the Philippines (see contacts below).

Study opportunities are also limited. There are a number of language schools, mostly in Manila, where you can learn **Tagalog**; one of the biggest is Languages Internationale at 926 Arnaiz Ave in Makati (T02/810-7971, W www.languagesintl.com).

Useful resources

UK

Coral Cay Conservation T020/8545 7710, W www.coralcay.org. Nonprofit organization that trains volunteers to collect scientific data to aid conservation in sensitive environments around the world, particularly coral reefs and tropical forests. At the time of writing marine expeditions were offered in southern Leyte.
VSO (Voluntary Service Overseas) T020/8780 7200, W www.vso.org.uk. Charity that sends qualified professionals to work on projects beneficial to developing countries. In the Philippines, VSO has a small number of volunteers working within the fields of sustainable agriculture and aquaculture, or with displaced communities in Mindanao.

US

Peace Corps T1-800/424-8580, W www .peacecorps.gov. Places people with specialist qualifications or skills in two-year postings in many developing countries, including the Philippines.

Australia

Australian Volunteers International T03/9279 1788, W www.australianvolunteers.com. Short-and long-term postings for professionals interested in working in the developing world. Volunteers in the Philippines have helped introduce sustainable fishing and marine conservation programmes and campaigned for the rights of minority groups.

Mail and couriers

Airmail letters from the Philippines (W philpost.gov.ph) take at least five days to reach other countries, though in many cases it's a lot longer. Postcards cost P13 while letters up to 20 grams cost P30 to P45 depending on the destination. Ordinary domestic mail costs P20 for letters up to 20 grams. **Post offices** are open from 9am to 5pm, Monday to Friday.

If you have to post anything valuable, use registered mail or pay extra for a **courier**. DHL

(W www.dhl.com.ph), Fedex (W www.fedex .com.ph), and the locally based LBC (W www .lbcexpress.com) and 2Go (W www.2go.com .ph) have offices throughout the country, listed on their websites, and can deliver stuff internationally. Sending documents overseas this way will cost from around P1000 (US and Australia) to P2000 (UK) and take two to three working days.

Maps

The best **maps** of the Philippines are in this book, but many smaller towns and cities in the Philippines haven't been mapped at all. The best map the Philippine Department of Tourism (DoT) offers locally is the free *Tourist Map of the Philippines*, which includes a street map of Manila, contact numbers for all overseas and domestic DoT offices and listings of hotels, embassies and bus companies. Road maps and country maps can be bought at branches of the National Book Store in all major cities and towns, although supply is unreliable.

Many bookshops sell the Accu-map range of **atlases** (W www.accu-map.com), A to Z-like pocketbooks that cover the whole of Metro Manila and detailed maps that cover Baguio, Subic Bay, Cavite, Angeles City, Puerto Galera, Boracay and other destinations. United Tourist Promotions publishes a range of decent maps called **EZ Map**, covering Manila and the country's regions, with each sheet featuring a combination of area and town maps.

If you want to seek out Philippines maps at home, you'll probably only find maps of Manila and Cebu City, in addition to country maps. **Nelles Verlag** (W www.nelles-verlag .de) publishes two good maps – a country map with a scale of 1:1,500,000 and a Manila city map. They are sometimes available in Manila bookshops, but can be hard to track down. The 1:1,750,000 **Hema** map (W www.hemamaps.com.au) of the Philippines is another to look out for before you arrive.

For a more varied selection of **area maps** and **sea charts** of the Philippines, try the National Mapping and Resources Information Authority (T02/810-5466, W www .namria.gov.ph) in Lawton Avenue, Fort Bonifacio, 10 minutes by taxi from Makati.

Money

The Philippine currency is the peso. One peso is divided into 100 centavos, with notes in denominations of P20, 50, 100, 200, 500 and 1000. Coins come in values of 25 centavos, P1, P5 and P10. At the time of writing the exchange rate was around P43 to US$1, P67 to £1 and a little less than P58 to the euro.

It's best to arrive with some local currency. Otherwise you can easily withdraw cash at **ATMs** found in cities and tourist destinations all over the country, but not in less visited areas such as the interior of Mindanao, the northern mountains, areas of Palawan outside Puerto Princesa and Coron Town, and in remote parts of the Visayas. It's best to use ATMs at major banks, and preferably in big cities, because these machines tend to be more reliable than provincial ones, which are often "offline" – because there's no cash in them, the computer has crashed or a power cut has affected their operation. **Credit cards** are accepted by most hotels and restaurants in cities and tourist areas, though the smaller hotels may levy a surcharge if you pay by card.

Travellers' cheques are safer to carry than cash, though note that you can only change them at a limited number of banks in Manila and in a few tourist haunts such as Malate and Boracay. It's best to bring US-dollar denominations from the major issuers – Thomas Cook, Visa or American Express.

Banks are normally open from 9am to 3pm, Monday to Friday and all major branches have ATMs and currency exchange. The best established local banks include **BPI** (Bank of the Philippine Islands), **DBP** (Development Bank of the Philippines), **Metrobank** and **Equitable PCI**; Citibank and HSBC also have branches in major cities. Most banks only change **US dollars**, and though many hotels will change other currencies, they offer poor rates. It's easy to change dollars in Manila, where there are dozens of small **moneychangers' kiosks** in Malate and P. Burgos Street, Makati, offering better rates than the banks; ask around at a few places and compare. In rural areas there are few moneychangers and banks don't always change money, so if you're heading off the beaten track, be sure to take enough pesos to last the trip.

Opening hours and public holidays

Most government offices are open Monday to Friday from 8.30am to 5.30pm, but some close for an hour-long lunch break, usually starting at noon, so it's best to avoid the middle of the day. Businesses generally keep the same hours, with some also open on Saturday from 9am until noon. Banks are open Monday to Friday from 9am to 3pm and do not close for lunch, except for some of the smallest branches in rural areas. Shops in major malls open daily from 10am until 8pm or 9pm, later during the Christmas rush or "Midnight Madness" sales; the latter take place every two weeks, on the first Friday after each pay day. Churches are almost always open most of the day for worshippers and tourists alike. Typically, the first Mass of the day is at around 6am, the last at 6pm or 7pm.

Government offices and private businesses close on **public holidays**, though shops and most restaurants remain open except on Good Friday and Christmas Day. Holidays are often moved to the closest

---

Public holidays

January 1 New Year's Day

February 25 Anniversary of the EDSA revolution

March/April (variable) Maundy Thursday, Good Friday

April 9 Bataan Day

May 1 Labor Day

June 12 Independence Day

August 21 Ninoy Aquino Day

August 29 National Heroes Day

August (31 August in 2011, 19 August in 2012 and 9 August in 2013) Eid 'l Fitr, the end of Ramadan

November 1 All Saints' Day (see box, p.37)

December 25 Christmas Day; the following day is also a holiday

December 30 Rizal Day, in honour of José Rizal (see p.427)

Friday or Monday to their original date (given below), so that people in the cities can use the long weekend to get back to the provinces to spend a few days with their families. This moving of public holidays is done on an ad hoc basis and is announced in the press just a few weeks – sometimes only a few days – beforehand.

Phones

The Philippines has embraced the **mobile-phone** age with vigour, partly because sending text messages is cheap and because mobile networks provide coverage in areas where landlines are limited. If you want to use a cellular phone bought abroad in the Philippines, you'll need a **GSM/Triband** phone and to have global roaming activated. Ask your service provider what the charges are for making and receiving calls when abroad. For local calls it will probably work out cheaper to buy a local **SIM card**, available at dozens of mobile-phone outlets in malls for any of the country's four mobile networks: Smart Communications, Globe Telecom, Talk 'N Text and Sun Cellular. Local SIMs start at just P55–200 and you can top up your credit for P100 to P500. Note that your phone must be "unlocked" to use a foreign SIM card (this can be done at local electronics shops). Standard-rate domestic calls from mobiles cost from P6.50–7.50 a minute (US$0.40 per minute for international calls); there are no charges for receiving calls. There are card outlets and dispensing machines in malls and convenience stores and at airports.

Basic mobiles in the Philippines are inexpensive, starting at less than P3000, so it can be worth buying one if you plan to stay for any length of time. Unless you have a permanent address in the country for home billing, you'll be funding your calls with prepaid cards.

Time

The Philippines is eight hours ahead of Universal Time (GMT) all year round.

Tipping

Keep your purse or wallet well stocked with P10 coins and P20 notes for tips. In cafés, bars and hotel coffee shops many Filipinos

Useful numbers and codes

☏ **117** Emergency
☏ **108** International operator
☏ **109** Assistance with long-distance domestic calls
☏ **114** or **187** Nationwide directory assistance

Calling abroad from the Philippines

To make an IDD call, dial ☏ 00, then the relevant country code, area or city code and then the number. Note that the initial zero is omitted from the area code when dialling to the UK, Ireland, Australia and New Zealand from abroad.

Australia 61
New Zealand 64
Republic of Ireland 353
UK 44
USA and Canada 1
South Africa 27

Calling the Philippines from abroad

Dial your international access code, then 63 for the Philippines, then the number.

simply leave whatever coins they get in their change. For good service in restaurants and bars you should leave a tip of about ten percent. In more expensive restaurants where the bill could be a couple of thousand pesos, it's okay to leave a somewhat smaller tip in percentage terms – P100 is a reasonable amount. Bellhops and porters get about P20 each and taxi drivers usually expect to keep the loose change.

Tourist information

The Philippine Department of Tourism (DoT; ⓦwww.wowphilippines.com.ph and www .tourism.gov.ph) has a small number of **overseas offices** where you can pick up glossy brochures and get answers to general pre-trip questions about destinations, major hotels and domestic travel. These offices are not so helpful, however, when it comes to information about places off the beaten track. The DoT has offices throughout the Philippines, but most of them have small budgets and very little in the way of reliable information or brochures. The best source of up-to-date information on travelling in the Philippines is guesthouses and hotels that cater to travellers, most of which have notice boards where you can swap tips and ideas.

Travelling with children

Filipinos are extravagant in their generosity towards children, but because so much of the country lacks infrastructure, specific attractions for them are often hard to find. Major hotels in big cities such as Manila and Cebu City have playrooms and babysitting services, but even in popular tourist destinations such as Boracay there are few special provisions in all but the most expensive resorts.

This doesn't mean travelling with children in the Philippines is a nightmare – far from it. Filipinos are very tolerant of children so you can take them almost anywhere without restriction, and children help to break the ice with strangers. They'll be fussed over, befriended and looked after every step of the way.

Supermarkets in towns and cities throughout the Philippines have well-stocked children's sections that sell fresh and formula milk, nappies and baby food. Department stores such as Rustan's and SM sell baby clothes, bottles, sterilizing equipment and toys. And travelling with children in the Philippines needn't be a burden on your **budget**. Domestic airlines give a discount of around fifty percent for children under twelve and hotels and resorts offer family rooms, extra beds for a minimal charge, or don't charge at all for a small child sharing the parents' bed. Most restaurants with buffet spreads will let a small child eat for free if he or she is simply taking nibbles from a parent's plate. Try asking for a special portion – the staff are usually happy to oblige.

One potential problem for young ones is the torpid **climate**. You'll need to go to extra lengths to protect them from the sun and to make sure they are hydrated. A hat

and good sunblock are essential. If your child requires **medical attention** in the Philippines, there are good paediatricians at most major hospitals, in five-star hotels and many resorts.

Travellers with disabilities

Facilities for the disabled are rare except in the major cities. Taxis are cramped, while bangkas are notoriously tricky even for the able-bodied. For wheelchair users the pavements represent a serious obstacle in themselves. Often dilapidated and potholed, they are frustrating at the best of times and simply impassable at the worst, when pedestrians are forced to pick their way along the gutter in the road, dodging cars and motorcycles.

In Manila, Cebu City, Davao and some other big cities, the most upmarket hotels cater to the disabled and so do malls, cinemas and restaurants. Elsewhere, the good news for disabled travellers is that Filipinos are generous when it comes to offering assistance. Even in the remotest barrio, people will go out of their way to help you board a boat or lift you up the stairs of a rickety pier. Of course once you're on board a ferry, for example, ramps and disabled toilets are likely to be nonexistent.

The government agency the **National Council on Disability Affairs or NCDA** (☎02/951-6033, ⓦwww.ncda.gov.ph) is mandated to formulate policies and coordinate the activities of all agencies concerning disability issues, but it doesn't have much practical advice for disabled travellers. Staff at the group's Quezon City office can give general pointers on transport and where to stay.

More useful are local websites such as **Cebu on Wheels** (ⓦwww.cebuonwheels .com.ph), and **Handi Divers** (ⓦwww.handi divers.com) of Alona Beach (Panglao Island, Bohol), which specializes in scuba diving for disabled travellers.

Guide

Guide

1

Manila

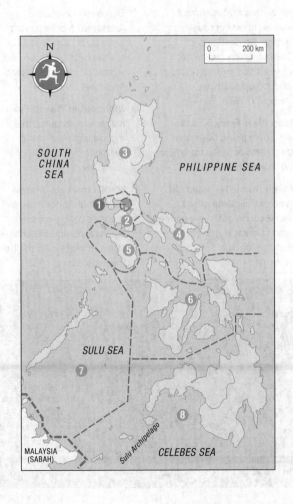

CHAPTER 1 # Highlights

✻ **Intramuros** The atmospheric old Spanish city, with cobbled streets, the elegant San Agustin Church and poignant Rizal Shrine inside Fort Santiago. See p.74

✻ **The National Museums** Two neighbouring museums housing the paintings of Filipino masters, relics from sunken ships and fascinating anthropology displays. See pp.77–78

✻ **Pasig River Ferry** Beat the traffic by cruising down the Pasig River between Intramuros and Makati. See p.78

✻ **Manila Hotel** The grand old dame of Philippine hotels. Even if you're not staying here, come to enjoy a drink in the sparkling lobby. See p.79

✻ **Ayala Museum** One of the best museums in the Philippines, an enlightening and innovative introduction to the history of the islands. See p.89

✻ **Barbecue chicken at Aristocrat** Manila's most famous restaurant still knocks out the best barbecue, along with a full roster of Filipino favourites. See p.93

✻ **Night out in Makati** From megaclubs to pubs, there's a good night out to suit everyone in Makati. See p.99

✻ **Manila markets** Whether you're looking for native crafts or pearl jewellery, Manila's vibrant and chaotic street markets offer the best bargains. See p.105

▲ Makati district, Manila

Manila

I f you like big cities you'll love **MANILA**: it's a high-speed, frenetic place, where you can eat, drink and shop 24 hours a day and where the Filipino heritage of native, Spanish, Chinese and American cultures are at their most mixed up. Like many capital cities, Manila bears little resemblance to the rest of the country – something to remember if this is your first taste of the Philippines. With 12 million residents, much of it is chronically overcrowded, polluted and suffers from appalling traffic jams, yet in between the chaos lie tranquil gate-guarded "subdivisions" that resemble affluent parts of the US. There's extreme poverty here, with young children cleaning car windows, dancing or just begging for food at every interchange; while in enormous shopping malls thousands of wealthy, middle-class Manileños are as fashionable and hooked up with iPhones as any of their contemporaries in London or New York. And while the older parts of the city remain shabby and run-down, sparkling districts like Makati, Ortigas and Fort Bonifacio are smart and skyscraper-smothered, like any other booming Asian metropolis.

Technically sixteen cities and one municipality make up what is officially known as **Metro Manila** covering a vast 636 square kilometres. However, you can explore the key sights in and around **Intramuros**, the city's only notable historical enclave, Manila Bay and Makati in a few days. Manila also prides itself on the quality of its restaurant scene, **nightlife** and the ability of its residents to whip up a good time. For many tourists, this will be their enduring memory of the place: fabulous food, funky bars and nightclubs in areas such as Malate and Makati. And don't forget, Manila is still a great place to pick up bargains, from the latest goods cranked out by Chinese factories to intricate native handicrafts.

Some history

Manila started life as a tiny Tagalog settlement called **Maynila**; after coming under the sway of the Sultanate of Brunei in the fifteenth century the area was converted to Islam. The village fell under **Spanish rule** in 1571 when Miguel López de Legazpi defeated the local ruler Rajah Sulaiman II and established the colony of Manila. Spanish Augustinian and Franciscan **missionaries** subsequently established themselves in villages around the city. The Jesuits arrived in 1581 and set up more missions, forming outlying centres of population – embryonic settlements that became the sixteen cities of today. Manila's central location on the biggest island, Luzon, made it the obvious choice as the **colonial capital**, and it became the hub from which the Spaniards effected the political, cultural and religious transformation of Philippine society. From 1571 until 1815, while the rest of the country remained economically stagnant, Manila prospered from the **galleon trade**.

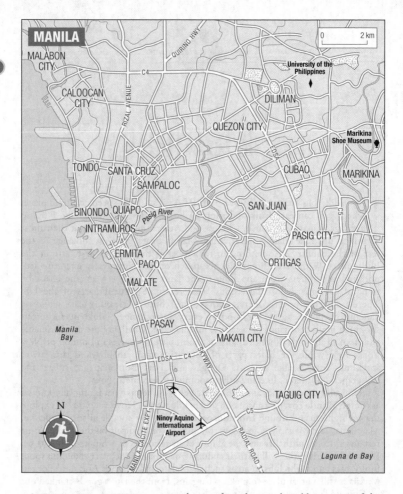

At 7pm on June 3, 1863, a catastrophic **earthquake** struck and large areas of the city crumbled, burying hundreds in the ruins. The new Manila that grew in its stead was thoroughly modern, with streetcars, steam trains and American-style public architecture, a trend that continued under American rule in the early twentieth century.

Manila suffered again during World War II. The **Japanese Imperial Army** occupied Manila from 1942 until it was liberated by the US at the **Battle of Manila** in 1945. The battle lasted 29 days and claimed 1000 American lives, 16,000 Japanese soldiers and some 100,000 Filipinos, many of them civilians killed deliberately by the Japanese or accidentally by crossfire. Once again, Manila was a city in ruins, having undergone relentless shelling from American howitzers and been set alight by retreating Japanese troops. **Rebuilding** was slow and plagued by corruption and government inertia.

In 1976, realizing that Manila was growing too rapidly for government to be contained in the old Manila area, President Marcos decreed that while the area around Intramuros would remain the capital city, the permanent seat of the national government would be Metro Manila – including new areas such as Makati and Quezon City. It was tacit recognition of the city's expansion and the problems it was bringing. **Imelda Marcos**, meanwhile, had been declared governor of Metro Manila in 1975 and was busy exercising her "edifice complex", building a golden-domed mosque in Quiapo, the Cultural Center of the Philippines on Manila Bay and a number of five-star hotels. Her spending spree was finally ended by the EDSA revolution in 1986 (p.432).

In the 1990s popular police officer Alfredo Lim won two terms as Manila mayor – his crime-fighting efforts certainly improved security in the city and he was elected a third time in 2007. He immediately and controversially set about undoing much of the work of his predecessor Lito Atienza (mayor 1998–2007), who had spent millions on city beautification projects. Though congestion and pollution remain huge and apparently intractable problems, Lim has presided over a booming economy, managed to remove squatters in Quiapo and has cleaned up the Baywalk area along Roxas Boulevard. Manileños rewarded him with a fourth term as mayor in May 2010, just months before the Manila bus hostage crisis, when a dismissed police officer hijacked a bus of Hong Kong tourists, eventually killing eight of them; the mayor's handling of the tragedy was highly criticized in the subsequent enquiry.

Arrival

Almost everyone visiting the Philippines arrives at **Ninoy Aquino International Airport** (T 02/833-1180, W www.manila-airport.net) or NAIA, named after the anti-Marcos politician who was assassinated here in 1983, on the southern fringes of Manila. The airport has four separate and unconnected terminals, making it seem, confusingly, as if there are several different airports (you may hear locals refer to them this way). Most international flights arrive at Terminal 1; Terminal 2, relatively nearby, serves only Philippine Airlines (international and domestic); the tiny Domestic Passenger Airport Terminal is 3km away on the other side of the airport and serves Zest Airways and Seair flights; further around is Terminal 3, serving Cebu Pacific and Airphil Express (international and domestic). A free shuttle bus connects all the terminals, running frequently throughout the day, but traffic congestion means transfers can take over one hour in some cases – leave plenty of time. Remember that if you are connecting to a domestic flight, you'll need to pay P200 departure tax. Note also that there is a long-standing plan to transfer all international flights to Terminal 3 – this may finally take place in 2012.

Terminal 1 has a small **Department of Tourism** reception desk (T 02/832-2964), open to meet all flights, where you can pick up maps and current information. There are **banks** and ATMs at all terminals (BPI is just outside the domestic terminal).

Airport transportation

The roads around the airport quickly become gridlocked in heavy rain or at rush hour; it can take anything from twenty minutes to one hour to travel the 7km to the main tourist and budget accommodation area of Manila Bay. To head into the centre, the best thing to do is to take an official yellow **airport taxi**; these charge higher rates than normal white taxis but they still use the meter (insist on the meter). The meter starts at P70 (for the first 500m) and adds P4 per 300m; reckon on P150–250 to Malate or Makati and P250–300 for Ermita, depending on traffic. The alternative is to take a fixed-rate taxi (you get tickets for these at desks outside the terminal), but these are expensive unless you have a large group (the "taxis" are big Toyota vans); the fixed-rate fare is P440 to Malate, P530 to Ermita, P330–440

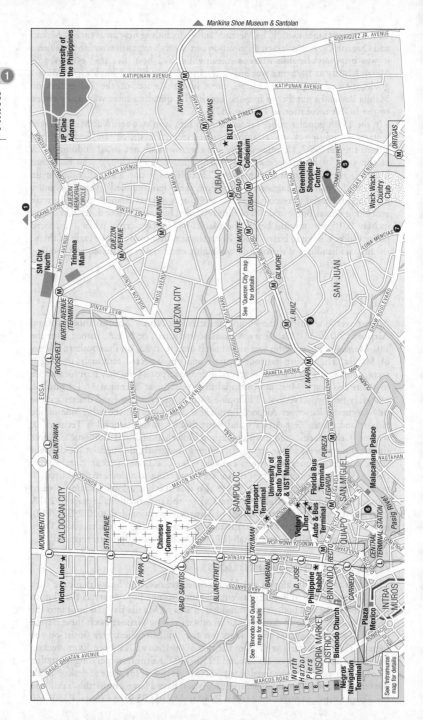

▲ Marikina Shoe Museum & Santolan

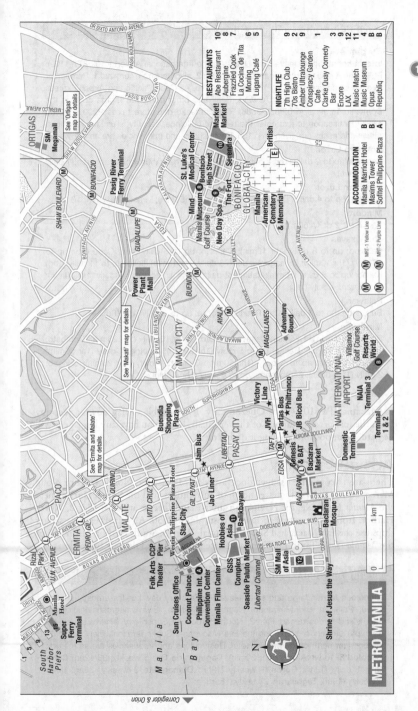

MANILA

RESTAURANTS
Abe Restaurant	10
Aubergine	8
Frazzled Cook	7
La Cocina de Tita Moning	6
Lugang Café	5

NIGHTLIFE
7th High Club	9
70s Bistro	2
Amber Ultralounge	9
Conspiracy Garden Cafe	1
Clarke Quay Comedy Bar	3
Encore	9
LAX	12
Music Match	11
Music Museum	4
Opus	B
Republiq	B

ACCOMMODATION
Manila Marriott Hotel	B
Maxims Tower	B
Sofitel Philippine Plaza	A

(M)—(M) MRT-1 Yellow Line
(M)—(M) MRT-2 Purple Line

METRO MANILA

0 ———— 1 km

N

Manila Bay

South Harbor Piers

▲ *Corregidor & Orion*

Moving on from Manila by air

By plane

International flights leave from Ninoy Aquino International Airport (☎02/877-1109); Philippine Airlines flights depart from Terminal 2, all others from Terminal 1. Remember to save some cash for the P750 departure fee. All Cebu Pacific and Airphil Express flights use Terminal 3; Zest Airways, Seair and other **domestic flights** go from the Domestic Terminal (☎02/832-3566). The domestic departure tax is P200 and you need identification to just enter the terminal buildings; security is usually very tight. Airline addresses are given on p.105. Destinations and frequencies are as follows:

Northern Luzon
Batanes: up to 2 daily (1hr 45min); Laoag: up to 3 daily (50min); Tuguegarao: 1 daily (1hr 15min).

Southern Luzon
Legazpi: up to 4 daily (1hr 10min); Naga: 1 daily (55min); Virac: 1 daily (1hr 10min).

Mindoro
San José: 2 daily (50min).

The Visayas
Bacolod: up to 8 daily (1hr 10min); Caticlan: up to 8 daily (1hr); Cebu City: up to 16 daily (1hr 10min); Dumaguete: up to 5 daily (1hr 15min); Iloilo: up to 11 daily (1hr); Kalibo: up to 6 daily (50min); Tablas: 2 daily (40min); Tacloban: 5 daily (1hr 10min); Tagbilaran: 4 daily (2hr).

Palawan
Busuanga: up to 3 daily (1hr); Puerto Princesa: up to 5 daily (1hr 10min).

Mindanao
Butuan: 1 daily (1hr 25min); Cagayan de Oro: up to 10 daily (1hr 25min); Cotabato: 1 daily (1hr 35min); Davao: up to 5 daily (1hr 50min); Dipolog: 1 daily (1hr 30min); General Santos: up to 3 daily (1hr 50min); Ozamiz: 1 daily (1hr 25min); Surigao: 2 daily (1hr 40min); Zamboanga: up to 4 daily (1hr 40min).

to Makati and P610–940 to Quezon City. It is possible to flag down a **jeepney** from the main roads near any of the terminals, but if you have any luggage it will be hard (or impossible) to drag it on board.

Arrival by ferry

There are two main passenger dock areas in Manila, the **North Harbor** along Marcos Road, a few kilometres north of Intramuros, and the **South Harbor** near the *Manila Hotel*. Negros Navigation inter-island **ferries** arrive at Pier 2, North Harbor, from where a taxi to Ermita costs about P150. All SuperFerry passenger ships use the Eva Macapagal Super Terminal, Pier 15, South Harbor, just north of the *Manila Hotel*. Taxis into Ermita/Malate from here should be P100 or less.

Moving on from Manila by ferry

Numerous **ferries** large and small leave Manila every day, but they mostly service Cebu, Palawan and Mindanao. Negros Navigation (🌐www.negrosnavigation.ph) inter-island ferries depart Pier 2, North Harbor. All SuperFerry (🌐www.superferry.com.ph) passenger ships use the Eva Macapagal Super Terminal, Pier 15, South Harbor, just north of the *Manila Hotel*. Destinations and frequencies are as follows: **Bacolod** 8–10 weekly (7hr/9hr 30min); **Cagayan de Oro** 5 weekly (33/42hr); **Cebu City** 1 daily (12hr); **Coron** 1 weekly (12hr); **Dumaguete** 3 weekly (36hr); **Iloilo** 6 weekly (19hr); **Tagbilaran** 1 weekly (18hr).

Arrival by bus

Dozens of buses serve Manila from the provinces. As a general rule, if you're arriving from the south, you'll end up in the **Pasay** area of EDSA, in the south of the city near Taft Avenue, while if you're arriving from the north you'll find yourself at the northern end of EDSA in **Cubao** (Quezon City). From Pasay you can take the LRT (see p.68) north to the Malate area (get off at Pedro Gil station) or the MRT (see p.68) northeast to Makati and beyond. A taxi from the Pasay area to Malate costs less than P100. From most bus stations in Cubao it's a short walk to the Cubao MRT station; a taxi from Cubao to Makati costs around P150. The "Moving on from Manila" box, pp.66–67, gives details of the various bus operators and terminals.

Orientation

The key tourist district is the area fronting **Manila Bay** along **Roxas Boulevard**, taking in the neighbourhoods of **Ermita** and **Malate**, and stretching north to the old walled city of **Intramuros** and over the Pasig River to **Chinatown**, also known as **Binondo**. **Makati**, 8km southeast of Manila Bay, is the city's central business district, built around the main thoroughfare of Ayala Avenue, and home to banks, insurance companies and five-star hotels. Just to the east of Makati (and almost an extension of it), lies the city's newest business and retail hub, **Fort Bonifacio**. The artery of Epifaño de los Santos Avenue, or **EDSA**, curves east of Makati stretching from Pasay in the south to Caloocan in the north. Up EDSA and beyond Makati is the commercial district of **Ortigas**, which is trying to outdo Makati with its hotels, malls and air-conditioned, themed restaurants. Beyond that is **Quezon City**, which is off the beaten track for most visitors, though it has some lively nightlife catering to students of the nearby University of the Philippines.

Information

The **Department of Tourism** is in Room 106 of the Department of Tourism Building, T.M. Kalaw Street, Ermita (daily 7am–6pm; ℡02/523-8411 ext 146, ℡02/525-2000 or 02/524-2384, ⓦwww.wowphilippines.com.ph), at the northern end of Rizal Park close to Taft Avenue. The entrance is not at the front beneath the grand Doric columns, but through a double door at the rear, where a guard will ask you to sign a visitors' book. Staff are helpful, but resources are thin on the ground.

Many bookshops (see p.103) sell the Accu-map range of **atlases** (ⓦwww .accu-map.com), A to Z-like pocketbooks that cover the whole of Metro Manila. Daily newspapers such as the *Philippine Daily Inquirer* (ⓦwww.inquirer.net) and the *Philippine Star* (ⓦwww.philstar.com) have entertainment sections with details of movies, concerts and arts events in Manila. Online, ClickTheCity (ⓦwww .clickthecity.com) has an events calendar, movie and gig guides and listings of restaurants and hotels.

City transport

There are so many vehicles fighting for every inch of road space in Manila that at peak times it can be a sweaty battle of nerves just to move a few hundred metres. **Walking** is usually out of the question, except for short distances, because **buses**

Moving on from Manila by bus

Leaving Manila by bus is confusing as there's no central bus terminal. Each company has its own station, but most of these are clumped together in two areas: along EDSA in Cubao, Quezon City, and EDSA around Taft Avenue MRT station in Pasay. Both areas are easily accessed via MRT/LRT trains. Often, if you tell your taxi driver your destination, they will bring you to the right station.

Baguio
Cable Tours 276 Rodriguez Ave, Quezon City ☎02/257-3582. Nightly (6–8hr).

Dagupan New York St, Cubao, Quezon City ☎02/727-2330. During the day (6–8hr).

Genesis EDSA, corner Taft, Pasay ☎02/853-3115. Hourly 11am–8pm (6–8hr).

Philippine Rabbit Rizal Ave, corner Recto ☎02/734-9836. Destinations north including Baguio (6–8hr).

Victory Liner Five terminals: Rizal Ave, Caloocan ☎02/361-1506 to 1510; EDSA, Pasay ☎02/833-5019; EDSA, Cubao ☎02/727-4534; EDSA, Quezon City ☎02/921-3296; and 551 Earnshaw Ave, a short walk from Legarda LRT station; ⊛www .victoryliner.com. Regular buses to Baguio (6–8hr).

Bataan, Bulacan and Pampanga
Baliwag Transit EDSA corner New York St, Quezon City ☎02/912-3343. Buses north to Bulacan province including Baliwag and San José.

Victory Liner See Baguio entry for terminal details. Buses to Mariveles (4hr).

Batangas and Tagaytay
Alps Transit Araneta Center Bus Terminal, Cubao and Pasay (EDSA) ☎02/911-2186, ⊛www.alpsthebus.com. Operates a useful bus service that departs every thirty minutes to the ferry terminal in Batangas City (2–3hr) and Lipa (for Taal).

Batman Star Express (BSC), EDSA, corner Taft, Pasay. Buses to Tagaytay (2hr) and Nasugbu (3hr).

Jac Liner Taft Ave and Sen Gil Puyat, Pasay City ☎02/831-8977, ⊛jacliner.com. Every thirty minutes to Lucena (via Alimos) and Lemery in Batangas. Also has a terminal at EDSA, Cubao.

JAM Transit Taft Ave at Sen Gil Puyat, Pasay ☎02/520-8734; with a second terminal near the corner of Timog Ave in Cubao. To various destinations in Batangas.

Clark/Angeles City
Partas 816 Aurora Blvd at EDSA ☎02/851-4025. Daily to Clark Airport (2hr), 6am, 10am, noon, 4pm.

Swagman Travel *Swagman Hotel Manila*, 411 A. Flores St, Ermita ☎02/523-8541 or 045/322-2890, ⊛www.swaggy.com. Runs small buses to Angeles City; daily 11.30am, 3.30pm and 8.30pm (2hr).

Victory Liner See Baguio entry for terminal details. All five terminals serve destinations north of Manila, including Dau (for Clark; 2hr).

La Cordillera and Banaue
Autobus Cayco and Valencia sts, Sampaloc ☎02/493-4111. Direct to Banaue (7–9hr).

Cable Tours 276 Rodriguez Ave, Quezon City ☎02/257-3582. Nightly to Bontoc (7–9hr).

GV Florida Transport Corner Extremadura and Earnshaw sts, Sampaloc ☎02/731-5358 or 749-4862, ⊛gvfloridatransport.com. Direct nightly services to Cagayan Valley.

Victory Liner 551 Earnshaw Ave, a short walk from Legarda LRT station. Regular buses north to the Cagayan valley (Santiago, Roxas, Tuguegaroa, Aparri, Ilagan, Tabuk and Tuao).

Laguna

Greenstar Express Taft Ave and Sen Gil Puyat, Pasay City ☎02/831-3178. Buses to Santa Cruz (for Pagsanjan; 2–3hr) via Calamba (2hr) and Los Baños (3hr).

JAM Transit Taft Ave at Sen Gil Puyat, Pasay ☎02/520-8734; with a second terminal near the corner of Timog Ave in Cubao. To various destinations in Laguna.

Mindanao

Philtranco EDSA, corner Apello Cruz St, Pasay ☎02/851-8078, ⓦwww.philtranco .com.ph. Daily a/c buses to Surigao and Davao at 1pm.

Pangasinan

Dagupan New York St, Cubao, Quezon City ☎02/727-2330. Services to Dagupan (6–7hr) and Lingayen (6–7hr).

Five Star Bus Lines Aurora Blvd, Pasay ☎02/853 4772. Regular departures for Pangasinan.

Victory Liner See Baguio entry for terminal details. All five terminals serve Alaminos (from 4.30am; hourly) and Dagupan (6–7hr).

Samar

Philtranco EDSA, corner Apello Cruz St, Pasay ☎02/851-8078, ⓦwww.philtranco .com.ph. Daily a/c buses to Tacloban.

Southern Luzon

Philtranco EDSA, corner Apello Cruz St, Pasay ☎02/851-8078, ⓦwww.philtranco .com.ph. Daily a/c buses to Legazpi (10.30am, 5pm, 7.45pm; 8–10hr), Daet (7.15am, 8pm; 7–8hr), Naga (7am, 8.30am, 10.30am, 5pm, 6.30pm, 7.30pm, 8.45pm; 6–8hr), Iriga (8.30am, 5pm, 6.30pm, 7.30pm; 7–9hr).

Superlines EDSA and Aurora Blvd, Cubao ☎02/912-3449. Small bus company operating to Daet (7–8hr) and Legazpi (8–10hr).

Subic Bay

Victory Liner See Baguio entry for terminal details. All five terminals serve Olongapo (daily 4am–8pm; hourly; 3hr).

Tuguegarao and far northern Luzon

Baliwag Transit EDSA, corner New York St, Quezon City ☎02/912-3343. Buses north to Tuguegarao (10–12hr).

La Union, Vigan and Laoag

Autobus Cayco and Valencia sts, Sampaloc ☎02/493-4111. Direct to Vigan (8–10hr).

Dominion EDSA, corner East Ave, Cubao ☎02/741-4146. Hourly to Vigan (8–10hr) and San Fernando (La Union; 6–8hr).

Fariñas Transit Corner Laoag Laan and M de la Fuente sts, Sampaloc ☎02/731-4507. Daily to Vigan (8–10hr) and Laoag (8–10hr).

Genesis EDSA, corner Taft, Pasay ☎02/853-3115. Hourly to to La Union until 5pm; San Fernando (6–8hr) via Dau, Tarlac; Baler, Carmen, Pangansinan and Mariveles.

Philippine Rabbit Rizal Ave, corner Recto ☎02/734-9836. Destinations north including Vigan (8–10hr), Laoag (8–10hr) and San Fernando La Union (6–8hr).

and **jeepneys** belch smoke with impunity, turning the air around major thorough-fares into a poisonous miasma. Fortunately, Manila's **taxis** are not expensive and are mostly air-conditioned – many visitors use them all the time. Manila's two light railway lines, the **LRT** and the **MetroStar Express** (MRT) are cheap and reliable, but they use mutually exclusive ticketing and the interchanges are poorly designed. Often very cramped and uncomfortable during the day, try to avoid them completely during rush hour (Mon–Fri 7–9.30am & 5–8pm) when you'll have to line up just to get into the stations, let alone the jam-packed trains. For the comparatively serene Pasig River Ferry, see p.78.

MetroStar Express (MRT)

The **MetroStar Express** (daily 5am–11pm; every 5–10min; Ⓦdotcmrt3.weebly.com) is also known as MRT-3 (or blue line): it runs for 16.95km along EDSA from Taft Avenue in Pasay City in the south to North Avenue, Quezon City in the north, connecting with the LRT (see below) at both ends. A single-journey **ticket** costs P10–15, or you can buy a multiple-journey ticket covering P100 worth of travel; if you plan to use the MRT a lot, you'll save a lot of time buying the latter (you'll still have to line up for a bag check before entering the station, but will avoid having to line up again for a ticket). Security guards patrol stations (and the first carriage is usually reserved for women), but watch out for pickpockets and the more brazen "snatchers", who rip phones, bags and wallets from your hand and make a run for it.

Manila Light Rail Transit (LRT)

The **LRT** (Ⓦwww.lrta.gov.ph) is an elevated railway system with two lines: the 17.2km Yellow Line (LRT-1); and the 13.8km Purple Line, which confusingly is known as MRT-2. The Yellow Line runs from Baclaran in the south to North Avenue in Quezon City in the north, where it connects with MRT-3. The Purple Line runs from Santolan in Pasig City to Recto in Quiapo, close to the Yellow Line's Doroteo Jose station. Trains on both lines run frequently from 5am to 11pm and tickets range from P12 to P20. P100 stored value tickets are also available.

Jeepneys and FX taxis

Jeepneys are the cheapest way to get around, and they run back and forth all over the city: fares start at P7 for the first 4km, and increase by P1.40 per kilometre thereafter. Destinations are written on signboards at the front. You'll also see tiny minivans or FX Taxis, usually labelled UV Express, that zip between fixed points, usually without stopping, for around the same price. While sometimes useful (linking SM Mall of Asia and Baclaran, for example), both forms of transport are usually incredibly cramped, and traffic congestion can make even short journeys last hours.

Wow Manila hop on hop off

Manila's transport system can be intimidating for first-time visitors, so the **Wow Manila Hop On Hop Off Bus** (℡02/631-1045, Ⓦmanilahoponhopoff.com; 1-day pass P700; 2-day pass P900) can be a good idea; their minivans connect all the major sights starting at Glorietta mall in Makati and include the Cultural Center, SM Mall of Asia and Intramuros. Buses depart the Ayala car park (in between the *Intercontinental Hotel* and SM Makati) at 9am, 11am, 1pm & 3pm, taking 2 hours 30 minutes to complete the loop. Note that heavy traffic will affect these vans the same as other forms of road transport, and that if you have a group taking taxis will probably be cheaper.

Buses

Local **buses** in Manila bump and grind their way along all major thoroughfares, such as Taft, EDSA and Buendia Avenue, but are not allowed on most side streets. The destination is written on a sign in the front window. Most vehicles are ageing contraptions bought secondhand from Japan or Taiwan, and feature no particular colour scheme; it's a matter of luck whether any one bus has air-conditioning. **Fares** start at P11 for the first 5km, and increase P2.20 per kilometre thereafter for air-conditioned buses (non a/c buses start at P9 and go up P1.85 per km after the first 5km). As with jeepneys, traffic congestion will add travel time and even larger buses will often be packed.

Taxis

Manila **taxis** come in a confusing mix of models, colours and shapes, though it's relatively easy to use them to get around – most drivers are honest these days and use the meter, though some may still try and set prices in advance or "forget" to switch it on (insist on the meter). Fares are good value and you'll save a lot of time using taxis over any other form of transport. The metered rate is an initial P30 (for the first 500m), plus P2.50 for every 300m thereafter (every two minutes waiting adds P1).

Accommodation

Most of Manila's budget accommodation is in the Manila Bay area, specifically in the enclaves of **Ermita** and **Malate**, which also have a high density of cheap restaurants, bars and tourist services. In recent years a number of reasonably priced mid-range hotels have sprung up, as well as several five-star places along Manila Bay, joining the historic *Manila Hotel*.

In the business district of **Makati**, there's some mid-range accommodation in and around P. Burgos Street at the northern end of Makati Avenue, beyond the *Mandarin Oriental Manila*. This is close to the red-light district, so if you want somewhere else in Makati try the somewhat anaemic but comfortable boutique hotels in Arnaiz Avenue, behind the Greenbelt mall. Most of these hotels are aimed at travelling executives who don't want to fork out for a five-star, and are an affordable, safe option in a convenient location.

The hotels in **Quezon City** are almost all around Timog Avenue and Tomas Morato Avenue, close to the nightlife; if you're planning to catch an early bus from Cubao it might be worth considering staying here. If you have an early flight and a bit more cash to spend there are some convenient and luxurious options close to the airport.

Airport area (Pasay City)
See map on pp.62–63.

Manila Marriott Hotel 10 Newport Blvd, Newport City Complex ☎02/988-9999, ✺www.marriott .com. Fabulous luxury hotel, right across from Terminal 3 (with free shuttle bus to all terminals). Stylish rooms come with flat-screen TVs and funky bathrooms with glass walls (with shades for the modest) and big tubs. The pool is a great place to chill out during the day. ❽

Maxims Tower Newport Blvd, Newport City Complex ☎02/836-6333, ✺www.rwmanila.com.

Self-styled "six-star" hotel almost lives up to the hype, with no front desk (check-in is conducted at your suite), futuristic Avaya Guest Media Hubs (touch-screen control panels), huge TVs that can surf the net and a personal butler on call 24hr. Part of the Resorts World Manila complex and casino. ❼

Intramuros
See map on p.75.

White Knight Hotel Intramuros Cabildo St at Urdaneta St, Plaza San Luis Complex ☎02/526-6539, ✺whiteknighthotelintramuros.com.

Nineteenth-century building with heaps of character and 29 simple but spacious rooms tastefully furnished in period style, with bathroom, a/c, flat-screen TV and free wi-fi. Worth considering for the novelty of staying in the most historic part of the city. ❹

Ermita

See map on p.83.

Best Western Hotel La Corona 1166 M.H. Del Pilar St at Arquiza St ☎02/524-2631, ⓦwww .bestwesternhotelmanila.com. Solid choice featuring stylish double a/c rooms with a modern Filipino theme, cable TV and free wi-fi. Good location and the rate includes a buffet breakfast for two. ❼

Chillout Guesthouse 1288 M.H. del Pilar St ☎02/450-8023 or 0939/517-7019, ⓦwww.manila-guesthouse.com. This fourth-floor hostel run by an enthusiastic young French crew has proved a real hit, with a choice of fan (❷) or a/c en-suite rooms (❸; the back rooms are quieter) and dorms (P350 a/c, P300 fan). There's a common kitchen area for self-caterers, and free wi-fi.

City Garden Suites Hotel 1158 A. Mabini St ☎02/536-1451, ⓦwww.citygardenhotels.com. Standard hotel with sparsely furnished but clean a/c rooms and a reasonable coffee shop in the lobby; Filipino buffet breakfast included. ❹

Ermita Tourist Inn 1549 A. Mabini St ☎02/521-8770. Decent budget choice on the edge of Ermita close to Malate, with thirty relatively spacious a/c rooms with shower. There's a travel agent downstairs for flights and visas. ❷

Gran Prix Econotel Tesoro Building, 1325 A. Mabini St ☎02/353-2993, ⓦwww.granprixhotel -manila.com. Spotless budget boutique hotel with bright, modern a/c rooms with cable TV, internet in the lobby and cheap rates online. ❹

Hotel H2O Manila Manila Ocean World (Behind the Quirino Grandstand) ☎02/238-6100, ⓦwww .hotelh2o.com. Most original boutique in Manila, with a chic "aqua" theme and fabulous views of the bay or Ocean World pool (for the nightly fountain shows). Rooms sport a trendy minimalist design and LCD TVs; some even have stunning wall-sized in-room aquariums, but on the downside the hotel is a bit cut off from the rest of the city. ❻

Lotus Garden Hotel 1227 A. Mabini St at Padre Faura St ☎02/522-1515, ⓦwww.lotusgarden hotelmanila.com/lotus. Swish modern rooms, excellent location and decent buffet breakfast make this chain hotel a good deal – book online for the best rates. ❹

Manila Hotel One Rizal Park ☎02/527-0011, ⓦwww.manila-hotel.com.ph. Esteemed

establishment that is undoubtedly past its best but nevertheless reeks of history, at least in the old wing where General Douglas MacArthur stayed during World War II; if you've got P32,000 to spare you can stay a night in his suite. The lobby is a grand affair with black-and-white-tiled flooring and oxblood velvet sofas. The rooms, many in need of a revamp, remain stubbornly traditional, with dark wood and four-poster beds. ❾

Southern Cross Hotel 1125 M.H. del Pilar St ☎02/521-2013, ⓦwww.thesoutherncrosshotel manila.com. Friendly budget hotel with small but comfy rooms equipped with a/c, cable TV, bathroom and fridge. It's owned by an Australian national and there's an Aussie-style bar and food, large-screen TV and billiard table downstairs. ❹

Malate

See map on p.83.

Adriatico Arms 561 J. Nakpil St ☎02/521-0736. A pleasant refuge of a hotel in an unbeatable location. The 28 a/c rooms are smallish, but well kept and functional, with TV but no breakfast. Nearby is *Café Adriatico*, where you can sit and watch the beautiful people stroll by. ❹

Aloha Hotel 2150 Roxas Blvd ☎02/526-8088, ⓦwww.alohahotel.net.ph. A Manila Bay stalwart, the *Aloha* is in a fine location with views of the bay from the front, but the rooms (all a/c) have seen better days – ask to see a selection before you hand over any money. There's a small café and a Chinese restaurant. ❼

Baywatch Luxury Condos 2057 M.H. del Pilar St ☎0919/490-1330, ⓦwww .baywatch1403.com. These studio apartments (identical units 1403 and 1903) are fabulous deals, with handsome interiors and spectacular views over Manila Bay from the balconies. There's a small kitchen too. ❼

Bianca's Garden Hotel 2139 M. Adriatico St ☎02/525-2846, ⓦwww.biancasgarden hotel.com. This idyllic provincial-style retreat on the southern edge of the tourist area is understandably popular with backpackers and divers stopping off in Manila for a few nights on their way to the beach. Rooms are spacious and elegant, decorated with Philippine antiques evoking the building's former incarnation as a wealthy Spanish-style home. There's a small swimming pool in the shady garden. ❸

Friendly's Guesthouse 1750 M. Adriatico St at Nakpil St ☎02/474-0742, ⓦwww.friendlysguest house.com. The chilled-out balcony common area, bird's-eye view over Malate and free wi-fi and hot drinks at this backpackers' hostel are plus points, but it's not the cleanest. Self-catering cooking facilities available. Many rooms have shared bathrooms. Fan dorms P325, a/c P375; singles from P500, doubles P900. ❷

Malate Pensionne 1771 M. Adriatico St ☎02/523-8304, ⊛www.mpensionne.com.ph. Tucked behind *Starbucks* in an unbeatable position, this has been one of the area's most popular guesthouses for years. Rooms are furnished in Spanish-colonial style and book up quickly. Dorm P350 (fan only), doubles ❷

🏃 **Pan Pacific Manila Hotel** M. Adriatico at General Malvar St ☎02/318-0788, ⊛www .panpacific.com/manila. This is the top choice in Malate for superlative service (each room comes with 24hr butler service), luxurious rooms and a buffet breakfast that could feed an army. Passing from the chaos outside to the soothing outdoor swimming pool and jacuzzi is a surreal but pleasant experience. ❼

Pearl Garden Hotel 1700 M. Adriatico St ☎02/525-1000, ⊛www.pearlgardenhotel.net. One of the best mid-range hotels on the block, with 83 small but clean and smart boutique-style rooms. The main downside (for non-smokers) is that the whole hotel is smoker friendly, and the free wi-fi is a bit unreliable. ❻

Pension Natividad 1690 M.H. Del Pilar St ☎02/521-0524, ⊛pensionnatividad.multiply.com. Spacious, impeccably clean rooms in a quiet old family house that was built before the war and partially destroyed by bombing. The terrace café is a good place to meet other travellers, and there's free wi-fi. One of the best budget places to stay in the area and handy for the airport. Dorm P400. Doubles with fan (❷), a/c (❸).

Sofitel Philippine Plaza CCP Complex, Roxas Blvd ☎02/551-5555, ⊛www.sofitel.com. See map on pp.62–63. If you can afford it and want a room with a balcony and a view of the Manila Bay sunsets, this is the place to stay. The *Sofitel* is big, brash and has a number of pricey bars and restaurants. First choice for many Japanese and Korean tour groups. ❼

Paco Park
See map on p.83.

Garden Plaza Hotel 1030 Belen St ☎02/522-4835, ⊛www.gardenplazamanila.com. Congenial and well managed, the *Garden Plaza* is right next to Paco Park and has a/c rooms, a lovely little swimming pool on the roof and the excellent *Old Swiss Inn* restaurant. ❺

Paco Park Oasis Hotel 1032–1034 Belen St ☎02/521-2371, ⊛www.oasispark.com. Next door to the *Garden Plaza* (see above) outside the walls of Paco Park. Economy, standard, deluxe and superior rooms, some with four-poster bed and whirlpool bath. Not as plush as its neighbour, but

the rooms are slightly cheaper and good value. Large swimming pool, pleasant terrace area, restaurant and a travel agency in the lobby. ❹

Makati
See map on p.88.

El Cielito Inn 804 Arnaiz Ave (formerly Pasay Rd) ☎02/815-8951, ⊛www.elcielito-makati.com. Small but clean glass-fronted mid-range hotel close to Makati's malls, with modern, carpeted a/c rooms and a coffee shop. ❼

🏃 **Makati Shangri-La Manila** Ayala Ave at Makati Ave ☎02/813-8888, ⊛www .shangri-la.com. If you fancy a splurge, this is the best choice in town, a top-notch establishment in the heart of Makati with chic rooms, fabulous service, waterfalls on every floor and the closest beds to the drink-all-you-can happy hour at *Conway's*, the bar upstairs. ❾

Mandarin Oriental Manila Makati Ave ☎02/750-8888, ⊛www.mandarinoriental.com/manila. Five-star establishment that serves as a good landmark in Makati, opposite Citibank and a short walk from the shops. Rooms are spacious, with all the comforts you'd expect from this luxury chain. The hotel's *Captain's Bar* is a popular venue for watching showbands, every night from 9pm. Good deals online. ❾

The Peninsula Manila Ayala Ave at Makati Ave ☎02/887-2888, ⊛www.peninsula.com/Manila. Ostentatious five-star that takes up a city block and has a cheesily opulent lobby where people go to drink coffee and to see and be seen. There are no fewer than seven restaurants, running the gamut from Asian to French. Rooms are as you'd expect at this price, with soft furnishings and all mod cons. ❾

Pensionne Virginia 816 Arnaiz Ave (Pasay Rd) ☎02/844-5228. Budget option in a convenient location at the business end of Makati, close to malls and offices; it's situated between ACA Video and a branch of the popular bakery, *Goldilocks*. Rooms all have a/c, cable TV, telephone and mini-bar but no wi-fi. ❹

Robelle House 4402 Valdez St ☎02/899-8061, ⊛www.robellehouse.net. This rambling family-run pension has been in business since 1977 and is still the most atmospheric Filipino budget accommodation in the business district. The location isn't great though: it's a good walk from the Makati shops in a desolate backstreet area. The floors are polished tile and the wooden staircases are authentically creaky, although the rooms are no more than serviceable. Ask for one on the first floor overlooking the small pool. With bath ❹; shared bath ❸

Tower Inn 1002 Arnaiz Ave (Pasay Rd) ☎02/888-5170, ⊛www.towerinnmakati.com. Modern business hotel with 48 rooms, coffee shop and small Mediterranean restaurant. It's within walking distance of Makati's shops and restaurants. ❺

Around P. Burgos Street
See map below.

City Garden Hotel Makati 7870 Makati Ave at Kalayaan Ave ℡02/899-1111, ⓦwww.citygardenhotels.com/makati. A comfortable, modern boutique hotel with spacious and well-maintained a/c rooms, small rooftop swimming pool and giddy views from the rooftop café. Good location, the staff are efficient and you can negotiate a discount off-season. ❻

🏃 Clipper Hotel 5766 Ebro St ℡02/890-8577, ⓦwww.theclipperhotel.com. This Art Deco gem is more South Beach than south Manila, an atmospheric budget hotel that opened in 2009. Rooms are simple but spacious, and there's cable TV, free wi-fi and a desktop in the lobby for guests (10min free). The only catch is its relative proximity to girlie bars and clubs, and the street outside can be noisy at night. ❸

Jupiter Suites 102 Jupiter St, at Makati Ave, close to *McDonald's* ℡02/890-5044, ⓦwww.jupiterarms.com. Offers spacious a/c singles and doubles, all en suite and with cable TV. Ask for a room at the back – those at the front overlook the busy street and you'll wake to the sound of jeepneys honking their horns at 5am. ❺

Our Melting Pot Unit 18-N&O, A. Venue Suites, 7829 Makati Ave at General Luna St ℡02/659-5443, ⓦwww.ourmeltingpot.hostel.com. Friendly hostel in an apartment building, with two dorms (❷), and a couple of private rooms with shared bathroom (❸). The two rooms are in another building five minutes away, in what's basically a private apartment with a kitchen and some of Makati's best views. Free wi-fi.

Oxford Suites P. Burgos St at Durban St ℡02/899-7988, ⓦwww.oxfordsuitesmakati.com. One of the best hotels on the P. Burgos strip, with 232 spacious rooms and suites, gym, 24hr coffee shop and fourth-floor restaurant. Some rooms have kitchenette, living room and terrace. Buffet breakfast included. ❻

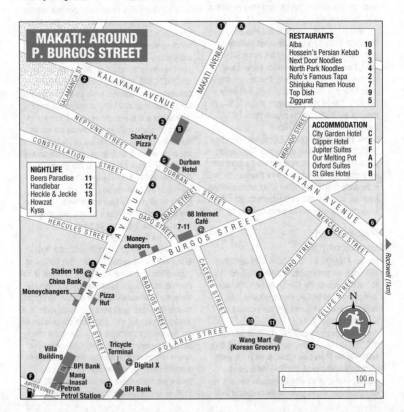

MAKATI: AROUND P. BURGOS STREET

RESTAURANTS
Alba	10
Hossein's Persian Kebab	8
Next Door Noodles	3
North Park Noodles	4
Rufo's Famous Tapa	2
Shinjuku Ramen House	7
Top Dish	9
Ziggurat	5

ACCOMMODATION
City Garden Hotel	C
Clipper Hotel	E
Jupiter Suites	F
Our Melting Pot	A
Oxford Suites	D
St Giles Hotel	B

NIGHTLIFE
Beers Paradise	11
Handlebar	12
Heckle & Jeckle	13
Howzat	6
Kyss	1

KALAYAAN AVENUE
SALAMANCA ST
MAKATI AVENUE
NEPTUNE STREET
CONSTELLATION STREET
Shakey's Pizza
Durban Hotel
DURBAN STREET
MERCADO STREET
KALAYAAN AVENUE
DAPO STREET
ABACA STREET
88 Internet Café
7-11
P. BURGOS STREET
HERCULES STREET
Money-changers
MERCEDES STREET
EBRO STREET
Station 168
China Bank
Moneychangers
Pizza Hut
CACERES STREET
BADAJOS STREET
ANZA STREET
FELIPE STREET
N
Villa Building
Tricycle Terminal
Digital X
POLARIS STREET
Wang Mart (Korean Grocery)
BPI Bank
Mang Inasal
Petron Petrol Station
BPI Bank
JUPITER STREET
Rockwell (1km)

0   100 m

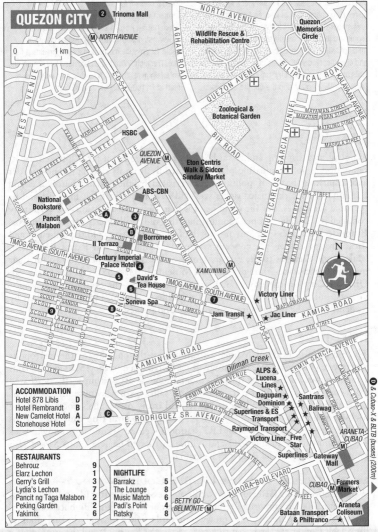

QUEZON CITY — Trinoma Mall, NORTH AVENUE, University of the Philippines (1km)

Wildlife Rescue & Rehabilitation Centre

Quezon Memorial Circle

Zoological & Botanical Garden

HSBC

Eton Centris Walk & Sidcor Sunday Market

ABS-CBN

National Bookstore

Pancit Malabon

Il Terrazo

Borromeo

Century Imperial Palace Hotel

David's Tea House

Soneva Spa

Victory Liner

Jam Transit

Jac Liner

KAMIAS ROAD

KAMUNING ROAD

Diliman Creek

ALPS & Lucena Lines

Dagupan

Santrans

Superlines & ES Transport

Baliwag

Raymond Transport

Victory Liner

Five Star

Superlines

Gateway Mall

ARANETA-CUBAO

Farmers Market

Araneta Coliseum

Bataan Transport & Philtranco

& Cubao-X & BLTB (buses) (200m)

ACCOMMODATION

Hotel 878 Libis	D
Hotel Rembrandt	B
New Camelot Hotel	A
Stonehouse Hotel	C

RESTAURANTS

Behrouz	9
Elarz Lechon	1
Gerry's Grill	3
Lydia's Lechon	7
Pancit ng Taga Malabon	2
Peking Garden	2
Yakimix	6

NIGHTLIFE

Barrakz	5
The Lounge	8
Music Match	6
Padi's Point	4
Ratsky	8

St Giles Hotel Makati Ave at Kalayaan Ave ☏02/988-9888, ⓦwww.stgilesmanila.com. Smart hotel that opened in 2010, close to all the action. There's a pool and gym, and the rooms are elegantly furnished in light neutral tones. Free wi-fi in the lobby. ⑥

Quezon City

See map above.

Hotel 878 Libis 878 E. Rodriguez Jr. Ave ☏02/709-0154, ⓦwww.hotel878libis.com. Fine mid-range option, with 29 stylish doubles all with verandas, cable TV and free wi-fi. The super-cool lofts (P3445) and suites (P4185) are also worth considering. ⑥

Hotel Rembrandt 26 T. Morato Ave Extension ☏02/373-3333. Medium-sized, modern hotel with a/c rooms, a gymnasium, a cosy piano bar on the top floor with views of the metropolis and a branch of *TGI Friday's* on the ground floor.⑦

New Camelot Hotel 35 Mother Ignacia Ave ☏02/373-2101, ⓦwww.camelothotel.com.ph.

You can't miss it: look out for the mock Arthurian spires rising above one of Quezon City's shanty-towns near the ABS-CBN television studios. The rooms are like a bad medieval dream with their imitation-silk sheets, plastic-flower arrangements and chairs carved with Gothic quatrefoils. There are suits of armour in the lobby, the coffee shop is called the *Winchester*, and the bar the *Dungeon*.

Need a present for someone special? Look no further than Lady Guinevere's Gift Shop. ⑤ **Stonehouse Hotel** 1315 E. Rodriguez Ave Ⓦwww.stonehouse.ph. Cosy budget hotel with cable TV, en-suite rooms and a tasty breakfast for two. The nightly live bands provide plenty of on-site entertainment. Free wi-fi in café area only. Rates start at P1100, a real bargain. ❸

The City

Manila is an intriguing and rewarding city to explore but it takes some effort; its reputation as an intimidating place stems mainly from its size, apparent disorder and dispiriting levels of pollution, exacerbated by the equally fierce heat and humidity. To see the major sights you will have to sweat it out in traffic and be prepared for delays, but the good news is that the main attractions are essentially confined to Manila proper, comprising the old walled city of **Intramuros**, **Binondo** – Manila's Chinatown – north of the Pasig River, and the museums and parks grouped along the crescent sweep of Manila Bay and Roxas Boulevard. **Makati** and **Ortigas** to the east are glossy business districts best known for their malls and restaurants, though the Ayala Museum in Makati should not be missed. **Quezon City** on the city's northern edge is a little out of the way for most visitors, but it does boast some lively nightlife (see p.96), most of it fuelled by students from the nearby University of the Philippines.

Intramuros

The old Spanish heart of Manila, **Intramuros** is the one part of the metropolis where you get a real sense of history. It was established in the 1570s and remains a monumental, if partially ruined, colonial relic, a city within a city, separated from the rest of Manila by its overgrown walls. It's not a museum; plenty of government offices are still located here, and many of Manila's poorest call the backstreets home. A good way to see it is by arranging a **walking tour** with Carlos Celdran (see below). The nearest LRT station is Central Terminal, from where it's a ten-minute walk to the walls and a little further to General Luna Street (also known as Calle Real del Palacio), the main drag.

Silahis Center and the Light & Sound Museum

Walking north along General Luna you'll pass the **Silahis Center** (daily 10am–7pm; free) at no. 744, an emporium selling arts, antiques and cultural publications from all over the Philippines. Across a pretty courtyard reached through the back door of the Silahis Center are the elegant *Ilustrado* restaurant (see p.92) and the atmospheric

---

Walk with the locals

If sightseeing in Manila on your own seems a little intimidating try **Walk This Way**, run by the highly entertaining Carlos Celdran (☎0920/909-2021 or 02/484-4945, Ⓦwww.carlosceldran.com). Carlos takes weekly history-lesson-cum-magical-mystery tours around the city, and as well as the classic Intramuros circuit (P1200), there are tailor-made trips through different Manila eras (from P900). Also recommended is Ivan Man Dy of **Old Manila Walks** (☎0917/329-1622, Ⓦwww.oldmanila walks.com), who runs fun tours of Binondo, and the Malacañang Palace.

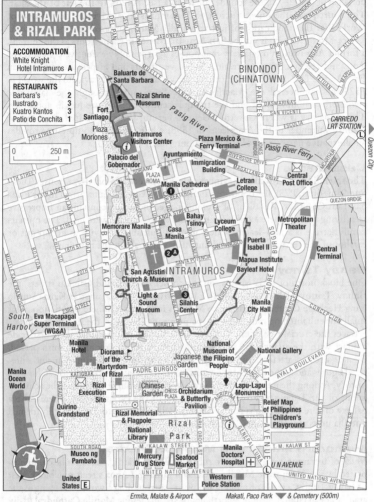

INTRAMUROS & RIZAL PARK

ACCOMMODATION
White Knight
Hotel Intramuros **A**

RESTAURANTS
Barbara's 2
Ilustrado 3
Kuatro Kantos 3
Patio de Conchita 1

Kuatro Kantos Bar (see p.92). One block west along Victoria at Santa Lucia Street is one of the city's more unusual attractions, the **Light & Sound Museum** (Tues–Sun 9am–6pm; P100; ℡02/524-2827), which contains a series of dioramas enlivened by a light-and-sound dramatization of all the key moments in Philippine history. The site opens on demand during the hours listed above, but only for a minimum of ten people; smaller groups can enter but they must pay a total P1000.

San Agustin Church and museum

A few hundreds metres north of the Silahis Center on the west side of General Luna Street stands **San Agustin Church** (daily 8am–noon & 1–5pm; P100, includes admission to the museum), with a magnificent Baroque interior, *trompe l'oeil* murals and a vaulted ceiling and dome. Dating back to 1587, it's the oldest stone church in the Philippines, and contains the modest tomb of Miguel López de Legazpi (1502–72), the founder of Manila (see p.426), to the left of the altar. The church was the only structure in Intramuros to survive the devastation of World War II, an indication of just how badly Manila suffered under occupation.

Access to the church is via the **San Agustin Museum** (same hours as the church), a former Augustinian monastery that houses a surprisingly extensive collection of icons and artefacts, rare porcelain, church vestments and a special exhibition on Fray Andrés Urdaneta (who led the second voyage to circumnavigate the world in 1528, and pioneered the Manila–Acapulco sea route), though the handsome two-storey building itself and the tranquil central cloisters are just as appealing. The old vestry is where Governor-General Fermín Jáudenes drafted the terms of Spanish surrender to the Americans in 1898, while the oratorio upstairs provides an alternative perspective of the church interior.

Casa Manila

The splendid **Casa Manila**, a sympathetically restored colonial-era house (Tues–Sun 9am–6pm; P75), lies opposite San Agustin on General Luna Street in the Plaza San Luis Complex. Redolent of a grander age, the house contains an impressive *sala* (living room) where *tertulias* (soirees) and *bailes* (dances) were held. The upstairs family latrine is a two-seater, which allowed husband and wife to gossip out of earshot of the servants while simultaneously going about their business.

Bahay Tsinoy

One block north of Casa Manila, on the corner of Anda and Cabildo streets, the **Bahay Tsinoy** (Tues–Sun 1–5pm; P100; ☎02/527-6083) in the Kaisa-Angelo King Heritage Center is a tribute to Manila's influential Chinese population. This small but enlightening museum – the name means "house of the Filipino Chinese" – traces the crucial role of the Chinese in Philippine history from their first trade contact with the archipelago in the tenth century to the colonial Spanish period. Besides assorted artefacts and multimedia presentations, the displays include life-sized figures and authentic reproductions of objects related to Tsinoy (or "Chinoy") history. Among the items of interest are a large hologram representing the achievements of the Tsinoys and a charming diorama of the Parian ghetto. There's also a gallery of rare photographs and a Martyrs Hall dedicated to Tsinoys who formed guerilla units against Japanese occupation.

Memorare Manila and Manila Cathedral

Much of Intramuros was reduced to rubble in World War II, a catastrophe commemorated by the **Memorare Manila** at General Luna and Anda streets one block west of Bahay Tsinoy, a series of moving sculptures surrounding a woman weeping as she cradles a dead child. One block north lies the Romanesque **Manila Cathedral** (daily 6.20am–5.30pm, or 7.30pm if special event/mass; free), originally just a nipa and bamboo chapel built in 1571 by Legazpi, and destroyed seven times down the centuries by a combination of fire, typhoon, earthquake and war. It was comprehensively flattened during World War II, but the Vatican contributed funds to have it rebuilt. The present structure was completed in 1958 from a design by Fernando Ocampo, one of the nation's finest architects, and is similar in style to the cathedral that stood here in the nineteenth century. It lacks the rich historical ambience of San Agustin, but the interior is impressive in its simplicity, with a long aisle flanked by marble pillars, stained-glass rose windows and a soaring central dome. Exhibitions in chapels around the nave throw light on the tumultuous history of the cathedral, and even tackle weighty theological questions such as "what is a cathedral?" and the meaning of the Immaculate Conception. Check out also the faithful reproduction of Michelangelo's *La Pietà* in a special chapel to the left of the entrance.

Fort Santiago and Rizal Shrine

The ruins of **Fort Santiago** (daily 8am–6pm; P75) stand at the northwestern end of Intramuros, a five-minute walk from the cathedral on the opposite side of busy A. Soriano Jr. Street. The first log fortress was built by Legazpi in 1571 on the remains of Rajah Sulaiman's base, but was rebuilt in stone twenty years later. The seat of the colonial power of both Spain and the US, Fort Santiago was also a prison and torture chamber under the Spanish regime and the scene of countless military-police atrocities during the Japanese occupation.

Just past the entrance to the fort, on the left, is the Baluartillo de San Francisco Javier, built in 1663 and now housing the Intramuros Visitors Center (same hours as the fort; ℡02/527-2961), a shop and a café. From here you can stroll through the gardens of Plaza Moriones to the fort proper, marked by a stone gate, walls and a moat – most of what you see today has been rebuilt in stages since the 1950s, after being virtually destroyed in 1945. Plaza de Armas forms a pleasant green square inside the fort (with a noble-looking statue of José Rizal in the middle), while the eighteenth-century Baluarte de Santa Barbara overlooking the Pasig River now houses the mildly interesting Rizaliana Furniture Exhibition (same hours as the fort; P10). This is the infamous dungeon where around six hundred American and Filipino POWs were incarcerated and left to drown by the rising tide. There is a cross and memorial outside to mark their final resting place.

For most visitors the real highlight is on the left side of Plaza de Armas, where the **Rizal Shrine** (Tues–Sun 9am–noon & 1–5pm; entry included with fort ticket) occupies a reconstruction of the old fort barracks (the brick ruins of the original are next door). The site is dedicated to José Rizal, the writer and national hero who was imprisoned here before being executed in what became Rizal Park in 1896. On the ground floor, the Chamber of Texts preserves some original copies of Rizal's work, while exerts are artfully displayed on iron girders. You can also peer into a reproduction of the room where he spent the hours before his execution. Upstairs the Reliquary Room displays some of Rizal's clothing and personal effects, while a larger hall houses the original copy of his valedictory poem, *Mi Ultimo Adios*, the greatest, most poignant work of Philippine literature. The poem was secreted in an oil lamp and smuggled out to his family; here it is displayed in various languages around the walls (the original was written in Spanish). While even the best English translations fail to capture the felicity of the original, they do give a sense of the sacrifice Rizal was about to make and of his love of the country:

Farewell, my adored country, region beloved of the sun,
Pearl of the Orient Sea, our Eden lost,
Departing in happiness, to you I give the sad, withered remains of my life;
And had it been a life more brilliant, more fine, more fulfilled
I would have given it, willingly to you.

National Gallery

Just beyond the southern walls of Intramuros (the closest LRT station is UN Avenue), the **National Gallery** (Wed–Sun 10am–4pm; free; ℡02/527-1215) is the foremost art museum in the Philippines, housed in the grand old Legislative Building on the northern edge of Rizal Park. Galleries are laid out thematically in rather desultory fashion over two floors, but each one is relatively small and easy to digest. The highlights are paintings by Filipino masters including Juan Luna (1859–99), Félix Hidalgo (1855–1913), José Joya (1931–95) and Fernando Amorsolo (1892–1972), with the most famous works displayed in the Hall of the Masters near the entrance; Luna's vast and magnificent *Spolarium* (1884) is here, a thinly veiled attack in oils on the atrocities of the Spanish regime, portraying fallen gladiators being dragged onto a pile of corpses.

Manila's river road

Inching along Manila's fume-choked streets is a grim but usually inevitable part of the capital experience, but you can escape the gridlock and the crowded metro by taking to the river. The **Pasig River Ferry** (☎0926/5232) connects Plaza Mexico (☎02/394-1841) on the north side of Intramuros (behind the Immigration Building) to San Joaquin (☎02/641-5810) in Pasig (16.82km), via Escolta, Quezon Bridge, Guadalupe (next to EDSA and the metro line station, in between Makati and Ortigas; ☎02/882-5734) and several other stops. The Seine it is not, but from the Pasig you'll get to see Metro Manila relatively fume- and hassle-free, from ramshackle shanties, thick clumps of floating water hyacinth and small kids fishing and (gulp) swimming in the murky waters, to the neoclassical buildings of Escolta, the Malacañang Palace (photos strictly forbidden) and shiny skyscrapers rising from the sprawl.

From the convenient stop at Guadalupe to Intramuros takes around one hour and costs P45; from Guadalupe it's just P35 (50min) to Quezon Bridge. Rates range P25–60 depending on distance. Monday to Friday boats depart Guadalupe at 6.30am, 7am, 7.30am, 8am then roughly every hour or every 90min until 4.36pm. Boats depart Intramuros at similar intervals between 9am and 6.45pm (Sat 8.30am–7pm). On Saturdays departures are scaled back to just seven in either direction, and there's no service on Sundays or public holidays. Boats are air-conditioned.

Other galleries are dedicated to National Artist award winners (Amorsolo was the first in 1972), showcasing Joya's *Origins* and Amorsolo's *Portrait of President Manuel Roxas*. There's also a section on architect Juan Arellano (1888–1960), who designed the building (completed in 1926), and a special gallery dedicated to the large Juan Luna collection; look out for his haunting *Mother in Bed* and the simple naturalism of *Study for Rice Harvesting*. The second floor contains mostly minor works from modern Filipino artists, and also a Bones Gallery where a huge sperm whale skeleton takes pride of place.

National Museum of the Filipino People

A short walk from the National Gallery on the opposite side of Finance Avenue, the absorbing **National Museum of the Filipino People** (Wed–Sun 10am–4pm; P100) occupies what used to be the Department of Finance Building, a stately Greek Revival edifice completed in 1940. Much of the priceless collection of artefacts on display has been retrieved from shipwrecks, most notably the *San Diego*, a Spanish galleon that sank off Fortune Island in Batangas after a battle with the Dutch in 1600. Recovered in 1992, the ship yielded over five thousand objects, not all intrinsically valuable: you'll see chicken bones and hazelnuts from the ship's store, as well as tons of Chinese porcelain, storage jars, rosaries and silver goblets. Other rooms contain objects from wrecked Chinese junks, going back to the early eleventh century – compelling evidence of trade links that existed long before the Spanish arrived.

The well-labelled anthropology section on the third floor is equally engrossing, with displays from almost every region and tribal group in the Philippines, including the enigmatic anthropomorphic jars discovered in Ayub Cave (Mindanao) that date back to 5 BC. These jars were used to hold the bones of ancestors.

Rizal Park

Still referred to by its old Spanish name of "Luneta", **Rizal Park** is a ten-minute walk south of Intramuros across busy Padre Burgos Street, or a short stroll north of UN Avenue LRT station. In a city notoriously short of greenery, the park was where the colonial-era glitterati used to promenade after church every Sunday. These days Rizal Park is an early-morning jogging circuit, a weekend playground for children and a refuge for couples and families escaping the clamour of the city. **Hawkers** sell everything from balloons and mangoes to plastic bags full of *chicheron*, deep-fried pigskin served with a little container of vinegar and chilli for dipping. The park is often busy, with many distractions and activities, but few visitors report any problems with hustlers, pickpockets or what Filipinos generally refer to as "*snatchers*".

At the far eastern end of the park is an impressive Marcos-era giant relief map of the Philippines. Walking west from here, the park's other sundry attractions include the **Orchidarium & Butterfly Pavilion**, though funding problems meant this was closed at the time of writing (it may reopen sometime in 2011). Walk a little further and you'll see the entrance to the peaceful Japanese Garden (daily 6am–10pm; P10), and the Chess Plaza beyond, where amiable seniors challenge each other to games of chess. The tranquil Chinese Garden (daily 6am–10pm; P10) is next on the right, but this western end of the park is most associated with its namesake, José Rizal. The main focus is the stolid looking **Rizal Memorial**, raised in 1912, where Rizal is entombed, and the 31-metre flagpole where Manuel Roxas, first President of the Republic, was sworn in on July 4, 1946. Just to the north is the site of Rizal's execution, marked by a memorial that also commemorates the execution of three priests garrotted by the Spanish for alleged complicity in the uprising in Cavite in 1872. Nearby is the Diorama of the Martyrdom of Rizal (daily 8am–5pm; P10; light show at 8pm in English P50) containing a series of eight life-size sculptures dramatizing the hero's final days; if the gatekeeper is around you should be able to wander around, but to run the light-and-sound presentation they need at least fifteen people.

Along Manila Bay

When Manila was in its heyday, **Manila Bay** must have been a sight to behold, with its dreamy sunsets and sweeping panorama across the South China Sea. The promenade has been cleaned up in recent years, but the area still feels past its peak. Nevertheless, the waterfront boasts several enticing attractions, from the *Manila Hotel* to Manila Ocean World and several museums – if it's too hot to walk taxis are the best way to get around this area.

Manila Hotel

The **Manila Hotel**, just northwest of Rizal Park, is the most historic of the city's luxury hotels, perhaps though now a little careworn. It's still the best place to get a sense of early twentieth-century Manila, those halcyon days when the city was at its cultural and social zenith; you can even stay (see p.70) in the General Douglas MacArthur Suite, residence from 1936 to 1941 of the man Filipinos called the Caesar of America. If even the standard rooms are beyond your means, you can at least sip a martini in the lobby while listening to a string quartet and watching the capital's elite strut by.

When the hotel opened in 1912 it represented the epitome of colonial class and luxury. Lavish dances known as **rigodon balls** were held every month in the Grand Ballroom, with high-society guests dancing the quadrille in traditional *ternos* (formal evening dresses) and dinner jackets. Today staff glide around in similarly elegant attire.

The hotel has its own historical **archive**, containing signed photographs of illustrious guests, from Marlon Brando, looking young and slender in a native *barong* (formal shirt), to Ricky Martin and Jon Bon Jovi. The archive is available to guests only, but if you eat or drink at the hotel, one of the guest relations officers should be able to show it for you. South of the hotel is the Quirino Grandstand where various official functions take place, including a military parade on Independence Day.

Manila Ocean World

Just behind the Quirino Grandstand is **Manila Ocean World** (Mon–Fri 10am–7pm, Sat & Sun 9am–8pm; P400), one of the city's newest and most popular attractions. At the time of writing the site still had a few glitches – the various shows, prices and packages on offer are a tad confusing and the whole thing is wrapped into yet another shopping mall, euphemistically dubbed Sunset Quay (daily 10am–9pm). The undoubted highlight is the **Oceanarium**, a huge saltwater tank viewed via a 25m-long walkway, packed with some 20,000 sea creatures. There are also spectacular light shows (P150), musical fountain shows (P250–300) and the *Liquid Bar & Pool* (Mon, Tues & Thurs 5pm–midnight, Wed & Fri 5pm–2am, Sat 1pm–2am, Sun noon–9pm; P180, P200 Sat & Sun, includes two drinks; for over-18s only). Shuttle buses (P30) run between the entrance and UN Avenue LRT station.

Museo ng Pambata

On Roxas Boulevard south of the *Manila Hotel*, the **Museo ng Pambata** (Children's Museum; April–July Tues–Sat 9am–5pm; Aug–March Tues–Sat 8am–5pm, Sun 1–5pm; P100 adults and children; ☎02/523-1797, ⓦwww.museopambata.org), has several hands-on exhibitions designed to excite young children; at the Maynila Noon exhibit they can get a feel for history using interactive displays – replicas of ships, churches and native Filipino homes – and there's also a simulated rainforest and seabed. On the first Saturday of every month there's shadow puppetry; on the third Saturday you can see music and dance (both start at 10am).

Metropolitan Museum

One of Manila's best-maintained museums, the **Metropolitan Museum** (Mon–Sat 10am–6pm; P100; ☎02/521-1517, ⓦwww.metmuseum.org) is located at the Bangko Sentral ng Pilipinas Complex on Roxas Boulevard, around 1.5km south of Museo ng Pambata. This arts museum houses a fine permanent collection of contemporary and historic works from Asia, America, Europe, Africa and Egypt, plus temporary displays of paintings, photographs and pottery from high-profile contemporary Filipino artists. The real highlight for history buffs lies in the basement, where the Central Bank's collection of **pre-colonial gold and pottery** is a stunning ensemble of magnificent jewellery, amulets, necklaces and intricate gold work. Most of it dates from between 200 BC and 900 AD, long before the Spanish Conquest. Look out for the extraordinary Kamagi Necklaces (long threads of gold), Islamic art from Lake Maranao, ancestral death masks and items from the Surigao Treasure (see p.425). The pottery section is dull by comparison, though some of the pots here are very ancient.

Cultural Center of the Philippines (CCP)

The **Cultural Center of the Philippines** (Tues–Sun 10am–6pm; free) on Pedro Bukaneg, was one of Imelda Marcos's grand plans for bringing world-class arts

Manila Bay by boat

Sun Cruises (☎02/527-5555, ⓦwww.corregidorphilippines.com), CCP Terminal A, Pedro Bukaneg Street, near the Cultural Centre, runs daily jaunts around Manila Bay, which can be fun despite the often distressing amounts of rubbish floating around – the views at sunset, surrounded by the volcanoes of Bataan and Batangas, are magical. Most cruises include a meal on board and run 4.30–5.45pm, 6.15–7pm and 8–9.15pm. Boats depart the wharf next to Jumbo Palace at the end of Pedro Bukaneg. Tickets are P550 per person.

to the Philippines. The main building stands on reclaimed land just off Roxas Boulevard, opposite the junction with Vito Cruz. Conceived during the early, promising years of her husband's presidency and opened on a night of great splendour in 1966, it's a slab-like construction typical of those built on Imelda's orders when she was suffering from her so-called "edifice complex". Various productions by Ballet Philippines and occasional Broadway-style hits such as *Miss Saigon* are staged in the main theatre, and there is a decent contemporary art gallery (free) on the third floor, showing temporary exhibits from Filipino artists. Upstairs on the fourth floor the **Museo ng Kalinangang Pilipino** (Tues–Sun 10am–6pm; P40) holds small but engaging temporary exhibits on various aspects of Filipino native cultures, as well as housing the permanent Asian traditional musical instruments collection. The CCP also encompasses several other properties beyond the main complex, further along Pedro Bukaneg, such as the **Folk Arts Theater**, which is the venue for occasional pop concerts, jazz and drama (see p.102), the **Manila Film Center** (see box below) and the **Coconut Palace** (see below). Note that ferries to the island of **Corregidor** (see p.109) leave from near the CCP.

The Coconut Palace

Built in 1978 on the orders of Imelda Marcos for the visit of Pope John Paul II three years later, the **Coconut Palace** is one of Manila's less visited gems, an outrageous but strangely compelling edifice, 70 percent of it constructed from coconut materials. The pope rightly gave Imelda short shrift when he arrived, saying he wouldn't stay in such an egregious establishment while there was so much poverty on the streets of Manila, and suggested she spend taxpayers' money (the equivalent of some US$10 million) more wisely. At the time of writing the palace looked set to become the official office of Vice President Jejomar Binay after a major renovation; ask at the Cultural Center to see if public tours will still be permitted.

The Manila Film Center

If bricks could talk, those at the Manila Film Center would have a sinister story to tell. Back in the 1970s, Imelda Marcos wanted to stage an annual **film festival** that would rival Cannes and put Manila on the international cultural map. But the centre she commissioned for the purpose was jerry-built and a floor collapsed in 1981, allegedly burying workers under rubble and killing many. No one knows exactly how many (some claim around 170), because most were poor labourers from the provinces and records were not kept of their names. Police were told to throw a cordon round the building so the press couldn't get to it, and work continued round the clock. The centre was completed in 1982, some say with dead workers still entombed inside, in time for the opening night of the Manila International Film Festival. Imelda celebrated by walking onto the stage to greet the audience in a black and emerald green *terno* (a formal gown) thick with layer upon layer of peacock feathers that were shipped specially from India.

The centre staged just one more film festival – some say it was haunted and Imelda herself had it exorcized – and it soon had to make ends meet by showing soft-porn (*bomba*) films for the masses. It was briefly rehabilitated in the late 1980s when it was used as a centre for experimental film-making, but after an earthquake hit Manila in 1990 it was abandoned. In 2001 it was partially renovated and now hosts transvestite song and dance extravaganzas organized by Amazing Philippine Theater (Tues–Sun 7.30pm & 9pm; P2000; ℡02/834-8870), especially popular with Korean tourists.

Ermita and Malate

Two of the city's oldest neighbourhoods, **Ermita** and **Malate**, nestle behind Roxas Boulevard within ten minutes' walk of Manila Bay. Ermita was infamous for its go-go bars and massage parlours up until the late 1980s, when tough-guy mayor Alfredo Lim came along and boarded up most of them, alleging that they were fronts for prostitution. Sadly, since 2000 the massages and KTV hostess bars have slipped back in, this time to serve busloads of Japanese and Korean high-spenders, and there has been a resurgence of prostitution in Ermita; it is now the Philippines second largest centre for paid sex after Angeles City. At the time of writing it looked like the government was starting to crack down on this, beginning the cycle all over again. Ermita and Malate otherwise remain in most part a ragbag of budget hotels, choked streets, fast-food outlets and bars, with street children all too prevalent on every corner, though the area does look to be changing; several high-end residential developments and hotels have already jazzed up some streets. There's not much in the way of traditional sights here, though Paco Park, just to the east, is worth a look if you have time.

Paco Park and Cemetery

One of the loveliest spots in Manila, **Paco Park and Cemetery** (Wed–Sun 8am–5pm; P5) is off a quiet street called San Marcellino at the end of Padre Faura, between Pedro Gil and UN Avenue LRT stations. It takes about fifteen minutes to get there on foot from central Ermita or Rizal Park.

A circular walled cemetery with an aged and beautiful garden dominated by a classical rotunda, Paco Park was built in 1820 just in time for victims of a cholera epidemic. After his execution in 1896 **José Rizal** was buried here in an unmarked grave. The story goes that his sister, Narcisa Rizal-Lopez, saw a group of guards standing beside a mound of freshly turned earth the length of a man; guessing this must be her brother's grave, she convinced the cemetery guardian to mark the site. Two years later Rizal's remains were exhumed and left in the custody of his family until 1912, when they were deposited beneath the Rizal Memorial (see p.79). A monument marks the location of the original grave.

The park's serenity has made it a favourite setting every Friday at 5pm and 6pm for free **open-air concerts**, usually classical recitals by Filipino artists or students. It's worth timing your visit to take in one of these performances – they're rarely packed, and it's pleasant to sit amid the greenery at sundown listening to Chopin sonatas or a Monteverdi madrigal.

The Museum at De La Salle University

Established in 1911, **De La Salle University** remains one of the most prestigious private Catholic colleges in the Philippines, tucked away in the southern end of Malate at 2401 Taft Ave (next to Vito Cruz LRT station). The **DLSU Museum** (Mon–Fri 8am–6pm, Sat 9am–noon; P50; ℡02/524-4611, ⓦthemuseum.dlsu .edu.ph) is really just a small gallery with revolving exhibits showing work from its substantial collection of modern Filipino artists such as Diosdado Lorenzo and Araceli Dans. Even if you're not an art fan, it's worth a quick look just to get a pass to wander the elegant neoclassical DLSU campus, far more redolent of classical Spain than the city outside. Register at the main entrance first (bring photo ID), then pay at accounting before heading to the gallery in Yuchengco Hall.

Binondo and Quiapo

Manila's Chinatown, **Binondo**, exercises a curious, magnetic pull. This is city life *in extremis*, a rambunctious ghetto of people on the make, the streets full of

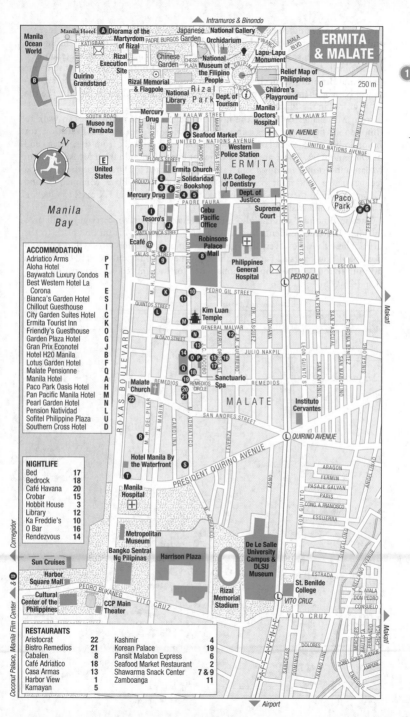

ERMITA & MALATE

0 — 250 m

Intramuros & Binondo

Manila Ocean World

Manila Hotel

A Diorama of the Martyrdom of Rizal

Japanese Garden

National Gallery

Orchidarium

PADRE BURGOS

FINANCE

AYALA BLVD

KATIGBAK

Rizal Execution Site

Chinese Garden

CHESS PLAZA

National Museum of the Filipino People

Lapu-Lapu Monument

Quirino Grandstand

Rizal Memorial & Flagpole

National Library

Relief Map of Philippines

B

SOUTH ROAD

Dept. of Tourism

Children's Playground

Rizal Park

i

Mercury Drug

M. KALAW STREET

T. M. KALAW ST

Museo ng Pambata

1

ALHAMBRA STREET

QUERINO ST

ORTIGAS ST

M. H. DEL PILAR

C Seafood Market

2

UNITED NATIONS AVENUE

A. BACOSI ST

Manila Doctors' Hospital

UN AVENUE

L

E United States

D

FLORES STREET

Western Police Station

UNITED NATIONS AVENUE

GENERAL LUNA

SAN MARCELINO

Manila Bay

ARQUIZA ST.

Ermita Church

E

Solidaridad Bookshop

3

F

4 5

Mercury Drug

ERMITA

TAFT AVENUE

U.P. College of Dentistry

Paco Park

H G

BELEN ST.

PEREZ

PADRE FAURA

Dept. of Justice

I

Tesoro's

J

Cebu Pacific Office

Supreme Court

LEON GUINTO ST

G. APACIBLE

J. L. ESCODA

SANTA MONICA STREET

Ecafé @

7

SALAS STREET

9

Robinsons Palace Mall

8

Philippines General Hospital

PEDRO GIL

L

M. H. DEL PILAR

K

10

PEDRO GIL STREET

SAN PEDRO

F. AGONCILLO

SAN MARCELINO

QUINTOS STREET

11

Kim Luan Temple

DR. VASQUEZ

INDIANA

L

M

GENERAL MALVAR

MARIA OROSA

M. GUERRERO

12

JULIO NAKPIL

LEON GUINTO

SAN ANTONIO

DIONYSIUS

SAN MARCELINO

ROXAS BOULEVARD

ALDAZO STREET

N

L.C. LOCOBO

13

14

O P

15 16

17

Sanctuario Spa

Q

18

19

Malate Church

REMEDIOS

20

REMEDIOS CIRCLE

MALATE

Instituto Cervantes

21

22

SAN ANDRES STREET

M. H. DEL PILAR

CAROLINA

ADRIATICO

ZEFERINO

R

L QUIRINO AVENUE

ARAGON

FERMIN

PASAJE GALVAN

PARIS

CONG. A. FRANCISCO

ESGUERRA

Hotel Manila By the Waterfront

S

PRESIDENT QUIRINO AVENUE

T

Manila Hospital

Metropolitan Museum

Bangko Sentral Ng Pilipinas

Harrison Plaza

De Le Salle University Campus & DLSU Museum

St. Benilde College

Sun Cruises

Harbor Square Mall

PEDRO BUKANEG

VITO CRUZ

Rizal Memorial Stadium

L VITO CRUZ

ESTRADA

DON PEDRO

CONSUELO

Cultural Center of the Philippines

CCP Main Theater

DOLORES

VITO CRUZ

ACCOMMODATION

Adriatico Arms	P
Aloha Hotel	T
Baywatch Luxury Condos	R
Best Western Hotel La Corona	E
Bianca's Garden Hotel	S
Chillout Guesthouse	I
City Garden Suites Hotel	C
Ermita Tourist Inn	K
Friendly's Guesthouse	O
Garden Plaza Hotel	G
Gran Prix Econotel	J
Hotel H20 Manila	B
Lotus Garden Hotel	F
Malate Pensionne	Q
Manila Hotel	A
Paco Park Oasis Hotel	H
Pan Pacific Manila Hotel	M
Pearl Garden Hotel	N
Pension Natividad	L
Sofitel Philippine Plaza	U
Southern Cross Hotel	D

NIGHTLIFE

Bed	17
Bedrock	18
Café Havana	20
Crobar	15
Hobbit House	3
Library	12
Ka Freddie's	10
O Bar	16
Rendezvous	14

RESTAURANTS

Aristocrat	22	Kashmir	4
Bistro Remedios	21	Korean Palace	19
Cabalen	8	Pansit Malabon Express	6
Café Adriatico	18	Seafood Market Restaurant	2
Casa Armas	13	Shawarma Snack Center	7 & 9
Harbor View	1	Zamboanga	11
Kamayan	5		

Corregidor

*Coconut Palace, Manila Film Center & *

83

Airport

merchants and middlemen flogging fake watches and herbs, sandalwood incense and gaudy jewellery. You can lose yourself for an afternoon wandering through its mercantile centre, snacking on dim sum at one of its many fan-cooled teahouses, and exploring the busiest thoroughfare in Binondo, **Ongpin Street**. A visit to the sepulchral **Binondo Church** will give you some idea of the area's historical significance. Nearby is the district of **Quiapo**, whose **Quiapo Church** is said to be the most visited in the Philippines.

From Magellanes Drive on the northern edge of Intramuros you can walk to Binondo in fifteen minutes across **Jones Bridge**. The best **LRT station** for Binondo is Carriedo at Plaza Santa Cruz, only a short walk from the eastern end of Ongpin Street. There are plenty of **jeepneys** to Binondo from M. Adriatico in Malate and Ermita, and also from Taft Avenue marked for Divisoria; the Divisoria jeepneys take you right past Binondo Church. From Plaza Miranda, behind Quiapo Church, there are buses to Makati, and jeepneys and FX taxis to Quezon City, Ermita and Malate.

Once in Binondo, you can also hire a **calesa** (horse-drawn carriage) – still used by some Binondo residents instead of taxis – to take you from one place to the next. These days, however, they generally serve tourists and rates will depend on how hard you bargain. Fares for short journeys should only cost P40, while a 30-minute tour of the whole Binondo area (or Intramuros) should cost no more than P250.

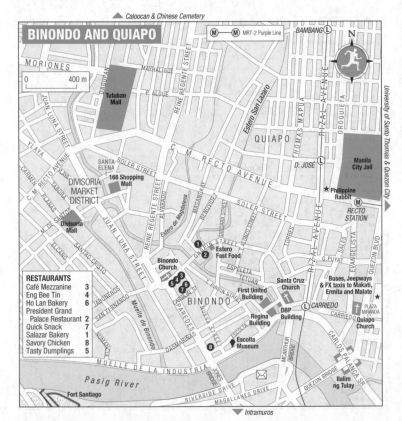

Binondo Church

The Minor Basilica of San Lorenzo Ruiz in Plaza de la Basco, at the western end of Ongpin Street, is commonly known as **Binondo Church** (daily 5am–6.30pm). It stands on the spot where Dominican priests established their church when they first came to Binondo in the seventeenth century, though the original building was destroyed by shelling in 1762 when the British invaded Manila and the Chinese were expelled. The Dominicans left with the Chinese but returned in 1842 and completed the church you see today, a solid granite structure with an octagonal bell tower and elaborate retable, in 1854.

The church was badly damaged by bombing during World War II and new features include the canopy at the entrance and the strikingly colourful murals on the ceilings. Depicting the life of Christ and the Assumption of the Virgin, these murals were not actually painted on the ceiling but were executed at ground level, then hoisted up.

The church is well known in the Philippines because it was where **Saint Lorenzo Ruiz**, the Philippines' first saint, served as a sacristan. Of Filipino and Chinese parentage, Ruiz was falsely accused of killing a Spaniard in 1636. It was probably because of this that he was encouraged to go to Japan, where he was arrested in Nagasaki in 1637 for spreading Christianity, and was executed for refusing to renounce his faith. The Vatican canonized him in 1987.

Ongpin Street

Behind Binondo Church is **Ongpin Street**, which is about 2km long and runs eastwards to Santa Cruz Church. It was originally called Calle Sacristia but was renamed in 1915 after Roman Ongpin, a fervent nationalist who was said to be the first Chinese-Filipino to wear the *barong tagalog*, the formal shirt that became the national dress for men. Ongpin Street is at the heart of Chinatown, chock-full of restaurants, noodle parlours, apothecaries and shops selling goods imported from China, though it tends to shut down early these days; you'll find the nearby Benavidez Street more lively at night.

Santa Cruz Church and Escolta

The eastern end of Ongpin Street empties into Plaza Santa Cruz near the Carriedo LRT station and **Santa Cruz Church** (daily 6am–10pm), an immense white Baroque structure. Originally built in the seventeenth century for the swelling ranks of Chinese in the area, it was most recently rebuilt in 1957 after damage from earthquakes and war. The most revered image inside is a 250-year-old replica of the Nuestra Señora del Pilar (the original image of this apparition of Mary is in Zaragoza, Spain), but the interior is otherwise unexceptional. Leading southwest off the plaza is **Escolta**, a once prestigious shopping street named after the horse-mounted military escorts of the British commander-in-chief during the British occupation of 1762. In the nineteenth century this was where Manila's elite promenaded and shopped, but its dizzy days as a Champs Elysées of the Orient are long gone. Only a few examples of the street's former glory remain; just across the river on the right is the **First United Building**, a pink and white Art Deco gem designed in 1928 by Andres Luna de San Pedro, the son of painter Juan Luna. Opposite is another of his buildings, the all-white **Regina Building** of 1934, at 400–402 Escolta, with its Art Nouveau cupolas (both buildings are occupied by shops and small businesses today). Further along in the beaux-arts Calvo Building, the quirky **Escolta Museum** (daily 9am–5pm; P50; ☎02/241-4538) is usually open by appointment only, but if the guard is around he should let you in. The main attraction is an extensive collection of multicoloured vintage bottles, but there are also scale models of Escolta's buildings, old photos and paper advertisements from the 1930s.

Quiapo Church

East of Plaza Santa Cruz lies **Quiapo**, a labyrinth of crowded streets and cheap market stalls, a universe away from the city's plush megamalls. Officially called the Basilica of St John the Baptist, **Quiapo Church** (daily 5am–7pm; ℡02/733-4434 ext 100) – as everyone in Manila calls it – is a short walk along Carriedo Street from Plaza Santa Cruz. The church is the home of the Black Nazarene, a supposedly miraculous wooden icon that came to the country on board a galleon from Spain in 1606 (it was enshrined here in 1767). The venerated life-size image carries a cross and is on display under glass at the back of the church (behind the altar to the left). On the edge of the nave, hunched old women will, for a fee, tell your fortune, pray the rosary for you or light candles for lost loved ones. The church burnt down in 1928 and was expanded in the 1980s to accommodate the crowds that gather every year on January 9 for the **Feast of the Black Nazarene**, when 200,000 barefoot Catholic faithful from all over the Philippines come together to worship the image.

The area around the church is a good area for bargain-hunters. Several stores that sell **handicrafts** at local prices are squeezed beneath the underpass leading to Quezon Bridge (aka Quiapo Bridge) on Quezon Boulevard, a place known as Ilalim ng Tulay ("under the bridge" or just Quiapo Ilalim).

Santo Tomas Museum of Arts and Sciences

The **Santo Tomas Museum of Arts and Sciences** (Tues–Sat 8.30am–4.30pm; P30; ℡02/781-1815), on the second floor of the main building of the University of Santo Tomas (UST), is a Victorian throwback, an old-fashioned but fascinating private collection of historic documents, rare books and dusty displays on ethnology, natural history, archeology and arts. Indeed, the collection dates back to 1871 and includes a stuffed orang-utan, a chair used by Pope John Paul II and a macabre pair of two-headed calves. There's also some medieval coins, an assemblage of religious statues, a rather incongruous collection of Chinese porcelain, and some decent art, including *Pounding Rice* (1940) by Vicente Manansala (who also created the stunning, Cubist-influenced *History of Medicine* murals adorning the lobby of UST's medicine faculty in 1958).

UST itself has an interesting history. It was founded in 1611, making it the oldest university in Asia, and served as an internment camp during World War II. The campus is much larger than it seems from the entrance, with the Main Building an impressive Spanish Revival pile completed in 1927, and the elegant Arch of the Centuries above the main entrance, combining the ruins of the original arch of 1611 and its replica, facing España Boulevard.

The university is about twenty minutes' walk (or a short ride on any jeepney marked UST) from Recto LRT station on the northern edge of Quiapo, via Lerma and España Boulevard.

The Chinese Cemetery

Four kilometres north of Chinatown, a short walk from Abad Santos LRT station, is the monumental **Chinese Cemetery** (use the South Gate entrance off Aurora Blvd; daily 7.30am–7pm; free), established by affluent Chinese merchants in the 1850s because the Spanish would not allow foreigners to be buried in Spanish cemeteries. Entire streets are laid out to honour the dead and to underline the status of their surviving relatives. Many of the tombs resemble houses, with fountains, balconies and, in at least one case, a small swimming pool. Many even have air conditioning for the relatives who visit on All Saints' Day, when lavish feasts are laid on around the graves with empty chairs for the departed. It has become a sobering joke in the Philippines that this "accommodation" is among the best in the city.

Malacañang Palace and Museum

Home of the governor-generals and presidents of the Philippines since the 1860s, the Malacañang Palace is a fittingly grand and intriguing edifice, well worth the minor hassle involved in arranging a visit. Much of the palace is permanently off-limits to the public, but you can visit the wing that houses the **Malacañang Museum** (Mon–Fri 9am–4pm; P50; ℡02/784-4286, ⓦwww.president.gov.ph) by making an appointment at least seven days in advance. You'll need to email or fax a letter of request to the palace, stating your name, preferred date and time of visit, and attaching a photocopy or scan of your passport; call first to confirm the latest procedure. You can also join a tour run by Ivan Man Dy of Old Manila Walks (℡0917/329-1622, ⓦwww.oldmanilawalks.com), which saves you the bother.

The Malacañang occupies the site of a smaller stone house dating from 1750. In 1825 the Spanish government bought it and, in 1849, made it the summer residence of the governor-general of the Philippines. After the governors' palace in Intramuros was destroyed in the earthquake of 1863, the move to Malacañang was made permanent and the property was extended several times over the years. The museum occupies the beautifully restored Kalayaan Hall, completed in 1921, and traces the history of the palace and of the presidency from Emilio Aguinaldo to the present day. The palace is in J.P. Laurel Street in San Miguel district, a short taxi ride east of Intramuros and Quiapo.

Makati

Makati, 5km east of Manila Bay, was a vast expanse of malarial swampland until the Ayala family, one of the country's most influential business dynasties, started

---

De-stressing Manila: spas, steam and shiatsu

After a day sweating it out on Manila's congested streets a couple of hours in a **spa** can be extremely tempting, especially now there are plenty of reputable ones serving stressed-out locals rather than sex-starved tourists. Note also that most of the five-star hotels listed in "Accommodation" (p.69) have excellent spas.

Neo Day Spa G/F, Net One Center Building, 26th St at 3rd Ave, Bonifacio Global City ℡02/815-8233, ⓦwww.neo.ph. Serene modern spa inspired by Zen minimalism, with elaborate Japanese-style massages from P1550 (90min), shiatsu (P950/1hr) and P420 head and neck massages (20min). Sun–Thurs 1–11pm, Fri & Sat noon–11pm.

Sanctuario 1826 J. Bocobo St, Malate ℡02/450-1127, ⓦwww.sanctuariospa.com. Fabulous spa that, unusually, has a Filipino theme; housed in a colonial-style mansion built in the 1940s, it's studded with Filipino artwork, antiques and tribal artefacts, and treatments feature indigenous as well as oriental styles and therapies. Try the traditional *hilot* (P855/1hr) a form of deep-tissue massage using coconut oil and performed by a genuine "medicine man". All treatments come with unlimited access to the dry sauna, steam room and the tranquil back garden, which has an outdoor pool and two jacuzzis. Sun–Thurs 3pm–midnight, Fri & Sat 3pm–3am.

Soneva Spa 4th Forum Building, Tomas Morato Ave, Quezon City ℡02/926-6249, ⓦwww.sonevaspa.com. Right on the main strip in Quezon City, this offers great value for your peso – come on a weekday afternoon and it's a dreamy, tranquil place with a huge roster of Xiamen (Chinese)-style massages from P699 (1hr) to P380 (feet) and P599 (back and feet combos). Daily 1pm–midnight.

The Spa G/F, Paseo de Roxas Drop-off Entrance, Greenbelt I, Makati ℡02/840-1325, ⓦwww.thespa.com.ph. One of a popular chain of deluxe spas, with the full range of massages and treatments, from Swedish massage (P820/1hr) to volcanic rock massages (P1500 for 1hr 15min). Daily noon–9pm.

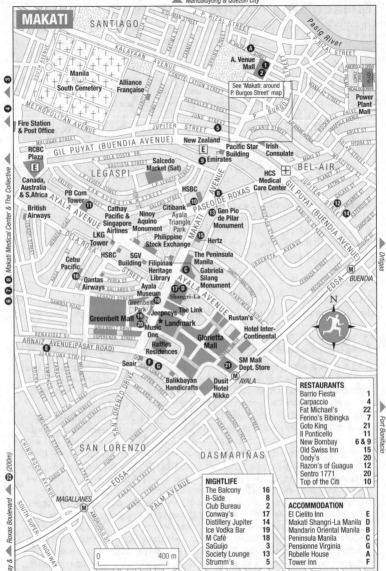

MAKATI

SANTIAGO

Mandaluyong & Quezon City

Pasig River

A. Venue Mall

Power Plant Mall

Manila South Cemetery

Alliance Française

See 'Makati: around P. Burgos Street' map

Fire Station & Post Office

RCBC Plaza

GIL PUYAT (BUENDIA AVENUE)

New Zealand

Pacific Star Building

Irish Consulate

Emirates

LEGASPI

Salcedo Market (Sat)

BEL-AIR

HCS Medical Care Center

HSBC

Canada, Australia & S.Africa

PB Com Tower

British Airways

Cathay Pacific & Singapore Airlines

Citibank

Ninoy Aquino Monument

Ayala Triangle Park

Gen Pio de Pilar Monument

LKG Tower

Philippine Stock Exchange

Hertz

Cebu Pacific

HSBC

SGV Building

Filipinas Heritage Library

The Peninsula Manila

Gabriela Silang Monument

Qantas Airways

Ayala Museum

Greenbelt Park

Shangri-La

Greenbelt Mall

Music One

The Link

Jeepneys

Landmark

Rustan's

Hotel Inter-Continental

Raffles Residences

Glorietta Mall

ARNAIZ AVENUE(PASAY ROAD)

Seair

SM Mall Dept. Store

AYALA

Balikbayan Handicrafts

Dusit Hotel Nikko

SAN LORENZO

DASMARIÑAS

MAGALLANES

Makati Medical Center & The Collective

Ortigas

BUENDIA

N

Fort Bonifacio

Pasay & Roxas Boulevard

(200m)

RESTAURANTS	
Barrio Fiesta	1
Carpaccio	4
Fat Michael's	22
Ferino's Bibingka	7
Goto King	21
Il Ponticello	11
New Bombay	6 & 9
Old Swiss Inn	15
Oody's	20
Razon's of Guagua	12
Sentro 1771	20
Top of the Citi	10

NIGHTLIFE	
The Balcony	16
B-Side	8
Club Bureau	2
Conway's	17
Distillery Jupiter	14
Ice Vodka Bar	19
M Café	18
SaGuijo	3
Society Lounge	13
Strumm's	5

ACCOMMODATION	
El Cielito Inn	E
Makati Shangri-La Manila	D
Mandarin Oriental Manila	B
Peninsula Manila	C
Pensionne Virginia	G
Robelle House	A
Tower Inn	F

0   400 m

developing it in the 1950s. It is now Manila's premier business and financial district, chock-full of plush hotels, international restaurant chains, expensive condominiums and monolithic air-conditioned malls, easily accessible via Ayala MRT station.

Opposite the station, the biggest mall is **Glorietta**, which has a central section and side halls numbered 1–5, and heaves with people seeking refuge from the traffic and heat. A short walk from Glorietta to the other side of Makati Avenue is

Greenbelt Park, a landscaped garden with the pleasant, modern, white-domed Santo Niño de Paz Chapel in the centre. The park forms part of Makati's other main mall, **Greenbelt**, which, like Glorietta, is divided into various numbered halls; on the north side is the excellent Ayala Museum (see below).

Just to the north is the pleasant green swathe of Ayala Triangle, bordered by Ayala Avenue, Paseo de Roxas and Makati Avenue. On the southeast corner facing Makati Avenue, the **Filipinas Heritage Library** (Tues–Sat 9am–6pm; ℡02/892-1801, ⓦwww.filipinaslibrary.org.ph) is an interesting little piece of history: it was Manila's first airport terminal, the Art Deco Neilson Tower, built in 1937 (Paseo de Roxas, the road to the north, was built where the runway used to be). Inside there's a bookshop that runs various literary-themed workshops. Further along Ayala Avenue, at the junction with Paseo de Roxas, is the **Ninoy Aquino Monument**, built in honour of the senator who was assassinated in 1983, while a block further on, the shimmering PBCom Tower (259m) at 6795 Ayala Ave is the tallest building in the Philippines (closed to the public).

Ayala Museum

Makati's one real attraction is the **Ayala Museum** (Tues–Fri 9am–6pm, Sat 9am–7pm; P425; ℡02/757-7117, ⓦwww.ayalamuseum.org) on Makati Avenue at De La Rosa Street (10min walk from Ayala MRT), by far the best place in the Philippines to get to grips with the nation's complex history. The mighty Ayala family donated much of the initial collection in 1967, and this modern building was completed in 2004. There are no dreary exhibits here, or ponderous chronological approach – the permanent exhibitions just highlight the key aspects of Philippine history beginning on the fourth floor with an extraordinary collection of pre-Hispanic goldware, created by the islands' often overlooked indigenous cultures between the tenth and thirteenth centuries. Over one thousand gold objects are on display, much of it from the Butuan area in Mindanao, including the "Surigao Treasure" (see p.425). Don't miss the astonishing gold regalia, a huge 4kg chain of pure gold thought to have been worn by a *datu* (chief). Other displays emphasize pre-Hispanic trade links with Asia, especially Song dynasty China, with a huge collection of porcelain and ceramics. On the third floor the "Pioneers of Philippine Art" showcases the museum's particularly strong collections of Juan Luna Realism, Fernando Amorsolo Impressionism and Fernando Zobel's more abstract work. On the second floor an extensive display of sixty dioramas dramatizes all the key events in Philippine history from prehistory to independence, while three audiovisual presentations tackle the postwar period, the Marcos years and People Power in 1986.

Manila American Cemetery and Memorial

On the southeastern edge of Makati, on the east side of EDSA and 3km away from Glorietta mall, is the serene **Manila American Cemetery and Memorial** on McKinley Road (daily 9am–5pm; free), containing 17,202 graves of American military dead of World War II, most of whom lost their lives in operations in New Guinea and the Philippines. The headstones are aligned in eleven plots forming a generally circular pattern, set among a wide variety of tropical trees and shrubbery. There is also a chapel and two curved granite walkways whose walls contain mosaic maps depicting the battles fought in the Pacific, along with the names of the 36285 American servicemen whose bodies were not recovered (rosettes mark the names of those since found and identified). From the Ayala LRT station you can walk to the cemetery in about twenty minutes, heading across EDSA near its junction with Ayala Avenue and along McKinley Road, passing the Santuario de San Antonio (the white church) and the Manila Polo Club on your right. The cemetery entrance is at the big roundabout about 1km past the polo club. A taxi from the centre of Makati will cost around P100.

Ortigas

Ortigas is a dense huddle of malls and offices, 5km north of Makati on EDSA, and can be reached by taking the MTR to Shaw Boulevard or Ortigas station. Ortigas began to come to life in the early 1980s, when a number of corporations left the bustle of Makati for its relatively open spaces; the Asian Development Bank moved here in 1991 and the old Manila Stock Exchange followed one year later.

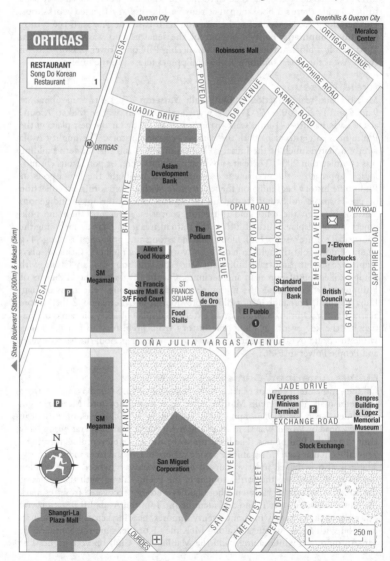

Today its biggest draw for Manileños is the SM Megamall, one of the region's largest shopping malls.

There is one genuine attraction in Ortigas, the **Lopez Memorial Museum** (Mon–Sat 8am–5pm; P100; ℡02/631-2417, Ⓦwww.lopez-museum.org), on the ground floor of the Benpres Building, on Exchange Road at Meralco Avenue (a brisk 15-minute walk from Ortigas station). The museum was founded in 1960 by Don Eugenio Lopez to provide scholars and students with access to his personal collection of rare books, the oldest of which is a priceless 1524 copy of the account of Magellan's circumnavigation of the world by Maximilianus Transylvanus. The museum's art collection includes important paintings by nineteenth-century Filipino masters Juan Luna and Félix Hidalgo, as well as selected works by artist Fernando Amorsolo, who gained prominence during the early 1930s and 1940s for popularizing images of Philippine landscapes and beautiful rural Filipinas. The museum's Rizaliana includes some ninety letters written by José Rizal to his mother and sisters in the 1890s, along with the national hero's wallet and paint-brushes, his flute and personal papers. Exhibits rotate every six months, as there's not enough space to display everything at once, but the library section always contains some of the best rare books, artwork and letters.

Marikina Shoe Museum

Nothing symbolizes the vanity of Imelda Marcos more than her collection of shoes, which numbered in the thousands on the eve of the EDSA revolution in 1986 (it's not known how many she owns today). This ghastly (but admittedly stylish) legacy is preserved at the **Marikina Shoe Museum** (Mon–Sat 9am–5pm; P40) on the eastern side of the city, where 749 pairs of the former first lady are displayed under her giant portrait, along with pairs owned by each president of the Philippines (the worn-out-looking shoes owned by Ferdinand Marcos make quite a contrast) and several other local celebrities. The history of shoemaking is explained upstairs. The museum is on J.P. Rizal Street in Marikina; take a taxi from the Katipunan LRT station.

Eating

Eating in Manila is a real treat; there's a full range of international and Filipino cuisine on offer, and budget eats available on every street corner and in every mall in the form of vast food courts (see box, p.92). Filipinos are big fans of fast-food franchises, with national chains such as *Jollibee*, *Chowking*, *Mang Inasal* (with unlimited rice) and *Max's* (for fried chicken) dotted all over the city. You should also pay a visit to one of the ubiquitous *Goldilocks* (Ⓦwww.goldilocks.com.ph) stores, purveyors of the best *polvoron* (peanut candy) and cakes since 1966.

Intramuros

The old walled city of Intramuros doesn't have many restaurants, but those it does have are mostly in old colonial buildings and are significantly more atmospheric than anything beyond the walls. For cheap eats, try the stalls (plates from P45) within the walls on the eastern edge of Intramuros or in nearby San Francisco Street, in an area known as **Puerta Isabel II**. See map on p.75.

Barbara's Plaza San Luis Complex ℡02/527-408. Elegant dining in a colonial setting, with woody interiors and rich Filipino food. This is a popular venue for lavish wedding receptions (it might be closed on Sat afternoon). Dishes average P250–400. Mon–Sat 11am–2pm & 6–10pm.

Top Manila food markets

Salcedo Community Market Jaime Velasquez Park, Bel-Air, Makati (see map on p.88). One of Manila's culinary highlights, featuring a dazzling display of gastronomic delights from all corners of the Philippines to take away or enjoy at one of the communal tables. Sat 7am–2pm.

Market! Market! Bonifacio Global City, east of Makati (see map on p.88). This spotless high-end market comes with tempting fresh fruit stalls and a massive covered food court. Daily 11am–8pm.

Power Plant Mall Rockwell Drive and Estrella St, Makati (see map on p.88). For a large and slightly more upmarket selection of restaurants and stalls check out this plush mall on the edge of Makati. There's also a huge **Rustan's** supermarket (ⓦwww .rustansupercenters.com), a good choice for self-catering (it has 20 branches in Manila). Open daily.

St Francis Square Mall Ortigas (see map on p.90). During the week the alley along the east side of this budget mall is cheap-eats paradise at lunchtime, with huge pots of delicious Filipino food dolled out for a few pesos; at the back there's **Allen's Food House**, with similar setup but more room to breathe, charging P40 for a meal. Inside St Francis Mall itself, the 3/F Food Court is another excellent place for local food (with a/c). Open daily.

Seaside Paluto Restaurants & Market Macapagal Ave, facing Manila Bay (see map on pp.62–63). Choose your fresh seafood at one of the stalls here (shrimps cost around P330/kilo, crabs P350/kilo, fish from P160/kilo), before proceeding to a restaurant to get it cooked (*Claire de la Fuente* at the entrance is a smart choice). Open daily.

SIDCOR Sunday Market Centris Walk, Quezon City, just off EDSA near Quezon Ave MRT station (see map on p.73). Featuring 450 stalls selling a variety of fresh veg, fruit, meat and seafood. Sun 6am–2pm.

SM Department Store Food Court Makati, close to Ayala MRT Station (see map on p.88). Offers a solid and cheap selection of standard food court options. Mon–Thurs & Sun 10am–9pm, Fri & Sat 10am–9.30pm.

Ilustrado 744 General Luna, at the back of Silahis Center, facing Carildo ☎02/527-3674, ⓦwww .ilustradorestaurant.com.ph. Nothing compares to *Ilustrado* if you are looking for the ambience of colonial Manila. The floors are polished wood, the tables are set with starched linen, ceiling fans whirr quietly and the cuisine is grand. Signature dishes include paella, Filipino beef stew, venison *adobo* and a three-course set dinner with steak (P1000) or fish (P800) as the main course. Mon–Sat 11.30am–3pm & 6–10pm.

Kuatro Kantos 744 General Luna (Calle Real). This charming little bar and café in the same old building as *Ilustrado* opens for

breakfast and stays open until 7pm – perfect for a good cup of coffee or a bite to eat while you're wandering around Intramuros. The hot *pan de sal* with corned beef or *carabao* cheese makes an excellent and very affordable snack, and their pesto is home-made and organic. Daily 8am–7pm.

Patio de Conchita 681 Beaterio St ☎02/527-1324. This great find is off the beaten path but an excellent place to have lunch; food is served buffet style, with a range of top-notch Filipino dishes. Try the *sinigang na baboy* (sour soup with pork) and freshly barbecued squid from P120. Mon–Sat 11.30am–3pm & 6–10pm.

Ermita and Malate

Almost everyone who dines out in **Ermita** and **Malate** does so either in one of the big hotels or in the area around J. Nakpil Street and Remedios Circle, where most of the restaurants are small, intimate and not owned by big corporations. Bear in mind that J. Nakpil is a fickle, faddish area, and restaurants come and go. See map on p.83.

Aristocrat 432 San Andres St, facing Roxas Blvd ⊕02/524-7671. Established out of an old van in 1936, *Aristocrat* is an institution among Filipinos for its justly lauded barbecued chicken (P195) and pork (P159), as well as the whole spread of Filipino comfort food. The special *halo-halo* (P100) here is an extravagant concoction of taro ice cream, sliced banana, beans, *nata de coco*, ice and evaporated milk. Don't miss the famous *bibingka* stall outside. Daily 24hr.

Bistro Remedios 1911 M. Adriatico St, just off Remedios Circle ⊕02/523-9153. Informal and homey little restaurant with pretty Filipiniana interior and charming staff. The food is exclusively Filipino, with cholesterol-filled fried pig's knuckles, beefy stews and hefty chunks of roast pork. There's also good fish and prawns, but not a great deal for vegetarians, although pineapple fried rice is on the menu (average meals P300). Mon–Fri 11am–3pm & 6–11pm, Sat & Sun 11am–3pm & 6pm–midnight.

Cabalen Robinsons Place, Level 2 Padre Faura Wing ⊕02/536-7987. Hugely popular chain of restaurants famed for their gut-busting buffets (P298) of traditional dishes from the province of Pampanga, including *camaru* (rice-field crickets), *batute* (fried pigs' trotters), *kuhol* (escargots), *sinigang tiyan ng bangus* (milkfish belly) and desserts such as *tibok-tibok*, *tibok-mais* and *halayang ube*, all made from root crops. There are six other branches, including one in Glorietta, Makati and at the SM Mall of Asia (P392, with extra Chinese and Japanese dishes). Daily 10am–9pm.

Café Adriatico 1790 M. Adriatico St ⊕02/738-8220. This chic but casual stalwart of the Malate nightlife scene opened a quarter of a century ago and was at the forefront of the area's revival. Light Spanish-Mediterranean themed meals include salads, omelettes and fondues (dishes average P150–300). Try the authentic *chocolate-eh*, a thick chocolatey drink served as an anytime "snack". Mon–Sat 7am–6pm, Sun 7am–4pm.

Casa Armas 573 J. Nakpil St at J. Bocobo St ⊕02/523-5763. Fashionable tapas bar serving big plates of sautéed shrimps in olive oil and garlic (P365), fried Spanish sausage (P285) and Galician octopus (P280), as well as omelettes, soups and salads. Mon–Sat 11am–midnight Sun 6pm–midnight.

Harbor View South Gate A, Rizal Park (between the US Embassy and *Manila Hotel*) ⊕02/524-1532, ⓦwww.harborview-manila.com. Located right on the harbour, perfect for sunset viewing, cool breezes, fresh seafood from the tank and all the classic Filipino dishes (from P200). It's a bit like a posh beach bar. Daily 11am–midnight.

Kamayan Merchant Building, 523 Padre Faura St at Adriatico St ⊕02/528-1723, ⓦwww.kamayan.com.ph. Excellent-value buffet restaurant with three sections: a traditional selection of unpretentious native dishes such as grilled fish, spicy crab, roast chicken and some good vegetables; a Western section with more conventional roast beef and the like; and a Japanese area with sushi, tempura and noodles. The staff are dressed in elegant Filipino costumes and strolling minstrels work the tables doing requests. Mon–Thurs lunch is P545, dinner P645; on Fri & Sat it's P645 all day. Daily 11am–2pm & 6–10pm.

Kashmir Merchants Center Building, 523 Padre Faura St (next to *Kamayan*) ⊕02/524-6851, ⓦwww.kashmirmanila.com. Curry, chicken tikka, a mouthwatering selection of breads and wonderfully cheesy ersatz Raj decor. Be warned, the *Kashmir* chefs can be liberal with the spices, so think twice when the waiters ask if you want it very hot. Main dishes range P350–500. There's another branch at Fastejo Building, 816 Arnaiz Ave in Makati. Daily 11am–11pm.

Korean Palace 1799 M. Adriatico St at Remedios St ⊕02/521-6695. One of a number of excellent Korean restaurants in the area, in part serving the growing numbers of Koreans here on a night out. Large menu that includes some good dishes to share, such as fried beef, chicken or fish with piping-hot rice and various side dishes including tangy pickled cabbage (mains P200–550). Daily 10am–midnight.

Pansit Malabon Express 103 B. Ermita Center Building, 1350 Roxas Blvd ⊕02/521-7403, ⓦwww.pansitmalabon.com. Famed purveyor of tasty fried noodles (*pansit Malabon*) in servings large enough for four people (from P300), as well as barbecue chicken meals (P120) and *bangus* (milkfish; P150). Daily 9am–9pm.

Seafood Market Restaurant 1190 J. Bocobo St ⊕02/521-4351. Here the day's catch is laid out on ice and you pick from whatever the boat brought in. The choice typically includes giant prawns, lapu-lapu, lobster, fish lips and sea slug, all cooked as you watch by wok chefs in a glass-fronted kitchen. A huge meal for two with a few beers will cost around P800. Daily 11am–2pm & 6–11pm.

Shawarma Snack Center 45 Salas St ⊕02/525-4541. Two branches of the *SSC* face each other across Salas St, so take your choice of plastic tables or a more rarefied atmosphere with table-cloths. The Middle Eastern dishes in both are superb and plentiful, with possibly the best falafels (P95) and kebabs (P165) in the city, and certainly the hottest chilli sauce. Mains mostly under P150. Located in a small Muslim enclave in Malate, replete with halal food and a small mosque just off the road. Daily 24hr.

Zamboanga 1619 M. Adriatico St, Malate ☎02/521-7345. Fresh seafood from the deep south of the Philippines, a trio of crooning guitarists and nightly cultural shows at 8.30pm (mostly folk dance). This is the restaurant that features on many travel agents' night-time city tours, but still lots of fun after a few drinks (mains range P250–475). Daily 11am–11pm.

Binondo and Quiapo

Binondo has no fancy restaurants and no bistros or wine bars; people come here for cheap, nourishing Chinese food in one of the area's countless Chinese restaurants or hole-in-the-wall noodle bars. Binondo and Quiapo also have a number of bakeries that are known in the Philippines for their *hopia*, a sweet cake-like snack with a soft pastry coating and thick yam paste in the middle. You can load up with Chinese snacks, dried squid and other packed foods at Bee Tin Grocery, 735 Ongpin St (daily 7.30am–7.30pm). See map on p.84.

Eng Bee Tin 628 Ongpin St ☎02/288-8888, ⓦwww.engbeetin.com. Filipinos often come to Binondo just to make a pilgrimage to this well-known bakery, which has specialized in various kinds of sweet, sticky mooncake and *hopia* since 1912. The bakers here invented *ube hopia*, made with sweet purple yam and now imitated throughout the country, and you can also buy *tikoy*, the sweet rice cake that is traditionally served during Chinese New Year. Daily 7.30am–8.30pm. Its *Café Mezzanine* (daily 6am–10pm) further along the street serves Chinese fast food from P85.
Ho Lan Bakery 551 Yuchengco St ☎02/242-9709. Classic bakery serving *hopia* rolls for P38, but also squidballs and savoury treats. Mon–Sat 7.30am–8pm, Sun 7.30am–5pm.

🏃 La Cocina de Tita Moning 315 San Rafael St, San Miguel ☎02/734-2146, ⓦwww.lacocinadetitamoning.com. See map on pp.62–63. Located in an ancestral home (the Legarda House) east of Quiapo, near the Malacañang Palace, this is an exceptional dining experience (expect to spend P1500/head). Guests get a tour of the house before eating in the antique dining room; expect sumptuous home-cooked dishes such as slowly roasted pork with crackling and candied sweet *camote*, or *kare kare de pata* (peanut stew with pig's trotters) with organic brown rice. Reservations required, 24hr in advance (minimum two persons). Open daily by appointment for lunch and dinner.
President Grand Palace Restaurant 746–750 Ongpin St ☎02/243-4988. Plush Cantonese restaurant with an extensive and occasionally elaborate menu that includes bird's nest and shark's fin (from P300). More mundane and ecologically uncontentious dishes include excellent crab, lemon chicken, spicy pork with bean curd and a good selection of fresh vegetables. Best experienced with a group (so you can order multiple dishes to share), but they also serve hearty noodle and rice dishes suitable for single diners (from P140). Daily 10.30am–11pm.

🏃 Quick Snack 637–639 Carvajal St ☎02/242-9572. Tucked away down a side alley crammed with wet market stalls, it doesn't get better than this for a cheap, home-cooked Hokkien-style meal. It's best known for its *lumpia* (spring rolls; P40) and *kuchang-an*, a sort of meat pie, *machang* (*zongzi* or rice wrapped in banana leaf) and oyster omelette (*e-a jian*; P170). Daily 8am–6.45pm.
Salazar Bakery 783 Ongpin St ☎02/733-1392. This bakery dates from 1947 and does a tasty *hopia* (P35), but is also great for savoury *asado* rolls and small chicken pies – the hefty mooncakes (P115) are also worth a try. Daily 5am–10pm.
Savory Chicken 201 Escolta St ☎02/243-0336. Legendary masters of fried chicken and sensational gravy since 1950 (half chicken P170, whole P320), with branches in SM Mall of Asia. Also do superb *bagoong* rice (P150) and noodles (P180). Daily 8am–midnight.
Tasty Dumplings 620 Ongpin St ☎02/242-5195. No-frills diner with justly popular pork dumplings going for P70; also does great pork chops (P99) and fresh soybean milk (P28). Mon–Sat 10am–9pm, Sun 9am–9pm.

Makati

Makati is the best place in the city when it comes to quality and variety of restaurants, with most options in or around the **Glorietta** or Greenbelt malls, or Burgos Street further north where there are a growing number of Korean and Japanese places. Bonifacio Global City, to the east, is an emerging destination for mostly high-end restaurants. See map on p.88.

Barrio Fiesta Makati Ave at Valdez St ☎02/899-4020. There are various branches of this colourful Filipino restaurant dotted around the city, all serving favourites such as pork *adobo* and *lechon* (roast pig) with hefty portions of rice and daily buffet options. P300 gets you a meat/seafood main and a singing waiter. Daily 9am–midnight.

Carpaccio 7431 Yakal St ☎02/843-7286. Popular but never uncomfortably busy, this casual little restaurant tucked away down a side street behind Makati Fire Station serves excellent regional Italian food and has a good, affordable wine list. The speciality is carpaccio – the beef carpaccio (P370) is delicious – but almost everything is good (pasta and pizza P340–520), including the home-made ice creams and sorbets. Expats love this place, and it's also got a loyal following among the local office crowd. Daily 11am–2.30pm & 6–10pm.

Fat Michael's 1354 Gen Lacuña St at Rodriguez Ave, Bangkal (near Magallanes MRT station) ☎02/843-1953. The main reason to make a pilgrimage to this cosy restaurant is not the food (which is so-so) but the lovely interiors, furnished with gorgeous antique lamps, paintings, and other bric-a-brac (many from the nearby thrift shops), and most available for purchase. The rosemary-herbed chicken (P145) and beef salpicao (P295) are solid choices for a meal. Mon–Sat 11am–10.30pm.

Ferino's Bibingka Cash & Carry Mall (Osmena Hwy and Gil Puyat); also on Makati Ave near Jupiter St (see map on p.88); ⊛www.ferinos bibingka.com. This *bibingka* franchise hails back to a family business established in 1938. Look out for their small carts in malls, worth trying for the tasty charcoal-cooked rice cakes (P95), daubed with coconut and salted egg. Usually 24hr.

Goto King 8 SM Food Court, Lower Ground Floor, SM Makati ⊛www.gotoking.com.ph. Beloved *congee* (rice porridge) chain established in 1984 with basic *congee* P39, and other varieties (egg, *chicharon* or fried pig skin) at P48–70. Has expanded in recent years to serve a wider merienda (snack) menu (*baboy*, *lugaw* etc), with branches in just about every SM mall. Daily 10am–8pm.

Il Ponticello 2/F Antel 2000 Building, 121 Valero St ☎02/887-7168. A bit tricky to find, tucked away in the backstreets of Makati between rows of anonymous office blocks, but worth the effort. This agreeable Italian restaurant serves excellent pizzas (from P240) – a refreshing change from the fast-food pizzas that Manila loves so much – and superb risotto from P280. The best tables are by the window, but you'll have to book to get one of those. There's also a fashionable bar inside called *Azzuri*. Mon–Fri 11am–2pm & 5.30pm–3am, Sat 5.30pm–3am.

New Bombay G/F, Sagittarius Building III, 312 H.V. Dela Costa St ☎02/819-2892. Speak to Indian residents in Manila and most will tell you this functional little restaurant is peerless for authentic Indian food. The menu is extensive and includes snacks such as mixed pakora, samosas, curries and freshly prepared naan, roti and chapati. Cheap, cheerful and very tasty (mains from P150). Branch in Glorietta and Greenbelt 2. Daily 9am–11pm.

Old Swiss Inn 7912 Makati Ave at Olympia Towers ☎02/818-0098, ⊛www.oldswissinn.com. Traditional food (heavenly Gruyère fondue from P650), funky alpine decor and waitresses in milkmaids' costumes – this place is as Swiss as cheese with a 24hr menu that also includes Hungarian sausages (P250) and Zurich *geschnetzeltes* (shredded pork; P350). Daily 24hr.

Oody's Level 2, Greenbelt 3 ☎02/757-4259. Excellent choice for a quick, affordable light meal. The speciality here is noodles in all forms, including Thai, Japanese, Italian pasta and Filipino. The rice meals are good value at P200–250; the *bagoong* (salty fish paste) rice (P198) is very fishy, but goes down well with a glass or two of fresh fruit juice (P65–75). Daily 11am–11pm.

Razon's of Guagua 22 Jupiter St ☎02/899-7841. Famous Pampanga *halo-halo* (P85; shaved ice dessert) and pancit *luglug* (P85; fried noodles) chain, with pork *adobo* from P165. Daily 10am–9.30pm.

Sentro 1771 Level 2, Greenbelt 3 ☎02/757-3940. Well-run, modern Filipino restaurant that's packed with office workers at lunchtime and the pre-cinema crowd in the evenings. The affordable menu (P230–520) includes modern variations of classics such as pork *adobo*, pancit (noodles) and Bicol Express (spicy stew); the specialty is *sinigang na* corned beef (sour stew with corned beef; P310). Daily 11am–11.30pm.

Top of the Citi 34/F Citibank Tower, 8741 Paseo de Roxas ☎02/750-5810, ⊛www.chefjessie.com. Mingle with Manila's upper class in this temple to fine dining with soaring views of the city and office workers below. Top chef Jessie Sincioco crafts modern Filipino cuisine such as crunchy pork *sisig* with mayonnaise, Japanese dishes, pasta, steaks and her famous dessert soufflés (the chocolate flavour is hard to beat), while the trendy bar gets all the attention from 5pm with the best cocktails in the city. Mains average P300–450. Mon–Fri 8am–10pm.

Around P. Burgos Street
See map on p.72.

Alba 38-B Polaris St ☎02/896-6950. Cosy Spanish restaurant with faux adobe walls and a wandering guitarist who croons at your table. Dishes include tasty tapas from P150, a large menu of paellas (from P410), and plenty of fish and stuffed squid from P300. Mon–Sat 11am–11pm.

Hossein's Persian Kebab 2/F, 7857 LKV Building, Makati Ave ☎02/890-6137, ⓦwww.hosseins.com. This glitzy take on a kebab house has froufrou decor and prices to match. If you're not in the mood for a brain sandwich, you can choose from dozens of Persian, Arabian and Indian dishes (with a huge range of curry and kebabs). Daily 11am–midnight.

Next Door Noodles 7876 Makati Ave ☎02/899-1893. Cheap-and-cheerful Chinese place, almost opposite its sister restaurant, *North Park Noodles*, which has a similar menu at the same low prices. Fantastic value – almost everything on the menu is under P200 (dim sum P40–75, noodles in soup P126 to P175 and fried rice P128). Daily 24hr.

Rufo's Famous Tapa 4736 Kalayaan Ave at Salamanca St ☎02/899-4207. Chain best known for its *tapa*, tender Batangas beef, marinated and served in a rich, sweet sauce with a side order of fried egg and garlic rice (P89). Their boneless *bangus* (milkfish; P89) and *tocino* (cured pork; P85) is also excellent. Daily 24hr.

Shinjuku Ramen House 7853 Makati Ave at Hercules St ☎02/890-6107. Some of the best Japanese noodles (*ramen*) in the city, with a vast choice ranging from basic *miso ramen* (P195) to more fancy pork and mushroom versions (P280). Daily 10am–1am.

Top Dish 4890 Durban St, near P. Burgos St ☎02/758-1122. The best hole-in-the-wall Korean restaurant in town, with reasonable prices, big

portions and excellent *kimchi* (pickled cabbage). Daily for lunch and dinner.

Ziggurat G/F Sunette Tower Building, Durban St at Makati Ave ☎02/897-5179. A seemingly endless menu featuring exotic dishes from all over the Middle East, Mediterranean and East Africa (try the mezze combos from P650), with flavoured hookahs to round things off. Count on about P150–300 for most dishes. Open 24hr.

Bonifacio Global City (Fort Bonifacio)

See map on pp.62–63.

Abe Restaurant Serendra, Bonifacio Global City ☎02/856-0526. Most taxi drivers will know this much-loved Filipino restaurant (Capampangan-style), with the two highlights Abe's chicken supreme (chicken stuffed with *galapong* rice, chestnuts and raisins; P840 for two) and mutton *adobo* with popped garlic (P395). Other dishes utilize forest ferns, banana plant, tiny crabs and fabulous pork knuckle. Daily 11am–11pm.

Aubergine 32nd & 5th Building, 5th Ave at 32nd St ☎02/856-9888, ⓦwww.aubergine .ph. The best reason to jump in a taxi and head over to Fort Bonifacio, this top-notch restaurant and patisserie delivers fresh ingredients and crisp flavours; the French-inspired international menu features pan-fried Norwegian salmon (P860), honey-glazed French duck breast (P950) and red-wine-braised Australian lamb shank (P820). Daily 11.30am–2pm & 6–10pm.

Ortigas and Greenhills

The malls at Ortigas and Greenhills are chock-full of small restaurants and fast-food outlets, while most of the **budget stalls** surround St Francis Square Department Store at the back of SM Megamall. See map on p.90.

Frazzled Cook 916 Luna Mencias St (near Shaw Blvd) ☎02/782-5980. See map on pp.62–63. Shabby-chic purveyor of legendary *paella negra* (P400 for two people), a short taxi ride west of Ortigas proper. Serves an otherwise eclectic menu including steaks (P380), spicy lamb kebabs (P450) and scampi pizza (P320). Tues–Sun 11am–10.30pm.

Lugang Café 116 Connecticut St, Greenhills, San Juan ☎02/721-9100. See map on pp.62–63. Tucked away in Greenhills, between Ortigas and Quezon City (Santolan MRT), this is arguably the

best Chinese restaurant in the city, part of the Shanghai-based Bellagio group and best known for its magnificent Taiwanese food, pork buns and *xiaolong bao* (pork dumplings; P158). Daily 6–11pm.

Song Do Korean Restaurant El Pueblo Real, ADB Ave at Julia Vargas St, Ortigas ☎02/636-4821. Top-notch Korean food in the entertainment hub of El Pueblo, serving a wide range of dishes from barbecued eel (P450) to *bulgogi* (P300) and a classic *bibimbap* (vegetables, ground beef and fried egg with spicy sauce and steamed rice; P340). Daily 10am–10pm.

Quezon City

Quezon City is a burgeoning alternative to Makati and the Manila Bay area for restaurants and nightlife. Most of the restaurants are on **Tomas Morato Avenue**, which runs north and south from the roundabout outside the *Century Imperial Palace Suites* hotel. See map on p.73.

To get to Quezon from the south of the city (from Malate and Makati, for example) you can take the MTR and get off either at Kamuning station or Quezon Avenue station, a journey of about 25 minutes.

Behrouz 63 Scout Tobias St (Scout is abbreviated Sct on most maps) ☏ 02/374-3242. Great late-night hole-in-the-wall snack place, run by a family of Iranians who cook authentic food, though alcohol isn't served. The lamb kebabs, beef *kobideh* (ground-beef kebab) and aubergine-based *moutabal* (a bit like baba ghanoush) are all superb – reckon on P200–300 for a meal. Daily 5pm–5am.

Gerry's Grill Tomas Morato Ave at Eugenio Lopez St (close to the ABS-CBN studios) ☏ 02/415-9514, ⓦ www.gerrysgrill.com. This is the original outlet of the now popular chain, serving provincial Filipino dishes such as crispy *pata* (pig's knuckle; P425) and *sisig* (fried pig's ear and pig's face; P175). Sun–Thurs 11am–2am, Fri & Sat 11am–3am.

Lydia's Lechon 118 Timog Ave ☏ 02/921-1221, ⓦ www.lydias-lechon.com. The *lechon* at this local favourite is delicious (especially the boneless *lechon* stuffed with paella), but the secret is the sauce, a sweet, barbecue concoction that will have you hooked. Slightly better than rival *Elarz Lechon* at 151 Quezon Ave (☏ 02/732-4116). Daily 9am–9pm.

Pancit ng Taga Malabon G/F Food Center, Landmark-Trinoma Mall, EDSA ☏ 02/703-2229. The chain that claims descent from the original "pancit Malabon" stall in the 1890s, when the addictive concoction of oysters, squid, shrimp, smoked fish (*tinapa*), *chicharon*, crab and duck eggs over thick rice noodles and golden sauce (P80) became known as "*pancit bame*" – Malabon was the location of the stall and has since been applied to noodle dishes nationwide.

Peking Garden 3/L TriNoma Mall ☏ 02/901-0502. Best Peking duck in the Philippines, a crispy, juicy delight served up to three ways (soup, in pancakes, and minced in lettuce leaves). Set menus start at around P1500. Daily 11.30am–2pm & 6–10pm. Also in Greenbelt 5, Makati.

Yakimix Tomas Morato Ave ☏ 02/332-8073. This all-you-can-eat Japanese and Korean food buffet is a fabulous deal (P499 lunch and P580 dinner). Add P65 to drink as much San Miguel as you like. Daily 11am–2pm & 6–11pm.

Drinking and nightlife

Few visitors to Manila are disappointed by the buoyant, gregarious nature of its **bars** and **clubs**. This is a city that rarely sleeps and one that offers a full range of fun, from the offbeat watering holes and gay bars of Malate to the chic wine bars of Makati. Manila also has a thriving **live music** scene, with dozens of bars hosting very popular and accomplished local bands almost every night. Clubs are especially prone to open, close and change names with frequency, so check before you head out – websites such as ⓦ www.mag24-7.com and ⓦ guestlist.ph are good places to get the latest information.

Karaoke Manila style

Forget cheesy versions of "My Way" and "Yesterday", Filipino KTV joints offer the latest hits for your crooning enjoyment (or embarrassment); think Green Day and Beyonce. A good place to start is **Music Match**, with great facilities, choice of songs and cheap snacks and booze. It has three branches; 3/F Forum Building, 270 Tomas Morato Ave (at Scout Limbaga), Quezon City (☏ 02/927-8531); Ortigas Home Depot, Julia Vargas Ave, Pasig City (☏ 02/470-2745) and Unit no. M1M2, Hobbies of Asia, 8 Macapagal Ave, Pasay City (☏ 02/556-1295). Rates start at around P400 for up to 3 hour (you get your own room), with packages including drinks and food starting at P1500.

Ermita and Malate

Ermita and Malate nightlife is a somewhat confusing mixture of budget restaurants, genuine pubs and a once again flourishing girlie bar scene, with as many Asian (mostly Korean) male patrons as Westerners. Adding to the melee at the intersection of J. Nakpil and Maria Orosa streets is the centre of Manila's gay club scene. If none of that appeals the Roxas Boulevard end of Remedios Street is full of cheap-and-cheerful places popular with students for their cover bands and drinks. Don't make the mistake of arriving early because most places don't even warm up until after 10pm and are still thumping when the sun comes up, with crowds in summer spilling out onto the streets. Friday, as always, is the big night, with many places closed on Sunday. See also *Ka Freddie*'s on p.83.

Bedrock 1782 M. Adriatico St, Malate ☏02/522-7278, ⍾bedrockmalate.moonfruit.com. A vaguely Flintstones-esque interior, lack of a cover charge and better-than-average cover bands have made this an Adriatico St institution. Two bands play three sets each of poppy hip-hop nightly. Mon–Wed & Sun 6pm–4am, Thurs–Sat 6pm–5am.

Café Havana 1903 M. Adriatico St, Malate ☏02/524-5526. Live samba music, a cigar lounge and Cuban food and cocktails all add to the classy atmosphere. Once dinner's over everyone leaps up to put their salsa skills to the test. There's another branch on the ground floor of Greenbelt, Makati. Daily 5pm–2am (Adriatico St), 11am–2am (Greenbelt).

Crobar 620 Julio Nakpil St at Maria Orosa St, Malate ☏02/710-7768. Malate's premier dance club starts the night as a restaurant before Manila's top DJs pump out house, r'n'b and electro till the early hours. Daily 6pm–late.

Hobbit House 1212 Del Pilar at Arquiza St, Ermita ☏02/484-0982, ⍾www.hobbithousemanila.com. In 1973 entrepreneur Jim Turner decided to open a bar that would pay homage to his favourite book, *The Lord of the Rings*. He staffed it with twenty midgets and a legend was born. *Hobbit House* has somehow endured, still employing short people, a huge list of bottled beers, Tex-Mex food and nightly appearances at 9pm by a variety of local bands, some good, some miserably bad. It has also become a notorious tourist trap, with busloads of visitors brought in every night to have their photographs taken alongside the diminutive staff. Daily 5pm–2am.

Library 1739 Maria Orosa St, Malate ☏02/522-2484, ⍾thelibrary.com.ph. Nightly stand-up/karaoke from veteran Manila drag queens where audience participation is very much part of the show. P100 cover charge.

Rendezvous (formerly *Koko's Nest*) Adriatico St, Malate. Friendly little bar next door to *Malate Pensionne* – no girls, no shows. A great first stop on a night out; the pavement-side tables offer unbeatable people-watching, and a bucket of San Miguel will set you back just P200.

Gay nightlife in Manila

The **gay scene** in Manila is vibrant and becoming more so. Even bars and clubs that aren't obviously gay are unreservedly welcoming and gay, straight, transvestite and transgender people mix easily and boisterously in the same nightclubs and bars. The whole area around Maria Orosa St and Julio Nakpil St in Malate are lined with gay bars and other places are scattered throughout the city. The best **bars** are not hard to find; *Bed* (J. Nakpil St at Maria Orosa St ☏02/536-3045, ⍾www.bed.com.ph) was Malate's biggest and boldest gay club, but sadly burnt down in 2010; at the time of writing the plan was to reopen the club bigger and better than before, but check the website for the latest. The *O Bar* at 1801 J. Nakpil St and Orosa St (Mon–Thurs 7pm–4am, Fri & Sat 7pm–6am, Sun 8pm–3am) is always crowded – especially on weekends – and there are sometimes drag shows and go-go dancers. Over in Pasig City, the *Clarke Quay Comedy Bar* at 405 Lope K. Santos St, San Joaquin (☏0915/612-9385) is a gay- and lesbian-friendly sing-along bar with nightly performances by gay entertainers and comedians. The nightly transgender extravaganzas put on by the **Amazing Philippine Theatre** at the Manila Film Center (see p.81) are extremely popular, and the shows at the *Library* are also worth checking out (see above). A useful website for Manila gay listings is Utopia (⍾www.utopia-asia.com). See p.44 for other gay resources.

Makati

Makati nightlife has traditionally revolved around office workers spilling out of the nearby banks and skyscrapers, but these days much of middle-class Manila party's in the bars and clubs here, with plenty of expats and travellers thrown in – it's generally smarter, safer and more fashionable than Malate. The area around Burgos Street is a bit seedier, though the girlie bar scene here is being driven more by Korean and Japanese KTV-style joints these days, and there are several genuine pubs in between offering cheap beers and snacks.

The Balcony G/F, Doña Angela Gardens, 110 C. Palanca Jr. St, Legazpi Village ☎02/810-7832. Fashionable bar/dance club, with massive Wednesday parties, a mostly well-heeled local clientele and creative DJs. Wed, Fri & Sat 9.30pm–5.30am.

B-Side The Collective, 7472 Malugay St, near Buendia Ave, Makati ☎0922/998-9512. Bar/club venue for cutting-edge hip-hop, soul and dance DJs from all over the world. Cover usually P200–300. Tues–Sat 9pm–4am.

Club Bureau A. Venue Mall, Antel Lifestyle City, 7829 Makati Ave ☎02/383-6660. Cool bar and club with a decent roster of resident DJs spinning an eclectic mix of music for weekend dance parties, a solid sound system and funky lighting. Daily 6pm–midnight.

Conway's *Makati Shangri-La Hotel*, 2/F, Makati Ave ☎02/840-0884. The most popular happy hour in Makati, with all-you-can-drink San Miguel for P500 (5.30–8.30pm) and live music (Mon–Sat 8.30pm–1am, 1hr on, 30min off) from some excellent middle-of-the-road bands. The crowd is a happy and hard-drinking mix of young Filipino *corpies* (corporate types), expats and travelling executives staying at the hotel. Mon–Sat 5pm–2am, Sun 5pm–midnight.

Distillery Jupiter 20 Jupiter St ☎02/403-5293. Bar with the widest variety of vodka, tequila, single malt Scotch and rare foreign beers. Happy hour runs 6–9pm and DJs get people dancing at the weekends, with especially crazy Friday nights. Mon–Sat 5pm–4am, Sun 5pm–1am.

Ice Vodka Bar Level 3, Greenbelt 3, Makati Ave ☎02/757-4472. Limitless free-flowing Vodkatinis for P395 between 7 and 10pm (and a free pizza thrown in for good measure) helps loosen up the image-conscious young crowd. Sun–Thurs 5pm–2am, Fri & Sat 6pm–4am.

M Café Ayala Museum, Greenbelt 4, Makati Ave ☎02/757-3000. *Museum Café*, or *M Café*, as it's known, is a swish little place serving drinks and snacks all day, and snazzy cocktails at night. On Thurs and Fri it's open till 3am with DJs. Light meals P200–400. Sun–Wed 8am–midnight, Thurs & Fri 8am–3am, Sat 8am–4am.

Society Lounge G/F Atrium, Makati Building, Makati Ave at Paseo de Roxas ☎02/408-1852.

Plush French-Asian fusion restaurant that morphs into trendy lounge bar every night, with plenty of fine wines and champagnes on offer. DJs spin house music at the weekends when it becomes more like a club. Daily: restaurant 11am–3pm & 6–11pm; lounge bar 11pm–3am.

Around P. Burgos Street

Beers Paradise 36 Polaris St at Durban St ☎02/895-9272. Small, informal place in which to quaff serious Belgian beers (they also claim to have over 100 brands from around the world), from the sledgehammer-in-a-glass 12 percent Bush Ambrée ale to the comparatively tame Duvel and Chimay brands (P130–300). Daily 5pm–3am.

Handlebar 31 Polaris St ☎02/898-2189, ⓦwww .handlebar.com.ph. Hospitable biker bar owned by a group of Harley fanatics. It's primarily for drinkers (with lots of sport on the TVs) but the food also makes it worth a visit. The menu is nothing exotic, just solid, satisfying pizzas, burgers and pasta, or Big John's BBQ from P200–600. Mon–Thurs 3pm–2am, Fri & Sun 11am–3am.

Heckle & Jeckle Villa Building, Polaris St at Jupiter St ☎02/890-6904, ⓦwww.heckleand jeckle.org. *Heckle & Jeckle* scooped everyone when it became the first bar in the Philippines to show live English Premier League football on Saturday and Sunday nights from 10pm. Live bands on Fridays and pool tournaments on Thursdays are enhanced by the decent Belgian and German beers that make a change from San Miguel. Happy hour runs 4–10pm (Mon–Fri; 4–7pm Sat & Sun). Free wi-fi. Mon–Thurs 4pm–6am, Fri–Sun 2pm–6am.

Howzat 8471 Kalayaan Ave at Fermina St ☎02/890-6904, ⓦhowzat.ph. Popular sports bar showing all major global sports events in wide TV screens via satellite (including Premier League games). Daily specials include San Miguel all you can drink for just P295 (local spirits for P325), curry buffets on Friday (P375) and a scrumptious Sunday roast for P495. Mon–Thurs 10am–2am, Fri–Sun 8am–2am.

Kyss 5343 Gen Luna St at Makati Ave ☎02/519-6925. Trendy fusion restaurant (Mon–Sun 7–11.30pm) and lounge bar that opened in 2010 with popular club nights that have raised the standard in the Burgos area – check to see if "Beauty Lokal" Thursdays is still on. Club open Wed–Sat 10pm–4am.

Bonifacio Global City (Fort Bonifacio)

See map on pp.62–63.

7th High Club B3, Quadrant 4, The Fort Entertainment Center, Bonifacio Global City ☎02/856-1785. Ultra-stylish club where the emphasis is on drinking and mingling (the dancefloor is quite small) and the elegant lounge area and tables come with a hefty price tag. Scarlet Wednesdays is the most happening midweek party in the city. Wed–Sat 10pm–4am. Cover P500.

Amber Ultralounge Unit F, The Fort Entertainment Center, Bonifacio Global City ☎02/887-6838. Another über-hip bar and lounge that morphs into a club later on, with spacious interiors, two floors, thumping sound system and a tempting array of cocktails (think pineapple mojitos and Coco Lychee Smash). Cover P500. Mon–Sat 7pm–2.30am.

Encore Unit D, The Fort Entertainment Center, Bonifacio Global City ⓦwww.encore superclub.com. New incarnation of the notorious Embassy superclub which opened in November 2009 with a promise to city officials to be better behaved. International DJs play Mon (from 7pm; P650 cover includes drinks), Wed (P400 with 3 drinks), Fri and Sat (from 9pm; P500 with 3 drinks).

Quezon City

Quezon City's entertainment district is focused on Tomas Morato and Timog avenues, which intersect at the roundabout in front of *Century Imperial Palace Suites* hotel. The area has a growing reputation for quality live music (see below), while for more mainstream nightlife there are plenty of chic bars and franchised hangouts at the southern end of Tomas Morato Avenue, near the junction with Don A. Roces Avenue. See map on p.73.

Barrakz 295 Tomas Morato Ave at Scout Rallos St ☎02/928-5683. This multi-level military-themed bar, restaurant (Filipino food) and club looks a bit like a whimsical theme park ride from the outside, with servers dressed in camouflage fatigues that salute each customer. DJs spin mostly techno and recent pop hits. Daily noon–4am.

Conspiracy Garden Cafe 59 Visayas Ave ☎02/453-2170, ⓦwww.conspi.net. See map on pp.62–63. This wonderfully ethnic little performance venue and café is a meeting place for artists, musicians, poets, songwriters and women's groups. *Conspiracy* was set up by the artists who perform there, among them luminaries of the independent Filipino music scene such as Joey Ayala, Cynthia Alexander and Noel Cabangon, who all

perform regularly. Well worth the taxi ride out there, but check first to see who's on. Daily 5pm–2am.

The Lounge 2/F, 243 Bellagio Square, Scout. Fuentebella St at Tomas Morato Ave ☎0917/5367-113. Swish lounge bar and club with excellent theme nights ranging from "Old Skul Tuesdays" (r'n'b and hip-hop) and "Stiletto Thursdays" (ladies' night) to "Scandalous Saturdays" (house). Tues–Sat 7pm–late.

Padi's Point G/F *Century Imperial Palace Suites*, Tomas Morato Ave ☎02/920-7864, ⓦwww .padispoint.com. Boisterous beer hall that serves very average Filipino food, although most guests are too drunk to care. Thursdays and Saturdays are disco nights, with happy hour (P100 for 3 bottles) Sun–Thurs 6–10pm. There are several branches scattered around the city, listed on the website.

Pasay City

See map on pp.62–63.

LAX Structure C, SM Mall of Asia ☎02/215-2659, ⓦwww.laxmanila.ph. Big, glamorous nightclub popular with a younger crowd and featuring plenty of hip-hop and r'n'b. Ladies' nights on Wed have open bar to 11pm. Wed, Sat & Sun 10pm–5am.

Republiq Atrium, Newport Mall, Resorts World Manila ☎0917/550-8888, ⓦwww.republiqclub.com. New generation of megaclub (with a strong claim to be the best club in the nation) and party central for Manila's beautiful people, with giant LCD screens, top-notch

DJs, plush lounge area and a whopping great sound system. Cover usually P500 (includes two drinks). Wed, Fri & Sat 9.30pm–5.30am.

Opus 2/F, Newport Mall, Resorts World Manila ☎02/856-0128. This jaw-dropping restaurant lounge bar has to be seen to be believed, with shiny silver sofas and vast Italian Renaissance-like murals on the walls, glass-encased booths, veined marble bar and an array of glamorous cocktails. Daily 5pm–2am.

Live music venues

Quezon City in particular has a reputation for live music, especially from up-and-coming bands formed by students from the nearby University of the Philippines who offer an eclectic range of music – from pure Western pop to grunge, reggae and indigenous styles. Many of the venues in the area are dark, sweaty places that open late and don't close until the last guest leaves. In Makati and Malate too, you're never far from a club with a live band, especially at weekends. Again, the music covers a range of genres.

70s Bistro 46 Anonas St, Quezon City ☎02/434-3597, ⓦwww.70sbistro.com. See map on p.73. Legendary (in the Philippines) live music venue playing host to some of the country's best-known bands as well as to impromptu jam sessions with big local names who happen to turn up. A great Manila experience and a cheap one too. Admission is rarely more than P100 and beers are P30. The only problem is it's a bit tricky to find: Anonas St is off Aurora Blvd on the eastern side of EDSA, Quezon City. Mon–Sat 5pm–2am.

Ka Freddie's M. Adriatico St at Pedro Gil St, Malate ☎02/526-7241, ⓦfreddieanakaguilar.com. See map on p.83. Music bar and restaurant opened summer 2009 by Filipino folk legend Freddie Aguilar. Check out their Facebook page for who's playing. Daily 11am–2am.

Music Museum Service Rd, Greenhills, San Juan ☎02/722-4532, ⓦwww.musicmuseum.com.ph. See map on pp.62–63. This "leisure-entertainment hub" hosts concerts, comedy shows, ballet, theatre and poetry readings, but the music is still the main

attraction; the acts are mostly popular Filipino pop and rock acts.

Ratsky 243 Tomas Morato Ave at Scout Fuentebella St, Quezon City ☎02/373-9883. See map on p.73. On your right a short walk south along Tomas Morato from the *Century Imperial Palace Suites*. Perhaps the most famous live music venue in QC, the club that gave a number of popular acts their break. There are live rock and alternative bands every night except Sunday from 9pm. Sun–Thurs 6pm–2am, Fri & Sat 6pm–3am.

SaGuijo 7612 Guijo St, San Antonio, Makati ☎02/897-8629, ⓦwww.saguijo.com. See map on p.88. This hip, arty bar is currently the best indie place in Manila, with both its live music (from 10.30pm nightly) and art gallery supporting up-and-coming talents. Effortlessly cool, but not pretentious with it. Tues–Sun 6pm–1am.

Strumm's 110 Jupiter St, Makati ☎02/895-4636. See map on p.88. Party-like atmosphere greets nightly bands at this Makati stalwart, mostly pop and indie but also old-school jazz on Tuesdays. Daily 5.30pm–2am.

Entertainment

When it comes to traditional performing arts – **dance and theatre**, for example – Manila hosts daily performances at the Cultural Center of the Philippines and a handful of other venues. The **Araneta Coliseum** in Cubao is the usual venue for large-scale events and concerts. As for **films**, every mall seems to have half a dozen screens. A good place to check upcoming events and buy tickets in advance is Ticketworld (☎02/899-9991, ⓦwww.ticketworld.com.ph) or TicketNet (☎02/911-5555, ⓦwww.ticketnet.com.ph).

Theatre, dance and classical music

The Philippines has a rich **folk arts** heritage, but a scarcity of funds and committed audiences with money to spend on tickets means it's in danger of being forgotten. Folk dances such as *tinikling*, which sees participants hopping at increasing speed between heavy bamboo poles which are struck together at shin-height, are seen in cultural performances for tourists, but are only performed occasionally in theatres. The same goes for *kundiman*, a genre of music that reached its zenith at the beginning of the twentieth century, combining elements of tribal music with contemporary lovelorn lyrics to produce epic songs of love and loss.

Most performances at the following theatres are listed in the Manila English-language daily press, usually the *Philippine Daily Inquirer* and the *Philippine Star*. It's also worth checking listings websites such as ⓦwww.clickthecity.com and the ticketing websites listed above.

Cultural Center of the Philippines Roxas Blvd, Ermita ⓣ02/832-1125 to 1139, ⓦwww.culturalcenter.gov.ph. Events here range from art exhibitions to Broadway musicals, pop concerts, classical concerts by the Philippine Philharmonic Orchestra, *tinikling* and *kundiman*. The CCP is also home to the Tanghalang Aurelio Tolentino (CCP Little Theater), where smaller dramatic productions are staged and films shown; Ballet Philippines (ⓣ02/832-3704, ⓦballetphilippines.org for box office); Bayanihan, the National Folk Dance Company (ⓦwww.bayanihannationaldanceco.ph); and the CCP's resident theatre group, Tanghalang Pilipino, dedicated to the production of original Filipino plays (July–March). Nearby is the Folk Arts Theater, built for the Miss Universe Pageant in 1974 and now staging occasional rock concerts and drama.

Globe Theatre at Onstage Greenbelt 1, Makati. Small venue mainly staging drama by local theatre groups, including Repertory Philippines (ⓣ02/571-6926, ⓦwww.repertory.ph), Manila's premier English-speaking theatre group (Jan–April).

Meralco Theater Meralco Ave, Ortigas. Stages everything from ballet by overseas companies to pantomimes with local celebs.

Paco Park and **Rizal Park** Paco Park has free classical concerts at 6pm on Friday, performed under the stars in the historic cemetery; Rizal Park stages similar free concerts every Sunday at 6pm.

Cinemas

Most shopping malls in Manila house **multiplex cinemas** that show all the Hollywood and Asian blockbusters in the original languages, including The Podium mall (18 ADB Ave in Ortigas; ⓣ02/633-8976), with late-night screenings on Fridays and Saturdays; Greenbelt 3 (ⓣ02/729-7777) in Makati and Power Plant Mall, Rockwell Drive, Makati (ⓣ02/898-1440). Tickets are usually around P150. In the Malate area, try Robinsons Place in M. Adriatico Street (ⓣ02/536-7813).

Sport in Manila

For a general overview of sport in the Philippines, see p.41. In Manila you'll have quite a bit of choice if billiards, bowling or golf is your thing. In Malate you can try Bowling Inn (daily 10am–1am), 1941 Taft Ave; in Makati, Coronado Lanes, 2/F Anson's Arcade, A. Arnaiz Ave (daily 10am–1am); in Ermita, Paeng's Midtown Bowl, Level 2, Robinsons Place. There are three **golf** courses in Manila where non-members can turn up and pay for a round. The Army Golf Club, in what was the Fort Bonifacio base south of Makati (ⓣ02/812-7521), has some of the lowest green fees in the country (P530–770). Nearby is the Villamor Golf Course (ⓣ02/833-8630), home of the Philippine Masters, which charges green fees of P1200–1900. Club Intramuros east of Bonifacio Drive (ⓣ02/527-6612 or 6613) has a compact eighteen-hole course that runs along the walls of the old city. A caddie here costs P300, club rental P520, while green fees for non-residents are P1400.

Spectator sports

Because the PBA (Philippine Basketball Association) teams are owned by corporations, and do not play in a home stadium, most **basketball** games are played at the Araneta Coliseum in Cubao, or the Cuneta Astrodome on Roxas Boulevard, Pasay City (games usually run Wed, Fri & Sun, Oct–July). Tickets in the cheap seats, the "bleachers", cost as little as P10, while a ringside seat will set you back P250 to P600. Tickets are available from Ticketnet (see p.101) or ⓦwww.pba.com.ph.

Major **cockfighting** venues in Manila include the huge air-conditioned Pasay City Cockpit (Dolores St), where "derbies" take place most weekends from noon (around P20 entry fee).

Tickets for Greenbelt and Glorietta cinemas can be reserved online at ⓦwww .sureseats.com for collection at the venue.

A venue for arthouse and independent films is the **UP Cine Adarna** (☎02/981-8500), UPFI Film Center building at Magsaysay and Osmeña avenues to the northeast of Quezon Memorial Circle, but screenings don't take place every day, so call ahead.

Shopping

The combination of intense heat and dense traffic means many Manileños forsake the pleasures of the outdoors at weekends for the computer-controlled climate of their local **mall** – there can be few cities that have as many malls per head of population as this one. Note that the developers rarely pay as much attention to the surrounding roads as they do to their precious real estate, which means that traffic is especially gridlocked in these areas. Despite the growth of malls there are still plenty of earthy markets in Manila where you can buy food, antiques and gifts at rock-bottom prices, as well as some decent bookshops and fashion boutiques. One trendy local brand to look out for is Bench (ⓦwww.benchtm.com), which sells Ben Chan's men's and women's lines in stores all over the city.

Books

The best general bookshop in Manila is **Powerbooks** (ⓦwww.powerbooks.com .ph), which has seven branches around the city including those at Glorietta 3 (Sun–Thurs 10am–9pm, Fri & Sat 10am–10pm) and Greenbelt 4 in Makati (daily 10am–10pm), and Level 4 Manila Midtown, Robinsons Place, Ermita (Sun–Thurs 10am–9pm, Fri & Sat 10am–10pm). There are branches of **National Bookstore**, the country's major bookshop chain, in Quezon City (Quezon Ave), Fort Bonifacio, Ermita and Malate – at Harrison Plaza and Robinsons Galleria – but as ever their stock is limited to contemporary thrillers, literary classics and *New York Times* bestsellers, with much of what's on offer stocked specifically for students. The bookshop with the best literary section in town is **Solidaridad Bookshop**, 531 Padre Faura St, Ermita (Mon–Sat 9am–6pm). It's owned by the novelist

---

Life beyond the mall – indie retailers

Megamalls haven't completely taken over Manila. **Cubao-X** (Cubao Expo) is a hub of independent retailers on General. Romulo Avenue in Quezon City (a short walk from Cubao MRT station), with numerous indie clothing stores, creative furniture stores, art galleries and thrift shops. Similarly in Makati, some of Manila's coolest designers have established the **Collective** (7274 Malugay St, San Antonio). The hub of 22 independent shops includes:

Longboards Manila Unit L ☎0917/850-2025, ⓦwww.longboardsmanila.com. Skateboarder heaven. Tues–Sat 1–9pm.

Ritual Unit A ☎0926/645-9478, ⓦwww.ritualshop.com. Organic grocery selling pink rice, local salts, sugar, lemongrass and coffee (bring your own containers). Tues–Sat noon–9pm.

Skitzo Unit M ☎0917/882-0114, ⓦwww.skitzomanila.com. Costume shop crammed with garish outfits, glasses and accessories. Tues–Sat noon–9pm.

Vinyl on Vinyl Unit H ☎0922/848-7427, ⓦwww.vinylonvinyl.blogspot.com. Sells old records and collectable vinyl toys (cartoon and anime characters). Tues–Sat 3–11pm.

F. Sionil José and, apart from stocking his own excellent novels, has a small selection of highbrow fiction and lots of material on the Philippines.

Handicrafts and souvenirs

The first stop for tourists looking for indigenous gifts and **handicrafts** is usually **Balikbayan Handicrafts** (ⓦ www.balikbayanhandicrafts.com). They sell a mind-boggling array of souvenirs, knick-knacks, home decorations, reproduction native-style carvings and jewellery, plus some larger items, such as tribal chairs, drums and musical instruments; staff can arrange to ship your purchases if requested. The biggest of their outlets is the cavernous Pasay branch along Macapagal Avenue, just south of the cultural centre (ⓣ02/831-0044), with the other at 1010 Arnaiz Ave (Pasay Rd) in Makati (ⓣ02/893-0775), both open daily 10am–7pm. **Teosoro's** 1325 A. Mabini St, Ermita (daily 9am–7.30pm; ⓣ02/524-3936, ⓦ www.tesoros.ph) is another handicraft chain selling woven tablecloths, fabrics, *barongs* and reproduction tribal crafts such as *bulol* (see below). Not as big as Balikbayan, but more convenient to budget hotels in Ermita. The other main branch is at 1016 Arnaiz Ave (Pasay Rd), Makati (ⓣ02/887-6285). There are tourist shops all over the place selling reproduction tribal art, especially *bulol* (sometimes spelt *bulul*) – depictions of rice gods, worshipped by northern tribespeople because they are said to keep evil spirits from the home and bless farmers with a good harvest. Genuine *bulol* are made from narra wood and are dark and stained from the soot of tribal fires and from blood poured over them during sacrifices. Opposite San Agustin Church in Intramuros is the Silahis Center (see p.74), a complex of small art and tribal shops selling everything from *bulol* and oil paintings to native basketware and jewellery. See also markets opposite.

Malls

Bonifacio High Street Bonifacio Global City, Taguig ⓦ www.ayalamalls.com.ph. Manila's newest and most lavish mall development, which links to the Market! Market! development of themed retail zones, fruit and flower markets, and a regional food and hawker's area. The Fort Bus (Mon–Sat 6am–10pm; every 30min) connects Ayala MRT station with the shopping centre. Daily 11am–11pm.

Glorietta Makati ⓦ www.ayalamalls.com.ph. A maze of passageways spanning out from a central atrium, Glorietta has five sections, a large branch of Rustan's department store, and heaps of clothes and household goods. At the Makati Ave end of the complex is Landmark, a big, functional department store that sells inexpensive clothes and has a whole floor dedicated to children's goods. Most of the restaurants are near the atrium and there's a food court on the third floor, above Marks & Spencer. Daily 10am–10pm.

Greenbelt Off Makati Ave, Makati, ⓦ www .ayalamalls.com.ph. This whole area has undergone – and is still undergoing – extensive redevelopment. Greenbelt 3 and 4 on Makati Ave are the most comfortable for a stroll and a spot of people watching. Most of the stores are well-known chains – Greenbelt 3 has the affordable stuff (including Nike, Adidas and Marks & Spencer) and Greenbelt 4 is full of expensive big names such as Ferragamo and DKNY. There are some excellent restaurants in Greenbelt 3 for all budgets, and coffee shops such as *Seattle's Best* and *Starbucks*. Daily 10am–9pm.

Power Plant Mall Rockwell Dr, about 1km west of Guadalupe MTR (from P. Burgos you can walk it in 15min), ⓦ www.powerplantmall.com. Upscale mall home to Rustan's supermarket, as well as some furniture shops selling imported teak items from Indonesia. Most of the mid-range brand names are also here, along with small shops selling fashion items for teenagers, a couple of good baby clothes shops, and electronics shops selling mobile phones and cameras. Daily 10am–10pm.

SM Mall of Asia End of EDSA in Pasaty City, facing Manila Bay ⓦ www.smmallofasia.com. Hard to believe that this vast complex is just the second largest in the Philippines (SM City North EDSA is the biggest), containing the first ever IMAX in the city, a seafront promenade, bowling alley, ice rink and hypermarket as well as numerous restaurants and stores that appeal to a younger crowd. You can get handy minibuses to here from Baclaran Market (below). Open daily 10am–10pm. SM also has the two megamalls in Ortigas (daily 10am–midnight), and the smaller department store (Sun–Thurs 10am–9pm, Fri & Sat 10am–10pm) in Makati, among many locations in Metro Manila.

Markets

Taking a taxi from one of Manila's opulent malls to a more traditional market district such as Quiapo or Divisoria is like going from New York to Guatemala in thirty minutes – the difference between the two worlds is shocking. Needless to say, prices in Manila's markets are a lot cheaper than the malls.

168 Shopping Mall Santa Elena and Soler sts, Binondo. Technically a two-section mall but more like a market with over 1000 stalls, flooded with mostly Chinese-made leather handbags, jackets, T-shirts, wallets, caps, toys, shoes and clothes for incredibly low prices. Forms part of the Divisoria market district (see below).
Baclaran Market Pasay City. This labyrinthine street market is spread tentacle like around the Baclaran LRT station; little stalls huddle under the LRT line as far as the EDSA station, and fill Dr Gabriel St as far west as Roxas Blvd. The focus throughout is cheap clothes and shoes of every hue, size and style, though you'll also come across fake designer watches and pirated CDs and DVDs. The market is a big, noisy, pungent place, and often incredibly crowded, but lots of fun. On Roxas you can pick up yellow minivans that will whisk you to SM Mall of Asia for P7. The market is open all week, but especially crowded every Wednesday, the so-called Baclaran Day, when devotees of Our Mother of Perpetual Help crowd into the Redemptorist church on Dr Gabriel St for the weekly *novena*.
Divisoria Market District Claro M. Recto Ave, North Binondo. For a range of bargain goods, from fabric and Christmas decorations to clothes, candles, bags and hair accessories, try fighting your way through the crowds at the immense market district. The pretty lanterns (*parols*) made from *capiz* seashells that you see all over the country at Christmas cost half what you would pay in a mall. The actual Divisoria Mall is at Tabora and Santo. Cristo streets, but it's the warren of streets around it that are good for bargains (especially Juan Luna, Ylaya, Tabora, Santo Cristo and Soler).
Greenhills Tiangge Greenhills Shopping Center, Ortigas Ave, San Juan Ⓦ www.greenhills.com.ph. Sprawling market inside this mall north of Makati and notorious for its illegal bargains: fake designer goods as well as pirated software and DVDs. There's also an area full of stalls selling jewellery made with pearls from China and Mindanao; a good-quality bracelet or necklace made with cultured pearls will cost from P1000, depending on the style and the number of pearls used. There's also attractive costume jewellery on sale. Other sections of the mall offer cheap mobile telephones (some secondhand), household goods and home decor. Daily 10am–10pm.
Ilalim ng Tulay Quezon Blvd, Quiapo. You can hunt down the cheapest woodcarvings, *capiz*-shell items, *buri* bags and embroidery in Manila among the ramshackle stalls beneath the underpass leading to Quezon Bridge in Quiapo (literally "under the bridge"); tell drivers "Quiapo Ilalim".

Listings

Airlines The main Philippine Airlines ticket offices are at the *Century Park Hotel*, P. Ocampo St, Malate (Mon–Fri 8.30am–5pm, Sat 8.30am–noon; ☏02/523-1554) and 2/F, Power Realty Building, 1012 Arnaiz Ave in Makati (same hr; ☏02/892-7339). Cebu Pacific (☏02/702-0888) has offices at Robinsons Place (Adriatico entrance) in Malate (daily 7am–9pm) and Robinsons Galleria, West Lane, Level 1, Ortigas Ave (daily 10am–9pm). Seair is at 2/F, La'O Centre, Arnaiz Ave in Makati (☏02/849-0239) and Zest Airways is at the Philippine Business Bank Building, Yakal St in Makati (☏02/888-2002). Other airlines with offices or representatives in Manila include: Air Canada, G/F, Unit 14-A, Colonnade Residences Condominium, 132 Carlos Palaca Jr. St, Legazpi Village, Makati ☏02/840-4626; Air New Zealand, 10/F, Rufino Pacific Tower, 6784 Ayala Ave, Makati ☏02/856-1366; American Airlines, *Century Park Hotel*, P. Ocampo St, Malate, ☏02/524-8625; British Airways, 135 Filipino Building, Dela Rosa St, Legazpi Village, Makati ☏02/817-0361; Cathay Pacific, 22/F LKG Tower, 6801 Ayala Ave, Makati ☏02/757-0888; Emirates, 18/F Pacific Star

Building, Gil Puyat Ave at Makati Ave, Makati ℡02/858-5300; Qantas, 10/F, Salustiana D Ty Towers, 104 Paseo de Roxas, Legazpi Village, Makati ℡02/812-0607; Singapore Airlines, 33/F LKG Tower, 6801 Ayala Ave, Makati ℡02/756-8888.

Banks and exchange Most major bank branches have 24hr ATMs for Visa and Mastercard cash advances. The moneychangers of Ermita, Malate, P. Burgos St (Makati) and in many malls offer better rates than the banks. Citibank is at 8741 Paseo de Roxas, Makati (℡02/813-9101); HSBC has branches at 6766 Ayala Ave, Makati (℡02/635-1000) and also in SM Mall of Asia, Binondo (Uy Su Bin Building, 535 Quintin Paredes St) and Quezon City (Nexor Building, 1677 Quezon Ave).

Car rental Avis is at *Traders Hotel Manila*, 3001 Roxas Blvd, Pasay City (℡02/527-9162); Budget is at Sanchez Centre, 2703 Taft Ave, Pasay City (℡02/812-2277); Hertz has an office on Makati Ave, Olympia Building ℡02/897-5179 and at the *Sofitel Philippine Plaza* (℡02/551-5555). All three have desks at the airport.

Dive operators Dive Buddies, G/F Robelle Mansion, 877 J.P. Rizal St ℡02/899-7388, Ⓦwww.divephil.com; Adventure Bound G/F, GBI Building, 2282 Pasong Tamo Extension, Makati ℡02/813-2067, Ⓦwww.adventurebound.com.ph; Scuba World, 1181 Pablo Ocampo St ℡02/895-3551, Ⓦwww.scubaworld.com.ph.

Embassies and consulates Australia, Level 23, Tower 2, RCBC Plaza, 6819 Ayala Ave, Makati ℡02/757-8100, Ⓦwww.australia.com.ph; Canada, Levels 6–8, Tower 2, RCBC Plaza, 6819 Ayala Ave, Makati ℡02/857-9000; Ireland, 3/F, 70 Jupiter St, Bel-Air 1, Makati ℡02/896-4668; New Zealand, 23/F, BPI Buendia Center, Gil Puyat Ave, Makati ℡02/891-5358; UK, 120 Upper McKinley Rd, McKinley Hill, Taguig City ℡02/858-2200, Ⓦukinthephilippines.fco.gov.uk; US, 1201 Roxas Blvd ℡02/301-2000, Ⓦmanila.usembassy.gov.

Emergencies ℡117. The Department of Tourism also has a 24hr security division (℡02/524-1660).

Hospitals and clinics Makati Medical Center, 2 Amorsolo St, Makati (℡02/815-9911, Ⓦwww.makatimed.net.ph) is the largest and one of the most modern hospitals in Manila. In the Manila Bay area, there's the Manila Doctor's Hospital, 667 United Nations Ave (℡02/524-3011, Ⓦwww.maniladoctors.com.ph), while St Luke's Medical Center, 279 E. Rodriguez Sr Blvd, Quezon City (℡02/723-0101, Ⓦwww.stluke.com.ph) is also highly regarded.

Immigration For visa extensions, head to the Immigration Building, Magallanes Dr, Intramuros (Mon–Fri 8am–noon & 1–5pm; ℡02/527-3257 or 3280).

Internet access The entire Robinsons Place mall in Ermita is a free wi-fi zone. *Ecafé*, 1415 MH del Pilar St, Ermita has a wider-than-average range of services. In the P. Burgos area try *Station 168* on Makati Ave, *Digital X* (24hr) at 48 Polaris St or *88 Internet Café* (24hr) on Burgos St. Rates are usually P40–60/hr.

Laundry Faura Laundry opposite *Midtown Inn* at 551 Padre Faura St and J. Bocobo St in Ermita (℡02/526-7579; daily except Wed; 8am–7.30pm), charges P33 per kilo.

Pharmacies You're never far from a Mercury Drug outlet in Metro Manila – at the last count there were two hundred of them. In Ermita, there's one at 444 T.M. Kalaw St (daily 7am–10pm) and 24hr branches at 660 San Andres St, Malate; Plaza Miranda in Quiapo; and Ayala Center, Park Square 1 in Makati.

Post Makati Central Post Office at Sen Gil Puyat Ave near Ayala Ave (Mon–Fri 8am–5pm; ℡02/844-0150); Ermita Post Office at Pilar Hidalgo Lim St, Malate.

Travel agents Bridges Travel & Tours, Unit 801 Liberty Center Building, 104 Dela Costa St, Makati ℡02/750-3372 to 3375, Ⓦwww.bridgestravel.com; Filipino Travel Center, G/F Ramona Apartment Building, 1555 M. Adriatico St, Malate ℡02/528-4507 to 4509, Ⓦwww.filipinotravel.com.ph.

Around Manila

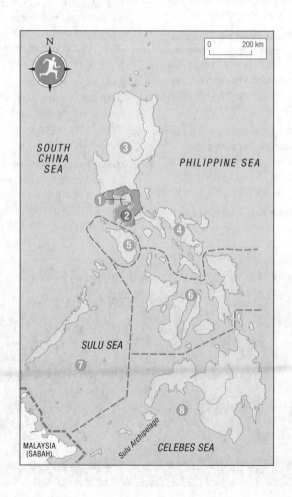

CHAPTER 2 # Highlights

✳ **Corregidor** Take the fast ferry to this idyllic, jungle-smothered island at the mouth of Manila Bay, also a poignant monument to World War II. See p.109

✳ **Pagsanjan Falls** The home to rough rapids, a towering cascade and the best *buko* pie in the Philippines is an enticing day-trip from Manila. See p.115

✳ **Tagaytay** Clinging to a high volcanic ridge, this town offers mesmerizing views of Lake Taal and some of the best food in Luzon. See p.116

✳ **Lake Taal** Take a bangka across this gorgeous lake and scramble up to the crater at the top of one of the world's smallest volcanoes. See p.117

✳ **Taal** Wonderfully preserved colonial town, with *bahay na bato* houses, ivy-clad churches and vibrant markets. See p.118

✳ **Anilao** A scenic stretch of coast with some choice resorts and the best scuba diving in the region. See p.121

✳ **Mount Pinatubo** One of the most enticing peaks in Luzon, with a pristine crater lake at the top, perfect for a refreshing dip. See p.124

▲ The view from Tagaytay

Around Manila

The areas of Luzon around Manila encompass some of the country's most popular tourist destinations – as well as a number of undeveloped provinces that few visitors take the time to see. The island of **Corregidor**, out in Manila Bay, is easily accessed by ferry from the capital. Littered with thought-provoking museums and monuments to World War II, its inviting hotel makes for a tranquil overnight break from the city.

South of Manila the real highlight is stunning **Lake Taal** and its **volcano**, best approached from the heights, restaurants and refreshing breezes of Tagaytay. Along the coast **Anilao** offers outstanding scuba diving, while south of **Laguna de Bay**, the nation's largest lake, Los Baños is best known for its delicious *buko* pie, hot springs and mountain pools. Further around the lake are the churning waters of the **Pagsanjan Falls**, where you can take a thrilling (and wet) canoe ride downriver across a series of rapids.

North of Manila you can enter northern Luzon on fast roads via historic **Malolos**, where the Revolutionary Congress was convened in 1898, and the town of **Obando**, scene of the intriguing festival known as the Obando Fertility Rites. For a little more adventure and scintillating views, climb the lush slopes of Mount Pinatubo or Mount Arayat. **Bataan** province, the peninsula northwest of Manila, is far more isolated and was the site of fierce fighting during World War II, commemorated by the **Shrine of Valor** atop Mount Samat. Come this way and it's a straight shot north to **Subic Bay**, once a major US navy base and now being developed into a series of relaxed beaches and adventure parks.

Corregidor

The tadpole-shaped island of **CORREGIDOR**, less than 5km long and 3km wide at its broadest point, is a living museum to the horrors of war. Lying 40km southwest of Manila, it was originally used by the Spanish as a customs post. In 1942 it was defended bravely by an ill-equipped US and Filipino contingent under continual bombardment from **Japanese** guns and aircraft. Some 900 Japanese and 800 American and Filipino troops died in the fighting; when the Americans retook the island in 1945, virtually the entire Japanese garrison of over 6000 men was annihilated. Little wonder Corregidor is said to be haunted. The island was abandoned after the war, and was gradually reclaimed by thick jungle vegetation – it wasn't until the late 1980s that the Corregidor Foundation began its transformation into a national shrine.

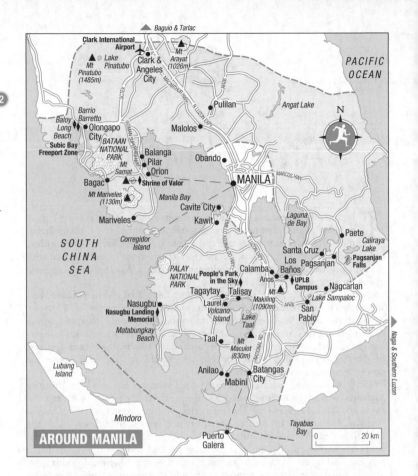

Most visits to Corregidor are by **guided tour**; the only way to wander around on your own is to stay the night (see opposite). Perhaps understandably, the tours tend to focus on the heroism, bravery and sacrifice of the men who fought here, rather than the grisly nature of the fighting itself, but it is still a moving experience – Japanese tourists also come here in numbers to pay their respects to the dead of both sides.

Touring the island

Tours begin near the ferry dock, with the statue of **General Douglas MacArthur**, who was reluctantly spirited away from the island before its capitulation. His famous words, "I shall return," adorn the statue's base, though he actually made the pronouncement in Darwin, Australia. From here tours take in all the main sights on the island, including the **Filipino Heroes Monument**, commemorating Philippine struggles from the Battle of Mactan in 1521 to the EDSA Revolution of 1986, and the **Japanese Garden of Peace**, where the Japanese were buried in 1945. Overgrown and lost, it was discovered in the 1980s, when the remains were cremated and brought back to Japan. A statue of the Buddhist bodhisattva Guanyin (or "Kannon" in Japanese) watches over the site. At some point you'll reach the **Malinta Tunnel**, a 253-metre-long chamber and connected network of damp underground bunkers where MacArthur (and President Manuel Quezon) set up temporary headquarters. Access is through an optional light-and-sound show that dramatizes the events of 1942 and is well worth the extra P150.

Elsewhere you'll see the ruined concrete shells of the once vast barracks that dotted the island, and the remains of various gun batteries, peppered with bullet and shell holes. You can also visit the **Pacific War Memorial** and its small **museum** containing weapons, old photos and uniforms that were left behind. Finally, clamber the 57 steps to the top of the old **Spanish Lighthouse** at the island's highest point (191m), for stupendous views across to Bataan and Mount Mariveles.

Away from the reminders of one of the war's most horrific battles, Corregidor is unspoiled, peaceful and a great break from the city: you can walk marked **trails** that meander through the hilly interior (look out for the monkeys and monitor lizards), rent a mountain bike or circle the island in a bangka and do some fishing.

Practicalities

Sun Cruises (☎02/527-5555, ⓦ www.corregidorphilippines.com) has a monopoly on **transport to the island**. It runs day-trips for P1999, and overnight packages for around P2250 per person. It's best to make reservations in advance, but you can buy tickets on the day before 7.30am – check-in takes place at the Sun Cruises office, CCP Bay Terminal A on Pedro Bukaneg Street, near the Cultural Centre in Manila (just beyond Harbour Square mall). Shuttle buses take you to the wharf from here (which is at the end of Pedro Bukaneg) for the 8am departure and 1 hour 15 minute ride to the island. Tours usually run on trolley buses that meet the ferries at around 9.30am, returning to the dock in time for the 2.30pm departure – a buffet lunch at the *Corregidor Inn* (see below) is included. You'll be back in Manila at around 3.45pm. Overnighters stay at the *Corregidor Inn* (☎0917/527-6350; contact Sun Cruises, see above), a creaky but atmospheric little place with polished wooden floors, thirty air-conditioned rooms and a decent pool.

South of Manila

The provinces to the south of Manila – **Cavite**, **Laguna** and **Batangas** – are prime day-trip territory, easy to get to and rich in attractions. The star is **Lake Taal**, a mesmerizing volcanic lake with its own mini volcanic island in the centre, but there are plenty of less visited natural wonders that provide a break from the city; you can ride down the river to the **Pagsanjan Falls**, soak in the **Laguna hot springs** or clamber up forested **Mount Makiling** for scintillating views. Divers should check out **Anilao** for the best reef action near the capital.

Getting around south of Manila

Without a car you'll need to take buses to explore this area. All the attractions between Calamba and the lakeside town of **Santa Cruz**, are served by buses from the Green Star Express terminal on Taft Avenue (in the MRT-Taft area, Pasay) and the HM Transport terminal in Cubao (Quezon); fares are P132 all the way to Santa Cruz. Numerous jeepneys also ply the National Highway between Calamba and Santa Cruz for around P17. From Santa Cruz you can catch jeepneys on to San Pablo, Paete and also Pangsanjan (P10). Note that all the Santa Cruz bus terminals line the National Highway outside the town itself, in the barangay of Pagsawitan.

The region also serves up a healthy dose of history. The romantic houses where national heroes **Emilio Aguinaldo** and **José Rizal** were born have been preserved as museums, **Paete** has retained its woodworking heritage and **Taal** itself is one of the most beautiful colonial towns in the Philippines. Lastly, many Mileños come here just to eat; **buko pie** is an especially prized treat made in Laguna.

Getting around the area is straightforward by bus, though you'll save a lot of time with a car. The easiest places to reach by public transport are the attractions to the south of Laguna de Bay, though Batangas City and Tagaytay are also well served by buses.

The Emilio Aguinaldo Shrine and Museum

For most Filipinos, the province of Cavite ("ka-vee-tay") will forever be associated with the revolution: in 1872 the Cavite Mutiny precipitated the national revolt against the colonial authorities (see p.427), and the area was also the birthplace of **Emilio Aguinaldo** (see p.428). That legacy is preserved at the **Emilio Aguinaldo Shrine and Museum** (Tues–Sat 8am–noon & 1–4pm; free; ⊕046/484-7643) in **KAWIT**, 23km south of Manila. This is the house in which Aguinaldo, first President of the Republic, was born in 1869, and also where he is buried, in a simple marble tomb in the back garden on the bank of the river. Philippine independence was proclaimed here and the Philippine flag first raised by Aguinaldo on June 12, 1898, commemorated on this day every year with the president waving the flag from the balcony. With its secret passages and hidden compartments, the house is testimony to the revolutionary fervour that surrounded Aguinaldo and his men. A number of the original chairs and cabinets have secret compartments that were used to conceal documents and weapons, while the kitchen has a secret passage that he could use to escape if the Spanish came calling. In the general's bedroom, one of the floorboards opens up to reveal a staircase that led to his private one-lane bowling alley under the house and an adjoining hidden swimming pool. Downstairs, the museum displays various Aguinaldo memorabilia including clothes, journals and his sword, while upstairs there is the general's bedroom, a grand hall, a dining room and a conference room.

You can get to Kawit on any Cavite-bound jeepney or FX taxi from Baclaran LRT station in Manila.

Calamba

The city of **CALAMBA**, just 54km from the capital, is best known today as the birthplace of national hero and revolutionary **José Rizal**. Once a rural backwater, Calamba is now the largest city in Laguna province and a choked extension of Manila – there's nothing to see in the modern section, but the old town of **San Juan Bautista** was built in Spanish colonial style, with a shady plaza in front of a town hall and an attractive church. A marker inside the church indicates that Rizal was baptized here by Fray Rufino Collantes on June 22, 1861.

Opposite the church on J.P. Rizal Street is the site of the house where Rizal was born on June 19, 1861. Now the **Rizal Shrine** (Tues–Sat 8.30am–noon & 1–4.30pm; free), the building here is a 1950s reproduction of a typical nineteenth-century Philippine *bahay na bato*, with lower walls of stone and upper walls of wood, narra wood floors and windows made from *capiz* shell. All the rooms feature period furniture and there are displays of Rizal's belongings, including the clothes he was christened in and a suit he wore as a young man. In the garden is a *bahay kubo* (wooden) playhouse, a replica of the one in which Rizal used to spend his days as a child.

Laguna hot springs

The area between Calamba and Los Baños touts heavily for tourist custom on the health properties of its **hot springs**, which bubble from the lower slopes of Mount Makiling. There are dozens of resorts of varying quality that use the hot springs to fill their swimming pools. Many cater to company outings, Korean tour groups, day-trippers and conferences, but visit on a weekday and the best ones (listed below) can make for a relaxing few hours. *Makiling Highlands Resort* (℡049/545-9703, ⓦwww.montevista.com.ph; standard rooms ❸; villas ❻), just off the main highway on Captain Mamon Road, has villas and very large air-conditioned rooms, hot pools spread out over many hectares of ground (day rates are P95–125), and – just in case you should start feeling too healthy – 24-hour room service from *Max's*, the fried chicken restaurant. You can also rent small wooden *kamaligs* (traditional huts) for P1300–1600 for 12 hour. *Monte Vista Hot Springs & Conference Resort* (℡049/545-1259, ⓦwww.montevista.com.ph; standard rooms ❸; villas ❻), on the right as you're heading south from Calamba, has eighteen hot mineral pools, assorted giant slides and enough room for 1500 day visitors (day rates P95–125). Rooms are air-conditioned and en suite.

Los Baños

The small lakeside town of **LOS BAÑOS**, around 60km south of Manila, attracts a steady stream of domestic tourists who primarily come to gorge on its delectable **buko pies** (stuffed with young coconut), said to have first been cooked up here in the 1960s by a food technologist from nearby UPLB. The best is still baked at ⌖ *Orient - the Original Buko Pie Bakeshop* (daily 5am–8.30pm; ℡049/536-3783) in Anos on the National Highway, on the left just before you reach the town centre from Calamba (note the double-parked cars and buses blocking the road). You should also try the tasty version at *Lety's Buko Pie*, next door (daily 4am–8pm; ℡049/536-1332), or at *Collete's* further along; there are numerous other brands around here, all priced at around P140 per pie. Note that *Lety's* will close early if it runs out of pies. Other specialty stores have set up here to cash in on the crowds: ⌖ *Net's Cassava Cake* (daily 5am–9pm; ℡049/827-3575) produces some of the most addictive cassava pudding in the Philippines (P90–180).

UPLB

Just outside Los Baños is the **University of the Philippines Los Baños** (UPLB; ⓦwww.uplb.edu.ph) campus at the base of Mount Makiling. There are a number of attractions on the campus itself, including the **UPLB Museum of Natural History** (Mon–Sat 8am–5pm; P20; ℡049/536-2864), which has more than 200,000 biological specimens of Philippine plants, animals and micro-organisms. Next door is the equally tranquil International Rice Research Institute, which is home to the unexpectedly absorbing **Riceworld Museum** (Mon–Fri 8am–5pm; free; ℡049/536-2701 ext 2201; ⓦwww.irri.org), showcasing the importance of the staple that feeds half the world's population. Apart from an overview of the developing world's food shortages, the museum has a number of small but intriguing displays on the history, production and types of rice, including one where visitors can inspect live paddy-field insects under a microscope, including damselflies, wolf spiders and aggressive fire ants.

Mount Makiling

The dormant volcano of **Mount Makiling** (1090m) is identifiable by its unusual shape, which is rather like a reclining woman. The mountain is named after Mariang Makiling (Mary of Makiling), a young woman whose spirit is said to protect the mountain. On quiet nights, tribespeople say, you can hear her playing the harp, although the music is rarely heard any more because Makiling is rumoured to be angry about the scant regard paid to the environment by the authorities. UPLB (see p.113) now manages the forest reserve that blankets the mountain and is hoping to develop its eco-tourism potential.

There is a well-established and strenuous trail to the summit starting at the Makiling Center (℡049/536-2577) at the College of Forestry on the UPLB campus (4–5hr up; P5 registration fee). The trail is safe and easy to follow, but be prepared for sudden downpours and flashfloods. **Guides** are not required. Most climbers start early and complete the hike in one day; you can pitch tents at the Malaboo and Tayabak campsites on the way up, but not near the summit. From the Los Baños Crossing on the National Highway (accessible via buses/jeepneys from Manila or Calamba, see box, p.111), take a jeepney to the College of Forestry (P7.50). Heading back to Manila from Los Baños, the last bus departs around 8.30pm.

San Pablo

Known as the "City of Seven Lakes", **SAN PABLO** was a prosperous hamlet named Sampaloc before the Spanish arrived, and where *sampalok* (tamarind) trees grew in abundance. It lies southwest of six of the lakes and is a five-minute jeepney ride from the seventh and largest of them, **Lake Sampaloc**, which you can circumnavigate on foot in a few hours. There are trails leading through lush jungle and farmland to all of the lakes, and the Lake Sampaloc shore boasts floating restaurants serving native freshwater fish such as tilapia, *bangus*, carp and several species of shrimp.

San Pablo is also home to *Colette's Buko Pie at Pasalubong*, 52 San Rafael (℡049/562-6754; 24hr), the coconut pie chain that was established here in 1989.

Practicalities

There are plenty of **resorts** in the area to choose from if you feel a day-trip here is too rushed. The best is *Villa Escudero Plantations & Resort* (℡02/523-2944, ⓦwww.villaescudero.com; ❼ full board), half an hour by road south of San Pablo near **Tiaong**. A working coconut plantation in a beautiful location surrounded by mountains, it has pretty cottages with verandas overlooking a lake, and the price includes all meals plus a tour of the plantation on a cart pulled by a carabao (**day rates** start at P1105). Also inside the plantation, within walking distance of the cottages, is the **Escudero Private Museum** (daily 8am–5pm) with a treasure trove of religious art, consisting of silver altars, gilded *carrozas* (ceremonial carriages), ivory-headed *santos*, oriental ceramics, costumes, dioramas of Philippine wildlife and ethnography, rare coins and antique Philippine furniture.

Around 10km to the west of San Pablo, on the road to Santo Tomas, is the town of **Alaminos**, site of the *Hidden Valley Spring Resort* (℡02/818-4034; ❾), which sits amid rainforest in a volcanic crater 100m deep. There are air-conditioned cottages and seven natural spring pools at the resort, some deep enough for swimming. The entrance fee for day-trippers is P1800, which includes a welcome drink, buffet lunch, afternoon snacks and use of all the pools. To get to Alaminos catch a local bus or jeepney from San Pablo or Los Baños.

Pagsanjan and the falls

Serving as the capital of Laguna province from 1688 to 1858, the town of **PAGSANJAN** lies 101km from Manila and is home to a few old wooden houses, an unusually ornamental stone gate – or **Puerta Real** – and a pretty Romanesque church. The gate sits on the road to Santa Cruz (Rizal St) and was completed in 1880, while **Our Lady of Guadalupe Church**, dating from 1690 but remodelled in the nineteenth century, is at the end of Rizal Street. The town's main claim to fame these days is as the staging point for the dazzling **Pagsanjan Falls**, chosen by Francis Ford Coppola as the location for the final scenes in *Apocalypse Now* in 1975. Most tourists come not for the Hollywood nostalgia value, however, but to take one of the popular **bangka trips** (daily 7am–5pm; minimum P970) down the fourteen **rapids** of the Bombongan River. The rapids are at their most thrilling in the wet season; during the dry season the ride is more sedate. You don't need to be especially daring to do the trip, though you will get wet, so bring a change of clothes. All ticket sales are supervised by the local **tourism office** in the municipal building (daily 8am–5pm; ☎049/808-3544) in the centre of town, opposite the church; ignore touts who try and sell tickets on the street. Most visitors pay P1000 for the ride; boats leave from the bridge behind the building.

It usually takes around 45 minutes to shoot 5.38km through the dramatic gorge; when you get closer to the actual 30m-high falls, you can ride a bamboo raft (*balsa*) to go directly below the cascade into the cavern known as Devil's Cave, another thirty minutes or so (this is an additional P250 per head).

Practicalities

It can take up to four hours to get to Pagsanjan from Manila if you hit bad traffic (around 2hr normally) – avoid weekends and public holidays (see p.111 for bus details). If you need cash there's a branch of BDO with an ATM in the centre of town.

There's no shortage of **accommodation** in and around Pagsanjan. *La Corona de Pagsanjan*, on the road from Pagsanjan to Cavinti (☎049/808-1753 or 808 1793, ⓦwww.hotellacoronapagsanjan.com; ❼), is the best in the area. It has en-suite air-conditioned doubles, triples and quads, a nice pool and includes breakfast in the room rate. *Pagsanjan Falls Lodge* in the barangay of Pinagsanjan (☎049/501-4251, ⓦwww.pagsanjanfallslodge.com.ph; ❸) has a good range of very ordinary but clean and spacious rooms including fan rooms, air-conditioned doubles plus fifteen rooms for up to three people. To get to Pinagsanjan, take a jeepney from General Luna Street in Pagsanjan.

J.P. Rizal Street in Pagsanjan is the place to look for budget **restaurants**, with *Pagsanjan Bakery* at no. 24 (towards Santa Cruz) best for cheap cakes, buns and bread. *Calle Arco* (daily 10am–10pm; ☎049/808-4584) further along the National Highway towards the falls is an old wooden house serving quality Filipino food such as *sinigang na baka* (beef tamarind soup with jackfruit). At 169 General Luna St, near the Municipal Building, *Aling Taleng's* (daily 9am–6pm; ☎915/531-4944) has been serving refreshing seven-ingredient *halo-halo* (P50) since 1933. For a real treat seek out 🍴 *Tio Casio's Bibingka* (daily 7am–6.30pm; ☎049/810-3829) on the National Highway round 5km west of Pagsanjan in Bubukal, for sumptuous slices of coconut-enriched *bibingka* (rice cake).

Paete

Sleepy **PAETE** ("pa-e-te"), is Luzon's **woodcarving capital**, packed with stores selling woodcarvings, oil paintings, wooden clogs (*bakya*) and the gaily painted papier-mâché masks that are used in fiestas. Most of the stores (usually open daily 8am–6pm) are on **Quesada Street** in the centre of town. At the southern end of Quesada, the town's crumbling but atmospheric Baroque **Santiago Apostol Parish Church** (daily 7am–8pm) dates right back to 1646, but in common with many Philippine churches built by the Spaniards, it has been reduced to rubble by earthquakes on a number of occasions and rebuilt. The present structure dates from 1939, has an ornate carved facade, weathered bell tower and a beautifully sculpted altar finished in gold leaf. Check out also the wonderfully vivid mural paintings near the main entrance, dating from the 1850s. During the second week of January every year Paete marks its **salibanda festival**, the feast of the Santo Niño (Holy Child) which includes a parade on the lake and a rowdy procession along the main street, with participants and spectators splashing water over each other. Paete is also well known for its sweet **lanzones** (harvested Oct–Dec).

Practicalities

Paete is 10km north of Pagsanjan, just off the main highway that hugs the east coast of Laguna de Bay, and is best approached by jeepney from Pagsanjan or Santa Cruz (take any one going to Siniloan). There is no **accommodation**, but you can visit it easily in a day. On Quesada Street there are several places **to eat**, including *Kape Kesada Art Gallery & Café* (Tues–Sun 9am–6pm; ☎0916/362-4015), which looks like a wooden Japanese house and serves decent sandwiches and brewed coffee.

Around 2km south of Paete, on the main road in the barangay of Longos, *Exotik* (daily 7am–9pm; ☎049/820-0086) is an enchanting restaurant modelled on a native village. The menu features frog (P285), shark (P295), eel (P295) and stingray (P295), but ask about seasonal dishes such as snake, wild boar and monitor lizard (which really does taste like chicken). Meats are cooked *adobo* style, "sizzling" or in coconut milk. There's also plenty of less exotic dishes such as noodles (P120), fish (P230) and *halo-halo* (P75).

Tagaytay

The compact and breezy city of **TAGAYTAY**, 55km south of Manila, sits on a dramatic 600-metre-high ridge overlooking Lake Taal and the volcano, a magical location that serves as the gateway to the lake area. The ridge road (known as Aguinaldo Highway west of the central Rotunda) can become very congested, particularly on weekends and holidays when the crowds can be overwhelming, but you still might consider spending the night to enjoy those entrancing vistas. Most day-trippers enjoy the views from the **Tagaytay Picnic Grove** (daily 6am–midnight; P50 per person; P35 for cars; tables P100) a ridge-top park 5km east of the Rotunda. Further along, around 7.5km east of the Rotunda, the **People's Park in the Sky** (daily 6am–6pm; P15) is the highest point in the area (750m) offering magnificent panoramas of the lake, the sea, Laguna de Bay and the smog that hangs over Manila to the north. It's topped by a collection of abandoned concrete buildings which are a bit of an eyesore; until they are redeveloped, the only other attraction up here is the modest **Shrine of our Lady, Mother of Fair Love**, constructed in 2003.

Accommodation

The gasp-inducing views from the ridge at Tagaytay make it more expensive to stay here than in one of the barangays by the lake around Talisay, where it's quieter and more convenient if you intend to climb the volcano.

Sonya's Garden Barangay Buck Estate, Alfonso ☎0917/532-9097, ⓦwww .sonyasgarden.com. Romantic cottage accommodation in a blossom-smothered garden. Cottages are *bahay na bató*-style, with antique beds, lots of carved wood and shuttered windows. The rate includes a delicious breakfast. If you're not staying the night, drop by for lunch or dinner: daily set lunch and dinner menus cost P610 (breakfast is P427 for non-guests) and include delights such as pasta with sun-dried tomatoes and banana rolls with sesame and jackfruit for dessert. Book ahead.

Sonya's is 12km beyond Tagaytay, so is tricky to reach without private transport: go past Splendido golf course and then look out for the signs on the right. ➐

Theodore Hotel Aguinaldo Hwy Km 54, Silang Crossing ☎046/483-0350, ⓦwww .thetheodorehotel.com. Best of a new generation of boutique hotels on the ridge, this centrally located hotel offers ten stylish rooms each with its own design theme (from New York to Japan), flat-screen TVs, spa, a tranquil garden and viewing deck. The restaurant serves fabulous food. ➒

Eating and drinking

Tagaytay has dozens of restaurants, though it has also been rather overrun by big chains and fast-food joints; better are the rows of fruits stalls along the ridge (the local pineapples are especially good).

Antonio's Grill Aguinaldo Hwy km 54 ☎046/483-4847. Hands-down the best Filipino food in town, though the views are marred somewhat by the fast-food joints below. Highlights include the huge pots of richly stewed *bulalo* (P680), a meal for two people, plates of fried *tawalis* (P200), a fine *adobo* (P290) and the barbecue chicken (P110). Daily 11am–9pm.

Josephine's Aguinaldo Hwy km 58 ☎046/413-1801. An institution among Filipinos, serving good Filipino dishes such as *sinigang* with mounds of steamed rice to go with those special views (they also do a weekday "pinoy bento" set meal tray for P200). Mon–Fri 9am–10pm, Sat & Sun 7am–11pm.

Maryridge Good Shepherd Convent East of the Rotunda, on the main road ☎046/483-4287. This religious institution attracts a steady stream of visitors for its small takeaway food counters run by Bahay Pastulan; the main draw is the pots of addictive *ube* jam (more like frozen ice cream; from P120), but the peanut brittle (P140), mango jam (P105), coconut juice (P20) and *halo-halo* (P50) are also worth gorging on. It's clearly signposted off the main road. Daily 10am–7pm.

Pink Sister's Convent of Divine Mercy Off the Aguinaldo Hwy, north of the Rotunda (heading back to Manila) – look for the Pink Sister signs. Tranquil religious institution (said to be popular with late President Cory Aquino), that sells home-baked food from a tiny gift shop to the left of the entrance. The nuns' cloister cookies – aka "angel cookies" (tasty oat biscuits that sell for P170 per large jar) – bring in the foodies. Daily 9am–5pm.

Rowena's 152 Barangay Francisco (on the Santa Rosa road) ☎046/860-2481. Delicious *buko* pies that have almost eclipsed *Colette's* in popularity; stop by for blueberry or strawberry cheese tarts, or the classic *buko* pie, for around P160 each. Daily 8am–6pm.

Lake Taal and Talisay

The country's third largest lake, awe-inspiring **LAKE TAAL** sits in a caldera below Tagaytay, formed by huge eruptions between 500,000 and 100,000 years ago. The active **Taal Volcano**, which is responsible for the lake's sulphuric content, lies in the centre of the lake, on **Volcano Island**. The volcano last erupted in 1965 without causing major damage, but when it blew its top in 1754, thousands died and the town of Taal was destroyed; it was rebuilt in a new location on safer ground an hour by road from Tagaytay to the southwest of the lake (see p.118). Before 1754 the lake was actually part of Balayan Bay, but the eruption sealed it from the sea, eventually leading to its waters becoming non-saline.

The departure point for trips across the lake to the volcano is the small town of **TALISAY** on the lake's northern shore, some 4km southeast of Tagaytay; this is a much more typical Filipino settlement, with a bustling market, fishermen

Getting to Lake Taal

From Manila you can approach Lake Taal from two directions: from the north **via Tagaytay**, or **via Tanauan**, east of the lake. Frequent Batman Star Express (BSC) buses run daily from Giselle's Park Place near MRT-Taft (Pasay) on EDSA to Tagaytay (P78). From Tagaytay, take one of the jeepneys (40min; P50) that shuttle back and forth all day to **Talisay** to get to the lakeshore. Green Star and JAM Transit buses from Taft Avenue (LRT Gil Puyat station aka "Buendia-Taft") for Lipa City stop at Tanauan (around P80). In Tanauan take a tricycle to the Talisay jeepney terminal (P8 per person); frequent jeepneys (P20) take around thirty minutes to reach Talisay from there. Once in Talisay tricycles should take you to nearby hotels or bangka operators for P8 per person, or P25–30 per ride. Some groups take a **taxi** from Manila or the airport all the way to Talisay; reckon on at least P5000.

doubling as tourist guides and nary a fast-food chain in sight. You can arrange a bangka and a guide at the waterfront market in town, or at any of the resorts listed below (*Taal Lake Yacht Club* is a dependable choice). Hiring a bangka to take you out to the island will cost around P1500 if you arrange it independently, plus another P700 or so for a guide to take you up to the volcano. You can ride a horse up to the top for an additional P850 – most tourists do this because of the heat. If you're staying the night by the lake, your hotel can arrange all this for you, with food and refreshments included, typically for P2000–3000.

With an early start, you can climb to either the new crater or the old crater (which has 2km-wide Crater Lake inside it) and be back in Talisay in time for lunch (the old crater takes around thirty minutes depending on fitness level). There isn't much shade on the volcano, so don't go without sunblock, a good hat and plenty of water. On the island itself is a basic restaurant, vendors selling overpriced drinks and a small **information office** where you must pay an entry fee of P50.

If you want to spend more time on the water, make for the *Taal Lake Yacht Club* (about 1km east of Talisay; ☎043/773-0192, ⓦwww.sailing.org.ph/tlyc/), where you can **rent** sailboats (Toppers from P1200/day) and kayaks (P750/day).

Practicalities

Most of the lakeside resorts are between Talisay and the village of Laurel a few kilometres to the south. Hotels are busiest September to February (the coolest months) so book ahead if travelling at these times. Weekdays are always much cheaper year-round. ⚲ *Club Balai Isabel* Barangay Banga, Talisay (☎043/728-0307, ⓦwww.balaiisabel.com) is a fashionable lakeside boutique resort, built around a century-old coconut and mango plantation just east of the town. The cosy hotel rooms (❼) and suites (❽) come with breakfast, while the luxurious lakeshore suites (❽) and villas (❾) are self-catering (all have kitchens) and can accommodate up to six people. A swimming pool, a variety of watersports and even a lake cruise are laid on for guests. A solid budget option is the quiet *Talisay Green Lake Resort*, next to *Taal Lake Yacht Club* (☎043/773-0247; ❸) which offers a range of rooms with bath and TV, set in a large, private compound right on the lakeshore.

Lake Taal is famed for its delicious **fresh fish**, especially *tawilis* (a freshwater sardine only found here), tilapia and increasingly rare *maliputo* (a larger fish, also only found in Lake Taal). The other speciality is piping-hot *bulalo*, a rich beef bone-marrow soup. Down by the lakeshore in and around Talisay, there are simple eating places selling barbecued meat and fish, but quality can be hit and miss; the numerous bakeries in Talisay are a safer bet for a snack. Try *Ronnie & Au* on the main street (☎0918/564-0349), one of the better sit-down options in town, a rustic diner knocking up all the usual favourites and 3-in-1 coffee (breakfast for P50). Staples include *adobo* (P120), tilapia (P110), *tawilis* (P60) and *bulalo* (P200). Ask what's been freshly caught; they sometimes have *maliputo* (not on the menu) for P380.

Taal

The town of **TAAL**, 130km south of Manila and a further 10km south of the lake, is one of the best preserved colonial enclaves in the Philippines and one of the few places you can get a real sense of its Spanish past. Founded in 1572 by Augustinians, it was moved to this location (and away from the deadly Taal volcano) in 1755 and today boasts a superb collection of endearingly weathered Spanish colonial architecture and *bahay na bató*-style homes, as well as one of the finest basilicas in Luzon.

The Town

Taal's compact centre is easy to explore on foot, but if it's too hot you can easily hire a **tricycle** to whisk you around (P100–120 depending on how many sights and hours you take). On the northern side of the plaza lies the elegantly weathered bulk of the **Basilica of St Martin de Tours** (daily 7am–8pm; free), said to be the biggest church in Southeast Asia, its facade visibly cracked, peeling and studded with clumps of weeds. The present church, built in 1856, has a magnificent interior and is often jam-packed for masses throughout the day. Taal is a major pilgrimage site thanks to an aged pinewood image of the Virgin Mary known as **Our Lady of Caysasay** (only 20cm high). The statue is said to have been fished out of the Pansipit River in 1603; it was lost then found again in a freshwater spring. The **Chapel of Caysasay**, located on the banks of the river on the edge of town, is a beautiful coral-hewn chapel where the image is transferred from its shrine in the basilica every Thursday and returned on Saturday afternoon. The ruined **Twin Wishing Wells of Santa Lucia**, a short walk from the chapel, are still reputed to have miraculous healing powers. Locals will point you in the right direction.

Several of the town's Spanish-era buildings are open to the public. The **Leon Apacible Historic Landmark** (Wed–Sun 8am–4pm; free) along M.N. Agoncillo Street is the ancestral home of Leon Apacible (1861–1901), lawyer and Filipino revolutionary. It has the best-preserved interior in town, and although remodelled several times, the wide, highly buffed narra floorboards, as well as the wide sweeping staircase (with its curved balustrade) are still original. The sliding doors and oriel windows betray American Art Deco influence while the transom filigree, featuring swirling chrysanthemums is Chinese style.

Further along Agoncillo Street, the **Marcela N. Agoncillo Historical Landmark** (Wed–Sun 8am–4pm; free) is the most evocative and visibly ageing house, with creaky wooden floors, a dusty library and old-fashioned *sala* upstairs. The house is the ancestral home of Marcela Mariño de Agoncillo (1860–1946), sewer of the first Philippine flag in 1898; an exhibit of flags from the days of the Philippine revolution adorns the lower half of the structure, and her statue (holding the flag) graces the garden.

Marcela's husband Felipe (1859–1941) was a lawyer who helped negotiate the Treaty of Paris in 1898. He once lived at the pristine all-white **Felipe Agoncillo Mansion,** along J.P. Rizal Street. It's still privately owned, but ring the bell and the housekeeper will give you a short tour of the faithfully preserved interior for P50 (daily 9am–4pm); Felipe's statue stands in the garden.

The **market** in the centre of Taal is a good place to eat and to look for local **embroidery**, including cotton sheets, pillowcases and tablemats. They're all made by hand in the town's small workshops and are much cheaper here than in Manila's department stores, as long as you're prepared to do some haggling. The area is also well known for the manufacture of **balisong**, traditional knives which have a hidden blade that flicks out from the handle (P150–1000).

Practicalities

Note that there is no direct road link between Taal and Talisay/Tagaytay on the northern side of the lake. From Manila the best option is to take a bus from the LRT-Gil Puyat area (JAM Transit) to Lemery and get off at the northern edge of Taal (2–3hr from Manila), not far from the plaza. You can get basic information at the **tourist information desk** (Mon–Fri 8am–5pm) inside City Hall, on the main town square. For **accommodation**, *Casa Punzalan*, at C. Ilagan and P. Gomez streets (☎043/408-0911) is the best budget option in the area, a beautiful and historic property in the town square overlooking the basilica. It contains three fan rooms (❶) and two air-conditioned rooms (❷), all with four-poster beds and shared bathrooms. *Casa Cecilia* (☎043/408-0046; ❺), just outside the town on Diversion Road, is a modern, cosy seven-room hotel sporting Spanish-style architecture and a patio overlooking the garden. Rooms are all en suite with parquet floors, tiled bathrooms, free wi-fi and cable TV, and there's a good **restaurant**, *La Azotea*, on the ground floor. Rates include breakfast.

Mount Maculot

Close to the town of **Cuenca**, on the southeastern side of Lake Taal, some 50km east of Taal itself, **Mount Maculot** (830m) is relatively wild and less of a tourist attraction than Taal Volcano. If you set out from Manila very early – as most local climbers do – you can climb its lush slopes and be in Taal (or back in the capital) for dinner. One reason for Maculot's popularity is an area of sheer rock near the summit known as the **Rockies** (starting at 706m) rising vertically up from the jungle and with a platform at the top affording unbroken views across Lake Taal. There's a steep but walkable path around the Rockies that takes you to the platform.

From Cuenca (where buses will drop you), walk or get a tricycle (P20) 2km to the trailhead via the **Barangay No. 7 Outpost**, a small hut marked by a barrier across the road. Here you must register and pay a small fee (P10); you can organize a guide here (payment is up to you, but give a minimum P500), but it's not necessary – the trail is easy to follow, with steps and handrails most of the way. From the nearby trailhead (behind the little sari-sari shop known as the "mountaineer's store") it takes about two hours to reach the summit, depending on your fitness level, via the **Grotto of the Blessed Virgin Mary**, a small shrine.

To get to Mount Maculot from Manila, take one of the hourly JAM Transit buses from Pasay to **Cuenca** (2hr; P120), or a Lemery-bound bus from Taft-Buendia or Cubao LRT stations (2hr 30min; P130) and get off in Cuenca. It's easy to flag down buses or jeepneys in Cuenca for the short ride on to Taal.

Nasugbu and Matabungkay Beach

The coastline around **NASUGBU**, 37km west of Tagaytay, is lined with resorts, mostly clearly signposted from the main road and grouped in three areas: to the north of Nasugbu on the white sand beach stretching to Fuego Point; around Nasugbu itself on Nasugbu Beach, which has darker sand and is more crowded; and about 12km and twenty minutes south of Nasugbu by road along the similarly darker sands of **MATABUNGKAY BEACH**, often marred by the *balsas* (rafts rented by resorts) that line the shore. Other than the beach, the only real sight is the **Nasugbu Landing Memorial** (a steel landing craft and statues of soldiers coming ashore), commemorating the second American landing in the Philippines in 1945.

From Manila, there are frequent Batman Star Express (BSC) **buses** to Nasugbu from the EDSA (MRT-Taft) terminal at Giselle's Park Place. There are jeepneys every few minutes between Nasugbu and Matabungkay. **Accommodation** prices at many of the establishments here increase by ten to twenty percent at weekends; the price codes below represent weekday rates.

Accommodation

Coral Beach Club Matabungkay Beach, Lian ☎0917/901-4635, ⓦwww.coralbeach.ph. A quiet, attractive place with restaurant (which is a bit overpriced), bar, pool tables, beachside pool and a/c rooms, all with cable TV and hot showers. Free wi-fi. ❺

Lago de Oro Cable Ski Park & Resort National Highway, Balibago, Calatagan 4215 (near Matabungkay) ☎0917/504-2685 or 0926/710-4754, ⓦwww.lago-de-oro.com. Modern hacienda-style resort, notable for the cable wakeboard system in its lagoon (daily 9.30am–12.30pm & 1.30–4.30pm;

P460/1hr); a cable drags you around the lake rather than a boat. There's also good food in the European-style restaurant and a pool for lounging. Vans to Nasugbu are P400. **⑦**

The Sanctuary at Maya-Maya Spa Barangay Natipuan, north of Nasugbu ☎0918/909-7170, ⊛www.mayamaya.com. This spa-cum-upmarket resort offers 14 thatched cottages with a/c rooms. It's good value and reasonably priced, with excellent service, boat transfers to and from local

beaches and speedboat rentals. The spa offers massage (from P450) and body treatments from P1800. **⑦**

Twins Beach Club 5km south of Lian ☎0912/322-8163, ⊛www.twinsbc.de. Homely German-managed pension on the seafront, offering en-suite doubles with tiled floors. Small beach, swimming pool and alfresco bar. Some of the best-value accommodation in the area if you're content with the simple life. **④**

Anilao

Some 140km south of Manila, the resort of **ANILAO** (the name refers both to the village and the 13km peninsula beyond it) is primarily a diving destination, popular with city folk at weekends, when the area can get a little busy. During the week it's much more peaceful and you can often negotiate a discount on your accommodation. The best time for diving is March through June; there's little point in coming just for the beach.

To reach Anilao by public transport, take a bus to Batangas City and then a jeepney west to Mabini or the wharf at Anilao village, then continue by tricycle along the coastal road to your resort. All the **accommodation** reviewed here is on the road beyond the wharf at Anilao, along the west coast of the Calumpan peninsula.

Accommodation

Aquaventure Reef Club Barangay. Bagalangit ☎02/584-1328, ⊛www.aquareefclub.com. Comfortable, unpretentious resort 3km along the coastal road beyond Anilao. Operated by Manila-based dive outfit Aqua One, it's primarily a scuba resort, though it also offers island-hopping and snorkelling trips in rented bangkas. Double rooms come with fan or a/c and bath; buffet-style meals are served in a nice open restaurant overlooking the sea. **⑥**

🏃 **Casita Ysabel** Barangay. San Teodoro ☎917/610-0005, ⊛www.casitaysabel.com. Preferred hideaway for non-divers (as well as divers), with its Tree Earth Spa and cosy *casitas* just off the beach (and local reef). Owner Linda Reyes-Romualdez has used Bali as inspiration for the nicest *casitas*, most of which have ocean views. Meals included. **⑥**

🏃 **Dive Solana** Barangay. San Teodoro ☎02/721-2089, ⊛www.divesolana.com. Along the coastal road beyond the *Aquaventure Reef Club*, this is a charming and slightly bohemian little retreat popular with divers and owned by Filipina film-maker Marilou Diaz-Abaya. There are

a/c and fan rooms (but no TV), some right on the beach, with an ethnic touch, and the rate includes three buffet meals a day. It's always full at weekends because people keep going back, so book in advance. Prices rise ten percent at weekends. **⑥**

Planet Dive Barangay. San Teodoro ☎0916/704-3718, ⊛www.planetdive.com.ph. The last of the resorts along the Anilao strip, these native-style cottages are opposite the Twin Rocks dive site, where the bay is sheltered enough for good snorkelling. You can have candlelit dinners on the shore and there's a viewing deck from which to take in Anilao's wonderful sunsets. Accommodation ranges from the very basic to cottages for six, all of it clean and comfortable. **④**

Vivere Azure Barangay. Aguada, San Teodoro km 108 ☎02/771-7777, ⊛www.vivereazure.com. Elegant boutique resort with the best views in Anilao and 14 luxurious suites, each featuring lots of earthy tones, stone and wood furnishings. Rates include all meals, use of pool, kayaks and snorkelling gear. **⑨**

Batangas City

BATANGAS CITY lies on the other side of Batangas Bay from Anilao, a 1 hour 30 minute drive from Manila via the STAR Tollway. The city has one of the fastest growing populations in the Philippines but there's not much to see and its

Moving on from Batangas City

Batangas Port lies 2km west of the centre of Batangas City. Regular **ferries** to Puerto Galera (2hr) depart Terminal 3, where various companies sell tickets; you can also catch Supercat ferries to Calapon further along the Mindoro coast. At nearby Terminal 2 (but with a separate entrance) you can buy tickets for Odiongan (from P560) and Romblon via Montenegro Lines (☏043/723-8294) as well as various ferries to Calapon, Roxas, Caticlan and Dumaguit. For both terminals you need to pay an additional **terminal fee** before boarding. There is a jeepney station outside Terminal 3, with rides into Batangas costing P7; tricycles will charge P50. If you're heading to Nasugbu (2hr), San Pablo (1hr 30min), Santa Cruz (3hr), Taal (1hr 30min) or Tagaytay (1hr 30min), take a jeepney to one of the bus terminals in town: You'll find the JAM, ALPS and Ceres Transport terminals on P. Burgos Street, a short ride from the port. Numerous **buses** wait at Terminal 2 for the frequent trip to Manila (3hr).

significance for most visitors is as a transit point on the journey to Puerto Galera on Mindoro (see box above).

Though there's little point in spending the night here, there are some tempting **places to eat**. The ordinary-looking 🍴 *A&M Village Restaurant* (daily 8am–9pm; ☏043/723-1118) off Del Pilar Road in the Hilltop area, near the University of Batangas (any taxi or tricycle driver will know it) is best known for sumptuous native cuisine such as *bulalo* (beef bone-marrow soup; P240), *kare-kare* (peanut stew; P240), *buko* juice (P50) and *leche* flan (P150). Another store with a cult following is the *Hungry Hippo* (daily 8am–8pm; ☏043/300-2323), right next to the University of Batangas (Hilltop Campus entrance on Del Pilar St), a chain beloved for its juicy hamburgers (P65). A final must-try is the pancit *tikyano* (red stir-fried noodles; P120) at 🍴 *Letty's* (daily 7am–9.30pm; ☏043/723-3388), a no-frills canteen on Dandan Street near the basilica and leafy plaza in the centre of the city.

North of Manila

Most travellers zip through the provinces **north of Manila** – Pampanga, Bulacan and Bataan – to the justly famed attractions of northern Luzon, but there are a few reasons to break the journey. **Malolos** has some historic distractions, while **Mount Pintatubo** and **Mount Arayat** provide energetic hikes and gasp-inducing scenery. **Bataan** is a surprisingly wild province, with some excellent beaches and World War II monuments, while **Subic Bay** is turning into an appealing beach, dive and outdoor activity centre (see p.129). Buses connect all the main attractions with Manila, though fast ferries are much quicker to Bataan – if they are running (see p.125).

Malolos

MALOLOS, capital of Bulacan province, is known for its impressive **Barasoain Church** (Tues–Sun 8.30am–noon & 1–4.30pm; ☏044/662-7686), on Paseo del Congreso. The current structure dates back to the 1880s; it was in this church that the Revolutionary Congress convened in 1898. The church houses the **Ecclesiastical Museum** (which displays religious relics such as a bone fragment of San Vicente Ferrer encased in glass, and antique prayer cards), and a light-and-sound presentation depicting events leading to the Philippine Revolution and the Philippine-American War. Aguinaldo made his headquarters at the nearby

Malolos Cathedral, aka the Basilica Minore de Immaculada Concepcion (daily 7am–8pm). In between the two churches on Paseo del Congreso is the **Casa Real** (Mon–Fri 8.30am–noon & 1–4.30pm; free), a gorgeous Spanish house built in 1580, and the site of the Imprenta Nacional, the printing press of the 1896 Constitution. It's now a small museum, with displays of priceless sixteenth-century Spanish religious artefacts and various incendiary pamphlets published by the revolutionaries. The helpful provincial **tourist office** is in the Capitol Building (Mon–Fri 8am–5pm; ☏044/791-7335, ⓦwww.bulacan.gov.ph).

Victory Liner buses have hourly departures to Malolos (P54 a/c; P45 non-a/c), from their terminals in Cubao in Manila.

Clark and Angeles City

Some 80km north of Metro Manila, **CLARK** (or more formally Clark Freeport Zone; ⓦwww.clark.com.ph) is an odd mix of converted barracks, unappealing duty-free malls, IT industrial zones, golf courses and prostitution. Indeed, Clark and adjacent **ANGELES CITY** remain one of the Philippines' most notorious sun and sex destinations, with dozens of "girlie bars" catering to high-spending Western, Korean and Taiwanese males. Clark was the site of an American military base between 1903 and 1991, and like Subic has been transformed into a "freeport zone" (a tax- and duty-free zone) since the departure of the US Air Force. It's been far less successful in shedding its sleazy image, however, though the **airport** has proved popular with budget airlines. If you are travelling to the airport or aiming to climb **Pinatubo** or **Arayat** you may end up spending some time here, but otherwise there's little reason to linger.

The name "Clark" is generally used to refer to the former base and the tourist area of Angeles City around it, particularly **Fields Avenue** on the south side where most of the bars are.

Practicalities

Several carriers connect **Diosdado Macapagal International Airport** (ⓦwww .dmia.ph) inside the former base area with Singapore, Taipei, Seoul, Kuala Lumpur, Macau, Cebu and other regional destinations. Outside the terminal there's a small convenience store and an ATM. Plenty of fixed-rate **taxis** meet each flight, but these are expensive: anywhere within Clark (including Fields Ave) is P300, the Dau bus terminal is P400 and Angeles City P500. They'll drive you to Manila (1hr 30min with traffic) for P3496, Manila airport for P4316 or Makati for P3916. San Fernando is P1200. **Jeepneys** (with a/c) run from the airport when full (minimum eight people) and charge P50 to anywhere in Clark or to the Dau bus terminal. Philtranco runs direct **buses** to **Manila** from the airport at 11.45am, 1pm, 4pm and 8.30pm. Coming in the other direction, buses depart Manila at 6.30am, 7am, 11.30am and 2.30pm.

For other destinations head to the **Dau Bus Terminal** (pronounced "Da-oo") in nearby Mabalacat, served by almost continual buses from Manila. Partas and Victory Liner have frequent departures north from Dau to Baguio, La Union, Aliminos and Vigan. Another option for travelling between Manila and Clark is the Fly-the-Bus service operated by Swagman Travel (☏02/523-8541 or 045/322-2890; ⓦwww.swaggy.com). The bus leaves the *Swagman Hotel* in A. Flores Street, Ermita, at 11.30am, 3.30pm and 8.30pm daily and serves a number of hotels in Clark for P600 one-way (it heads back to Manila at 8am, noon and 3pm).

If you have to overnight in Clark keep in mind that the **hotels** are almost universally geared to prostitution. Your best bet is probably the *Holiday Inn Clark Field* (☏02/845-1888, ⓦwww.holidayinn.com; ⓞ), on Mimosa Drive, not far from the airport but slightly isolated from the rest of Angeles City (a good thing). Internet is P500 per 24 hour.

When it comes to **eating**, Angeles City is known as the "Sisig Capital of the Philippines". The dish (made from parts of a pig's head and liver, usually seasoned with calamansi and chilli) was first cooked up at *Aling Lucing Sisig* (daily 6am–3am; ☎045/888-2317) on Valdez Street in 1974, still the best place to sample it.

Mount Pinatubo

On April 2, 1991, people from the village of Patal Pinto on the lower slopes of **Mount Pinatubo** (1485m), 25km east of Clark, witnessed small explosions followed by steaming and smelt rotten egg fumes escaping from the upper slopes of the supposedly dormant volcano (the last known eruption was 600 years before). On June 12, the first of several major explosions took place. The eruption was so violent that shockwaves were felt in the Visayas and nearly 20 million tons of sulphur dioxide gas were blasted into the atmosphere, causing red skies to appear for months after the eruption. A giant ash cloud rose 35km into the sky and red-hot blasts seared the countryside. Ash paralysed Manila, closing the airport for days and turning the capital's streets into an eerie, grey, post-apocalyptic landscape. By June 16, when the dust had settled, the top of the volcano was gone, replaced by a 2km-wide caldera containing a lake. Lava deposits had filled valleys, buildings had collapsed, and over 800 people were dead.

Pinatubo is quiet once again, except for tourist activity. Until August 2009, the one- or two-day trek through the resultant moon-like lahar landscape of Pinatubo was one of the country's top activity highlights. However, due to heavy landslides that caused the deaths of eleven tourists, the trail has been indefinitely closed off. At the time of writing the only trek on offer went like this: from **Santa Juliana** where you register, a 4WD takes you for an hour or so across flat lahar beds and over dusty foothills to the start of a 45-minute gentle climb to **Lake Pinatubo** (around 960m). The lake itself is admittedly stunning, with emerald-green waters, and spectacular surrounding views, but those looking for some serious exercise, or even a close look at the moonscape will be disappointed. Bring a picnic and your swim stuff, and spend the day up there, to make the most of the trip (you can rent boats for P350).

Practicalities

The North Luzon (toll P2.13/km) and SCTEX expressways (toll P2/km) make getting to Pinatubo easy enough, and it's feasible to visit as a day-trip from Manila. Several companies run Pinatubo trips, though none will volunteer the information that the longer treks are closed, so question them carefully about what's open to trekkers at present. Try the Mount Pinatubo 4x4 Club (☎0919/608-4313, ⓦwww .pinatubo.tk), which operates from the small town of Santa Juliana about 40km from Clark. Coming from Manila or Clark on any Tarlac/Baguio bus, ask to be let off in Capas, where you can catch a jeepney to Santa Juliana. Prices for the "trek" are dependent on group size but count on at least P2000 per person. Swagman Travel in Clark (see p.123) runs overnight tours for US$150, shorter day excursions for US$47 and one-hour flights over the crater for US$80 (minimum two people).

Mount Arayat

Mount Arayat (1026m), a dormant volcano 42km east of Pinatubo, rises from the lowlands of Pampanga in solitary and dramatic fashion, the only mountain for miles around. It is said to be inhabited by Mariang Sinukuan (Maria the Abandoned), a *diwata* (fairy) of Tagalog folklore, and that when Mariang comes down from the mountain and visits the lowlands, her presence can be felt because the air turns fragrant. From the summit all of central Luzon is visible, from the snake-like Pampanga River to the mountains of Zambales, Bataan and beyond.

Practicalities

It takes just three to four hours to **climb** Arayat and get back down, depending on your fitness level. Companies such as Swagman in Clark will arrange a guide and transport for you (from US$37; see p.123), but it is possible to arrange the climb independently. Contact local guide Allan Sun (℡0923/428-2284) in advance and make your way to the foot of the mountain, a dilapidated former resort area known as Mount Arayat National Park, effectively occupied by villagers from nearby San Juan. Allan will help you get the local barangay permit back in the village (P20), and the DNER permit further up the trail (P100), before guiding you to the top of what's known as Peak 1 for P1500 (total, not per person). To **get to Mount Arayat** from Manila take a Sierra Madre or Arayat company bus from Monumento, EDSA in Caloocan to Arayat town (2hr; P120), then a tricycle to the National Park entrance (P30/person). A taxi from Clark Airport will cost an exorbitant P1800, but hotels should be able to arrange a driver for much less.

Bataan peninsula

With 85 percent of it covered in mountainous jungle, the **Bataan peninsula** is one of the most rugged places in the country. The province, forming the western side of Manila Bay, will always be associated with one of the bloodiest episodes of World War II. For four months in 1942, 65,000 Filipinos and 15,000 Americans – "the battling bastards of Bataan" – held out here against the superior arms and equipment of the Japanese. After their surrender in April 1942, the Filipino and American soldiers, weakened by months of deprivation, were forced to walk to detention camps in Tarlac province. About 10,000 men died along the way.

A poignant memorial to those that died, the "Dambana ng Kagitingan" or **Shrine of Valor** (daily 8am–5pm; P20) occupies the summit of **Mount Samat** (564m), a little inland from the provincial capital **Balanga**. The shrine has a chapel and a small museum of weapons captured from the Japanese, but the centrepiece is a 92-metre **crucifix** (P10) with a lift inside that takes you to a gallery at the top with views across the peninsula and, on a clear day, to Manila. Jeepneys ply the mountain highway between Balanga and Bagac, passing Mount Samat, but unless you find someone to give you a lift, it's a 7km walk (1hr) from the nearest stop to the shrine. Hiring a van from Balanga should cost around P1000.

Getting to Bataan

From **Manila**, Baatan is a convenient 1hr zip across Manila Bay – assuming the ferries are running. In late 2010 services from the SM Mall of Asia to the Mount Samat Ferry Terminal just south of the town of **Orion** on Bataan's east coast were cancelled – ask at the tourist office to see if another service has replaced it. From Orion, you can get a bus or jeepney south to **Mariveles** (42km), or north to **Pilar** (for the Shrine of Valor, 6km) and the provincial capital **Balanga** (8km).

The time-consuming alternative to the ferry is to take a **bus** all the way from Manila. Bataan Transit, 599 Kaunlaran St, runs the most frequent air-conditioned services to Balanga (3hr) and Mariveles (4hr) – they also run from their Pasay terminal. Genesis Transport (℡02/421-1413) runs a similar service to Balanga and Mariveles, while Victory Liner (℡02/361-1506) connects Balanga with Olongapo for Subic Bay (1hr) every hour. Genesis also runs buses between Mariveles and Baguio every 2hr.

Mariveles

There are some picturesque **beaches** on Bataan's southwest coast between **MARIVELES**, some 50km south of Balanga, and **BAGAC**. Of a number of resorts used mostly by Filipinos for weekend breaks, the best is *Montemar Beach Club* (☎047/888-4719, ⊛www.montemarbeach.com; ⑥) in Barrio Pasinay, Bagac. It's a large, well-established place on a five-hundred-metre stretch of clean sandy beach, with watersports facilities and a swimming pool. The rooms have air-conditioning and a private balcony overlooking either the beach or the gardens. Take a jeepney from Balanga to Bagac.

From Mariveles itself you can strike out for the summit of **Mount Mariveles** (1130m), a tricky overnight climb that starts with a twenty minutes' tricycle ride (P100) from Mariveles to the barangay of **Alasasin**, where you need to register at the barangay hall (P20) and ask for a guide. Apart from food and water, you'll need a good tent or bivouac, a sleeping bag and a warm jacket – it can be surprisingly chilly when night falls.

Subic Bay

Since the closure of Subic Bay Naval Base in 1992, the **Subic Bay area** has been re-invented as a gate-guarded playground for the rich, with golf courses, a yacht club, a casino and smart hotels. For most foreign travellers, the main appeal is the wide range of watersports, diving and tranquil beaches on offer. Subic Bay is vast, and is best thought of as four distinct areas.

The Subic Bay **Freeport Zone** (a tax- and duty-free zone) encompasses the old base, accessed by "gates" manned by security guards, and comprises two parts. Most of the banks, restaurants, shops and hotels are located on a small island known as the **Central Business District**. On the mainland to the south lie the beaches and most of the outdoor activities, theme parks and attractions.

To the north of the CBD, linked by gates and bridges across the drainage channel (the **Main Gate** is also known as the Magsaysay Gate), **Olongapo City** lies outside the Freeport Zone but is generally considered part of the Subic Bay area. It is a typical Philippine provincial town, streets crammed with stalls and smoke-belching tricycles. This is where the bus terminals are located, but you won't spend much time here otherwise.

Finally, around 5km north of Olongapo along the coast (also outside the Freeport Zone), **Barrio Barretto** is gradually shaking off its go-go bar days, though it still attracts its share of the ageing expat/Filipina "girlfriend" scene. Nearby **Baloy Long Beach** is a better place to crash, a laidback row of bars and hotels right on the sand.

Arrival and information

Most of Subic lies in Zambales province, an hour southwest of Clark via the SCTEX highway (P115 toll for cars), and some 110km northwest of Manila. At the time of writing **Subic Bay International Airport** wasn't serving passenger traffic, though Cathay Pacific and Air Asia were considering reopening flights. Until that happens the only way to get here is by bus or to rent a car. Most **buses** arrive in Olongapo City at either the Saulong Transit terminal just across the drainage channel from the main gate, or at the Victory Liner terminal further north at Rizal Avenue and West 18th Street.

The Subic Bay Tourism Department (daily 8am–5pm; ☎047/252-4154, ⊛www.greatersubic.com or www.sbma.com) is next to the Subic Bay Exhibition

& Convention Center at 18 Efficiency Ave, just off the main highway to Manila at the edge of the zone. Staff here can help book tours, hotels and provide the latest on what's happening; you'll also need to arrange hikes here (see p.129).

Major hotels in Subic have wi-fi or business centres where you can access the **internet**, but they charge more than the many hole-in-the-wall internet cafés in Olongapo, most of them along Rizal Avenue and Magsaysay Avenue. In Barrio Barretto popular resorts and restaurants such as *Mango's*, *Barts* and *Johansson's* have reliable internet.

Subic Bay transport

Jeepneys and tricycles are banned within **Subic Bay Freeport Zone**, so transport is provided by Megatsai **taxis** (24hr; ☎047/252-8102) and Winstar Transport **buses**; both have their terminals in the CBD in a car park (known as "park and shop") off the Rizal Highway, close to the Main Gate and a short walk from the Saulong Transit terminal over in Olongapo. **Taxis** charge fixed rates from here, with most fares P40–90 within the CBD. Elsewhere it's P140 to JEST, the airport, Pamulaklakin and Cubi, P250 to All Hands Beach, P325 to Subic Safari and

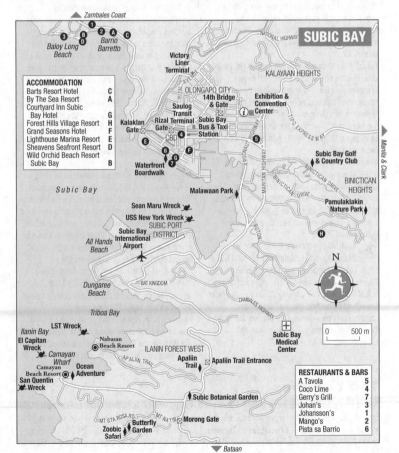

ACCOMMODATION
Barts Resort Hotel	C
By The Sea Resort	A
Courtyard Inn Subic Bay Hotel	G
Forest Hills Village Resort	H
Grand Seasons Hotel	F
Lighthouse Marina Resort	E
Sheavens Seafront Resort	D
Wild Orchid Beach Resort Subic Bay	B

RESTAURANTS & BARS
A Tavola	5
Coco Lime	4
Gerry's Grill	7
Johan's	3
Johansson's	1
Mango's	2
Pista sa Barrio	6

Nabasan Pier and P350 to Ocean Adventure. Buses run every thirty minutes but are not that useful; they charge P7 within the CBD, P11 for the Binictican area (Pamulaklakin) and P13 to Cubi (for JEST).

In **Olongapo** all jeepneys are colour-coded; from just outside the Victory Liner bus terminal you can take frequent blue jeepneys (direction "Castillejos") to Barrio Barretto and Baloy (P10). To travel between Olongapo and the Freeport, you'll have to walk across the Main Gate (the two systems are mutually exclusive). To **rent a car** contact Avis (Mon–Sat 8am–5pm; ℡047/250-0357) at Unit 116, Charlie Building, Subic International Hotel Compound.

Accommodation

You can stay at one of the **hotels** within the perimeters of the old base itself, or look for bargain beachside options at **Barrio Barretto**.

Subic Bay Freeport Zone

Courtyard Inn Subic Bay Hotel Waterfront Rd ℡047/252-2366, ⊛www.courtyardinn-subic.com. Modern hotel, rather soulless, but very clean and with comfortable rooms with cable TV and breakfast included at mid-level rates. The location is good, close to restaurants in the central business district. ❺

Forest Hills Village Resort El Kabayo Rd, Binictican Heights ℡047/252-1406. Self-catering accommodation in low-rise buildings that used to house naval officers: there is a kitchen and three bedrooms that sleep six (as well as a pool and tennis courts). *Forest Hills* is perched on a hill overlooking Subic, so you'll need to have a car to get around. ❽

Grand Seasons Hotel Canal Rd ℡047/645-0357, ⊛www.subicgrandseasonshotel.com. The 84 deluxe rooms here are simple and comfortable, with muted decor and no unnecessary frills (though TV and wi-fi are standard). There's a casino, various restaurants and an outdoor pool. ❻

🏃 **Lighthouse Marina Resort** Moonbay Marina Complex, Waterfront Rd ℡047/252-5000, ⊛www.lighthousesubic.com. Lavish 34-room boutique topped with a replica of an actual lighthouse (not working). The room theme is "aqua", with soothing blue and green tones, contemporary furnishings, DVD players, flat-screen TVs and a glass-walled bathroom with an old-fashioned tub. ❽

Barrio Barretto and Baloy Long Beach

Barts Resort Hotel 117C National Hwy ℡047/223-4148, ⊛bartsresortsubic.com. Comfortable budget doubles in a grey motel-style building around a small garden and swimming pool, but close to the beach. Attic rooms are the cheapest (fan only), while all other rooms have a/c, but note that *Barts* is a popular nightlife hangout, so can be a little noisy. It's located at the north end of the Barrio Barretto beach. ❷

By The Sea Resort 99 National Hwy ℡047/222-2888, ⊛www.bythesea.com.ph. Fifty a/c rooms with cable TV and free wi-fi either right on the beach or set back around a quiet garden. Convivial restaurant and bar overlooking the sea, live music Wed–Sat. ❷

🏃 **Sheavens Seafront Resort** Baloy Long Beach ℡047/223-9430, ⊛www.sheavens.com. Big but peaceful resort-hotel in an unbeatable location right on the water. Immaculate rooms, good food (the menu includes European and Thai dishes) and helpful staff who can arrange bangka trips and scuba diving. Wide range of rooms, starting from budget (fan only; ❷). Deluxe rooms ❻

🏃 **Wild Orchid Beach Resort Subic Bay** Baloy Long Beach ℡047/223-1029, ⊛www.wildorchidsubic.com. Justly popular choice, with standard "deluxe" rooms equipped with king-size beds, flat-screen TVs, DVD players and free internet. Fabulous extras include *Captain Rob's Steakhouse* and *Barefoot Bar* on the beach, and an enormous pool (with jacuzzis and swim-up bar). ❼

The beaches

Most travellers come here for the **wreck diving**, which is superb (see box opposite), but there are plenty of peaceful, clean **beaches** inside the former base if you just want to chill out. **Dungaree Beach** (daily 6am–6pm; P150, P100 children; ℡047/252-4032) on the southern side of the airport is closest to the CBD, a tranquil stretch of sand and beach huts (P1500/day) shaded by trees; during most weekdays you'll have it to yourself. Popular **Nabusan Beach** further to the south is being developed into a posh resort by businessman Antonio Tony "Boy" Cojuangco – day visitors may be allowed access for a fee, but check with the tourist office on the latest. The best beach in the Freeport Zone is **Camayan Beach** (formerly Miracle Beach) and now part of the *Camayan Beach Resort* (T 047/252-8000, W www.camayanbeachresort.com) offering diving, snorkelling, kayaking and swimming; day visitors can access the beach for P300 (children P250).

Barrio Barreto has a scrappy beach that leads into the much nicer **Baloy Long Beach**, one of the better strips of sand in Luzon; locals charge a nominal entry fee of P30, but you can skip this if you stay the night.

Activities

If you're feeling energetic, there are numerous other activities on offer around Subic Bay. To go **hiking**, you'll need to contact the Tourism Department in advance (see p.126) to arrange mandatory guides; there's a standard fee of P50 per hike. The **Apaliin Trail** runs along the banks of the Apaliin River to the coast (2hr), while visits to the rainforest trails within the **Pamulaklakin Nature Park** include orientation from members of the **Aeta tribe** ("eye-ta"). These are the so-called Negritos, who are thought to have arrived here long before the Austronesian majority; they receive no help or recognition from the government and their situation remains controversial. The Aeta were one of the few groups sad to see the Americans leave – Aeta warriors trained US Marines here for service in Vietnam and were generally well treated.

Other than a few groups of monkeys, the most visible wildlife in the hills around Cubi is a colony of around 10,000 bamboo bats, golden-crowned flying foxes and fruit bats – the so-called **Bat Kingdom**. They tend to move around, so just ask a

---

Dive Subic

Subic Bay is a popular **diving** site, and has nineteen wrecks in still waters, all no more than thirty minutes by boat from the waterfront area. The **USS New York**, is the star attraction of Subic's underwater world, a battle cruiser launched in the US in 1891. When World War II broke out, she was virtually retired, and when the Japanese swept the US Marines out of the Philippines, the Americans had no choice but to scuttle her as they departed from Subic in early 1942. The ship now lies on her port side in 27m of water between Alava pier and the northern end of Cubi Point runway. For experienced divers, the 120-metre-long hull presents excellent opportunities for what scuba divers call a "swim-through" – an exploration of the inside of the wreck from one end to the other.

The **El Capitan**, a Spanish-era wreck lying 20m down in a pretty inlet on the east coast of Subic Bay is a much easier wreck dive, suitable for novices. The **San Quentin** (16m) is the oldest known wreck in Subic, a wooden gunboat scuttled by the Spanish in 1898 in a futile attempt to block the channel between Grande and Chiquita islands against invading Americans. Other Subic wrecks include the Japanese POW ship *Oryoku Maru* and the *Seian Maru*, a Japanese cargo vessel sunk by the American Navy in 1945.

For **diving trips** try Johan's Adventure Dive Center (T 047/224-8915, W www .subicdive.com), right on the shore at Baloy Beach; Moby Dick Watersports (T 047/252-3773); or Subic Bay Aqua Sports (T 047/252-6048) on Waterfront Drive at Building 249. Boardwalk Dive Center (T 047/252-5357), is at Building 664, Waterfront Road, in the same building as the *Boardwalk Inn*. Two-dive packages start at around P2200 at each place.

local where they are; during the day bats hang from trees asleep, but at dusk thousands of these giant, harmless creatures take to the air to look for food. If you don't have your own transport, most hotels can arrange **tours** with guides for around P2000 (including other sights).

Ocean Adventure and Zoobic Safari

Next to Camayan Beach, **Ocean Adventure** (daily 9am–6pm; P500, children under 12 P420; ☎047/252-9000, ⑩www.oceanadventure.com.ph) is one of Subic's major tourist draws, where you can swim (45min; P4200) or have a brief encounter on the beach (30min; P2800) with the park's friendly dolphins (all prices include site entry). Nearby **Zoobic Safari** (daily 8am–4pm; P495; ☎047/252-2272, ⑩www.zoobic.com.ph) offers tiger safaris via jeep (where the guides feed chicken to the "wild" tigers), a serpentarium with iguanas, crocodiles, snakes and lizards, and a petting zoo. The tigers are well treated, but if you don't like zoos you really won't like this. Taxis here from the CDB are P400.

Eating and drinking

The best places to **eat** and **drink** line the CBD waterfront or beaches to the north and south. The restaurants in Olongapo City are on the main drag, Magsaysay Drive, and tend towards the usual range of fast-food joints. Much of the nightlife in Barrio Barretto still revolves around girlie bars, but there are plenty of places in the CBD trying to attract families and a more mixed clientele.

Subic Bay Freeport

A Tavola Palm St, at the Argonaut Hwy (near the big duty-free stores ten minutes east of the Main Gate along Rizal Ave) ☎047/252-6556. If you crave authentic Italian food in Subic the undisputed king is this gem of a restaurant owned by an Italian chef, offering huge plates of home-made pasta dishes (from P240), wood-fired pizza (from P320) and a good selection of affordable wines. Daily noon–3pm & 6–10pm.

Coco Lime Rizal Hwy, CBD ☎047/252-2412. Decent Philippine, Thai and Japanese dishes that taste good if not always totally authentic; great adobo rice and lapu-lapu (P160–200). Daily 11am–2pm & 5–10pm.

Gerry's Grill Waterfront Rd, near Labitan St ☎047/252-3021. Big, brash chain restaurant that sells local food in immense portions; think fried chicken (P225), pork sisig (P175) and crab rice (P175). Sun–Thurs 11am–midnight, Fri & Sat 11am–1am.

Pista sa Barrio Building 141, Waterfront Rd at Espiritu St ☎047/252-3187. Solid Filipino cuisine – pork adobo for P170, half fried chicken P190 and a huge range of sinigang (Filipino sour tamarind soup)

from P150), especially good seafood, served inside or on the breezy covered deck; you can also stay the night here (from P1750). Free wi-fi. Daily 24hr.

Barrio Barretto and Baloy Long Beach

Johan's Baloy Long Beach ☎047/224-8915. Smartest bar and diner in Baloy, right on the beach, with rooms from P700 and plenty of knowledge-able expats dispensing sage advice at the bar. Daily 24hr.

Johansson's 128 National Hwy, Barrio Barretto ☎047/223-9293. Popular Swedish-owned hangout, with omelettes for breakfast a bargain P40, and a lunch and dinner menu that includes blue marlin steak (P140), boiled veal with dill sauce (P140), schnitzel, beef stew (P125) and an interesting take on sinigang using salmon (P95). Daily 24hr.

Mango's 116 National Hwy, Barrio Barretto ☎047/223-4139, ⑩www.mangossubic.com. Beach bar, restaurant, cheap inn and local landmark (look out for the neon sign) serving both Filipino and European cuisine. Breakfast from P150, and burgers from P195. Daily 7am–10pm.

Northern Luzon

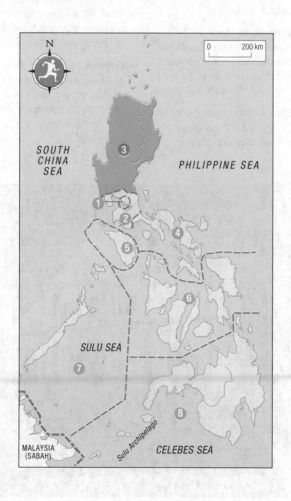

Highlights

CHAPTER 3

* **Surfing in La Union** The sweeping beach at San Juan has big breakers, magical sunsets and resorts for every budget. See p.142

* **Vigan** Atmospheric old Spanish outpost with cobbled streets, horse-drawn carriages and, if you're there at the right time, lively festivals. See p.144

* **Sagada** Celebrated mountain Shangri-La with hanging coffins, cave exploration, exceptional trekking and very cheap lodgings. See p.175

* **Trekking around Banaue** Wonderful walks through tribal villages and rice terrace scenery – don't miss the trek to nearby Batad. See p.184

* **Batanes** Enchanting group of little-visited rural islands off the northern tip of Luzon, offering unforgettable scenery and terrific trekking. See p.186

▲ St Paul's Cathedral, Vigan

3

Northern Luzon

North of Manila, the island of Luzon tempts visitors with some wonderful mountainous areas, volcanic landscapes and a beautiful coastline dotted with heavenly beaches. Heading up the west coast from Subic, the **Zambales coast** is dotted with laidback resorts, while the Lingayen Gulf is the location of the **Hundred Islands** – a favourite weekend trip from Manila. Further along the coast, the province of La Union draws visitors particularly for its surfing. North of here is **Ilocos Sur**, known primarily for the old colonial city of **Vigan**, where horse-drawn carriages bounce down narrow cobblestone streets. The area around the capital of Ilocos Norte province, **Laoag**, features a number of sites related to former dictator Ferdinand Marcos, who was born in the nearby village of Sarrat. And on the northwestern edge of Luzon there are excellent beaches around **Pagudpud**.

The northeast of the island is one of the archipelago's least visited wildernesses. Those who head this way usually do so for the excellent surfing on the east coast at **Baler**, but further north is **Palanan** – the jump-off point for the barely explored **Northern Sierra Madre Natural Park**. For many visitors, though, the prime attraction in Northern Luzon is the mountainous inland **Cordillera** region. Highlights here include the mountain village of **Sagada** with its caves and hanging coffins, and the stunning rice terraces around **Banaue** and **Bontoc**. In the village of **Kabayan** in Benguet province it's possible to hike up to see mummies, discovered in caves in the early twentieth century. Kabayan also provides access to **Mount Pulag**, the highest mountain in Luzon. Finally, far off the northern coast lie the scattered islands of **Batanes** province.

The Zambales Coast

Zambales is an undeveloped rural province, known for its succulent mangoes, which is still largely undiscovered by foreign tourists. It is, however, worth a stop for its scenic beaches, good surfing and relaxing resorts. For a break from beaches you can head inland to **Lake Mapanuepe**, formed after Mount Pinatubo erupted in 1991.

Travel along the coast is straightforward, with a large number of buses running along the main road. Victory Liner has services straight up the coast from Manila, stopping at major towns like Iba and Santa Cruz but able to drop you between if you request it. There are also dozens of local buses and jeepneys, so it's easy to make short trips from one place to the next.

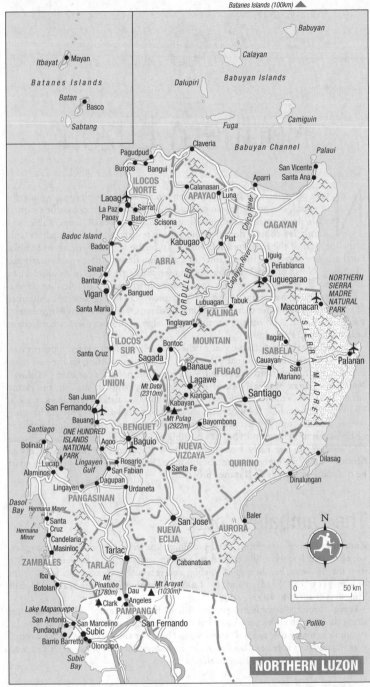

Batanes Islands (100km)

Babuyan

Calayan

Itbayat Mayan

Batanes Islands

Dalupiri

Babuyan Islands

Batan Basco

Sabtang

Fuga

Camiguin

Claveria

Babuyan Channel

Palaui

Pagudpud

San Vicente

Burgos Bangui

Santa Ana

ILOCOS
NORTE

Calanasan

Aparri

Laoag

Luna

La Paz Sarrat

Calco River

CAGAYAN

Paoay Batac

Scisona

Kabugao

Piat

Badoc Island

ABRA

Iguig

Badoc

Peñablanca

Cagayan River

Tuguegarao

Sinait

NORTHERN
SIERRA
MADRE
NATURAL
PARK

Bantay

Lubuagan Tabuk

Vigan Bangued

KALINGA

Maconacan

Santa Maria

Tinglayan

ILOCOS
SUR

Bontoc

MOUNTAIN

Ilagan

ISABELA

Santa Cruz

Sagada

Banaue

Cauayan

LA
UNION

*Mt Data
(2310m)*

Lagawe

IFUGAO

San
Mariano

Palanan

Kiangan

Santiago

San Juan

Kabayan

San Fernando

*Mt Pulag
(2922m)*

Bayombong

Bauang

Santiago

ONE HUNDRED
ISLANDS
NATIONAL
PARK

Agoo

BENGUET

Baguio

Bolinao

NUEVA
VIZCAYA

QUIRINO

Lucap

*Lingayen
Gulf*

Rosario

Santa Fe

Dilasag

Alaminos

San Fabian

Lingayen Dagupan

Dinalungan

Urdaneta

PANGASINAN

*Dasol
Bay*

Hermana Mayor

Santa
Cruz

Baler

*Hermana
Minor*

Candelaria

San Jose

Masinloc

NUEVA
ECIJA

AURORA

ZAMBALES

Tarlac

TARLAC

N

Iba

Cabanatuan

Botolan

*Mt
Pinatubo
(1780m)*

Dau

*Mt Arayat
(1030m)*

0   50 km

Lake Mapanuepe

Angeles

San Antonio San Marcelino

Clark

Pollilo

Pundaquit

Subic

PAMPANGA

Barrio Barretto

San Fernando

Olongapo

*Subic
Bay*

NORTHERN LUZON

The beaches

The beaches along the coast benefit from wonderful sunsets and views of the South China Sea. One lovely long stretch of white sand lies close to the fishing village of **Pundaquit** (sometimes spelled Pundakit); it's also the access point for Capones Island (P800 by bangka), a great place to camp. To get to Pundaquit you need to catch a jeepney or tricycle from San Antonio, which is 5km to the north on the main highway.

If your passion is for surfing, make a beeline for **Crystal Beach Resort** just north of San Antonio, near the town of San Narciso. The best surf is between September and February. Further north in **Botolan** are a couple of sleepy but well-run resorts on the wide beach of the barangay of Binoclutan; they are reachable by jeepney (P10–15) in less than ten minutes from where buses drop you on the main highway. Another thirty minutes north of Botolan, the provincial capital **Iba** boasts an attractive brown sand beach, reached by jeepney and tricycle from town. Iba has a **tourist office** on the second floor of the Capitol building (☎047/811-7216), which can arrange tours focusing on mango production, or activities such as mangrove planting.

Uacon, just north of Candelaria town on the National Highway, has a resort that makes a good base for visiting tiny Potipot Island, an idyllic little white sand getaway. At times you may have the island to yourself, although it can get busy at weekends and during school summer holidays (mid-March to early June). Close to the border with Pangasinan province, **Santa Cruz** is the main access point for two islands in Dasol Bay: **Hermana Mayor** and **Hermana Menor**. Neither island has accommodation for visitors, but both have some picturesque coves of fine white sand and good snorkelling. They are privately owned but *SeaSun* resort (see p.136) can arrange a day-trip for P1200.

Accommodation

The resorts in Zambales tend to be on the expensive side. The crowd here is usually a mix of expatriates and Filipino tourists.

Pundaquit

Nora's Beach Resort ☎0918/278-8188. A basic but clean place where the a/c rooms are better value than the fan-cooled nipa huts. The resort hires out bangkas at P1500 for a day exploring nearby Camara and Capones islands, as well as Anawangin Cove where there's some good snorkelling. Surfing is possible from July to February, although the first half of the season is usually more reliable. ❺

Punta de Uian ☎0918/800-8426, ⓦwww .puntadeuian.net. Probably the most upmarket place to stay on the whole Zambales coast. Several of the buildings on the large site are arranged around a lagoon and there's a spa, tennis court, mini-golf and even plans for a motocross circuit. Island-hopping trips can be arranged. ❼

Crystal Beach

Crystal Beach Resort ☎0918/800-8426, ⓦwww.crystalbeach.com.ph. A range of rooms popular with surfers in season and evangelical groups for the rest of the year. Travellers on a budget can hire a tent with bedding (❷), or pitch

their own for P150. In addition to surfing lessons with qualified instructors (P200 per hour) and board hire (P200/hr or P400/half a day), the resort can also arrange sea kayaking and island-hopping. No alcohol is served in the resort. ❺

Botolan

Botolan Wildlife Farm 3km inland from a turning on the National Hwy just south of Botolan ☎0917/734-2206, ⓦwww.botolanwildlifefarm.com. A quirky accommodation choice, this private zoo is run by a Swiss zoologist and home to rescued animals including macaques, pig-nosed turtles, Philippine egrets and a Siberian tiger. The rooms are good value; some have views of mountains and trees, others overlook the tiger pen. ❷

Rama International Beach Resort ☎0918/910-1280, ⓦwww.ramabeach.com. The best beach resort around Botolan, with clean, rustic cottages on the shore and wi-fi in public areas. The owners can arrange trips to limestone caves near Santa Cruz, the old hilltop gold-mining town of Acoe or nearby Mount Binoclutan. ❹

Iba

Café Tolyo Pension House Close to the Capitol Building in town ℡047/811-1266. The rooms are uninspiring but acceptable as a cheap alternative to the beach resorts; upstairs there are no showers (only buckets of water), while the downstairs double has its own bathroom with shower. The café serves Chinese and Filipino dishes, and is decorated with antiques and knick-knacks. ❶

Palmera Garden Beach Resort 5min north of Iba in the barangay of Bantangalinga ℡047/811-2109, Ⓦwww.palmeragarden.com. Large place with concrete a/c rooms – some with bamboo exteriors – and a lovely swimming pool set in gardens overlooking the ocean. The free wi-fi reaches some of the bedrooms. ❺

Uacon

Dawal ℡0919/573-0952, Ⓦwww.dawal.com.ph. This resort has fifty rooms at various prices, including nipa huts, poolside rooms and a couple of houses suitable for families. There's a dark sand beach, an area for guests to barbecue their own food, and a live band and disco from 8pm–2am on Saturday nights. The resort arranges trips to Potipot (P400 for up to 6 people) but has no snorkelling equipment for hire. ❹

Santa Cruz

SeaSun Beach Resort About 7km south of Santa Cruz ℡0917/409-3347, Ⓦwww.seasun.com.ph. The cheapest rooms here are basic and cooled by fans, while there are also more comfortable a/c (❹) rooms available. The resort has a long and clean stretch of beach, with a coral reef which is good for snorkelling. ❷

Lake Mapanuepe

One of the most interesting side-trips from the coastal route is inland to **LAKE MAPANUEPE**, formed after Mount Pinatubo erupted in 1991 and dammed the Mapanuepe River. The waters partly submerged the barrios of Aglao, Buhawen and Pili, requiring the evacuation of hundreds of people. Their homes remain beneath the water and a church cross still breaks the surface.

The displaced residents settled on the shores of what they commonly call Ang Lawa (simply "the lake"), in the remains of their barrios or in new settlements. The main access point to the lake is Aglao, which can be reached from San Marcelino on the National Highway. On the way to Aglao from San Marcelino you'll pass the Macarang viewpoint, a concrete structure with a great view of the lake. Down at the lake itself, it is possible to hire a boat to go out to the submerged church (around P500) or right across to Aeta villages such as Lomibao.

Aglao is a 45-minute journey by jeepney from San Marcelino. Unfortunately the last jeepney back is around noon, so you'll probably need to stay the night, walk back (2–3hr) or hitch a lift. A better plan is to contact Leah Villajuan at the municipal tourist office (℡047/623-2123) in San Marcelino, who can organize very good-value trips by 4WD for just the cost of fuel (around P400–500). You'll also need to pay for the boat across the lake if you take it. The trip can include a visit to one of the Aeta tribal villages, either across the river or on the near side – it's a more meaningful trip if you are with someone who can translate.

There are a few very basic places to **stay** in the area; the tourist office can help. The barangay hall in Pili may be able to arrange a homestay, while the barangay hall in Buhawen accepts overnight visitors at its day care centre for a small donation. Alternatively contact Pastor Jerry de la Cruz (℡0999/785-8934) – who is also a tribal chieftain – about his resthouse in the village of Pawan.

The Lingayen Gulf

Many of the beaches dotted along the western stretch of the **Lingayen Gulf**, between Bolinao and Dagupan, are working beaches, where people fish in the gulf's rich waters and mend their nets. The sand is generally grey and unappealing and the water likewise; much of the coral has been destroyed by dynamite and cyanide fishing. It certainly isn't all bad news though. The gulf's primary attraction, the **Hundred Islands National Park**, is worth the trip here alone. There's more though: at the western end of the gulf around Bolinao you'll find good beaches and some excellent snorkelling areas, while at the northeastern end of the gulf the capital of La Union province, **San Fernando**, provides access to beaches and resorts as well as opportunities for trekking and climbing. There is also some excellent surfing if you time it right, with surfers congregating in the resorts of **San Juan**.

Buses from Manila, run by Five Star and Victory Liner, ply the route along the gulf although you'll probably need to change bus – with Dagupan one of the main hubs – even if you are passing straight through.

Hundred Islands National Park

These tiny, emerald-like islands – actually there are 123, but that doesn't have quite the same ring to it – are part of a **national park** covering almost twenty square kilometres in the Lingayen Gulf. Some islands have beaches, but many are no more than coral outcrops crowned by scrub. Sadly, much of the underwater coral in the park has been damaged by a devastating combination of cyanide and dynamite fishing, typhoons and the El Niño weather phenomenon. The authorities are, however, going all out to protect what coral is left and help it regenerate, meaning you can only snorkel in approved areas. Marine biologists from the University of the Philippines have been at the forefront of the protection movement, replanting hundreds of *taklobos* (giant clams).

The best place to base yourself for exploring the islands is the small town of **Lucap**, from which you can island-hop by day before returning to a shower and a comfy bed in the evening. Lucap can be reached by tricycle (15min; P60) from the city of **Alaminos**, which is on the National Highway.

Arrival and information

Tricycles from Alaminos can drop you at your hotel in Lucap – they are all in a single strip – or at the small **national park office** (open 24hr; ☎075/551-2505) at the nearby pier. You can pay your **park entrance fee** and arrange **camping permits** at the office, and they also hire out snorkelling equipment and camping gear although it would be wise to call ahead to check on availability of the latter. The office has a handy ATM. If you're looking to do something other than island-hopping, contact the Hundred Islands OceanSports Center (☎075/551-2246) in Lucap: activities include parasailing (from P1250/15min) and sea kayaking (P150/hr or P500/day).

Accommodation and eating

There are three islands where you can **camp** overnight for P200 per tent: Governor's Island, Children's Island and Quezon Island. On Governor's Island there is also a **guesthouse** ideal for a family but it isn't cheap at P10,000 per night. Most people stay in Lucap, where all the hotels listed below are located. Most of the hotels on the strip have **restaurants**; there are also overpriced canteens on the three developed islands.

Helden Resthouse ☎0981/731-2151. One of the few really low-budget options in Lucap, so it tends to fill up quickly. The cheapest rooms are just P500, with shared bathrooms and fans. ❷

Island Tropic ☎075/696-9405, ⓦwww.islandtropichotel.com. The twin and matrimonial rooms here are excellent value, while the penthouses (❻) are fabulous. Be sure to try the Alaminos-style longganisa (garlicky sausage) in their popular restaurant. ❹

Maxine by the Sea ☎075/551-2537, ⓦwww.maxinebythesea.com. On the pier with minimalist but appealing doubles with either a/c or fan and private bathrooms. The restaurant serves freshly caught seafood. ❹

HUNDRED ISLANDS NATIONAL PARK

Cathedral Island
Scout Island
Quezon Island
Marcos Island
Cuenco Island
Quilne Island
Children's Island
Marta Island
Governor's Island
Shell Island

Vigan, Laoag & Pagudpud

San Juan

San Fernando

San Fernando Airport

Burgos

Bauang

N

Baguio

Baguio

Patar Beach

Bolinao

Tandol Beach

Anda

Agoo

See Inset for details

Hundred Islands National Park

Lucap

Lingayen Gulf

Rosario

Baguio

Alaminos

San Fabian

Burgos

Daguran

Manila

Dasol

Lingayen

Urdaneta

San Carlos

Infanta

0   20 km

HUNDRED ISLANDS AND LINGAYEN GULF

Zambales Coast & Subic

Tarlac & Manila

Seaside Haven ☎075/551-2711. A collection of simple rooms and nipa huts right by the water. ❹

Villa Milagrosa ☎075/551-3040. The first hotel you come to on the main drag, with rooms that are adequate and reasonably priced by Lucap standards. ❸

Vista de las Islas ☎075/551-4455, ⓦwww .vistadelasislas.com. Probably the classiest place in town, with a large L-shaped pool and a spa on site. The rooms are not quite as fancy as you might expect from the public areas, but do have some

nice touches. The newer rooms in the Emerald wing are worth the extra expense. ❺

Restaurant

The Boat House This octagonal restaurant on the waterside is an impressive addition to the strip, owned by the proprietor of the OceanSports Center. It isn't the cheapest restaurant in town, with mains such as yellow fin tuna for P275, but the cooking is accomplished and the atmosphere relaxed. Fri–Sun 5.30pm–midnight.

Island-hopping

The only three islands with any form of development are **Governor's Island**, **Children's Island** and **Quezon Island**. A day-trip to all three costs P800 for a small boat for five people (larger boats are also available). You'll need to choose one island on which you will spend most of your time – the boatman will leave you there for a few hours then return, and you'll visit the other two more briefly.

A much more appealing option is to pay P1400 for a "service boat" allowing you to visit the more interesting undeveloped islands. Some of these dots of land are so small and rocky it's impossible to land on them, while others are big enough to allow for some exploring on foot, with tiny, sandy coves where you can picnic in the shade and swim. One of the prettiest islands is **Marta**, actually two tiny islets connected by a thin strip of bright white sand that almost disappears at high tide. **Marcos Island** has a blowhole and a vertical shaft of rock; you can clamber to the top and then dive into a seawater pool about 20m below. A number of islands, including **Scout Island** and **Quirino Island**, have caves; on **Cuenco Island** there's a cave that goes right through the island to the other side. Shell Island has a lagoon in which you can swim at high tide, while birdwatchers should ask to stop beside **Cathedral Island**.

Boats are available from 6am and will return to Lucap no later than 5.30pm; if you are planning to stay overnight on one of the islands then you need to leave Lucap by 5pm, and you will be charged P1400 for a small boat to drop you off and pick you up next day. Whatever your plans, the park office may be able to arrange for you to join another group if you do not have enough people to fill a boat and want to save some money.

Bolinao and around

The landscape around the town of **BOLINAO** is one of cascading waterfalls, rolling hills and white beaches, including the popular **Patar Beach** and the little-known **Tondol Beach**. In town you can visit the small **Bolinao Museum** (Mon–Fri 8am–5pm; free), on Rizal Street opposite Cape Bolinao High School, which contains art, geology, botany and zoology displays. The **Church of St James** in the main square was built by the Augustinians in 1609 and boasts a good collection of wooden *santos* figures. It was devastated by a typhoon in 2009 and at the time of writing still had a temporary roof.

If you are interested in finding out more about the local marine life, contact the University of the Philippines Marine Science Institute (℡075/541-8022, Ⓦwww .msi.upd.edu.ph/bml). In addition to arranging a visit to their lab, they can offer snorkelling trips to an area where giant clams are cultivated. For scuba diving try Cape Bolinao Diving Centre (℡0929/307-7515) on D. Celino Street Prices start at P3000 for two dives.

Practicalities

The **tourist office** (℡075/554-4284) is in the town hall. Although you are probably better moving on to one of the nearby resorts on Patar Beach, there are

---

Moving on from the Hundred Islands

Victory Liner and Five Star have daily bus services from Alaminos to Manila (5hr 30min; P350) or to Santa Cruz (1hr 30min; P80) for connections to Zambales. They also have buses eastwards to Lingayen (45min; P40–45), and to Dagupan (1hr 30min; P65–70) where you can change for Baguio or San Fernando, La Union. Air-conditioning vans make the same journeys more quickly for only a few more pesos. Heading west, Bolinao can be reached in 30–45min by van (P50), jeepney (P40) or bus (P50).

3

a couple of places to **stay** in Bolinao: the best is the good-value *El Pescador* (℡075/554-2559; ❸), with a swimming pool. As well as the usual basic **restaurants**, Bolinao has a surprise in the form of *Yumi Yuki* – a Japanese restaurant serving sushi, sashimi and noodles. It's located close to the Victory Liner terminal, on the way out of town past the city hall.

Patar Beach

The best-known beach in the Bolinao area is **Patar Beach**, about thirty minutes west of town, which has fine white sand and good surf. On the road to Patar there are some pleasant, relaxed beaches and resorts; you can stay either in one of them or on Patar Beach itself. The resorts can arrange trips to a large **barrier reef** offshore, near **Santiago Island**, where there is some wonderful solitary snorkelling. Another popular attraction is the **Enchanted Cave**, close to the *Dutch Beach Resort*, where you can descend steep and slippery steps to swim in an underground pool of exceptionally clear water.

If you're going all the way to Patar then tricycles (P150) and jeepneys from Bolinao will drop you in a car park at the most developed part of the beach. Close to the beach is the old **Cape Bolinao Lighthouse**, constructed in 1905 and the second tallest lighthouse in the country. There's an easy path to the base of the building, and the views across the South China Sea are well worth the climb. Not far offshore lie a number of old Spanish galleons and Chinese junks that local wisdom says contain treasure.

Accommodation

Other than *Treasures of Bolinao*, the listed resorts are all on the road from Bolinao to Patar Beach. If you're on a budget and want to stay on Patar Beach itself, try one of the very basic nipa huts (❷) close to the main entry point.

Puerto del Sol Ilog Malino barangay ℡075/696-0530, ⓦwww.puertodelsol.com.ph. Simple nipa huts and appealing villas in landscaped grounds, with facilities including a jacuzzi under an open-sided hut. There are many activities on offer, including kayaking, volleyball and badminton. Wi-fi is a steep P120 per hour. ❻

Punta Riviera Ilog Malino barangay ℡075/696-1350, ⓦwww.puntarivieraresort.com. With well-tended grounds, an infinity pool and plans to open a spa, this is one of the most relaxing resorts in the area. The cheapest accommodation – the *cabañas* – is pretty basic for the price, so if you're really after comfort then you may want to pay the extra (❽) for a Riviera Room. ❻

Rock Garden Arenda barangay a 10min drive along the road west of Bolinao ℡075/554-2876, ⓦrockgardenbolinao.com. This resort may not have the best beach in the area but it is a comfortable place to stay, with spick-and-span double rooms and a swimming pool. The cheapest rooms are fine as long as you don't need a/c. ❷

Solomon's Paradise Patar barangay, close to the main beach ℡0905/398-1470, ⓦwww.solomonsparadise.multiply.com. Located between two rocky promontories, this resort feels quiet and private. The rooms are better value than most along this stretch of coast, and the owners are welcoming. They also arrange excursions to the Enchanted Cave and the Cape Bolinao lighthouse. ❹

Treasures of Bolinao Beach Resort Patar Beach ℡0916/372-1979, ⓦwww.treasuresofbolinao.com. This resort is pricey but has some very appealing rooms; try suite 3 (❽) for glorious views of the sea, sand and sunset. ❼

Villa Carolina y Juan Just across from *Punta Riviera* ℡075/696-9405. This friendly place is owned by a Belgian and Filipina couple and serves some Belgian dishes in the restaurant. Rooms are prohibitively expensive in high season; at other times there are significant discounts. ❼

Tondol Beach

Southeast of Bolinao on the island of Anda – linked by bridge to the mainland – is the magnificent **Tondol Beach**, which remains largely off the tourist radar. It may have no facilities but it's absolutely stunning, with water shallow enough at low tide for you to wade out as far as Tanduyong Island a kilometre away. To reach Tondol take a bus to the barangay of Tara from either Bolinao or Alaminos, then another bus to Anda but check the tides before setting out, as the beach is only at its best during low tide. Also note that as on many beaches in the area, there can be a lot of seaweed on the beach from October to May. For more information contact Tito Garibay, Anda's tourist officer (℡0929/160-8757).

Lingayen

The main reason to visit **LINGAYEN**, the capital of Pangasinan province about an hour east of Alaminos, is for its historical resonance. The grey, volcanic sand beach close to the Provincial Capitol building was where American forces landed on January 9, 1945, paving the way for the liberation of Luzon from Japanese occupation. There is a small open-air **museum** within the Provincial Capitol complex, which includes photographs as well as a fighter plane, two tanks and an anti-aircraft gun.

Practicalities

The helpful and well-organized provincial **tourist office** (Mon–Fri 8am–5pm; ℡075/542-6853) is in the Malong Building; if you happen to have a strong interest in *bangoong* (shrimp paste) then they can arrange a visit to a local producer. The office also sells a good range of local products and souvenirs. Most of the **hotels** are also around here, including the *Hotel Consuelo* (℡075/542-8932; ❹) in Alvear Street, which has modern air-conditioned rooms, a swimming pool and a spa. Also close to the Capitol is the government-owned *Capitol Resort Hotel* (℡075/542-5871; ❷), with overpriced cottages but great-value rooms and a dorm in the main building. *El Puerto Marina* (℡075/542-5328; ❻) – a short drive west – is a significantly more upmarket beach resort, with a spa and pool as well as a range of activities such as kayaking.

San Fernando and around

The coastal road from Lingayen passes through Dagupan, San Fabian and Agoo, none of which have much to detain visitors. The next major hub is **SAN FERNANDO**, the capital of La Union province and site of a former US air base, which has little of interest to tourists other than the new *Thunderbird Poro Point* casino and hotel (see p.142). It is, however, the access point for two beach areas: **Bauang** is a short tricycle ride to the south, while **San Juan** is a slightly longer jeepney ride north but is preferable for most visitors (and particularly surfers).

Arrival and information

San Fernando **airport** is around 3km south of the city centre. Different bus companies have their own terminals: Dominion (℡072/888-2997) stops near *McDonald's* just south of the city centre and Partas (℡072/242-0465) stops north of the plaza on Quezon Avenue. There are two **tourist offices** just off the main plaza; the city tourist office (Mon–Fri 7.30am–5pm; ℡072/888-6922) is in the city hall, and the provincial tourist office (Mon–Fri 9am–5pm; ℡072/242-5550) is in the Provincial Capitol building. The main drag is Quezon Avenue where there are a number of **banks** with ATMs, as well as a police station behind La Union Trade Center. If you're interested in scuba diving in the area, contact Ocean Deep Diver Training Centre (℡072/700-0493, ⓦwww.oceandeep.biz) on Poro Point just west of the airport.

Accommodation

Unless you're here for the luxury of *Thunderbird Poro Point*, or just staying the night before moving on, then you're better off heading for the resorts in Bauang (see opposite) or San Juan (see below).

Sea and Sky ☎072/607-5579, ⓦwww.sea andskyhotel.com. The more expensive rooms at the back look out onto the sea, but those at the front face the busy road. The sea-facing basement rooms are the cheapest of all and represent good value for money. ❸
Thunderbird Poro Point ☎072/888-7777, ⓦwww.thunderbirdresorts.com. This swanky hotel has brought in enough well-heeled tourists to

justify resuming scheduled flights to the city from Manila. The resort's white walls and blue domes take their inspiration from Santorini in Greece, and it has exceptionally comfortable rooms. Many people come for the casino – which is in a separate building reached by shuttle – and there is also a 9-hole golf course, but other than that it's really a place simply to relax. ❾

The City

If you have a few hours to spare between bus connections then take a walk uphill to Freedom Park and the **Chinese–Filipino Friendship Pagoda**. You can either take Zigzag Road past the popular *Zigzag Disco*, or use the steps up Hero's Hill from Quezon Avenue. The pagoda boasts great views across the rooftops and out to the South China Sea. Along Quezon Avenue on the northern outskirts of the city is more evidence of the Chinese influence in the area, the impressive **Ma–Cho temple**.

Eating and drinking

Most of San Fernando's **nightlife** is on the road to Poro Point, where the *Thunderbird* resort is located, but the legacy of the (now closed) US air base on the point means that it's pretty sleazy. There are a few **restaurants** worth trying in town.

Café Esperanza Dishing up good Filipino food, this café is located up a short flight of stairs next to St William Cathedral in the main plaza.
Halo Halo de Iloko Corner of Zandueta & P. Burgos sts. Although it serves very good main

courses, locals flock here for its *halo-halo* (shaved ice with evaporated milk and toppings including fruit and purple yam). Daily 10am–10pm.

San Juan

A dramatic crescent with big breakers that roll in from the South China Sea, the coast just north of **SAN JUAN** in the barangay of Urbiztondo is a prime surfing beach. Most of its resorts have surfboards to rent (P200/hr) and offer tuition (another P200). There are two breaks in **Urbiztondo**, one a beach break close to the main huddle of resorts and the other the **Mona Liza** point break at the northern end of the beach. Both are more suited to experienced surfers, while the best spot for **beginners** is the **Cement Factory** break in the nearby barangay of Bacnotan. The peak season is November to March, and at other times there may be no waves but you can get significant discounts on accommodation.

Buses and minibuses travelling between San Fernando and Loaog, Vigan or Abra province pass through San Juan; ask the driver to let you off at one of the resorts. Alternatively take a jeepney (P13) from the junction of P. Burgos Street and Quezon Avenue in San Fernando.

Accommodation

All the resorts listed below are right on the beach and within walking distance of each other.

Moving on from San Fernando

Numerous bus companies have routes from San Fernando: Partas serve Manila (6hr; P384), Laoag (6hr; P323), Vigan (3hr; P207) and Baguio (90min; P92); and Dominion have buses to Vigan (3–4hr; P207) and Manila (4–5hr; P391). Zest Airways provides flights to Manila three times a week.

Ganaden's Nook ☎072/720-0636. A family-run place, which at the time of research had only a couple of affordable a/c rooms; there were plans to build cheaper fan rooms. It's also possible to camp on the site, at P750 including hire of a 4-person tent. The only downside is that it can get noisy down this end of the beach when videoke is in full flow. ❷

Kahuna Beach Resort and Spa ☎072/607-1040, ⓦwww.kahunaresort.com. It may not be entirely in keeping with San Juan's laidback surfer vibe, but this new resort certainly has verve. The rooms are stylish and comfortable, and the infinity pool is a great place to sip cocktails. ❻

Little Surfmaid ☎072/888-5528, ⓦwww .littlesurfmaidresort.com. At the northern end of the string of resorts, close to the Mona Liza point break, this Danish-owned place is a very good option. Rooms have attractive wooden furniture and the more expensive ones have balconies; the restaurant is one of the best around. There is free wi-fi throughout. ❻

Lola Nanny's Surf Retreat ☎0915/418-4034. The restaurant at this budget resort is right on the beach and a great place to hang out; it helps that the staff are very friendly. The cheapest accommodation is in fan-only rooms or nipa huts, while an a/c room for four people costs P1500. Discounts for long stays. ❷

Monaliza Surf Center ☎072/888-4075. The first resort on the beach has been open for over 30 years and is still going strong with the same family owners. It isn't the flashiest place around, and there's no food available, but the rooms are good value. The cheapest have no a/c. ❷

San Juan Surf Resort ☎072/720-0340, ⓦwww.sanjuansurfresort.com. This place is squarely aimed at surfers: there is a shop selling board shorts, boards and other kit, and surf conditions are posted by the bar. The place has a wide range of rooms, with the cheapest having no a/c. Wi-fi around the bar and restaurant. ❷

Bauang

The long stretch of brown sandy beach north of **BAUANG** ("ba-whang") town and south of San Fernando is nice enough for a stroll and a swim, but it isn't as appealing as San Juan. Bauang has a reputation as a sex tourism centre and several of the resorts along the beach, though not all, have nightclubs attached. Buses heading north from Manila pass through Bauang town before reaching San Fernando.

Accommodation

China Sea ☎072/607-6607. A relaxed family resort at the southern end of the beach with a swimming pool and spacious a/c cottages. ❹

Coconut Grove Beach Resort ☎072/607-6604, ⓦwww.coco.com.ph. Appealing family option on

the southern half of the beach with fine standard doubles, spacious deluxe doubles and large family rooms. There's also a bar, large swimming pool and bowling green. ❹

Ilocos

Between them making up half of the Ilocos region (La Union and Pangasinan provinces make up the other half), Ilocos Sur and Ilocos Norte line Luzon's northwestern coast. Long and narrow, **Ilocos Sur** is sandwiched by the sea on one side and the Cordillera Mountains on the other. For most tourists its highlight is undoubtedly **Vigan**, one of the most atmospheric and enjoyable cities in the country. Walking its cobbled streets and exploring its heritage homes gives an inkling of the former importance of this trading city. **Ilocos Norte** is still strongly associated in Filipino minds with former President Ferdinand Marcos, and his family continues to wield considerable political power in the province. Sites related to the Marcos family in the area include Ferdinand's birthplace in Sarrat, the mansion known as the **Malacañang of the North** beside Paoay Lake and Ferdinand's **mausoleum** in Batac. Getting away from the Marcoses, on the northern coast the town of **Pagudpud** draws visitors from across Luzon with some of the best beaches on the island.

Vigan

An unmissable part of any North Luzon itinerary, **VIGAN** is one of the oldest towns in the Philippines. Lying on the western bank of the Mestizo River, Vigan was in Spanish times an important political, military, cultural and religious centre. The old town, with Plaza Salcedo and Plaza Burgos on the northern edge and Libertad (Liberation) Boulevard to the south, is characterized by its cobbled streets and some of the finest old **colonial architecture** in the country – it mixes Mexican, Chinese and Filipino features. Various governmental and non-governmental organizations have joined forces to preserve the old buildings; many are still lived in, others are used as curio shops, and a few have been converted into museums or hotels. Vigan's time-capsule ambience is aided by the decision to close some streets to traffic and allow only pedestrians and *kalesas*. A ride in one of these horse-drawn carriages makes for a romantic way to tour the town.

Some history

In pre-colonial times, long before Spanish galleons arrived, **Chinese** junks came to Vigan and helped it to become a major trading port. They arrived with silk and porcelain, and left with gold, beeswax and mountain products brought down by inhabitants of the Cordillera. Stories of Vigan's riches spread and before long immigrants from China arrived to settle and trade here, intermarrying with locals and beginning the multicultural bloodline that Biguenos – the people of Vigan – are known for.

The **Spanish** arrived in 1572. Captain Juan de Salcedo – a conquistador born in Mexico – conquered the town and named it Villa Fernandina de Vigan in honour of King Philip's son, Prince Ferdinand, who died at the age of 4. Salcedo then rounded the tip of Luzon and proceeded to pacify Camarines, Albay and Catanduanes. In January 1574 he returned to Vigan, bringing with him **Augustinian missionaries**. Salcedo himself set about the task of creating a township his king would be proud of, with grand plazas, municipal buildings and mansions for the governing classes.

One of the potentially incendiary results of Spanish political domination of Vigan was the rise of a *mestizo* (mixed ethnicity) masterclass, whose wealth and stature began to cause resentment among landless natives. In 1763 things came to a head when revolutionary **Diego Silang** and his men assaulted and captured Vigan, proclaiming it capital of the free province of Ilocos. When Silang was assassinated by two traitors in the pay of the Spanish, his wife, Maria Josefa Gabriela Silang, assumed leadership of the uprising. She was captured and publicly hanged in the town square.

Unlike in Manila, many of Vigan's fine **old buildings** managed to survive World War II. However, the combination of the destructive humidity and the fact that they're primarily built of wood makes their preservation difficult. Many of the town's rich left Vigan in favour of a new life in Manila, allowing their ancestral homes to fall into partial ruin, though Vigan's 1999 inclusion on the **World Heritage Site** list at least guarantees it some level of protection and funding.

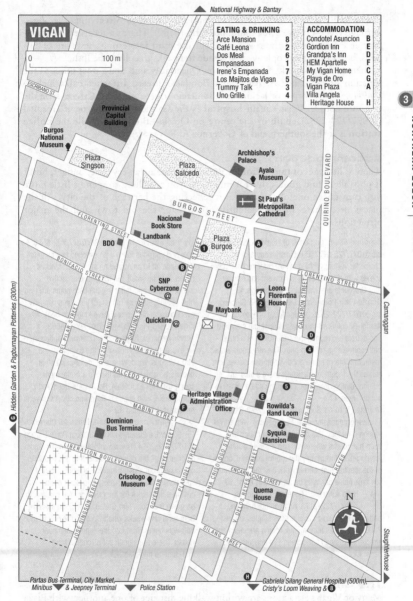

VIGAN

0	100 m

EATING & DRINKING

Arce Mansion	8
Café Leona	2
Dos Meal	6
Empanadaan	1
Irene's Empanada	7
Los Majitos de Vigan	5
Tummy Talk	3
Uno Grille	4

ACCOMMODATION

Condotel Asuncion	B
Gordion Inn	E
Grandpa's Inn	D
HEM Apartelle	F
My Vigan Home	C
Playa de Oro	G
Vigan Plaza	A
Villa Angela	
Heritage House	H

National Highway & Bantay

ESCRIBANO ST

Provincial Capitol Building

Burgos National Museum

Plaza Singson

Plaza Salcedo

Archbishop's Palace

Ayala Museum

QUIRINO BOULEVARD

BURGOS STREET

St Paul's Metropolitan Cathedral

FLORENTINO STREET

Nacional Book Store

Landbank

BDO

Plaza Burgos

FLORENTINO STREET

Camanggan

BONIFACIO STREET

SNP Cyberzone @

Leona Florentina House

CALDERON STREET

DEL PILAR STREET

QUEZON AVENUE

SIKATUNA STREET

JACINTO STREET

Quickline @

Maybank

GEN. LUNA STREET

SALCEDO STREET

Hidden Garden & Pagburnayan Potteries (300m)

Heritage Village Administration Office

Rowilda's Hand Loom

MABINI STREET

Dominion Bus Terminal

Syquia Mansion

QUIRINO BOULEVARD

LIBERATION BOULEVARD

Crisologo Museum

GOVERNOR A. REYES STREET

PLARIDEL STREET

MENA CRISOLOGO STREET

ENCARNACION STREET

V. DELOS REYES STREET

Quema House

E. REYES

JOSE SINGSON STREET

SILANG STREET

N

Slaughterhouse

Partas Bus Terminal, City Market, Minibus & Jeepney Terminal

Police Station

Gabriela Silang General Hospital (500m), Cristy's Loom Weaving & **8**

Arrival and information

Partas buses arrive at a terminal near the market, while Dominion's terminal is at the southern end of Quezon Avenue. Other buses stop on the National Highway in the nearby town of Bantay, P10 from Vigan by tricycle.

The **tourist office** (daily 8am–5pm; ☎077/732-5705) is in Leona Florentina House, near *Café Leona* on Plaza Burgos. The Heritage Village Administration

145

Office (daily 8.30–11.30am & 1–4.30pm) on Crisologo Street runs the Vigan heritage **river-cruise**, a 30–45min boat trip (P100). There's a recorded commentary and dioramas on the riverbanks, but the most interesting views are of fish pens, boatyards and people wading beside the banks to collect shellfish.

There are many **banks with ATMs** on Quezon Avenue, and a **post office** at the junction of Governor A. Reyes and Bonifacio streets. **Internet cafés** include *Quickline* at the corner of Jacinto and Bonifacio streets, and *SNP Cyberzone* on the opposite corner. Vigan's main **hospital** is the Gabriela Silang General Hospital (☎077/722-2782), south of the centre on Quirino Boulevard, while the **police station** is at the southern end of Governor A. Reyes Street.

Accommodation

There is little **accommodation** in Vigan for those on a very strict budget, but it is possible to find good value for money. If you're willing to spend a little more you can stay in one of several places reflecting the heritage of the city. All the places listed here are conveniently situated for the old town and the major attractions.

Condotel Asuncion Corner of Florentino & Jacinto sts ☎077/722-8777. Quiet, restful and a great choice for visitors wishing to self-cater, as each room comes with a stove, oven, microwave and refrigerator. Discounts are available for long stays. ❺

Gordion Inn Corner of V. Delos Reyes & Salcedo sts ☎077/722-2526, ⓦvigangordionhotel.com. A brightly coloured place with appealing standard and deluxe a/c rooms; the suite (❾) has a huge bathroom with a roll-top bath. The airy brick-walled restaurant offers some good vegetarian dishes and serves the included breakfast; there's also an outdoor dining area with a teppanyaki bar. Wi-fi in public areas. ❺

Grandpa's Inn 1 Bonifacio St ☎077/72-2118, ⓦwww.grandpasinn.com. Very popular with travellers on a budget, this place is full of curios and even has rooms where you can sleep in a *kalesa* (carriage). Unfortunately the rooms are tired, some of the electric fans barely work and the bathrooms are tiny; noise can also be an issue at night. ❷

🏃 **Hem Apartelle** Governor A. Reyes St ☎077/722-2173. An absolute bargain, particularly for solo travellers, as singles are just P600. Offered as apartments, rooms are clean and simple, with small flat-screen TVs and very firm beds. ❸

My Vigan Home 14 Plaridel St ☎077/722-6528. A cool and spacious lobby with exposed beams gets this place off to an appealing start. The standard rooms may be small, but they have attractive wooden floors and furniture; the bathrooms are also high quality. Superior rooms (❻) are on a veranda overlooking a garden and have king-size beds. ❹

Vigan Plaza Plaza Burgos ☎077/722-8553, ⓦwww.viganplazahotel.com. Charming option in an excellent location close to the cathedral and Plaza Burgos. Windows are made of *capiz* shell, floors are hardwood and there's a pretty inner courtyard with a fountain. Rooms are fresh and comfortable, with spotless linen and clean showers; breakfast is included. ❻

🏃 **Villa Angela Heritage House** 26 Quirino Blvd, a 20min walk south from Plaza Burgos ☎077/722-2914, ⓦwww.villangela.com. The most colonial of all the colonial hotels, this is a beautiful old museum of a place and the billet of choice if you want to wallow in history and don't mind paying a little extra for the privilege. You can ask to be given the room Tom Cruise slept in: he stayed here for a few weeks when *Born on the Fourth of July* was being filmed on the sand dunes near Laoag. There are significant discounts from mid-June to mid-Sept. ❹

The City

Many of Vigan's attractions are within walking distance of one another, with Plaza Burgos the most obvious reference point, although it's cheap enough to take a tricycle (from P10) or a *kalesa* (from P20) around town. The latter can also be used to tour the city (P150/hr) – tell the *kutchero* (driver) where you want to visit, or let them suggest a route.

Vigan's festivals

The biggest secular festival is the **Vigan Town Fiesta**, a week-long celebration consisting of carnivals, parades, musical extravaganzas, beauty contests and nightly cultural shows. It culminates on January 25 with the celebration of the conversion of St Paul the Apostle, the town's patron saint. Almost straight after that comes the **Kannawidan Ilocos**, a recent addition to the festival calendar at the end of January celebrating the culture of the whole of Ilocos Sur, not just Vigan. It includes a "battle of the bands" and a beauty contest.

The **Viva Vigan Festival of Arts**, held during the first week of May, includes dancing and music, and the highlight is the religious celebration on **May 3** (Tres de Mayo), which starts with a Mass at Vigan's cemetery chapel and continues with dancing in Crisologo Street and a *kalesa* parade. **Holy Week** is also a special time in Vigan, with candlelit processions through the old streets and a *visita iglesia* that sees devotees doing the rounds of churches and cathedrals.

The old town

Vigan's **old town** is where most of the beautiful ancestral houses are located. Also known as the Mestizo District or Kasanglayan (where the Chinese live), the old town runs roughly from Plaza Burgos in the north to **Liberation Boulevard** in the south. The most important thoroughfare is elegant old Crisologo Street, which has been given a makeover and is closed to traffic – a rarity in the Philippines. Architecturally, the houses are fundamentally Chinese or Mexican, influenced either by the immigrant architects from China's eastern seaboard who prepared the plans, or by ideas picked up by the Spanish in their South American colony. But they have flourishes such as sliding *capiz*-shell windows and *ventanillas* (ventilated walls) added by local artisans.

Although most houses are still private homes, a few are open to the public. These offer an intimate view of *ilustrado* life at the turn of the nineteenth and twentieth centuries. The **Crisologo Museum** (Tues–Sat 8.30–11.30am & 1.30–4.30pm; P15) on Liberation Boulevard has displays about the history of the influential – and sometimes controversial – Crisologo family, including the car in which Governor Carmeling Crisologo was ambushed in 1961. **Syquia Mansion** on Quirino Boulevard (Tues–Sun 9–11.30am & 1.30–4.30pm; P20) is the ancestral home of former President Elpidio Quirino, an eye-catching red-brick colonial house that has been restored and furnished in nineteenth-century style and contains a collection of presidential memorabilia. **Quema House** (⊕077/722-2542), at the junction of Liberation and Quirino boulevards, can only be seen by appointment. It is chock-full of beautiful old polished wood furniture, curios and oil paintings.

St Paul's Metropolitan Cathedral and the Archbishop's Palace

Built by the Augustinians between 1890 and 1900, **St Paul's Metropolitan Cathedral** (daily 6am–9pm) is like something from a Mexican fairy tale. Standing between Plaza Burgos and Plaza Salcedo on the city's northern edge, it is an "earthquake Baroque" church, with thick ramparts and a belfry built 15m away so that it stood a chance of surviving if the church itself collapsed. Given Vigan's history, it's not surprising that there's some Chinese influence: see, for example, the brass communion handrails.

Across the road is the **Archbishop's Palace** (*Arzobizpado*), completed in 1783 and still the official residence of the Archbishop of Nueva Segovia (the old Spanish name for what is now Ilocos Sur). Inside is the **Museo Nueva Segovia** (Mon–Fri

147

9.30–11.00am & 1.30–4pm; P20), which showcases ecclesiastical artefacts, antique portraits of bishops and religious paraphernalia from all over Ilcos Sur.

Burgos National Museum

To the west of Plaza Salcedo, the **Burgos National Museum** (Tues–Sun 8.30–11.30am & 1.30–4.30pm; P10) is in a captivating if dilapidated eighteenth-century colonial house that was once home to one of the town's most famous residents, Padre José Burgos, whose martyrdom in 1872 galvanized the revolutionary movement. It contains Burgos memorabilia including much of his original furniture, his clothes and his diaries. Non-Burgos exhibits include a small ethnological collection and fourteen paintings by the artist Villanueva, depicting scenes such as the violent 1807 Basi Revolt prompted by a Spanish effort to control the production of *basi* (sugar-cane wine).

Eating, drinking and nightlife

Don't leave Vigan without trying the local empanada – a crispy deep-fried tortilla of rice-flour dough containing cabbage and green papaya. Some empanadas – sometimes known as "special" – also contain an egg and *longganisa* (garlic sausage). Either way, eaten with sugar-cane vinegar and chopped shallots they are a delicious snack. The stalls on the western side of Plaza Burgos, known collectively as **Empanadaan**, sell empanadas along with *okoy* (egg, prawn, tomato and onion frittata) – again, dip it in vinegar. For **breakfast**, if you're feeling adventurous then copy the locals and head out bright and early to the Vigan Slaughterhouse near the barangay of Mindoro (a 15min tricycle ride from the centre). A bowl of exceptionally fresh *liempo* (beef, innards and onions in broth) costs just a few pesos. **Nightlife** in Vigan is pretty limited and quiet, with the startling exception of *Legacy Super Club* (see below).

Arce Mansion 87 Quirino Blvd ☎02/725-0819 or 0917/824-6900. Step back in time at this heritage home by donning costumes from the Spanish era and dining on Vigan specialities such as *pipian* (chicken soup thickened with crushed and roasted rice) and *bagnet* (deep-fried pork complete with fat and skin). The experience costs P1500 and includes souvenir photos; men may want to wear their own black trousers as the sizes available are quite small. Usually open 10am–6pm but call or text ahead.

Café Leona Crisologo St, just south of Plaza Burgos. Tourists are drawn to the outdoor tables here in the evenings. Serves native Ilocano dishes such as *bagnet*. Daily 10am–midnight.

Dos Meal Corner of A Reyes & Salcedo sts. The owners of this wi-fi-equipped café previously lived in Thailand, so as well as standard fare they have dishes such as *tom yum* and *pad thai*. On Sundays they offer a more extensive Thai menu including *laab* and Thai curries. Their vegetarian options are cooked in separate pans, they don't use MSG and everything is freshly cooked. To round things off there are several imported beers available. Daily 10am–midnight.

Irene's Empanada Just around the corner from the Syquia Mansion, this simple place has many local devotees who say it makes the best empanada in Vigan (and, by extension, anywhere).

Legacy Super Club Corner of Crisologo & Mabini sts. Owned by one of the influential local families, this rather incongruous nightclub has somehow been given permission to open within the heritage district. At weekends the bass thump can be heard from a couple of streets away. Mon–Thurs 8pm–2am, Fri & Sat 8pm–4am.

Los Majitos de Vigan General Luna St near Quirino Blvd. This street restaurant is only open in the evenings, when its candlelit tables are almost always full. The food is mostly *inihaw* (grilled), with a few Ilocano dishes.

Tummy Talk Crisologo St, close to Plaza Burgos. Simple, clean, with no sign – just a blackboard outside listing the day's offering. For breakfast P20 will get you soup made from *miki* (flat egg noodle) and *bagnet*; lunch try meat, veg and rice for P50.

Uno Grille Opposite *Grandpa's Inn*, and with the same owners, this courtyard restaurant has an open kitchen. There are two menus, one covering grilled food and the other a variety of Asian dishes including some unusual options such as mountain ants and eel *adobo*. Most dishes are for sharing, although solo diners might try the *molo* (a vegetable and pork soup). Daily 6–10pm.

Shopping

Souvenir-hunters after something more than the usual bulk-produced tourist gewgaws should head for Rowilda's Hand Loom, on Crisologo Street near the *Cordillera Inn*, which offers the kind of old-style **textiles** traded during colonial times. If that whets your appetite then head out of the centre. In the barangay of Mindoro, to the south near the airport, you can buy blankets called **binakol**, which have distinctive geometric patterns, while in Camanggaan, to the east, you can watch women at Cristy's Loom Weaving (daily 7am–6pm) using old looms to make bedsheets, tablemats and runners. Both Mindoro and Camanggan can be reached in fifteen minutes by tricycle.

Vigan is also known for its **pottery**. The massive wood-fired kilns at the Pagburnayan Potteries in Gomez Street, at the junction with Liberation Boulevard, produce huge jars known as *burnay* which are used by northerners for storing everything from vinegar to fish paste. They also make simple U-shaped pots called *tapayan* on which salt is dried. Carabao are used to squash the clay under hoof, although you'll need to arrive between 4–6am to see them in action.

A little further southwest beyond Pagburnayan, the **Hidden Garden** – a P20–30 tricycle ride from the old town – is a shady spot popular with families at the weekend. It's primarily a nursery, selling ferns, palms, bonsai and bamboo among others, but it also has a café and is simply a pleasant place to wander around.

Around Vigan

The town of **BANTAY**, close to Vigan on the National Highway (P10 by tricycle), is a popular stop on *kalesa* tours (see p.144) thanks to the bell tower of **Saint Augustine Parish Church**. Built between 1590–92, it has five bells each associated with a different occasion (but they are no longer rung as there are concerns about the strength of the structure). The tower is famous as one of the locations in the Filipino fantasy movie *Ang Panday* (*The Blacksmith*, 1980). It is usually locked, but someone from the church will give you a short tour in return for a small donation.

Another worthwhile trip from Vigan is to the UNESCO World Heritage-listed **Santa Maria Church**, about an hour's drive south and dating from 1769. It's a solid structure with a brick facade, set on a hill and reached via 83 steps; unsurprisingly it was used as a fortress during the Philippine Revolution. The interior is quite plain with the exception of its geometric floor tiles, and it's inhabited by birds and bats. While in the area you may want to take the 45-minute walk to **Pinsal Falls**; ask at the tourist office in the grounds of the town hall for details. To reach the church from Vigan, take any of the Manila-bound buses (P50–60), or catch a minibus (slow) or van (faster) in the direction of Candon from Bantay.

The coastal road north of Vigan to Laoag is sealed all the way and the journey time is only two hours. If you do want to break the journey then you might try

---

Moving on from Vigan

The Partas (☎077/722-3369) bus terminal for buses north and south along the coastal road is located near the market: destinations include Manila (8–9hr; P585), Laoag (2hr; P121), Baguio (5hr; P294) and San Fernando (3hr; P207). For other destinations in the Lingayen Gulf – Lingayen, Dagupan or Alaminos – you should change at Urdaneta (5hr; P335). Dominion (☎077/722-2084) buses to Manila (9–10hr; P450 for older vehicles, P600 for the newer ones) leave from the terminal at the junction of Quezon and Liberation boulevards, and many other bus companies have services heading north and south from the Caltex petrol station on the National Highway.

stopping at **BADOC**, the birthplace of the Filipino painter Juan Luna. His reconstructed house, known as the **Juan Luna Historical Landmark** (daily 10am–4pm; donation), stands in a side street close to the seventeenth-century Virgen Milagrosa de Badoc church. About a kilometre off the coast of Badoc lies **Badoc Island**, which is gaining a reputation for good surfing – the seasons are late October to early March and late June to early September – and can be reached by hiring a bangka from the little wharf in Badoc town.

Laoag

The busy and congested streets of the Ilocos Norte provincial capital, **LAOAG**, can't compete with Vigan's historical core when it comes to aesthetic appeal, but there are a handful of things to do and see in Laoag including one of the country's best museums. The city also makes an excellent base for exploring the beautiful coast at nearby La Paz and Suba or touring sights associated with former dictator Ferdinand Marcos.

Arrival and information

Laoag **airport** is close to the city, just ten minutes by jeepney (P10). Many of the bus and jeepney terminals are clustered to the west of Aurora Park, with minibus terminals (for services from Pagudpud and Vigan) to the north of the park. There is a Partas terminal on J.P. Rizal Street. All are within walking distance of the central hotels, although you may want to hop on a tricycle from the Partas terminal.

Laoag City **tourist office** (☎077/773-1676) is in the City Hall, on the southwestern side of Aurora Park in the city centre. There is a provincial tourism office in the Provincial Capitol building (☎077/770-4242). **Banks**, **convenience stores** and **pharmacies** lie to the east of Aurora Park on Rizal Avenue. There are numerous **internet cafés** in the centre, including one in the Gym Carry building opposite *Max's* fast food outlet on General Segundo Avenue.

Accommodation

The streets of Laoag are busy, so try to get a room away from the road if you're staying in the city. If your budget will stretch to them, there are also some pleasant places to stay outside the centre.

Fort Ilocandia On the beach in the barangay of Calayab, 3km south of the airport ☎077/670-9101, ⓦwww.fortilocandia.com.ph. Built in 1983 and hastily completed for the wedding reception of Ferdinand and Imelda Marcos's youngest daughter Irene, this expansive resort aims for classic elegance rather than modern chic. Its casino is a magnet for Taiwanese tourists, while other amenities include a golf course, spa and an array of activities including hot air balloon flights and quad bike rides on the nearby dunes. It's a long way from the city, and inconveniently there's no shuttle service. Wi-fi is expensive. ❽

Hotel Tiffany General. Segundo Ave ☎077/770-3550, ⓦwww.hoteltiffany-laoag.com. Budget glamour is the order of the day here: the rooms are simple and candy-coloured, while the common areas are decorated with photos of the Beatles and Marilyn Monroe. The building itself has Art Deco curves and there's a lip-shaped sofa in reception; the diner downstairs is metal-plated in old-fashioned US style. ❷

Java Hotel Behind the Caltex petrol station, Bacarra Rd ☎077/770-5996, ⓦjavahotel.com.ph. A P10–20 tricycle ride from the centre, this place has simple but modern standard rooms; the suites make more of the loose Balinese theme. The *Eagle's Nest* restaurant, on stilts and under a nipa roof, is popular for its excellent baby back ribs as well as its Filipino dishes. ❺

La Elliana Corner of Rizal St & Ablan Ave ☎077/771-6008. A tall block with a restaurant on the ground floor and good-value rooms. Ask for a room on one of the upper floors if you want to escape the noise of traffic. ❷

LAOAG

ACCOMMODATION	
Fort Ilocandia	D
Hotel Tiffany	B
Java Hotel	A
Le Eliana	C

EATING & DRINKING	
Cockhouse	4
La Preciosa	2
Papa Pau	1
Saramsam	3

Pagudpud & **A**

Partas Bus Terminal (250m)

M. H. DEL PILAR STREET

ARADILLA STREET

JUAN LUNA STREET

RCBC

BDO

MANUEL NOLASCO STREET

DON ACOSTA STREET

DON ELEUTERIO RUIZ

GENERAL SEGUNDO AVENUE

GOVERNOR J. LIGOT STREET

SEN. S. FONACIER STREET

BPI

JOSE RIZAL AVENUE

F.R. CASTRO AVENUE

PACO ROMAN STREET

LAGASCA

Minibuses to Vigan ★

Metrobank

National Department **B**
of Tourism Office

ℹ

@ Gym Carry

Ilocano Heroes Hall

Sinking Bell Tower

St William's Cathedral

GOVERNOR J. ARCOD STREET

VILANES STREET

Minibuses to Pagudpud ★

Ilocos Norte Capitol Building

ℹ Provincial Tourist Office

TRES MARTIRES

Police

TRES MARIAS

Aurora Park

BALINTAWAK STREET

GOVERNOR DOMINGO S. MONTE STREET

DON M. FARINAS STREET

Museo Ilocos Norte

BPI

Food Court

Marcos Hall of Justice

TRES MARIAS

City Hall ℹ

GOVERNOR PRIMO LAZARO AVENUE

GENERAL HERNANDO AVENUE

SENATOR ANTONIO LUNA STREET

Maria de Leon Transit Bus Terminal

GENERAL GIRON

GOVERNOR MAURICIO CASTRO AVENUE

Farinas Bus Terminal

RCJ Transport Bus Terminal **4**

DON R. GUERRERO

3

Z. FLORES

RIZAL STREET

A.G. TUPAZ AVENUE

F.R. CASTRO

H. STREET

JUAN LUNA STREET

1

DON ROQUE B. ABLAN AVENUE

DON C. PERALTA STREET

DON E. JULIAN STREET

BITANGA STREET

ROMERO STREET

RIZAL STREET

2

C

La Paz

Laoag River

Sarrat, Batac, La Paz, Paoay, Airport (3km), Vigan, Suba & **D**

0   100 m

N

NORTHERN LUZON

3

151

Moving on from Laoag

The fastest way to reach Manila is on one of the daily Cebu Pacific flights. The streets around Aurora Park are the hub for **transport within the province**, with vans and jeepneys leaving when they are full for Sarrat, La Paz, Batac and Pagudpud. There are also a number of bus terminals in Laoag such as RCJ (☎077/771-3308) and Maria de Leon (☎077/770-3532), from which non-air-conditioned buses head to Vigan, San Fernando, Dau and occasionally as far as Manila. For a greater degree of comfort, Partas (☎077/771-1514) and Farinas (☎077/772-0126) air-conditioned buses also make the long trip to Manila (12hr; P500–600). Partas also runs buses to Vigan (9hr; P585) and San Fernando (6hr; P384). GMW runs a service to Tueguegaro (6–7hr; P455) – there are numerous buses in the morning and a couple in the evening. You can take any Tuguegarao-bound bus to Pagudpud (1hr 30min; P60).

The City

The most interesting attraction in the city is the **Museo Ilocos Norte** (Mon–Sat, 9am–noon & 1–5pm; Sun 10am–noon & 1–5pm; P20), which provides an overview of the province's history and culture. Close to the main plaza, it's housed in a restored Spanish-era tobacco warehouse. Exhibits include vintage costumes, farming equipment and tribal artefacts. There's even a replica of an *ilustrado* (educated middle class) ancestral home complete with antiques, and the souvenir shop has some interesting books and gifts.

Close by are the **Sinking Bell Tower** and **St William's Cathedral**. The bell tower was built by Augustinian friars with a door big enough for a man on horseback to pass through. The tower has sunk so much that today you can only get through the door by stooping. The cathedral, one of the biggest in the Philippines, was built in 1880 on older foundations. The **Marcos Hall of Justice** (daily 9am–4pm; free), the square white building on the west side of Aurora Park, was where a young Ferdinand Marcos was detained in 1939 after being accused of the murder of one of his father's political opponents. Marcos wanted to graduate in law and used his time in detention wisely, swotting for the bar examination and successfully preparing his own defence.

Eating, drinking and nightlife

There are some good **restaurants** in Laoag, while for cheap local dishes you could try the food court tucked away behind a white building close to the Shell station on Rizal Avenue. The local version of the empanada (see p.148) is more famous than Vigan's, with a thicker crust and orange in colour. Laoag has more in the way of **nightlife** than many other cities in Luzon.

Cockhouse Near the bus stations on F.R. Castro Ave. The best bet for live music in Laoag, putting on local bands as well as some from further afield in the Philippines.

La Preciosa Rizal St ☎077/773-1162. The most popular restaurant in town, with a sign that proclaims "fine dining" but it's more relaxed than that suggests. The kitchen prepares excellent Ilocano dishes such as *pinakbet* (vegetables sautéed in fish paste), but the place is really famous for its carrot cake. Daily 8am–11pm.

Papa Pau Serves some interesting dishes such as *binalot* (various meat dishes served wrapped in a banana leaf) and crispy sizzling *sisig*.

Saramsam Rizal St. The menu at this informal restaurant includes *poque-poque* (grilled aubergine with egg, tomatoes and onions, with a name which is commonly used but causes amusement for its rude literal meaning) and award-winning *pinakbet*. Daily 11am–10pm.

Sarrat

Thirty minutes due east of Laoag by jeepney or FX van is the sleepy and pretty village of **SARRAT**. Ferdinand Marcos was born here on September 11, 1917, and his former home has now been turned into a **museum** (daily 6am–6pm although opening is erratic; donations). It showcases a number of hagiographic displays charting Marcos's "brilliant" law career and his ascent to the presidency, but is really for Marcos completists only.

Sarrat's attractive **Santa Monica Church** was the wedding venue of Marcos's youngest daughter Irene in 1983, in a ceremony that cost US$10.3 million. Preparations for the wedding involved thousands of men remodelling the town and 3500 contracted employees renovating the 200-year-old church. Large parts of Sarrat were reconstructed, with houses torn down and rebuilt in the old Spanish colonial style.

Ferdinand Marcos Mausoleum

Marcos spent his childhood in the pretty town of **Batac**, about 15km south of Laoag, before moving to Manila to take up law. The Marcos mansion is not open to the public, but there is a small museum (Tues–Sun 9am–noon & 1–4pm; free) with photographs, quotations and framed medals. The real attraction is the **mausoleum** (daily 9am–noon & 1–4pm; free) opposite, which contains the former dictator's refrigerated corpse. There are rumours that it's nothing more than a wax model, and few people would be surprised if that turned out to be true. Imelda wants to bury him in the *Libingan ng mga Bayani* (Heroes' Cemetery) in Manila, a proposal that has failed to find favour with successive governments.

To reach Batac from Laoag you can catch a jeepney from Hernando Avenue or a minibus from General Luna Street at the corner of Lagasca Street.

Paoay

A few kilometres west of Batac, **Paoay** is the location of a UNESCO-listed **church** as well as the **Malacañang of the North**, the opulent mansion where Marcos stayed during presidential holidays. The church is in the town of Paoay itself, and is perhaps the best-known "earthquake Baroque" church in the Philippines. Begun in 1804, it took ninety years to build and has twenty-six immense side buttresses designed to keep it standing. Nearby is a bell tower dating from 1793, which you can climb for views of the area.

Malacañang of the North (Tues–Sun 9am–noon & 1–4.30pm; P20), named after the presidential palace in Manila, is beside Paoay Lake on the road between Paoay and Laoag. The mansion had seven bedrooms, two living rooms, several studies, kitchens on both floors and a private clinic used by Ferdinand in his later years. In 2010 the building was renovated: the clinic became a small museum, and one of the guest rooms is now a souvenir shop. The house is set on a vast estate of gentle lawns and has its own golf course – Marcos was an avid golfer – which is now part of the *Fort Ilocandia* resort. A trail around the edge of the lake makes for a pleasant 3km-long walk, taking you through quiet lakeside barrios.

Paoay is served by regular jeepneys (P34) from Laoag via Batac, which can set you down at the church. The lake is most easily reached by tricycle (P60) from Paoay church.

Ilocos Norte Sand Dunes

The coastline west of Laoag is a sight to behold. More like desert than beach, it measures almost one kilometre across at some points and reaches as far as the eye can see, fringed by huge sand dunes. The area has become a favourite among Manila film crews who drive north to film love scenes in the surf for trashy Tagalog movies. The stretch at **La Paz** – known locally as "Bantay Bimmaboy" due to the shape of some of the dunes, said to resemble a pig's back – is just fifteen minutes west of Laoag. Also impressive are the **Suba** dunes further south, close to the *Fort Ilocandia* resort, where Oliver Stone shot segments of *Born on the Fourth of July*. The LEAD Movement (☎0919/873-5516, ⊛leadmovement.wordpress.com/) arranges trips combining a 4WD ride and sandboarding (P2500/1hr for up to four people).

Pagudpud and around

From Laoag it's a couple of hours by bus to **PAGUDPUD**, a typical provincial town providing access to several wonderfully picturesque beaches. The Pagudpud area is deservedly becoming known as a destination that has all the beauty of Boracay, but only a fraction of number of tourists and none of the nightlife.

Arrival and information

Buses from all directions arrive on the main road in Pagudpud town, from where plenty of tricycles can take you the rest of the way to **Saud Beach** for P40. If you've booked at a resort then ask them about transfers. The **tourist office** (Mon–Fri 8am–5pm; ☎0921/558-6254) is in the town hall. There are no ATMs and the banks do not change currency, so bring enough pesos.

Accommodation and eating

Resorts around Pagudpud are a little pricier than similar establishments elsewhere, and many of them double their prices during high season (April–May, Holy Week and Christmas). It's always worth asking for a discount at other times. Budget travellers should consider a homestay. The tourist office has accredited more than 30, with fixed prices of P250/350 per head for fan or air-conditioning, and there are at least another 40 unofficial homestays in the area. Contact the tourist office for details, or just wander along the road behind the main resorts on Saud Beach.

The resorts offer the best **food**, particularly *Evangeline* (at the southern end of Saud Beach) and *Kapulan* (at the Blue Lagoon), but for something a bit different try *Bergblick* (Mon 5–11pm, Tues–Sun 8am–11pm), a German-owned restaurant on the highway between Saud Beach and the Blue Lagoon. It serves dishes such as *Wiener schnitzel* and *schweinbraten* (roasted pork) as well as Filipino favourites.

Saud beach

Apo Idon ☎077/676-0483 or 0917/510-0671, ⊛www.apoidon.com. If you're seeking luxury on Saud Beach, then look no further than the tropical suite (**7**) at this resort on the southern end of the beach. The cheaper rooms are good too, and there's a restaurant overlooking the sea. Wi-fi throughout. **6**

Arinaya White Beach Resort ☎0921/558-1366. With double, triple and family rooms right in the middle of the beach, this is a pleasant choice that raises its prices less than most during peak season. Travellers on a budget can ask about their tents (**2**) for four people. **4**

🏃 **Polaris Beach House** ☎0919/307-8803, ⊛polarisbeachhouse.wordpress.com. Friendly owners and very reasonable prices make

this resort – close to *Saud Beach Resort* in the centre of the beach – a real winner. Arranges day-trips by tricycle for P600, and there's free wi-fi in the restaurant. **2**

North Ridge Southern end of the beach ☎0920/220-5089, ⊛northridgeresort.com. The cool and quiet rooms here are better value than the popular nearby *Jun & Carol* resort, and with less of a price hike during the high season. The resort has wi-fi. **3**

Other beaches

Agua Seda Blue Lagoon ☎0920/243-1832. A little family-run wooden place close to the hard-to-miss *Hannah's Beach Resort*, with seven decent rooms. **4**
Hidden Treasure Ayoyo Beach ☎0908/929-2806. The rudimentary huts may not represent great value

for money, but the stunning location makes up for it. The huts are on stilts and arranged on a hillside overlooking the sea, and there are concrete viewing decks. Out of season it's practically deserted. ④

🏃 **Kapuluan Vista** Blue Lagoon ☎ 0920/952-2528, ⓦ www.kapuluanvista.com. An absolute gem hidden away at the western end of the beach, with lovely grounds, appealing rooms, an alluring pool and friendly staff. The cheapest rooms are the dorms for two or six people, and while much more basic than the standard (⑤) or deluxe (⑥) they are a real bargain as you have full

use of the facilities. The restaurant uses organic fruit and vegetables grown in the grounds, and the resort is big on recycling. It's popular with surfers and offers board hire (P200/hr) and tuition. ③

Surf Homestay (AKA Wally's World Homestay) Blue Lagoon, between *Hannah's* and *Kapulan Vista* ☎ 0938/615-8791. If you're just here for the sea and sand, and you don't mind staying in a makeshift hut, then this could be what you are looking for although as in most places the prices rise (②) during peak season. The owner also hires out longboards (P300/hr) and arranges instruction (P200/hr). ①

The beaches

Saud Beach ("Sa-ud"), a few kilometres down a narrow road to the north of town, is a beautiful long arch of white sand backed by palm trees. Resorts on the beach hire out snorkelling equipment, and can provide bangkas (P5–600 for half a day) so that you can head to the best spots. Birdwatchers should check out the area behind the Saud Beach Resort.

East of Saud (30min tricycle ride; P200–250) is the glorious **Blue Lagoon** (also known as Maira-ira Beach). The setting is stunning, with dazzling water lapping a sugary crescent of sand; the breaks also attract surfers from July to January. One stretch of the beach has been overdeveloped with a large and incongruous resort, but it's possible to get away from that and still enjoy the sand and sea. From March–June, boats offer dolphin-watching trips (P300).

To the west of Pagudpud and accessible by tricycle (P70–100) is the beach at **Ayoyo**. It's not sandy, but it's still beautiful and it rarely sees foreign tourists – there's little here except palm trees and sea, overlooked by a single resort.

West of Pagudpud

Thirty minutes west of Pagudpud by road is the **Cape Bojeador Lighthouse** (daily 8am–5pm; free) in the town of **Burgos**. Built in 1892, the lighthouse is the tallest in the country, and from the top there are unobstructed views of the coastline and across the South China Sea. It's still in use and its keeper, Vicente Acoba Jr, will be happy to give you a tour.

To get to Burgos from Pagudpud take a jeepney from the main road. Once in Burgos itself, you can take a tricycle to the lighthouse; a tricycle all the way from Pagudpud would cost about P300. On the way to the lighthouse you'll pass the **Bangui Wind Farm** on the shore. The first facility of its kind in the Philippines, the twenty turbines are said to provide 40 percent of the power requirements of Ilocos Norte and have also become a tourist attraction.

The northeast

The **northeast** of Luzon, comprising the provinces of Nueva Vizcaya, Quirino, Aurora, Isabela and Cagayan, is one of the archipelago's least explored regions, with miles of beautiful coastline and enormous tracts of tropical rainforest. Following the National Highway from Ilocos as it curves south brings you to the biggest city in the region, **Tuguegarao**, the starting point for trips to the **Peñablanca Caves**. Alternatively turn off the highway and follow the north coast road to reach **Santa Ana**, home to the country's best game-fishing and the departure point for boat trips to the rugged and isolated **Babuyan Islands**.

The coast south of Santa Ana and east of Tuguegarao is cut off from the rest of Luzon by the **Sierra Madre** mountains. One of the only significant settlements is **Palanan**, jump-off point for the barely explored **Northern Sierra Madre Natural Park**. The climbing and trekking possibilities here are exciting, but the area is so wild and remote that it's also potentially hazardous, with poor communications and areas of impenetrable forest. Further south on the coast – but unreachable by road from Palanan – is **Baler**, the best-known tourist destination in the northeast. This coastal town has become a popular surfing destination, but its location six hours from Manila means that it isn't swamped with weekenders.

There's only one major **airport** for the whole region and that's at Tuguegarao, served by Philippine Airlines from Manila. There is also a small airport in Cauayan, from which it's possible to take a twin-engine aircraft to the airstrips in Palanan and Maconacon. Buses run regularly from Manila to Baler via Cabanatuan, about three hours north of the capital.

Santa Ana

The northern coast of Luzon, part of Cagayan province, is skipped over by many visitors in their haste to head either west to Ilocos Norte or south to Tuguegarao. Yet the untouristy fishing town of **SANTA ANA** – on the northeastern point of Luzon – has much to offer, including some terrific white sand beaches and a number of enticing offshore islands. It is also the departure point for boats to Maconacon and the North Sierra Madre Natural Park (see p.159).

There is little to do in Santa Ana itself but the **tourist office** (℡0780/858-1004) in the municipal building can offer advice on island-hopping and arrange homestays. You can also hire a bangka (P1500) or van (P2000) for the day from the barangay of **San Vicente**, 6km northeast of Santa Ana town centre, to the lovely and secluded **Angib Beach**. There is no accommodation on the beach, but it's a great place to pitch a tent.

The seas around Santa Ana offer marvellous **game-fishing**, thanks to the currents that run through the Luzon Strait from the Pacific. The season is from March to July and for details you can contact the Philippine Game Fishing Foundation (℡02/634-9187). The best place to stay is *Jotay Resort* (℡078/372-0560 or 0906/478-1270, Ⓦwww.jotayresort.com; ❸) on Santa Ana town's beach. The rooms are simple but comfortable, and the resort offers activities including humpback whale- and dolphin-watching, fishing, snorkelling, hiking and island-hopping.

Palaui Island

The closest island to Santa Ana is **Palaui**, which has no roads or hotels and only limited electricity. Contact the Palaui Environmental Protectors Association (PEPA; ℡02/933-3147 or 0927/279-5807, Ⓦwww.palaui.net), a community-based project that runs a homestay on the island as well as offering a two-day eco-tourism itinerary including snorkelling, hiking, planting mangroves and cleaning up the beach. Don't miss **Siwangag Cove** on the island's northern coast, a beautiful crescent lagoon watched over by an old but still operating Spanish lighthouse.

Moving on from Santa Ana

There are regular vans to **Tuguegarao** (3hr), while Florida Bus Liner runs a twice-daily service all the way to **Manila** (14hr; P750). Non-air-conditioned buses make the trip to Laoag (7hr; P500). Boats to **Maconacon** in the North Sierra Madre Natural Park leave from San Vicente.

To reach Palaui you need to hire a bangka from the port in San Vicente (see opposite). It costs P1200 for a return trip to the main settlement Punta Verde on the south of the island, from where there's a trail heading north to Siwangag Cove – the walk will take about three hours. Alternatively it's a P1500 bangka ride from San Vicente to the cove.

The Babuyan Islands

The MV *Eagle* ferry (☏0909/651-5595) makes the often rough crossing from San Vicente to the isolated and undeveloped **Babuyan Islands**, a cluster of 24 volcanic and coralline islands 32km off the coast. Only five of the islands – Camiguin, Calayan, Fuga, Babuyan and Dalupiri – are inhabited and even Calayan, the most developed, has limited electricity. There are some beautiful beaches on several of the islands including Fuga and Dalupiri, and there are hot springs on the volcanic Camiguin.

The ferry costs P700 to Camiguin (3hr) or P800 to go all the way to Calayan (4hr), and runs when the weather permits. Ask at the inhabited islands' barangay halls for homestay accommodation; for somewhere to stay on Calayan you can also contact Tes Singun (☏0929/837-5737) who owns a small lodge with two non-air-conditioned rooms.

Tuguegarao and around

The capital of Cagayan province, **TUGUEGARAO** ("Too-geg-er-rao") is a busy city of choked streets lined with pawnshops and canteens, offering little of interest for travellers. It is, however, convenient to fly to Tuguegarao if you intend to explore the east coast around the Sierra Madre or the northernmost coast near Santa Ana, or head west into Kalinga province and its capital Tabuk. There are also small aircraft flights from Tuguegarao to Batanes.

Don't head off straight away, though, as Tuguegarao is also the best starting point for a visit to a remarkable cave system at **Peñablanca**. In addition a number of travel agents in Tuguegarao offer **whitewater rafting** and **kayaking** trips on the Pinacanauan and Chico rivers, usually from August until February. Try Anton Carag at Adventure and Expeditions Philippines (☏0917/532-7480), for more adventure activity options.

Practicalities

Tuguegarao **airport** lies 2km south of the city centre along the National Highway, easily reached by tricycle or jeepney. **Buses** stop in several locations, including Diversion Road (for Florida buses) and the barangay of Leonarda on the National Highway (for Victory Liner).

The regional **tourist office** (Mon–Fri 8am–5pm; ☏078/844-1621, ⓦwww.dotregion2.com.ph) is at 29 Rizal St. You can ask here about permits and guides for the Peñablanca caves, or book trips in other parts of Northeast Luzon such as tours of the Sierra Madre Natural Park (see p.159). There is also a provincial tourist office (Mon–Fri 8am–5pm; ☏078/846-7576) in the Provincial Capitol complex on the city plaza. For more information on activities, contact the Sierra Madre Outdoor Club (☏0917/272-6494) whose members have reliable firsthand information about caving, trekking, abseiling and climbing.

The best **accommodation** in the centre is *Hotel Roma* (☏078/844-1057; ❹) at the corner of Luna and Bonifacio streets, which is unappealing from the outside but has spacious rooms equipped with flat-screen TVs. A cheaper option is *Hotel Ivory* (☏078/844-2249; ❷) on Buntun Highway, 10 minutes north of the city centre by tricycle. There's a restaurant and a large, clean swimming pool.

Moving on from Tuguegarao

Buses to **Manila** (12hr; P630) run day and night, operated by companies including Victory Liner (☏078/844-0777), Baliwag (☏078/844-4325), Ballesteros Liner, Dagupan Bus and Dalin Liner. Every bus going to Manila stops in the transport hub of Santiago (3hr; P175–350), where there are buses to Dilasag (for Palanan, see p.159) and also into Ifugao province. GMW has a service from Tuguegarao to **Laoag** from a terminal along Diversion Road (6–7hr; P455). Destinations served by vans include Santa Ana (4hr), Claveria (3hr 30min) and Tabuk (1hr 30min).

Cebu Pacific and Airphil Express fly to Manila, while Batanes Airlines operates **flights** to Basco in Batanes province.

Tuguegarao has the usual fast-food **restaurants** along the main drag Bonifacio Street. At lunchtime, try the buffet (11am–2pm) at *Adri-Nel's*, close to the tourist office. For P170 you get unlimited quantities of dishes such as *caldereta* (beef and tomato stew) and *dinuguan* (pork and pig's blood stew) as well as local specialities like *poso ng saging* (banana hearts with shrimp). In the evening it's à la carte only.

Peñablanca Caves

The major tourist attraction around Tuguegarao is the marvellous **cave system** at Peñablanca, 24km to the east and reachable in an hour. Peñablanca, officially known as the Peñablanca Protected Seascape and Landscape, is riddled with more than 300 caves, many of them deep and dangerous, and a good number still largely unexplored. You might want start by visiting the Cagayan Provincial Museum and Historical Research Center (Mon–Fri 8am–5pm) in the Provincial Capitol complex on the road between the city and the caves; it's worth a few minutes there to learn about what has been found in the various caves.

Callao Cave

The easiest cave to visit is **Callao Cave** (P20), which has seven immense chambers – previously there were nine but an earthquake in the 1980s cut off the last two. The main chamber has a natural skylight and a chapel inside where Mass is celebrated on special occasions. No guide is needed for this cave, although you can ask for one at the entrance. There are 184 steps before you reach the entrance of the cave, and inside the rocks can be quite slippery during the rainy season.

The cave is reached by jeepney (P45) from Don Domingo market. If you want to be certain of transport for the return trip you can hire a tricycle (P500) or jeepney (P1000) – prices include waiting. This is particularly worthwhile if you want to make a day of it by taking a **boat trip** after the cave. There is a pier close to the cave entrance and boatmen charge P600 for a return trip including waiting: they will start by taking you under a spot where water drips from tree roots – a good way to cool off after the exertion of the caves. They will then leave you on the riverside to relax; it's best to bring your own food. In season there are kayaks for rent at P200 per hour. Ask your boatman to leave you somewhere with a good view of the bat cave where at dusk you can see great flocks of the creatures leaving to hunt.

The only **resort** in the protected area is the *Callao Caves Resort* (☏078/846-7576; ❸) near Callao Cave, a large and dated complex with a range of accommodation, from simple bunk beds in a dorm (P200) to two-bedroomed air-conditioned cottages. Staff here also organize guides for caving and kayaking trips.

Other caves

A **guide** is essential for all caves except Callao: contact the Sierra Madre Outdoor Club or the tourist office in Tuguegarao (see p.157). Rates for guides are P1000 per day plus food, and you'll need one guide per three people. Porters charge P200–500 a day depending on what they are carrying. Most of the caves are protected, but it's possible to visit three – Callao, Musang and Lattu-Lattuc – without permission; all three can be done in a single day. There are several other caves – including Jackpot, Odessa-Tumbali and San Carlos – that can be visited with permission from the tourist office in Tuguegarao. Note that typhoons between August and October can flood the caves and make them impossible to visit.

Northern Sierra Madre Natural Park

At almost 3600 square kilometres, the **Northern Sierra Madre Natural Park** remains one of the country's last frontiers. Said by conservationists to be the Philippines' richest protected area in terms of habitat and species, the park is eighty percent land and twenty percent coastal area along a spectacular, cliff-studded seashore.

One of the reasons for the health of the park's ecosystems is its inaccessibility from outside. To the east lies the Pacific, which is too rough for boats during much of the northeast monsoon (Dec–Feb) and typhoon (July–Oct) seasons; to the west, no roads cross the park or lead towards the more populated, rice-growing valleys. Small aircraft connect the towns of Palanan and Maconacon to the outside world, but that doesn't make the area any less remote and for those unable or unwilling to pay for flights it's very time-consuming to reach. If you do make it, however, then you'll have no regrets.

Getting to the park

The small town of **Palanan** is the main gateway to the park. Cyclone Airways (℡078/652-0913, @www.cycloneairways.com) has four scheduled flights a week from Cauayan City in Isabela Province to Palanan. Tickets typically cost P2500–3000 single; the planes are six-seaters, so reserve ahead. Cauayan can be reached from Manila by air (Cebu Pacific) or night bus (Victory Liner, Florida Bus Line and Baliwag). To avoid flying, it's possible to take a long **boat** journey from San Vicente Port in Santa Ana to Maconacon town (8hr) and then change onto a second boat to Palanan via Divilacan (another 8hr). Alternatively, take a **minibus** from Santiago City in Isabela province (itself a 9hr trip from Manila) to Dilasag in Aurora province (non-a/c; 8hr; P400). The minibus leaves about 6am on weekdays, daily in April and May, and passes through Quirino province. From Dilasag, there are boats to Palanan (7hr; P350).

For hardy visitors, the most interesting option is to **trek** into the park from San Mariano. It's a three-day walk that requires a guide – contact Alma and Albert Gonzales at the Palanan Wilderness Development Cooperative (see p.160). To get to San Mariano, take a bus from Ilagan, Naguilian or Cauayan (all in Isabela province).

The Dumagats

The people known as the **Dumagats** are among the original inhabitants of the Philippines. The word Dumagat translates roughly as "those who moved to the ocean", and the area around Palanan is the last stronghold of their vanishing culture and way of life. Some have now settled but others are still nomadic, living in small camps on the beaches around Palanan where they build temporary sloping shelters from bamboo and dried grass. Life for the Dumagats is simple in the extreme: they survive by hunting and gathering, using little modern equipment. The main threats to their continued existence are through the commercialization and exploitation of their homelands, along with exposure to diseases previously unknown to them.

Information

The park's **tourism officer**, Myrose B. Alvarez (☎0916/525-4545), is based at the town hall in Palanan. Along with offering advice and information, she can help with arranging a homestay – there are no guesthouses or hotels in Palanan – and inform the Department of Environment and Natural Resources (DENR) that you are planning to hike in the area. Another useful contact is the **Palanan Wilderness Development Cooperative** (☎0915/935-0028, ⓔamgpalanan @yahoo.com) based in the town, which can help with guides and homestays. If you are interested in seeing the resident but endangered Philippine **crocodiles**, contact the Cagayan Valley Programme on Environment and Development (☎078/622-8001, ⓦwww.cvped.org). Every March members of the nomadic Dumagat community (see box, p.159) join with the settled inhabitants of Palanan for the **Sabutan festival**.

Visiting the park

The park has few wardens and no fences for boundaries, so you can visit any time you want without restriction; it is essential, however, to take a **guide** if you are to visit safely. A guide can take you down the Palanan River to the village of **Sabang**, from where you can walk through farmland and forest to **Disadsad Falls**, a high cascade that crashes through dense forest into a deep pool. For some of the trip there's no trail, so you'll have to wade upriver through the water. Another memorable trip from Palanan takes you northwards along the coast to the sheltered inlets around the towns of Dimalansan and Maconacon. On the isolated beaches here the **Dumagat** people establish their temporary homes (see box, p.159).

Baler

The laidback east coast town of **BALER** is known for its excellent if intermittent surfing: it was the location for the surfing scenes in Francis Ford Coppola's *Apocalypse Now*. The shots were filmed at a break known as Charlie's Point located at the mouth of the Aguang River, which is a 45-minute walk north of the main surfing beach of Sabang. When the film crew departed they left the surfboards behind, kick-starting local interest in the sport.

Arrival and information

There is a **tourist office** in the Provincial Capitol compound, about 500m east of where buses terminate. You can hire surfboards on Sabang Beach for around P200 per hour; lessons cost another P200 per hour.

Accommodation and eating

All the best **accommodation** in Baler is on or around the beach at Sabang, which is a short tricycle ride (P10) from the town. Apart from during the annual Aurora Cup in February, you won't have any problem finding somewhere to stay.

AMCO Beach Resort ☎0921/411-7671. A low-rise colonial-style building off the beach. Rooms have a/c and private hot showers, while the restaurant offers a modest menu of Filipino and Chinese dishes. ❷

Bahia de Baler Garden Resort ☎0921/576-5655, ⓦbahiadebaler.com. Right on the beach, this mid-range resort is good value, with a choice of single, double, family and group a/c rooms. ❹

Bay's Inn ☎0908/982-3509, ⓦbaysinnbaler .multiply.com. Arguably the most popular resort among tourists and out-of-town surfers, *Bay's Inn* boasts panoramic views of Baler Bay, the Pacific Ocean and surrounding cliffs and beaches. It has clean fan or a/c doubles with private cold showers and a popular restaurant with views, plus you can rent surfboards. ❷

Moving on from Baler

Genesis Transport (☎0919/650-6997) has several buses each day to Pasay in Manila (8hr; P420), while to get to other parts of Luzon – such as Baguio – you'll need to change in Cabanatuan (4hr; P230) in Nueva Ecija province. There are no road links north along the coast to the North Sierra Madre Natural Park, but you can catch D'Liner buses north to Dilasag where you can get a boat to Palanan.

3

Beaches

You can **surf** year-round at Baler although the best waves usually come between October and February, especially early in the morning. While it's the most convenient, Sabang Beach isn't the only good spot for surfing: **Cemento Beach**, 6km east of Baler, sees waves of up to 4m. To get there, take a tricycle from Baler town to the river outlet south of Sabang Beach and then either hire a bangka for the ten-minute ride to Cemento or make the forty-minute walk.

If you aren't looking for surf then you could try the white beach at Dicasalarin Cove, which can be reached by bangka from Baler (P3500 for a day-trip) or on foot from Digisit (2–3hr) which is 5km beyond Cemento. Further afield, Casiguran Sound is a calm and picturesque inlet around 3–4 hours north of Baler by either road (P162 ordinary bus, P595 a/c bus, P200 van) or sea. Protected from onshore winds and waves by a finger of hilly land, it is perfect for **swimming** and very undeveloped.

The Cordillera

To Filipino lowlanders brought up on sunshine and beaches, the tribal heartlands of the north and their spiny ridge of inhospitable mountains, the **CORDILLERA**, are still seen almost as another country, inhabited by mysterious people who worship primitive gods. It's true that in some respects life for many tribal people has changed little in hundreds of years, with traditional ways and values still very much in evidence. If anything is likely to erode these traditions it is the coming of tourists: already an increasing number of tribal people are making much more from the sale of handicrafts than they do from the production of rice.

The **weather** can have a major impact on a trip to the Cordillera, not least because landslides can cause travel delays during the rainy season (particularly May–Nov, but continuing until Jan or Feb). Since the rains come in from the northeast it's the places on the eastern side of the mountains – such as Banaue and Batad – that are usually worst hit, and fog can roll into those areas any time from October to February. Throughout the region it can get cold at night between December and February. It's worth noting that the rice terrace planting seasons vary significantly; the lower-lying areas typically have two plantings a year while the highlands have one. Terraces are at their greenest in the month or so before harvesting, although their barren appearance after a harvest can also look impressive.

Baguio and around

Many Filipinos speak of **BAGUIO** with a certain reverence, but it's fair to say that its heyday as an escape from Manila is far behind it. The city centre, particularly Session Road, is blighted by a polluted tangle of smoke-belching jeepneys and the arrival of a large shopping mall has hardly improved the scenery. Still, there are

Trekking in the Cordillera

Since the road network is poor in many parts of the region, and there are so many jungled peaks and hidden valleys, trekking is the only way to see some of the region's secrets: burial caves, tribal villages and hidden waterfalls. Gentle day hikes are possible, particularly in the main tourist areas of Banaue and Sagada, but there are also plenty of two- or three-day treks that take you deep into backwaters. Don't be tempted to wander off into the Cordilleran wilderness without a guide: good maps are almost nonexistent and it's easy to become disoriented and lost. Medical facilities and rescue services are few and far between, so if you get into trouble and no one knows where you are then you'll have a long wait for help to arrive.

Most of the best trails are around Sagada, Banaue, Bontoc, Tabuk and Tinglayan. In all of these towns there is a tourist office or town hall where someone will be able to help arrange **guides**. In smaller barrios a good place to look for a guide is at the barangay hall. In many places the guides won't have any official certification, but will know the area like the backs of their hands. Your guide may also agree to carry equipment and supplies, but don't expect him to have any equipment himself. Most guides happily wander through inhospitable landscapes with only flip-flops on their feet – don't follow suit. Rates start from around P500 a day but they vary from place to place; ask in advance if the guide is expecting you to provide food for him. The guide will expect a tip, even in the form of a few beers and a meal, for getting you home safely.

---

some interesting sights in and around Baguio plus a number of excellent restaurants and interesting nightlife stemming from the fact that this is a university city. Its position as a major hub for the Cordillera means that you're likely to pass through Baguio, and unless you are pushed for time it's worth spending a couple of days exploring the city.

Some history

In the sixteenth century, intrepid **Spanish friars** had started to explore the region, finding a land of fertile valleys, pine-clad hills and mountains, lush vegetation and an abundance of minerals such as copper and gold. Soon more friars, soldiers and fortune-hunters were trekking north to convert the natives to Christianity and profit from the rich natural resources. In the nineteenth century, **colonizing Americans** took over and developed Baguio into a modern city, a showcase recreational and administrative centre from which they could preside over their precious tropical colony without working up too much of a sweat. In 1944, when American forces landed in Leyte, the head of the Japanese Imperial Army, **General Yamashita**, moved his headquarters to Baguio and helped establish a puppet Philippine government there under President José Laurel. In 1945 the city was destroyed and thousands lost their homes as liberating forces flushed out Yamashita and his army. The general quickly fled north into the interior.

The city is also etched on the Filipino consciousness as the site of one of the country's worst natural disasters, the earthquake of July 16, 1990, which measured 7.7 on the Richter Scale and killed hundreds, mostly in the city's vulnerable shanty towns, many of which cling precariously to the sides of steep valleys.

Arrival and information

Baguio's **airport** lies 7km south of the city beyond Camp John Hay, but at the time of research there were no regular commercial flights using it. Most **buses** from Manila drop passengers on Governor Pack Road on the eastern side of Burnham Park; Victory Liner's terminal is to the southeast of the centre just off Upper Session Road.

The **tourist office** (daily 7am–6pm; ☎074/442-7014) is in the DoT Complex on Governor Pack Road, a ten-minute walk south of Session Road. There is also a small office in Burnham Park. There's a **post office** with a poste restante service at the junction of Session and Governor Pack roads. There are plenty of ATMs in the centre and you shouldn't have much trouble finding banks with currency exchange; for emergency cash transfers try the branch of Western Union on Session Road down from the post office. The main **police stations** are near City Hall on Abanao Street and on Governor Pack Road near the junction with Session Road. Several **internet cafés** remain open 24 hours a day on Session Road, including *South Park* in La Azotea Building and *Naver Internet* opposite the post office. They typically charge P20 per hour.

Accommodation

Hotels in the centre can get quite noisy, so ask for a room away from the road; there are also some good choices further out, including the chance to stay in traditional huts at the artist-run Tam-awan Village (see p.168).

Bloomfield 3 Leonard Wood Rd ☎074/446-9112, Ⓦwww.bloomfieldhotel.com. The thirty rooms here have modern, restrained decor and are good value given the central location near the SM Mall. Deluxe rooms have no views, while the superiors benefit from balconies but as a result are a bit noisier. Staff are friendly and helpful, and there's wi-fi throughout. ❺

Burnham Hotel 21 Calderon St ☎074/442-2331, Ⓦwww.burnhamhotelbaguio.com. One of the few budget or mid-range options close to Burnham Park and Session Rd, the rooms here are frayed around the edges but at least they have character. Thin walls mean it can be noisy, so get a room away from the road and hope that your neighbours don't talk too loudly. Wi-fi is free but doesn't reach all rooms. Note that some taxi drivers don't know this place and may try to take you to a more upmarket place called *Burnham Suites* instead. ❸

Casa Vallejo Upper Session Rd ☎074/424-3397, Ⓦcasavallejobaguio.com. Built in 1909 to house government employees, this Baguio landmark became the city's first hotel in the 1920s. It was one of very few buildings to survive World War II, but by the 1990s it had fallen into disrepair. It reopened in 2010 after extensive renovation with bags of US colonial-era charm; the rooms here are tasteful, modern and a bargain even in peak season. The windows are not double-glazed, so ask for one away from the road. The *Hill Station* restaurant serves impeccable dishes, and the block also has a bookshop and spa. ❺

Harrison Inn 37 Harrison Rd ☎074/442-7803. There's little to recommend the dark and tiny rooms here other than the prices, but if you want an exceptionally cheap room in the centre (for as

little as P400 with shared bathroom) then look no further. ❷

Holiday Villa Court 10 Legarda Rd ☎074/442-6679, Ⓦwww.baguioholidayhotel.com. The apartments here have two bedrooms and a kitchen, making them great for families. All the rooms are overpriced at peak times (Christmas and Holy Week); at other times expect at least a 25 percent discount. ❻

The Manor Camp John Hay ☎074/424-0931, Ⓦwww.cjhhotels.com. Probably the poshest place in town, where the excellent restaurant even has a dress code. The rooms are of a very high standard and the surroundings are beautiful. There's a gym and sauna, a deli and a branch of Narda's handicraft store, and live bands play in the bar in the evening. Significant discounts are available outside of high season. ❽

PNKY Home Leonard Wood Rd ☎074/444-5418, Ⓦwww.pnkyhome.com. Wonderfully quiet and cosy bijou bed-and-breakfast accommodation with only four rooms, so book in advance; rates include full breakfast in the neighbouring *PNKY Café*. The owners are very clued-up and can arrange everything from car rental to massage. There is also a fantastic, well-equipped cottage for six people, with two bedrooms, fitted kitchen and open fireplace. ❻

YMCA Post Office Loop ☎074/442-4766. As the address suggests, it's in a circular side street behind the post office at the top end of Session Rd. The rooms were recently renovated, improving the standards of both the dorms (P400 per head) and private rooms (which now have flat-screen TVs). Good location and popular with students, although it can be noisy during the day as there is a gym on the premises. ❹

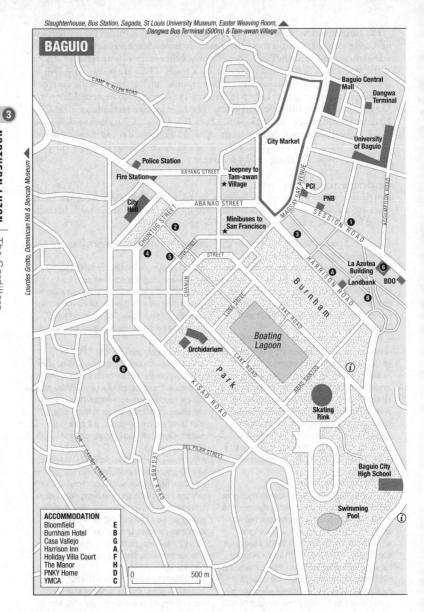

Slaughterhouse, Bus Station, Sagada, St Louis University Museum, Easter Weaving Room, Dangwa Bus Terminal (500m) & Tam-awan Village

Lourdes Grotto, Dominican Hill & Bencab Museum

BAGUIO

Baguio Central Mall

Dangwa Terminal

CAMP N' ALLEN ROAD

City Market

University of Baguio

Police Station

Fire Station

KAYANG STREET

Jeepney to Tam-awan ★ Village

MAGSAYSAY AVENUE

PCI

PNB

SESSION ROAD

ASSUMPTION ROAD

City Hall

CHUNTUG STREET

2

ABANAO STREET

Minibuses to San Francisco ★

3

1

HARRISON ROAD

La Azotea Building

6

4   5

OTEK STREET

STREET

Landbank

A

BDO

B

CHANUM

LINE DRIVE

Burnham

LAKE ROAD

Orchidarium

Boating Lagoon

F

8

LAKE ROAD

Park

ABAD SANTOS

KISAD ROAD

Skating Rink

(i)

DEL PILAR STREET

Baguio City High School

LEGARDA ROAD

DR. CARINO STREET

Swimming Pool

(i)

ACCOMMODATION	
Bloomfield	E
Burnham Hotel	B
Casa Vallejo	G
Harrison Inn	A
Holiday Villa Court	F
The Manor	H
PNKY Home	D
YMCA	C

0   500 m

The City

Baguio's municipal centre – the area around **Burnham Park** – was designed by American architect Daniel Burnham and based loosely on Washington DC. The main drag is **Session Road**, which is lined with restaurants and shops, while on a hill above Session Road stands the eye-catching **Baguio Cathedral**. Rather more prominent these days is the SM Mall, which looms incongruously over the city centre from the southern end of Session Road. From Session Road and Burnham

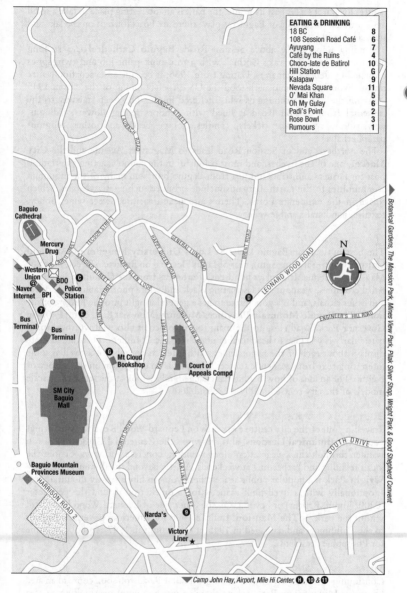

Botanical Gardens, The Mansion Park, Mines View Park, Pilak Silver Shop, Wright Park & Good Shepherd Convent

EATING & DRINKING	
18 BC	8
108 Session Road Café	6
Ayuyang	7
Café by the Ruins	4
Choco-late de Batirol	10
Hill Station	G
Kalapaw	9
Nevada Square	11
O' Mai Khan	5
Oh My Gulay	6
Padi's Point	2
Rose Bowl	3
Rumours	1

Camp John Hay, Airport, Mile Hi Center, **H**, **10** & **11**

Park you can easily reach many attractions on foot. If you're going a little further afield, to Camp John Hay, the Botanical Gardens, Mines View or Wright Park for example, it's easy and cheap to take a taxi.

Burnham Park and Session Road

Despite the efforts of the SM Mall the city's centrepiece is still **Burnham Park**, a hilltop version of Rizal Park in Manila with a man-made boating lake at the centre. Even if it's a bit past its prime, the park is an interesting place to take a stroll and to watch the people of Baguio at play: there are boats for rent on the lake and tricycles for kids.

Standing imperiously above Session Road, **Baguio Cathedral** is a striking example of "wedding cake Gothic" with a rose-pink paint job and twin spires crowned by delicate minarets. Dating from 1936, it became an evacuation centre during World War II and withstood the US carpet-bombing of the city in 1945 – saving the lives of thousands who sheltered inside. The steep stairway to the cathedral from Session Road is lined with vendors selling flowers, balloons, newspapers, sweepstake tickets, candles, rosary beads and other religious paraphernalia.

The northern end of Session Road leads to Magsaysay Avenue and the **City Market**, one of the liveliest and most colourful in the country, acting as a trading post for farmers and tribes not just from Baguio but from many of the mountain communities to the north. Bargains include produce such as strawberries, which thrive in the temperate north. There's also peanut brittle, sweet wine, honey, textiles, handicrafts and jewellery.

The museums

The best museum in Baguio is the **St Louis University Museum of Arts and Culture** (Mon–Sat 8am–5pm), near St Louis Hospital on Bonifacio Street, north of Magsaysay Avenue. It displays hundreds of artefacts from the Cordillera including tribal costumes, weapons and fascinating black and white photographs of sacrifices and other rituals, and is a good place to get a general insight into the history of the north. The **Baguio Mountain Provinces Museum** (Mon–Sat 8am–5pm; P40), on Governor Pack Road close to the main tourist office, is also well worth visiting, particularly if you plan to head further north into the Cordillera. There are separate displays about each of the major tribes, with artefacts and photos as well as some interesting text from academic sources. Upstairs is an exhibition on the history of Baguio. For an idea of how Baguio has changed, take a look at the set of three scale models of the city centre in 1909, 1928 and 2009.

Botanical Gardens and Wright Park

Travelling out of the city centre eastwards on Leonard Wood Road for 4km brings you to the **Botanical Gardens**, also known as the Centennial Gardens. You can wander through thick vegetation along winding concrete pathways, or join the locals relaxing and barbecuing at weekends. A little beyond the Botanical Gardens, **Wright Park** is a popular public space where you can hire a sturdy mountain nag – optionally with a dyed-pink mane – for a quick trot around the perimeter (P200/30min, P30/hr) or beyond. On the other side of Leonard Wood Road, still within the park, is **The Mansion**. Built in 1908 for American governor-generals to the Philippines and damaged in 1945, it was rebuilt in 1947 as a holiday home for Philippine presidents.

Mines View Park

Continuing east from Wright Park along Gibraltar Road you soon come to an area known as **Mines View Park**, where there's a viewing point overlooking an area that used to be the location of mining operations. To get there you have to make your way past countless souvenir stalls and hawkers, and if you ever wanted to have your photo taken with a sunglasses-wearing St Bernard dog then this is the place to fulfil your dream. A short walk up the hill from the viewpoint is the **Good Shepherd Convent**, with a store inside the main gate where you can buy products made by the nuns, including strawberry, coconut or *ube* (purple yam) jam and cashew or peanut brittle. If you need *pasalubong* – souvenirs, usually food, which Filipinos always pick up as gifts on their travels – then this is a great place to buy them. There's also a café, and the far end of the convent's car park, an observation deck with views across the Cordillera mountains.

Camp John Hay

Named after American President Theodore Roosevelt's secretary of war, this green space south of the Botanical Gardens used to be a rest and recreational facility for employees of the United States military and Department of Defense. During World War II the property was used by the Japanese as a concentration camp for American and British soldiers. In 1991 Camp John Hay was turned over to the Philippine government for development into an upmarket country club, with hotels (including *The Mansion*), a golf course (☎074/444-2131, ⓦwww.cjhhotels.com), private mountain lodges and sundry restaurants and clubhouses.

The expansive, undulating grounds have some nice walks through the pine trees and are also ideal for jogging. Jeepneys can't enter the park itself, so it's best to get a taxi from the city centre (P50). If you don't have a particular destination in mind then ask to be dropped at the entrance to the **Historical Core**. Here you can buy a ticket (P50) to see the Bell Amphitheatre, the Ambassador's Residence (which is still US-owned) and the site where General Yamashita formally surrendered to US forces. At weekends, Filipino families congregate close to the entrance to the Historical Core to enjoy picnics away from the city centre's traffic.

Also close by is the **Tree Top Adventure** (daily 8am–5pm; ⓦwww.treetop adventuresubic.com), where you can try a zip line (P200–300) and abseiling (P150), or join guided walks. If you need something to eat, try the friendly *Chocolate de Batirol* near the entrance to the golf club. Alternatively head over to the Mile Hi Center where you will find duty-free outlet stores, several restaurants, a hotel and a handy ATM.

Lourdes Grotto and Dominican Hill

High on a hill in the western part of the city, off Dominican Hill Road, is **Lourdes Grotto**, a Catholic shrine watched over by an image of Our Lady of Lourdes and reached by 252 steps. Beyond the grotto at the summit of the road is **Dominican Hill**, from where the views across the city are superlative. The crumbling hotel that stands there was built by the Dominican Order then later owned by a controversial entrepreneur and faith healer; locals claim that it is haunted by his former patients. It's possible to take a taxi to the top, or to walk from the grotto.

BenCab Museum

One of the best art galleries in the Philippines, the **BenCab Museum** (Tues–Sun 9am–6pm; P100; ⓦwww.bencabmuseum.org) is well worth the short trip out of the centre. Built to house the collection of local artist Ben Cabrera, who has a home and studio next door, it's an airy modernist structure with lots of natural light and great views of the surrounding scenery. One gallery has temporary exhibitions while the other eight contain permanent displays, including everything from Ifugao artefacts and old prints of the Philippines to paintings and sculptures by contemporary Filipino artists.

On the lowest floor is a café, which is a pleasant place to relax with a drink for an hour or two. If you are feeling more active, there's a path to a viewpoint on the hillside at the back of the building. To get to the museum from central Baguio, take a jeepney (P20) in the direction of Asin hot springs or hop in a taxi (around P100).

On the northwest outskirts of Baguio, **Tam-awan Village** (T 074/446-2949, W tam-awanvillage.com; ●) is a replica tribal village established in 1996 by a group of Filipino artists, including Ben Cabrera and Jordan Mang-osan. If you want to spend the night in a tribal hut, and are not going further north, then this is a good chance. There is a small gallery with changing exhibitions, a gift shop and café, and a cultural show (P50) with dancing every Saturday from 2–5pm. If you happen to be around on a Saturday night there's a good chance that a few of the artists will be around eating, drinking and enjoying some live music.

Take a jacket if you're staying because it can get surprisingly cold. On a clear evening, you'll see magnificent China Sea sunsets and even the Hundred Islands in the distance; hence the name Tam-awan, which means "vantage point". You can reach Tam-awan Village by taxi for P50 or so, or by jeepney for around P10; it's past the Easter Weaving Room on the road to La Trinidad (the provincial capital, which has little for tourists).

Eating

In addition to the usual fast-food outlets in the SM Mall, Baguio has some of the best **restaurants** in the country. There is also a good selection of street food, including a couple of places beside *Casa Vallejo* hotel serving *bulalo* (beef on the bone in a broth). Alternatively, if you're feeling brave then take a five-minute taxi ride to the slaughterhouse and try one of the exceptionally cheap dishes in the eateries there; if you want to try *azucena* (dog meat) then here's a chance – there will be more if you're heading north.

Café by the Ruins 25 Chuntug St T 074/442-4010. Try not to leave Baguio without eating here. It's far and away one of the city's culinary highlights, with excellent organic food prepared with home-grown herbs and served either indoors or in the shady yard. The shrimp and mango curry, served with an array of side-dishes, is exquisite. Other dishes include crispy *tapa* (fried shredded beef), home-made bread and handmade pasta. Daily 7am–9pm.

Choco-late de Batirol Camp John Hay, near the country club entrance. The owners of this café are passionate about introducing customers to their hot chocolate, using family recipes based on Spanish traditions. The chocolate is stirred with a wooden stick called a *batirol* before being served with a flourish, and there are various flavoured mixes; all contain peanuts. There's food too – try the rich but gorgeous *taba ng talangka* (crab fat) with tomato and mango salsa. 8.30am until around 9.30pm.

Hill Station Upper Session Rd T 074/423-9100. Part of the *Casa Vallejo* hotel, with a smart but unpretentious dining room and waiting staff in military-style uniforms to reflect Baguio's history as a US hill station. The menu includes a collection of stews from other famous hill stations in countries such as India. There is also a café bar open until 11pm.

Jinhox Nook Jose de Leon Building, Session Rd. One of many Korean restaurants in Baguio, catering to tourists as well as the thousands of Korean students who stay in the city for periods of several months to learn English. You can smell the pork BBQ from the stairwell. 10am–11pm.

Kalapaw 117 Martinez St. Offering "a taste of Laoag", this native-style restaurant close to the Victory Liner terminal has an Ilocano chef and an array of regional specialities on the menu. Two or more people can order the "boodle fight", a set menu designed to be eaten with your hands, but there are also meals for one. 8am–9pm.

O' Mai Khan 12 Otek St. Feast on the Mongolian BBQ, a buffet of several meats with 18 sauces, at P195/head (P135 for children). Alternatively, try the Mongolian hot pot where you dip meat and veg into a soup to cook it at your own table (P160/person, cheaper in bigger groups). Daily 10am–10pm.

Oh My Gulay La Azotea Building, Session Rd. Not the easiest place to find – it's upstairs in a small shopping complex – but an unmissable fixture on Baguio's dining scene. The food is vegetarian, but even committed carnivores will love the outdoors-indoors feel. 11am–8.30pm.

Rose Bowl 7 Harrison Rd. A Baguio institution since 1969, the *Rose Bowl* continues to serve quality Chinese dishes including pancit (noodles) which many locals claim are the best in the country. Daily 6.30am–11pm.

Drinking and nightlife

Baguio's large student population demands a good **nightlife**. Most bars with live music charge an entry fee of around P50.

18 BC 16 Legarda Rd. The walls are decorated with wagon wheels and deer-head trophies, but the music in here is more likely to be acoustic rock than country.

108 Session Road Café Packed at weekends, this place serves food and alcohol to the strains of live reggae from 5pm–midnight.

Ayuyang Under *Baden Powell Inn*, 26 Governor Pack Rd. Popular with students and artists, this friendly bar often has live acoustic and reggae music in the evenings.

Nevada Square 2 Loakan Rd. With something of a reputation for drunken antics, this collection of

bars and clubs is packed with students at the weekend.

Padi's Point Fernando G. Bautista Dr, on the edge of Rizal Park. Part of a chain with branches across Luzon, this bar has live and loud music until 4am on weekdays and 5am at the weekend. Happy hour is 5–9pm.

Rumours 55 Session Rd. A straightforward place to enjoy a drink, without intrusive music or other distractions. There's a better than usual choice of beers and snacks to enjoy with them. Open until 2 or 3am.

Moving on from Baguio

Most bus companies use one of three locations: Governor Pack Road, the Dangwa terminal off Magsaysay Avenue behind Baguio Central mall, or the Slaughterhouse compound on Magsaysay Avenue. Victory Liner has its own terminal on Upper Session Road. Those mentioned below are some of the most popular routes; other destinations include Santa Ana, Cavite, Aparri and Baler.

Dagupan Bus (6hr; P350), Philippine Rabbit (5hr; P350) and Genesis (5hr; P390) all have hourly buses to **Manila** from Governor Pack Road. The Victory Liner (5hr; P455 regular, P615 deluxe, P715 with bathroom) service is the most comfortable, with five buses per day.

Buses to **Bontoc** cost P212 and take 5–6 hours. Services are run by GL Lizardo (Slaughterhouse; 4 daily), D'Rising Sun (Slaughterhouse; hourly from 5am–4pm) and Jack Dulnuan (Dangwa; 3 each morning).

There are four GL Lizardo buses each morning from Dangwa (5–6hr; P220) to **Sagada**, while A-Liner buses operate three services each day (5hr; P123), departing from the Slaughterhouse compound. One Ohio Liner bus leaves each morning from Dangwa (5hr; P128).

It's an 8- to 9-hour journey to **Banaue** by bus; due to the route taken, it takes almost as long as it does to go from Manila to Banaue direct. It therefore makes more sense to go via Bontoc and Sagada if those are on your itinerary. If, however, you want to take a direct vehicle to Banaue then there are several options. The Jack Dulnuan service (P330) leaves Dangwa in the early evening. Two other companies depart from Chanum Street: Ohayami Trans (P460) and KMS Lines (P415) each have a bus in the morning and one in the early evening. A quicker option for this route, albeit one requiring more changes, is to take a van from Dangwa to Bambang in Nueva Vizcaya province (4hr; P200) then travel to Banaue by jeepney.

To get to **San Fernando (La Union)** there are hourly services from 5am–8pm with Eso–Nice Transport (2hr; P60) departing from the corner of Otek and Chagum streets. For **Laoag**, Partas has one bus early morning and one mid-afternoon (5–6hr; P274) to **Vigan**. Partas also runs hourly services (P382) from Governor Pack Road. There are several options for **Tuguegarao**: Dalin has one service each evening via Ilagan (11–12hr; P550) from Gov. Pack Road; Dalin JD runs two buses via Roxas each evening (10–12hr; P550); and Dangwa Pine Tree has two buses each day from Dangwa (12hr; P550).

Shopping

The SM City Baguio at the top end of Session Road is home to the usual array of chain stores. The city does, however, still have plenty of interesting little cottage-industry outlets where you can rummage for souvenirs and inexpensive home decor.

Apart from the City Market (see p.166) and Good Shepherd Convent (see p.166), one of the most popular shopping pilgrimages is to the **Easter Weaving Room** (daily; ℡074/442-4972, ⓦwww.easterweaving.com) in Easter Road, on the northwestern outskirts of the city. The shop produces hand-woven articles such as rugs, tablemats, wall hangings, textiles, cushion covers and bed linen. You can watch the weavers at work on old hand looms and, if you've got a few weeks to wait, place a personal order. Take a jeepney heading in the direction of Guisad from Kayang Street, at the northern end of Burnham Park, or a taxi for around P50.

In Upper Session Road, a short walk from the eastern end of Session Road and just before you reach the Victory Liner terminal, **Narda's** manufactures and sells attractive clothes, bags, rugs, linen and tablemats. There's a good café too, with wi-fi access. **Pilak Silver Shop** on Leonard Wood Road, near the *Baguio Vacation Hotel*, has bargain-basement silver jewellery. For **books**, visit 🏛 Mt Cloud in the same building as *Casa Vallejo* (see p.163). It's a small place but with an excellent selection and friendly, knowledgeable staff.

Kabayan and around

An isolated mountain village 85km north of Baguio, **KABAYAN** in Benguet province makes a thrilling side trip, although because of the rough road you'll need to spend at least one night in the village. There was no road here until 1960 and no electricity until 1978, and this extended isolation has left the village rural and unspoilt, a good place to involve yourself in the culture of the **Ibaloi**, who are friendly and helpful if a little prone to shyness in the company of foreigners (and that means anyone from further afield than Baguio). Hikers are also drawn to Kabayan for the chance to climb Mount Pulag, the highest peak in Luzon.

Kabayan came to the attention of the outside world in the early twentieth century when a group of **mummies**, possibly dating back as far as 2000 BC was discovered in the surrounding caves. When the Americans arrived, mummification was discouraged as unhygienic and the practice is thought to have died out. Controversy still surrounds the Kabayan mummies, some of which have disappeared to overseas collectors, sold for a quick buck by unscrupulous middlemen. One was said to have been stolen by a Christian pastor in 1920 and wound up as a

---

Making a mummy

The history of the Ibaloi **mummies** is still largely oral. It is even uncertain when the last mummy was created; according to staff at the town's museum, mummification was attempted most recently in 1907 but the wrong combination of herbs was used. It's possible that the last successful mummification was in 1901, of the great-grandmother of former village mayor Florentino Merino.

What is known is the general procedure, which could take up to a year to complete. The body would have been bathed and dressed, then tied upright to a chair with a low fire burning underneath to start the drying process. Unlike in other mummification rituals around the world, the internal organs were not removed. A jar was placed under the corpse to catch the body fluids, which are considered sacred, while elders began the process of peeling off the skin and rubbing juices from native leaves into the muscles to aid preservation. Tobacco smoke was blown through the mouth to dry the internal tissues and drive out worms.

sideshow in a Manila circus. Some mummies remain, however, and some have been recovered. Officials know of dozens of mummies in the area, but will not give their locations for fear of desecration. You can, however, see several of them in designated mountaintop caves.

Kabayan is most easily approached from Baguio, as the road to the north of the village (which joins the Halsema Highway at Abatan town) is very rough and suitable only for 4WD vehicles.

Arrival, information and accommodation

On arrival you should register at the Municipal Hall, where you will also find the tourist office. There is a branch of Rural Bank but no ATM so you will need to bring enough pesos from Baguio. There are just two **accommodation** options in Kabayan, although at the time of writing another was being constructed: the newcomer may be named the *Pine Cone Lodge* and all signs are that it will be the most comfortable option in town once open; it will also have a restaurant. Call Gertrude Manguson on ☎0929/327-7749 for an update.

Kabayan Coop Lodge ☎0920/356-990. Very neat, clean rooms with doubles or bunk beds (P200/ person) with a shared bathroom and toilet. It's a friendly place but there's not much hot water. ❶

Municipal Guesthouse No phone. Near the Municipal Hall, this place has two single-sex dorms each sleeping six people at P200 a head. ❶

The village

Before heading on to the other burial sites, be sure to visit **Opdas Cave** (P20 donation) at the southern end of the village. It contains around 200 skulls and bones estimated to be up to 1000 years old, discovered in a pile but now arranged. Nobody knows why they were buried together, but one theory is that they died as a result of an epidemic. Follow the signs from the main road and call at the caretaker's house (it's the green corrugated iron building). A member of the family will open the gate to the cave and will encourage you to pray to the spirits, asking them to allow you to enter and leave safely.

It's also worth visiting the small branch of the **National Museum** (Mon–Fri 8am–noon & 1–5pm; P30), at the western end of Kabayan beyond the bridge. The curators are helpful and can give you a personal guided tour of the exhibits, which include a mummy in a foetal position inside a coffin.

Eating and drinking

There are half a dozen sari-sari stores in Kabayan where you can get snacks, but only a couple of places to **eat** a meal. Local officials have banned the sale (but not the consumption) of alcohol.

Brookside Café Next to the *Kabayan Coop Lodge*. The owner here can rustle up cheap and simple dishes such as pork soup and rice, as well as sugary Benguet coffee which is just the tonic on a cold Cordillera morning.

Kabayan Mini-mart This popular combined grocery store and café has tables both inside and on a balcony with attractive views of the surrounding fields.

Timbac Cave

The area around Kabayan is excellent trekking country, and it's possible to hike up to see the collection of mummies in **Timbac Cave** (P20 plus P100 per group) and return within the day. It's essential to bring an Ibaloi guide not only to ensure you don't get lost but also to respect local sensibilities: locals believe that unaccompanied outsiders will attract the wrath of the spirits. As one local puts it, "If ever there is a curse, it will not be on you but on us." The tourist office can arrange an accredited guide at P1000 for up to five people.

It's a strenuous four- to five-hour climb to the cave. Take food and drink and aim to set off around 6am. On the way ask your guide to point out the **Tinongchol Burial Rock** (P20 donation plus P10 barangay fee), in which deep niches were carved to inter the mummified dead in coffins. On the way to the cave there are also a number of **lakes** and **rice terraces** where farmers grow *kintoman*, an aromatic red rice. Your guide will retrieve the key to Timbac Cave from a caretaker who lives close by, and say the necessary prayers before you enter.

The walk back down to Kabayan takes three hours, or you can walk for an hour or so beyond the cave to the Halsema Highway and flag down a bus (the guide will charge an extra P200 for this). This means a shorter and more comfortable journey back to Baguio, or you can head north to Bontoc. The last bus will pass around 5pm but don't cut it too fine. It is not recommended that you do this in reverse and approach the cave from the highway, since you risk finding that the caretaker isn't there or offending locals by arriving without a guide.

Finally, if you don't want to walk at all – and it isn't the rainy season – you can hire a 4WD to take you up to the cave. This can be arranged at the *Coop Lodge* for P2500–3000 (plus an extra P500 if you want to carry on to the Halsema Highway).

Bangao Cave

If you don't have time to trek to Timbac Cave, or just want to see as much as possible while in the area, consider visiting the caves around Bangao village. The **Bangao Cave** (P20/person, plus P100/group) has a handful of mummies in coffins, although they are in worse condition than those in Timbac. It's a two-hour walk from Kabayan, although you can reduce this to thirty minutes by hiring a jeepney (P1500–2000) to take you some of the way.

Mount Pulag

Standing 2922m above sea level, **Mount Pulag** is the highest mountain in Luzon and unless you are experienced you shouldn't try it alone. The terrain is steep, there are gorges and ravines, and in the heat of the valleys below, it's easy to forget it can be bitterly cold and foggy on top. Despite what villagers may flippantly say, don't underestimate the difficulty of this mountain. It's essential to treat the area with respect: a number of indigenous communities including the Ibaloi, Kalanguya, Kankana-eys and Karaos live on Pulag's slopes and regard the mountain as a sacred place. They have a rich folklore about ancestral spirits inhabiting trees, lakes and mountains, and while they're friendly towards climbers you should stick to the trails. For up-to-date information on which trails are most accessible, contact the tourist office in Baguio.

The two best **trails** for first-timers are those that start from Ambangeg and Kabayan. Whichever way you choose to climb Pulag, take a tent and expect to spend the night on top. Ambangeg is a regular stop on the Baguio to Kabayan bus route; ask the driver to drop you at the visitor centre in the Bokod barangay of Ambangeg, where you must **register** and pay a P850 entrance fee. It's a two- to three-hour walk from here to the ranger station where the hike officially begins, although it's also possible to get a lift to the ranger station on a jeepney or motorcycle (around P150). At the ranger station you can hire a **guide** at P500 per group of up to five. It is best to spend the night at the furthest campsite, about three hours from the ranger station, and ascend to the summit for dawn the next day. If you arrive in Ambangeg too late to ascend then staff at the visitor centre can find you a bed in the local school or a private home.

The trail from Kabayan, known as the **Akiki** or **Killer Trail**, starts 2km south of Kabayan on the Baguio–Kabayan road. Guides are available at the trailhead and trekkers should also register there; if you are staying in Kabayan then the tourist office can take care of this for you. Expect to pay a guide P2000 for a round trip. As the name suggests this is a more difficult route, taking at least seven hours to reach the saddle camp near the summit. The next morning you will go to the peak, then descend. Another, less-used option is the **Enchanted Trail** starting in Tawangan, a two-hour drive north of Kabayan; contact the tourist office in advance to arrange this route.

Bontoc and around

The road from Baguio to **BONTOC** is the **Halsema Highway** or "Mountain Trail", a narrow, serpentine gash in the side of the Cordillera that's sometimes no more than a rocky track with vertical cliffs on one side and a sheer drop on the other. Although the surface of the road has been greatly improved in recent years, it can still be an uncomfortable trip by public transport as some of the buses are crowded and not especially well maintained. The views are marvellous, especially as you ascend out of Baguio beyond La Trinidad and pass through deep gorges lined with vegetable terraces.

BONTOC lies on the banks of the Chico River about an hour east of Sagada. Primarily used by tourists as a transport hub, the town is also a good base for **trekking** and has easy access to the beautiful **Maligcong** rice terraces. Some of the local tribes can be nervous of foreigners and it would be unwise to approach them without a guide to help smooth the way (P300–500/day). One well-known local is Francis Pa-in (☏0915/769-0843), who can also act as a guide in Tinglayen; ask at the *Churya-a Hotel* if you can't get him on the phone.

There isn't much to see in the town itself but don't miss the **Bontoc Museum** (Mon–Sat 9.30am–noon & 1–5pm; P20), next to the post office close to the town plaza. It includes photographs of headhunting victims and of zealous American missionaries, and there is a small collection of indigenous buildings outside. The museum shop sells items including handmade jewellery and CDs of traditional music.

Practicalities

The **accommodation** in the town centre is mostly very uninspiring. The best option is *Sonnorah's Inn, Café and Restaurant* (☏0930/194-2503; ❶), although *Churya-a* (☏0906/430-0853; ❷) is worth a look mainly for its balcony café, which is a good place to meet other travellers. Otherwise you are better off heading across the bridge on the eastern side of town to *Archog* (☏0918/328-6908; ❷). It's probably the best hotel in the area; try rooms 7 & 16, which have good views of the rice fields.

The best places to **eat** are the hotel restaurants, particularly *Churya-a* and *Ridgebrook* (which is close to *Archog* hotel). Otherwise there are several unexceptional

---

Moving on from Bontoc

Cable Tours (☏0918/521-6790) has one air-conditioned bus a day from Bontoc to Quezon City in **Manila** (11hr; P650), and one bus via the spectacular road to **Banaue** (1hr 30min; P150). Von Von also runs buses to Banaue. Several companies – including D'Rising Sun, GL Lizardo and Jack Dulnuaun – have services to **Baguio** (5–6hr; P212).

From the market you can get occasional jeepneys or minibuses north to **Tinglayan** (3hr; P120) and **Tabuk** (7hr; P200) in the province of Kalinga. Jeepneys to **Sagada** (P40) leave hourly 8am–5.30pm and take around 45 minutes.

places on the main drag. Look out for *inasin* (salted pork) which is a local delicacy; it is also combined with specially prepared chicken for *pinikpikan*. This involves beating the bird with a stick before it is killed in the belief it brings blood to the surface, making the meat more tender and tasty. Once dead, the chicken is put on an open fire to burn off the feathers; this adds to the flavour of the dish. The mountain tribes then traditionally use the innards for fortune telling, before eating the meat. The only regular **nightlife** in town is the *Cable Café* on the main drag, where there's live music every night

Maligcong and Mainit

The stone-walled rice terraces of Maligcong are only a short trip from Bontoc, and are at their best in June and July immediately before the harvest. From the point where public transport stops, a path descends into a valley and follows the contour of the terraces to Maligcong village. There's a sari-sari store in Maligcong but no café so it's best to bring your own food; ask around about homestays if you want to spend the night.

From Maligcong it is a strenuous ninety-minute walk to Mainit ("Ma-i-nit"), a village known for its hot sulphurous springs. There are two simple lodges (no phone; ❶), each with shared bathrooms and with access to hot springs. *Bendict's Inn* has concrete buildings, a swimming pool and warm spring water. *Geston Hot Spring* offers nipa huts and cooler water.

Jeepneys to Maligcong (45min; P25) from Bontoc run from early morning until early afternoon; the last return journey is at around 4pm. There are also two jeepneys direct to Mainit (1hr; P35) each day.

Alab Petroglyph and Ganga Cave

A huge rock with etched drawings of humans with bows and arrows, the **Alab Petroglyph** is at the end of a two-hour hike uphill from the barangay of Alab, 9km south of Bontoc on the Halsema Highway. Although it was declared a national cultural treasure in 1975, little is known about who created the carvings or why. An hour further along is the **Ganga Cave**, a burial cave containing coffins and jars of bones. You'll need to find a guide in Alab for either destination.

Regular jeepneys to Alab (P20) leave from in front of Aglipay General Merchandise or near the XiJEN Business Center in Bontoc. Buses to Baguio can also let you down in Alab.

Barlig, Kadaclan and Natonin

These three villages east of Bontoc are well off the normal tourist route, but their wonderful rice terraces are certainly worth the trip. The closest village to Bontoc is **Barlig**, which is also the starting point for a trek up Mount Amuyao (2702m). The trek can be done in a day, or you can continue on to Batad (see p.184) making it a two-day trip – enquire about guides at the Barlig town hall. There are two no-frills lodges in town, the *Halfway Inn* (❶) and *Sea World* (❶).

Kadaclan and **Natonin** are rarely visited by tourists, but are situated among beautiful scenery and are ideal for getting away from it all for a day or two. In Natonin there is basic accommodation at the *San Roque Lodging House* (❶) or *Arang Multi-Purpose Cooperative* (❶).

Jeepneys head from Bontoc to Barlig (P70) each afternoon, taking an hour and a half. The first return trip is very early in the morning, before 6.30am, while a later trip at 9am depends on passenger numbers. Kadaclan is an hour and a half by jeepney from Barlig, or 3–4 hours from Bontoc (jeepneys depart after lunch and cost P150; return trips are early in the morning). Natonin is another hour on from Kadaclan on a very bad road; jeepneys cost P170.

Sagada

The small town of **SAGADA**, 160km north of Baguio, has long attracted curious visitors. Part of the appeal derives from its famous hanging coffins and a labyrinth of caves used by the ancients as burial sites. But Sagada also has a reputation as a remote and idyllic hideaway where people live a simple life well away from civilization. Sagada's distance from Manila, and the fact that the quickest way to reach it from the capital involves at least one buttock-numbing bus journey on a terrifyingly narrow road, means it has kept mass tourism at bay. Sagada's lofty beauty is given added resonance by its very un-Filipino-ness. The landscape is almost alpine and the inhabitants are mountain people, their faces shaped not by the sun and sea of the lowlands, but by the thin air and sharp glare of altitude.

Arrival and information

All **buses** and **jeepneys** arriving in Sagada from Baguio and Bontoc terminate in a small market square opposite the commercial centre, close to the main junction. There's a small **tourist information centre** (℡0920/919-0708) in the nearby old municipal building, where all visitors must register. They have a long list of guided tours with fixed prices, as does the Sagada Genuine Guides (℡0929/556-9553, ⓦsagadagenuineguides.blogspot.com) office close to *Yoghurt House* (see p.178).

You'll find a **post office** in the municipal building, as well as a branch of the Sagada Rural Bank (Tues–Sun 8am–4pm) with an ATM. There are no other banks for miles around, so it's best to bring enough pesos rather than rely on the ATM. The police outpost is next to the old municipal building, and there's one small **hospital**, St Theodore's, on the eastern edge of the village. Sagada also has a few small internet cafés, such as *Tripple J* which has one branch uphill from the Ganduyan Inn and in the commercial centre.

Accommodation

Most of the village's restaurants and **guesthouses** are located on the main road, which runs through the town centre past the market, the town hall, the municipal

Moving on from Sagada

Jeepneys leave for **Bontoc** (45min; P40) every hour from 6am to around midday, or when they are full to the brim. There are no direct buses from Sagada to **Banaue**, but you can take a jeepney to Bontoc and then another from Bontoc market to Banaue, a two- to three-hour trip over a mountain pass that even in the dry season can be enveloped in mist. GL Lizardo runs buses (5–6hr; P220) to the Dangwa terminal in **Baguio** six times a day.

buildings and the police station. Guesthouses in Sagada are on the whole great value. The town gets packed out at Christmas and Easter, so if you're planning to visit at these times try to book ahead.

Ganduyan Inn & Cafe ☏0921/273-8097. The main building has six small but comfortable rooms in a good central location, 50m from the municipal building. There is also an extension up the hill with better rooms for the same price; rooms 5, 6 and 8 have good views from their balconies. **②**

George Guest House ☏0918/548-0406. A good choice of cosy, clean rooms each with two double beds, private showers and hot water; the price depends on how many people sleep in the room. Some have small, private balconies, so ask to see a selection before you choose; there's also free wi-fi for guests. An annexe down the hill has more rooms plus cottages. **②**

Rock Inn ☏0920/909-5899, ⓦwww.rockfarmsagada.com. A fantastic place located in an orange grove a fifteen- to twenty-minute walk from the centre of Sagada; for P50 entrance plus P50 per kilo, you're welcome to pick their fruit. There's a choice of rooms ranging from triples to an attic where you can sleep under a duvet on a tatami mat (P250/head); you can also hire a tent for three at P500 per night. Delicious meals in the sunny restaurant use vegetables from the gardens. The owner, Bang, is an entertaining host and a mine of information. **④**

Sagada Guesthouse & Café ☏0921/969-4053. Central if slightly noisy location above the bus station and the little open-air market. Economy rooms with shared bathrooms are just P200 per head; more comfortable standard doubles (**②**) are also available. **①**

Sagada Homestay ☏0919/702-8380. A hotel rather than a homestay, although with a more homely feel than most. It's a friendly place made from pine, with a kitchen for guests – you just pay for any gas used. Rooms are available with or without private bathrooms, while a separate cottage (**④**) sleeps four people. There's wi-fi in the main building for P40 per day. **②**

St Joseph Resthouse ☏0918/559-5934. On the right-hand side just before you reach Sagada approaching from Bontoc. Converted from a convent and still owned by the Anglican church, this guesthouse has the best-maintained grounds in town. Economy rooms are small and simple, with shared cold showers although hot water buckets can be ordered. Rooms with private bathrooms (**❸**) have much more character, while cottages (**❸**) offer additional space. Amenities include a large restaurant. **②**

The Town

Sagada only began to open up as a destination when it got electricity in the early 1970s, and intellectuals – internal refugees from the Marcos dictatorship – flocked here to write and paint. They didn't produce much of note, perhaps because they spent, it is said, much of their time drinking the local rice wine *tapuy*. European hippies followed and so did the military, who thought the *turistas* were supplying funds for an insurgency. Today the place still has a very relaxed atmosphere, which continues to be enhanced – for some – by the locally grown marijuana, which (while very definitely illegal) is easy to come by and generally tolerated.

There isn't a lot to do in the town itself although there are plenty of **activities** close by. The **Ganduyan Museum** (8am–7pm; P25), next to the *Ganduyan Inn*, is worth visiting for its collection of Kankanay artefacts. Other than that there's plenty of scope for just hanging around and enjoying the tranquillity of the town, while in the evenings you can settle down by a log fire in one of the wooden cafés or restaurants. A curfew means you can't drink after 9pm, but by then almost everyone has gone to bed anyway.

If you have time then it's worth wandering down to the village of **Demang**, reached from a turning on the right just beyond the *George Guest House* and *Pinik-pikan Eatery*. The village is older than Sagada and remains practically untouched by tourism. It's a quiet residential area with several *dap-ay* (stone circles where community matters are resolved).

Filipino food

Philippine cuisine is a delicious and exotic blend of Malay, Spanish, Chinese and American traditions. Dishes range from the very simple, like grilled fish and rice, to more complex stews, paellas and artfully barbecued meats, many using local ingredients such as calamansi, coconuts and mangoes. Seafood is especially rich – expect anything from meaty crabs and milkfish to grouper and stingray on the menu. Most meals are served with San Miguel, the local beer, and are followed by sumptuous tropical fruits and decadent desserts.

Rice paddies ▲

Grilled seafood ▼

The staples

Rice is the key Filipino staple, often accompanied by little more than freshly caught fish with a vinegar sauce. Lapu-lapu (grouper) and *bangus* (milkfish) are commonly served, while squid, crabs and prawns are especially good and cheap in the Philippines. **Chicken** is another key staple – competition for the best fried or barbecued chicken (*lechon manok*) is fierce. Popular dishes on virtually every menu include **sinigang**, a refreshing tamarind-based sour soup, **kare-kare** (a stew made from delicious peanut sauce with vegetables and usually beef) and sizzling **sisig**, fried pig's head and liver, seasoned with *calamansi* and chilli peppers. Filipino Chinese dishes such as pancit (noodles) and *lumpia* (spring rolls) are common. Probably the most popular meat is **pork**, transformed into dishes such as crispy *pata*, *adobo* and *lechon*.

Adobo

It might seem simple – stewed pork and chicken – but it's hard to resist the justly revered national dish of the Philippines. *Adobo* originally meant "sauce" or "seasoning" in Spanish, but its use has morphed throughout Spain's former colonies – the Filipino version is actually indigenous to the islands, dating back to a dish cooked up here long before Magellan's arrival. Philippine *adobo* is pork, chicken or a combination of both slowly stewed in soy sauce, vinegar, crushed garlic, bay leaf and black peppercorns – it's the latter two ingredients that gives true *adobo* its distinctive flavour and bite. No two *adobos* are exactly alike however – you'll discover different versions all over the country.

Shrimp *sinigang* ▼

Roast masters

Evolving from the merging of indigenous and Spanish cooking traditions is **lechon**, roasted pig cooked whole on a spit over a charcoal or wood fire. In the Philippines, *lechon* is usually served with vinegar or special sauce (unique to each *lechon* shop but normally made from fruits or liver pâté, garlic and pepper). The meat is deliciously fragrant and juicy, but the real highlight is the crispy smoked skin, a fatty, sumptuous treat. *Lechon* is usually sold by specialist roasters, and ordered by the kilo. The term has expanded on the islands to cover roast chicken (*lechon manok*), and versions such as *lechon kawali* (small pieces of pork that are boiled then fried) and *lechon paksiw* (leftover *lechon* boiled in vinegar or sauce, then stir-fried with vegetables).

▲ *Lechon*

▼ Filipino pastries

Ices and pies

Filipinos adore sweets and desserts. Sold all over the Philippines, **halo-halo** (from the Tagalog word *halo*, meaning "mix") is a mouthwatering blend of shaved ice, evaporated milk and various toppings such as sweetened beans, fruits and taro, served in a tall glass or bowl – the "special" version usually has taro ice cream on top. A specialty of Laguna Province, **buko pie** is made by layering strips of young coconut and cake mix into a crispy pie crust – the addictive dessert has cult status in the Philippines and an intense rivalry exists between many pie-makers. The most popular traditional Filipino sweet is **polvorón**, a sort of shortbread made with flour, sugar and milk, and often sold in flavours such as cashew nut, chocolate and *pinipig* (crispy rice). Sold on every street corner, **turon** is a crispy deep-fried banana in a spring roll wrapper, while **leche flan** (caramel custard) is a staple on every restaurant menu.

▼ Ice-cream seller

Beef *adobo* ▲

Tropical fruits ▼

Barbecued chicken ▼

A regional menu

▶▶ **Around Manila** Laguna is celebrated for its *buko* pie makers, while Batangas is known for *bulalo* (beef stew), and Lake Taal's tasty *tawilis* (freshwater sardines). Pampanga is the home of Kapampangan cuisine, *kare-kare*, and a native version of *longganisa* (sausage). Sizzling *sisig* was "invented" in Angles City in 1974. See p.122.

▶▶ **Ilocos** (northern Luzon) Ilocano cuisine features plenty of vegetables, freshwater fish and liberal use of *bagoong* (salty fish paste). Local specialties include *dinengdeng*, a *bagoong* and vegetable soup and *pinakbet* (vegetable stew). See p.143.

▶▶ **Cordillera cuisine** (northern Luzon) Eating in the mountains is all about smoked and grilled meats; *pinikpikan* is chicken grilled over an open fire, while *etag* is salted meat that tastes like blue cheese and *pinuneg* is a native blood sausage. See p.168.

▶▶ **Bicol** (southern Luzon) Bicolano cuisine is heavy on the chilli peppers and coconut milk, though Bicol Express (a spicy coconut stew) was actually invented in Manila; local dishes include *pinangat* (blend of taro leaves, chilli, meat and coconut milk). See p.208.

▶▶ **Cebu** Cebu's *lechon* is considered the best in the country; the island is also famed for its mangoes and *otap* (oval-shaped puff pastry). See p.270.

▶▶ **Mindanao** Davao is the tuna and *kinilaw* (ceviche) capital of the Philppines. The island is also the centre of pineapple and durian production, spicy Moro (Muslim) food and some of the best seafood in the Philippines. See p.414.

▶▶ **Iloilo** (Panay) Illongo food is known for its rich, complex flavours; dishes include pancit *molo* (dumplings with chicken, pork and shrimp); *La Paz batchoy* (noodle soup with pork, liver and *chicharrón*); and *binakol* (chicken soup with coconut stock). Celebrated barbecue chain *Mang Inasal* also hails from Iloilo. See p.319.

Trekking

There are dozens of wonderful **treks** around Sagada. One of the most popular day hikes, taking about three hours in all, is to see the **hanging coffins** in **Echo Valley**. It's only a 25-minute walk to the coffins themselves, and it can be done alone with a map (souvenir shops sell sketch maps for around P20), but there are numerous paths and it isn't unknown for people to get lost even on such a short walk. On the whole, it's better to take a guide (P400/group) who can also fill you in on local history and traditions. After the coffins, the route takes you along a short stretch of an underground river at Latang Cave. It ends at the **Bokong Waterfall** on the eastern edge of Sagada, where you can swim. The waterfall can also be reached from the town without a guide in about half an hour, although it's easy to miss the steps on the left about 500m beyond Sagada Weaving. Other hikes on offer by the tourist office and Sagada Genuine Guides (see p.175) include one to the **Bomod-ok Waterfall**, Fidelisan rice terraces and villages north of Sagada (P600); a dawn trip to a scenic area of rice terraces known as **Kiltepan** (P450); and a trek on **Mount Ampacao** (P600).

Caving

Caving in Sagada's deep network of limestone channels and caverns is an exhilarating but potentially risky activity. Many of the caves are slippery and have ravines inside that plunge into the bowels of the earth. A small number of tourists have been killed in these caves, so if you want to explore them you must get a reliable accredited guide.

The most commonly visited cave is **Sumaging** (P500 per four visitors, plus P350 for transport), also known as Big Cave, a 45-minute walk south of Sagada. The chambers and rock formations inside are eerie and immense, and have all been named after the things they resemble – the Cauliflower, the King's Curtain, the Rice Granary and a few which are more risqué. Guides equipped with lanterns will take you on a descent through a series of tunnels you'll only be able to get through by crawling, ending in a pool of clear and cold water where you can swim. Ideally you should wear trekking sandals, but otherwise shoes can be left at an appropriate point and the final sections negotiated barefoot.

Like many caves in the area, Sumaging was once a burial cave, although there are no coffins or human remains there now. However, the standard itinerary also includes a visit to the entrance of **Lumiang Burial Cave**, a short walk south of Sagada and then down a steep trail into the valley. Around a hundred old coffins are stacked in the entrance. Don't point at any of them as it's considered the worst kind of bad luck; lizards, on the other hand, are portents of good luck and their images have been carved onto some of the coffins.

Lumiang is also the starting point for the **Cave Connection** trip (P800 for one or two people, plus P400 for each additional person; transport is P400), which heads through passages linking it to Sumaging. It's a three- to four-hour trip and not for the faint-hearted; if you are not experienced then try Sumaging first and see how you fare. At points you'll need to descend a few feet vertically without ropes, jamming your limbs against the rock walls and inching down.

Rafting

Set up by American expat Steve Rogers, Raft Sagada (℡0919/698-8361) is an outfit that trains locals to work as rafting guides. Trips are possible on the Chico River from July until early January, although at the beginning of the season it may only be possible to raft the upper sections. October and November see the most pleasant weather, but the highest water is in December and early January making it possible to go further downstream. You normally spend 1 hour 30 minutes to

The Igorots

The tribes of the Cordillera – often collectively known as the **Igorots** ("mountaineers") – resisted assimilation into the **Spanish Empire** for three centuries. Although they brought some material improvements, such as to the local diet, the colonizers forced the poor to work to pay off debts, burned houses, cut down crops and introduced smallpox.

The saddest long-term result of the attempts to subjugate the Igorots was subtler – the creation of a distinction between highland and lowland Filipinos. The peoples of the Cordillera became minorities in their own country, still struggling today for representation and recognition of a lifestyle that the Spanish tried to discredit as unChristian and depraved. The word Igorot was regarded as derogatory in some quarters, although in the twentieth century there were moves to "reclaim" the term and it is still commonly used.

Though some Igorots did convert to Christianity, many are still at least partly animists and pray to a hierarchy of **anitos**. These include deities that possess shamans and speak to them during seances, spirits that inhabit sacred groves or forests, personified forces of nature and generally any supernatural apparition. Offerings are made to benevolent *anitos* for fertility, good health, prosperity, fair weather and success in business (or, in the olden days, tribal war). Evil *anitos* are propitiated to avoid illness, crop failure, storms, accidents and death. Omens are also carefully observed: a particular bird seen upon leaving the house might herald sickness, for example, requiring that appropriate ceremonies are conducted to forestall its portent. If the bird returns, the house may be abandoned.

2 hours in the water and the price is P4500 per person for four or fewer, P3000 if there are five or more. If there are just two of you then they might be able to offer a bare-bones trip as a training exercise for their team, at P3500 per person. Alternatively, they will try to add you onto a larger group.

Eating and drinking

The choice of **food** in Sagada is among the best in the country, partly because fresh produce is available on the doorstep.

Kimchi Opposite the *Igorot Inn*, this restaurant has two buildings – one a concrete-floored hut and one a more atmospheric log cabin next door to *Persimoon*. The menu has Korean dishes alongside its standard Filipino selection.

Lemon Pie House On the road towards Sumaging Cave, before the *Village Bistro*. The famous lemon meringue pie is P20 a slice or P150 for the whole thing, and is worth every peso; there are also other seasonal fruit pies if that doesn't tempt you. Take away or sit in at low tables; you're supposed to reserve takeaway orders in advance. Daily 6am–8pm.

Log Cabin Up the hill past the *Sagada Guesthouse*, the *Log Cabin* does some of the best food in town. On Saturday evenings there's a popular buffet (P250) prepared by an expatriate French chef, with ingredients always bought fresh from the market that morning. Reserve in the morning if you plan to dine in the evening; for the buffet you should reserve a couple of days in advance. Sun–Fri 6–10pm, Sat 7–10pm.

Masferré Café and Restaurant The food here is good, but the main reason to visit is for the wonderful set of photographs of Sagada taken by Eduardo Masferré in the mid-twentieth century. Daily 6.30am–9pm.

Persimoon Café and Bamboo Grill Popular for a drink in the evening, particularly with foreign visitors, and also serving a range of Filipino dishes.

Pinikpikan Eatery If you want to try *pinikpikan* – also known as "killing me softly" as it involves beating a chicken with a stick before killing it, so that the meat is tender – then it may as well be here at just P80 including rice. That is if you can bear seeing all the soon-to-be-eaten chickens in the coop out front.

Yoghurt House On the main street past the town hall heading west, this wood cabin is renowned for its breakfast of pancakes and home-made yoghurt. Its main courses at lunch and dinner are pretty good too: try the roasted aubergine with basil and pasta.

Shopping

The tiny **Cosmic Tea**, located close to *Kimchi* and *Persimoon,* is run by owner Madhu who sells three different herbal tea blends and a selection of handmade jewellery, paints T-shirts and offers both yoga and meditation lessons. The former costs P500 for 90 minutes, the latter is free for 15 minutes but only if she thinks you're serious about learning. Drop in and chill out, or call her on ☎0919/604-9467 to arrange a lesson at your hotel.

At **Sagada Weaving**, a short walk east of the centre, you can buy fabrics and clothes produced using traditional tribal designs. Around a dozen people work at sewing machines in the shop itself, while next door you can see the weaving being done on wooden looms. It's a good place to pick up a gift such as a *bahag* (loincloth), an exquisitely hand-loomed piece of long cloth wrapped around a man's middle but increasingly bought by tourists as a throw or table runner.

Around 1.5km north of the centre, a fifteen-minute walk or P10 jeepney ride in the direction of Besao, **Sagada Pottery** specializes in high-quality stoneware. One of the potters will demonstrate their craft for P100, including a chance to have a go yourself. Call ahead to Siegrid Anne Bangyay (☎0919/671-9875) out of season; she also organizes local tours.

Kalinga province

The mountains, rice fields and villages in the province of **Kalinga** rarely see visitors, never mind foreign tourists. This is real frontier travel, with massive potential for hiking and climbing. Outside of the towns of Tinglayen and Tabuk the only accommodation is in simple lodges or local homes, the only shops are roadside stores, and electricity is a rarity so make sure you bring a good torch.

The Kalinga, once fierce **headhunters**, are still called the Peacocks of the North because of their indomitable, fiery spirit and their refusal to be colonized. Most Kalinga communities live on levelled parts of steep mountain slopes, where a small shrine called a *bodayan* guards the entrance to the village.

In the dry season Tinglayen and Tabuk can both be reached by jeepney heading north from Bontoc, although services in this area are anything but regular and it's a bumpy road, so the trip can take many hours. In the rainy season (particularly from July–Oct) it may be impossible to travel between Tinglayen and Tabuk due to the road conditions, in which case Tinglayen is best approached from Bontoc while Tabuk is reached via Tuguegarao.

Tinglayan

The town of **TINGLAYAN**, about halfway between Bontoc and Tabuk, is a good place to base yourself if you want to explore Kalinga. From here you can strike out on mountain trails originally carved by the Spanish when they tried, and failed, to bring the Kalinga people into the Catholic fold. There are trails through tribal villages and rice terraces at Lubo and Mangali, to the crater of the extinct volcano Mount Sukuok, and to a number of mountain lakes including Bonnong and Padcharao. Rice is planted twice a year around Tinglayen, and the fields are at their greenest from March to April and September to October.

Wherever you go hiking you'll need a **guide**. Staff in the municipal building will usually refer you to either Victor Baculi (barangay captain of nearby Luplupa) or Francis Pa-in (see p.173). Guide rates are not fixed and could be anything from P500 to P1000 per day; a guide is essential not only to avoid getting lost but also to ensure that you respect local sensibilities. Occasionally there are disputes – over water rights, for instance – that result in violence, and a guide will stop you stumbling into any areas where tensions might be high. Law and order in the province still relies very much on tribal pacts (*bodong*) brokered by elders. If you're interested in tattoos then ask your guide about visiting a tattoo artist who still uses traditional materials and designs; it may even be possible to have a piece done yourself (from P500 for a small design).

Practicalities

A couple of jeepneys and buses pass through each day in each direction on the Bontoc–Tabuk route (although see p.161 for advice on the rainy season). There are no banks in Tinglayen, and no internet access. Accommodation is also limited. The slightly grubby bedrooms at *Sleeping Beauty* (**①**) are downstairs from a decent enough restaurant, but a better bet is to cross the suspension bridge to Luplupa and stay in the *Riverside Inn* (**②**). You'll probably need to ask for directions as you pass through the village. Run by barangay captain (and tourist guide) Victor Baculi, it's a clean and simple place where bedding is provided but you need to bring your own towel.

There is generally no formal accommodation outside of the town, but there are homestays (donate around P200–300/day for food and lodging).

Lubuagan

They don't see many tourists in **LUBUAGAN**, an hour north of Tinglayen on the road to Tabuk, but it makes for a worthwhile stop. The town itself has a makeshift air, with grey concrete buildings and livestock in the street, but it's beautifully located amid rice terraces. Remarkably it was the capital of the free Philippines for 35 days in 1900, when the revolutionary President Aguinaldo established his headquarters in the town before being forced to flee the US army.

The barangay of Mabilong is known for its **textiles** and you can arrange to visit one of the women who weave at home, sitting on the floor using rudimentary hand looms. Ask at the town hall to arrange a visit, or for advice about hiking routes and guides. You might also ask about the cultural village, around thirty minutes from the town, where traditional dance performances occasionally take place.

Practicalities

The town hall may be able to arrange a homestay; otherwise the only official **accommodation** in town is the *Pines* (no phone; **①**), with five non-air-conditioned rooms and cold-water bathrooms. There's a restaurant downstairs, where there's no menu but they'll cook what is available. This will usually include the local red rice. While in town don't miss *ilangila*, a tasty mix of glutinous rice and coconut.

There are a handful of buses and jeepneys each morning to Lubuagan from either Tinglayen (1hr; P100) or Tabuk (3hr; P80). The last vehicles out of Lubuagan leave at noon (for Tinglayen) or 2pm (for Tabuk). There are also buses running between Lubuagen and Bontoc (3–4hr; P180).

Tabuk

The provincial capital **TABUK**, 50km north of Tinglayan, is the place to sign up for whitewater **rafting trips** with Chico River Quest (℡0920/205-2680, ⓦwww.chicoriverquest.com). The best run for beginners starts at the confluence of the Pasil and Chico rivers, and lasts for about two hours; it costs $50 per head for a minimum of five people, including transport and food. More experienced participants should ask about a longer run which starts upriver in Tinglayen. The company has seven rafts and uses one or two guides per raft, running trips from July until around Christmas.

While in Tabuk, take the time to visit **Ryan's Farm** (P50; ☎0916/755-7078) owned by Corazon and Jeremy Ryan. They have a prawn hatchery and fish ponds, and experiment with vermiculture (worm composting) and organic agriculture, but most of all it's just pleasant to enjoy their conversation – possibly over a glass of home-made *bugnay* (local berry) wine. They can also prepare a meal and possibly even put you up for the night if you call in advance. A tricycle to the farm will cost around P50–70.

Practicalities

The **accommodation** options are surprisingly good for such a remote place; all three listed here have swimming pools. *Grand Zion Garden Resort* (☎0916/373-4366; ❹) is the most stylish place in town, resembling an alpine lodge with pleasant gardens at the back. *The Davidson Hotel* (☎0926/412-6018; ❸) also has comfortable rooms and a popular restaurant; no alcohol is served. Finally, at *Golden Berries Hotel* (☎0915/844-4119, ⓦgoldenberrieshotel.com; ❸), the owner roasts and grinds locally grown coffee on the premises.

Banaue and around

It's a rugged but spectacular trip from Bontoc to **BANAUE** in Ifugao province, along a winding road that leads up into the misty Cordillera and across a mountaintop pass. It may only be 300km north of Manila, but Banaue might as well be a world away, 1300m above sea level and far removed in spirit and topography from the beaches and palm trees of the south. This is the heart of **rice terrace** country: the terraces in Banaue itself are some of the most impressive and well known, although there are hundreds of others in valleys and gorges throughout the area, most of which can be reached on foot. At nearby **Batad** there is rustic accommodation so you can stay overnight and hike back the next morning.

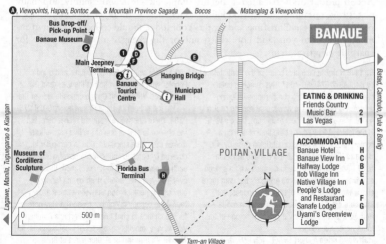

NORTHERN LUZON | Banaue and around

Banaue's stairways to heaven

The **rice terraces** around Banaue are one of the great icons of the Philippines, hewn from the land 2000 years ago by Ifugao tribespeople using primitive tools, an achievement in engineering terms that ranks alongside the building of the pyramids. Called the "Stairway to Heaven" by the Ifugaos, the terraces would stretch 20,000km if laid out end to end. Not only are they an awesome sight, but they are also an object lesson in **sustainability**.

The terraces are on the UNESCO World Heritage list, and they will not last forever if they are not protected. They have always been subject to constant deterioration, due to weather erosion, imperfect irrigation systems and the actions of earthworms. Today, however, there's a shortage of young people to help carry out repairs – rice farming has little allure for many of them; they are understandably tired of the subsistence livelihood their parents eked from the land and are either working in tourism or packing their bags for Manila. Alongside this, another recent pressure is the conversion of the rice terraces into vegetable terraces or into residential and commercial areas.

Arrival and information

Other than Florida Bus services which stop a short walk or jeepney ride south of the town centre, all long-distance buses terminate close to the Banaue Museum. From here, most accommodation is within walking distance. As well as the **tourist office** (⊕074/386-4052 or 0929/270-5695) in the town hall, there is an unofficial **Banaue Tourist Information Centre** (daily 7am–7pm; ⊕074/386-4010) on the main square. You can hire an accredited guide (P1200/day) or porter (P700/day) at either of them. Motorcycle hire is P1000 per day. There are no banks in Banaue, but some hotels **change money**. It's better, though, to bring enough pesos. If you get really stuck, there's a branch of PNB with an ATM in the provincial capital Lagawe – but that's 25km away. The **post office** is near the Florida Bus drop-off point, and there are several **internet cafés** in town.

Accommodation

Accommodation in Banaue is generally simple but clean and friendly, and many places have restaurants attached. Finding somewhere without a reservation is not a problem, except at Christmas and Easter. Your lodge should collect a P20 environmental fee from you, and note that some of the cheaper places have a fee for charging electrical items.

Banaue Hotel Ten minutes south of the marketplace by jeepney ⊕074/386-4087. This rambling hotel has pleasant grounds, big comfy rooms including deluxes (❼) with terrace views, a swimming pool, a souvenir shop and a decent restaurant; there's wi-fi in the lobby at P150/day. At the time of writing a hostel building was being constructed close by. ❺

Banaue View Inn Next to the Banaue Museum ⊕074/386-4078. Big, clean doubles with a shared or private bathroom. Rooms are boxy but with more character than in some of the other lodges, and there are great views from the shared veranda – or from your private balcony if you choose one of the more expensive rooms. ❷

Halfway Lodge A short walk beyond *Uyami's Greenview* ⊕074/386-4082. A good budget bet with simple singles (P300), doubles and quads. Popular with Filipino groups at the weekend. ❶

Ilob Village Inn On the opposite side of the valley from *Uyami's Greenview* ⊕0929/276-0304. There are twelve standard rooms here, but the chance to stay in one of the five native huts makes this place stand out. One in particular is covered by carabao skulls, a symbol of wealth as each was slaughtered at a celebration; this hut is over 100 years old and is used by the family although in peak season they sometimes allow tourists to occupy it. Another reason to stay here is for the chance to chat to owner Perfecta Dulnuan, who is very knowledgeable about local customs. ❷

Native Village Inn Uhaj, 9km west of Banaue on the road to Hapao ⊕0916/405-6743,

ⓦwww.nativevillage-inn.com. The rice terrace views here are stunning, and the accommodation is in comfortable if rudimentary native huts. The food is another highlight, including fresh bread baked on the premises. A tricycle to the inn from Banaue costs P150 and takes 30 minutes; between 4–6pm there are jeepneys to Hapao (P25) which can drop you just outside. ❹

People's Lodge and Restaurant Right beside the main square Ⓣ📞074/386-4014. Cheaper rooms share showers and toilets, while more expensive rooms are big with private hot showers. Some of these more expensive rooms also have excellent views across the valley. There's a small internet café in the building, close to the entrance. ❷

🏃 **Sanafe Lodge** Just beyond the public market in the direction of the town hall Ⓣ📞074/386-4085, ⓦsanafelodge.com. Run by the

cheerful and helpful owner Susan Paredes, this is a homey and atmospheric wooden lodge. All the rooms are spacious and comfortable, with hot water in the bathrooms; if you take one of the new deluxe rooms (❹) at the back you'll have marvellous rice terrace views. The place also has one of Banaue's better restaurants, serving European and Filipino food. There's no wi-fi but there is a PC with internet. ❷

Uyami's Greenview Lodge Just north of the main square Ⓣ📞074/386-4021. Twins, doubles and family rooms, some with private showers; the rooms with views (❹) are much more expensive. Together with a comfortable restaurant boasting good views and wi-fi, this place is understandably popular with foreigners despite quirks such as a fee for hot water if you're in one of the cheaper rooms. ❷

The Town

Banaue is a small and mostly unimpressive town centred on a marketplace, with a few guesthouses, some souvenir shops and a couple of good museums. The fascinating **Museum of Cordillera Sculpture** (daily 8am–5pm; P100; Ⓣ📞0908/9140-6122, ⓦcordilleranmuseum.weebly.com) displays the collection of American expat George Schenk. Formerly a renowned horticulturalist, Schenk settled in the Philippines and ran an antiques store; concerned that so many Ifugao cultural objects were ending up in private collections overseas he founded this fascinating museum.

The small **Banaue Museum** (daily 8am–5pm; P50) has old tribal tools, costumes and a collection of photographs of Banaue and its people at the beginning of the twentieth century. It was assembled by American anthropologist Henry Otley Beyer, the grandfather of the current owner. If the museum is closed then ask at the neighbouring *Banaue View Inn* for the key.

Two kilometres north along the road from the marketplace is a series of five **lookout points** for the rice terraces, where Ifugao elders in traditional costume hang out and ask for a small fee if you want to take their photograph. The third lookout point has the view depicted on the P1000 banknote, while the final one has the best view. A tricycle up will cost P180.

Moving on from Banaue

The easiest way to reach **Manila** is by night bus (9hr; P400–450) operated by Ohayami (Ⓣ📞0917/506-0817), Auto Bus (Ⓣ📞0999/712-4633) and Florida Lines (Ⓣ📞074/386-4042); make sure you book in advance. During the day, take a jeepney to Solano in Nueva Vizcaya province (3hr; P50) and then take a Baliwag bus (7hr; P346).

Jeepneys run to **Bontoc** (3hr; P90) and **Sagada** (4hr; P100) each morning; there are also buses to Bontoc run by Von Von. Direct buses to **Baguio** (8–9hr) are operated by Jack Dulnuan (Ⓣ📞0908/291-2126; P330), Ohayami (P460) and KMS Lines (P415), or you can take a jeepney to Bambang then a van (4hr; P200) to Baguio. It's slow going however you do it, though, and if you plan to visit Bontoc and Sagada then it makes sense to go to them first and then continue on to Baguio. For **Vigan**, take a bus bound for Baguio and change in Rosario (La Union province).

Eating, drinking and nightlife

Most of the best food is served in lodges: *People's Lodge and Restaurant*, *Uyami's Greenview Lodge* and *Sanafe Lodge* have some good dishes, while *Banaue Hotel* is the most upmarket choice.

Friends Country Music Bar The best of the little nightlife in Banaue, where local men listen to live country music, drink Red Horse beer and occasionally get into a minor fracas. The music stops at 9pm and it closes an hour later due to a curfew.

Las Vegas Opposite the row of lodges just north of the main square. The cheap Filipino dishes here are popular with backpackers and groups of local tourists. It's one of the few stand-alone restaurants in Banaue, although the owners do have a lodge of the same name a little outside the centre.

Batad

The trek to the remote little village of **BATAD** has become something of a pilgrimage for visitors looking for rural isolation and unforgettable rice terrace scenery. Although you could walk from Banaue, most people cut out the first 12km by taking a jeepney (1hr; P50) from the market to Batad Junction. From there it is a strenuous 3km walk northwards up a steep, marked trail to the saddle then 45 minutes downhill to Batad. If you really want to shorten the hike, you can arrange a private jeepney (P2500 return including waiting) all the way up to the saddle.

Batad nestles in a natural amphitheatre, close to the glorious **Tappia Waterfall**, which is 21m high and has a deep, bracing pool for swimming. There are signs that life in Batad is slowly beginning to change – the village now has electricity and a dozen simple **guesthouses** have sprung up – but it remains peaceful. Each guesthouse offers basic rooms with shared bathrooms and charges around P150–200 per head; hot water is available in buckets if not in the showers. For views try the *Hillside Inn* or *Rita's Mount View Inn*. One interesting project is the *Batad Kadangyan Lodges*, two old native huts maintained by the local community.

There are several good hikes around this area (including to Cambulo and Pula, see below); ask around at the lodges for a guide. One way back to Banaue is by backtracking south for about two and a half hours to the tiny village of **Banga-an**, no more than a few dozen Ifugao homes perched between rice terraces close to the National Highway. A local woman called Virginia Hangdaan has opened one of the huts as the *Banga-an Village Inn* (℡0907/789-7853; ❶), also providing food on request. There is also a more established lodge, the *Banga-an Family Inn* (℡093/9567-7332; ❶), overlooking the village from the highway. It's a good idea to book ahead if you're relying on one of these places after a hike.

Cambulo and Pula

From Batad you can trek north through fields and terraces to the villages of **CAMBULO** and **PULA**. There are some unforgettable sights along this route, including waterfalls, steep gorges and a hanging bridge near Cambulo that requires a bit of nerve to cross. The journey from Batad to Cambulo takes about two hours and from Cambulo to Pula it's another hour. Either camp or spend the night at one of the small **inns** or homestays – such as the *Pula Village Inn* – in Pula for around P150–200 per person. The owners should be able to brew you strong coffee and rustle up some tinned food or vegetables. The path from Pula back to Banaue will bring you out at Awan-Igid, near the Banaue rice terraces viewpoints, from where you can walk a final 8km or hop on a jeepney back to your hotel.

Pula is also the start of a hike up **Mount Amuyao** (2702m), a full day's walk and not something to be attempted without a guide and plenty of stamina. You'll need to sleep at the top and return next day, or you can continue on to Barlig (see p.174) and eventually Bontoc.

Hungduan and Hapao

Less than 10km from Banaue as the crow flies but reached by a protracted looped road, the small town of **HUNGDUAN** is a two-hour jeepney journey away (P55). The trip is well worth it, though, as it's the location of the Bacung spider web terraces, at their best in April and May. Ask about hiking guides (P700/day) and accommodation at the town hall. The rice terraces in the barangay of **HAPAO**, around 30 minute back towards Banaue, are also spectacular.

Mayoyao

The site of another set of beautiful rice terraces, **MAYOYAO** is rarely visited due to its remote location – it's three hours by bus from Banaue, or five hours from Santiago City (P140) if you're coming from Manila. The terraces are punctuated by distinctive pyramid-roofed local houses, and by stone burial mounds called Apfo'or. They are at their greenest from April to May and October to November. There is a simple **hostel** (no phone; ➊) in the town. If you're around at the right time of year then it's worth contacting Pochon Youth Group (☎0906/530-8242, ✉josh21010@gmail.com), a small community project that offers visitors the chance to get involved in rice planting twice a year (Jan–Feb & June–July).

Kiangan and around

On September 2 1945, General Yamashita of the Japanese Imperial Army surrendered to US and Filipino troops in the town of **KIANGAN**, 10km from the provincial capital Lagawe (which is itself 24km south of Banaue). The surrender is commemorated with a large shrine although the actual site of the surrender (marked with a plaque) is now occupied by the library of the nearby Kiangan Elementary School. The hill on the right as you look out from the front of the shrine is where the Japanese holed up for their last stand; it is known as the Million Dollar Hill, named for the supposed cost of the artillery with which the US shelled it. Across from the shrine is the **Ifugao Museum** (Mon–Fri 8am–5pm; P20), which displays everyday local artefacts and religious objects.

The **rice terraces** around Kiangan are at their best in April and May. You can take a tricycle to the terraces at either **Nagacadan** (20min; P200 return with waiting) or **Julungan** ("Hul-ungan"; 30min; P600). Ask at Kiangan tourist office if you need a guide.

An hour from Kiangan by jeepney, the Pula barangay of Asipulo town is the stopping-off point for visits to the **Julia Campbell Agroforest Memorial Park** (☎0905/732-2942, ⓦwww.bantaicivetcoffee.com or juliacampbellpark .wordpress.com). The park grows organic coffee made from beans that have been eaten and excreted by civets, a product considered particularly flavourful and sold at a premium price. There are also walking trails and some very basic accommodation in huts (➊) without running water or electricity, and it's possible to stay for free if you agree to work as a volunteer in the park. Either contact them direct or make arrangements through Worldwide Opportunities on Organic Farms (ⓦwww.wwoof.com.ph).

Practicalities

Kiangan is twenty-five minutes from Lagawe by jeepney (P15), and frequent jeepneys connect Lagawe to Banaue (1hr; P30). There are also buses from Lagawe to Manila (P382). The provincial **tourist office** (Mon–Fri 8am–5pm) – covering

Banaue as well as Kiangan – is in the barangay of Baguinge at the Kiangan-Lagawe junction, a few minutes by tricycle from the town itself. The best **guesthouse** in the Kiangan area is *Ibulao, Ibulao* (☏0908/874-1722, ✉totokalug@yahoo.com .ph; ❹), close to the tourist office on the site of a World War II lookout post. The family room (❻) is particularly impressive, decorated with Ifugao wood carvings and built around exposed rocks. Other rooms are more conventional, including a dorm for P500 per head, but the whole place is homely and cosy; owner Roberto Kalungan also arranges caving and rafting trips. Bookings are essential as no walk-in guests are accepted. If you're looking for something cheaper then the *Kiangan Youth Hostel* (☏0910/324-3296; ❶) close to the shrine and museum in town has three simple double rooms and single-sex dorms at P100 per person.

Batanes

Almost 100km off the northern coast of Luzon, **BATANES** is the smallest, most isolated province in the country. This is a memorable place with otherworldly scenery, where doors are rarely locked and welcomes are warm even by Filipino standards. The people are different, the language is different, even the weather is different. The coolest months (Dec–Feb) can get chilly with temperatures as low as 10°C, while the hottest months (April–June) are searing. For visitors, the islands are at their best from February to May.

Batanes can be idyllic, but it would be wrong to portray it as a tropical utopia as the realities of life this far away from the rest of the world can sometimes be harsh. Petrol and provisions are brought in by ship, which means they cost more, and when typhoons roar in from the east (July–Sept) it may be impossible for ships or aircraft to reach the islands. Boredom can set in and locals joke that during the typhoon season the cargo ship brings 50,000 sacks of rice but 60,000 crates of gin.

Only three of the ten islands in the Batanes group are inhabited: **Batan** – the location of the capital **Basco** – **Sabtang** and **Itbayat**. The native inhabitants of Batanes, the **Ivatan**, trace their roots to prehistoric Formosan immigrants and latter-day Spanish conquistadors. Most still make a living from the cultivation of yams and garlic or the raising of goats and cows; if you visit a village during the daytime, be prepared to find that almost everyone is out in the fields. Some women still wear rain capes called *vakul*, made from the stripped leaves of the *voyavoy* vine. The main dialect, Ivatan, includes some pidgin Spanish: "thank you" is *dios mamajes*

Getting to Batanes

The quickest way to get to Batanes from Manila is on the SEAIR thrice-weekly **flight** from Manila to Basco. Book well in advance. Unfortunately, the flights are regularly cancelled at short notice so there's a good chance that you won't depart on the day for which you have a ticket; you should allow for at least three or four days either side, or more if bad weather is likely. There's also a chance that your check-in luggage will not be taken on your flight but instead brought along at a later date. It's a measure of the appeal of Batanes that it genuinely is worth the hassle.

An alternative – albeit one which also suffers cancellations due to poor weather – is to take a small twin-engine aircraft from Tuguegarao to Basco. Scheduled flights are usually operated by Batanes Airlines (☏0915/940-4823 or 0939/198-6918), but at the time of writing they had been suspended. It was unclear when they would resume.

and "goodbye" is *dios mavidin* (if you are the person leaving) or *dios machivan* (if you are staying behind).

Batan Island

The island of **Batan** is the biggest in the group and site of the tiny capital, **BASCO**. The town boasts a spectacular location right on the lower slopes of Mount Iraya, a volcano that hasn't erupted since the fifteenth century but is still officially active. You can walk around the town in half an hour, and there are no specific attractions, but it's a pleasant and friendly place to spend time.

Arrival and information

There is a tiny airport within walking distance of Bascol; a tricycle will take you for just a few pesos. The town is built around a rectangular plaza with the municipal buildings and church on the north side and the sea to the south. Opposite the church is a small **police station**. At the time of writing there was no full-time tourist office, but the very helpful part-time official – Dan Esdicul (℡0918/206-8345) – could be reached through the governor's office (Ⓦwww.purocastillejos.com)

Siayan, Mabudis, ▲ North & Y'ami Islands

BATANES

Mt Santa Rosa ▲ (277m)

Chinapoliran Landing

Mayan

Torongan Hill

Raile ✈ ▲ Mt Riposed (229m)

Itbayat Island

Dinem Island

SOUTH CHINA SEA

N

Batan Island ▲ Mt Iraya (1099m)

Basco

Radar Tukon

Mahatao

Mt Matarem ▲ (459m)

Diura
Rakuh-a-Payaman (Marlboro Country)

San Vicente

Nakabuang Beach

Imnaibu

Ivana

Itbud

Dequey Island

Centro

Uyugan

Songsong

Nakanmuan

Ibujos Island

Savidug

Sumnaga

Sabtang Island

Chavayan

0   5 km

in the Provincial Capitol building on the main plaza. He can arrange guides for P700 per day. On arrival you may spot purple-shirted employees of the Batanes Cultural Travel Agency (℡02/546-1197, Ⓦbatanestravel.com). They have an office on Castillejos Street, and are the official ticket agents for SEAIR as well as offering tours and bicycle hire. Batanes Airlines has an office at the airport. If you'd like to explore the reefs around Batan, contact Chico at Dive Batanes (℡0929/131-2051, Ⓦwww.divebatanes.com).

Make sure you take **pesos** to Batanes because credit cards are not accepted, other than at *Fundacion Pacita*. You should be able to change US dollars at one of the banks in town, but not at a favourable rate, and there are no ATMs.

Public transport

If you are in a group then the easiest way to get a quick overall picture of the beauty of Batan is to hire a **jeepney** with driver for the day (P2500) through your accommodation. It's also possible to travel in public jeepneys which connect towns along the coastal road, but you'll have to be prepared to wait and probably to do some **walking** and **hitching**. Alternatively hire a bicycle or scooter (try your lodging or the Petron petrol station for the latter) – the roads are very quiet, the only real issue is the blind bends so take it easy.

Accommodation

The potential for trekking and **camping** on Batan is enticing. There are no campsites, but as long as you respect the landscape no one minds if you pitch a tent for the night near a beach. Whatever you do, take food and water, because there are few places to get provisions. All the accommodation listed below is in or around Basco.

Batanes Resort 2km south of Basco ☎0908/548-2907. In a fantastic location, this resort is made up of six tidy little stone duplex cottages sitting on a breezy hillside, with steps leading down to a marvellous black sand cove. The restaurant has good food and a pleasant terrace while the cottages have hot showers; ask for one with a sea view. ❸

Brandon's ☎0929/541-7786. Owned by the provincial governor, this lodge was being renovated at the time of research. There are two buildings, with one on top of a small hill boasting great views. ❸

Fundacion Pacita Chanarian-Tukon barangay ☎0927/290-2404, ⓦwww.fundacionpacita.ph. The home of artist Pacita Abad until her death in 2004, this beautiful stone building has been turned into an exceptional hotel. It isn't cheap, and there's a minimum stay of two nights, but a portion of the proceeds go to educating local artists. The common areas exhibit Abad's art, while the rooms have been impeccably designed and some have magnificent views. The restaurant serves traditional Ivatan cuisine. ❾

Ivatan Lodge ☎0908/178-2809. Faded yellow building on the seafront side of the National Rd, with some of the cheapest accommodation in town. On the ground floor are various small offices and storerooms, while on the first floor are seven dusty, dilapidated rooms with shared facilities. ❶

Pension Ivatan ☎0999/562-4395, ⓦpensionivatan.net. You'll see the sign as you leave the airport, but that's just the restaurant – the rooms are actually a short walk into town in an unstaffed building. So for food, or just to check in, you need to go to the airport location. The comfortable rooms are good value and include breakfast. ❸

🏃 **Shanedel's Inn & Café** Corner of National Rd & Abad St ☎0920/447-0737, ⓦwww.shanedels.com. This is a congenial little guesthouse where the non-a/c rooms are the best budget accommodation in Basco, and the a/c rooms are good too. Grab yourself a cold beer in the terrace restaurant at the rear and watch the sun set over Basco harbour, while helpful owner Dely and her staff rustle you up a dinner of local dishes such as grilled flying fish. There's reasonably reliable wi-fi for a small daily charge. ❷

The island

Most organized tours start by heading south from Basco along the coastal road to the *Batanes Resort* (see above), before turning left up a narrow road to an abandoned weather station called **Radar Tukon**. This can also be done on foot as a day hike: it's about an hour from Basco and from here the whole island is spread at your feet. Beyond the weather station is *Fundacion Pacita* (see above), and there are also some tunnels nearby created by the Japanese army during World War II.

After heading back to the coastal road you can return to Basco, or continue south through the pretty old Spanish village of **Mahatao** and on to **Ivana** ("Ih-va-na") with its eye-catching yellow church. Just opposite the church is the pier for ferries to Sabtang Island.

Following the coastal road round the southern end of the island, you'll find that if anything the east coast is even more breathtaking than the west. The road takes you to the village of **Uyugan** before turning north to **Song Song**, where you can see the remains of stone houses that were washed away by a tidal wave. After Itbud there is a turning inland and uphill taking you through **Rakuh-a-Payaman** (known to tourists as "Marlboro Country"), elevated pastures populated by Ivatan bulls and horses, grazing against the backdrop of Mount Iraya and the Pacific Ocean. Jeepney tours typically stop here for lunch.

After passing through the pastures you can either return to Mahatao (and from there to Basco) or continue to Diura, where there are signs for a fishing village – they lead to a small shop that sells an entrance ticket for a few local attractions.

These include the Spring of Youth feeding into a concrete pool, a pleasant spot in hot weather. Another possibility is the Crystal Cave, although many of the crystals have been damaged or removed so it isn't really worth the 30-minute walk. There's no route for vehicles up the coast from Diura so unless you're hiking you'll need to head back to Basco via Mahatao.

Eating and drinking

Several of the lodges in Basco have **restaurants** or can make food to order, while elsewhere on the island you'll be reliant on the occasional small canteen so it's best to travel with at least a snack and some water.

Hiro's Café Abad St, Basco. This place serves Filipino and Ivatan dishes as well as pancakes for breakfast. Specialities include *venes*, salty dried taro leaves with meat. 6am–midnight.

Honesty Café Ivana, close to the pier. This café is renowned for being unstaffed – you help yourself and leave money in a box. There's instant coffee, cup noodles and little else other than souvenir T-shirts. Daily 6am–6pm.

Kanan du Ivatan Lizardo St, Basco. A hut serving beer and rice wine, along with a few snacks and simple dishes. Daily 9am–11pm.

North Spirit Café On the plaza close to the harbour. The only real bar in town at the time of writing, with a cocktail list and videoke.

Sabtang Island

Don't miss the opportunity to spend at least a day exploring **Sabtang**, a peaceful island dotted with Ivatan stone villages where life seems to have altered little in a hundred years. Ferries arrive in the port on the island's northeast coast, in an area known as **Centro** where there's a Spanish church, a school and a few houses.

You can do a circuit of the island on foot, but with a vehicle it's necessary to double back and visit the eastern and western parts of the island separately. You could start by heading south from the port to Chavayan, about 10km away. On the way there are the remains of a fortress (*idjang*), although you're unlikely to find them without a guide. It's possible to head up there for views of the area and a motorbike can go most of the way to the base. It's pretty overgrown and the path is steep in places, so take it slowly. Chavayan itself has some of the island's best-preserved traditional homes and a small chapel, as well as the Sabtang Weavers' Association.

From here you can take a trail to **Sumnaga** if you are on foot. The walk takes about two hours to **Nakanmuan**, from where you may be able to hire a boat (around P600) to visit Ivuhos Island – it's inhabited only by grazing cows. From Nakanmuan it's another hour to Centro via **Nakabuang Beach** (or less along an inland path). If you're on a scooter or in a jeepney, you must return to the port and then continue along the coastal road to Nakabuang.

Practicalities

Sabtang lies southwest of Batan, a one-hour journey by **ferry** (P50) from the pier at Ivana. Ferries usually leave at 7am but inconveniently the earliest jeepneys to Ivana only depart from Basco around 7–8am, so the best option is to take a tricycle (30min; P200). Avoid the crossing in rough weather, as the channel is known for its strong currents and big waves. The last ferry returns to Batan at around 1pm, but be sure to double check this.

The **tourist centre** (usually daily 6am–5.30pm; ☏0908/399-7873) is to the left as you leave the port. They have no maps or brochures but can provide advice on routes, and will collect your P100 registration fee. The building also has three double **rooms** at P300 per head; it is often full from March to June, so try to book ahead. You can also try the dormitory next door at the School of Fisheries for the same price. If you want a **tour** of the island, the best plan is to call the tourist office in advance or to organize it in Basco. You should be able to book a jeepney for a group (P1500–2200 depending on distance), or possibly a scooter with driver (around P1000) if you're alone.

Itbayat Island

Of the three inhabited islands in the Batanes group, **Itbayat** is the least accessible. There's no public transport on the island so you'll have to get around either on foot or by asking one of the residents who owns a motorbike to give you a lift. It's crisscrossed by trails made by farmers and fishermen, making for superb trekking in good weather. You can stay in a dormitory (P150/person) at the municipal guesthouse – enquire at the town hall in the pretty little capital, **MAYAN** – or ask around for a homestay.

A daily **ferry** to Itbayat leaves Basco between 5–7am (2hr 30min; P450) and returns the same day; you won't have enough time to see much without staying the night. Be warned that it can be a very uncomfortable and rough crossing, and that the ferries can be cancelled for several days in a row if sea conditions are particularly poor. At the time of research the airstrip was being upgraded and there were plans to resume flights between Batan and Itbayat. The ferry lands at the west coast harbour of Chinapoliran, from where you can walk or hitch a lift to Mayan. There are great views of the island, and the others nearby, from Mount Karububan on the northern side of the island. Alternatively go looking for the stone boat-shaped burial markers at Torongan Hill, above a cave where the first inhabitants of the island are believed to have lived.

Southern Luzon

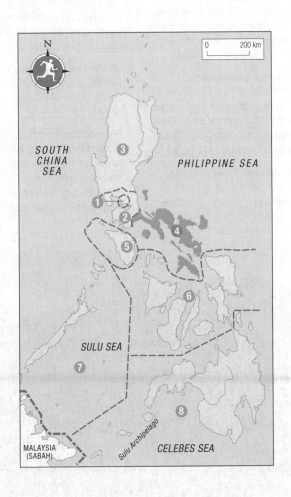

CHAPTER 4

Highlights

✳ **Moriones festival** Every Easter the beautiful little island of Marinduque lays on a boisterous religious pageant celebrating the life of Longinus, the Roman soldier who pierced Christ's side at the Crucifixion. See p.201

✳ **Camsur Watersports Complex** Try your beginner's luck at wakeboarding here, or – if you're already an expert – test out the world-class set of rails and ramps. See p.209

✳ **Caramoan Peninsula** See for yourself what attracts international TV productions – limestone cliffs, remote islands and beautiful secluded beaches. See p.211

✳ **Mayon Volcano** Even if you don't climb it, you can't miss its almost symmetrical cone standing imperiously above Legazpi. See p.215

✳ **Whale shark-watching in Donsol** Snorkel with the gentle giants of the sea. See p.220

✳ **Puraran Beach, Catanduanes** It may be a prime surfing beach, but it's not only for surfers; the offshore coral reef is thick with marine life. See p.231

▲ The Caramoan Peninsula

Southern Luzon

Lying southeast of Manila, the provinces that make up **Southern Luzon** are home to some of the country's most popular tourist destinations – both active and natural. As well as snorkelling with whale sharks, trekking up active volcanoes and surfing waves whipped up by typhoons, Southern Luzon also offers a number of glorious white sand beaches and some lovely islands.

The National Highway south from Manila takes you down to **Quezon province**, home to Mount Banahaw, a revered dormant volcano that presents one of the most rewarding climbs in the country. Quezon is linked by ferry to the beautiful, heart-shaped island province of **Marinduque**, still largely untouched by mass tourism and best known for its Easter festival, the Moriones. Beyond Quezon is the **Bicol** region, a narrow finger of land studded with volcanoes including Mount Bulusan and Mount Mayon. The coastline is often stunning, too, with some great beaches and island-hopping opportunities particularly around **Legazpi** and **Sorsogon City**. Best of all, though, is the **Caramoan Peninsula** where tourism is developing apace but where it's still possible to find little deserted hideaways. There are also attractions offshore and although it can't rival the Visayas for scuba diving, Bicol does have an ace up its sleeve in the form of **Donsol**, home to huge whale sharks. Other water-based activities in Bicol include surfing in **Daet** and wakeboarding at **CamSur Watersports Complex**. Two island provinces add further variety: **Masbate** is the Philippines' wild east, where cattle are raised and the biggest tourist draw is the annual rodeo in May. Known as the "Land of the Howling Winds", **Catanduanes** is infamous for its exposure to passing typhoons, but this extreme weather is, however, what attracts surfers to its beaches.

Getting to South Luzon

Given the distances involved it is worth considering entering the region by **air**: there are commercial airports in Naga, Legazpi, Virac (Catanduanes), Boac (Marinduque) and Masbate City. There is a **train line** between Manila and Legazpi via Naga, but consult the Philippine National Railway website (Ⓦ www.pnr.gov.ph) to see whether it is operating. There are plenty of **buses** running from Manila down the National Highway via Naga and Legazpi, some going as far as Sorsogon City or beyond. In addition to **ferries** between the Luzon mainland and the islands of Catanduanes, Marinduque and Masbate, there are also regular services across the Bernardino Strait between Matnog in Sorsogon province and Samar in the Visayas. Masbate has ferry links to several provinces including Romblon, Panay and Cebu; there are also plans to link Masbate City to Manila by sea.

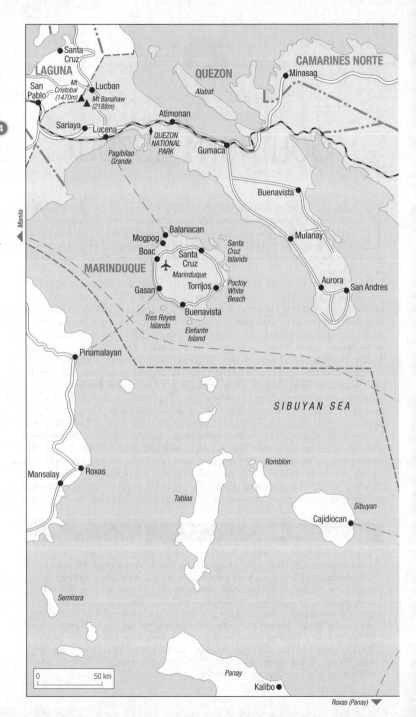

Santa
Cruz

LAGUNA

San
Pablo

*Mt
Cristobal
(1470m)*

Lucban

*Mt Banahaw
(2188m)*

Sariaya

Lucena

QUEZON

Alabat

Atimonan

QUEZON
NATIONAL
PARK

Gumaca

CAMARINES NORTE

Minasag

L.

*Pagibilao
Grande*

▲ *Manila*

Balanacan

Mogpog

Boac

MARINDUQUE

Gasan

Santa
Cruz

Marinduque

Torrijos

*Santa
Cruz
Islands*

*Poctoy
White
Beach*

Buenavista

*Tres Reyes
Islands*

*Elefante
Island*

Buenavista

Mulanay

Aurora

San Andres

Pinamalayan

SIBUYAN SEA

Romblon

Mansalay

Roxas

Tablas

Sibuyan

Cajidiocan

Semirara

0   50 km

Panay

Kalibo

Roxas (Panay) ▼

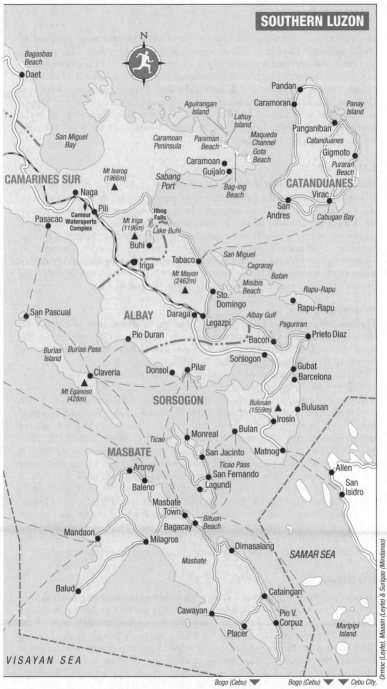

4

N

Bagasbas Beach

Daet

Pandan

Caramoran

Panay Island

Panganiban

Aguirangan Island

Lahuy Island

Catanduanes

San Miguel Bay

Caramoan Peninsula

Paniman Beach

Maqueda Channel

Gota Beach

Gigmoto

Mt Isarog (1966m)

Puraran Beach

CAMARINES SUR

Naga

Pili

Caramoan

Guijalo

Sabang Port

Bag-ing Beach

CATANDUANES

Virac

Pasacao

Camsur Watersports Complex

Mt Iriga (1196m)

Itbog Falls

Lake Buhi

San Andres

Cabugao Bay

Buhi

Iriga

Tabaco

San Miguel

Cagraray

Batan

Mt Mayon (2462m)

Misibis Beach

Rapu-Rapu

Rapu-Rapu

San Pascual

ALBAY

Sto. Domingo

Daraga

Legazpi

Albay Gulf

Paguriran

Pio Duran

Bacon

Prieto Diaz

Burias Island

Burias Pass

Sorsogon

Gubat

Claveria

Donsol

Pilar

Barcelona

Mt Eganoso (428m)

SORSOGON

Bulusan (1559m)

Bulusan

Ticao

Monreal

Bulan

Irosin

MASBATE

San Jacinto

Matnog

Allen

Aroroy

Ticao Pass

San Fernando

San Isidro

Baleno

Lagundi

Masbate Town

Bagacay

Bituon Beach

Mandaon

Milagros

Dimasalang

SAMAR SEA

Balud

Masbate

Cataingan

Pio V. Corpuz

Cawayan

Placer

Maripipi Island

VISAYAN SEA

Ormoc (Leyte), Maasin (Leyte) & Surigao (Mindanao)

Bogo (Cebu) ▼   Bogo (Cebu) ▼ ▼ Cebu City,

Quezon

Much of the northern part of Quezon province is mountainous and hard to reach, although there are isolated communities on the coast. The southern portion of the province serves mainly as a staging post on the road from Manila to the Bicol region, though it does have attractions such as a couple of excellent climbs, **Mount Banahaw** and **Mount Cristobal**. Further east you can explore **Quezon National Park**, which has some fairly easy marked trails. If you happen to be in Quezon in mid-May, check out what is by far the biggest festival in the province, the **Pahiyas**, held in and around **Lucban**, not far from the very ordinary provincial capital, **Lucena**.

Lucena

The bustling town of **LUCENA** is worth considering for a stop on the route south, as a useful base during the Pahiyas festival in nearby Lucban or for those on their way to Marinduque via Dalahican port. The only thing to see in the town itself is the **Museo ng Quezon** (Mon–Fri 9am–noon & 1–4.30pm; donations), a small repository of the personal belongings of former president Manuel Quezon, including clothing and books. Quezon served from 1935–44 and is considered by Filipinos to have been the country's second president, following Emilio Aguinaldo's leadership during the failed revolution (see p.428). The museum is inside the Provincial Capitol building at the eastern end of Quezon Avenue.

Practicalities

The **bus station**, called Grand Central, is on the northern edge of the city on Diversion Road. It's a fifteen-minute jeepney ride (P8) to Quezon Avenue, the main thoroughfare. The **Quezon Tourism Association** has an office in the Provincial Capitol Building (☎042/373-7510).

The best **accommodation** in town is at the modern *Star Garden Tower* (☎042/710-4437; ❹) on Quezon Avenue, which has clean, modern rooms and a small but well-equipped gym. Its *Sky Bar*, with views of the town, is a good place for a drink. The *Sir Josh* (☎042/660-2481; ❷) hotel near the corner of Bonifacio and Zamora streets caters to lower budgets with boxy but brightly painted air-conditioned rooms. If you don't need to be based in the town itself, the *Queen Margarette Hotel* (☎042/373-7171; ⓦ www.queenmargarettehotel.com; ❹) is a good choice; it's on Diversion Road, a five-minute drive east of the city in the Domoit barangay, and has comfortable rooms and a swimming pool.

There are a couple of decent places to **eat**. *Precious Eastern Cuisine* (daily 8am–11.30pm) on Quezon Avenue serves a mixture of Filipino and Chinese dishes, and is particularly known for its *siopao* (steamed buns, the Filipino version of Chinese *baozi*). A cosier option is *Eduvgis*, at the corner of Magallanes and Bonifacio, with BBQ on offer alongside pizzas, burgers and other fast food. The most famous foods in Lucena are its *chami* (noodles) and *tinapa* (smoked fish).

Lucban

Quezon province's major tourist draw is the **Pahiyas thanksgiving festival**, held every year on May 15 in **LUCBAN**, which sits at the foot of Mount Banahaw, 26km north of Lucena. There isn't much to see in Lucban itself, apart from **St Louis Church**, which dates from the 1730s. You could join the faithful as they climb **Kamay ni Hesus** – a hill on the edge of town peppered with tableaux depicting the stations of the cross – in the hope of being healed of various ailments. At the top of the hill there's a large, open-armed statue of Christ; the route up is exposed and can be tiring on a hot day but worth it for the wonderful views. Although a church stands at the base of the hill and masses are regularly held, the whole site has something of a theme-park feel, with a children's playground and replica Noah's ark (under construction at the time of research), which will eventually provide accommodation. The hill can be reached by jeepney from Lucban (5min; P8); from Lucena the twenty-minute trip will cost P30 by jeepney or P50 by van.

Practicalities

Jeepneys and buses from Lucena stop on Quezon Avenue. From Manila, you could either travel via Lucena or take a bus to San Pablo (see p.114) or Santa Cruz (see p.111) in Laguna province, where you can change for a local bus to Lucban.

If you're staying in town during the festival then book by January and expect the prices to be inflated. The most comfortable **hotel** in town is *Patio Rizal* on Quezon Avenue (☎042/540-2107; ❹), which has decent standard and superior rooms; the suites, except perhaps the VIP suite, aren't really worth the extra expense. *Summer Capital* (☎042/540-3421; ❶), on the main plaza above a shop, has affordable fan rooms but is pretty grubby. There are a few **restaurants** close to the town plaza. Popular places for local dishes include *Buddy's* (daily 9am–10pm) on the plaza and *Abcedes* (daily 8am–9pm) at 51 Quezon Ave. Be sure to try pancit *habab* (a local noodle dish traditionally eaten with your hands) and the famous garlicky *Lucban* longganisa (sausage), particularly delicious when served with *achara* (pickled papaya). For dessert try the *budin* (cassava cake).

Mount Banahaw

Northwest of Lucena, the town of **Dolores** is the starting point for treks up **Mount Banahaw** and **Mount Cristobal**, which lie either side of the town. Both mountains are protected areas and some trails have been closed for the past few years to reduce human impact on the environment. Other trails, however, are open. Considered sacred, 2188-metre Mount Banahaw has spawned a vast number of legends and superstitions: one says that every time a foreigner sets foot on the mountain it will rain. Before the protection order, every Easter thousands of pilgrims used to climb Mount Banahaw in the belief that bathing in its waterfalls would cure their ailments. Members of various sects still live around the base of the mountain, claiming that the mountain imbues them with supernatural and psychic powers. Its slopes thick with jungle, Banahaw is a challenging but rewarding climb with panoramic views of the surrounding country from the crater rim. Treat this mountain seriously because although the trail looks wide and

The Pahiyas festival

Each May Lucban is transformed into something from a fairy tale, the houses decorated in the most imaginative fashion with fruit, vegetables and brightly coloured *kiping* (rice paper), which is formed into enormous chandeliers that cascade like flames from the eaves. There is good reason for this creativity: every year the winner of the best-decorated house wins a cash prize and is blessed for twelve months by San Isidore (the patron saint of farmers). The festival starts with a solemn Mass at dawn and goes on well into the night, with much drinking of liquor and dancing in the streets. There is a parade, a beauty contest, a marching band and a carabao parade in which enormous water buffalo, more used to rice fields and mudholes, are led through the streets in outrageous costumes. It's open-house for visitors during Pahiyas, and everyone is especially honoured to have foreigners at their table.

well trodden, it soon peters out into inhospitable rainforest – even experienced climbers allow three days to reach the summit and get back down, while a crater descent should only be attempted by experts.

If you haven't time to reach the summit, you might prefer to trek to **Kristalino Falls** (Crystalline Falls) and back, which can be done in a day. One and a half hours further on is a second waterfall, whose surroundings make an ideal **campsite**.

Nearby **Mount Cristobal** is seen as the negative counterpart to the positive spiritual energy of Mount Banahaw. It takes up to six hours of serious trekking along an awkward trail to reach Jones Peak, which is 50m lower than the inaccessible summit. The climb isn't recommended for beginners or unaccompanied trekkers.

Practicalities

To reach the access town of Dolores, take one of the JAM Transit, Green Star or Lucena Lines buses running between Manila (Buendia or Cubao) and Lucena. Get off at San Pablo, from where there are irregular buses and vans (P80–100) to Dolores. Take a jeepney to the barangay of Kinabuyahan where you can hire **guides** (P200–300/day), and, very importantly, sign the logbook. There are also souvenir stalls selling amulets, herbs and other mystical paraphernalia here.

Dolores is the home of the renowned *Kinabuhayan Café* (℡0916/221-5791, Ⓦkinabuhayancafe.multiply.com), owned by artist Jay Herrera. Set meals cost P600 per head. The café also arranges hikes in the area.

Quezon National Park

Quezon National Park, less than two hours east of Lucena by road near the town of **Atimonan**, is off the well-beaten trail, far from the picture-postcard beaches of the Visayas and too distant from Manila to make it a viable weekend trip. Though relatively small at just ten square kilometres, the park is so dense with flora and fauna that you have a good chance of seeing anything and everything from giant monitor lizards to monkeys, deer and wild pigs. This is also home to the *kalaw*, a species of hornbill.

A paved trail leads to the highest point, 366m above sea level, which has a viewing deck from which you can see both sides of the Bicol peninsula. The summit is known as Pinagbanderahan, meaning "where the flag is hoisted", because both Japanese and American flags were flown there before the Philippine flag was raised in 1946. The walk to the summit takes about an hour. There are also numerous **caves** in the park that can be explored with guides, experience and the right equipment.

Practicalities

The turning for the park is on the Maharlika Highway, which runs from Lucena to Atimonan. The winding approach road to the park, known locally as *bituka ng manok* (chicken's intestine), is a challenge for buses: from Lucena's Grand Central station, you can get any bus heading east through Bicol (to Daet, for instance) or an Atimonan-bound bus, as all these vehicles pass the park entrance. Enquire about **guides** at the Quezon Tourism Association in Lucena (see p.196) or at the Atimonan Municipal Tourism Council (℡042/316-6905). There are some places to **eat** in the pavilion at the entrance to the park but no accommodation, though you can **camp** overnight with a permit (P50) from the warden. There are also **hotels** in Antimonan, including the *Dona Rosario Sea Breeze* resort (℡042/316-6916, Ⓦwww.donarosarioresorts.com/seabreeze.html; ❹), which has a swimming pool and its own bowling alley.

Marinduque

The heart-shaped island of **MARINDUQUE** (pronounced "mar-in-DOO-kay") is a great place to get away from it all – work your way slowly around the coastal road to the pretty beaches south of **Boac**, then across the island to **Torrijos** and **Poctoy White Beach**, where you can live cheaply in the shadow of majestic **Mount Malinding**. There's some good island-hopping around Marinduque too, with beaches and coves to explore around the **Tres Reyes Islands** off the southwest coast and the **Santa Cruz Islands** off the northwest coast. The island is known for its **Moriones festival**, an animated Easter tradition featuring masked men dressed like Roman soldiers (see box, p.201). If you plan to visit during Holy Week then you should book ahead.

For all its geographical closeness to Manila, Marinduque might as well be a world away, with most of the 230,000 residents leading a life of subsistence coconut farming and fishing. When copper mining was begun here in 1969, many thought it was the dawn of a new era for the island. Sadly, the dream ended in disaster and recrimination as on two separate occasions, waste from disued pits flowed into the island's rivers, destroying agricultural land, the livelihood of the locals and marine

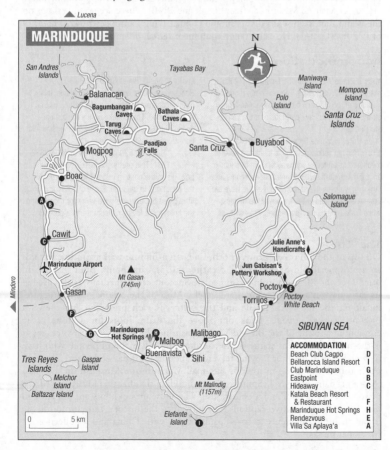

life, which is still trying to recover today. More recently a luxury resort opened on a small island off Marinduque, providing jobs – around 80 percent of the staff are locals – but otherwise having little impact on the lives of most islanders.

Boac

BOAC ("bow-ak") is an orderly, compact town with neat streets and low-rise buildings laid out around a central plaza. The area around the cathedral has numerous typical Filipino *bahay ng buto* (wooden houses), the windows boasting carved wooden shutters instead of glass and the balconies exploding with bougainvillea and frangipani. Many of these houses were built in the nineteenth century and are now a photogenic, if faded, reminder of a style of architecture that is rapidly disappearing.

Information

The **tourist office** (☎042/332-1498, ⓦwww.boac.gov.ph/tourism_page.htm) in the Capitol Building complex (on the road between Boac and the airport) is helpful and has a handful of leaflets, but once on the road be prepared for a lack of reliable information regarding destinations and methods of getting around. There are banks with ATMs in Boac (Land Bank and PNB). There are no dive shops on the island, but keen scuba divers should contact Ding Pampola (☎042/332-2779 or 09208/917-041). He can arrange equipment rental, divemasters and air refills.

Accommodation

Abby's Place Magsaysay St, facing the public market ☎042/332-2643. The seven a/c rooms here are all good value, but they face onto a busy street – fine if you have earplugs or are a heavy sleeper. ❷

Boac Hotel Opposite Boac Cathedral ☎042/332-1121. This big yellow building is the oldest hotel in town, and its antiques and wooden furniture lend it an appealing atmosphere. The cheapest rooms are fan-only, while standard rooms and above have a/c. Suite A is decorated with pictures of the Beatles, while Suite B has a four-poster bed. Free wi-fi. ❶

Lucky 7 Gov D. Reyes St ☎042/332-2777. Reached via stairs among a row of shops, this orange concrete building has decent rooms in a noisy location. The videoke on the rooftop bar doesn't help matters, particularly for the cheapest non-a/c rooms with bunk beds. ❶

🏃 **Tahanan sa Isok** Canovas St ☎042/332-1231. This pretty, plant-festooned white building on the eastern edge of town is probably the best hotel in the area. Some of the rooms are a little dated but they are good value for money, and the hotel has a lovely restaurant and a pool. ❷

The Town

On top of the hill on the town's north side, a ten-minute walk from the plaza, is an atmospheric old Spanish Gothic **cathedral** (5.30am–6pm). Built in 1666 in honour of the Blessed Virgin of Immediate Succour, the cathedral was also used in its early days as a refuge from pirate attacks. Most of the original main structure, including the red-brick facade and the belfry, is well preserved and there's a pleasant garden outside. Look out above the main doors for a stone niche containing a statue of the Blessed Virgin, enshrined here in 1792. Devotees say it is the most miraculous statue in the country and tell of blind people who have regained their sight after praying fervently underneath it day and night. The only other tourist attraction in town is the small **Marinduque Museum** on the plaza (Mon–Fri 8am–noon & 1–5pm; free), in a building that has previously served as a prison, a boys' school and a courthouse. The museum's exhibits are limited and have too few descriptive captions, but introduce the history and culture of the island including evidence of pre-Spanish trade with China and a collection of Moriones masks.

Getting to and from Marinduque

Marinduque is connected to Manila by **air**, and the airport is just north of Gasan. Zest Airways has a few flights a week – check the most recent timetables. If you aren't flying then the only direct option between Manila and Marinduque is to take the JAC Liner (T 02/927-6139) daily roll-on/roll-off (RORO) bus service (8–10hr; P700 including bus and ferry). Other standard **ferry services** include those run by Montenegro Lines (T 09178/672-337), Starhorse Shipping Lines (T 09212/745-340), Santa. Cruz Shipping Lines (T 042/824-5340) and Boac Ferries (T 09166/977-112). The quickest of these is the Montenegro Lines fastcraft (1hr 50min; P260). Boac Ferries also has a service between Gasan on Marinduque and Pinamalayan in Mindoro (2hr 30min; P300).

Island transport

Public transport on the island is limited to jeepneys, tricycles for shorter distances and small boats for island-hopping. It is possible to make the trip around the island in two days, but four or five would be more comfortable particularly since if you miss the last jeepney (most services stop around 4–5pm) you can easily find yourself stranded. An easier way to get around is by hiring a van for around P3500 per day. Enquire at the tourist office in Boac.

Eating

Most of the places to eat in Boac are *carinderias*, simple establishments where you choose from a selection of dishes displayed in pots.

Cely's Kitchenette De Octubre St. Expect to pay P60 for a meal including rice at this carinderia set over two floors. Daily 6am–8.30pm.

Good Chow De Octubre St. A snack bar selling tasty *siopao* (steamed buns) as well as Western fast food such as pizza. Daily 7am–7pm.

Kusina sa Plaza Overlooking the plaza on Mercader St. The most popular place in town, serving Filipino dishes such as *kare kare* (peanut stew with oxtail and beef). There's also a café attached. Daily 5.30am–8pm.

Gasan

The west coast from Boac south to **GASAN** and a little beyond boasts a number of **resorts**. The beaches are pebbly but they do offer fine views of the sunset and across the sea towards Mindoro in the distance. These resorts are often full for the Moriones festival and at Christmas, but at any other time you might find that you are the only guest. It's much better to stay in the resorts than in Gasan itself, but the town has a few small souvenir shops selling Moriones-themed products and tasty arrowroot biscuits (which, along with *bibingka* rice cakes, are a Marinduque speciality).

Moriones festival

The **Moriones festival** celebrates the life of Longinus, the Roman soldier who pierced Christ's side during the Crucifixion. Blood from the wound spattered Longinus's blind eye, which was immediately healed. Converted on the spot, he later attested to the Resurrection and, refusing to recant, was executed. The Marinduqueyo version is colourful and bizarre, involving fanciful masked figures dressed as centurions chasing Longinus around town and through nearby fields. Several Moriones pageants are staged in Marinduque during **Holy Week**, with extra events added in recent years for the benefit of tourists (see W www.marinduque.gov.ph for more information). Although the festival originated in Mogpog, and other towns including Santa Cruz have their own versions, these days the major Moriones festival is in **Boac**.

Accommodation

Club Marinduque Near the barrio of Pingan ℡0920/852-2667. The a/c rooms are spacious and there's a pleasant swimming pool and outdoor jacuzzi (P150/hr). Island-hopping can be arranged and the snorkelling off the beach is decent, although you'll need to bring your own equipment. ❸

Eastpoint Barangay Balaring ℡042/332-2229, Ⓦwww.eastpointhotel.com. This quirky family-run place has an array of different types of room and provides a large kitchen for guests' use. There's a wellness centre with massage and other treatments on the premises, plus a library and wi-fi in the garden. The restaurant offers some healthy choices and uses vegetables grown on site. ❷

Hideaway Behind Cawit port ℡0906/693-8451. Look out for the surfboard leading you to this resort with more character than most. Accommodation is in huts made from different local materials, or in a concrete building. There is no restaurant; eat at the simple places in the port. ❷

🏃 **Katala Beach Resort & Restaurant** 3km south of Gasan, approximately 45min by jeepney from Boac ℡0915/512-4784. This modern concrete place lacks the rustic charm of the resorts closer to Boac, but it does have spick-and-span fan and a/c rooms with balconies at very reasonable rates. The restaurant, on the water's edge, has a good range of food and drink. There's a boat you can rent at P1500 for day-trips (this is the closest resort to the Tres Reyes Islands). ❷

Villa sa Aplaya'a (formerly Villa Carlos) ℡042/332-1882, Ⓦwww.villasaaplaya.blogspot .com. A good choice close to Boac, with tastefully decorated rooms with balconies – ask for a sea view. There is a badminton court although getting hire equipment may be tricky. ❸

Eating

Barbarossa Pub San José St. Popular with expats as well as locals, and serves Filipino and Italian dishes. Daily 9am–9pm.

The Tres Reyes Islands

The beautiful **TRES REYES ISLANDS** – popularly known as **Baltazar**, **Melchor** and **Gaspar** after the biblical Three Kings – lie a few kilometres off Marinduque. There is some good scuba diving here; see p.200 for contact details, or try one of the resorts. On the far side of Gaspar Island there's a white beach with good coral for snorkelling; a small fishing community is located on the eastern tip of the island, but there's no formal accommodation. Getting to any of the islands takes about thirty minutes from Marinduque. Many of the resorts can arrange a boat for you or you can ask around among the fishermen in Buenavista; expect to pay P1500 upwards for a day-trip depending on the distance travelled.

Buenavista and Mount Malindig

South of Gasan lies the sleepy town of **BUENAVISTA**, where jeepneys usually terminate – so you'll have to wait here for onward transport. Buenavista itself has little to detain visitors, but it sees a steady flow of tourists as it is close to the departure point for boats to the *Bellarocca Island Resort* (℡02/817-7290, Ⓦwww.bellaroccaresorts.com; ❾) on Elefante Island just offshore. The resort attracts well-heeled Filipinos and Korean honeymooners, and offers extremely stylish rooms, an indulgent spa and impeccable service. It's more a place for couples than families, with only a small beach but a selection of waterborne activities and a golf course on the mainland.

There is a rather more modest accommodation option on the mainland. *Marinduque Hot Springs* (℡0910/848-4947, Ⓦwww.marinduquehotsprings.co .cc; ❸), 2km east of Buenavista in Malbog barangay (P50 by tricycle) has five rooms. The family room (❻) has its own pool fed by the spring. There are also five public pools, free for guests or with a small fee for day visitors (8am–10pm), and a restaurant with driftwood tables. There is a less developed hot spring, with more sulphurous water, a fifteen-minute walk away – ask at the resort for directions. If you're continuing east from the resort, make sure you arrange for the tricycle driver to collect you on the morning of your departure, so you can get back to Buenavista in time to get a comfortable seat on the jeepney.

Another reason to visit Buenavista is to climb **Mount Malindig**, a 1157m volcano that's considered active. The hike can be done in a day starting from barangay Sihi, with the ascent taking about three and a half hours and the descent significantly less. There is a military post partway up and a permit is sometimes required: make enquiries at the tourist office in Boac or at the barangay hall in Sihi. Either of these should also be able to arrange a guide for around P500.

The road to Torrijos

There are **two routes** from Buenavista to Torrijos, although only the main route across the hills has public transport. The more scenic coastal road is feasible only in a hired jeepney (P2000) or van (P3000), which is quite an expense for a one-hour journey although drivers may be open to haggling. Even on the standard route direct jeepneys are few and far between, so you may need to change transport on the way – for example you could travel from Buenavista to Malibago (P30), and then to Torrijos (P45). You may even need to change in Digui between Mailibago and Torrijos. After 5pm vehicles are scarce and the cost goes up significantly.

TORRIJOS itself is a friendly little town but it has no beaches. If you miss the last jeepney out of town (at around 3–4pm) and need to stay the night, the best place is the motel-style *Village Sunrise* (℡0920/909-3674; ❸). It has no restaurant but is only a five-minute walk from the town centre. A cheaper option is *Mixt Apartelle* (℡0920/862-3038; ❶) where the ordinary rooms are simple boxes with fans, but clean enough. The *Garden Grille* in town serves typical Pinoy dishes from an open-sided hut with a shady yard.

Poctoy White Beach

Just 2km from Torrijos is **POCTOY WHITE BEACH**, where the sand is not as pale as the name suggests but is still much better than the pebbles on the west coast. The views across the bay to Mount Malindig can also be spectacular. Passing through a concrete arch – guarded by two centurions – from the main road brings you to a car park. To the right is *Rendezvous* (℡0907/289-7878; ❸), a concrete complex with adequate rooms and a collection of Moriones costumes belonging to the owner. The videoke is open 24 hours for guests, but at least it's a little away from the bedrooms. The nearby stretch of beach is packed with huts which can be rented for the day, and has a small market where you can buy the catch of the day by weight and have it cooked for an extra P25. The beach is quieter if you go further along to the right.

To move on from Poctoy White Beach, take a tricycle back into Torrijos and board a jeepney at the crossroads for Santa Cruz. The jeepneys do pass Poctoy White Beach, but by the time they get there are so crowded that you won't get on, short of clinging perilously to the roof.

A little north of Poctoy is the excellent ⫿ *Beach Club Cagpo* (℡0921/993-2537, ⓦ www.beachclubcagpo.com; ❸). Located on an attractive stretch of beach, it's a great place to relax – there's a no videoke policy, a wood-fired pizza oven and a barbecue. The cheapest accommodation is the "backpacker room" with two bunk beds (P500 for two people, P150 per additional person) and a fan, but there are also larger rooms and cottages with air conditioning.

The road to Santa Cruz

On the road from Torrijos to Santa Cruz, there are a couple of worthwhile stops for anyone interested in **handicrafts**. Within the barangay of poctay, a short distance from the beach, is pottery workshop of Jun Gabisan (☏0918/774-5533), who learned the craft from his father and has been making pots since he was twelve. He and his father (who speaks better English) offer tuition on the potter's wheel at P300 per hour for a small group. Further along the coastal road in barangay Bonliw is Julie Anne's Handicrafts (☏0919/465-6992), a popular stop with the few tour groups who make it to Marinduque. Employing 38 women, the company produces placemats and other textiles on traditional looms. The weavers are happy to receive visitors and allow photographs, but may not speak much English.

Santa Cruz and around

If you're interested in exploring the caves and islands in the northeast of Marinduque, **SANTA CRUZ** is the best base for a day or two. The town is unmemorable, the only sights a whitewashed Spanish-era church and the dilapidated wooden convent next to it, while the narrow streets in the centre are choked with tricycles and jeepneys from dawn to dusk – be prepared for noise. There are a handful of hotels, including *Oromismo 898* (☏042/321-1283; ❷) on Gomez Street.

From the town centre it's a bumpy thirty-minute tricycle ride (P1000 return including waiting) to the **Bathala Caves**. There are seven caves; four are accessible and one contains human bones believed to be the remains of World War II soldiers. You've a good chance of seeing pythons here, along with the thousands of bats that call the caves home. There is also a natural pool for cooling off after the rigours of the journey. The caves are privately owned and you have to pay the caretaker P150 per person for a guided tour. Another option is the 2km-long, **Bagumbongan cave** (price not available at time of writing), which can be reached by jeepney to barangay San Isidro. To arrange a guide contact Efren Delos Reyes in the Provincial Environment and Natural Resources Office (☏0920/474-9674 or 0999/744-7496), or visit the barangay hall in San Isidro. It's a bit more challenging than the Bathala Caves, with some fixed ropes and spots where water reaches chest height. Helmets, lights and gloves are provided.

There are few tourist facilities on Maniwaya, Mompong and Polo, collectively known as the **Santa Cruz Islands**, but there are a number of white sand beaches good for snorkelling. Freddie Pelaez (☏0912/815-0802), former barangay captain of Maniwaya, can assist with accommodation and camping on the island. There are regular boats to Maniwaya (P75) and Mompong (P100) from Buyabod, 10km southeast of Santa Cruz and accessible by tricycle or jeepney.

Mogpog

The main reason to visit the hillside town of **MOGPOG**, a few kilometres north of Boac, is the **Tarug Caves**, actually one enormous cave with three chambers set inside a 300-metre-tall limestone spire that's barely 3m wide at the top. You can climb to the top, where the reward is a panoramic view of the Bondoc peninsula to the east and the Tablas Strait to the west. Another trip to consider is to Paadjao Falls, a series of gently cascading falls with a large pool at the bottom, where you can swim. The falls are in Bocboc barangay and can be reached by jeepney (P20) or tricycle (P30).

Mogpog is considered to be the birthplace of the Moriones festival and holds its own festivities – smaller in scale than those in Boac – during Holy Week. One of the most famous Moriones **costume makers**, Dick Malapote, lives and works in the town's Janagdong barangay, and has been creating the outfits for 25 years, selling whole sets of armour for as much as P12,000. He welcomes visitors, but he doesn't speak much English so the best bet if you are interested is to enquire at the Boac tourist office. If you're coming independently, take a tricycle from Mogpog to barangay Sibucao (P10) a kilometre away, then ask around – locals know where he lives. Arrive around 7–8am to see him at work.

The only **place to stay** is the pleasant colonial-style *Hilltop Hotel* (☎042/332-3074; ●), a P100 tricycle ride from Balanacan. There are simple but spacious double fan rooms and more expensive double air-conditioned rooms. The communal balcony, with views over the hinterland, is perfect for relaxing with a drink. Try to call in advance to tell the owners of your arrival.

Bicol

Known throughout the Philippines as an area of great natural beauty, **Bicol** ("bee-col") comprises the mainland provinces of Camarines Norte, Camarines Sur, Albay and Sorsogon, and the island provinces of Catanduanes and Masbate. The area is rich in **adventure sports**, from surfing in Camarines Norte and volcano-climbing in Albay to whale shark-watching in Sorsogon. Another highlight is the **cuisine**, which is some of the best in the country, characterized by the use of chillies and coconut milk.

Daet

The capital of Camarines Norte province **DAET**, 200km southeast of Manila, is overrun with tricycles but the nearby coastline has more than its fair share of unspoiled beaches and islands. Surfers are drawn to the fickle waves at Bagasbas Beach (see p.206) and San Miguel Bay.

Daet's busy little central plaza is a popular meeting place in the evenings. One block north is the 1950s Provincial Capitol, in front of which is Kalayaan (Freedom) Park with the tallest statue of **José Rizal** outside Manila. Erected in 1899, this was the first monument to Rizal in the country and set the trend for thousands of others in town and barrio plazas across the archipelago.

Practicalities

Buses arriving in Daet stop at the edge of the city on the National Highway, from where it's less than 2km into town; plenty of tricycles travel the route for P30. The **tourist office** (Mon–Sat 8am–5pm, Sun 8.30am–noon) is on the ground floor in the Provincial Capitol complex.

Accommodation in Daet is basic, with a handful of hotels offering a similar choice of functional rooms. On the whole you're better off heading straight to Bagasbas Beach, but if you want to stay in town then try Vinzons Avenue where there are a number of hotels within walking distance of each other. *Prime Suite* (☎054/571-3531; ●) is the pick of the bunch with very cheap fan-only doubles and slightly more expensive air-conditioned triples. *Villa Mila* (☎054/721-5107; ●) is another good choice, with small, clean rooms – including fan-only singles for P250 – and a swimming pool.

For **food**, there are hole-in-the-wall canteens all over town selling various dishes for just a few pesos. For something more special, locals rate *KFisher* (daily 10am–10pm; Ⓦwww.kfisherseafooddaet.com), which specializes in seafood ranging from tuna or *pusit* (squid) *sisig* to a mixed sushi platter for P260. *Alvino's Pizza* is on Dasmarinas Street and is known for its tasty pizzas as well as pasta, salads and roast chicken.

Bagasbas beach

Lovely **Bagasbas Beach** is 4km northeast of Daet and accessible by tricycle (P40). The waves crash in from the Pacific and are sometimes big enough for **surfing**, particularly from November to March. In fact, the whole area of coast east of Daet has become something of a surfers' hangout; the shore can be pretty much deserted by all but stray dogs on weekdays.

Several places on Bagasbas Beach rent out surfboards and offer tuition, including most of the hotels and the friendly *Hang Loose* (T054/440-1946). Surfboard hire is P150–200 per hour or P500 for a whole day, and lessons cost around P200 per hour on top of that. There is a **tourist information** desk, run by the Camarines Norte Surfing Association, on the stretch of beach to the left of the public transport drop-off point. **Experienced surfers** who want to look beyond Bagasbas should ask about the breaks in nearby San Miguel Bay, which often has very good waves close to the town of Mercedes and around the seven islands known as the Siete Pecados.

Kiteboarding can be arranged at Mike & Jay's Kite Bar (W www.mikes-kites .com) starting at $65 for a day's equipment hire or $60 for a two-hour introductory session. If the wind and waves are not cooperating, they also hire out sea kayaks and organize island-hopping trips.

Accommodation and eating

Until recently, development on Bagasbas Beach was limited to a couple of small lodges and plenty of noisy, tatty videoke bars. The opening of the ✤ *Bagasbas Lighthouse* (T054/441-5855, W www.bagasbaslighthouse.com; ❹) on the sea front may change all that, offering stylish accommodation in rooms or cheaper converted shipping containers and with plans to open backpacker dorms for around P500 per head. The restaurant, with seating beside the swimming pool, is excellent and open to non-guests. It serves Filipino favourites and Western fast food plus Bicol specialities such as *tinuktok* (coconut and prawn wrapped in taro leaves). Other accommodation options on the seafront include the friendly *Surfers Dine-Inn* (T0916/475-9053 or 0908/463-0547; ❶), with a range of simple fan and air-conditioned rooms. Set one street back from the beach is *Zenaida's Palace* (T054/441-6286; ❸) with large rooms set around a swimming pool, some of them with balconies.

Other than *Bagasbas Lighthouse,* the best place to eat is *Kusina ni Angel* (Angel's Kitchen), set back from the beach close to the junction where tricycles drop new arrivals. It's a lovely, down-to-earth little restaurant serving dishes such as seafood pancit *canton* (noodles with shrimp, octopus and fish fillet).

Naga

Centrally located in the province of Camarines Sur, the lively university city of **Naga** was established in 1578 by Spanish conquistador Pedro de Chavez. Although there's not a great deal to see in the city itself, it has found itself on the tourist map in the last few years partly due to the success of the CamSur Watersports Complex (also known as CWC; see p.209) in nearby Pili. Although there's accommodation at CWC, Naga offers an alternative base with more choices for sleeping and eating. It also has a fun nightlife partly due to its large student population: opened in 1948, the University of Nueva Caceres is the oldest in Southern Luzon.

Arrival and information

Buses to Naga arrive at the Central Terminal, which is situated across the river to the south of the town centre, close to the SM mall; you'll have to take a tricycle from here (from P7). **Naga Airport** is located 12km out of town to the east, in the provincial capital Pili; there are jeepneys (P10) into Naga. If you plan to go to the CamSur Watersports Complex then you don't need to go into Naga at all as it's closer to Pili. The **Naga City Visitors Center** is in the DOLE Building, City Hall Complex, J. Miranda Avenue (Mon–Fri 8–11am & noon–4pm; ☎054/473-4432), 1km east of the Naga River to the east of the city centre. The building isn't easy to find: head round the left-hand side of the main building, past the Senior Citizens' Centre. There is no shortage of **internet cafés** in the city centre. Numerous banks line General Luna (alongside Plaza Rizal) and Peñafrancia

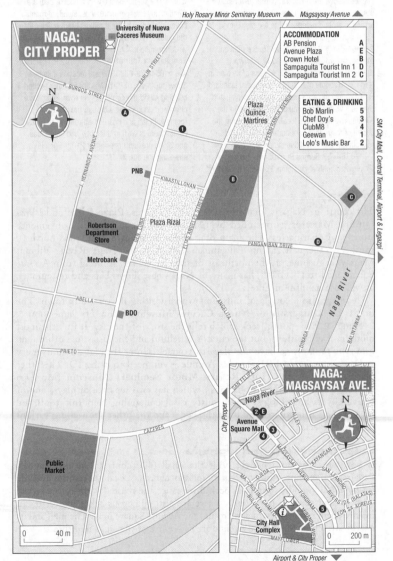

Avenue; there are also useful **ATMs** in the Avenue Square mall. The main **post office** is in the City Hall complex. Air Philippines has an office at 2/F Galleria de San Francisco, Peñafrancia Avenue (☎054/473-2277).

Accommodation

During the **Peñafrancia festival** in September many hotels, particularly the budget ones, are fully booked so plan ahead.

AB Pension P. Burgos St ☎473/2991-0909. Located above the Aristocrat barber, this reasonably priced option has a handful of simple rooms arranged around reception; the a/c single room for P500 is a bargain. ❸

Avenue Plaza Behind Avenue Square mall on Magsaysay Ave ☎054/473-9999, ⓦwww .theavenueplazahotel.com. In a class of its own in Naga, with rooms of a truly international standard. Facilities include a swimming pool and gym, and there's low-key piano music in the lobby in the evenings. Although the location is away from the centre of town, there are numerous bars and restaurants within walking distance. ❼

Crown Hotel P. Burgos St ☎054/473-8305, ⓦwww.crownhotelnaga.com. Low-rise hotel right

in the noisy centre of Naga, with a good range of rooms. The single rooms (with a double bed) are significantly cheaper than twins; standard rooms have no window but that makes them quieter than the deluxe. There's a small bar and a coffee shop; wi-fi throughout. ❹

Sampaguita Tourist Inn 1 and 2 42 Panganiban Ave ☎054/473-8893. Central location a stone's throw southeast of Plaza Martinez, with a second building round the corner on the river. Rooms are clean and good value, although the cheapest rooms with fan and shared bathrooms are pretty basic. There is wi-fi in the lobby and café areas, and blood pressure checks for P10 if Naga is stressing you out. ❶

The City

The centre of Naga is focused on two main squares, **Plaza Rizal** and **Plaza Quince Martires**, surrounded by fast-food restaurants, banks, convenience stores and pharmacies. The main drag, **Elias Angeles Street**, runs north to south; to the east, along Panganiban Drive, is the Naga River. Vibrant Magsaysay Avenue, to the northeast of the city centre, running from Avenue Square mall to City Hall, has many of Naga's best shops, bars and restaurants, as well as a handful of hotels.

There are also a couple of museums worth visiting if you are in town. The first is the **University of Nueva Caceres Museum** (Mon–Fri 9am–noon & 2–5pm, Sat 9am–noon; free), which tells the story of the city. It isn't the most modern of exhibitions, but the curator is helpful and enthusiastic – other than him, you're likely to have the place to yourself. Enter through the university campus entrance on J. Hernandez Avenue – you need to bring ID. The other place to visit is the **Holy Rosary Minor Seminary Museum** (Mon–Fri 8.30am–noon & 1–5pm; donations), which has two separate displays, one of which covers archeology – with dusty cases containing Neolithic tools and objects such as decorative gold tooth pegs – and the other showcasing various religious objects.

Eating, drinking and nightlife

If you want **eat** on a budget, visit the small food court in an alleyway off Peñafrancia Avenue close to San Francisco church. Local specialities include *log-log kinalas* (noodle soup with pork, liver sauce and roasted garlic) often served with toasted *siopao* (a pork bun). There are also numerous other places to eat, mainly chain restaurants, in and around the Avenue Square mall. The mall and its nearby stretch of Magsaysay Avenue are the centre of the city's nightlife.

Bob Marlin Magsaysay Ave. Famous for its crispy *pata* (deep fried pork leg), which receives lots of praise on the wall-mounted plates signed by famous visitors, this small and laidback place mixes great Filipino food with reggae music. It's further south on Magsaysay than the cluster of restaurants near Avenue Square mall. Daily 10am until 10pm inside or midnight outside.

Chef Doy's Behind 37 Magsaysay Ave. This restaurant promises "fusion, flares and a twist of Filipino cuisine" – so it has familiar Pinoy dishes with unexpected techniques or ingredients such as quail eggs. It's a little more expensive than the average, with most mains costing P190–360.

ClubM8 Corner of Magsaysay Ave & Catmon St. This is one of the places where students go to let their hair down until close to dawn (Thurs–Sat 7pm–4am).

Geewan P. Burgos St. A good place in the city centre to try spicy Bicolano dishes such as *pinangat* (shrimp paste, coconut and chilli wrapped in a taro leaf). Daily 8am–9pm.

Lolo's Music Bar Upper floor of Avenue Square mall. Fun bar that serves pasta as well as Bicolano food, and has a stage for regular live music performances. Tues–Sun 4pm–midnight.

CamSur Watersports Complex (CWC)

A major new tourist destination located roughly halfway between Naga and Pili, **CWC** (☏054/477-3344, ⓦwww.cwcwake.com) is an international-standard wakeboarding course. There is a beginners' winch park, where you can practise standing up on a straight run, and it's also possible to use a kneeboard on the main course. The main course involves six turns and an assortment of ramps and rails for those who know what they are doing. Prices vary depending on what you want to do, for example P370 for half a day on the main course including rental of a beginner's wakeboard and other equipment.

Building something like this with taxpayers' money was certainly a gamble, but it seems to have paid off. Within a few years of opening CWC has helped CamSur to become second only to Boracay in terms of tourist arrivals, and international competitions are already being held here. There are ambitious plans for further development, including a golf course and mountain biking track. The complex already has a swimming lagoon and a small skatepark.

There is also a range of **accommodation**, from tiki huts (❸) and converted shipping containers (❹) to private villas (❻). Hardcore wakeboarders tend to favour the *cabañas* (❹) as they are right beside the cable park, while if you're on a tight budget you might try fan-cooled huts at the *Ecovillage* (❶), which is a little further from the action. The site also has a bar (3pm–7am) and a café (6am–midnight). There is wi-fi on site and in some of the rooms.

CWC is located within the Provincial Capitol complex in Pili. From Naga, take a bus or jeepney to the Capitol Junction (15min from the main terminal; P10) then a tricycle (10min; P10). Alternatively there are shuttles running from the SM City mall and along Magsaysay Avenue – contact CWC for the current timetable. From the airport, a tricycle will charge you a rather steep P150.

Lake Buhi

Mostly enclosed by hills that rise to 300m in places, Lake Buhi lies 52km from Naga. To reach the town of **BUHI**, the only realistic access point for the lake, take a Filcab Express van from Naga (1hr 10min; P70–80). Located on the south shore of the lake, the town is a surprisingly busy little place.

You can charter a **bangka** at the lakeside market in Buhi and take a trip across the water (P700–1000), perhaps stopping for a picnic on Roca Encantada, the island in the middle. Don't miss **Itbog Falls** in the barangay of Santa Cruz, 5km from Buhi and north of the lake; these wonderful twin falls come crashing through thick rainforest vegetation into deep pools that are perfect for swimming. Once you're across the lake, the boatman can guide you (for around

P700 extra) on the terrific one-hour trek to the falls through rice paddies and along rocky trails.

There are several places to **stay** in Buhi, including *Lake Buhi Resort and Country Club* (☎0927/249-1614; ❹), which has a swimming pool, restaurant, videoke bar and an enclosed fishing village on the lake.

Mount Isarog National Park

One of the Philippines' richest and least trampled areas, **Mount Isarog National Park** covers forty square kilometres in the heart of Camarines Sur, about 40km east of Naga. At its centre stands **Mount Isarog** (1966m), the second highest peak in southern Luzon and part of the Bicol volcanic chain that also includes Mayon. Isarog is considered potentially active, although it is not known when it last erupted.

The park is relatively easy to reach, but once on the lower slopes of the mountain you may feel as if you have stepped through a portal into the Jurassic Age. The jungle is thick and steamy, and the **flora and fauna** are among the most varied in the archipelago. Long-tailed macaques and monitor lizards are a pretty common sight, while with a little luck you may also spot the indigenous shrew rats, reticulated pythons and rare birds such as the bleeding-heart pigeon, red-breasted pitta and blue-nape fantail. Reaching the summit takes two days of strenuous climbing. At the top are two craters, the lower of the pair containing a number of fumaroles steaming with sulphurous gas.

A number of paths on Isarog's lower slopes lead to **waterfalls** – including Mina-Ati, Nabuntulan and Tumaguiti – all of which are surrounded by thick rainforest and have deep, cool pools for swimming. The easiest waterfall to reach is beautiful Malabsay, a powerful ribbon of water that plunges into a deep pool surrounded by forest greenery. It's a delightful place for a dip. There are also some hot springs in Panicuason (admission P200).

Practicalities

The best time to trek is between March and May, but it is possible at other times weather allowing; September to December is particularly wet. The most commonly used route to the summit takes three days and is called the **Panicuason trail**, starting at the barangay of Panicuason. There are also four other recognized routes on the mountain: the PLDT Trail (2 days), Curry Trail (3 days), Patag-Patag Trail (3 days) and Hiwakloy Trail (4 days). They vary in character and difficulty.

There's a Protected Area Office (contact Yolda Abante on ☎0910/482-4615) at the park entrance used for the Panicuason trail, where you can get a permit (P80); if you are taking a different trail then you should instead request a permit at the Mount Isarog Protected Area Superintendent Office, 35 Panganiban Drive in Naga at least three days in advance.

A good place in Naga to glean additional information about the climb is the Kadlagan Outdoor Shop (☎054/472-3305, ⊛kadlagan.i.ph), 16 Dimasalang St, where you can rent basic equipment. You will also need to secure the services of a local **guide** (P250–400/day); ask at Kadlagan, the Naga City Visitors Center or the Protected Area Office.

To get to Panicuason, take a jeepney (P20) from close to the market in Naga. It's a four-kilometre walk from Panicuason along a well-marked trail to the ranger station, Malabsay Waterfall and the entrance to the park proper. There are no jeepneys from Panicuason back to Naga after 4pm, so keep an eye on the time. If you get stuck you'll have to pay to rent one privately, usually costing around P1000.

Caramoan Peninsula

The wild and sometimes windswept **CARAMOAN PENINSULA**, 50km to the east of Naga, is blessed with limestone cliffs and blue-water coves to rival the Visayas or Palawan. Until recently its relative isolation and lack of infrastructure meant that it attracted only a handful of tourists. Then in 2008 the French production of the *Survivor* TV show was filmed here, and other international productions followed suit. While today the area hardly rivals somewhere like Boracay in terms of development, it is attracting increasing numbers of people to its rugged, scenic landscape. The dry season here runs from February to October, while November sees the most rain.

Caramoan Town

There isn't much to delay you in **CARAMOAN TOWN** other than a few souvenir shops, a couple of simple restaurants and *Planetbiz* (daily 8am–9pm) internet café on the main road. There are no banks and no ATMs. If you're keen to **stay**, the best choice is the homely ☩ *La Casa Roa* (☎054/811-5789; ❹) on Sirangan Street. The oldest hotel in Caramoan Town, the building was levelled by a typhoon but rebuilt with salvaged original features, such as its beautiful wooden floors. *Rex* (☎0915/329-5658; ❷) on Real Street is a very popular choice which fills up quickly; rooms are bright, clean and good value.

Gota Beach

The most developed spot on the peninsula is **GOTA BEACH**, 6km from Caramoan Town and reachable in about ten minutes by tricycle (P40) along a surfaced but damaged road. Although it's possible to visit just for the day (P300 adults, P150 children), it's worth considering a stay at the *Gota Village Resort* (☎02/818-0831; ❺). This camp of 81 comfortable *cabañas* was originally built to house the *Survivor* television crews. The resort is often block-booked in summer for filming, but the rest of the time the *cabañas* are available to the public. In addition to a lovely, golden-sand cove with crystal-clear water – and, sometimes, crashing waves – there are activities such as kayaking, island-hopping, caving, hiking, rock climbing and mountain biking. The list goes on, so contact the resort to find out about the current options. You can also visit the abandoned sets of different TV productions.

Several tiny islands lie just off Gota Beach, including **Lahos Island** (or Bichara Island), which has deep, clear water, stunning limestone formations and a beach cutting through from one side of the island to the other. Also nearby is **Matukad Island**, which has some of the whitest sand in the area and a hidden lagoon.

Other beaches and islands

If Gota is too pricey or too developed for your tastes, then it's worth checking out the resorts on **Paniman Beach**: ☩ *Breeze and Waves* (☎0908/291-1072; ❸) is a friendly family-run place, while *La Playa* (☎0919/813-6766; ❷), a little further down the beach, has a range of accommodation options – guests can pitch their own tents or hire them (P600 with bedding), and there are fan-cooled huts and a/c rooms. Other beaches well worth striking out for include **Bag-ing Beach**, a scenic crescent of white sand on a lagoon-like deserted bay.

It's easy to arrange **island-hopping trips** through most accommodation; alternatively you can hire a bangka direct from Bikal Wharf just outside Caramoan Town, at around P1500–3000 for a full day depending on the distance covered. There are

4

The easiest way to reach the peninsula is by **boat** from the small port of Sabang, an hour east of Naga by minivan or jeepney (P70–85). Visitors coming direct from Manila can take a Raymond Transport bus from Cubao direct to Sabang (10–12hr; P560). From Sabang, bangkas make the two-hour trip (P120–150) east along the coast to Guijalo ("Gee-ahlo") port on the Caramoan Peninsula; there are views of Mount Mayon on a clear day. If you miss the last ferry at around 1pm, you can hire a boat for P1500–2000 (for five people) or P3500–4000 (for twelve). At low tide the boats cannot stop at the jetty in Guijalo, so you either get wet or pay a porter P5–10 to carry you ashore. From Guijalo it's then a 15 to 20 minute hop by tricycle (P40) to Caramoan Town.

If you're staying at Gota Beach then things are a little quicker and easier; there's a fast 65-seat catamaran (1hr 15min; P375) departing from Nato port (south of Sabang in Sagñay town) at 10.30am during high season. A free shuttle runs from Guijalo to the resort.

The other alternative is to skip the sea journey and instead take a Raymond Transport **bus** all the way to Caramoan Town from Naga or Pili (P300). In the rainy season, however, this route may be impassable. Even in the dry season the road is poor and the trip takes four hours; on the whole the sea route is a better option until the road is eventually upgraded.

several islands grouped together close to the mainland, including the V-shaped **Bagieng**, which has long stretches of white sand and good snorkelling. A little further from shore is the wonderful **Lahuy Island**, also known as "Treasure Island" because of its history of gold mining. There is still small-scale gold panning in the barangay of Gata, and visitors can try their hand for a small fee; this is most easily arranged through the *Gota Village Resort* (see p.211) or one of the resorts in Paniman. Aim to arrive at low tide and expect to pay around P2000 for a bangka. Lahuy has a fine stretch of seemingly endless white beach on one side and some scenic coves on the other. There's no accommodation, but it's possible to camp out for the night on the beach, as long as you make sure the boat will be back for you the following day. Nearby is **Aguirangan Island**, which has a stunning coral reef for snorkelling.

Legazpi and around

About four hours south of Naga, the busy port city of **LEGAZPI** (sometimes spelt Legaspi) is a convenient base for exploring the area, including **Mount Mayon** whose almost perfect cone-shaped bulk rises from paddy fields to the north of the city. Other attractions include quiet beaches around the town of **Santo Domingo**, the eerie remains of a church at **Cagsawa** that was buried in the devastating eruption of Mayon in 1814, and **Hyop-Hoyopan** and **Calabidongan caves**.

Arrival and information

Long-distance **buses** arrive at the Grand Central Terminal on the western edge of the newer part of town (known as the city proper). The airport is only a couple of kilometres northwest of the city proper; incoming flights are met by tricycles at the airport (P20 to the city).

Legazpi has two **tourist offices**, close to each other in the Albay district. One, run by the city government (Ⓦwowlegazpi.com), is in the City Hall; the other is the Albay provincial tourist office (☎052/820-6314), part of the Astrodome complex on Captain F. Aquende Drive. Enquire at either about arranging a guide

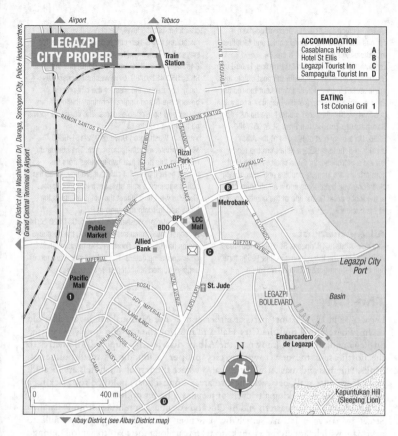

LEGAZPI CITY PROPER

Airport ▲   Tabaco ▲

Train Station

Albay District (via Washington Dr), Daraga, Sorsogon City, Police Headquarters, Grand Central Terminal & Airport

DON B. ERQUIAGA

RAMON SANTOS EXT

RAMON SANTOS

PEÑARANDA

QUEZON AVENUE

T. ALONZO

MAGALLANES

P. AGUINALDO

Rizal Park

ACCOMMODATION
Casablanca Hotel   A
Hotel St Ellis   B
Legazpi Tourist Inn   C
Sampaguita Tourist Inn   D

EATING
1st Colonial Grill **1**

Metrobank

BPI   LCC Mall
BDO

Public Market

Allied Bank

F. IMPERIAL

Pacific Mall

ROSAL

LOS BAÑOS AVENUE

RIZAL AVENUE

GOV. IMPERIAL

ILANG-ILANG

MAGNOLIA

ROSE

DAHLIA

DAISY

CAMIA

P. ELIZONDO

QUEZON AVENUE

LAPU-LAPU

St. Jude

LEGAZPI BOULEVARD

LEGAZPI Basin

Legazpi City Port

Embarcadero de Legazpi

N

0   400 m

Kapuntukan Hill (Sleeping Lion)

▼ Albay District (see Albay District map)

for Mount Mayon (see p.215), while for car hire, private tours, trekking (including Mount Mayon) and other adventure tourism try On-Trail Adventures (☏052/486-1265 or 0915/590-5980) or Bicol Adventures and Tours (☏052/480-2266), which is in the same building as the *Legazpi Tourist Inn*.

The **post office** is on Lapu-Lapu Street at the junction with Quezon Avenue, and there are a numerous **banks** on Rizal Avenue as well as ATMs in the shopping malls. In the Albay district, you can find ATMs in the Provincial Capitol Annex and at the branch of BPI close to *Lita's Lodge* on Rizal. The main **police station** is on the F Imperial Extension to the west of the centre. There are plenty of **internet cafés** in the city proper.

Accommodation

Most of the **accommodation** in Legazpi lies along the main roads, so rooms at the front can be noisy.

City proper

Casablanca Hotel Peñaranda St ☏052/480-8334, ⓦwww.casablancahotel.ph. A popular hotel with large rooms decked out in a mildly dated "Mediterranean" style. There is a tour desk

downstairs that can book tickets for Cebu Pacific and Zest flights. ④

Hotel St Ellis Rizal St ☏052/480-8088, ⓦwww.hotelstellis.com.ph. The only truly high-end hotel in the city proper, this is a seriously

4

SOUTHERN LUZON | Legazpi and around

213

classy addition to Legazpi's accommodation options. The rooms are impeccable, and facilities include a luxurious spa and a crèche. **7**

Legazpi Tourist Inn 3/F, V&O Building, Lapu-Lapu St ☎052/480-6147. Opposite the post office, this small and friendly place has well-kept fan rooms for a reasonable price. Not the height of luxury, but good value; the cheapest rooms have no a/c. **2**

Sampaguita Tourist Inn Rizal St ☎052/480-6255. On a busy part of Rizal St at the Albay district end, but set back a little from the road behind a petrol station. Good choice of boxy but comfortable a/c singles, doubles and triples, with clean en-suite bathrooms and a small coffee shop in the lobby area. Go for one of the quieter rooms at the back. **2**

Albay district

Casa de Abuela 18 Vinzons St ☎052/480-4066. While decent, the three rooms in this 1950s family home-cum-"eco-hostel" don't have much

character, but the lovely garden and vegetarian restaurant more than compensate. Discounts for stays of a week or more. **2**

Casablanca Suites Alternate Rd (Benny Imperial St) ☎052/481-0789, ⓦwww.casablancasuites.com. Located to the west of the city proper, beyond the Grand Central Terminal, this hotel has stylish and comfortable rooms. The cheapest rooms all have twin beds. **6**

Venezia Washington Drive ☎052/481-0888, ⓦwww.hotelvenezia-legazpi.com. The standard rooms in this hotel just two minutes from the airport ooze minimalist chic but are tiny, while the suites sacrifice a little style for a lot more space. There is wi-fi throughout the hotel, a café in the lobby and in-room massage at P750. **7**

Vista al Mayon Washington Drive ☎054/820-5814. A decent hotel with a swimming pool; the executive rooms have wooden floors, wicker furniture and other appealing details. The deluxe rooms are more simply outfitted but completely acceptable. **3**

The City

Legazpi is in two distinct parts at either end of the National Highway. The old town, where you'll find the City Hall and most of the top-end hotels, is centred on Peñaranda Park and known as the **Albay district**. A couple of kilometres to the northeast is the new town, or **city proper**, a muddle of small businesses, banks, cinemas and market stalls, and also where the rest of the hotels are located. It's a 25-minute walk between the two areas along a busy, polluted road lacking a decent pavement, making a tricycle or jeepney a better option.

The **wharf** is at the eastern end of Quezon Avenue, ten minutes from Peñaranda Street by tricycle. It isn't served by passenger ferries, although it's possible to negotiate with boatmen for a bangka to take you along the coast to Santo Domingo and even as far as the islands of San Miguel, Cagrary, Batan and Rapu-Rapu. This is also where you will also find the most ambitious recent development in Legazpi, the **Embarcadero de Legazpi** (ⓦwww.embarcadero.ph) waterfront complex. In addition to an array of shops and restaurants, there's go-karting, arcade games and regular live music. The Embarcadero is still a work in progress – there is even talk of creating a wakeboarding facility to compete with CWC (see p.209).

To the northwest of the city centre is **Lignon Hill**. Popular with local families, the hill is a great viewpoint for Mayon but also a destination in its own right. Quad bikes can be rented at the base of the hill from Your Brother Travel and Tours (☎052/821-1320;

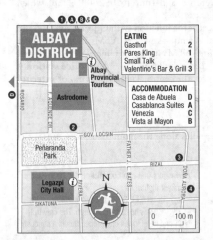

ALBAY DISTRICT

EATING
Gasthof	2
Pares King	1
Small Talk	4
Valentino's Bar & Grill	3

ACCOMMODATION
Casa de Abuela	D
Casablanca Suites	A
Venezia	C
Vista al Mayon	B

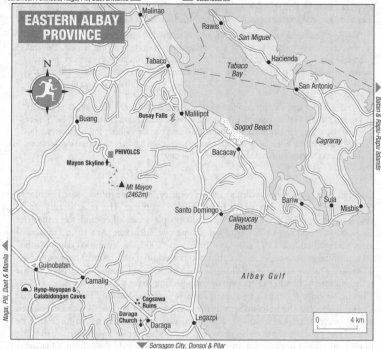

EASTERN ALBAY PROVINCE

N

Malinao

Rawis

San Miguel

Hacienda

Tabaco

Tabaco Bay

San Antonio

Buang

Busay Falls

Malilipot

Sogod Beach

Cagraray

PHIVOLCS

Mayon Skyline

Bacacay

Mt Mayon (2462m)

Bariw

Sula

Misbis

Santo Domingo

Calayucay Beach

Albay Gulf

Guinobatan

Camalig

Hyop-Hoyopan & Calabidongan Caves

Cagsawa Ruins

Daraga Church

Daraga

Legazpi

0   4 km

P1800/1hr) for tours to see volcanic rock formations. At the top of the hill are two zip lines (P200 for both) and a large concrete building containing souvenir shops and cafés including a small branch of *Chowking*.

Eating

In the city proper the options are largely limited to small carenderias (canteens) and the usual fast-food outlets; try *1st Colonial Grill* in Pacific Mall for decent renditions of Filipino and Bicolano favourites. Below are a handful of more interesting eating options, all in the **Albay district**.

Gasthof Gov Locsin St. A branch of the popular Boracay establishment, serving local favourites but also its famous spare ribs.

Pares King Washington Dr. Although it serves other dishes the reason to come here is for the beef *pares*, a satisfying dish of beef brisket served with rice and broth. Daily 7am–2am, later if there are customers.

Small Talk Doña Aurora St ☎052/480-1393. The most atmospheric dining experience in the city, located in an ancestral home complete with family pictures and old photographs

of Mayon. The menu covers all the standard Filipino fare, plus some twists on Bicolano cuisine including pasta with Bicol Express (spicy coconut milk and pork) sauce. Mains and pizzas cost around P200, with pasta from P100. Daily 11am–10pm.

Valentino's Bar and Grill Rizal St ☎052/481-7142. Set in an old building with wooden floors and stained-glass windows, this is one of the best restaurants in town. The biggest seller is the "Linkin Pork", although the "Killer Seafood" also goes down well. Daily 8am–midnight.

Mount Mayon

The elegantly smooth cone of **MOUNT MAYON** (2460m) in Albay province makes it look benign from a distance, but don't be deceived. Mayon is a devil in

The most comfortable way to reach Manila is to **fly** with Philippine Airlines, Air Philippines or Cebu Pacific. Each of the airlines has an office at the airport. Several companies run buses to Manila (10–12hr; P700 plus), mostly departing in the early evening and arriving around dawn. Try Philtranco (T02/851-8078, Wwww.philtranco .com.ph), Peñafrancia (T052/435-3012, Wwww.penafranciatours.com) or Isarog (T052/481-4744).

The quickest and easiest way to reach destinations in Bicol – such as Naga (2hr) or Tabaco (30min) – is by **minivan**. If there are no direct vans to Donsol (1hr; P60) then it may be necessary to change in Pilar. The vans run throughout the daytime, as do local buses which are slightly cheaper but slower; both types of transport depart from the Grand Central Terminal to the west of the city.

disguise. The most active volcano in the country, it has **erupted** more than forty times since 1616, the date of its first recorded eruption. The most deadly single eruption was in 1814 when around 1200 people were killed and the church at Cagsawa (see opposite) was destroyed; 77 people, including American vulcanologists, were killed in a 1993 eruption. In August 2006, an "extended danger zone" was enforced but the expected eruption did not occur. Three months later, however, Typhoon Durian caused mudslides of volcanic ash and boulders on Mayon that killed hundreds. Further eruptions and ash ejections have occurred since.

It's no wonder the locals spin fearful **stories** around Mayon. The most popular legend has it that the volcano was formed when a beautiful native princess eloped with a brave warrior. Her uncle, Magayon, was so possessive of his niece that he chased the young couple, who prayed to the gods for help. Suddenly a landslide buried the raging uncle alive, and he is said to be still inside the volcano, his anger sometimes bursting forth in the form of eruptions.

The presence of Mayon results in strange meteorological conditions in and around Legazpi, with the volcano and the surrounding area often blanketed in rain when the rest of the country is basking in unbroken sunshine. The traditional window of opportunity for an ascent is **February to April**, and even then you'll have to be well prepared for cold nights at altitude and the possibility of showers. At any other time of year you could be hanging around for days waiting for a break in the weather. Though the slopes look smooth, it takes at least two days to reach the highest point of the trail, working your way slowly through forest, grassland and deserts of boulders. Above 1800m there's the possibility of being affected by poisonous gases, although some guides will offer to take you to 2000m.

There are three recognized approaches to Mayon: via Legazpi's Buyunan barangay; via the Centennial Forest in Santo Domingo; and via San Roque barangay in Malilipot. The last of these is the most commonly used, starting at 762m above sea level on a ledge where the **Philippine Institute of Volcanology and Seismology** (PHIVOLCS) research station is located. Nearby are the abandoned **Mayon Skyline Hotel** and the Mayon Planetarium and Science Park (free), which has exhibits including photographs of space. It's worth heading up to this point even if you aren't climbing Mayon, just to see the views.

Practicalities

You can get to the PHIVOLCS research station by taking a **jeepney** or **bus** from Legazpi to **Tabaco** (see p.219), 26km north of Legazpi, then another heading west to **Buang**, where the narrow concrete road up the mountain is on the left just before you reach Buang itself. Whatever you do, don't attempt the climb without a **guide**. Local authorities have made guides mandatory and setting out without one would be foolhardy in the extreme. You can arrange one at the tourist offices in Legazpi and also check whether conditions are suitable for an ascent. Another good source of information is ⓦwww.phivolcs.dost.gov.ph. You'll have to bring all your food with you from Legazpi; there are sources of water on the volcano, but you'll need purifying tablets.

Daraga Church

Fifteen minutes northwest of Legazpi by jeepney, the busy market town of **DARAGA** is home to **Daraga Church**, an imposing eighteenth-century Baroque structure built by Franciscan missionaries from blocks of volcanic lava. The exterior was decorated by skilled stonemasons with statuary, carvings, alcoves and niches, but until recently had been falling into disrepair. It was declared a national cultural treasure in 2008 and a project was undertaken to restore the church to its former glory, although in the meantime the work has significantly reduced the appeal of the exterior.

To get there, take a jeepney to Daraga and then walk or take a jeepney (P7) to the church on the western edge of town. Before leaving it's worth taking a break at the *7 Degrees Grill and Restaurant* (daily 10am–midnight; ⓣ052/483-4171), which has a terrace overlooking Mayon and serves Bicolano and Filipino dishes such as *kilawing* tuna (raw fish cured in vinegar). In the evening the lights and candles on the terrace make it a romantic spot; reservations are wise for dinner at weekends.

Cagsawa Ruins

Eight kilometres northwest of Legazpi, beyond the town of Daraga, the **Cagsawa Ruins** (P10) are the remains of a Spanish church that was destroyed by the 1814 eruption of Mayon. Around 1200 people were entombed in lava and still remain there.

To get to the ruins, take a jeepney from Legazpi in the direction of Camalig, Ligao or Guinobatan. Jeepneys don't stop automatically near the ruins, so tell the driver where you want to get off. The ruins are small and there's not much to explore, but they are picturesque, standing in gardens close to paddy fields with marvellous views across the plain to Mount Mayon. This is a popular spot, so if you want peace and quiet – as well as to take photographs before the cumulus rolls in to obscure Mayon's tip – take an early jeepney. There are a number of souvenir stalls and sari-sari stores right outside the ruins where you can buy drinks and snacks, and there is also a swimming pool (daily 6am–6pm; P50) close by.

Hyop-Hoyopan and Calabidongan caves

Hyop-Hoyopan (daily 7am–8pm; guided tour P200) – meaning "Blowing Wind" due to the breeze inside – is the most easily accessible of 14 limestone caves in the area. It's a well-established attraction and guides hang around the entrance, although you could try Marife Nieva (ⓣ0915/286-7221) or Bam Nuylan (ⓣ0927/969-9855) if nobody is there.

Tours take about thirty minutes, with guides pointing out fragments of burial jars dating from 2000 years ago. There is also a concrete dancefloor built in 1972, when parties were held in secret to avoid the curfew of the martial law era. Hyop-Hoyopan is most easily reached with a private vehicle but if you're using public transport, take a jeepney from Legazpi to Camalig (30min; P15) and then hop on the back of a motorcycle (P50–100 depending on your negotiating skills). This mode of transport is known locally either as a "single" or a "door-to-door".

Calabidongan (Cave of the Bats; P550 including transport from Hyop-Hyopan) is a more serious proposition as it is always partly flooded and requires a very short swim at one point. It is best visited from **March to June**, as at other times the water level can be too high. Guides have torches, but if you have a waterproof one then bring it. Wear flip-flops or sandals and don't take a camera unless you have a waterproof bag. Guides at Hyop-Hyopan can arrange a door-to-door to Calabidongan, and the trip takes a total of three hours.

Santo Domingo and the nearby beaches

About thirty minutes northeast of Legazpi along the coastal road is the small town of **SANTO DOMINGO**, a tidy, friendly little barrio with an atmospheric old Spanish church on the north side of the narrow main street. On the way to Santo Domingo look out for three large concrete crosses commemorating the flash floods in 2006 which devastated a nearby barangay. A little beyond that, in the barangay of Buyuan, is a signposted turning for a nine-hole golf course and stables offering horseriding (P500 to ride to the lowest camp on Mount Mayon).

To the east of Santo Domingo a concrete road winds its way up and down through some delightful, pristine countryside, with the main destination being **Calayucay Beach**. It's pretty but not spectacular, though the views across Albay Gulf are attractive and its resorts are good places to relax. To the north of Santo Domingo, the main attraction is **Sogod Beach** near Bacacay – a pleasantly rustic stretch of black volcanic sand sometimes known as the Mayon Riviera. In addition to several sets of day-cottages for picnickers, there are a couple of resorts with accommodation.

There are jeepneys from Legazpi's market to Santo Domingo and to Bacacay. From Santo Domingo you can get a jeepney to Calayucay Beach, while for Sogod Beach you need to take a tricycle from Bacacay.

Accommodation

Coastal View Calayucay Beach ☎052/437-8170. The first resort you come to on Calayucay beach is also one of the best, with an attractive use of natural materials in the rooms. The standard rooms have no view, unlike the executive rooms which also have a more attractive decor. Jet skis, skimboards and quad bikes are available to rent. **❹**

Costa Palmera Calayucay Beach ☎052/481-9175, Ⓦwww.costapalmeraresort.com. The economy rooms here are boxy and windowless but fine as a place to lay your head. Much quirkier are the two poolside rooms, which share a pool and jacuzzi. There is also a tidal seawater pool for all guests. Wi-fi throughout and a generator in case of blackouts. **❷**

Manhattan Calayucay Beach ☎052/481-9524, Ⓦwww.manhattanbeachresortphils.com. Though the paintings of New York seem rather out of place, this is a good option. Standard rooms are arrayed above their own parking spaces and have views of the sea. There is also a pool with a slide, and wi-fi access. **❸**

Puerto Vista Calayucay Beach ☎0918/693-9765. The "suite room" is just a standard double and has no window, but this is a decent choice with a swimming pool. **❷**

Tanchuling Sogod Beach ☎052/820-2912. *Tanchuling* has simple rooms that can be either a/c or fan-only, and island-hopping can be arranged. The telephone number is for the related hotel of the same name in Legazpi, where bookings should be made. **❷**

Viento de Mar Sogod Beach ☎052/480-2266. Has a set of *cabañas* set in a grassy open space. The cheapest rooms are fan-only with no mosquito netting, while a/c rooms start at P1700; food is made to order. The place offers numerous activities including horseriding on the beach, fishing, biking, scuba diving, kayaking and island-hopping. Bookings must be made in advance through Bicol Adventure & Tours, on the number above, as there is no reception desk at the resort. **❷**

Tabaco and around

TABACO, 26km northeast of Legazpi, is a busy little port that functions as the gateway to **Catanduanes** (see p.229), and to four smaller **islands** – San Miguel, Cagraray, Batan and Rapu-Rapu – which all have lovely beaches and great scuba diving.

Most **buses** arrive at the integrated bus terminal on Rizal Street. The **jeepney** terminal is behind the indoor market, opposite the church on the main street; the **port** is a ten-minute walk down the road running next to the market. Several ferries run back and forth each day to Virac and San Andres, on the southwest coast of Catanduanes, which can be a rough crossing particularly from October to December.

If you need to spend the **night**, there are a few decent **accommodation** options: *HCG Residence Mansion* on Ziga Avenue (T 052/830-3206; ❺) is a comfortable and central hotel with wi-fi. Above a small shopping complex, the *JJ Midcity Inn* (T 0922/830-2858; ❸) is a pleasant surprise – its rooms are clean and good value, but ask for one away from the market.

Local **food** specialities include *ibos latik* (rice cake with reduced coconut milk). For coffee and a snack, try *She Lei Girl* (daily 7am–midnight) on the ground floor of the *Casa Eugenia Hotel* on Ziga Avenue. Combining a café and grocery store, it serves dim sum and other Chinese dishes either to eat in or take away. For something more substantial, *Solamente* on the National Highway (a 5min walk away from the centre) serves good Filipino dishes although most are in large portions for sharing.

Cagraray

The best island near Tabaco to visit, and the most accessible, is **Cagraray**, which has some wonderful white sand beaches in the barrios of **Sula** and **Misibis** on the southeast coast. The latter is the location of the luxurious *Misibis Bay* resort (T 02/661-8888, W www.misibisbay.com; ❾), with 37 stylish villas at prices to match. The resort has quad bikes, mountain bikes and dune buggies to hire, as well as various waterborne activities. Otherwise if you want to stay overnight you'll either need to camp or ask locals whether anyone can put you up (offer a token of your appreciation, at least P100 a night). If you aren't taking advantage of a resort transfer, **San Antonio** barangay on Cagraray can be reached from Tabaco by ferry (2hr; P55) or using a bridge from the peninsula east of Santo Domingo. This latter route can be more reliable during the typhoon season; jeepneys run from Tabaco and Legazpi (1hr; P50–60). Hiring a bangka to see the beaches and coves should cost around P500 for a full day.

Sorsogon province

A toe of land with a striking volcanic topography and some little-known beaches, lakes, hot springs and waterfalls, **Sorsogon province** lies south of Albay and is the easternmost part of mainland Bicol. The province is best known to tourists for the chance to snorkel with whale sharks off the coast near **Donsol**, but it's also a great area for activities such as hiking and caving. **Sorsogon City** makes a good base for exploring the area's many lovely beaches – the nicest stretch of sand being **Rizal Beach**, in the barrio of Gubat to the east of Sorsogon City. There are many pristine coves to explore along the coast around **Bacon** while south of Sorsogon City, **Mount Bulusan** is a climbable, active volcano.

Driving through Sorsogon province you will pass many stalls selling items made from the fibre of *abacá*, the fibre of a species of banana tree and one of the major products of the province. Sometimes known as Manila hemp, although it also grows in Malaysia and Indonesia, it is processed to make everything from banknotes to teabags.

Donsol

The area around Donsol is best known for one of the greatest concentrations of **whale sharks** in the world. The number of sightings varies: during the peak months of February to May there's a good chance of seeing ten or fifteen whale sharks a day, but on some days (particularly early or late in the season, which stretches from mid-November to June) you might strike out and see none. Holy Week is extremely busy and best avoided.

Arrival and information

Jeepneys and air-conditioned **minivans** arrive at a terminal on the southern edge of town. **Ferries** from Masbate arrive at Pilar port, 20min away from Donsol town by jeepney. The **Visitor Centre** (daily 7.30am–5pm; ☎0919/707-0394 or 0917/868-1626) is northwest of Donsol town among the resorts in **Dancalan** barangay, P25 away by tricycle from the centre of town. There are **no ATMs** in Donsol, and the only place offering currency exchange at the time of research was the *Elysia* resort (see below) – it would be unwise to rely on this, so bring enough pesos. Some of the accommodation options, including *Giddy's Place* (see below), will take credit cards. **Internet** is available in Donsol town.

Accommodation

The **resorts** are about 2km northwest of the town centre and many close outside of the whale shark-watching season. The town itself is becoming more tourist-oriented as locals aim to capitalize on growing visitor numbers; although there are few hotels, there are numerous homestays. Contact the tourist office for an up-to-date list.

Donsol Town

Agu-Luz San José St ☎0918/942-0897. The rooms here are within the family home, and are impeccably clean. There is a garden at the front with tables and a hammock, and wi-fi is available. ❷

Giddy's Place 54 Clemente St ☎0917/848-8881, ⓦwww.giddysplace.com. The deluxe and family rooms in this hotel are pretty good although on the expensive side, but there are also cheap fan-only "backpacker rooms" each with two bunks at P500 per head. It's fine to arrive solo as long as you are willing to share. Facilities include free wi-fi, a spa and a dive shop with training pool. ❻

Santiago Corner of San José St & Tres Marias Drive ☎0917/861-9918. A long-standing homestay in a noisy spot, offering decent fan or a/c rooms with shared bathrooms. Guests can use the kitchen. ❷

Resorts

AGM ☎0919/688-2264 or 0917/381-3404, ⓦwww.agmresort.com. The first resort you come to on the strip, *AGM* has two rows of clean and tidy a/c concrete rooms with hot and cold showers. ❹

Elysia ☎0917/547-4466 or 0926/475-9762, ⓦwww.elysia-donsol.com. This Korean-owned place is easily the most upmarket choice along the strip, with prices to match. All rooms are poolside, and Rooms 1 and 15 have ocean views. US dollars can be exchanged here. ❼

Vitton ☎0927/912-6313. Among the best of the resorts: the cottages are clean and comfortable, with spacious bathrooms, and the grounds are well tended. The restaurant overlooks the sea and attracts plenty of customers from outside. The *Woodland Resort* next door is owned by the same people, with similar rooms and grounds – not quite as high a standard but a little cheaper. ❺

Whale shark watching

At the Visitor Centre you can complete all the formalities of **hiring a boat** for a whale shark-watching trip. Queues can start to form before the centre opens during peak season, particularly at weekends, so arrive early.

Tourists are not allowed to board a boat without first being briefed by a **Butanding Interaction Officer** (BIO), who explains how to behave in the water near a whale shark. The number of snorkellers around any one shark is limited to six; flash photography is not allowed, nor is scuba gear, and avoid the animal's tail because it can do you some serious damage. Some boatmen flout these rules in order to keep their passengers happy, but this risks distressing the whale sharks and should not be encouraged. Check that your boat has one of the mandatory propeller guards.

Boats cost P3500 for up to seven people, and there's also a registration fee of P300 for foreigners (P100 for Filipinos). **Snorkelling equipment** can be hired from outside the visitor centre at P150 for mask and snorkel plus P150 for flippers. Each boat has a crew of three, the captain, the BIO and the spotter, each of whom would welcome a token of your appreciation. All this makes it an expensive day out by Philippine standards, but take heart from the fact that your money is helping the conservation effort. Take plenty of protection against the sun and a good book. Once a whale shark has been sighted you'll need to get your mask, snorkel and flippers on and get in the water before it dives too deep to be seen.

Other activities

Although the snorkelling is Donsol's number one draw, there's also scuba diving at the infamous **Manta Bowl**; actually closer to Ticao (see p.228), it is best reached from the dive shops attached to several of the resorts in Donsol. The site is far from shore, and requires divers to descend rapidly and cling onto rocks – try to get a reef hook or gloves. You then use the strong drift to move towards the Manta Bowl, and if you are lucky you will be rewarded with close-up views of mantas or even whale sharks. Be warned that this is not a dive for beginners, whatever the dive shops may tell you when trying to get your business. Also be on the lookout for shoddy equipment.

If all this sounds too intense, then a day **island-hopping** can be arranged through resorts. *Giddy's Place* (see opposite) can also sort out **kayaking** trips on the Ugod River for P1500 per person. Another popular attraction is **firefly watching** (P1250/boat, for up to 5 people) in the early evening. There are two starting points, one beside the bridge on the main road and the other on the Ugod River.

Whale sharks

Known locally as the *butanding*, the **whale shark** is a timid titan resembling a whale more than the shark it is. It can grow up to 20m in length, making it the largest fish in the seas. These gentle giants gather around Donsol every year around the time of the northeastern monsoon to feed on the rich shrimp and plankton streams that flow from the Donsol River into the sea, sucking their food through their gills via an enormous vacuum of a mouth.

Whale sharks were rarely hunted in the Philippines until the 1990s, when demand for their meat from countries such as Taiwan and Japan escalated. Cooks have dubbed it the tofu shark because of the meat's resemblance to soybean curd. Its fins are also coveted as a soup extender. Tragically, this has led to its near extinction in the Visayas and further south in Mindanao. Though the government is trying to protect the whale sharks by fining fishermen who catch them, it's an uphill battle, largely because enforcement is difficult and a good whale shark can fetch enough to keep a rural family happy for months. In Donsol, however, attitudes seem to be changing, with locals beginning to realize that the whale sharks can be worth more alive than dead, attracting tourists and thus investment and jobs.

The former is a little more convenient, but the latter is a narrower stretch of water and provides a better experience. Trips start at 7pm; you can just show up at the starting point in good time, but it's better to enquire at the Visitor Centre. April and May are said to be the best months, as the air conditions are at their calmest.

Eating and drinking

The resorts in Dancalan each have a restaurant, open to non-guests. In town, there are simple places serving *turo-turo* (where you select from an array of pre-cooked dishes on display).

Barracuda On the waterfront between *Vitton* and *Woodland* resorts. Overlooking the sea, *Barracuda* serves the catch of the day and good cold beer.

Giddy's Butanding Bar Part of *Giddy's Place* hotel. A pleasant spot serving both local and international dishes, at around P120 for a main course. The bar also has wi-fi. Daily 6am–1am.

Shanley's Beside the bus and jeepney terminal in Donsol town. The smell from the mangroves takes a little getting used to, but locals are drawn to this bar for live music on Friday and Saturday nights. Expect dancing and plenty of drinking; snacks like pancit *canton* (noodles) are served.

Sorsogon City

There are not many attractions in Sorsogon City itself, although it's worth visiting the small **Museum and Heritage Center** (Mon–Fri 9am–5pm; free) housed in the old provincial hospital building, just behind the Hall of Justice. Alongside old pottery and photographs, the most prized exhibit is the backbone of a whale shark found washed up on a nearby beach. The creature was originally around 10m in length, but the cartilage decayed before the bones were recovered. If you're staying for the night then the **boardwalk** on the pier is a good place to watch the sun set, with views of Mount Pulag and Mount Bulusan.

The city's most established annual event, the **Kasanggayahan festival** (roughly Oct 17–31), celebrates the town's history with street parades, bangka races and beauty pageants.

Practicalities

From 7am–10pm buses are forbidden to enter Sorsogon City, instead stopping at Pangpang junction on Diversion Road; the plan is eventually to build a new terminal near the city hall. In the meantime tricycles take passengers into town for P8. There are also plans to open a **tourist information office** beside the town's museum, but until then the owners of *Fernando's Hotel* (see below) are the best sources of local knowledge. Also check out the website of the Sorsogon Provincial Tourism Council (Ⓦwww.sorsogontourism.com). There are a number of **banks** (including BPI, PNB and UCPB) and small **internet cafés** on Rizal Street.

The best place to **stay** is ⚞ *Fernando's Hotel* (Ⓣ056/211-1357, Ⓦwww .fernandoshotel.com; ❷), a cosy two-storey white building one block west of Rizal Park on N. Pareja Street. It has a lovely eating area and helpful, informative owners. The Deluxe A rooms (❼) are worth a look for their creative use of natural materials, the standard rooms (❹) have a bit of character, and the cheapest rooms with shared bathrooms are fine but a bit gloomy – room 217 is the brightest.

Another good option is *Villa Kasanggayahan* (Ⓣ056/211-1357; ❷), a low-rise mint-green building with a well-tended and quiet garden on Rizal Street. If you're on a very tight budget then consider the *Mercedes Country Lodge* (Ⓣ056/211-5560, Ⓦwww.mercedes-country-lodge.com; ❶) at the corner of V.L. Peralta and Rizal streets. The name could hardly be less appropriate, but the fan and air-conditioned rooms in this concrete block are acceptable.

Food in Sorsogon Town is mostly of the quick and cheap variety; as well as *Fernando 168 Bistro* next to *Fernando's Hotel*, try *Jane's Fastfood* at the corner of Rizal and De Vera for decent Filipino dishes.

Rizal Beach

A short tricycle ride beyond the barrio of **Gubat**, about 12km east of Sorsogon City on the eastern tip of the province, Rizal Beach stretches for 2km in a perfect crescent. It's an idyllic spot, a rustic corner of the world in which to idle away a day or two. It is also sometimes suitable for **surfing** between September and May; call Jeorge Duana (℡0917/930-9930) from the *Rizal Beach Resort* for more information.

The two resorts on the beach are a little careworn, but the *Veramaris Resort* (℡056/211-2457; ❸), a four-storey white building, is marginally the better of the two. Make sure to get a room with a sea view, even if you pay a little extra. The *Rizal Beach Resort* (℡0917/418-8233 or 0922/883-1032; ❷) is just next door.

Bacon and Paguriran

The small town of **BACON** (pronounced "Backon"), half an hour north of Sorsogon City by jeepney, has a grey sand beach with a handful of resorts. Only ten minutes by tricycle west of Bacon is the black sand **Libanon Beach**, where surf hammers dramatically against immense, black rocks that were spewed centuries ago by Mayon. The volcano is visible in the distance.

Bacon is also a good base for exploring some of the islands in the eastern half of Albay Gulf. The best of these is **Paguriran**, about forty minutes by bangka or thirty minutes by jeepney from Bacon. For the latter option you'll need to arrive at low tide and walk across to the island; make sure that you check your timings. Paguriran is nothing more than a circle of jagged rock, much like the rim of a volcano, inside which is a seawater lagoon, a great place to swim and snorkel – you may spot turtles – although you'll need to bring your own equipment. Diving can be arranged through *Sirangan* resort (see below) or through *Fernando's Hotel* (see opposite) in Sorsogon City.

There isn't any true budget **accommodation** on Bacon Beach. *Fisherman's Hut* (℡0909/515-8758; ❺) is a small resort with – appropriately enough – simple huts, and the more expensive ones have kitchenettes. Cheaper are the small fan rooms at *Sea Breeze* (no phone; ❸), where the beachside buildings have concrete floors and bamboo furniture. The most luxurious resort by far is *Sirangan* (℡0919/818-8080, ⓦwww.sirangan.com; significant discounts in low season; ❽), a boutique hotel

---

Moving on from Sorsogon province

The main link between Sorsogon and the north is Legazpi. **Minivans** (1hr; P60) leave from the terminal in Donsol when full until about 4pm; if there's no direct van then it may be necessary to change in Pilar. Pilar is also the departure point for **ferries** to Masbate and Ticao: for Masbate, take one of the four daily Montenegro Lines services (2hr; P360); for Ticao there is a ferry departing at noon and making the return trip at 7am (90min; P100).

From Sorsogon City, vehicles to **Legazpi** run from two temporary van terminals at the corner of Rizal and Burgos St near the Development Bank of the Philippines (DBP) and Land Bank. Jeepneys to Matnog, Bacon, Prieto Diaz and Gubat run along Rizal St and Magsaysay St. Ferries leave from Matnog, on the southern tip of Sorsogon province, every hour from 4am to midnight heading to Allen and San Isidro in Samar (90min; P120).

with a dozen spacious and tastefully appointed rooms. Natural materials such as granite and rattan are used throughout and each room has its own character; some have fabulous sea views from their four-poster beds. There is snorkelling out in front of the resort and there's also a dive shop.

Bulusan Volcano National Park

Mount Bulusan is one of three active volcanoes in the Bicol region. On November 6, 2010 a series of ash explosions and earthquakes began, reaching their peak on November 21. At the time of research, a 4km-wide "Permanent Danger Zone" was still being enforced around the volcano and many families had been evacuated; crops in the surrounding villages were destroyed by the ashfall and there were concerns about possible lahar flows in the case of heavy rain. Trekking on the volcano was certainly not on the cards, and it is essential to check the situation before considering an ascent.

If the park is open then visitors can explore lush rainforest, waterfalls, hot springs and caves. There are several decent trails and a concrete path around Lake Bulusan, the most accessible of a number of lakes in the park at 600m above sea level. At Bulusan's peak (1559m) is a crater lake and, a short walk away through tricky terrain, the small Blackbird Lake.

Practicalities

When open the park is relatively easy to reach, as a motorable road leads right up to Lake Bulusan. From Sorsogon City you can take a jeepney to the town of **Irosin** (45min; P50) and then another to the lake. Coming from Rizal Beach, Gubat or Matnog, take a jeepney down the scenic coast road through the towns of **Barcelona** and **Layog** to Bulusan town, then another to the lake.

If you want to reach the peak, take a lakebound jeepney from Irosin and get off in the village of **San Roque**, where you'll find the trailhead. Hikers will be refused access by rangers if an eruption warning is up; for **guides** and up-to-date details about the state of the volcano, inquire at *Fernando's Hotel* (see p.222) in Sorsogon City. You should also consult the Philippine Institute of Volcanology and Seismology website (Ⓦwww.phivolcs.dost.gov.ph). If you need to spend the night in Bulusan town, try *Villa Luisa Celeste* (Ⓣ0920/906-0969; ❸) close to Dancalan beach. The owners have converted part of their home into comfortable lodgings for guests.

Masbate

The province of **Masbate** ("Maz-bah-tee") lies in the centre of the Philippine archipelago. It is comprised of the **island of Masbate** with its small capital city of the same name, two secondary islands called **Burias** and **Ticao**, and numerous smaller islands. There are a number of exceptional beaches on Masbate, such as Bituon and immense caves in thick jungle such as **Kalanay** and **Batongan**. It's the infrastructure that's lacking. This is slowly changing, however, with an increased emphasis on tourism and developments such as an anticipated new ferry route to Manila via Caticlan (and therefore Boracay).

The position of Masbate at the heart of the Philippines leads to some complicated **cultural blending**, with a mix of **languages** including Cebuano, Bicolano, Waray, Ilonggo, Tagalog and Masbateño. The province has long had something of a reputation for violence, with an image throughout the Philippines as a lawless "Wild East" frontier province. Like many isolated areas of the archipelago, Masbate does seem a law unto itself and political killings are certainly not unheard of, but its reputation for goonish violence is mostly unfair. In any case it is highly unlikely that tourists will feel any less safe here than in most other parts of the country.

The Wild East moniker is, however, apt for reasons other than lawlessness: Masbate ranks second only to the landlocked province of Bukidnon, Mindanao, in raising **cattle**. There's even an annual rodeo in Masbate City in May, where cowpokes do battle for big prize money. Farming is the second most common form of livelihood, fishing the third.

Masbate City

The provincial capital of **MASBATE CITY** is attractively situated, nestling between the sea and the hills, but spoiled slightly by unstructured development and the nerve-jangling presence of the ubiquitous tricycles. The main thoroughfare is Quezon Street, running behind the port area, and there's a busy **market** seven days a week in Zurbito Street. To the northeast of the centre is an area of reclaimed land where several hotels, restaurants and bars have been built.

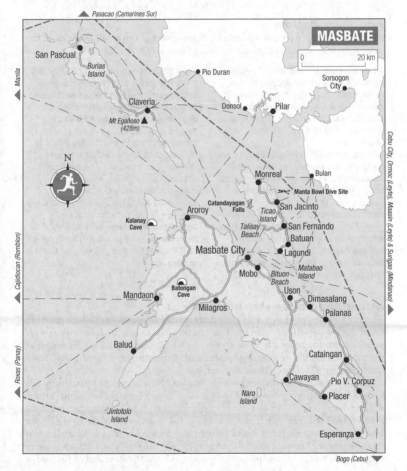

The most notable tourist attraction is the **Rodeo Masbateño**, a four-day orgy of bull-riding and steer-dogging which takes place every year in May (usually May 6–9).

Arrival and information

Masbate City is only a five-minute jeepney or tricycle ride from the **airport**. The **ferry** pier is also close to the town centre and within walking distance of many of the hotels. **Buses**, **jeepneys** and minivans leave from a terminal on Diversion Road on the southern edge of town, a little beyond the fishing port.

The **tourist office** (☎056/333-5608) is in the city hall building, and can advise on itineraries although it has little in the way of printed material. It's also worth dropping into the **Coastal Resource Management Interpretative Centre** (☎0906/212-5684), also in the city hall complex. It doesn't offer tourist information as such, but the displays give plenty of details about the island's coastal areas. There are places to eat, convenience stores, **internet cafés** and several **banks** with ATMs and currency exchange on Quezon Street. There's a **police** outpost beside the main pier.

Accommodation

Most of the cheaper **accommodation** is in the centre of town, while several of the more upmarket options are on the reclaimed land to the northeast.

Alburo's Lodging House ☎0922/421-8937 or 0999/364-0907. If you're just staying the night waiting for a ferry, this may be just the thing: tiny rooms for one or two people with bunk beds and shared bathrooms for P150 a head. Turn right out of the port and take the first right, down a narrow alleyway. ❶

Backpack Ibingay Rd ☎056/333-2682. This small hotel has something of a family feel and good-value rooms including cheaper singles. It's located between the city centre and the hotels on the northeast coast. ❸

Balay Valencia Ibanez St ☎056/333-6530. An old home which now has nine guest rooms, designated ordinary (shared bathroom) and VIP but none especially inspiring. The common areas retain some old-fashioned charm though, with wooden floors and carved air vents over the doors. ❶

MG Hotel Punta Nursery ☎056/333-5614. This place is out on the reclaimed land to the northeast of the centre, but well worth the mild inconvenience of the odd tricycle trip. Rooms are clean and spacious, the restaurant is good and there's a small pool. ❸

Rendezvous Punta Nursery ☎056/582-0496 or 0916/454-5643. Antiques and quirky features – like flying ducks on one wall – make the common areas interesting to explore, and all but the cheapest rooms have the same feel. ❷

Sampaguita Tourist Inn Quezon St ☎056/333-4729. Dark, boxy a/c or fan rooms in a noisy location. Some of the twins and doubles are a reasonable size, but there's hardly room to swing a cat in the singles so it's a good thing that they're so cheap. ❶

Attractions near Masbate City

There are a number of activities and sights around Masbate City, which together make a good day-trip by bangka. The tourist office should be able to help with arrangements for bangka hire, or you could bargain directly with a fisherman at the pier close to the main transport terminal. Expect to pay around P1000 for a small boat, or P2500 for a medium-sized one.

You'll see numerous **fish pens** within Masbate Bay; many are operated by the Crown Bee company, whose employees are used to receiving the occasional visitor at their warehouse. They can usually offer a short tour of the *bangus* (milkfish) pens, where you can watch the fish being fed. Southwest of here, the **Pawa boardwalk** was built primarily to shorten the distance to school for students in Pawa barangay. The path extends into protected mangroves at each side, where migratory birds can be seen particularly at low tide. At the Pawa end of the bridge there is also a very basic cottage on stilts over the water (☏0908/575-2336; ❷). There's just one double bed, a toilet and little else; if you're looking for solitude and don't mind roughing it then it's worth considering. Meals are provided on request but bring some supplies along.

Leaving the bay and heading out into the pass between Masbate and Ticao islands, stop at the **Buntod Sandbar**. A popular spot at the weekend but empty during the week, it has little shelter so bring sun cream and a hat. There are a couple of floating platforms for lazing around, and some decent snorkelling. To reach the sand bar straight from town, take a tricycle to the barangay of Nursery (P40), where there are ferries at the weekends or boats for private hire at P500–600 for a round trip including waiting.

Eating

Masbate City has plenty of small carinderias where the day's choices are laid out in aluminium pots. For fresh fruit there's a **wet market** at the northern end of Quezon Street where, depending on the season, you'll find coconuts, bananas and *ponkan* (small oranges).

Felix Piazza Ibanez St, opposite *Balay Valencia* hotel. With an array of gazebos and other open-sided seating areas, this restaurant serves Filipino favourites until late into the night.

Minlan Osmeña St, on the edge of Rizal Park. A restaurant serving a wide range of Chinese and Filipino dishes, such as sweet and sour pork for P130. Daily 9.30am–9pm.

Port Zirteas 41 Mabini St. Set on two floors, with a clothes boutique occupying the top floor, this popular restaurant serves Filipino dishes to share for around P120 and value meals for one at P70–85. Daily 7am–9pm.

Tio Jose Ibanez St. A stab at a US-style bar, with walls covered in the logos of international brands; the dishes are largely fast food.

Aroroy

The ramshackle little fishing village and gold-panning town of **AROROY** is 20km northwest of Masbate City along the coast road, and easy to reach by jeepney. Its beach isn't suitable for sunbathing but is an interesting place to watch fishermen making boats and mending nets. The village also has a more eccentric attraction in the form of the **Aroroy Wacky Rodeo**, held every October to test participants' skill at handling that notoriously bad-tempered and uncontrollable

Moving on from Masbate

Zest Airways (☏056/582-0407) has five flights a week to **Manila**, while Air Philippines (☏056/333-5689) flies daily.

The island's central location in the archipelago means that it has numerous maritime connections: from Masbate City, Romblon Shipping Line runs one ferry a week to **Manila** (19hr). There are also sailings to **Cebu**, **Surigao** (Mindanao), **Ormoc** and **Maasin** (both Leyte). Smaller ferries run daily from Masbate City to the port towns of **Bulan** and **Pilar** on the southwestern coast of Sorsogon province. Montenegro Lines has two RORO (roll-on/roll-off) services from the island to **Bogo** (Cebu) each day; one departs from Cataingan and the other from Cawayan. Both take six hours and cost P650. Rosalea also runs cheaper ferries from Cataingan to Bogo (Cebu), departing early in the morning, but the RORO is generally preferable as it avoids the need to spend a night in Cataingan where there are no good accommodation options.

From Mandaon, there are bangkas to **Cajidiocan** in Romblon scheduled to run on Wednesdays and Sundays at 6am, but they are not very reliable so be prepared for significant delays. Similarly unpredicatable are the pumpboats to Roxas in Panay.

beast, the crab. The crustaceans are a major livelihood source for the area and this day-long festival, after the usual parades and street dances, includes crab catching, crab tying, crab races and, of course, crab eating. The culmination is the crowning of a beauty queen, Miss Crab.

Bituon Beach

The sand at **Bituon Beach** (aka Bagacay Beach), 14km south of Masbate town and 2km down a dirt road from the barangay of **Bagacay**, is not as blindingly white as some, but that's a minor quibble. Some 2km long, the beach, with palm trees at the edge and beautifully clear shallow water, is still an exceptionally pretty crescent bay. The only **place to stay** is *Bituon Beach Resort* (☎056/333-2342; fan ❷, a/c ❹), an extensive development of bamboo huts and concrete rooms. During the week it's a quiet place to unwind, but at weekends half the population of Masbate City seems to descend to eat, drink and be merry.

If you are staying at the resort then ask them about their shuttle service from the airport or city. It's a 15-minute jeepney ride to Bagacay from Masbate City; they stop on the main road and from there you can either walk to the beach or take a tricycle down the track. A tricycle all the way from Masbate City should cost P300.

Kalanay and Batongan Caves

The town of **Mandaon** is 64km west of Masbate City on the opposite coast of the island. The trip by jeepney (P40) takes you along a scenic road that passes through pastureland, paddy fields and a number of isolated barrios inhabited by subsistence farmers. There's not much in Mandaon itself, but it's a good base for exploring two of the island's most noted natural wonders, **KALANAY CAVE** on the northwest coast 40km from Mandaon, and **BATONGAN CAVE**, 20km inland from Mandaon. Both make excellent day-trips, but Batongan is the better of the two, with immense caverns and a large population of bats whose guano is collected and used as fertilizer. About 100m away is an underground river, which you can swim in. It's easy to get lost in these parts and if you fall and get injured you might not be found for days, so don't explore the caves or the river without a **local guide** (P500). In Mandaon you can ask at the town hall; the mayor or his staff will appoint someone to take you.

Ticao Island

The island of **TICAO**, across the Masbate Passage from Masbate City, can be reached in less than an hour on one of the big bangkas (P100) that go back and forth from Masbate pier to **Lagundi**, on Ticao's southwest coast. From **Bulan** in Sorsogon province, there are four ferries each morning to **San Jacinto** (1hr; P100). There is also a daily ferry from Pilar to **Monreal**.

The infrastructure is mostly basic and the roads can be very difficult in the rainy season, but Ticao is well worth the trip. A convenient way to get around is to hire a bangka for around P2000 and explore the coast. Ask the boatman to take you to **Talisay**, the island's finest beach, and then on to **Catandayagan Falls**. In a country known for its waterfalls this is one of the most impressive, plunging more than 30m into a gin-clear pool at its base. It's ideal for swimming.

If you want to stay then there are two upmarket resorts operating in Ticao, each offering full board. Halfway between Monreal and San Jacinto, the *Ticao Island Resort* (☎02/893-8173, ⓦwww.ticao-island-resort.com; ❼) has nine lovely beachfront *cabañas* and a handful of cheaper rooms. It offers kayaking, snorkelling, island-hopping and diving at the Manta Bowl (see p.221). At the *Altamar Resort* (☎02/998-2378 or 0921/825-6809, ⓦwww.ticaoaltamar.com; ❻), reached by a ten-minute boat ride from San Jacinto, visitors can stay in cottages or the hilltop villa. Activities include horseriding and snorkelling. If these options are too expensive, you could try arranging a homestay through the tourist office in Masbate City (see p.226).

Burias Island

There is no formal accommodation for tourists on the remote island of **Burias**, a three-hour trip by ferry northwest of Masbate City. This is a backwater even by provincial Philippine standards, populated by subsistence fishermen, farmers and American missionaries who have established a number of churches here.

Burias's most prominent landmark is the dormant volcano **Mount Engañoso** (428m), which you'll see in the distance as you approach from the sea. From December to May keep your eyes peeled for **whale sharks**, which are often seen feeding in the Burias Passage. Given the lack of infrastructure the island is too big to explore in a day, so limit yourself to the area around Claveria which has some pretty beaches known for their impressive rock formations. If you do make it further north, you will find one of the oldest churches in the Philippines at **San Pascual**.

Twice a week a bangka makes the trip from Masbate City to Claveria and San Pascual. You can also reach Claveria on the daily morning ferry from Pilar in Sorsogon province, from Pasacao in Camarines Sur or from Pio Duran in Albay.

Catanduanes

The eastern island province of **Catanduanes** is ripe for exploration, a large, rugged, rural island with mile upon mile of majestic coastline. It has still barely felt the impact of tourism, although with eight flights a week from Manila and improvements to the main road around the island this is slowly changing. In fact **surfers** have known about Catanduanes for quite some time, attracted to the big waves off **Puraran Beach** on the wild east coast. There are also several good beaches within easy reach of the capital Boac, as well as other attractions like the immense caves in **Lictin**, while the undeveloped west coast offers the opportunity to blaze a trail into areas few travellers see. Most of all Catanduanes is a friendly, down-to-earth place to hang out for a few days, as long as you are willing to adjust to a slower pace of life and travel.

It isn't all good news though. Filipinos think mostly of bad weather when they think about Catanduanes, lying as it does on the exposed eastern edge of the archipelago smack in the middle

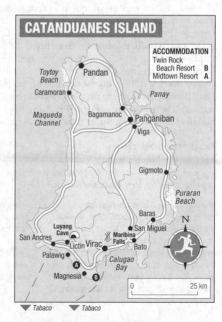

CATANDUANES ISLAND

ACCOMMODATION
Twin Rock
Beach Resort **B**
Midtown Resort **A**

Toytoy Beach
Pandan
Caramoran
Panay
Maqueda Channel
Bagamanoc
Panganiban
Viga
Gigmoto
Puraran Beach
Baras
Luyang Cave
San Miguel
San Andres
Maribina Falls
Lictin Virac
Bato
Palawig
Calugao Bay
Magnesia

N

0   25 km

229

▼ Tabaco   ▼ Tabaco

Getting around Catanduanes

Hiring a **car** with a driver is a good if expensive way to see the island; try the drivers at the airport, visit the tourist office or simply ask your accommodation to arrange it. For about P2000–3000, for instance, you can get a return trip to Puraran Beach including waiting time; for a full day exploring expect to pay P4000–5000. Otherwise, **buses** run from Virac up the east coast to Bagamanoc (90min; P100) or Pandan (3–5hr; P150). The going is significantly slower on the west coast road. **Jeepneys** are commonly used for shorter distances, such as from Virac to the nearby municipalities of San Andres, San Miguel and Bato; tricycles will also make these trips at a higher rate. Some locals offer trips around the island on their **motorcycles** for P1000–2000; the journey to Puraran would cost around P300–500.

of the "typhoon highway". Unless you are a surfer the best time to visit is from March to June, when the chances of rainfall are slight and the wind is less wicked. During the wet season (July–Nov) the island can be hit half a dozen times by typhoons, causing extensive damage to crops and homes and sometimes loss of life.

Virac

VIRAC is an anonymous provincial town, busy with mercantile activity and the noise of jeepneys. There is a small central plaza where the cathedral stands and a busy market, but for most visitors Virac will simply be a base for exploring the rest of the island.

Arrival and information

Virac's airport is 4km west of the town. A tricycle into town will cost around P50, or less if you walk away from the airport waiting area. The combined **bus** and **jeepney terminal** is near the central market on Rizal Street, a short distance across the Santo Domingo River from the town centre. The **wharf** on the eastern edge of town, at the end of Geronimo Tabuzo Street, is where ferries arrive from Tabaco, along with dozens of other small craft bearing cargo from Manila and Cebu, or fish and produce from other areas of Catanduanes.

The **tourist office** (Mon–Fri 8am–5pm; ☎052/811-1335) is in the Provincial Capitol Building in Rizal Street, a five-minute tricycle ride northeast from the plaza. There are three **banks** in Virac, which have ATMs and where you can change dollars. PNB is on the east side of the plaza and BDO is on the west side; Land Bank is north of the main roundabout on Rizal Avenue, opposite the Caltex station. The **post office** (Mon–Fri 8am–5pm) is at the back of the municipal building, and on Rizal Street there are a few **internet cafés**.

Accommodation

Each of the hotels listed in Virac have cheap fan rooms as well as air-conditioned options. If you're keen to stay out of town, but within reach of Virac's amenities, try the *Twin Rock* or *Midtown* resorts.

Marem Pension House 136 Rizal Ave ☎0917/515-3181 or 0928/237-5398, ⓦwww .marempensionhouse.com. This old favourite is a sprawling place with standard "singles" (with a bed for two) and "doubles" (with twin beds) as well as more spacious deluxe rooms with three singles. The non-a/c rooms are, while certainly cheap, also pretty grim. Wi-fi in bar/restaurant. ❶

Midtown Inn San José St ☎052/811-0527, ⓦwww.catmidinn.com. Located just off the town's main roundabout, this is the pick of the Virac bunch. Most rooms are a/c and have cable TV and private bathrooms with hot showers, and there's wi-fi in the restaurant. The owners also have a tiny resort (see below) close to Virac. ❶

Midtown Resort Batag Beach, 20min west of Virac ☎ 0927/804-8324, ⓦ www .catmidinn.com. A private resort on the delightful Batag Beach, with a one-bedroom a/c cottage which can sleep up to ten – a perfect, if basic, place to escape from it all. Meals can be cooked to demand for an extra fee, or you can cook your own. Island-hopping (P2000 upwards) and scuba diving can be arranged. Booking is essential, and there's a free shuttle from Virac. ❺

Rakdell San Pedro St ☎ 052/811-0881.The standard-suite rooms include a double bed and a sofa, while the cheaper non-a/c rooms are good value for solo travellers (or couples with an extra matress squeezed in) and still have private bathrooms. There is a pleasant restaurant and bar on the roof deck. ❷

Rhaj Inn Gogon ☎ 0929/129-9071. A 10min walk from the town centre but close to the main market, this place is mainly noteworthy for its budget options including very cheap singles. ❶

Twin Rock Igang barangay, 10km south of Virac centre. ☎ 052/811-3742, ⓦ www.twinrock.com.ph. The island's most developed resort. Rooms in the manicured grounds range from grubby fan-cooled boxes with shared bathrooms to unexceptional doubles (❸) and family rooms (❺). The real attractions are the beachside location and the huge range of facilities and activities including a zip line over the sea, a climbing wall, quad bikes, scuba diving, snorkelling and kayaking. The main drawback is the sound of videoke, particularly at weekends. ❶

Attractions near Virac

You will find some good, surfable beaches west of Virac in the villages of **Magnesia**, **Buenavista** and **Palawig**, although none is as pretty or as popular as **Puraran** (see below). Inland from Palawig there are enormous limestone **caves** near the village of **Lictin**. To get there you'll have to find a guide in Lictin (there are no established rates, but P500 is a reasonable amount to pay); contact the tourist office in Virac before setting out, or ask at the barangay hall or in any of the village stores. The best known is Luyang Cave, whose waters are said to have healing properties.

Another spot that makes a good short trip from Virac is the **Maribina Waterfall** in the barrio of **Maribina**, fifteen minutes inland by jeepney. The fall plunges more than 10m and the pool at the base is crystal-clear and good for swimming. A little further east in **Bato** it's worth taking a look at **Batalay Church**, an atmospheric Baroque structure built in the sixteenth century following the arrival of Spanish Captain Juan de Salcedo, who had been hunting for pirates on the coast.

Eating and drinking

Blossom's Salvacion St. With its wooden shutters, high ceilings with beams and lights all around the exterior, this two-floor restaurant is appealingly atmospheric. It serves a range of pasta and Filipino dishes. Mon–Sat 7am–10pm.

Chef de Leoj Ground floor of the *Midtown Inn*. One of the better places to eat in town, serving the usual Filipino dishes. If no staff seem to be around, knock on the kitchen door. Mon–Sat 7am–9pm, Sun 8am–noon.

Sea Breeze To the right of the pier, approaching from the town. The large wooden huts here are a hit with families and groups, while the videoke is mercifully confined to indoors. There's local and imported beer, a menu with lots of seafood options, and free wi-fi access.

SOG Opposite the *Rakdell*. The only real nightlife in town, where the nightly programme alternates live bands with videoke until well after midnight.

Puraran Beach

The first decent beaches you reach as you head north along the **east coast** from Virac are around **Baras**, a small trading and fishing town where the only visitors are surfers who come occasionally to spend the day. It's worth stopping to climb the hill to the radar station; it's a 30-minute scramble to the top, but when you get there you're rewarded with uninterrupted views of the coast and a vast area of

Moving on from the Catanduanes

Both Zest Airways (☎0917/597-7101) and Cebu Pacific (☎052/811-2809) **fly**
between Catanduanes and Manila; Cebu Pacific flies in the mornings, Zest Airways
in the afternoons.

Three **ferries** sail to Tabaco each day from San Andres, and one from Virac. The
latter is the biggest but slowest ferry, the M/V *Eugene Elson* (P200 or P250 a/c)
operated by Peñafrancia, which reaches Tabaco in four hours. Regina Shipping Lines
(☎052/811-1707) runs the boats from San Andres (3hr; P190 or P240 a/c).

narra trees. At the time of research the radar station, which had been derelict, was
undergoing renovation and there were plans to welcome visitors.

However, for many visitors the only stop on the east coast is at beautiful
PURARAN BEACH, with a break referred to as **Majestic** by surfers. Majestic is
fickle but it's generally thought that the best bet is from **July to October**, when
low-pressure areas lurking out in the Pacific help kick up a swell. Of course, these
areas can turn into tropical storms and typhoons that batter the coast, making
surfing impossible for all but experts and the foolhardy. Prices for board hire
(P150/hr shortboard, P200/hr longboard) and lessons (P150/hr) are set by the
Department of Tourism, although you may find locals willing to do a deal for
longer term hire.

You don't have to be a surfer to enjoy a few days on a beach as lovely as this one.
There are extensive **coral gardens** just offshore that make for wonderful snorkelling, and swimming is safe inside the line of the reef and away from the rocks – ask
for advice at your resort before heading out, as it is not unknown for swimmers to
get into trouble.

Puraran is still mercifully undeveloped, with only two basic resorts on the beach
as well a slightly more comfortable one (which was up for sale at the time of
research) up the hill close to the main road. At *Puting Baybay Resort* (☎0910/314-
5482; ❷) there are simple, clean cottages or concrete rooms with cold water only.
Elena's Majestic Resort (☎0919/558-1460; ❷), is another simple place with a
handful of rooms and six small cottages right on the sand, each with its own
rickety terrace where you can relax with a cold drink at the end of a day's surfing.
Electricity is often limited to a few hours a day and the nearest internet access is in
Virac. These are very laidback resorts, and it is not unusual for visitors to end up
staying for a couple of weeks.

There is only one morning jeepney (2hr; P35) direct to Puraran each day from
Virac. More vehicles make the trip to Baras, from where it's a P150 tricycle trip to
the beach. When you're ready to leave the resort owners can arrange a tricycle to
Baras, or all the way to Virac for P600 if you've missed the last jeepney.

5

Mindoro

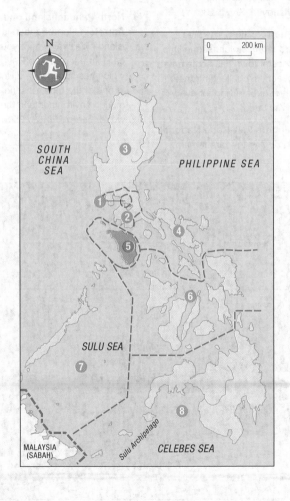

CHAPTER 5

Highlights

* **Tribal visits** Get an intriguing insight into a marginalized culture by meeting Mindoro's original inhabitants, the Mangyan. See p.239

* **Puerto Galera** The area around this picturesque little coastal town has some great beaches, challenging treks and scuba diving for every level. See p.239

* **Mounts Iglit-Baco National Park** See the rare *tamaraw*, a type of water buffalo, as you trek through some of the most beautiful countryside on Mindoro. See p.252

* **North Pandan Island and Apo Reef** North Pandan is an island hideaway where you can join a trip to Apo Reef, which has superlative diving in one of the most pristine marine environments in the world. See p.253 & p.254

▲ Sabang beach

Mindoro

W ithin a few hours of Manila, yet worlds away, **Mindoro** remains undeveloped even by Philippine provincial standards. Much of the island is wild and rugged, with some near-impenetrable hinterlands and an often desolate coastline of wide bays and basic fishing villges. The island, seventh largest in the archipelago, is divided lengthways into two provinces, **Mindoro Occidental** and **Mindoro Oriental**; the latter is the more developed and visited. Most travellers head this way only for the beaches, **scuba diving** and nightlife around the picturesque town of **Puerto Galera** on Mindoro Oriental's northern coast, a short ferry trip from Batangas, but there is much more to Mindoro than this. Few people, Filipinos included, realize that the island is home to several areas of outstanding natural beauty, all protected to some degree by local or international decree. As well as the incredible marine environ-ments of Puerta Galera, and the world-class **Apo Reef** on the west coast, Mindoro's interior offers the chance to experience genuine Mangyan culture, visit pristine wilderness, and maybe see endangered species such as the Mindoro dwarf buffalo, the *tamaraw* at the **Mounts Iglit-Baco National Park**.

Getting to Mindoro

San José **airport**, in the south of Mindoro Occidental, is served by daily Airphil Express, Cebu Pacific and Zest Airways flights. The main **ferry** port for departures to **Puerto Galera** is Batangas City (see p.121). MSL and FSL are the two main companies that work this route. A good way to reach Puerto Galera from Manila is to buy a combined **bus-boat ticket** with Si-Kat (☎02/521-3344; 4–5hr; P700); the bus departs from their office at **Citystate Tower Hotel** at 1315 Mabini St, Ermita.

There are also big bangkas from Batangas to **Sabang** and **White Beach**, and Montenegro lines operates a car ferry (2hr) to **Balatero**, 3km west of Puerto Galera. Supercat ferries (🌐www.supercat.com.ph) operate nine ferries per day from Batangas to **Calapan** (1hr), and Besta Shipping Lines have ten slower ferries daily (2hr), while Supershuttle operate two car ferry services per day. You can also make the two-hour crossing from Batangas to **Abra de Ilog** in Mindoro Occidental, with Besta Ferries (3 services daily) and Marina Ferries (6 services daily).

As for ferries other than from Luzon, there are several services every day between **Roxas** and **Caticlan** (for Boracay), which take around four hours and cost in the region of P330. Roxas is also served by a few weekly boats from Odiongan in Romblon, including Montenegro Shipping Lines and Supershuttle. **Pinamalayan** on Mindoro's east coast is linked by irregular ferries with Balanacan on Marinduque. There's meant to be a daily departure at 6.30am, but the boat will only leave if there are enough passengers.

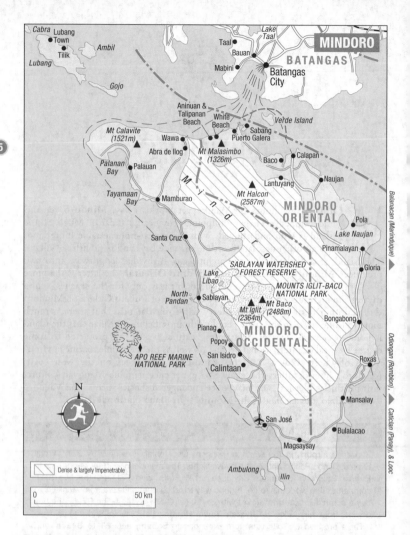

Dense & largely Impenetrable

0   50 km

Mindoro Oriental

More accessible and developed than its poorer neighbour across the mountains, most visitors head to **Mindoro Oriental** to dive in the marine reserve at **Puerto Galera**, in the north of the province. Nearby **Mount Malasimbo** is also protected because of the biodiversity of its thickly jungled slopes. To the east of Puerto Galera, near the port of **Calapan**, is **Mount Halcon**, at 2587m, Mindoro's tallest peak and a difficult climb even for experienced mountaineers, although it is currently off-limits. The south of the island is less populated than the north, with few tourists making it as far as **Roxas** on the southeast coast, aside from to take one of the regular boats to Caticlan (for Boracay).

Puerto Galera

PUERTO GALERA (meaning "Port of the Galleons") is actually the name of a small town (*poblacion*), but is generally used to refer to the area between **Sabang**, 5km to the east, and **White Beach**, 8km to the west.

Great **diving**, countless coves and beaches and a stunning natural harbour within a few hours of Manila make Puerta Galera a natural choice for escaping Manileños and travellers alike. During Easter, and summer weekends, the whole place seems full to bursting, and many hotels substantially raise their prices, so it's worth booking ahead if you're planning to visit during these times. There's also plenty on offer in addition to diving, including excellent snorkelling, trekking into the mountains and beach- and island-hopping by bangka. Most visitors head straight for Sabang and the nearby beaches of **Small La Laguna** and **Big La Laguna**. Between them, these locations offer a diverse range of accommodation, diving, restaurants and nightlife. There are also a number of family-friendly resorts near the village of **Palangan**, about halfway along the road from Puerto Galera to Sabang. Northeast of Palangan there's a small isolated cove at **Sinandigan** with a handful of very peaceful resorts. In the other direction, to the west of Puerto Galera, the nearest beach is the picturesque White Beach, which has plenty of accommodation, and is popular with partying Manileños at the weekends. For more of a remote experience, walk – or take a tricycle – round to beautiful **Aninuan Beach** and **Talipanan Beach**, both of which have comfort- able, affordable places to stay.

Arrival and information

Most travellers arrive by boat from Batangas at charming Muelle pier where there's a small **tourist office** (daily 8.30am–4pm; ☎043/287-3051). The **post office** is at the junction of E. Brucal and Axalan streets (alternatively some resorts will post mail for a small fee). **Internet** access is widely available from P25 per hour – try *Kaisser*, near the post office, or *Dhegz* on Concepcion Street. The Allied Bank near the turn-off for Muelle pier exchanges foreign currencies and has an **ATM**, but is not always online, so bring enough pesos, or dollars, for your time here. The well-stocked Candava Supermarket on Concepcion Street also changes dollars. The **police station** (☎043/281-4043) is inside the municipal compound a short walk from Muelle pier. The **immigration office** is in the same building, and can provide on-the-spot visa extensions on Mondays, Tuesdays and Wednesday mornings. The Puerto Galera **Medical Clinic** is in Axalan Street in town, a short walk up the hill from Muelle pier, opposite the church. There are a number of other rudimentary clinics in the town; if in doubt you can always ask the dive operators, who know where the best doctors are. There are also a few small **pharmacies** in town.

PUERTO GALERA AREA MAP (MINDORO ORIENTAL)

ACCOMMODATION
Blue Crystal Beach Resort D
Coco Beach Island Resort A
Coral Cove Resort B
Kalaw Place C

Python Cave, Tamaraw Falls, ▼ Calapan, Roxas & San José

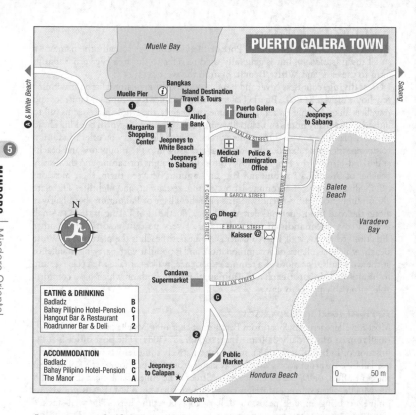

PUERTO GALERA TOWN

Muelle Bay

A & White Beach

Sabang

Bangkas

Muelle Pier

Island Destination
Travel & Tours

Puerto Galera
Church

Jeepneys
to Sabang

Allied
Bank

Margarita
Shopping
Center

Jeepneys to
White Beach

Medical
Clinic

Police &
Immigration
Office

H. AXALAN STREET

P. CONCEPCION STREET

E. DOBRAGLIBAS. SR STREET

Balete
Beach

Jeepneys
to Sabang

R. GARCIA STREET

Dhegz

E. BRUCAL STREET

Kaisser

Varadevo
Bay

N

Candava
Supermarket

LAXALAN STREET

EATING & DRINKING

Badladz	B
Bahay Pilipino Hotel-Pension	C
Hangout Bar & Restaurant	1
Roadrunner Bar & Deli	2

ACCOMMODATION

Badladz	B
Bahay Pilipino Hotel-Pension	C
The Manor	A

Jeepneys
to Calapan

Public
Market

0   50 m

Hondura Beach

Calapan

Accommodation

With direct boats from Batangas to Sabang and White Beach, there's really little need to stay in Puerto Galera. That said, if you want to escape the beach scene, there are a few decent places to stay here. **Power failures** are a regular occurrence in Puerto Galera, so it's worth asking resorts if they have a backup generator before committing yourself to staying.

Badladz On the hill above Muelle pier ☎043/287-3184, ⓦwww.badladz.com. Great bay views and spacious rooms with hot water, a/c and cable TV. There's also a dive shop and free wi-fi. ②
Bahay Pilipino Hotel-Pension In the centre of the *poblacion* opposite Candava Supermarket ☎043/442-0266. A friendly place run by Bavarian Dr Fritz and his Filipina wife Jasmin. The fan rooms are small and well kept, but have shared bathrooms. ①

The Manor A little out of town on the hill above the Yacht Club ☎043/442-0029.

The only upscale offering in the vicinity of the town is the *Manor*, a modern mansion which sits on a ridge above the Yacht Club, and enjoys spectacular views in all directions. Each room is individually decorated and features high-quality furnishings and modern art – the "Presidential Suite" and "Indonesian Room" are particularly impressive. There are also a couple of houses for rent, which are great for families. In the grounds you'll also find tennis courts and an infinity pool, and there's a free boat shuttle from the Yacht Club. ⑦

The Town

Arriving at Puerto Galera by ferry from Batangas is a memorable experience, the boat slipping gently through aquamarine waters past a series of headlands fringed with

haloes of sand and coconut trees. Brilliant white yachts lie at anchor in the innermost bay and in the background looms the brooding hulk of Mount Malasimbo, invariably crowned with a ring of cumulus cloud. The town itself is in a marvellous spot, overlooking Muelle Bay on one side and with green hills behind it, and you could sit for hours over a cool drink at the sleepy little cafés right on the waterfront on Muelle pier watching the bangkas phut-phut back and forth. The town has various souvenir shops, general stores and a handful of modest places to stay, but despite its beautiful views and appealingly sleepy tropical ambience, there are no compelling reasons to base yourself here and most tourists move straight on to the beaches and dive resorts.

Diving in Puerto Galera

The beauty of scuba diving around Puerto Galera is the number and variety of dive sites that can be reached by boat in a matter of minutes. These offer something for everyone, from exhilarating dives in raging currents to gentle drifts along sheltered coral reefs.

A good dive for **novices** is **Shark's Cave**, a drift dive along a reef that takes you past a cave where you might get a close-up of sleeping whitetip sharks. **Fish Bowl**, a blue-water descent to the top of a reef where sweetlips and rainbow runners are common, is another popular spot. **Sabang Point**, just off Sabang Beach, makes a good night dive, while **Monkey Wreck**, only five minutes from Sabang, is a local cargo boat that sank in 18m of water in 1993, and now plays host to large schools of batfish and snappers. Finally, don't miss the **St Christopher**, a retired diving boat that was deliberately sunk and is a refuge for the extraordinary frogfish, an ugly character with large fins and a flabby, drooping face.

More challenging dives include **Canyons**, which has a healthy reef split into three slab-like sections (hence the name) and some fierce currents that mean it's usually for advanced divers only. What makes it special is that it's the best place in

Day-trips around Puerto Galera

Tribal villages Some Mangyan tribal villages are easily accessible from Puerto Galera, while others require a bit more effort in the form of some stiff uphill hiking, but are rewarded with a more genuine experience. To get the most out of your visit it's worth organizing through one of the travel agents in Puerto Galera or Sabang (see below), who can provide an interpreter and cultural etiquette tips.

Tamaraw Falls Off the main road to Calapan lie a number of caves and thundering waterfalls, and thirty minutes from Puerto Galera, Tamaraw Falls is the mother of all cascades. Here cool mountain water plummets over a precipice and into a natural pool and man-made swimming pool. The falls have become a popular sight (hence the P20 entrance fee), so avoid going at the weekend, when they are overrun.

Mount Malasimbo One of the best day-treks is from White Beach into the foothills of Mount Malasimbo, where there are a number of tribal communities, as well as waterfalls with cold, clear pools big enough for swimming.

Python cave and hot springs This popular day-trek takes you 3km out of town along the Calapan road, from where a narrow, unsigned trail leads up to the immense cave through thick vegetation and piping-hot springs deep enough for a swim.

Tour operators

In Puerto Galera town, Islands Destination Travel & Tours (☏043/287-3184) can arrange all of the above trips, as can GPLP Tours (☏0927/326-0535) in Sabang on the main road next to Filipino Travel Centre (who also run day-trips). GPLP can also organize kayak expeditions and overnight treks into the tribal hinterlands. Expect to pay between P1000 and P2000 depending on the trip.

Moving on from Puerta Galera

By boat

Slow car ferries (2hr) for **Batangas** leave from Balatero port, 3km from Puerto Galera, or there are regular direct big bangkas (1hr; P200, plus P10 terminal fee) from Muelle pier between 5.45am and 4.45 pm. There are also less frequent big bangkas from Sabang (7 daily) and White Beach. Si-Kat (☏02/521-3344), operates combined bus and ferry Manila tickets which cost P700 and can be purchased from their office near Muelle pier For **Abra de Ilog** in Mindoro Occidental (the road to Abra is impassable except on foot or trail bike) there are daily bangkas from Muelle, providing the seas aren't too rough, although a safer way to get there is to head back to Batangas and then take a ferry from there.

By jeepney

For jeepneys to **Sabang** you need to walk up the hill to Concepcion Street, although these won't leave until they are overflowing. Jeepneys to **Calapan** (90min; P80) leave when full from the market on the edge of town from early morning until mid-afternoon. One Calapan-bound jeepney also leaves from Sabang each morning.

the area to encounter large pelagics such as sharks and barracuda. Occasionally manta rays, eagle rays and hammerheads pass through. For a real thrill there's not much to beat the **Washing Machine**, a notorious dive near Verde Island, where currents are so strong and the topography so tricky that divers report being thrown around underwater and disoriented.

Dive operators

There are dozens of dive operators in Sabang, Small La Laguna and Big La Laguna, and a smattering in White Beach and the beaches near here. Established firms include: Action Divers (☏043/287-3320, ⓦwww.actiondivers.com), next to *Deep Blue Sea Inn* on Small La Laguna; Asia Divers (☏043/287-3205, ⓦwww.asiadivers .com) next door to *El Galleon*, Small La Laguna; Badladz Adventure Divers (☏0906/221-4972, ⓦwww.badladz-adventure-divers.com), in the hotel of the same name at Muelle pier and Frontier Scuba (☏043/287-3077, ⓦwww .frontierscuba.com) near *Angelyn Beach Resort* in Sabang. Rates are around $32 for a dive with full equipment, or $27 if you bring your own wet suit and buoyancy control device, but the more dives you do, the cheaper it gets.

Eating and drinking

Badladz Muelle pier. Decent Mexican, Asian and European dishes in a lovely setting looking out over the harbour. Daily 7am–9pm.

Bahay Pilipino Hotel-Pension In the centre opposite Candava Supermarket. The restaurant serves simple German dishes, including mushroom schnitzel (P265). Daily 8am–8pm.

Hangout Bar & Restaurant Muelle pier. Popular spot for a drink or light meal as you watch the boats come and go in the beautiful natural harbour. The menu includes tasty pizzas, pancakes and toasted sandwiches. Daily 7am–7pm.

Roadrunner Bar & Deli On the edge of town. Popular bar frequented mostly by expats; it has a good selection of imported goods, including German sausage. Daily noon–10pm.

Sabang

Set in a pretty cove, **Sabang** is jam-packed with hotels, restaurants and dive schools, however, the beach itself is nothing special, and not great for swimming, while the very visible girlie bar scene comes as a shock to many visitors. If you arrive here by bangka from Batangas City, you'll be dropped in front of *At-Cans*, a little east of the main road.

At the **Filipino Travel Centre** office (daily 9am–6pm; ℡043/287-3108) on the main road opposite the *Tropicana Castle Dive Resort* in Sabang, staff can offer information as well as book local day-trips and plane and ferry tickets. Almost next door, GPLP Tours (℡0927/326-0535) runs an extensive range of local trips to waterfalls, Mangyan villages and even as far as Taal Volcano. Just across the road you can **change currency** at the Western Union, and around the corner from that is a small **supermarket**. There are a few small **internet cafés** dotted along the main alley through Sabang, and most hotels and resorts have wi-fi. For a **doctor**, head for the 24-hour Medical Clinic and Diagnostic Centre (℡043/287-3156) 100m up the alley across from the *Tropicana Castle*.

Accommodation choices in Sabang range from cheaper cottages in small hotels to more expensive dive resort options. Generally speaking the accommodation to the west of the main road, which is closer to the nightlife, is pricier than that to the quieter east. Most of the dive resorts have their own bars where divers tend to congregate – *Big Apple Sports Bar* and *Captain Gregg's* are popular spots. If you're feeling more adventurous, swim out to one of the **floating bars** on the main Sabang beach. Outside of the resorts and listings below, Sabang's night scene is dominated by the go-go bars, and gets seedier as the night progresses.

Accommodation

Angelyn Beach Resort Towards the far western end of the beach ℡043/287-3047, ⓦwww .angelynsdiveresort.com. Good location right on the beach and only a short walk from dive operators, bars and restaurants, with a choice of rooms and en-suite cottages, some with balconies and a/c. There's also a small open-air restaurant with wi-fi. ❸

Big Apple Dive Resort ℡043/287-3134, ⓦwww .dive-bigapple.com. Set back from the shore on the main footpath, this is one of Sabang's best-known resorts, with its own dive centre and rooms in a quiet garden surrounding a swimming pool. There's a choice of fan (❷), a/c deluxe and a/c superior rooms, the latter of which are worth the extra outlay. ❻

Captain Gregg's Divers Resort Turn left at the end of the road in Sabang then it's a couple of minutes walk along the beach ℡0917/540-4570. A popular, well-established resort catering mainly to divers, *Gregg's* offers acceptable rooms, decent food and useful advice from the resident divers in the dive shop, many of whom have lived in Sabang for years. There's free wi-fi in the bar, which looks straight out over the sand. ❷

Garden of Eden Turn right at the T-junction and the resort is a short walk along the beachfront ℡0917/812-6625, ⓦwww.cocktaildivers.com. There's a choice of nipa-style rooms with fan, a/c bungalows or lovely a/c suites with cable TV and private patios. Bathrooms are all tiled, and the furniture is simple bamboo. All accommodation is

The Mangyan

It's estimated that there are around 100,000 of Mindoro's original inhabitants, the **Mangyan** left on the island, their way of life not much changed since they fought against the invading Spanish in the sixteenth century. With little role in the mainstream Philippine economy, they subsist through slash-and-burn farming, a practice the elders insist on retaining as part of their culture, despite the destruction it causes to forests.

You may well see Mangyan as you travel around the island, often wearing only a loincloth and machete and carrying produce for market, but if you want to actually visit them in their villages, it's best to go with a guide who can act as an interpreter. You can break the ice with a few treats such as cigarettes, sweets and matches, but if you want to take photographs, make sure you have their permission. Treks to Mangyan villages are possible in several parts of the island (see p.239 & p.252).

set in a tropical garden planted with orchids, banana and papaya, and there's also a nice pool in the grounds. ⑤

🏃 **Steps Garden** Almost at the far western end of the beach ☎043/287-3046, Ⓦwww.stepsgarden.com. Discreetly tucked into the western end of the cove, Swedish-owned *Steps* has a wide variety of comfortable huts spread through the lovely hillside gardens, many of which have great balcony views. There's also an attractive pool, a good restaurant and friendly staff. ④

Tropicana Castle Dive Resort Right on the main road ☎043/287-3075, Ⓦwww.tropicanadivers .com. An extraordinary faux German *schloss* owned and operated by the Maierhofer family, *Tropicana* has medieval-themed rooms with all mod cons (including wi-fi) and four-poster beds that would make Lady Guinevere feel at home. There's a swimming pool, a small spa, and a restaurant offering marinated grilled chicken, pepper steak and snapper fillet in herbs and white wine. Many guests are on all-in packages from Europe that include diving. ⑥

Eating, drinking and nightlife

Eddie's Bar Right on the seashore, *Eddie's* is a great place for a sunset drink.

Grab & Go Opposite *Marti's* in the middle of the main alley ☎0915/4948-788. Run by the couple behind *Tamarind*, this place is another sure-fire winner, serving tasty sandwiches, burgers and shakes around the clock. 24hr.

Hemingway's Bistrot On the front towards the western end of the beach ☎0920/206-0553. Renowned for offering the finest Western cuisine on the strip, German-owned *Hemingway's* has an American chef, imported ingredients, and the highest prices in Puerta Galera – main courses start from P415, and run up to P1645 for the Porterhouse steak. Daily 10.30am–10.30pm.

Marti's Owned by an affable Antipodean, head to *Marti's* for a quiet drink and a chat, undisturbed by the sleaze outside. As well as San Miguel,

home-made Baileys (P45 per shot) is on offer, and food can be ordered in from a variety of local restaurants including *Grab & Go* and *Hemingway's*.

Relax Off the main alley through town, near *Grab & Go* ☎0920/708-4471. A friendly little restaurant serving mainly Asian dishes with a few Western offerings for under P200. Stays open late. Daily 6am–3.30am.

🏃 **Tamarind** On the front at the western end of the beach ☎043/287-3240. Offering tropical charm, wonderful ocean vistas, and tasty Thai and international dishes, *Tamarind* is Sabang's most popular restaurant. The spicy Thai salads (P180–190), *tom kha gai* (P200) and BBQs (P330–440) are all worth sampling. Daily 7am–10pm.

The Venue One of the few discos in town that isn't a girlie bar, *The Venue* is popular with both locals and tourists.

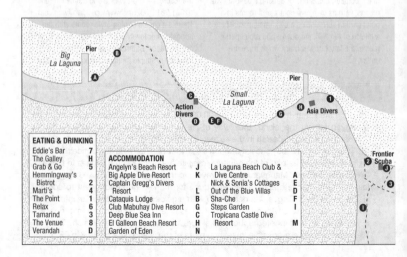

EATING & DRINKING	
Eddie's Bar	7
The Galley	H
Grab & Go	5
Hemingway's Bistrot	2
Marti's	4
The Point	1
Relax	6
Tamarind	3
The Venue	8
Verandah	D

ACCOMMODATION			
Angelyn's Beach Resort	J	La Laguna Beach Club & Dive Centre	A
Big Apple Dive Resort	K	Nick & Sonia's Cottages	E
Captain Gregg's Divers Resort	L	Out of the Blue Villas	D
Cataquis Lodge	B	Sha-Che	F
Club Mabuhay Dive Resort	G	Steps Garden	I
Deep Blue Sea Inn	C	Tropicana Castle Dive Resort	M
El Galleon Beach Resort	H		
Garden of Eden	N		

Small La Laguna

Just a few minutes' walk from Sabang, **Small La Laguna** is the ideal choice if you're looking for a range of friendly accommodation in a quiet location – most of it right on the beach – with good dive operators and a handful of informal bars and restaurants.

Accommodation

Club Mabuhay Dive Resort ☎043/287-3097, ⓦwww.mabuhay-dive-resort.com. Not to be confused with its near namesake (*Dive Resort Club Mabuhay*) over in Sabang, this is a substantial resort set in expansive tropical gardens and finished to a high standard. All rooms are a/c and have balconies overlooking the central swimming pool. Their stylish *Mabuhay Beach Restaurant* is right on the shore and there's a silent 24hr generator should the power fail. ❼

Deep Blue Sea Inn On the west end of the beach, 30m from Action Divers. No phone. Very comfortable a/c apartments, cottages and doubles with bathrooms. The upstairs restaurant has fine views across the sea towards Verde Island. An excellent budget choice in a quiet location. ❹

🏃 **El Galleon Beach Resort** ☎02/834-2974. Professionally run tropical-style hotel with airy bamboo a/c double rooms, many with balconies. Try to get one of the rooms on the upper level at the front, right on the beach. The pleasant seaside restaurant serves breakfast and a good range of lunch and dinner dishes including pasta, chicken, salads and seafood, produced by the resident French chef. ❺

Nick and Sonia's Cottages No phone. Simple rooms with a fridge, hot shower and their own cooking facilities; there's a choice of fan or a/c. ❷

Out of the Blue Villas ☎043/287-3357, ⓦwww .outoftheblue-villas.com. Sophisticated apartments set on the hillside above the beach, most of which feature huge windows and balconies looking out to sea. There's also a small pool, and a great restaurant, *Verandah* (see p.244). ❺

Sha-Che Roughly midway along the beach ☎0928/411-3748. Small but friendly place with a choice of clean a/c and fan rooms, with cable TV, fridge and wi-fi. ❸

Eating and drinking

The Galley At *El Galleon Resort*. Great views and excellent European and Filipino cuisine continue to make this one of the most popular restaurants in Small La Laguna. Daily 7am–10pm.

The Point On the headland between Sabang and Small La Laguna. Popular sunset drinks spot with a huge cocktail list and open until midnight. Daily noon–midnight.

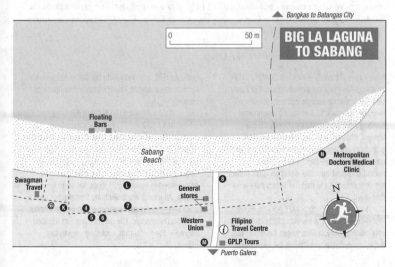

▲ Bangkas to Batangas City

```
0        50 m
```

BIG LA LAGUNA TO SABANG

Floating Bars

Sabang Beach

Ⓝ Metropolitan Doctors Medical Clinic

Swagman Travel

Ⓛ

@ Ⓚ ❹ ❼

❺ ❻

General stores

❽

Western Union

ⓘ Filipino Travel Centre

Ⓜ GPLP Tours

N

▼ Puerto Galera

Verandah At *Out of the Blue Villas*. Perched high above the beach this is the most upmarket restaurant in Small La Laguna and serves good salads and pizzas (from P200) either in the tasteful interior or out on a breezy terrace overlooking the ocean. There's also a decent wine list (from P750). Daily noon–3pm & 6–10pm.

Big La Laguna

Just around the corner from Small La Laguna, the sheltered cove of **Big La Laguna** has dive shops, a good choice of accommodation and a few convivial beach-style bars and restaurants at the resorts themselves.

Accommodation and eating

Cataquis Lodge ☎0916/31-9877. Brightly coloured concrete huts with a/c, cable TV and hot water, and the location is exceptional, just paces from the sea. There are cheaper wooden cottages at the back. ④

Coco Beach Island Resort Not actually in Big La Laguna, but a little further along the coast to the west ☎02/521-5260, ⓦwww.cocobeach.com. See map on p.237. Reachable only by private bangka (they'll collect you in Batangas or at Muelle pier), this is secluded and idyllic, with airy rooms built of indigenous materials and a full range of activities on offer, including day-trips, diving and tennis. There's also a large outdoor swimming pool in the well-kept grounds. The only problem is that you'll have to depend on the resort's bangkas to take you anywhere, even out for dinner at night. The resort does, however, have several restaurants of its own. ④

La Laguna Beach Club & Dive Centre ☎043/287-3181, ⓦwww.llbc.com.ph. Substantial resort with various palm-roofed rooms and cottages surrounding a beautiful swimming pool. All rooms have a/c, hot water, cable TV and DVD player. On site are a reputable diving school, a first-class restaurant serving Asian and European fare and the relaxing upstairs *Gecko Bar* with a large balcony for sunset-watching. ⑦

Palangan and Sinandigan Cove

There are some quiet and comfortable places to stay around the small barrio of **PALANGAN**, ten minutes by jeepney along the road from Puerto Galera to Sabang. Some are on the ridge above the road, with marvellous views across Puerto's bays and islets and just a short walk from the beach. Not all of these resorts have dive centres, but they can all help arrange diving through operators in Sabang. Quiet **Sinandigan Cove**, also known as Coral Cove, is twenty minutes northeast of Palangan by jeepney.

Accommodation and eating

Blue Crystal Beach Resort ☎043/287-3144, ⓦwww.bluecrystalbeachresort.com. For those seeking a remote escape without foregoing everyday luxuries, this imposing colonnaded building right on the seashore may be the answer. Rooms have a/c, cable TV and are grandly decorated with heavy furnishings, and some have kitchenettes. There's also a decent pool and beautiful coastal vistas. In fact the only downside is that the beach here isn't that great. ⑥

Coral Cove Resort ☎043/287-3320, ⓦwww.coral-cove.com. This excellent little resort is the only place to stay in Sinandigan Cove and has large, comfortable, sea-facing fan rooms and cottages (⑦), a friendly little bar and a restaurant right on the seafront. There's also a dive operator here. ④

Kalaw Place ☎043/422-0209 or 0917/532 -2617, ⓦwww.kalawplace.com.ph. This is something special, a gracious and relaxed family-run resort on a promontory to the north of the road just before you reach Palangan. Options range from rooms in the main house to whole wooden houses (⑦), good for up to 6 people. All rooms are beautifully furnished in native style and many boast expansive bamboo balconies with fabulous views. The owners prepare the food served in the restaurant, including vegetarian dishes. ④

White Beach

A once quiet crescent of sand, **White Beach** has in recent years been populated by many small resort hotels and cottage rooms. Unlike Sabang, this has no girlie bars and there are fewer scuba divers too, but it does have a number of lively discos and bars that can get a bit noisy. White Beach gets especially busy at peak times, notably New Year and Easter, when backpackers and students from Manila hold all-night rave parties on the sand. There are still some quieter spots on the beach, but those looking for an isolated and quiet beach experience should head around the corner to Aninuan, and Talipanan (see below).

There are no **banks** here, so bring cash; credit cards won't be accepted. **Internet cafés** include *Parkway Internet* near *Apartelle de Francesca*. From early morning until 2 or 3pm, big bangkas make the one-hour trip to Batangas (P200). White Beach has become very popular of late, and room prices have rocketed. For those on a budget it can be hard to find a decent room, particularly at weekends and holidays; it's definitely worth booking in advance.

Most of the resorts have their own simple **restaurants**, usually offering basic dishes such as grilled fish and *adobo*. The beach is also lined with small-scale cafés and restaurants which serve simple, often overpriced food.

Accommodation

Coco Aroma ☏0916/616-7337, ⓦwww .cocoaroma.com. At the quieter western end of the beach this is one of the few remaining simple beachside places and has basic fan rooms, a couple of nicely styled a/c cottages (❺), a laidback café, and lots of ambience. ❹

Lenly's ☏0915/408-0904. Set behind the first row of stalls back from the beach, *Lenly's* is one of the few bargains left at White Beach. There's a range of spacious a/c and fan cottages, some of which have kitchenette and fridge. ❸

Marco Vincent ☏02/813-6329, ⓦwww .marcovincent.com. Set a few hundred metres back from the beach, with plush a/c rooms set around a central courtyard with pool, this hacienda-style development is as grand as it gets here in White Beach. The resort has wi-fi throughout, and also has a dive centre. ❽

Summer Connection ☏0912/316-5910. Located at the attractive western end of the beach, *Summer Connection* has managed to retain much of its original charm, in spite of having added a modern concrete block. The new block has clean and functional a/c rooms with cable TV, fridge and hot water, or there are a few simpler rooms in the old nipa house at the back. ❻

Eating and drinking

Coco Aroma Western end of the beach. A pleasant exception to the uniformity of most of White Beach's restaurants, *Coco Aroma*, with its low tables looking out to sea, has good Western and Filipino dishes (P150–450), and delicious shakes. Daily 7am–10pm.

Peter's Restaurant & Bar Middle of the beach. Tasty curries (P150) and pasta dishes (P100–200) in a long-standing favourite on the beach. Daily 7am–10pm.

Aninuan and Talipanan beaches

With White Beach becoming increasingly busy, travellers looking for something more pristine are slowly moving further west along the coast. Both **Aninuan** and **Talipanan** beaches can be reached either by bangka from Muelle pier, tricycle from White Beach (P40) or by walking around the headland from White Beach. At low tide Talipanan is also reachable along the shoreline (20min walk from White Beach), and when the tide is in there's a pathway that leads up over the headland. Aninuan is more popular, while Talipanan is for those seeking real solitude – there's no nightlife and no karaoke – just you, the fishermen and the fireflies.

At both beaches you can charter a bangka to do some beach-hopping, or ask your accommodation to help you arrange a trek to the lower slopes of Mount Malasimbo to visit waterfalls and Mangyan people.

Accommodation and eating

Luca's At the far end of Talipanan ☎0916/417-5125, ⓦwww.lucaphilippines.com. *Luca's* has well-designed rooms with a/c, cable TV, fridge and hot water, plus genuine Italian food at the beautifully situated restaurant. ❺

Mountain Beach Resort Cottages In the middle of Talipanan Beach ☎0906/362-5406, ⓦwww.mountainbeachresort.com. A good choice of rooms, some of which have kitchens, cable TV and hot water, and there's free wi-fi in the restaurant. ❷

Sunset at Aninuan Beach Resort Halfway along Aninuan Beach ☎0920/931-8946, ⓦwww.aninuanbeach.com. This marble-floor complex right on the sand has tastefully styled, a/c rooms which look out over the sea. Staff are helpful, and there's a relaxing open-air bar and a good restaurant with wi-fi. A pool should be complete by the end of 2011. ❼

Tamaraw Beach Resort At the White Beach end of Aninuan ☎0921/279-5161, ⓦwww.tamarawbeachresort.com. *Tamaraw* has an unbeatable location on the beach and pleasant rooms with balconies overlooking the sea, perfect for watching the sunset. The main building is an ugly motel-style box, so go for a separate cottage (❼). They do good, reasonably priced food – mostly grills and salads with rice. ❷

Calapan

About 30km along an often unpaved road east of Puerto Galera, the busy port city of **CALAPAN** is the capital of Mindoro Oriental. It's not a tourist destination, depending for most of its livelihood on trade, but it is well connected transport-wise and is the base for a trek up **Mount Halcon**, the fourth highest mountain in the country and supposedly the toughest to climb; its trails are currently off-limits.

Arrival and information

Arriving in Calapan by **fast ferry** from Batangas City, the city centre is a fifteen-minute ride away by tricycle (P20). Calapan's main street is J.P. Rizal Street, which is only 500m long and runs past Calapan Cathedral south to Juan Luna Street. The main **tourist office** for Oriental Mindoro is in the Provincial Capitol building in J.P. Rizal Street (daily 9am–4pm; ☎043/288-5622). The **immigration office** (Thurs & Fri only), where you can extend visas, and the **post office**, are also in the compound. There are numerous banks with **ATMs** along J.P. Rizal Street, including BDO and Metrobank, which are opposite each other. Just along the street there's also a Mercury Drug pharmacy, as well as plenty of **internet cafés** including the *Galactic Internet Café* and *MPS Cybernet* at the junction with Bonifacio Street. For information on exploring Mount Halcon head for **Apak Outdoors** shop opposite the Land Transport Office on Quezon Drive (☎0916/241-1780, ✉richard.alcanices@yahoo.com) – see opposite for more.

Accommodation and eating

Accommodation options in Calapan don't set the pulse racing, but there are some decent budget hotels. Much more preferable to staying in town, however, is to take a tricycle out to the coast and stay near the Nautical Highway. As for **eating**, a walk along the traffic-clogged length of J.P. Rizal Street in town will take you past the usual Philippine fast-food outlets, including *Jollibee*, *Chowking*, *Greenwich* and *Mister Donut*. On the same street *Starmax Coffee* also serves light snacks.

By ferry

Calapan is served by numerous fast and slow ferries from Batangas. Supercat (☎043/288-3179) has 8–9 fast services daily (1hr), while Besta Shipping has services every 2–3hr around the clock (2hr), and Supershuttle runs two car ferries per day (2hr).

By bus, jeepney and van

If you're heading for **Puerto Galera**, many resorts will send transport to meet you if you book and pay in advance. Otherwise you can take a jeepney (90min) from the Flying V petrol station out beyond the Provincial Capitol building on J.P. Rizal Street. Services operate roughly every 45 minutes from 6am to 5.15pm. There are some terrific views during the second half of the jeepney ride as the road ascends into the hills above the palm-fringed coast. Note that many of these jeepneys don't stop at **Sabang**, for which you'll have to go all the way to Puerto Galera Town and then get a jeepney back. For the 3–4 hour journey to **Roxas**, jeepneys head out from the market, Alps buses leave from their terminal on the corner of Roxas and Magsaysay streets and there are also minivans from the Angel Star terminal on Mabini Street, while other buses leave from the ferry pier.

Calapan Bay Hotel On the Nautical Highway ☎043/288-1309. Bright and clean a/c rooms with cable TV and hot water, and free wi-fi in the lobby. There's also an atmospheric restaurant with a patio overlooking the ocean. ❸
Parang Beach Resort 15min southeast of town ☎043/288-6120, ⓦwww.parangbeachresort.com. A number of plain but comfortable and well-kept

rooms in tin-roofed cottages right on the shore, with a beachside restaurant. ❸
Riceland II Inn M.H. Del Pilar ☎043/288-55903. This place has a range of motel-style standard rooms in the main building, and more comfortable rooms in the annexe building at the back (❸). Choice of fan or a/c, and with or without cable TV determine the rate and there's free wi-fi. ❶

Mount Halcon

Rugged **Mount Halcon** rears up dramatically from the coastal plain of Mindoro Oriental, southwest of Calapan. At an altitude of 2587m, it's Mindoro's highest peak, distinguished by the dense tracts of rainforest that surround it, some of the most extensive forest on the island. A large tract of the mountain is under a UNDP reforestation programme, and trails up the mountain have been off-limits for the past few years. At the time of writing an alternate trail was being created.

Unusually for the Philippines, Halcon is not of volcanic origin, created instead by a massive geological uplifting millions of years ago. The lower slopes of Mount Halcon are about one hour from Calapan; chartering a jeepney at the market for the trip will cost around P700. At the town of **Baco** you'll take a turn-off up an unsealed track to the Mangyan settlement of **Lantuyang**, where you pay P50 to the barangay head. You can also approach the mountain from Puerto Galera, taking a jeepney for Calapan and getting off at the Baco turn-off.

The total climb – Dulangan and Halcon combined – is longer than that to the summit of Mount Everest from Base Camp; allow four to five days for the ascent and descent. There are many obstacles, not the least of which is the sheer volume of rain that falls on Mount Halcon. There is no distinct dry season here and heavy rain is virtually a daily occurrence, resulting in an enormous fecundity of life – massive trees, dense layers of dripping moss, orchids, ferns and pitcher plants – but also making the environment treacherous and potentially miserable for climbers.

Trails should reopen in May 2011, but don't even think about climbing Mount Halcon on your own – **Apak Outdoors** shop, a hole-in-the-wall outfit opposite the Land Transport Office on Quezon Drive in Calapan should be your first point of contact. The friendly owner, Richard (☎0916/241-1780, ⓔrichard.alcanices @yahoo.com), is a member of the Halcon Mountaineering Association, and can advise on the current situation, and if the trail hasn't reopened, he can suggest other trails, **bike routes** and **rivertubing** options (P500). If the trail is open, expect to pay P2000 per person (in a group), including permit, guide fees and transport but excluding food and water. You'll be sleeping on the mountain for at least three nights, so if you need a tent and other equipment, you can rent them at the shop, but they need to know in advance. Make sure you have good waterproof clothing and a waterproof cover for your backpack.

Roxas

Unless you just have a penchant for rough road driving and are planning to head across the mountains to San José and beyond, the main reason for heading down the east coast to **ROXAS** is to take the ferry to Caticlan (for Boracay) or Romblon. South of Calapan the road runs past the immense **Naujan Lake** and skirts the eastern edge of the Naujan National Park before hitting the rather drab and uninspiring coastal towns of Pinamalayan and Bongabong. These east coast towns depend on trade and fish rather than tourism for their livelihood, and there are no pristine beaches, just long, hot stretches of grey sand. Roxas itself is a busy market town, where there's a market, a few hotels and beach resorts out by the new port at Dangay, and not much else.

Arrival and information

Ferries to Caticlan leave around the clock, so there's really little reason to stay in Roxas unless you're too late to get onwards transport to San José or Calapan. **Buses** and **jeepneys** run north and south from Roxas, leaving from near the market on Administration Street, and **Dangay** pier which is on the eastern edge of town. There's a **tourist office** (Mon–Fri 8am–5pm; ☎043/289-2824) at the entrance to the pier. To get cash, there's an Allied Bank with **ATM** on Administration Street, or to **change currency** head for Moneygram on Bagobayan Street, and nearby you'll find *Route 168* **internet café**. There's a Mercury Drug **pharmacy** next to Roxas Villas, and a **doctor's** surgery at the *RL Ganan Hotel*.

Accommodation and eating

If you find yourself with a few hours to wait for a ferry, the best thing to do is camp out at one of the simple resorts on Dahlican Beach, just along the coast from

---

Moving on from Roxas

By ferry

Roxas is a key link on the Strong Nautical Highway route to Boracay, and there are ferries departing for **Caticlan** around the clock. Supershuttle (☎0922/880-2513) runs two services a day (12.30am & 12.30pm), as does Starlite (☎043/289-2886; 11am & 11pm) while Montenegro Shipping has five daily boats, and a host of other smaller companies also operate departures. There is also one weekly ferry for **Odiongan** in Romblon, at noon on Wednesday (3hr).

By road

Heading north to **Calapan** is a simple enough procedure and there are a series of minivan depots on Magsaysay Street which operate cramped but speedy trips (P150 for the 3–4hr journey). A couple of jeepneys attempt the journey west over the mountains to **San José** (4hr) every morning, or alternatively you can take a jeepney as far as Bulalacao and then take a bangka around the coast (see opposite).

Dangay pier, although most of these places get very busy on weekends. For something to eat, try *LYF Hotel* (see below), or *Mangyan's Place* next to Montenegro Shipping at Dangay pier.

Cruzsmart Beach Resort ☎043/289-2421. Has a pool (P75 for non-residents) and a/c rooms which are rentable in 4-, 12- and 24-hour segments. There are pergolas for rent (P200 per half-day), but the bad news is there is also karaoke. ❸

LYF Hotel Magsaysay St ☎043/289-2819. Painted a brilliant orange colour, this place has clean fan and a/c rooms with cable TV, although some have no windows, and the walls are very thin. The canteen serves up some good food. ❶

RL Ganan Hotel Bagumbaya ☎043/289-2421. The best hotel in town, with big and bright a/c rooms complete with cable TV. ❸

The road to Bulalacao

The coastal road south from Roxas trundles through **Mansalay** and on to **Bulalacao**, the jumping-off point for a bangka ride to some beautiful and remote islets, including Target, Aslom, Buyayo and Tambaron Island. On Tambaron you'll find the charmingly isolated *Tambaron Green Beach Resort* (☎0920/339-2595; ❹), which has dorm beds (P200) and large, simple family cabins set amid trees on a beach frequented by green sea turtles. There's night-time electricity and a communal kitchen.

Beyond Bulalacao the road fizzles out into a rough track that few vehicles can negotiate – apart, that is, from the trusty jeepney, and, in the rainy season, even these frequently end up having to swap passengers just before the crest of the pass. If you're not up for this kind of adventure, the three-hour bangka trip (P250) from Bulalacao along the coast to San José (see below) is almost as beautiful. The bangkas don't operate to a strict timetable, but there's usually one that leaves Bulalacao every morning. Alternatively you can charter your own bangka to San José at the wharf for about P2500 one-way.

Mindoro Occidental

Aside from a few intrepid wildlife enthusiasts and divers around Sablayan, **Mindoro Occidental** remains wonderfully undiscovered, and travellers with flexible travel plans and a penchant for bumpy jeepney rides will have their efforts rewarded with wild jungly mountains, remote beaches, and maybe meeting a few of the local Mangyan people along the way.

San José on the southwest coast has the only functioning airport on Mindoro and makes a logical starting point for trips north to the **Mounts Iglit-Baco National Park**, home to the *tamaraw*, a dwarf buffalo endemic to Mindoro and in acute danger of extinction. Further north, the fishing town of **Sablayan** is the jumping-off point for a sight no scuba diver should miss, the **Apo Reef Marine Natural Park**, a vast reef complex offering some of the best diving in the world. As well as organizing a trip from Sablayan, you can also do so in advance at a dive shop in Manila (see p.106) or Busuanga (see p.379). Sablayan is also a base for a visit to Mounts Iglit-Baco or the **Sablayan Watershed Forest Reserve**, a lowland forest with beautiful Lake Libao at its centre. The northwest of the island is little visited, though there are some unspoilt beaches around the town of **Mamburao**, the low-key capital of Mindoro Occidental.

San José

On Mindoro's southwest coast, the intensely sun-bleached and noisy port town of **SAN JOSÉ** is a quintessential Philippine provincial metropolis, with traffic-dense streets lined with drugstores, cheap canteens and fast-food outlets. Travellers usually only see San José as they pass through on their way from the airport to Sablayan or the **Mounts Iglit-Baco National Park**, for which **permits** can be obtained in San José. Though the Apo Reef is close by, there are no major dive operators in town and it's best to organize a trip there through the *Pandan Island Resort* accessed from Sablayan (see p.253). If you like the look of the **offshore islands** that can be seen from Sikatuna Beach, then *White House Beach Resort* (see opposite) can charter a boat to take you out to White Island (P1000 round trip for 4 passengers) or Ambulong (P3500 round trip for up to 10 passengers), but they need to know a day in advance.

Arrival and information

San José is bounded on its northern edge by the Pandururan River, beyond which are the **pier** and the **airport**. Arriving by jeepney from Roxas, or bus from Sablayan, you'll find yourself on Cipriano Liboro Street in the west of town. From here it's a short walk (or tricycle ride) to the main thoroughfare, **Rizal Street**, which runs across town and turns into the National Highway in the east, where it runs inland to Magsaysay. There are a number of **banks**, including PNB on M.H. Del Pilar, and Metrobank on Cipriano Liboro, both of which have ATMs. Close to PNB are the **police station**, town hall and **post office**. There are a handful of small **internet cafés** dotted around town – try *Elmo's*, opposite the *Sikatuna Town Hotel*.

For Mounts Iglit-Baco, you can apply for a **permit** (P50) and hire a guide at the Protected Area Office (Mon–Fri 8am–4pm; ☎043/491-4200) in the LIUCP Building on Airport Road. The park is a sixty-kilometre drive from San José: take a bus or jeepney along the coastal road to the barangay of **Popoy**, then a jeepney or tricycle the rest of the way.

▲ **A**, **B**, **C**, **D**, Protected Area Office & Airport

Pandururan River

ACCOMMODATION	
Mindoro Plaza	E
Mora Hotel	C
Sikatuna Beach Hotel	A
Sikatuna Town Hotel	D
White House Beach Resort	B

EATING & DRINKING	
Kusina ni Lea	3
Nice & Spice	2
Pilot's Lounge	1

**SAN JOSÉ
(MINDORO OCCIDENTAL)**

0   50 m

N

CAPT. COOPER STREET
Market
SIKATUNA STREET
BONIFACIO STREET
Metro Bank
Mercury Drug
Elmo's
HS Department Store
RIZAL STREET
Jeepney Depot
Caltex Gas Station
Dimple Star Bus Depot
Roxas Jeepneys
Regular Bus Depot
Land Bank
PNB
Police Station & Town Hall
St Joseph's Cathedral
P. ZAMORA ST
P. GOMEZ STREET
E. JACINTOS STREET
QUIRINO STREET
MAGSAYSAY STREET
LAPU-LAPU STREET
R. BURGOS STREET
DIEGO SILANG STREET
DAGOHOY STREET
TANDANG SORA STREET
CIPRIANO LIBORO STREET
BARRETTO STREET
LOPEZ JAENAS STREET
M. H. DEL PILAR STREET
QUEZON STREET
MABINI STREET
M. ELEUTERIO STREET
P. BURGOS STREET
SOLDEVILLA STREET

By plane

San José airport is a twenty-minute (P50) tricycle ride from town, or you could take one of the private cars that act as airport taxis, for which you'll pay P100. The airport is served by daily flights from Manila by Airphil Express, Cebu Pacific and Zest Airways. Cebu Pacific's office is at the airport, Airphil Express has an office next to the *Sikatuna Town Hotel*. If you plan to travel **northwards** from San José on the day you arrive, then the Airphil Express or Zest flights, both of which arrive early morning, are more convenient than the late-afternoon Cebu Pacific option.

By boat

Cheap flights have superseded boats to **San José**, and at the time of writing, there were no ferries at all, but this is set to change with the construction of a new pier, which is due for completion in early 2012 and should serve Batangas and Manila. For the meantime, the only boats to leave San José are the bangkas, which work their way around the southern tip of the island to Bulalacao. A bangka (P250) leaves from San José each morning and takes around three hours to make the trip, but if the seas are rough they don't run. If you miss the boat, you should be able to charter a bangka for P2000–2500.

By bus and jeepney

Buses leave from the Dimple Star depot (☏043/668-4151) opposite the Caltex Station on Cipriano Lobato street every couple of hours for **Sablayan** (3–4hr), **Mamburao** (5–6hr) and **Abra de Ilog** (7hr). Some of these services also continue on to Batangas by ferry, and then Manila by bus, but if you're not planning to stop anywhere along the way, it's almost as cheap, and much quicker to fly. If you want to reach **Puerto Galera**, you'll need to take a bus to Abra de Ilog, then a jeepney to Wawa on the north coast, and finally take (or charter) a bangka the rest of the way. Two minutes' walk south of the Dimple Star Terminal, another bus stand on the same side of the road also offers the same services, without air-conditioning. Dimple Star also run buses to **Roxas**, although these frequently involve transferring to a jeepney beyond Magsaysay. Jeepneys leave from just west of the Rizal Street and Cipriano Lobaro Street junction and run to Sablayan (3–4hr) and Roxas (4hr).

Accommodation

Unless you arrive too late to move on, there's little reason to stay in San José, but if you find yourself with a night here, the choices are between one of the budget options in town, or spending a little more out at the beach on the edge of town.

Mindoro Plaza Zamora St ☏043/491-4661. Friendly central option with shabby a/c rooms and a canteen. ❷

Mora Hotel San Roque ☏043/491-4869. A choice of themed rooms (Japanese, Filipino) with a/c and cable TV, and there's also a pool. ❺

Sikatuna Beach Hotel Airport Rd, San Roque 1 ☏043/491-4108, ⓦwww.sikatunabeachhotel.com. Nice place with friendly staff and some a/c rooms

that look out to the ocean. There's also a pleasant open-sided restaurant with wi-fi. ❷

Sikatuna Town Hotel Sikatuna St ☏043/491-1274. Slightly gloomy fan and a/c rooms with cable TV and private showers. ❶

White House Beach Resort Airport Rd, San Roque 1 ☏043/491-1656. The best place to stay in San José, with marble-floored, a/c rooms plus cable TV, ocean-view balconies, and wi-fi in the dining room. ❻

Eating

For snacks and supplies, look for HS Department Store on Rizal Street. Dining options in San José principally revolve around the hotels, and of these the restaurants at *Sikatuna Beach Hotel*, **Mora Hotel's** *Pilot's Lounge*, and the canteen at the *Mindoro Plaza*, are your best options.

Kusina ni Lea Opposite *Sikatuna Town Hotel.* Cheap soups, sandwiches and Filipino dishes in a pleasant wooden dining hall. Daily 8am–10pm.

Nice & Spice Sikatuna St. Focusing more on the nice than the spice, this canteen serves sandwiches, soups and burgers. Daily 8am–8pm.

Sablayan

A very bumpy forty kilometres north of San José, the unhurried fishing town of **SABLAYAN** is the perfect jumping-off point for several nearby attractions including Mounts Iglit-Baco National Park, the Sablayan Watershed Forest Reserve and Apo Reef. The town, small enough to cover on foot, has a central plaza with a town hall and a stretch of beach lined by bangkas.

Arrival and information

There are buses and jeepneys north to Mamburao (3hr; P123) and Abra de Ilog (4hr; P187), and south to San José (3–4hr; P113) from the **bus station** on the southern edge of town, on the National Highway, while slightly faster Dimple Star services (with onwards boat-bus connections for Batangas and Manila) leave from their terminal on the national highway. The **pier** is a five-minute walk south of the bus station. For **internet**, try *Kaboom* near the *Landmanz Hotel*.

To arrange **permits** for Mount Iglit-Baco (P50), guides, and boats to North Pandan Island, head to the friendly Sablayan Eco-Tourism Office (Mon–Sat 8am–noon & 1–5pm ℡0928/465-9585, Ⓦwww.sablayan.net) in the town plaza.

Accommodation and eating

Accommodation in Sablayan is pretty limited, as are eating options, which are generally best in the hotels. Otherwise head to the places around the town plaza: *GV Restaurant* serves egg sandwiches for breakfast and buffet meals for lunch and dinner, or for fast food, try a burger or hot dog from *Star Shake* on Urieta Street.

La Sofia Apartelle ℡0907/268-9685. The best rooms in town are in the new wing of *La Sofia Apartelle* which have a/c and cable TV. Fan-cooled rooms in the older main building are basic but clean. ❶

Landmanz Hotel Arellano St ℡0910/546-5004. Cheaper than *La Sofia Apartelle*, but the plumbing is sketchy. ❶

Sablayan Adventure Camp ℡0917/850-0410. Out by the pier, this cheery establishment has spacious fan rooms set in cottages looking out to the beach, although the walls dividing the rooms don't stretch to the ceiling, meaning you'll hear everything that your neighbours do. They also have a bar and restaurant and hire out mountain bikes (P50/hr) and motorbikes (P500/day). ❷

Mounts Iglit-Baco National Park

The **Mounts Iglit-Baco National Park** is dominated by the twin peaks of **Mount Baco** (2488m) and **Mount Iglit** (2364m), which offer some challenging climbs; it can take up to two days to reach the peak of Mount Iglit, so these climbs are tough and not to be underestimated. Vegetation is so dense there have been no officially recorded ascents of Mount Baco. This is also a New People's Army (NPA) area and while there have been no notable events involving tourists, it's worth asking around for the latest information.

There are also a number of more leisurely treks through the foothills to areas in which you are most likely to see the endangered *tamaraw* (*Bubalus mindorensis*), a dwarf bovine of which fewer than two hundred exist. The *tamaraw*, whose horns grow straight upwards in a distinctive "V" formation, has fallen victim to hunting, disease and deforestation, and to create more awareness of its plight there is talk of designating it the country's national animal. Apart from the *tamaraw*, the park is also prime habitat for the Philippine deer, wild pigs and other endemic species such as the Mindoro scops owl and the Mindoro imperial pigeon.

To visit the park, you'll first have to secure a **permit** (P50) and arrange a guide (P1000 for three days), either in San José at the Protected Area Office (see p.250) or the Sablayan Eco-Tourism Office. Both of these offices can help put together all of the logistics for your trip, including camping options, and can also advise on visits to the "Gene Pool", a small laboratory where scientists are trying to breed the *tamaraw* in captivity. Reaching the park by public transport from Sablayan means taking one of the regular buses or jeepneys south along the coastal road to the barangay of **Popoy**, then a jeepney up the bumpy and rutted track to the park itself.

Sablayan Watershed Forest Reserve

The **Sablayan Watershed Forest Reserve** is unusual among protected wilderness areas because it contains the Sablayan Prison and **Penal Farm**, a huge open prison for low-risk inmates, surrounded by agricultural lands worked by the prisoners. The inmates also produce handicrafts, and are distinguishable from the guards only by their orange T-shirts and the fact that they are not armed. Nearby are a number of villages where staff and prisoners' families live; beyond the last of these villages is a motorable track that ends on the edge of thick forest, close to **Lake Libao**. This shallow, roughly circular lake is covered in lilies and alive with birds, including kingfishers, bitterns, egrets and purple herons. An undulating footpath around the lake makes for some wonderful walking, taking you through the edge of the forest and through glades from where there are views across the water; you'll see locals balanced precariously on small wooden bangkas fishing for tilapia. If you're reasonably fit you can walk round the lake in three hours, starting and finishing at the penal colony, though allow an hour to get between the colony and the main road.

To reach the penal colony directly you'll have to hire a vehicle and driver in Sablayan (P2000 for a day-trip) or take a bus along the coastal road and ask to be dropped at the turn-off for the colony, near the town of **Pianag**. There are buses and jeepneys from Pianag if you need one for the return trip.

North Pandan Island

Idyllic **North Pandan Island** (P150 entrance fee), ringed by a halo of fine white sand, coral reefs and coconut palms, lies two kilometres off the west coast of Mindoro. In 1994 a sanctuary was established around the eastern half of the island so the **marine life** is exceptional; with a mask and snorkel you can see big grouper, all sorts of coral fishes, even the occasional turtle.

If you want to visit the island it's easy to arrange a **boat** to Pandan (20min; P600 return for a boat which can hold 15 passengers) from the Sablayan Eco-Tourism Office (see opposite). You'll need to pay a P75 fee to set foot on the island.

The island is the site of the well-run ⚓ *Pandan Island Resort* (☎0919/305-7821, Ⓦ www.pandan.com), a back-to-nature private hideaway developed by a French adventurer who discovered it in 1986. There are four types of **accommodation** at the resort: budget rooms (❷) standard double bungalows (❹), larger bungalows for four (❺), and family houses for up to six (❷). During the diving season (Nov–May) the island is so popular that all rooms are often taken, so it's important to book in advance. Guests are required to take at least one buffet meal at the resort **restaurant** every day, and this is no bad thing: the chef dishes up excellent

European and Filipino cuisine (try the tangy fish salad in vinegar) and the beach bar serves some unforgettable tropical cocktails.

On most days the resort's scuba-diving centre organizes day-trips to Apo Reef, and longer overnight safaris both to Apo and to Busuanga off northern Palawan (see p.377) if there are enough passengers. Even if you don't dive, there's plenty to keep you occupied on and around the island itself, including kayaking, jungle treks, windsurfing and sailing.

Apo Reef Marine Natural Park

Lying about 30km off the west coast of Mindoro, **Apo Reef** stretches 26km from north to south and 20km east to west, making it a significant marine environment. There are two main atolls separated by deep channels and a number of shallow lagoons with beautiful white sandy bottoms. Only in three places does the coral rise above the sea's surface, creating the islands of Cayos de Bajo, Binangaan and Apo. The largest of these, **Apo**, is home to a ranger station and a lighthouse. The diving is really something special, with sightings of sharks (even hammerheads), barracuda, tuna and turtles fairly common. Most of the Philippines' 450 species of coral are here, from tiny bubble corals to huge gorgonian sea fans and brain corals, along with hundreds of species of smaller reef fishes such as angelfish, batfish, surgeonfish and jacks.

If you're not staying at the *Pandan Island Resort*, you can head to the reef on one of the **liveaboard** trips offered by many dive operators in Coron Town (in Busuanga; see p.377) or Manila. Alternatively the Sablayan Eco-Tourism Office can organize a 10-person boat out to the reef for P6500. However you get here, to snorkel on the reef you need to pay a fee of P350, or P1300 to dive.

The northwest

It's hard to believe that the quiet, relatively isolated west coast town of **MAMBURAO**, 80km north along the coastal road from Sablayan, is the capital of Mindoro Occidental. With a population of 35,000, Mamburao is significant only as a trading and fishing town, although the coastal road is undeniably scenic, with blue ocean on one side and jungled mountains on the other. North of town there are some alluring stretches of **beach** which are slowly being developed for tourism. The best of these is **Tayamaan Bay**, 4km north of Mamburao, where you can rest and eat good, fresh food at the *Tayamaan Palm Beach Club* (☏043/711-1657; ❸). Cottages at the resort have twin or double beds, private bathrooms and verandas close to the sea. In Mamburao itself, you could stay at the *La Gensol Plaza Hotel* (☏043/711-1072; ❷), on the National Highway through town. The cheapest rooms are fan singles with tiny cold showers, though they also have larger, more comfortable doubles with air conditioning and cable TV.

North of Mamburao the road forks. From here, jeepneys and some buses head northwest along the coast to Palauan or northeast to **Abra de Ilog** near the north coast; the journey to Abra de Ilog takes you past dazzling green paddy fields and farmland planted with corn. In the town there's one small hotel, *L&P Lodging House* (☏0918/528-2173; ❶), about 1km before you reach the pier at **Wawa**. The easily motorable road ends here, although the track to Puerto Galera is a popular route with bike riders, and hikers have also made the trip.

The easiest way to get to **Puerto Galera** is to take a bangka. Sometimes there are morning passenger bangka services, but don't be surprised if you end up having to charter your own (about 2hr; P1500–2000).

The Visayas

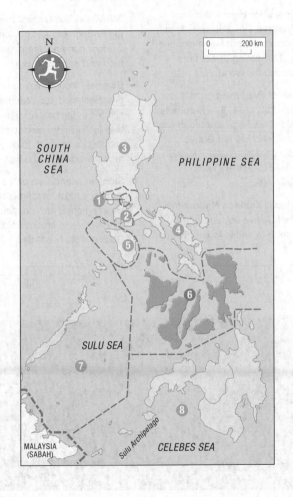

CHAPTER 6

Highlights

* **Malapascua** A little gem off the tip of Cebu, boasting the dazzling Bounty Beach, islets to explore and scuba diving with thresher sharks. See p.278

* **Pescador Island Marine Reserve** Tiny Pescador is only 100m long, but has a glorious reef attracting divers from around the world. See p.281

* **Bohol** Everything good about the Philippines in one compact island package: superb diving, fine beaches, old Gothic churches and, uniquely, the iconic Chocolate Hills. See p.283

* **Mount Kanlaon National Park** Active volcano at the centre of dense forest offering some extreme trekking and climbing. See p.302

* **Apo Island** Robinson Crusoe-esque hideaway off Negros, with excellent diving. See p.308

* **Ati-Atihan** The biggest bash in the Philippines: wild costumes outdoor partying and copious food and drink. See p.315

* **Boracay** Though verging on overdeveloped, the beach is still one of the best anywhere, the nightlife is tremendous fun, and there's so much to do you'll never be bored. See p.324

* **Sibuyan Island** One of the country's most intact natural environments, with dramatic forest-cloaked Mount Guiting Guiting at its heart. See p.338

▲ Chocolate Hills, Bohol

The Visayas

T he **Visayas**, a collection of islands large and small in the central Philippines, are considered to be the cradle of the country. It was here that Ferdinand Magellan laid a sovereign hand on the archipelago for Spain and began the process of colonization and Catholicization that shaped so much of the nation's history. The islands were also the scene of some of the bloodiest battles fought against the Japanese during World War II, and where General Douglas MacArthur waded ashore to liberate the country after his famous promise, "I shall return".

There are thousands of islands in the Visayas and everywhere you turn there seems to be another patch of tropical sand or coral reef awaiting your attention, usually with a ferry or bangka to take you there. There are nine major island groups – **Cebu**, **Bohol**, **Siquijor**, **Negros**, **Guimaras**, **Panay**, **Romblon**, **Samar**, and **Leyte** – but it's the hundreds in between that make this part of the archipelago so irresistible. Of the smaller islands, some are famous for their beach life (especially **Boracay**, off the northern tip of Panay), some for their fiestas, and some for their folklore.

No one can accuse the Visayas, and the Visayans who live here, of being a uniform lot. Visayan is the umbrella language, the most widely spoken form of which is Cebuano, but in some areas they speak Ilongo or Waray Waray, in others Aklan; all three languages are closely related Malayo-Polynesian tongues. The diversity of languages is a symptom of the region's fractured topography, with many islands culturally and economically isolated from those around them, part of the Philippine archipelago in little more than name.

Getting around the Visayas is fairly easy, with increasingly efficient transport links. Cebu, Bohol, Negros, Panay, Romblon, Leyte and Samar are all accessible by air, most with daily **flights** from Manila and, in some cases, Cebu City. Major **ferry** companies still also ply some routes between Manila and the Visayas, although with increasingly low airfares, these services are dwindling. Within the Visayas, the ferry network is so extensive it doesn't really matter if you can't get a flight. Ferries large and small, safe and patently unsafe, link almost every city and town in the Visayas with neighbouring islands, so it's unlikely you'll ever be stuck for long. But the beauty of the region is that there's no need to make formal plans. There's always another island, another beach, another place to stay.

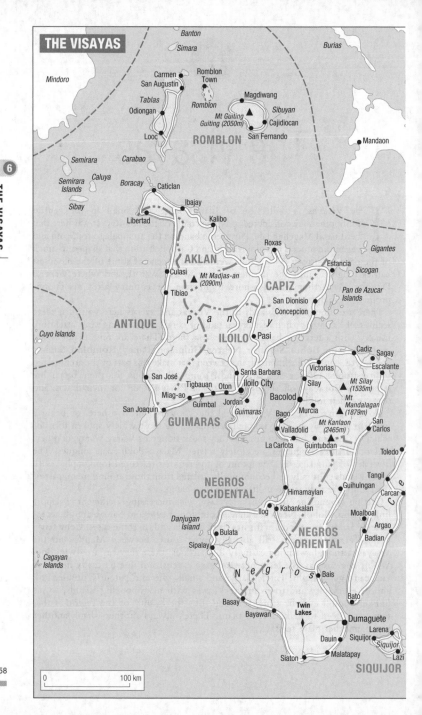

THE VISAYAS

Mindoro

Banton

Simara

Burias

Carmen
San Augustin

Romblon
Town

Magdiwang

Tablas

Romblon

Sibuyan

Odiongan

Mt Guiting
Guiting (2050m)

Cajidiocan
San Fernando

Looc

ROMBLON

Mandaon

Semirara

Carabao

Semirara
Islands

Caluya

Boracay

Caticlan

Sibay

Ibajay

Gigantes

Libertad

Kalibo

Roxas

Cuyo Islands

AKLAN

Estancia

Sicogan

Culasi

Mt Madjas-an
(2090m)

CAPIZ

Pan de Azucar
Islands

Tibiao

P a n a y

San Dionisio
Concepcion

ANTIQUE

ILOILO

Pasi

Cadiz

Sagay

San José

Santa Barbara

Victorias

Escalante

Tigbauan

Oton

Iloilo City

Silay

Mt Silay
(1535m)

Miag-ao

Guimbal

Jordan

Bacolod

Mt
Mandalagan
(1879m)

San Joaquin

Guimaras

Bago

Murcia

Mt Kanlaon
(2465m)

San
Carlos

GUIMARAS

Valladolid

La Carlota

Guintubdan

Toledo

NEGROS
OCCIDENTAL

Himamaylan

Guihulngan

Tangil

Carcar

Cuyo Islands

Ilog

Kabankalan

Moalboal

Danjugan
Island

Bulata

NEGROS
ORIENTAL

Argao

Sipalay

Badian

Cagayan
Islands

N e g r o s

Bais

Basay

Bató

Bayawan

Twin
Lakes

Dumaguete

Larena

Dauin

Siquijor

Siquijor

Siaton

Malatapay

Lazi

SIQUIJOR

0   100 km

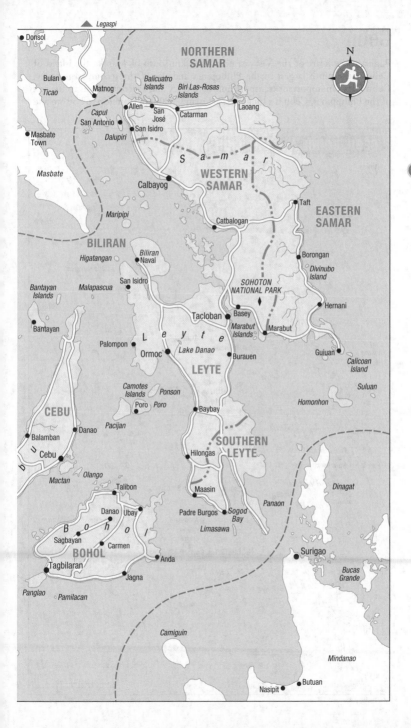

Cebu

Right in the heart of the Visayas, nearly 600km south of Manila, the island of **Cebu** is the ninth largest in the Philippines and site of the second largest city, **Cebu City**, an important transport hub with ferry and air connections to the rest of the Philippines. Cebu is a long, narrow island – 300km from top to bottom and

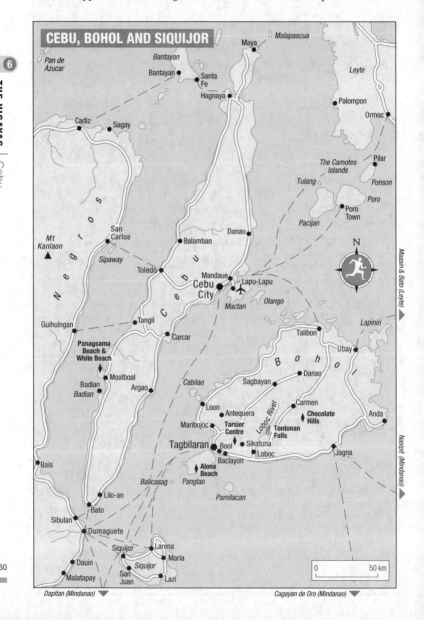

CEBU, BOHOL AND SIQUIJOR

Pan de Azucar

Bantayan

Bantayan

Santa Fe

Hagnaya

Maya

Malapascua

Leyte

Palompon

Ormoc

Cadiz

Sagay

Pilar

The Camotes Islands

Ponson

Tulang

Poro

Pacijan

Poro Town

San Carlos

Balamban

Danao

Mt Kanlaon ▲

Sipaway

Toledo

Mandaue

Cebu City

Lapu-Lapu

Olango

Mactan

N

Negros

Guihulngan

Tangil

Carcar

Talibon

Ubay

Lapinin

Panagsama Beach & White Beach

Moalboal

Cabilao

Sagbayan

Danao

Bohol

Badian

Badian

Argao

Loon

Antequera

Maribojoc

Tarsier Centre

Carmen

Chocolate Hills

Anda

Tagbilaran

Bool

Sikatuna

Loboc

Tontonan Falls

Baclayon

Jagna

Bais

Alona Beach

Balicasag

Panglao

Pamilacan

Lilo-an

Bato

Sibulan

Dumaguete

Siquijor

Larena

Maria

Dauin

San Juan

Siquijor

Lazi

Malatapay

0   50 km

Maasin & Bato (Leyte) ▶

Nasipit (Mindanao) ▶

Dapitan (Mindanao) ▼

Cagayan de Oro (Mindanao) ▼

A quick guide to Cebuano

Filipino (Tagalog) might be the official language and English the medium of instruction, but **Cebuano**, the native language of Cebu, is the most widely spoken vernacular in the archipelago, not only used in Cebu but also by most of the central and southern Philippines. Cebuano and Filipino have elements in common, but also have significant differences of construction and phraseology. It's quite possible for a native Manileño to bump into a native Cebuano and not be able to understand much he or she says. The complex web of languages and dialects that spans the Philippines is one of the reasons for its political and social fragmentation.

Cebuano is evolving as it assimilates slang and colloquialisms from other Visayan dialects, as well as from Filipino and English. Confused? You will be. Most Cebuano conversations veer apparently at random between all three languages, leaving even Filipino visitors unable to grasp the meaning.

Some Cebuano basics

Good morning	*Maayong buntag*	Yes	*O-o*
Good afternoon	*Maayong hapon*	No	*Dili*
Good evening	*Maayong gabi*	OK	*Sigi*
How are you?	*Kumusta?*	How much is this?	*Tag-pila ni?*
I'm fine	*Maayo man*	Expensive	*Mahal*
Very well	*Maayo ka'ayo*	Cheap	*Barat*
What's your name?	*Umsay pangalan ni mu?*	Idiot!	*Amaw!*
		Go away!	*Layas!*
Where are you from?	*Taga din ka?*	Who?	*Kinsa?*
Thank you	*Salamat*	What?	*Unsa?*
You're welcome	*Walay sapayan*	Why?	*Ngano?*
Goodbye	*Ari na ko*	Near/Far	*Duol/Layo*

only 40km wide at its thickest point – with a mountainous and rugged spine. Most tourists spend little time in the towns, heading off as soon as possible to the beaches and islands of the north or west. The closest beaches to Cebu City are on **Mactan Island** just to the southeast, although they are by no means the best. Head north instead to the marvellous island of **Malapascua**, where the sand is as fine as Boracay's, to tranquil **Bantayan** off the northwest coast, or to really get away from it all, to the isolated **Camotes Islands**. To the south of Cebu City, you can take a bus along the coast through the old Spanish town of **Carcar** and across the island to the diving haven of **Moalboal** and its nearby beaches.

Getting to Cebu is simple. There are dozens of **flights** daily from Manila and less frequent flights from a number of other key destinations in the Philippines and Asia. Cebu's position in the middle of the country makes it an excellent place to journey onwards by ferry, with sailings to Luzon, Mindanao and elsewhere in the Visayas.

Cebu City

Gateway to the Visayas, **CEBU CITY**, nicknamed the "Queen of the South" is the Philippines' third largest city, home to over 800,000 people. Peppered with historic attractions, it's worthy of a day or two's exploration before moving on to the beaches and islands beyond. While an easier introduction to urban life in the Philippines than Manila, Cebu is not without its problems and streets are often clogged with smoke-belching jeepneys, while "rugby-boys" (glue-sniffing street children) are a common sight. As always in the Philippines, wealth and poverty are never too far apart – the urban elite live in the greener northern suburbs and frequent the upscale malls of Ayala and Banilad.

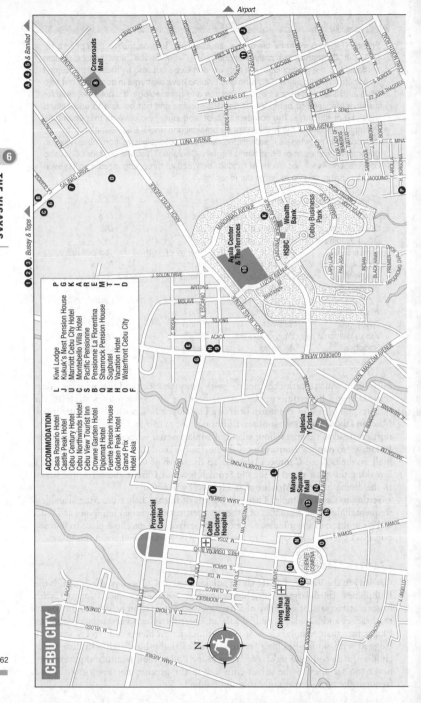

6

CEBU CITY

▲ Airport

◀ A · 4 · 5 & Banilad

◀ 1 · 2 · 3 Busay & Tops

ACCOMMODATION

Casa Rosario Hotel	L	Kiwi Lodge	P
Castle Peak Hotel	U	Kukuk's Nest Pension House	G
Cebu Century Hotel	J	Marriott Cebu City Hotel	K
Cebu Northwinds Hotel	C	Montebello Villa Hotel	A
Cebu View Tourist Inn	S	Pacific Pensionne	R
Crowne Garden Hotel	B	Pensionne La Florentina	E
Diplomat Hotel	Q	Shamrock Pension House	M
Fuente Pension House	N	Sugbutel	T
Golden Peak Hotel	H	Vacation Hotel	I
Grand Prix	O	Waterfront Cebu City	D
Hotel Asia	F		

Crossroads Mall **8**

Wealth Bank

Ayala Center & the Terraces **10**

HSBC

Cebu Business Park

Provincial Capitol

Cebu Doctors' Hospital

Mango Square Mall

Iglesia Y Cristo

Chong Hua Hospital

Fuente Osmeña

N

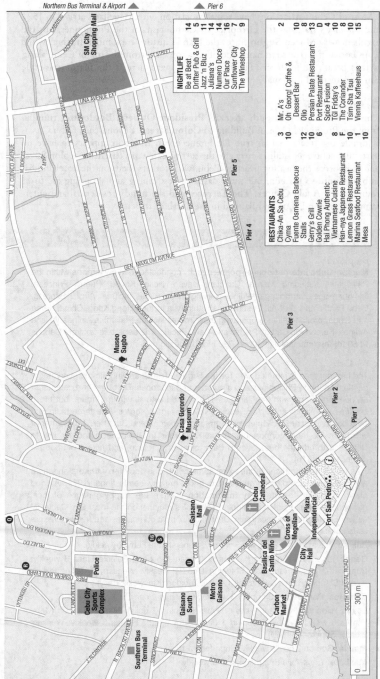

NIGHTLIFE
Be at Beat	14
Drifter Pub & Grill	5
Jazz 'n Bluz	11
Juliana's	14
Numero Doce	16
Our Place	7
Sunflower City	9
The Wineshop	

RESTAURANTS
Chika-An Sa Cebu	3	Mr. A's	2
Cyma	10	Oh Georg! Coffee &	
Fuente Osmena Barbecue	12	Dessert Bar	10
Stalls		Olio	8
Gerry's Grill	10	Persian Palate Restaurant	13
Golden Cowrie	6	Port Restaurant	D
Hai Phong Authentic		Spice Fusion	4
Vietnamese Cuisine	8	TGI Friday's	10
Han-nya Japanese Restaurant	F	The Coriander	8
Lemon Grass Restaurant	10	Tsim Sha Tsui	10
Marina Seafood Restaurant	1	Vienna Kaffeehaus	10
Mesa	15		

6

THE VISAYAS

Most of Cebu's attractions have some association with Magellan's arrival in 1521 and the city's status as the birthplace of Catholicism in the Philippines, but the excellent new **Museo Sugbo** traces the island's history back much further, while Tops Lookout is true to its name and offers a top view from the top of Cebu, along with a breath of fresh air. The main tourist event here is the mardi-gras-style **Sinulog festival** in January (see p.269).

Orientation

The city's main north–south artery is **President Osmeña Boulevard**, running from the Provincial Capitol Building to **Colon Street**. Beyond this, Cebu City is a jumble of streets that in true Philippine urban tradition appears to have no particular centre. Nostalgics may cite the earthy, careworn charms of Colon Street and the port as the beating heart of Cebu, while others focus on the hotel and bar hub of **Fuente Osmeña**, but these days the best dining and shopping are to be found at the **Ayala Center**, **The Terraces** and the trendy residential and entertainment area in Lahug and Banilad in the north of the city.

Moving on from Cebu City

By plane

Mactan-Cebu international airport is directly connected to many airports within the Philippines including Manila, Caticlan, Davao, Ilioilo, Kalibo, Puerto Princesa, Tacloban and Zamboanga. Airlines serving these routes include: Airphil Express, Cebu Pacific and Zest Air. Destinations within Asia include Hong Kong, China, Korea and Singapore, and airlines operating these routes include Philippine Airlines, Asiana Airlines, Korean Air, Cathay Pacific and Cebu Pacific. The departure tax from Cebu is P550 for international flights and P200 for domestic departures.

By ferry

The harbour area is jammed with **ferries** large and small serving almost every major destination in the Philippines and a number of minor ones. Fast boat and catamaran services link Cebu with the Camotes, Bohol and Leyte all within 3 hours, but these services are significantly more expensive than regular ferries. The three main fast boat companies are Oceanjet, Weesam and Supercat (and Superferry), the latter of which are the most comfortable. As well as ferries to Dumaguete, another way to Negros is to ride the bus down to Bato, or over to Toledo, and take a big bangka across (see p.276).

As well as ticket offices at the piers, some hotels can book **ferry tickets** and there are travel agents and ticket outlets throughout the city (see Listings, p.273). A good place to get up-to-date **ferry information** is from the shipping pages of local newspapers. There's also a shipping schedules channel on the local Sky Cable TV network, available in some hotels. Destinations, boat companies and frequencies are as follows:

Bilaran: Naval (Roble Shipping 3 weekly; Supershuttle Ferry 2 weekly).

Bohol: Tagbilaran (Cokaliong 1 weekly; Oceanjet 5 daily; Palacio Lines 3 weekly; Supercat 3 daily; Trans-Asia Shipping Lines 1 weekly; Weesam 3 daily), Talibon (Island Shipping Lines & Kinswell 1 daily), Tubigon (Kinswell 2 daily).

Camotes: Poro (Aznar Shipping 3 weekly; Oceanjet 1 daily).

Leyte: Hilongos (Kinswell 1 daily; Roble Shipping 2 daily), Maasin, Ormoc (Cebu Ferries 6 weekly; Roble Shipping 1 daily; Supershuttle Ferries 3 weekly; Weesam 2 daily; Supercat 3 daily).

Manila: Gothon Lines 3 weekly; Superferry 1 daily.

Masbate: Trans-Asia Shipping Lines 6 weekly.

Arrival

Cebu flights land at **Mactan Cebu International Airport** (☎032/340-2486) on Mactan Island. There is a **tourist information** counter in the arrivals hall where you can pick up the Department of Tourism's city and island map. The arrivals hall also has car rental booths for Avis, FastTransit and Friends, all reputable and offering a car with driver from P2000 per day. Metered airport **taxis** charge about P180 to take you to Cebu City, 8km away across the suspension bridge. Touts will also offer to take you straight to Malapascua or Moalboal, saving the expense of a night in a city hotel, though make sure you agree a price first.

The arrival point for ferries is one of six large piers in the **harbour** area beyond Fort San Pedro. Pier 1 is closest to Fort San Pedro, a matter of fifteen minutes on foot, and pier 6 furthest away. Jeepneys and buses line up along nearby Sergio Osmeña Boulevard for the short journey into the city. Taxis wait to meet arriving ferries and should agree to use the meter.

There are two bus terminals in Cebu. The **Northern bus terminal** on the coastal road, just east of the city, is used by buses and jeepneys for destinations north of

Mindanao: Cagayan de Oro (Cebu Ferries 3 weekly; Superferry 3 weekly), Dapitan (Cokaliong 6 weekly; Oceanjet via Tagbilaran & Dumaguete 1 daily), Iligan (Cebu Ferries 2 weekly), Nasipit (Cebu Ferries 3 weekly; Superferry 2 weekly), Ozamiz (Cebu Ferries 4 weekly), Surigao (Cokaliong Shipping Lines 6 weekly; Cebu Ferries 3 weekly; Superferry 1 weekly), Zamboanga (George & Peter Lines 1 weekly).

Negros: Dumaguete (Cokaliong 1 daily; George & Peter Lines 3 weekly; Oceanjet via Tagbilaran 2 daily).

Panay: Iloilo (Cokaliong 3 weekly; Trans-Asia Shipping Lines 1 daily).

Samar: Calbayog (Palacio Shipping Lines 3 weekly), Catbalogan (Roble Shipping 1 weekly).

Siquijor: Oceanjet via Tagbilaran and Dumaguete 1 daily.

Shipping Lines and Ferries

Aznar Shipping ☎032/234-4624; Gothong Lines, Pier 7 ☎032/232-9998; Cebu Ferries, Pier 4 ☎032/233-7000, ⓦwww.cebuferries.com; Cokaliong, Pier 1 ☎032/232-7211; George & Peter Lines ☎032/254-5154; Kinswell ☎032/416-6516; Oceanjet, Pier 1 ☎032/255-7560, ⓦwww.oceanjet.net; Palacio Lines, Pier 1 ☎032/253-7700; Supercat, Pier 4 ☎032/233-7000, ⓦwww.supercat.com.ph; Superferry, Pier 4 ☎032/528-7000, ⓦwww.superferry.com.ph; Supershuttle Ferry, Pier 8 ☎032/232-3150; Trans-Asia Shipping Lines, Pier 5 ☎032/254-6491, ⓦwww.transasiashipping.com; Weesam, Pier 4 ☎032/412-9562, ⓦwww.weesamexpress.com.

By bus and taxi

Buses run to the southern half of Cebu every thirty minutes or when they are full from Cebu City's Southern bus terminal. These vehicles serve the full length of the east coast through Carcar, Argao and on to the port of Lilo-An (where you can hop on a boat to Negros), terminating in Bato (4hr; P154). Buses for Toledo (90min; P60), and Moalboal (3hr; P91) and Badian also leave from this station, crossing the mountains and many of them continuing the length of the southwest coast to Bato. Buses heading north to Hagnaya (for Bantayan Island) and Maya (for Malapascua) leave from the Northern bus terminal.

You may prefer to charter a **car with driver** to get around the island; many tourists simply flag down a taxi and negotiate a flat rate with the driver, usually P2000–2500 for the day or a one-way trip to, say, Moalboal or Maya. Many of the bigger hotels have their own cars with drivers, but you'll pay significantly more.

the city. The **Southern bus terminal**, for buses and south, is in Bacalso Avenue, west of President Osmeña Boulevard.

Information

The main **tourist office** is the Department of Tourism's Cebu regional office (Mon–Fri 8am–5pm; ☎032/254-2811) in the LDM Building at the corner of Lapu-Lapu and Legaspi streets, near Fort San Pedro.

Of the **city maps** available, the best is *EZ Map* (P99), which is available at National Bookstore and some hotels, but the free one given out at the tourist offices and kiosks isn't bad. There are a number of English-language local **newspapers**, including the *Cebu Daily News* (Ⓦwww.cdn.ph), and the *Sun Star Cebu* (Ⓦwww.sunstar.com.ph), both of which contain ferry timetables, local events listings and restaurant reviews. As well as information about the festival, The Sinulog Foundation website (Ⓦwww.sinulog.ph) also has a wealth of information about the city.

City transport

Cebu City is reasonably compact with just a few buses operating within the city limits. There are, however, plenty of **taxis** in the city and it's not hard to find a driver who's willing to use the meter. The tariff is P2.5 per 200m plus a flagfall of P30; a typical cross-city trip costs P50–70 outside rush hour.

Jeepneys and open-sided Isuzu vans painted in outrageous colours ply dozens of cross-city routes. From Colon Street, jeepneys run almost everywhere: east to the piers and the SM City Mall, north to Fuente Osmeña, northeast to Ayala Center and south to Carbon Market. There are also jeepneys along N. Escario Street, north of Ayala Center, heading east to Mandaue and west and southwest to the Provincial Capitol Building, Fuente Osmeña and the Colon Street area.

Accommodation

Some of the cheapest accommodation in Cebu City is in the old **Colon Street** area, though the streets in this neighbourhood can be a little scary at night, with roaming pimps and a number of shabby massage parlours and girlie bars. Hotels around **Fuente Osmeña** are better, and further out, options near the **Ayala Center** and in **Lahug** and **Banilad** are close to the big malls and many of the city's more fashionable restaurants.

Colon Street and around

Cebu Century Hotel Colon St corner Pelaez St ☎032/255-1341. This hotel has seen better days, but is redeemed by its low prices. Deluxe rooms have fridge, cable TV and have been more recently renovated. ❷

Cebu View Tourist Inn 200 Sanciangko St ☎032/254-8333. Reasonably comfortable and secure, offering a/c rooms with cable TV, although it can be noisy. There are cut-price 9pm–7am rates. ❷

Fuente Osmeña and around

🏃 **Casa Rosario Hotel** 101 E Ramon Aboitiz St ☎032/253-5134, Ⓦwww.casarosario .multiply.com. Stylish mid-sized hotel in a quiet part of town but just minutes' away from Fuente

Osmeña. All of the boldly painted a/c rooms have cable TV and attractive furnishings. There's free wi-fi throughout and a nice breakfast bar in the lobby. ❸

Diplomat Hotel 90 F. Ramos St ☎032/253-0099, Ⓦwww.diplomathotelcebu.com. Substantial and popular hotel in a good location set back from F. Ramos St. Standard rooms are perfectly adequate, but often booked out long-term by Koreans, while superior rooms are bigger, brighter, and some have decent views. All rooms are a/c, and have hot water, cable TV, fridge, safe and (pay) wi-fi connection. ❸

Fuente Pension House 0175 Don Julio Llorente St ☎032/412-4989. Well-run place behind Fuente Osmeña in a quiet road offering ordinary but clean and comfortable doubles and trebles with a/c and cable TV. There's a restaurant and free wi-fi. ❸

Gran Prix Pacific Coast Building, Mango Ave ☎032/254-9169, ⊛www.granprixhotels.com /cebu. New economy hotel in a great location near Fuente Osmeña with small, modern rooms (many without windows though), free wi-fi and *Jollibee* vouchers for breakfast! ❸

Hotel Asia 11 J. Avila St ☎032/255-8536, ⊛www.hotelasiacebu.com. In a good location north of Fuente Osmeña, a 10min walk from the Cebu Doctors' Hospital, this neat, medium-sized and well-run hotel has an airy white-tiled lobby and small, well-appointed rooms, each with a high-tech Japanese toilet. Larger, deluxe rooms boast stone bathtubs. The Japanese restaurant is open 24hr and there's a rooftop bar. ❹

Pacific Pensionne 313-A President Osmeña Blvd ☎032/253-5271, ⊛www.pacificpensionne .com. Just off Osmeña Blvd, this is a welcoming, quiet little hotel with a bright café in the lobby and a range of rooms from very affordable singles to four-bed family options. Staff are charming and can help with travel arrangements. There's also a coffee shop with free wi-fi. ❷

Shamrock Pension House Fuente Osmeña ☎032/255-2900. Budget a/c accommodation in the hubbub of Fuente Osmeña, so close to the BBQ stalls that you can smell sizzling chicken from the lobby. Rooms range from standard and deluxe doubles to studios for two. ❹

Vacation Hotel Juana Osmeña ☎032/253-2766, ⊛www.vacationhotel-cebu.com. The best rooms at this charming little place, north of Fuente Osmeña, are on the second floor, with balconies overlooking the small pool, although the beds are very soft. Downstairs some of the rooms at the front have little verandas, but others are darker and less enticing – ask to see a few. ❸

Ayala Center and around

Golden Peak Hotel Gorordo Ave ☎032/233-8111, ⊛www.goldenpeakhotel.com. Good-value, mid-range hotel with efficient staff and rooms with views if you ask to be on one of the higher floors. The more expensive deluxe rooms aren't worth the extra outlay. Decent buffet breakfast included in the price. ❺

Kiwi Lodge 1060 G Tudtud St, Mabolo ☎032/232-9550, ⊛www.kiwilodge.org. Small and friendly well-run hotel in a residential area south of Ayala Center and Cebu Business Park. Range of comfortable a/c rooms at reasonable prices, with a restaurant serving hearty Western cuisine (including meat pies and fish and chips), and a bar where the usually expat clientele can offer all sorts of travel advice. ❸

Kukuk's Nest Pension House 157 Gorordo Ave ☎032/231-5780. This legendary, rather down-at-heel hangout for artists and beatniks is a ten-minute walk northwest of Ayala Center along busy Gorordo Ave. Tatty Rrooms, some with a/c, bathroom and cable TV, are kitted out with wooden antiques, and there's a café where you can eat and drink to the sound of thundering traffic. ❷

Marriott Cebu City Hotel Cardinal Rosales Ave, Cebu Business Park ☎032/411-5800, ⊛www.marriott.com. The *Marriott* is housed in a twelve-storey building just a short walk through parkland to the Ayala Center and fine dining at the Terraces. There are over 300 rooms, all remodelled in sleek modern style, plus three restaurants, a poolside café and a health club. For trips downtown there are taxis on the doorstep. Wi-fi internet access costs P250/hr. ❻

Pensionne La Florentina 18 Acacia St ☎032/231-3118. Friendly, family establishment in an attractive old building set back from Gorordo Ave. The coffee shop offers simple native dishes and the shops and restaurants of Ayala are a short walk away. ❷

Lahug and Banilad

Cebu Northwinds Hotel Salinas Drive (the continuation of J. Luna Ave) ☎032/233-0311, ⊛www.cebunorthwinds.com. Close to Lahug's bars and restaurants, this modern hotel has a/c, hot water, cable TV, wi-fi and a coffee shop, restaurant and bar. The more expensive superior rooms on the front side of the hotel are bigger but noisier. ❸

Crowne Garden Hotel Salinas Drive ☎032/412-7157. Formerly the *La Guardia*, this hotel has a good location close to the action on Salinas Drive. Rooms are bright, clean and comfortable and have a/c, hot water, cable TV, fridge and there's room service. Many rooms also have bathtubs. Wi-fi P200 for 4hr. ❹

Montebello Villa Hotel Banilad ☎032/231-3681, ⊛www.montebellovillahotel.com. Rambling, establishment set in its own neat gardens behind the popular Gaisano Country Mall, with an expansive outdoor and two swimmming pools. The renovated deluxe rooms are substantially nicer than the superior rooms. There are good dining and nightlife options in Banilad, but for downtown sightseeing you'll need to take a cab (or jeepney). ❻

Waterfront Cebu City Salinas Drive ☎032/232-6888, ⊛www.waterfronthotels.com.ph. A city landmark, the *Waterfront* is a world unto itself with a casino, several upscale restaurants, bars, gym and a large pool. The grandeur of the maritime themed lobby doesn't extend to the standard rooms, but the deluxe rooms are far more tastefully styled and have bathtubs. All rooms have free wi-fi, cable TV, fridge and hot water. ❻

Elsewhere in the city

Castle Peak Hotel F. Cabahug corner President Quezon st, Mabolo ☎032/233-1811, ⓦwww .castlepeakhotel.net. Clean and affordable hotel in a quiet area east of Ayala. Although starting to show signs of age, the rooms are spacious and the bathrooms are well maintained. Handily, there's a taxi rank right next to the hotel. Internet facilities are available and there's a decent restaurant. Free wi-fi in the lobby. ❸

Sugbutel S. Osmeña Blvd ☎032/232-8888, ⓦwww.sugbutel.com. The economy version of Japan's capsule hotels, this bizarre budget business stopover has the best dorms in the city. Large rooms have been subdivided into train-like compartments which house 2–6 bunk beds, each of which has an overhead light, small safety box, plug socket, shoe ledge and wi-fi. ❷

The City

The old part of Cebu City, known to bureaucrats as **Central Proper**, is a seething cobweb of sunless streets between Carbon Market and Colon Street, the latter said to be the oldest mercantile thoroughfare in the Philippines. You can explore the area on foot, picking your way carefully past barrow boys selling pungent limes, hawkers peddling fake mobile phone accessories and, at night, pimps whispering their proposals from dark doorways. A vibrant, humming, occasionally malodorous area of poorly maintained pavements and thick diesel fumes, it's not a mainstream tourist sight but worth some time for its spirit and vigour. About ten minutes' walk south of Colon Street, **Carbon Market** is no longer the coal unloading depot from which its name is derived, and is now an area of covered stalls where the range of goods on offer, edible and otherwise, will leave you reeling – shining fat tuna, crabs, lobsters, coconuts, guavas, avocados and mangoes. The market is alive from well before dawn and doesn't slow down until after dark.

The Cross of Magellan

Cebu City's spiritual heart is an unassuming circular crypt in the middle of busy Magallanes Street that houses the **Cross of Magellan** (daily 9am–7pm; free). The first of the conquering Spaniards to set foot in the Philippines, Magellan began a colonial and religious rule that would last four hundred turbulent years. The crypt's ceiling is beautifully painted with a scene depicting his landing in Cebu in 1521 and the planting of the original cross on the shore. It was with this cross that Magellan is said to have baptized the Cebuana Queen Juana and four hundred of her followers. The cross which stands here today, however, is a modern, hollow reproduction said to contain fragments of the famous conquistador's original.

Basilica del Santo Niño and Cebu Cathedral

Next to the Cross of Magellan on President Osmeña Boulevard is the **Basilica del Santo Niño**, built between 1735 and 1737, where vendors sell plastic religious icons and amulets offering cures for everything from poverty to infertility. Inside is probably the most famous religious icon in the Philippines, a statue of the Santo Niño. It's said to have been presented to Queen Juana of Cebu by Magellan after her baptism, considered the first in Asia, in 1521. Another tale has it that 44 years later, after laying siege to a pagan village, one of conquistador Miguel Lopez de Legazpi's foot soldiers found a wooden box that had survived the bombardment inside a burning hut. Inside this box was the Santo Niño, lying next to a number of native idols. If you want to see the statue, let alone touch it, you'll have to join a queue of devotees that often stretches through the church doors and outside. A short walk from the basilica is **Cebu Cathedral**, a sixteenth-century Baroque structure that's crumbling on the outside, though its interior has been restored.

Fort San Pedro

When he arrived in 1565, conquistador Miguel Lopez de Legazpi set about building **Fort San Pedro** (daily 8am–8pm; P30) to guard against marauding Moros from the south. It was here, on December 24, 1898, that three centuries of Spanish rule in Cebu came to an end when their flag was lowered and they withdrew in a convoy of boats bound for Zamboanga, their waystation for the voyage to Spain. The fort, near the port area at the end of Sergio Osmeña Boulevard, has been used down the centuries as a garrison, prison and zoo, but today is little more than a series of walls and ramparts with gardens in between. On Sundays, the park opposite, Plaza Independencia, seethes with locals playing ghetto-blasters and families enjoying picnics.

Casa Gorordo Museum

Built in the middle of the nineteenth century by wealthy merchant Alejandro Reynes, the marvellous **Casa Gorordo**, 35 Lopez Jaena St (off the eastern end of Colon St; Tues–Sun 10am–6pm; P70), is one of the few structures of its time in Cebu that survived World War II. Owned by a succession of luminaries, including the first Filipino Bishop of Cebu, Juan Isidro de Gorordo, it was acquired in 1980 from the bishop's heirs and opened as a museum three years later.

The house is a striking marriage of late Spanish-era architecture and native building techniques, with lower walls of Mactan coral cemented using tree sap, and upper-storey living quarters built entirely from Philippine hardwood held together with wooden pegs. The interior offers an intriguing glimpse into the way Cebu's rich once lived, elegantly furnished with original pieces from America and the Old World – a Viennese dining set, a German piano, American linen and Catholic icons from Spain and Mexico. In the ground-floor library are photographs of Cebu during the American regime.

Museo Sugbo

Housed in the former Carcer del Cebu (provincial jail), the **Museo Sugbo** (Mon–Sat 9am–6pm; P75) is arguably the best museum in Cebu. Exhibits are well laid out and labelled in English, tracing the island's history from early Chinese and Siamese trading to the arrival of the Spanish, and the modern era. The highlights

---

Sinulog

Almost as popular as Kalibo's Ati-Atihan (see box, p.315), the big, boisterous **Sinulog festival**, which culminates on the third Sunday of January with a wild street parade and an outdoor concert at Fuente Osmeña, is held in honour of Cebu's patron saint, the Santo Niño. Sinulog is actually the name given to a swaying **dance** said to resemble the current (*sulog*) of a river and is said to have evolved from tribal elders' rhythmic movements. Today, it's a memorable, deafening spectacle, with hundreds of intricately dressed Cebuanos dancing through the streets to the beat of noisy drums. Most of the action happens on President Osmeña Boulevard, but to escape the crowds, grab a spot on one of the smaller roads, such as N. Escario Street, where security is less zealous and you can slip underneath the velvet ropes and join the dancers. For information about Sinulog and details of the exact route, which varies every year as the festival grows, visit ⓦwww.sinulog.ph. If you plan to visit Cebu during Sinulog, make sure you book accommodation well ahead of time.

are the World War II exhibits, including banned "guerilla money"issued after the Japanese had instituted their own currency, and possession of which was punishable by death. There are also wartime notices detailing the types of foods Filipinos were allowed to eat: one of the few local staples not on the list was sweet potato, meaning that during the occupation, many people survived on these alone. Towards the rear of the complex, a separate room houses finds excavated from Plaza Independencia including a spooky fifteenth-century "death mask" made of gold leaf.

Busay

The road that winds northwards out of Cebu City eventually finds its way to **Busay**, the high mountain ridge that rises immediately behind the city. On the way up you'll pass *Mr A Bar & Restaurant*. There's a wide concrete lookout area known to locals as **Tops**, where you pay a P100 entrance fee, buy a stick of barbecued chicken from one of the vendors, and sit and watch the sunset. Tops is popular at dusk, so don't expect romantic solitude, but the view is great and the air cooler and cleaner than in the concrete jungle below. A taxi ride there and back will cost in the region of P900, including a wait while you admire the view. Some jeepneys from SM City and Ayala Center are marked for Busay, but they don't go all the way, leaving you with a hot uphill walk of almost 1km.

Jumalon Museum and Butterfly Sanctuary

On the western edge of the city, the **Jumalon Museum and Butterfly Sanctuary** (by appointment only 8.30am–5pm; P50; ☎032/261-6884), 20-D Macopa St, is lepidopteran heaven, with rooms full of glass display cases and a large garden at the back with live butterflies fluttering around. As well as everyday species such as monarchs and viceroys there are also rare examples such as albinos, melanics, dwarfs and Siamese twins. The museum is in **Basak**, a largely residential suburb about twenty minutes from the centre by taxi (P90). Alternatively, you can take any jeepney heading along the Cebu South Road to Friendship Village or Basak, get off at the Holy Cross Parish Church and look out for Macopa Street near Basak Elementary School.

Eating

Cebu's well-regarded dining scene has been boosted further with the opening of **The Terraces** at the Ayala Center, a tastefully designed food court, offering everything from Greek to Vietnamese cuisine, overlooking atmospheric gardens. **Banilad Town Center** (BTC) and **Gaisano Country Mall** also offer good mall restaurants, while other dining highlights include the roadside barbecues at **Fuente Osmeña** and lunch with a view at *Mr A*. Fast-food joints can be found all over the city and in the malls. For **coffee** and wi-fi access there's *Starbucks* on President Osmeña Boulevard and at the Terraces, plus *Bo's Coffee* at on F. Ramos Street and at Robinson's Cybergate on Fuente Osmeña.

Around Fuente Osmeña

Fuente Osmeña Barbecue Stalls Fuente Osmeña. Carnivore heaven. The cooking starts with a vengeance at dusk and the choice ranges from whole chickens cooked over coals to sticks of pork and street food delicacies such as chicken's feet and intestines. Daily dusk to late.
Han-nya Japanese Restaurant *Hotel Asia*, 11 J. Avila St. Authentic Japanese cuisine served around the clock in a lattice-screened restaurant with raised seating areas. Sushi starts at P120 and there's *ube* ice cream (P70) for dessert to remind you that you're in the Philippines. 24hr.
Persian Palate Restaurant Mango Square Mall. Very spicy Indian and Middle Eastern dishes, including chicken biryani (P195), samosas (P75), baba ganoush (P110) and nan bread which you can

wash down with a mango lassi (P85). Daily
10am–8pm.

Vienna Kaffeehaus General Maxilom Ave.
Founded more than 20 years ago by an expat
Austrian, the *Kaffehaus* is a little corner of imperial
Europe in the tropics. There are nine types of
coffee including Viennese iced coffee and excellent
espresso. The lunch and dinner menu is also
Austrian, with wholesome goulash, schnitzel (P280)
and delicious home-made sauerkraut and sausage.
Daily 10am–midnight.

Ayala Center and The Terraces

Cyma Garden Level, The Terraces
☎032/417-1351. Delicious Greek salads,
dolmadakia (stuffed vine leaves; P195), tzaziki and
souvlaki in an attractive Greek-themed restaurant.
They also have branches in Manila and Boracay.
Daily 11am–11pm.

Lemon Grass Restaurant Level 1, The
Terraces ☎032/233-8601. Bright restaurant
with garden views. Thai and Vietnamese dishes are
as close to authentic as they can be, with lots of
well-seasoned and spicy coconut curries. The *banh
xeo* (sizzling Vietnamese crêpes; P225) are also
delicious and to refresh your palate there's citrus
and herb lemonade (or Singha beer for P95). Daily
11am–11pm.

Mesa Level 1, The Terraces. This busy restaurant
serves traditional Filipino dishes with a modern
twist. Try *salpicao* ostrich (P280), pomelo salad
with *latik* (P250) or seabass steamed in *dayap* and
chilli (P80 per 100g). Daily 9am–10.30pm.

Oh Georg! Coffee & Dessert Bar Level 1, Ayala
Center. In a mall chock-full of fast-food restaurants
and coffee shops, this one deserves special
mention. The menu includes a delicious soup-of-
the-day, Greek salads (P190) and a Mexican salad
(P225) that's big enough to share. There's another
branch, called *Café Georg*, on the ground floor of
the MLD Building in Banilad. Sun–Thurs 10.30am–
10pm & Fri–Sat 10.30am–11pm.

Lahug and Banilad

Chika-An Sa Cebu Salinas Dr. A Cebu institution
that serves popular rustic food such as chicken,
pork barbecue, *lechon kawali* (crispy pork), sizzling
bangus (milkfish) and *bulalo* (beef bone stew).
There's another branch in SM City Mall. Daily
11am–10pm.

The Coriander Crossroads Mall ☎032/268-3510.
Authentic Indian, Malaysian and Indonesian dishes
prepared by the Singaporean Indian chef and
owner. Beef rendang (P299), coriander prawn and
squid, and chilli crab (P890/kilo) are all on the
menu, and there's masala chai (P85) to end your
meal. Tues–Sun 11am–2pm & 6–10pm.

Golden Cowrie Salinas Dr, Lahug ☎032/233-
4670. The interior is Philippine Zen with cream
walls and dark-wood furniture and there's a
pleasant outdoor dining area. Favourite dishes
include green mango salad (P65), blue marlin
(P159) and Bicol Express (P129). There are less
atmospheric branches at Robinson's Cybergate
Fuente Osmeña, and as *Hukad*, at The Terraces.
Daily 11am–2pm & 6–10pm.

Hai Phong Authentic Vietnamese Restaurant
Crossroads Mall, Banilad. Unpretentious place with
plastic tables offering promptly served and
appetizing Vietnamese dishes such as beef noodle
soup, spring rolls and spicy curries, all prepared
with fragrant herbs. Daily 11am–8pm.

Marina Seafood Restaurant Nivel Hills, Lahug
☎032/233-9454. Laidback native-style alfresco
restaurant on a hill above the city (a taxi from the
centre will cost P100). Two people can feast on
tuna belly, grilled marlin and shrimps with chilli
and coconut for about P250 a head. Daily
11am–8pm.

Olio Crossroads Mall, Banilad ☎032/238-2391.
High-end "fusion" restaurant specializing in
seafood and steaks, with a tempting but expensive
(P1100–4700) wine list. The 400-gram New York
Steak (P1100) is a carnivorous treat. Other good
meals include herb-crusted rack of lamb with
crispy potatoes (P1200), or for a light lunch there's
mozzarella and tomato salad (P550). Daily
11am–2pm & 6pm–midnight.

Port Restaurant *Waterfront Cebu City*, Salinas
Drive ☎032/231-7441. A tacky marine-themed
reinvention of the quintessential Filipino seafood
restaurant, though the food is undeniably good,
especially the baked mussels with butter and
garlic. Nightly buffet (P299), but you'll be charged
double if you leave anything on your plate! Daily
11am–2.30pm & 6–9.30pm.

Spice Fusion Banilad Town Center (BTC)
☎032/344-2923. A small, stylish and very
popular fusion restaurant with appealing dishes such
as crispy mango rolls (P120) and sizzling ginger fish
fillet (P280). Daily 11am–2pm & 6–10pm.

Drinking, nightlife and entertainment

Cebu, like its big brother Manila, is a city that never – or rarely – sleeps. You don't
have to walk far in the centre to pass a pub, karaoke lounge or a music bar,

although you'll want to choose your venue carefully. Bars and clubs near Mango Square including *Be at Beat*, *Juliana's* and *Numero Doce* are loud, lively and fun until 3 or 4am, but further down Mango Avenue almost all of the establishments near the Iglesia Y Cristo are girlie bars. Many of the nicest places for a drink are at the malls, and in the suburbs of Banilad.

Drifter Pub & Grill G/F, Gaisano Country Mall, Banilad ☎032/231-2531. Popular venue for live acoustic bands, close to good restaurants in Gaisano Country Mall and BTC.

Jazz 'n Bluz 27 F. Cabahug St, opposite the *Castle Peak Hotel* ☎032/232-2698. Cebu's best jazz bar is low-lit and sophisticated and has nightly jazz and blues from 9pm, after which time there's a cover charge (P110–160). Drinks and snacks are served to the lounge and bar tables while you enjoy the show.

Our Place Pelaez St, right on the junction with Sanciangko St. Under new management, *Our Place* remains a Cebu stalwart, straight from the pages of Graham Greene. A small upstairs bar is cooled by inefficient ceiling fans, where expat men swill San Miguel (P40) into the early hours and complain about the hardships of life in the tropics.

Sunflower City Salinas Dr. Entertainment complex where you can enjoy a cocktail at the bar, east-meets-west cuisine in the minimalist restaurant, and then move on to the nightclub for DJs and live bands. There are also private karaoke rooms. Regular admission is P100 and P150 on Friday and Saturdays.

The Wineshop Gorordo Ave, near *Castle Peak Hotel* ☎032/233-3744. Warm and convivial wooden bar-restaurant with a Spanish wine list (P400–1600) and European meals. Look for the suit of armour outside.

Shopping

The two biggest **malls** are the Ayala Center in the north of the city and SM City on J. Luna Avenue in the east on the way to Mandaue City, both of which have international brand names galore, restaurants, internet cafés and travel agents. Aside from the big two, Crossroads, Gaisano Country Mall and Banilad Town Center (BTC) are all worth checking out for their dining scenes. For good **souvenirs** your best option is the Artevalman Handicraft Market (☎032/346-0644) in Mandaue City, a short taxi ride away. There are also a half-dozen souvenir stalls inside the airport departure lounge. For handmade guitars and ukeleles, popular gifts in the Visayas, try Borremeo Street, a 10-minute walk south of Colon Street, or Mactan Island (see opposite).

Listings

Airlines All these firms have offices at the airport, and you can book tickets in Cebu City at most travel agents and Western Unions: Asiana Airlines ☎032/342-8062; Cathay Pacific ☎032/340-3254; Cebu Pacific ☎032/230-8888; Korean Air ☎032/340-5431; Philippine Airlines ☎032/340-0181; Silk Air ☎032/340-0042; Zest Air ☎032/341-0226.

Banks and exchange There is no shortage of places to change currency, particularly along the main drag of President Osmeña Blvd, on Fuente Osmeña and in all shopping malls. Beware the 24-hour exchanges in the bar districts unless you really have to – rates are often substantially lower than elsewhere. Also try to use guarded indoor ATMs if you need to withdraw cash late at night – ATM muggings are not unheard of. There are plenty of banks on President Osmeña Blvd including BDO, PNB and Allied, all north of Fuente Osmeña, a Metrobank just south, and a BPI opposite the *Gran Prix Hotel* on General Maxilom (Mango Ave). There also ATMs in all of the malls.

Bookshops National Book Store has branches in SM City Mall, Ayala Center and close to Fuente Osmeña. The choice of literature isn't vast, but you will find a good selection of paperback best-sellers, along with classics such as Dickens.

Car rental Many firms, including Avis, have kiosks at the airport. In town Alamo is at the *Waterfront Cebu City*, Salinas Drive ☎032/232-6888 and Hertz is at the *Marriott*, Cardinal Rosales Ave ☎032/232-6100.

Cinemas Ayala Center has the most comfortable movie theatre in Cebu, and shows the latest movies in English daily.

Consulates A number of countries have consular offices in Cebu, among them the UK, at Villa Terrace, Greenhills Rd, Mandaue City

(☎032/346-0525) and the US, *Waterfront Cebu City*, Salinas Drive (☎032/231-1261), though these are open only part-time and don't offer a full consular service.

Couriers Courier companies can be found in most of the city's malls; the Ayala Center contains offices for DHL, Fedex, UPS and TNT.

Emergencies ☎161.

Hospitals Among the best equipped are Cebu Doctors' Hospital, President Osmeña Blvd (☎032/253-7511); Chong Hua Hospital, J. Llorente St, just north of Fuente Osmeña (☎032/254-1461); and Perpetual Succour Hospital on Gorordo Ave (☎032/233-8620).

Immigration The Cebu Immigration District Office is in P. Burgos St, Mandaue (☎032/345-6442), a busy suburb 30min away by taxi. You can extend a 21-day visa to 59 days here in a few hours.

Internet access Most malls have internet cafés, often on higher floors; *Netopia* is on level 4 of the Ayala Center. There are also net cafés in Mango Square on General Maxilom Ave. Many hotels, restaurants and coffee shops have free wi-fi.

Pharmacies There are large pharmacies in all malls and you'll also find 24hr pharmacies that are often little more than holes in the wall, but carry a good stock of essentials. There's a big branch of Mercury drugstore at Fuente Osmeña, and a Watson's just round the corner on President Osmeña Blvd.

Police The main Cebu City Police Office is south of Fuenta Osmeña (☎032/231-5802 or 253-5636), close to Cebu State College. There's a small police outpost known as Police Station 3 at Fort San Pedro, close to the post office and another, Precinct 4, a short walk north of SM City in J. Luna Ave Extension.

Post The main post office (Mon–Fri 8am–noon and 1–5pm) on Quezon Blvd close to the port area (at the back of Fort San Pedro) has poste restante and a packing service. There's also a branch in the Capitol complex.

Travel agents To be found in most malls and many hotels. Cebu Holiday Tours & Travel, 4 AD Building, Tojong St ☎032/231-5391; Cebu Trip Tours, M.J. Cuenco Ave ☎032/268-5470; Grand Hope Ventures Travel, 4/F Ayala Center ☎032/268-9008; Land and Sky Travel, Rivergate Complex, General Maxilom Ave ☎032/253-9022; Rajah Travel, *Waterfront Cebu City*, Salinas Drive ☎032/232-2113.

Mactan Island

The closest beaches to Cebu City are on **Mactan Island**, linked to the main island of Cebu by the Mandaue–Mactan Bridge and the New Mandaue–Mactan Bridge. Off the southern coast of Mactan and linked by two short bridges is **Cordova Island**, a relatively undeveloped slab of land with a couple of secluded, upmarket resorts on the beach. While the beaches and scuba diving at these islands don't compare with Malapascua, for instance, they are easier to reach and there are plenty of other watersports on offer at the many resorts here. The small capital of **LAPU-LAPU** has a heaving central market, a mall, a post office and some small hotels, but not much for tourists.

Arrival and information

Mactan is a P14 jeepney ride from Cebu City's SM City Mall in J. Luna Avenue Extension, close to the *Sheraton Cebu Hotel*. From the airport to anywhere on Mactan is a short traffic-free journey that costs no more than P150 by taxi. Getting to Cordova takes a little longer and will cost up to P200.

Lapu-Lapu is on the island's northern shore, close to the Mandaue–Mactan Bridge and the oil depots that service visiting container ships. Jeepneys stop near the small market square in Lapu-Lapu, where you can catch another jeepney onwards towards the beaches of Mactan's east coast. The **police station** (☎032/341-1311) is on B.M. Dimataga Street facing Upon Channel, the thin stretch of water that separates Mactan from the Cebu mainland, and there's a Philippine National Bank on Quezon National Highway. The best **hospital** is the Mactan Doctor's Hospital in Basak.

Sights and shopping

Magellan's Marker and **Lapu-Lapu's Monument**, both memorials to the battle that ensued when Magellan landed here in 1521, are in the north of the island on

The death of Magellan

Everything seemed to be going well for Portuguese explorer **Ferdinand Magellan** when he made landfall in Samar early in 1521 and claimed the pagan Philippines for his adopted country, Spain, and the true religion, Catholicism. He stocked up on spices and sailed on, landing in Cebu. It was here that he befriended a native king, Raja Humabon and, flush with his conquest of the isles, promised to help him subdue an unruly vassal named Lapu-Lapu. Early on the morning of April 27, 1521, Magellan landed at Mactan and tried to coerce Lapu-Lapu into accepting Christianity. Lapu-Lapu declined and when Magellan continued to hector he angrily ordered an attack. As his men fled quickly to their ships. Magellan, resplendent in polished body armour, backed away towards safety, but was felled by a spear aimed at his unprotected foot. Lapu-Lapu's men quickly moved in for the kill. Seventeen months later, on September 8, 1522, the last remaining ship in Magellan's original fleet sailed into Seville with eighteen survivors on board. After three years and the loss of four ships and 219 lives, the first circumnavigation of the globe was complete.

the main road that goes to the *Shangri-La's Mactan Island Resort*. Neither is really worth a special trip. There are a few sorry-looking souvenir stalls here, but not much else and the trip from Cebu can be a hassle.

For many tourists the obligatory souvenir purchase is a handmade **guitar** from one of Mactan's diminishing number of small guitar factories, of which a couple remain on the old Maribago Road, the most famous of which is Alegre. The guitars are not so well constructed that you'd want to stake a musical career on one, but some of the smaller ukuleles and mandolins, starting from P1000, make novel gifts. A simple but full-sized steel-stringed acoustic can be picked up for upwards of P2000, but top-quality instruments cost far more.

Scuba diving

Simon Timmins (☏032/345-0071, ⊛www.sidive.com) is an experienced dive instructor based in Mactan who offers very competitive rates for dives and PADI packages – Open Water costs US$250–295 depending upon how many people are taking the course. Scotty's Dive Center at Punta Engano Road, Lapu-Lapu (☏032/231-0288, ⊛www.divescotty.com) is also reliable for dive trips from Mactan.

Accommodation and eating

The northern town of **Lapu-Lapu** has a handful of functional, affordable hotels with air conditioning and restaurants. On Mactan's eastern shore there are about twenty **beachfront resorts**, ranging from overpriced hotels to more affordable native-style establishments. The beach here is not especially attractive and in some cases has been expensively groomed and landscaped to make it look like a tropical beach should – with the predictable result that it looks fake. Most of the "upmarket" resorts are fenced, private enclaves, so **eating** means taking expensive resort transport into Cebu City, or staying in for middling, overpriced food. Most of the clientele at the resorts are rich Filipinos, and package tourists from Hong Kong, Japan and South Korea. If you're travelling independently room rates will be high if you simply show up without a reservation. You'll save some money if you book in advance either with a travel agent or online.

Lapu-Lapu

Bellavista Hotel Quezon Hwy, Lapu-Lapu City ☏032/340-7821, ⊛www.thebellavista-hotel.com. The bright blue box of the *Bellavista* has just had a makeover, and rooms are sleek and modern, with good amenities. There's a pool, travel desk, and room rates include breakfast and round-trip airport transfers. ❻

Hotel Cesario Quezon Hwy, Lapu-Lapu City ☏032/340-7480. Modern mid-range hotel with a/c rooms, use of the pool at the *Bellavista* next door, and a buffet breakfast included in the rate. Helpful staff can handle travel reservations. ❸

East coast

Club Kontiki Maribago ☏032/340-9934, ⊛www .kontikidivers.com. By far the best bet on Mactan's east coast if you're looking for somewhere with genuine charm and without the unnecessary frills and fuss of the five-stars. *Kontiki* is mainly geared to divers, with good simple rooms in a pretty building on the shore, which is rocky but has flat areas for sunbathing. The "house reef" is one of the best in the area. ❸

Costabella Beach Resort Buyong ☏032/232-4811. Expansive tropical-style resort with palm trees, swimming pool and a/c rooms on the shore. Friendly, less showy and a little cheaper than many other Mactan resorts, there's the usual range of activities, including jet-skiing and scuba diving. ❼

Shangri-La's Mactan Island Resort Punta Engaño ☏032/231-0288, ⊛www.shangri-la.com. Not as tasteful as its Boracay cousin, the Mactan *Shangri-La* is still super-comfortable and has every amenity imaginable. There are five hundred rooms, eight restaurants and bars and, if the traffic is getting you down, a helicopter to meet you at the airport. Plenty of recreation, some of which you pay extra for, including scuba diving, windsurfing, banana-boat rides, and for relaxation, the renowned Chi Spa. ❾

Olango Island

Five kilometres east of Mactan Island, **Olango Island** supports the largest concentration of **migratory birds** in the country. About 77 species, including egrets, sandpipers, terns and black-bellied plovers, use the island as a rest stop on their annual migration from breeding grounds in Siberia, northern China and Japan to Australia and New Zealand. Declared a **wildlife reserve** in 1998, the island is also home to about 16,000 resident native birds which live mostly in the northern half; the southern half of the island is made up of a wide, shallow bay and expanses of mud flats and mangrove. The reserve is at its best during peak migration months: September to November for the southward migration and February to April northbound.

Most resorts on Mactan can organize a day-trip here, though you could visit independently: there are hourly bangkas (P40) to **Santa Rosa** on Olango Island from the wharf near the *Hilton* on Mactan Island or you can hire your own bangka from the area around the *Tambuli Beach Resort* for around P2000 to the island and back. From the small Santa Rosa wharf it's only a short tricycle ride to the sanctuary. If you want a knowledgeable **guide**, make arrangements with the Coastal Resource Management Project of the Department of Environment and Natural Resources (☏032/346-9177) located in the Capitol Building in Osmeña Boulevard in Cebu City, which runs an Olango Birds and Seascape tour. Jump Off Point Outfitters (☏032/236-5678, ✉jump_offpoint@yahoo.com) can also arrange kayak trips to Olango and Sulpo islands.

The only **place to stay** is the lovely *Nalusuan Island Resort & Marine Sanctuary* (☏032/516-6432, ⊛www.nalusan.mencaresorts.com; ❺), a wonderful place on an islet rising out of Olango's western coastal reef with rooms and duplex cottages on stilts in the water. The open-air restaurant specializes in seafood caught on the doorstep and there are nightly campfire cookouts where you can barbecue food as you like it. The resort can collect you in Mactan if requested in advance and there are kayaks available to explore the area.

Toledo and Balamban

On the west coast of Cebu, less than two hours from Cebu City by road, **TOLEDO** has several daily ferries (P40) for **San Carlos** in Negros (see p.296). Buses leave Cebu City's Southern bus terminal for Toledo from 5am daily (P60) – make sure you get there before mid-afternoon as Toledo isn't a place you'd choose to stay though there is one rudimentary hotel, *Aleu's Lodge* (℡032/322-5672; ❷), on Polyapoy Street on the southern edge of town. If you're heading from Cebu City to Negros, catch an early bus to Toledo to make sure you don't miss the last ferry.

Twenty minutes out of Toledo, the town of **BALAMBAN** has slightly more to offer in its clutch of deserted black sand **beaches**. The German-owned *Sailor's Cabin* (℡032/465-2816; ❶) is located in the quiet residential area of Abucayan (look out for the big white and blue entrance). Accommodation here comprises three types of apartment, with cable TV and private bathroom. The menu at the restaurant includes German sausage, smoked ham with sauerkraut and Hungarian goulash. The proprietor can organize trips to some undiscovered areas of the rural west coast.

Bantayan Island

Bantayan Island, just off the northwest coast of Cebu, is quiet and bucolic, flat and arable, without the moody mountains of mainland Cebu. There's not a huge amount to explore, and divers might be disappointed with the lack of coral, but there are plenty of picture-perfect beaches to relax on and a few pleasant, low-key resorts. Most of the island's resorts and beaches are around the attractive little town of **SANTA FE** on the southeast coast, which is where ferries from mainland Cebu arrive.

Arrival and information

To reach Bantayan from Cebu City you can take a bus (P70–100) from the Northern bus terminal to the port town of **Hagnaya**, where you pay a P10 pier fee

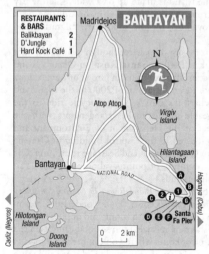

and P140 for the one-hour ferry crossing to Santa Fe; there are six or seven departures a day. Alternatively taxis from Cebu to Hagnaya can be negotiated for around P2000, or as little as P700 on the way back. From further afield, there are big bangkas to Bantayan from Cadiz on Negros. Coming from Malapascua, bangkas can be chartered for around P2500, but only take this route in good weather.

The only **local transport** is a *habal-habal*, or the trusty tricycle, known on Bantayan as a *tricikad*. It's fun to hire a motorbike or moped (P300) or bicycle and tour the island yourself by the coastal road, though inspect the bike thoroughly beforehand.

Next to the **police station** in Santa Fe there's a health centre and a small **tourist office** (9am–noon and 1–6pm) which has simple

(Map: BANTAYAN)

RESTAURANTS & BARS
Balikbayan 2
D'Jungle 1
Hard Kock Café 1

Madridejos

N

Atop Atop

Virgiv Island

Hilantagaan Island

Bantayan

NATIONAL ROAD

Hilotongan Island

Doong Island

0   2 km

Santa Fa Pier

Cadiz (Negros)

Hagnaya (Cebu)

ACCOMMODATION
Bamboo Oriental   F   Ogtong Cave   C
Budyong Beach Resort   D   Santa Fe Beach Club   B
Hoyohoy Village Resort   G   St Bernard's Resort   A
Kota Beach Resort   E

photocopied island maps (P5), and a few hotel brochures. The *Marque Internet Café* in Santa Fe market has **web access** for P20 per hour. For information about Bantayan before your trip Ⓦ www.wowbantayan.com is a good resource. There's a **post office** and an Allied Bank with **ATM** in Bantayan town, but it's best to bring enough cash to last your stay. Currency can be changed at some of the resorts and at an exchange office next to Palawan Pawnshop in Santa Fe.

Accommodation

If you intend to **stay** in Santa Fe, you can get a pedicab from the pier to your accommodation, though some resorts can send a representative to collect you at the pier.

Budyong Beach Resort A short ride west of Santa Fe by pedicab ☎ 032/438-5700. A good selection of fan and a/c cottages set in a coconut grove on one of the island's nicest stretches of beach. There's a simple restaurant here too. ❷

Hoyohoy Village Resort Just west of Santa Fe pier ☎ 032/438-9223. Spacious and solid concrete villas in pleasant gardens with a small central pool, *Hoyohoy* has some of Bantayan's best rooms, all of which have a/c, cable TV and fridge. The rooms and grounds are littered with antiques, and there's free wi-fi. The only downside to this place is that this stretch of beach is very close to the ferry pier. ❽

Kota Beach Resort A short ride west of Santa Fe by tricycle ☎ 032/438-9042. A range of different rooms and cottages set in attractive gardens on a lovely stretch of beach. The superior cottages are right on the sand, and for those on a budget, the economy and fan rooms at the back offer decent value. ❷

Ogtong Cave About 15min west of the Santa Fe pier by tricycle ☎ 032/438-9129. On a headland looking out over Sugar Beach, and set in pleasant gardens with a spring-fed swimming cave and pool, this is Bantayan's best hotel. As well as deluxe rooms, sea-view villas and budget row houses, exclusive deluxe suites (❾) have access to a separate private pool. A short walk takes you down to the beach, where you can arrange fishing expeditions with the locals and bring your catch back to the *Ogtong* chef to be cooked. Free wi-fi. ❹

St Bernard's Resort North of *Santa Fe Beach Club* on Alice Beach, and 5min by tricycle from the pier ☎ 0917/963-6162. Quaint little circular cottages set in narrow gardens leading down to a very local patch of beach. There's a small restaurant where you can get a good meal for P150–200. ❷

Bantayan town

Along the west coast, the port town of **BANTAYAN** has no decent accommodation but it's worth a quick visit; there's an elegant Spanish-style plaza on the south side of which stands the **SS Peter and Paul Church**. The original structure was torched by marauding Moros in 1640. Eight hundred local folk were taken captive and sold as slaves to Muslim chieftains in Mindanao. Every Easter Bantayan holds solemn processions of decorated religious *carozzas* (carriages), each containing a life-sized statue representing the Passion and death of Jesus Christ. Thousands of locals and tourists turn out to join in the processions, many setting up camp on the beaches because resorts are full.

Eating and drinking

Dining in Bantayan has a way to go before it becomes a culinary destination, but there are a few places to try after a hard day at the beach. A great cheap breakfast option is just to buy banana bread from the bakery and some fresh mangoes from the market.

Balikbayan Santa Fe. Friendly restaurant in the backstreets of Santa Fe with cosy pergolas dotted around a pretty garden. Great breakfasts, good pasta and the house coconut shake is as good as you'll find anywhere. Daily 7.30am–11pm.

D'Jungle Santa Fe. Near *Cou Cou's*, foreign-owned *D'Jungle* offers excellent buffets and Mongolian barbecue. Daily 11am–9pm.

Hard Kock Cafe Santa Fe. On the main strip, this café has a terrible name but a good atmosphere, and is usually the liveliest place for a drink in the evening. Daily 8am–midnight.

Malapascua Island

Eight kilometres off the northern tip of Cebu, the tiny island of **Malapascua** is often touted as the next Boracay, largely because of **Bounty Beach**, a blindingly white stretch of sand on the island's south coast. The island also has great diving, and is renowned for the chance to see thresher sharks. The nearest airport is Cebu, meaning that so far Malapascua has escaped overdevelopment, but it's changing fast, and many new resorts and dive shops have established themselves. The locals love to party and no matter when you visit, chances are there'll be some kind of fiesta or pageant.

Arrival and information

You can reach Malapascua from Cebu, Bantayan or San Isidro on Leyte. Most visitors head from Cebu City's Northern bus terminal to **Maya** by Ceres Liner bus (3–4hr; P90 ordinary or P136 a/c) or private taxi (P2500), and then take one of the hourly bangkas (P50) across to the island. The last boat to Maya is usually at 4pm, although boatmen may try and tell you earlier to get you to charter a bangka (P500–1000 depending on the boat and your bargaining). At either end you may need to transfer to a small paddle boat to the shoreline which should cost P10. From **Bantayan** you'll need to charter a bangka from Malapascua, which should take 2–3 hours and cost P2500; only undertake this trip if the weather is set fair. **From Leyte**, there is a daily boat at 7am from San Isidro to Maya (P180), returning at 10am.

There are **no banks** on Malapascua, and while you can change money at some of the resorts it's best to bring enough pesos with you. For **internet** there are terminals (and wi-fi) at *Maldito's Bar*, plus the tiny *N Café* at the bangka terminal on Logon village beach.

Accommodation

There are about a dozen **resorts** on Bounty Beach and a number of others dotted around the island; all are available to independent travellers and apart from during the busiest holidays (Christmas, New Year and Easter) you shouldn't have any problem turning up and finding a room.

Bounty Beach

Blue Corals Beach Resort Western end of Bounty Beach ☎032/437-1021. This blue concrete box doesn't exactly blend into the scenery, but its location at the end of the beach gives fantastic views in both directions. Large a/c rooms are nicely painted and have good balconies. Fan rooms are similar without the balcony. ❹

Danao Beach Resort Close to *Malapascua Exotic Island Dive & Beach Resort* ☎0915/666-1584. Some of the simplest huts on the beach nicely spread through extensive coconut grove grounds. Many of the huts have seen better days but they are slowly being renovated. ❸

Blue Water Beach Resort Middle of the beach ☎032/429-9011, ⓦwww.malapascuabeachresort .com. Hard to miss, *Blue Water* is a pretty sight, with a thatched main building, a restaurant overlooking the sea and a patio at the front for watching life go by on the beach. There's an Italian restaurant and a lovely little chill-out bar on the

beach – perfect for sundowners. The rooms are plain but tastefully furnished with white linen and mosquito nets on the beds, and all en suite. ❹

Exotic Island Dive Resort Far eastern end of Bounty Beach ☎032/437-0983, ⓦwww .malapascua.net. This is one of the most popular places to stay, especially for divers, with pleasant, clean cottages, a small restaurant and 24hr electricity. ❸

Mike & Diose's Close to *Malapascua Exotic Island Dive & Beach Resort* ☎032/254-2510. A couple of very simple beach huts plus two newer fully kitted out cottages with a/c, cable TV, DVD player, fridge and wi-fi. Both room types are in an excellent location tucked in a garden at the east end of Bounty Beach. ❷

Around the island

Bantigue Cove ☎032/437-0322 ⓦwww .bantiguecove.com. On a peninsula between two bays at the far northern end of the island, *Bantigue* is wonderfully remote and many of its ridge-top cottages have great views. There's a choice of fan or a/c rooms and also a small restaurant. To get here either charter a bangka or take a *habal-habal*. ❹

Logon Beach Resort Logon, Daanbantayan ☎0920/472-1451. On a headland just west of Bounty Beach, *Logon* has a lovely collection of huts, the best of which look straight out to the ocean. ❸

Mangrove Oriental Resort Logon, Daanbantayan ☎0906/469-0555, ⓦwww .mangroveoriental.com. A couple of kilometres along the west coast from Bounty Beach (P30 by *habal-habal*), this is a wonderfully romantic and secluded exotic hideaway with eight tastefully decorated cottages nestled around a small cove. Many of the cottages are uniquely styled, and the Kasbah, which is perched on top of the hill, is furnished with inlaid furniture from Mindanao. The budget cottages right on the sand have brightly painted exteriors and simple but comfortable furnishings. ❷

White Sand Bungalows At the southern end of Logon village beach ☎0927/318-7471, ⓦwww .whitesand.dk. There are only three huts left at *White Sand* after the DENR ordered the demolition of those too close to the sea. The remaining huts have been renovated, and this remains a lovely quiet spot, very close to delicious Italian food at *Angelina's*, and only a few minutes' walk from Bounty Beach. ❷

Diving and activities

Diving is Malapascua's main drawcard with a number of extreme dive sites that will get the adrenaline pumping and several top-quality outfits on the island including *Exotic Island Dive Resort* (see opposite), Divelink (☎032/231-4633, ⓦwww.divelinkcebu.com) and Evolution (☎0917/628-7333, ⓦwww .evolution.com.ph). Sightings of thresher sharks at **Monad Shoal** have been less common in recent years, but they are still around, and given a few early mornings you should get lucky. There are also plenty of wrecks in the vicinity, including the passenger ferry **Dona Marilyn**, which went down in a 1984 typhoon and is now home to scorpion fish, flamefish and stingrays. Overnight trips can be arranged to the tiny volcanic island of **Maripipi** (see p.349), where reef sharks and dolphins are common.

Back on land it's worth taking a stroll in the cool of the late afternoon to the lighthouse tower on Malapascua's northwest coast for tremendous views across the Visayan Sea. For more of an adventure, you can **walk** the entire circumference of the island in a few hours, a journey which will take you through sleepy fishing villages lined with mangroves, to remote white sand beaches where you'll feel as if you have the whole island to yourself. Take water, sunscreen and don't be afraid to ask directions – there are a bewildering array of trails for an island just 1km wide.

Whether you're diving or not, don't miss the opportunity for a day-trip to **Calangaman**, a beautiful, remote islet that consists of no more than a strip of sand just a few metres wide with a few trees at one end. Another gem in the area – two hours to the northeast by bangka – is the Robinson Crusoe-esque **Carnassa Island**, where you land at a picturesque bay fringed by palm trees.

Eating and drinking

Most of the resorts have their own restaurants, and *Exotic Island* is particularly good, but there are also some decent independent places.

Angelina's Logon Village Beach. Easily the best (and most expensive) place to eat on the island, *Angelina's* serves top-quality pizza and pasta dishes looking out over pretty Logon Village Beach. Daily 8am–10pm.

Ging Ging's In the maze of lanes which run behind Bounty Beach. Popular backpacker hangout with inexpensive sandwiches, soups and simple meals (P55–180). Daily 7am–10pm.

Maldito's Logon Village Beach. Set a little back from the beach *Maldito's* is a large bar-restaurant which serves overpriced European fare, but is better visited for a drink in the evening. Daily 8am–midnight.

The Camotes Islands

About 30km northeast of Cebu City, the friendly, peaceful **Camotes Islands**, which once sheltered Magellan's fleet, are gradually opening up to tourism, with fast boats from Cebu now bringing them within a couple of hours of the city. The two principal islands, **Poro** and **Pacijan**, are linked by a causeway, which makes exploring by motorbike an appealing prospect.

The main town on Pacijan is **San Francisco**, but most of the resorts are on the beaches of the northwest and southwest coasts. In the north beyond Lake Danao, **Tulang** is a picturesque islet lapped by turquoise waters, which has good snorkelling and diving. Over on Poro you can pay P10 to swim in a series of small underground caves in **Bukilat**, while easier swimming awaits at **Busay Falls** just a short walk from Tudela on the south coast. To get the lay of the land head up to **Arquis Viewing Deck** on Pacijan. From here you can see **Lake Danao**, site of Greenlake Park where you can take *sakanaw* (local boats; P500 for a 10-person boat) trips out to the mangroves.

Arrival and information

The Oceanjet fast ferry departs for **Poro** daily from Cebu City Pier 1. There are also daily bangkas and Supershuttle Ferry (⊕0928/371-3113) services from Danao to Poro and **Consueles** on Pacijan. Poro is also linked by public bangkas from Mandaue. Hiring a motorbike (P500/day) is the easiest way to get around, while short trips on a *habal-habal* cost P50. The easternmost (and smallest) Camotes island, **Ponson**, can be reached by small bangka from Poro.

There's a **tourist information desk** and **post office** at the town hall in Poro, but there are no banking facilities anywhere in the Camotes, so bring enough cash to last.

Accommodation and eating

For food, the better restaurants are mostly in the resorts, but the *Green Lake Restaurant* on Lake Danao does delicious tilapia.

Keshe Beach Resort In the northwest of Pacijan Island, next to *Borromeo* ⊕0929/892-5792. Situated on beautiful Bakhaw Beach, *Keshe* has attractive simple nipa huts. ❷

Mangodlong Rock Resort Heminsulan on Pacijan Island ⊕032/345-8599, ⓦwww.oceandeep.biz. Sister resort to *Santiago Bay*, *Mangodlong* has rooms set in a coconut plantation overlooking the beach, plus a dive centre. ❹

My Little Island Hotel In Esperanza on Poro Island ⊕032/497-095 ⓦwww.mylittleislandhotel .com. The best rooms on Poro, and a pool (P75 for non-residents), but it's not on the beach. ❹

Santiago Bay Garden and Beach Resort In the southwest of Pacijan Island ⊕032/345-8599 ⓦwww.camotesresorts.com.ph. Great views and comfortable a/c rooms with cable TV. ❸

Moalboal

Three hours by road and 89km from Cebu City, on the southwestern flank of Cebu Island, lies the once drowsy coastal town of **MOALBOAL**, now a boozy hangout for travellers and scuba divers (see box opposite). Sun-worshippers looking for a Boracay-style sandy beach will be disappointed – there isn't one. If being on the beach is top of your list, head 8km along the coast to **White Beach**, an attractive strip of sand with several mid-range resorts. In Moalboal, the shoreline is a little rocky in places and not generally suitable for recreational swimming. Moalboal makes up for this in other ways, with a great range of cheap accommodation, a marvellous view of the sunset over distant Negros, and some good discounts on diving and rooms. Besides diving, the jagged limestone peaks

Diving at Moalboal

Pescador Island, 30min by bangka from Moalboal, is one of the best dive sites in the country, surrounded by a terrific reef that teems with marine life, and renowned for its swirling sardine shoals. Barely 100m long, the island is the pinnacle of a submarine mountain reaching just 6m above sea level and ending in a flat surface, making it look from a distance like a floating disc. The most impressive of the underwater formations is the Cathedral, a funnel of rock that is open at the top end and can be penetrated by divers. Pelagic fish are sometimes seen in the area, including reef sharks and hammerheads, while at lesser depths on the reef there are Moorish idols, sweetlips, fire gobies and batfish.

There are at least ten other dive sites around Moalboal, including the gentle Balay Reef, Ronda Bay Marine Park, Airplane Wreck and Sunken Island. Arranging diving trips is easy, with a dozen operators at Panagsama Beach, including Blue Abyss Dive Shop (☏032/474-3036, ⓦwww.blueabyssdiving.com), Savedra Dive Center (☏032/474-0014), Seaquest (☏032/232-6010, ⓦwww.seaquestdivecenter.ph), and Visayas Divers (☏032/474-0018). Dives typically cost US$23 for a shore dive and US$28 for a boat dive, including equipment. For something a little different, Wolfgang Dafert (☏0928/263-4646, ⓦwww.freediving-philippines.com) arranges free-diving courses which aim to assist guests in holding their breath longer and diving deeper unassisted!

and lush river valleys of Cebu's central mountains offer canyoning, hiking, kayaking, mountain biking and horseriding all within easy reach of Moalboal.

Arrival and information

A number of **bus** companies, including Ceres, run regular services to Moalboal town from Cebu City's Southern bus terminal (3hr; P91), but make sure the driver knows where you want to get off, as most buses continue beyond Moalboal. The little town of Moalboal proper is on the road that follows the coast; what tourists and divers refer to as Moalboal is **Panagsama Beach**, a P50 tricycle ride from the point on the main road where buses drop passengers. A quicker option than the public buses is to negotiate a rate with a Cebu taxi – P2000–2500 is a reasonable price. Heading south for Santander and Negros, there are regular Ceres buses, or you can arrange a van through one of the resorts (P1500).

Within Moalboal sunbathing by resort pools, diving and drinking take centre stage, and there's little else to do except maybe visit the quirky **Naomi's Bottle Museum and Library**, where recycled bottles from the resorts adorn every available surface, each one filled with a message of goodwill. To get away from the dive scene and explore the wild hinterlands of western Cebu, head for **Planet Action Adventure** (☏032/474-0073, ⓦwww.action-philippines.com). Jochen and Jinky can organize caving, canyoning, kayaking and trekking trips (US$50–75/trip with a minimum of 2–4 guests) from their office at the *Tipolo Beach Resort*. The nearest **ATMs** to Moalboal are in Carcar on the other side of the mountains, so it's worth bringing enough cash to last your stay.

Accommodation

There's a wide range of accommodation in Moalboal, most of it huddled in the same area along the beach, but beach-lovers will prefer White Beach, or Badian.

Panagsama Beach

Hannah's Place At the northern end of the beach ☏032/474-0091. Pleasant rooms, some of which are right on the ocean, a 5min walk north of the restaurants. ⑤

Love's Beach & Dive Resort Right at the southern end of the beach, a 5min walk from *Quo Vadis* ☏032/474-0140, ⓦwww.loves beachresort.com. Attractive and well-cared-for resort on a quiet section of coast. There's a wide variety of fan and a/c rooms to choose from, a nice pool, free wi-fi in the public areas, and a lovely restaurant looking out to sea. ❸

Moalboal Backpacker Lodge Next to Moalboal Dive ☏032/474-3053, ⓦwww.moalboal -backpackerlodge.com. Cheapest place to stay in Moalboal with very simple dorms (P275) and a couple of private rooms. Dorms and rooms share clean bathrooms and there's free wi-fi. ❶

Quo Vadis Beach Resort Towards the southern end of the beach ☏032/474-0018, ⓦwww .moalboal.com. Attractive place with a good choice of rooms set in coastal gardens. Economy rooms are in a block at the back, while a/c huts and cottages (❹) are closer to the front. There's also a pool and a bar-restaurant looking straight out to sea. Wi-fi costs P200 for the duration of your stay. Visaya Divers is also located here. ❷

Sunshine Pension House 50m inland from the sea opposite *Marcosas Cottages* and Blue Abyss Dive Shop ☏0921/689-1865. Budget favourite, set in a pleasant garden with a pool. The simple rooms come with fan and private bathroom, but walls are very thin. ❷

Tipolo Beach Resort Just south of the centre of the beach ☏032/474-3016. Lovely little resort owned by the friendly folk behind Planet Action Adventure and *Last Filling*

Station. Rooms are tastefully furnished in bamboo, and look out onto an attractive garden, and the sea beyond. There's free wi-fi throughout. ❷

Badian Island

Badian Island Resort & Spa Badian Island ☏032/475-1102, ⓦwww.badianhotel.com. Luxurious resort on Badian Island south of Panagsama. There's a huge list of faciliities – as well as diving, tennis and glass-bottomed boat rides you can get a four-hand massage for $95. Round-trip transfers from Cebu City or the airport cost $60 per person. Alternatively make your own way to Badian town from where the resort can pick you up by private bangka. ❼

White Beach

Blue Orchid On a coral promontory at the far end of the beach ☏0939/270-5692, ⓦwww .blueorchidresort.com. Beautifully isolated property with a pool, dive school, well-designed rooms and a small animal shelter for rescued endemic species. ❻

Dolphin House Southern end of the beach ☏032/474-0073, ⓦwww.moalboal.net. The most sophisticated place to stay on White Beach has a lovely pool and free wi-fi, but the shoreline is rocky here.

Ravenala Beach Bungalows Roughly in the middle of the beach ☏032/254-9563, ⓦwww .ravenala-resort.com. Laidback resort right on a lovely stretch of beach, with comfortable wooden cottages set around a small garden. Attractive and well-cared-for resort on a quiet section of coast. ❻

Eating, drinking and nightlife

As well as the listings below, *Marina* at *Cabana Beach Resort* serves pretty decent pizza and also has free wi-fi. For drinks *Chief Mau's* away from the northern end of the beach is usually the liveliest place in town, but other popular spots include *Little Corner*, and nearby *Chili Bar*, where the sign on the wall warns "The Liver is Evil and Must Be Punished" reinforcing the fact that you can get three shots here for P99. If you find yourself in Moalboal on a Saturday night, *Pacita's Disco* (P30 cover charge) runs from 9pm to 3am.

At White Beach dining is principally at the resorts, while in Badian the resort is the only choice. Opening hours for the listings below are generally from around 7am to the time that the last customer goes home in the evening.

Panagsama Beach

Hannah's Place Northern end of the beach. Good seafood, tranquil ocean views and laidback service are the hallmarks of this small restaurant-bar.

Last Filling Station At *Tipolo Beach Resort*. *Last Filling Station* serves the healthiest and tastiest meals in town, with great breakfasts including

muesli and fruit (P145), baguettes and pitta sandwiches.

Ocean Globe Above the dive shop of the same name in the middle of the beach. For something completely different, *Ocean Globe* does decent Japanese, including yaki soba (P190), katsu curry (P230) and sashimi from P220.

Bohol

Bohol, a two-hour hop south of Cebu, is an attractive little island where life today is pastoral and quiet. The only sign of heavy tourist activity is on the beautiful beaches of **Panglao**, a magnet for scuba divers and sun worshippers, close to the utilitarian port capital of **Tagbilaran**. Most visitors only leave the beach for a day tour taking in the Bohol's most famous attractions: the much-touted **Chocolate Hills**, a glimpse of the **endangered tarsier**, lunch on the Loboc River and a visit to the Blood Compact site, memorial to Bohol's violent past. Those with more time will be rewarded by trips to other parts of the province, including the adventure centre at Danao, the attractive island of Cabilao and the pretty beaches of Anda. Bohol is also renowned for its wonderful old **Spanish churches**, many of them built with coral, which can be found all over the island, notably at Baclayon and Albuquerque. May is **fiesta month** on Bohol with island-wide celebrations including barrio festivals, beauty pageants, street dancing and solemn religious processions.

Tagbilaran

There are plenty of hotels and lodges in **TAGBILARAN**, the hectic port capital of Bohol, but with so many beaches and sights nearby, there's no real reason to stay here. From Tagbilaran you can be on Panglao Island in less than twenty minutes and even the Chocolate Hills, hidden in the hinterlands, are less than an hour away by road.

The only sights in Tagbilaran itself are the **Cathedral**, opposite the plaza in Sarmiento Street, a nineteenth-century hulk standing on the site of an original that was destroyed by fire in 1789, and the **Bohol Museum** (Mon–Fri 10am–4.30pm; P10) in Carlos P. Garcia Avenue, set in the former home of Carlos Garcia (fourth President of the Philippine Republic), and containing various presidential memorabilia and a collection of shells. The **Tagbilaran City Fiesta** takes place on May 1.

Arrival and information

Tagbilaran's main drag, **Carlos P. Garcia Avenue** (known as CPG), runs north from Plaza Rizal and is where you'll find hotels, fast-food joints, malls, convenience stores and banks. Island City Mall on the edge of town by the **Dao Integrated Bus Terminal** and Central Market, is also packed full of shops, cafés, restaurants, and has a post office. The **airport** lies less than 2km outside the city; tricycles from the airport into town cost P50, and taxis are only a little more on the meter. The **ferry pier** in Tagbilaran is off Gallares Street,

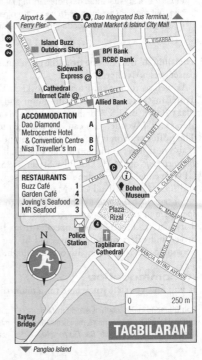

ACCOMMODATION

Dao Diamond	A
Metrocentre Hotel & Convention Centre	B
Nisa Traveller's Inn	C

RESTAURANTS

Buzz Café	1
Garden Café	4
Joving's Seafood	2
MR Seafood	3

Airport & Ferry Pier — Dao Integrated Bus Terminal, Central Market & Island City Mall

Island Buzz Outdoors Shop — BPI Bank — RCBC Bank — Sidewalk Express @ — Cathedral Internet Café @ — Allied Bank — Bohol Museum — Plaza Rizal — Police Station — Tagbilaran Cathedral

N — 0 — 250 m

Taytay Bridge

TAGBILARAN

Panglao Island

Moving on from Tagbilaran

By plane

Tagbilaran's small airport has daily flights to Manila (1hr 15min) with Airphil Express (2 daily), Cebu Pacific (2 daily), Philippine Airlines (3 daily) and Zest Air (2 daily).

By ferry

The Cebu route (1hr; P500–800) is operated by several fast ferry companies including Oceanjet (5 daily), Supercat (3 daily) and Weesam (5 daily). Other operators such as Cokaliong (1 weekly), Negros Navigation (1 weekly) and Trans-Asia (1 weekly) also have cheaper slower services (4–5hr; P170) between Tagbilaran and Cebu City. **For Dumaguete** there are two Oceanjet fast ferries (1hr 40min; P650) per day, and Weesam also have one service daily (2hr 10min). There's also a useful Oceanjet trip between Tagbilaran and Siquijor, via Dumaguete (2hr 40min; P700). **For Dapitan** in Mindanao there's one daily Oceanjet departure at (3hr 40min; P900). Finally, if you don't want to fly to Manila, Negros Navigation has one weekly boat service (32hr; from P1237).

By bus, jeepney and taxi

All bus journeys around the island start at **Dao Integrated Bus Terminal**, near Island City Mall and the Central Market, ten minutes outside Tagbilaran by jeepney or tricycle. Buses leave here every thirty minutes or hourly for all destinations along the coast from Baclayon and Loon to east coast towns such as Jagna (90min; P60), Anda (2hr 30min; P100) and Ubay (4hr; P109). They also travel the cross-island road via Carmen (90min; P60), passing close to the Chocolate Hills. Jeepneys likewise leave from Dao, making trips clockwise and anticlockwise around the coast, but they stop often and become uncomfortably overloaded, so are best used only for short trips. Travel agents and most hotels in Tagbilaran and Panglao can arrange car or van hire, but the cheapest way is to negotiate directly with a taxi which should cost cost P2000-4000 per day, dependent on your destinations.

---

a ten-minute tricycle ride from the city centre. Taxis and vans for hire wait to meet passengers arriving on ferries.

As well as tourist information kiosks at the airport and ferry pier, the **Bohol Tourism Office** (Mon–Fri 8am–noon and 1–5pm; ☎038/501-9186) is just off Plaza Rizal, on J.S. Toralba Street. ATMs can be found at a number of **banks** along CPG Avenue. You can also change money in Tagbilaran City Square Mall. The **police station** is near City Hall, behind St Joseph's Cathedral; the **post office** is also near here, at the end of the City Hall car park. To get **online**, try *Cathedral Internet Cafe* on M.H. Del Pilar Street, or *Sidewalk Express* around the corner on CPG Avenue. Many coffee shops have free wi-fi connection, including *Bo's Coffee*, and *Buzz Café* in Island City Mall.

For trips into the interior there are a few good **travel agencies** in Tagbilaran which specialize in adventure- and eco-tours. Barkada Tours (☎0920/901-2792, ⓦwww.barkadatours.blogspot.com) operates from Island Buzz outdoor shop on Gallares Street and offers mountain bike and hiking trips around Bohol from P1800 per person per day. They can also organize night kayaking trips to see fireflies.

Accommodation

If you find yourself stuck here for a night there are a few decent options.

Dao Diamond In Dao, north of Island City Mall ☎038/411-5568, ⓦwww.daodiamond.com. Away from the hustle of downtown, *Dao Diamond* has

good-value rooms with a/c, cable TV, fridge and microwave. The hotel is run by the Bohol Deaf Academy and it's easy to learn a little sign language during your stay. There's also a small pool in the grounds. ❸

Metrocentre Hotel & Convention Centre CPG Ave ☎ 038/411-2599, ⊛ www.metrocentrehotel .com. The marbled lobby has a coffee shop with wi-fi, and there's a gym and a small pool on the top floor. Rooms are tasteful and comfortable, all with cable TV and fridge, although the cheapest standard rooms are windowless (❸). The hotel has a well-stocked 24hr convenience store which also sells local handicrafts and *pasalubong*. ❹

Nisa Traveller's Inn 14 CPG Ave ☎ 038/412-3731, ⊛ www.nisatravellersinn.com. One of the better budget places in town, featuring good doubles with fan and clean bathroom, as well as more expensive a/c (❸). Rooms at the front are noisy. ❷

Eating

CPG Avenue is lined with fast-food outlets, and there's more of the same at Island City Mall.

Buzz Café Island City Mall. Owned by *Bohol Bee Farm* and featuring the same exquisite range of fresh dishes as the hotel restaurant, including organic garden salads (P120), and honey-glazed chicken (P160). They also have delicious ginger lemonade (P50) and sell packaged local delicacies. Free wi-fi. Daily 8am–9pm.

The Garden Café Plaza Rizal. Established by the Bohol Deaf Academy and providing training for deaf students, the café's menu has a mix of Mexican and Filipino dishes (P150–300) and you can communicate with the staff in writing, or with sign language (a few basic signs are listed in the menu). Downstairs you can buy tasty mango pies in the cake shop, and upstairs is a fun-filled

Wild West-themed restaurant with moose heads on the wall, wooden booths and cowboy-booted staff. Daily 7am–10pm.

Jovings Seafood By the pier. Immense menu that includes grilled tuna, marlin and lapu-lapu, chilli crab and king prawns. All dishes are served with a hefty mound of steaming hot rice; two people can fill up here for around P500. Next door *MR Seafood* offers similar fare. Daily 10am–10pm.

The Prawn Farm Island City Mall. Surprisingly chic for small town mall dining, *The Prawn Farm* serves excellent tilapia in lemon butter sauce (P155), and equally tasty prawns in garlic and chilli (P215). Daily 8am–9pm.

Panglao Island

Across the bridge from Taglibaran, **PANGLAO** boasts beautiful beaches, first-rate diving and historic Spanish churches. The whole island is enjoying increasing popularity, nowhere more so than **Alona Beach**, and while there is now a great choice of hotels and restaurants, this also means higher room and food prices. The best quieter stretches of white sand are Bolod Beach, San Isidro Beach, Bikini Beach and Doljo Beach.

Arrival and information

It's not hard to find a **taxi, van or tricycle** at the airport or pier in Tagbilaran to whisk you across the bridge and out to Panglao. If you negotiate a little you won't pay more than P500 for a taxi to Alona, or P250 for a tricycle. A cheaper but less convenient alternative is to take a bus from the Dao Integrated Terminal to Panglao. To get around the island (and Bohol) you can **rent a motorbike** in Alona or from your resort from around P400 per day.

Seashine Tours (☎038/502-9038) next to the tourist information centre can book all **ferry tickets**, as well as arrange day-trips around Bohol, van hire, and boat trips (P1500–2500 for a boat for the day). There's a BPI **ATM** next to *Jugali's* in Alona, but don't count on it having cash. There are also plenty of places to change money in Alona – Jad-ski, a small shop on the main road, offers competitive rates. The only place on Alona Beach which changes travellers' cheques is the **tourist centre** (daily 9am–9pm) near the beach opposite the *Alona Kew* restaurant. It's really just a glorified shop, but there's also **internet** avaible here for P60 per hour. Many beach resorts and restaurants also have wi-fi for customers. Laundry can be done at Dada's, next to the tourist information centre. In case of any trouble, head for the **tourist assistance centre**, opposite Rona's Corner.

Accommodation

Hotel prices have gone skywards in Alona, and there are hardly any budget options actually on the beach, but if you don't mind a short walk to the sea, there are still a few cheapies out there. For those who prefer to be away from the buzz at Alona, there are some fantastic resorts dotted around Panglao, although most are in the mid-range to high price bracket.

Alona Beach

Alona Grove Tourist Inn Set back from the western end of the beach ☎038/502-4200. One of a number of small budget resorts at the western end of the beach, *Alona Grove* has simple huts, some with a/c, fridge and cable TV. ❷

Alona Tropical Eastern end of the beach ☎038/502-9024, ⓦwww.alona-tropical.com. One of the better big resorts, with a wide selection of rooms spread along a quiet section of beach and up the hillside behind. A/c rooms (❾) have cable TV and hot water, but the budget fan rooms have the best location, right on the sand. There's a decent pool up the hill, and free wi-fi at reception and the beach bar. ❸

Alona Vida Halfway between the main access road and the eastern end of the beach ☎038/502-9180, ⓦwww.alonavida.com. Excellent rooms with all amenities decorated in earthy tones just a few metres back from the beach. There's one budget room but it's a little too close for comfort to the lively *Coco Vida* bar. There's a nice pool and free wi-fi throughout. ❺

🏃 **Charts Resort** By the turn-off for Ester Lim St ☎038/502-9095, ⓦwww.charts-alona.com. A beautifully designed boutique resort, *Charts* is intimate, well managed, and has some of the most tasteful rooms on the island, set around a compact garden with a dolphin-shaped pool. The luxurious suite has an expansive roof terrace, and there's also one budget fan room (❸) by the chill-out bar. The upstairs arts café showcases works by local artists and there's also a small handicrafts store near the reception. The only downsides are that it's not on the beach, and there can be a little road noise. Free wi-fi. ❼

Citadel Alona Inn On the main road ☎038/502-9424, ⓦwww.citadelalona.com. An interesting budget option with simple but stylish, brightly painted rooms spread through a large house. There are various sizes of standard rooms, plus family rooms, but none of them have en-suite bathrooms. The shared facilities are clean, and there's also a communal kitchen, wi-fi and a small café with local artwork on display. ❷

🏃 **Flower Garden Resort** On Ester Lim St ☎038/502-9012, ⓦwww.flowergarden-resort.com. Efficiently managed by a resident Swiss, this wonderful little resort has pretty chalet-style houses and spacious bungalows, plus a pool, all set in tropical gardens a short stroll inland from the beach. All rooms have a/c, cable TV, fridge and kitchen facilites. Excellent value. ❹

Peter's House Eastern end of the beach ☎038/502-9056, ⓦwww.genesisdivers.com. One of the last genuine budget options right on the beach, *Peter's* has simple and cosy nipa rooms above the bar. Owned by Genesis Divers, the hotel has an in-house divers-only policy during peak season. ❶

Bolod Beach

Amarela Barangay Libaong ☎038/502-9497, ⓦwww.amarelaresort.com. Perched on top of a hill looking out to the inviting sea, *Amarela* is an initimate, sophisticated hideaway with stylish rooms and good amenities. Heavy wood furnishings define the rooms, all of which have a/c, balconies, hot showers, cable TV and DVD players. The popular restaurant has wi-fi and enjoys wonderful views, and from here steps lead down to a pretty stretch of white beach, plus there's a pool. ❽

Bohol Beach Club Bolod Beach ☎038/502-9222, ⓦwww.boholbeachclub.com. Large resort split into two wings, Habagat with native-style cottage blocks, some with sea views, and the newer Amihan boasting more elegant rooms surround two swimming pools, with a few grand suites fronting the beach. There's free wi-fi in the business centre, but you need to pay to use it in your room. Water-sports are also on offer, along with a range of other facilities and services. Day visitors can use the beach and pool for P350–500 (all but P150 of which is consumable). ❼

Bohol Bee Farm Dao, Dauis ☎038/502-2288, ⓦwww.boholbeefarm.com. As the name suggests this place offers the unique opportunity to stay on a local bee farm. As well as getting to enjoy the farm's organic produce in the excellent restaurant, overnight guests are given a complimentary tour. Comfortable cottages with a/c, cable TV and hot and cold water are dotted throughout the property and there's also a pool and oceanside swimming platform. Free wi-fi in the lobby, and the store sells organic goodies and handicrafts produced here. ⑦

Doljo Beach

Ananyana Beach Resort Doljo Beach ☎038/502-8101, ⑩www.ananyana.com. Stylish, intimate resort on Doljo Beach with eight fashionably decorated double rooms and two family suites of two storeys. Breathtaking sea views from your balcony and less than fifty metres to a beautiful stretch of white sand beach that's nowhere near as busy as Alona Beach, add to the allure. Tasty Asian food in the restaurant, and the native-style beach bar is perfect for a drink at sunset. ⑨

Elsewhere on the island

Panglao Island Nature Resort Near Dauis, on the island's north coast ☎038/501-7288, ⑩www.panglaoisland.com. Upmarket resort that can be reached by taxi from Tagbilaran in 20min. Spacious villas are either on the beach or in a quiet garden, all with large *lanai* (veranda). A good restaurant, a large swimming pool, gym and massage are also available. ⑧

⑥

Diving and activities

The **reef** at the western end of Panglao, a few minutes by bangka from Alona Beach, has healthy corals, a multitude of reef fish and perpendicular underwater cliffs that drop to a depth of 50m. This is where most of the island's dive sites are, though you can go further afield to Doljo Point and Cervira Shoal, or use Alona Beach as a base for diving at Cabilao (see p.290). Dives typically cost around P1500 per time, plus equipment, but as always, the more dives you do the cheaper it gets. Dolphins, and sometimes whales, can also be seen off the coast of Panglao. Day-trips also run to the **Balicasag**, a beautiful halo of coral with steep drop-offs to the southwest and **Pamilacan**, a further 22km east, where mantas and whale sharks can be seen between January and April.

Given the dive boats filling the sea off Alona, the best sea **swimming** on the island is to be found at the exclusive resorts along the south coast: *Bohol Beach Club* charges P350 to P500 entrance fee. Alternatively you could head to one of the quieter north coast beaches at **Doljo or Momo**, both of which have good swimming at certain times of year.

Away from the reefs and beaches, Panglao has two main towns, **Dauis** and **Panglao**, on the east and west sides of the island, both of which hold pretty Spanish churches. The rest of the interior presents a verdant rural pastiche of nipa huts and towering palms, perfect for short walks, cycle rides or touring by motorbike. Near Dao on the island's southern coast, **Bohol Bee Farm** (☎038/502-2288, ⑩www.boholbeefarm.com) offers the chance to tour an organic bee and vegetable farm, and then sample the delicious produce at the restaurant, or buy some of the goodies to take home. You can also watch local handicrafts being made here, and even stay the night (see opposite).

Eating and drinking

In Alona itself, there is a good selection of **restaurants**, both on the beach and along the road into town. Many of the beachside places set up tables and chairs on the sand which make the perfect spot for a sunset beer, whether or not you choose to dine there. Nightlife mainly revolves around resort and dive-shop bars (*Coco Vida* and *Oops* are both popular), but there are a few independent places, such as *Helmut's*, on the Alona Kew junction, and *L'Elephant Bleu* (see below). Just down the street towards the beach, *One 4 Da Road* is a popular expat watering hole.

Alona Beach

Charts By the turn-off for Ester Lim St. Lovely daytime café where you can get a decent cup of coffee while looking at local artwork. Daily 7am–6pm.

L'Elephant Bleu On the main road, opposite just before the *Alona Kew* turn-off ☎038/502-8328. One of a new breed of trendy eateries to be found in Alona, French-owned *L'Elephant* serves healthy breakfasts (P40–200), croque monsieur (P140), a range of salted pancakes (P140–180), and illy coffee, in an attractive garden with comfy sofa areas. Catching on to the Boracay vibe, there are hookah water pipes (P450) to round off your meal. *L'Elephant* also has movie nights on Mondays and techno on Thursdays. Daily 8am–midnight.

Graziella On the *Alona Kew* turn-off road ☎0920/561-6169. Previously known as *Kamalig*, this Italian-owned restaurant continues to turn out the best pasta on the island with delicious carbonara (P235). Beef carpaccio (P215), caffe carretto (with amaretto) and Italian house wine are also on the menu. Open Tues–Sun 6–10pm.

Hayahay Eastern part of the beach ☎038/502-9288. *Hayahay* serves a mean pizza (try the Balicasag with salmon and tuna, P240) right on the beach. Daily 7am–10pm.

Jugali's Bistro On the main road, opposite just before the *Alona Kew* turn-off ☎0929/410-3189, ⓦwww.jugalibistro.com. Owned by a German chef and named after his son, *Jugali's* is a modest-looking place which serves fantastic food using super-fresh ingredients. Top choices include lapu-lapu in potato crust with buttered vegetables (P380) and mango chicken (P280). In the morning the heavy-duty breakfast (P300) packs enough Brazilian beef strip, potatoes, onion and egg to see you through until dinner. There's also free wi-fi for customers. Daily 7am–11pm.

The Interior

Apart from the famous Chocolate Hills, Bohol's **interior** hosts a range of sights worth exploring. The cheapest (and probably the best) way to see the island is to hire a motorbike and do it yourself, armed with a map and a sense of adventure. For a more comfortable trip, hiring a vehicle and driver is an easy option. Expect to pay P2000–3000 for a full day, dependent on your destinations. A car and driver should cost around P1500. There are also specialized operators in Tagbilaran which offer eco-tours and wilderness adventures (see p.284).

The Tarsier Visitors Center

Ten kilometres northeast of Tagbilaran, the **Tarsier Visitors Center** (Tues–Sat 8am–4pm; P60; ☎0912/516-3375, ⓦwww.tarsierfoundation.org) is dedicated to protecting what is left of the native tarsier population, a cuddly saucer-eyed creature you will see on posters throughout the country. Often mistakenly referred to as the world's smallest monkey, the **tarsier** – all 10–15cm of it – is more closely related to lemurs, lorises and bushbabies and has been around for a staggering 45 million years. Knowledgeable **guides** at the centre can usually lead visitors to their favourite haunts, though spotting them among the thick foliage is difficult during the day when these nocturnal creatures rarely move. When they are awake they study visitors with wide-eyed curiosity, sometimes swivelling their heads a disconcerting 180 degrees to get a better look.

To reach the Tarsier centre you can take a bus, jeepney (or taxi) from Tagbilaran to **Corella** and then a tricycle for the last 4km, or visit the centre as part of a day-trip. From the centre it is also possible to hike 15km along the **tarsier trail to Loboc**, where you could have some lunch and a boat trip, before continuing on to the Chocolate Hills or back to Tagbilaran, both of which can be reached by bus and jeepney. The trail is well marked, but it's best to contact the centre in advance to arrange a guide to point out wildlife along the way.

The Loboc River and around

Eleven kilometres east of Corella, the town of **LOBOC** is the start point for boat trips along the jungly **Loboc River** to **Tontonan Falls**. Private **boats** cost from P600 for the hour-long return trip, while seats on all-you-can-eat floating barge buffets cost P250 per person. Loboc Riverwatch (☎038/537-9460, ⓦwww.lobocriverwatch.com) is one of the most professional outfits. Whichever way you choose to cruise, it's a pretty journey past idyllic barrios, green paddies, twisted roots and towering palms. After rounding a bend you approach the falls themselves which are attractive, but not breathtaking. Some boat operators offer photo opportunities with captive tarsiers – note that this is illegal (visit the Tarsier Visitors Center instead).

There is a simple but beautifully located **resort** on the river, *Nuts Huts* (☎0920/846-1559; ❷). Run by two friendly Belgians, the resort's cottages are basic but charming and have balconies with river views. The outdoor restaurant is perched on a hill with views down the valley across a dense green canopy of rainforest. Activities on offer include rafting, trekking or mountain biking. The easiest way to get to *Nuts Huts* is to charter a boat from the Sarimanok Boat Company (P100 per person) in Loboc for the ten-minute trip to the resort.

Continuing inland from Loboc, it's worth stopping at **Simply Butterflies** (daily 8am–4.30pm; P30; ☎038/535-9400, ⓦwww.simplybutterfliesproject.com), a butterfly sanctuary which also serves delicious local snacks and has a few rooms.

The Chocolate Hills

The surreal **Chocolate Hills** are renowned throughout the Philippines and one of the country's biggest tourist attractions. Some geologists believe that these unique 40-metre mounds – there are said to be 1268 of them if you care to count – were formed from deposits of coral and limestone sculpted by centuries of erosion. Most locals, however, will tell you that the hills are the calcified tears of a broken-hearted giant while others prefer the idea that they were left by a giant carabao with distressed bowels. What you think of the hills will depend largely on the **time you visit**. During the glare of the day the light casts harsh shadows and the hills lose their definition. But at dawn or dusk they look splendid, especially during the dry season (Dec–May) when the scrub vegetation that covers the hills is roasted brown, and they really do resemble endless rows of chocolate drops.

Most visitors arrive by tour bus at the **Chocolate Hills Complex** (P50), where there's a **hotel** (☎038/416-0199; ❷) and a few small souvenir shops. From here there are 213 steps up to the **viewing decks** where you'll have the chance to pose for photos riding a broom and wearing a Harry Potter hat. To get here independently take one of the buses to **Carmen** (90min; P60) which leave hourly from the Dao terminal in Tagbilaran, often with every inch of bus space taken by locals returning from market with produce. From Carmen it's a pleasant 4km walk south up to the hills and then up the steps to the lookout area. You can also hop on a motorbike from Carmen for around P50.

For a different view of the Chocolate Hills, exploring the backroads by motorbike, bike or on foot is definitely worthwhile. Contact Barkada Tours (p.284) for hiking or biking trips. Alternatively you could head to **Sagbayan Peak**, northwest of Carmen, where there's another tourist complex which offers closer-up, quieter views. Take a bus from Tagbilaran to Sagbayan town, then rent a motorbike or walk to the peak complex.

Danao Adventure Park

Moving north from the Chocolate Hills to the small town of Danao, the limestone mounds swell into a rugged jungled massif cut by deep valleys, perfect for outdoors adventures. Established in 2006, **Danao Adventure Park** (P25 entry fee; ☎0921/759-4403, ⓦwww.eatdanao.com) has quickly become the centre for outdoors pursuits in Bohol offering everything from rivertubing (P200) to the white-knuckle inducing "plunge" (P700) which involves being lowered down a cliff on a rope and pendulum swung across the canyon. You can also try climbing (P400–600), caving (P350), kayaking (P200) and quad biking (P1800/hr). There's a canteen and simple rooms (❷) at the centre, or you can camp if arranged in advance

The easiest and quickest way to get here is to arrange a car and driver through your resort (around P3000 return), but if you want to go it alone take a bus from Tagbilaran to Sagbayan, where you'll need to change buses for the bumpy leg on to Danao. In Danao you can charter a tricycle (P100) to take you the final few kilometres to the park.

Along the north coast

The scenic road north from Tagbilaran takes you through the pretty coastal town of **MARIBOJOC**, 14km from Tagbilaran and not hard to reach by bus or jeepney. The town is the site of the old Spanish **Punta Cruz watchtower**, one of a number of old watchtowers of note on Bohol. Once a lookout for marauding pirates, Punta Cruz is now a viewing deck from where you can gaze across to Cebu and Siquijor.

Another 8km along the coastal road from Maribojoc is **LOON**, which has at its centre the imposing and atmospheric Loon Church. Built in 1803 by Recollect Friars, it's the largest church in Bohol and has a maw-like interior with three immense naves. On the outside it's equally impressive, with twin bell towers at the front and Corinthian architectural flourishes on its columns and pilasters. Loon can be reached easily via Maribojoc by bus or jeepney from the Dao terminal.

Cabilao Island

From Loon you can take a motorbike north to the pier at Mopoc, from where there are bangkas (20min; P20) to the tiny island of **CABILAO**, where there are a handful of modest but very comfortable resorts aimed largely at divers. *Cabilao Beach Club* (☎038/416-0463, ⓦwww.cabilao.com; ❸) has simple, clean wooden cottages set in green surroundings right on the beach, near the village of Cambaquiz on the island's northeast coast. The place is well run by a Swiss-German management team and the staff are helpful, plus there's wi-fi in the restaurant. *Polaris Dive Centre* on the main beach on the island's northwest coast (☎0918/903-7187; ❸), offers a choice of cottages ranging from simple wooden treehouses to more substantial air-conditioned doubles, bungalows and family houses. These resorts can arrange trips to local dive sites such as the **Wall at Cambaquiz**, where there are turtles and baby sharks, and **Shark View Point**, where one of the attractions – apart from sharks – is pygmy sea horses.

Ubay

On the opposite side of Bohol to Tagbilaran, about four hours away by bus, **UBAY** is a dull agricultural town notable for its ferry connections to Leyte. Just offshore, the undeveloped island of **Lapinig** offers some good diving, some of it extreme in subterranean caves. To explore you can rent a bangka for the day at the

---

Antiques at Antequera

A number of resorts offer half-day trips for around P2000 per person to the town of **Antequera**, north of Tagbilaran (you can get here independently by bus or jeepney from Tagbilaran). The attraction for tourists here is the lively **market**, twice a week on Thursdays and Saturdays. Craftsmen and traders from around the island congregate to sell locally made handicrafts such as baskets, hats and various home decor items such as linen tablecloths, mirrors and attractive bowls made from stone or coconut shells. Prices are significantly cheaper than in the cities and it's a fun place to haggle and pick up a few inexpensive souvenirs.

small pier in Ubay, but the easiest way to dive here is to arrange a trip through one of the dive operators in Panglao.

A number of **ferries and pumpboats** depart from Ubay, including trips to Maasin (3 weekly) and Bato (daily) on Leyte. Further along the north coast, in **Talibon**, there are daily Island Shipping and Kinswell ferries to Cebu.

Along the south coast

Heading east from Tagbilaran along the south coast takes you first to the coastal fishing town of **BOOL**, 5km away. Said to be the oldest settlement on the island, it's also the site of the **Blood Compact Site**, marked by an attractive bronze sculpture on the seafront. This is the spot where local chieftain Rajah Sikatuna and Miguel Lopez de Legazpi concluded an early round of Philippine–Spanish hostilities in 1565 by signing a compact in blood. Every year for one week in July, Boholanos gather in Bool for the **Sandugo** (One Blood) **festival** which, apart from the usual beauty pageants and roast pigs, includes a passionate re-enactment of the blood ceremony.

About 2km east of Bool, **BACLAYON** is the site of **Baclayon Church**, the oldest stone church in the Philippines. Much of the existing facade was added by the Augustinian Recollects in the nineteenth century, but the rest dates back to 1595 and was declared a national historical landmark in 1995. The church's convent has been transformed into an intriguing **ecclesiastical museum** (Mon–Sat 9am–4pm; P25) that houses a number of priceless religious icons. One of the most impressive collections is of Spanish colonial **santos** (statues of saints), including the Nuestra Señora de los Dolores, which has miracles attributed to it. Five kilometres further along the coast, **ALBUQUERQUE** (known as just "Albur") offers another impressive church and belfry, built in 1886 and set in an attractive palm-lined square.

Fifty kilometres east of Albur, **JAGNA**, is a pleasant enough place but all it really offers the traveller is an alternative port for getting away from Bohol. **Mindanao-bound boats** operated by Cebu Ferries leave for Cagayan de Oro (5hr 30min; P620–950) on Thursdays and Saturdays and for Nasipit (6hr; P660–990) at midnight on Sundays.

Anda

Around three hours by bus from Tagbilaran, the countless white sand coves near the town of **ANDA** in beautiful Guindulman Bay are an emerging choice for those looking to escape Panglao's commercialized beach and dive scene.

Of the resorts which have popped up in recent years, British-owned *Blue Star* (☎0919/453-4468, ⓦwww.bluestardive.com; ❼) stands out for divers and has a good pool, wi-fi, a tiny beach at low tide and good snorkelling on the house reef. There's a brand-new dive centre, and fan rooms are spacious and tastefully designed with lovely views out over the bay – air-conditioned rooms were nearly complete at the time of writing. For pure beach lovers, *Anda White Beach Resort* (☎0915/541-0507, ⓦwww.andabeachresort.com; ❼) can't be beaten and has attractive rooms, the best of which front onto a bright white strip of sand. There's also a pool, billiards and wi-fi (P100/hr). Two minutes' walk from here is one of the few cheaper options in Anda, *La Petra* (☎038/331-1316, ⓦwww.lapetraresort.com; ❹). Standard rooms are in a non-descript concrete block, but the cheaper nipa fan huts look right over the beach. A pool was under construction at the time of writing. All of the resorts in Anda have their own restaurants, and some offer half- and full-board rates.

Siquijor

Small, laidback **Siquijor** lies between the Cebu, Negros and Bohol islands and makes a worthwhile stop on a southern itinerary. Very little is known about the island and its inhabitants before the arrival of the Spanish in the sixteenth century who named it the Isla del Fuego ("Island of Fire") because of the eerie luminescence generated by swarms of fireflies. This sense of mystery still persists today, with many Filipinos believing Siquijor to be a centre of **witchcraft**. Shamans aside, Siquijor is peaceful, picturesque and a pleasure to tour, whether by bike, tricycle, motorbike or jeepney. The **beaches** alone make it worth a visit, but there are also **mountain trails**, waterfalls and old churches to explore as well as decent scuba diving.

Most places to stay are within half an hour of the port towns of **Siquijor** and **Larena**, notably around **San Juan**, south of Siquijor, and at **Sandugan**, north of Larena. A number of resorts have certified **dive operators** who will take you on trips to places such as Sandugan Point and Tambisan Point, both known for their coral and abundant marine life. At Paliton Beach there are three submarine caves where you can see sleeping reef sharks and at Salag-Doong Beach on the eastern side of the island divers have occasionally reported seeing manta rays and shoals of barracuda. Further afield but still within easy reach, Apo Island (see p.308) is another dive favourite, and is worth a visit even if you stay above water.

Arrival and information

Siquijor is not accessible by plane, but there are fast **ferry** connections to Siquijor town with Delta and Oceanjet. Oceanjet has a combined daily service from Dumaguete (45min; P200) and Tagbilaran (2hr 40min; P700), and a separate trip

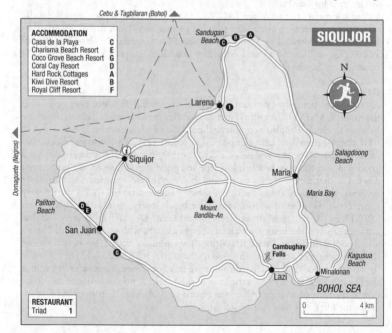

Sorcerors on Siquijor

Every Good Friday herbalists from around Siquijor and from the rest of the Visayas and Mindanao gather in **San Antonio**, in Siquijor's pea-green hinterlands, to prepare potions made from tree bark, roots, herbs and insects. The culmination of this annual Conference of Sorcerers and Healers – now rebranded the **Folk Healing Festival** because it sounds less menacing – is the mixing of a mother-of-all potions in a large cauldron. As the mixture is stirred, participants gather in a circle and mumble incantations said to imbue it with extraordinary healing powers (the ceremony takes place on Good Friday in the belief that on Christ's day of death, supernatural forces are free to wander the earth). It's evidently a strong brew, with wide-ranging powers that include provoking a good harvest, securing a spouse or getting rid of that troublesome zit.

from Cebu (3hr 40min; P950). Delta runs four fast boats to and from Dumaguete. A few slower Montenegro and Palacio ferries run from Dumaguete, Tagbilaran and Mindanao to Larena.

If you've booked accommodation in advance, you may get a free pick-up from the port, otherwise there are tricycles from the main port of Siquijor, and jeepneys from Larena. **Renting a motorbike** (or bicycle) is the cheapest and best way to get around the island, but tricycles and jeepeneys are also an option, or you could arrange a tour through your resort. The entire 72km **coastal road** is paved – a rare delight in the Philippines – and traffic is light. Motorbikes can be rented for P350 per day at Scandinavian Rent-A-Motorbike (☎0939/640-5132) on the National Highway in Siquijor Town, and also at some resorts. To take you along the coast by sea, bangkas can be chartered in Larena, Siquijor Town and Lazi. **Onwards boat tickets** can be arranged through most resorts, or directly at Siquijor and Larena piers.

Siquijor Town and the west coast

SIQUIJOR TOWN, where fast ferries from Cebu, Dumaguete and Tagbilaran dock, is a likeable enough place though without anything to keep you there for long. There is an atmospheric eighteenth-century **church** on the seafront, the Church of St Francis of Assisi, which was built in 1783 partly from coral and with a bell tower you can climb for views across the town and out to sea.

There's a **tourism assistance centre** (Mon–Fri 8am–noon & 1–5pm) at the pier which has a few maps and brochures and can also help arrange transport and guides. The main drag, **Rizal Street**, is chock-a-block with cheap canteens and bakeries selling fresh *pan de sal*. *Samyz Pizza* on Mabini Street does OK pizza and is a pleasant enough place to while away time if you find yourself waiting for a ferry. There are also a few small **internet cafés** in town, including the intriguingly named *Melbon Rub*.

Twenty minutes west of Siquijor you come to beautiful and undeveloped **PALITON BEACH**, 1km down a bumpy track from the main road (take the turn-off at the church in Paliton Town), but well worth the journey. A west-facing cove of sugary-white sand, Paliton is sheltered from big waves by the promontory of **Tambisan Point**, and has views of tropical sunsets you'll never forget.

A few kilometres further south the small town of **SAN JUAN** has an unusual focal point: the sulphurous **San Juan de Capilay Lake** where locals gather, especially at weekends, to wallow in the eggy water, said to have miraculous healing qualities. For more energetic activity, try the scenic but strenuous trek from San Juan along a jungled trail to San Antonio.

Accommodation

Charisma Beach Resort Solangon ☏035/481-5033, ⓦwww.charisma-resort.com. British-owned place with spick-and-span white motel-style rooms arranged around a swimming pool and right on the beach. ❸

Coco Grove Beach Resort Tubod ☏035/481-5008, ⓦwww.cocogroveresort.com. By far the island's most luxurious resort, Australian-owned *Coco Grove* occupies a prime stretch of palm-fringed beach. Rooms range from modest but tasteful standards to newer executive suites and luxury villas, all of which are a/c. There are two restaurants, two pools, a swim-up bar, dive centre, kayaks, massage and wi-fi among other amenities. The resort also runs daily dive trips to Apo Island. ❺

Coral Cay Resort On the beach at Solangon, 3km to the west of San Juan ☏035/481-5024, ⓦwww.coralcayresort.com. This resort is owned by an expat and his Filipina wife who can arrange jeepney tours, trekking, scuba diving, mountain bikes and anything else you care to ask for. Accommodation ranges from clean, simple rooms with fan and cold shower to spacious a/c cottages (❻) with a small living area and separate bedroom. The restaurant menu is surprisingly urbane for such an isolated place, featuring coq au vin and Australian Chardonnay. ❷

Royal Cliff Resort Close to *Coco Grove*, Tubod ☏035/481-5038, ⓦwww.royal-cliff-resort.de.tf. As its name suggests, this laidback resort sits on coral cliffs overlooking a tiny stretch of beach lapped by glass-clear water. Simple rooms are spread through a lovely garden and the restaurant looks out over the sea. ❷

The east coast

Siquijor's picturesque east coast is a rural littoral of sun-bleached barrios and hidden coves, some of the most secluded around **Kagusua Beach**, reached through **Minalonan** and then the sleepy little fishing village of **Kagusua**. There's a sealed road from the village to the edge of a low cliff, where steps take you down to the sand and a series of immaculate little sandy inlets. To proceed north from Kagusua you'll have to backtrack to the coastal road at Minalonan, where you can catch a jeepney through **Maria** and on to **Salag-Doong**, where there's a resort popular with locals at weekends. For Salag-Doong Beach, look out for the signposted turning about 6km north of Maria. You can walk it in about twenty minutes from the main road.

Heading to Minalonan from the west you'll pass through **Lazi**, with its delightful nineteenth-century church built of coral and stone and right opposite it, the oldest convent in the Philippines, a low-rise wooden building now sagging with age but still beautiful. A few kilometres inland from Lazi, **Cambughay Falls** are the island's most accessible and popular waterfalls. Steep steps lead down to the pretty falls which are a pleasant spot for a picnic or a swim.

Larena and Sandugan

Some slower ferries arrive at the port of **LARENA**, from where the beaches of Sandugan are only a brief jeepney or tricycle ride to the north. From the pier it's only a short walk to the town centre, which has a town hall, plaza, church, post office and an Allied Bank with **ATM**, but not much else.

There are a couple of basic lodges in Larena, but with plentiful jeepneys and tricycles to nearby Sandugan, there's really no need to stay. You can get **online** in Larena at *Mykel's Internet*, next to the pension house of the same name. In town there are a few simple places to eat, but for something more memorable, head for *Triad Restaurant* (☏0917/321-2124) perched atop a hill a short ride from Larena, from where there are expansive views over the coast. Dishes on offer include buttered shrimp (P270), *lechon kawali* (P90), and pancit (P95).

Sandugan

Six kilometres northeast of Larena is the village of **SANDUGAN**, where there's a beach and a number of resorts, one with professional scuba-diving facilities. To reach the beach, take a tricycle or jeepney from Larena to Sandugan and then negotiate the rutted path that leads to the shore. All the tricycle drivers know it, so you won't get lost.

Casa de la Playa ☎035/484-1170, ⓦwww .siquijorcasa.com. Owners Terry and Emily have established a New Age tropical spa that offers yoga sessions, food made with organic vegetables from the resort's own garden, and even massages from a local shaman. Accommodation is in a range of lovingly built fan and a/c huts; some are set back from the shore in a pretty garden bursting with frangipani and white *sampaguita* blossom, while others are on the beach and have sea views. ❹
Hard Rock Cottages East of Sandugan ☎0926/278-6070. Four very simple cottages in a lovely quiet spot overlooking the ocean. Two of the

cottages are on the clifftop, while the other two are down by the sea. There's a small bar and restaurant here. ❷
Kiwi Dive Resort At the eastern end of the beach (turn right at the end of the path) ☎035/424-0534, ⓦwww.kiwidiveresort.com. Pleasant, small-scale resort with attractive stone cottages on a low hill overlooking a private cove, all with bathrooms and hot water. Omelettes, nourishing stews, curry, fish, spaghetti and vegetarian dishes are some of the tasty options available at the restaurant. One of the owners is a dive instructor and can organize trips to nearby sites. ❶

Mount Bandila-an

At 557m (or 628m, depending upon who you ask), **Mount Bandila-an**, is Siquijor's highest point and accessible to anyone reasonably fit. It lies at the centre of the island in an area still recovering from damage inflicted during World War II, when acres of forest were razed by retreating Japanese troops. Now the entire area is part of the Siquijor Reforestation Project and while rehabilitation is not yet complete, wildlife such as the leopard cat and long-tailed macaque survive.

Mount Bandila-an can be climbed in a day; you can enquire about **guides** at the tourism assistance centre in Siquijor town, although many resorts can also offer advice and arrange for a local to show you the way. Access is via either the village of **Cantabon**, which can be reached by tricycle or jeepney from Larena on the north coast, or **Cangmonag** on the south. On the way to the peak you'll pass the **Stations of the Cross**, where a solemn religious procession re-enacting the Passion of Christ is held every Easter, and there are a number of springs and caves. Ask the guide to point out the huge old **balete tree** at the side of the trail, said to be home to spirits, imps and guardians of the forest. To ask their permission to pass, the polite thing to say is *tabi tabi lang-po*, which means "excuse me, please step aside".

Negros

The island of **NEGROS**, fourth largest in the country and home to 3.5 million people, lies at the heart of the Visayas, between Panay to the west and Cebu to the east. Shaped like a boot, it's split diagonally into the northwestern province of Negros Occidental and the southeastern province of Negros Oriental. The demarcation came when early missionaries decided the thickly jungled central mountain range was too formidable to cross, and is still felt today with each side of the island speaking different languages – Cebuano to the east and Ilonggo to the west.

Today Negros is known as "Sugarlandia", its rich lowlands growing two-thirds of the nation's sugar cane and you'll see evidence of this in the vast silver-green

Getting to Negros

The main **airports** on Negros are Bacolod, with daily flights from Manila and Cebu City, and Dumaguete, served by flights from Manila. Likewise, the biggest and busiest ports on the island are Bacolod and Dumaguete, which are connected by regular ferries with Manila, Cebu City and Mindanao. Bacolod also has **ferry connections** with Iloilo on Panay, and Dumaguete also has services to Tagbilaran on Bohol and Siquijor. Many other coastal towns on the island, including Cadiz, San Carlos and Guihulngan, have smaller ferries going back and forth to Iloilo, Cebu and Guimaras, as well as to other destinations on Negros itself. There are regular ferries on the useful crossing from the southerly tip of Cebu to the east coast of Negros. These ferries sail between Bato (Cebu) and Tampi (north of Dumaguete); and Lilo-an (Cebu) and Sibulan, also north of Dumaguete.

expanse of sugar-cane plantations stretching from the Gulf of Panay across gentle foothills and on to volcanic mountains of the interior. The mountains rise to a giddy 2465m at the peak of **Mount Kanlaon**, the highest mountain in the Visayas. For the intrepid this means there's some extreme trekking and climbing on Negros, from Mount Kanlaon itself to **Mount Silay** in the north. From **Bacolod**, the capital of Negros Occidental, you can follow the coastal road clockwise to **Silay**, a beautifully preserved sugar town with grand antique homes and old sugar locomotives. Much of the north coast is given over to the port towns through which sugar is shipped to Manila, but at the southern end of the island around **Dumaguete** there are good beaches and scuba diving, with a range of excellent budget accommodation. The **southwest coast** – the heel of the boot – is home to the island's best beaches, and remains charmingly rural and undeveloped, with carabao in the fields and chocolate-coloured roads winding lazily into the farming barrios of the foothills.

Some history

Among Negros's earliest inhabitants were dark-skinned natives belonging to the **Negrito** ethnic group – hence the name Negros, imposed by the Spanish when they set foot here in April 1565. After appointing bureaucrats to run the island, Miguel Lopez de Legazpi placed it under the jurisdiction of its first Spanish governor. Religious orders wasted no time in moving in to evangelize the natives, ripe for conversion to the true faith. The latter half of the eighteenth century was a period of rapid economic expansion for Negros, with its sugar industry flourishing and Visayan ports such as Cebu and Iloilo open for the first time to foreign ships. In the last century the rapacious growth of the sugar industry and its increasing politicization were to have disastrous consequences that are still being felt today.

Bacolod

On the northern coast of Negros, **BACOLOD** is a half-million-strong provincial metropolis, known as the "City of Smiles" and famed for its flamboyant **Masskara Festival** (third week of Oct). The old town is centred on City Plaza and San Sebastian Cathedral while government buildings, museums and the best dining options are to be found to the north. Its tourist attractions aren't significant enough to make you linger for more than a day or two, but it's a major transit point and a good base from which to visit the nearby historic towns, such as Silay and Victorias, or to arrange more adventurous excursions to Mount Kanlaon.

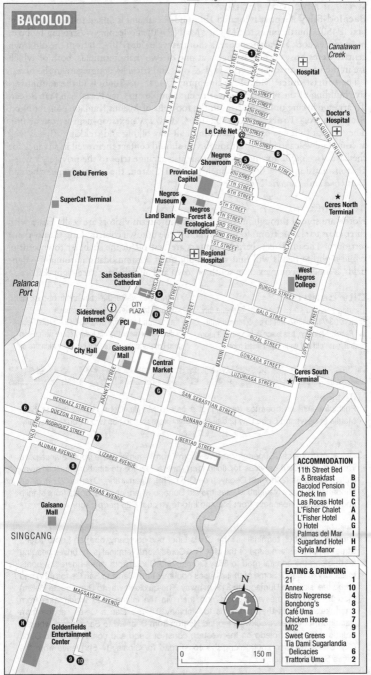

BACOLOD

Banago Wharf ▲   ▲ Cinema, The Ruins, Silay & Airport

Canalawan Creek

✚ Hospital

Doctor's Hospital ✚

Le Café Net @

Negros Showroom

Cebu Ferries

SuperCat Terminal

Provincial Capitol

Negros Museum 🏛

Land Bank

Negros Forest & Ecological Foundation ✉

✚ Regional Hospital

★ Ceres North Terminal

West Negros College

Palanca Port

San Sebastian Cathedral

Sidestreet Internet (i) @

City Plaza

PCI

PNB

City Hall F

Gaisano Mall

Central Market

Burgos Street

Galo Street

Rizal Street

Gonzaga Street

Luzuriaga Street

★ Ceres South Terminal

Hermaez Street

Quezon Street

Rodriguez Street

Alunan Avenue

Lizares Avenue

Roxas Avenue

San Sebastian Street

Ronano Street

Libertad Street

Gaisano Mall

SINGCANG

Magsaysay Avenue

H

Goldenfields Entertainment Center

N

0   150 m

ACCOMMODATION

11th Street Bed & Breakfast	B
Bacolod Pension	D
Check Inn	E
Las Rocas Hotel	C
L'Fisher Chalet	A
L'Fisher Hotel	A
O Hotel	G
Palmas del Mar	I
Sugarland Hotel	H
Sylvia Manor	F

EATING & DRINKING

21	1
Annex	10
Bistro Negrense	4
Bongbong's	8
Café Uma	3
Chicken House	7
M02	9
Sweet Greens	5
Tia Dami Sugarlandia Delicacies	6
Trattoria Uma	2

Arrival and information

Bacolod-Silay Airport is located 15km northeast and is linked to the Bacolod by taxi (P450), shuttle buses to SM City Mall (P100) and jeepneys. Arriving by boat, most ferries dock at **Palanca port**, a short tricycle ride (P10–20) from the old town centre. Ceres **buses** drop passengers at one of two main terminals, both of which are in the north of town. **Jeepneys**, FX vans and tricycles congregate in the plaza.

The **tourist office** (Mon–Fri 8am–5pm; ☎034/708-3066) is in the administrative building of the provincial government complex in City Plaza, San Juan Street. To arrange hiking or biking trips in the foothills of Mount Kanlaon contact **Next Stop Negros Tours** (☎034/702-1064, ⓦwww.nextstop-negros-tours.com). They operate a range of trips including half-day biking and trekking trips as well as complete volcano climbs, although you should contact them well in advance for the latter (see p.302 for more). They can also arrange trips to the privately owned Gaston mansion for a slap-up lunch by Jomi Gaston, the culinary talent behind *Café Uma* and *Trattoria Uma*.

Accommodation

Hotels are spread throughout the city, but short-term visitors are really faced with three areas to choose from: foodies will relish the uptown choices along the northern section of Lacson Street, bargain-hunters are best off in the shabbier town centre, while nightlife fiends will find surprsingly quiet accommodation around Goldenfields, a modern complex 3km south of town and also the city's red-light district.

City centre

Bacolod Pension Plaza Cuadra St, opposite City Plaza ☎034/433-4547. Not to be confused with the *Bacolod Pension*, this place is bigger and more central, with old but well-maintained rooms. There's free wi-fi in the lobby and front-desk staff can also book air and ferry tickets. ➋

Check Inn Luzuriaga St ☎034/432-3755. Decent-value option near the old town centre with clean and comfortable rooms, the best of which are on

Moving on from Bacolod

By plane

Philippine Airlines operates four flights a day to Manila. Cebu Pacific flies to both Manila (4 daily) and Cebu City (2 daily). Airphil Express also has two Cebu flights daily.

By ferry

Oceanjet, Supercat, Superferry and Weesam Express ferries leave from Palance port. There are frequent services for Ilolio (1hr), and a few for destinations further away including Manila (24hr) and Cagayan de Oro (17hr), Iligan (18hr), Ozamis (22hr), all on Mindanao. Negros Navigation uses the old Banago wharf, and has boats from Manila and Mindanao. Jeepneys from Banago into town cost P25 per person.

By bus

There are two bus terminals of the Ceres Liner bus company, both on Lopez Jaena Street on the eastern edge of the city. The Ceres North terminal is for buses heading north along the coastal road to Silay (30min) and Cadiz, from where there are boats to Bantayan Island. Some of these buses continue from Cadiz to San Carlos (3hr) and round the island to Dumaguete 313km away. The quickest way to Dumaguete (5–6hr) though, is down the west coast and then via the inland road which runs from Kabankalan across the mountains to Mabinay. There's also a Ceres service from Bacolod that travels clockwise around Negros from Bacolod to San Carlos, where it boards a ferry for Toledo on the western coast of Cebu and continues on to Cebu City. Buses heading south along the coast road for Sipalay (4–5hr) leave from the Ceres South terminal.

the business floor set around the roof garden. There's also free wi-fi and a gym. ❷

Las Rocas Hotel Gatuslao St ☎034/433-3190. Dark, small fan or a/c rooms with no views, but they're among the cheapest in Bacolod and at least it is right in the middle of the action, opposite City Plaza and the cathedral, a stone's throw from shops and restaurants. ❶

O Hotel 52 San Sebastian St ☎034/433-7401, ⓦwww.ohotel.com.ph. Large, modern motel-style hotel with decent rooms, although those facing the front are noisy. There's also an ATM in the hotel. ❸

Sylvia Manor St Juan St ☎034/434-9801, ⓦwww.sylviamanor.com. Boutique hotel in a central location one block south of the main city plaza. Wide range of comfortable, high-ceilinged a/c rooms and suites (❼), all tastefully decorated and with cable TV and, in some cases, a kitchenette. There's a laidback café-bar in the lobby. Free in-room wi-fi. ❹

Lacson Street

🏃 **11th Street Bed & Breakfast** 14, 11th Street St ☎034/433-9191, ⓦwww.bb11st.webeden.co.uk. A great-value little pension in a quiet location within walking distance of the plentiful restaurants on Lacson St. Rooms are clean and simple with cable TV and cold showers, and there's free wi-fi throughout. ❷

L'Fisher Chalet Lacson St ☎034/433-3730, ⓦwww.lfisherhotelbacolod.com. The budget wing of *L'Fisher* offers the best-value rooms in the city,

plus access to all of the hotel's excellent facilities. All rooms are a/c and feature modern furnishings, cable TV, fridge, safe, free wi-fi and balcony. ❷

🏃 **L'Fisher Hotel** Lacson St ☎034/433-3730, ⓦwww.lfisherhotelbacolod.com. One of Bacolod's best top-end hotels, this glass-fronted establishment has a great location amid the dining options on Lacson St. Deluxe rooms are comfortable and well maintained, but it's worth paying extra for one of the newly renovated superdeluxe rooms which are tastefully decorated in understated style. All rooms are a/c and have cable TV, fridge, safe and free wi-fi. There's also a 24hr poolside café that offers buffet lunches and dinners. ❼

Goldenfields and elsewhere

Palmas del Mar Resort J.R. Torres Ave ☎034/434-8987. Family resort in a residential area close to the sea, with a good range of accommodation, including regular a/c rooms, family rooms and cottages. There's a decent-sized pool and the restaurant serves local specialities and European dishes. Pleasantly quiet during the week, when you might have the pool to yourself, but weekends can get busy. ❹

Sugarland Hotel Araneta St ☎034/435-2690, ⓦwww.sugarlandhotel.com. Good-value modern hotel with stylish and well-kept a/c rooms with free wi-fi. There's also a small pool and a couple of good restaurants in the hotel. ❸

The Town

The old **city centre**, chaotic and choked with traffic, is best defined as the area around the City Plaza at the northern end of Araneta Street. North of here, Bacolod's main thoroughfare is **Lacson Street**, which runs past the capitol building and to the city's social hub, where there are good hotels, restaurants, shops and bars. There are more hotels, restaurants and nightlife 3km south of the town centre at the **Goldenfields Commercial Complex**.

About 300m north of the centre, the 1930s Provincial Capitol Building is one of the few architectural highlights. Next door is the **Negros Museum** (Mon–Sat 9am–6pm; P50), which details five thousand years of island history. Housed in an elegant Neoclassical building dating from the 1930s, the museum itself is only really worth a look for its "Iron Dinosaur" steam engine, once used to haul sugar cane, and exhibited on the first floor. Just around the corner, the **Negros Forest and Ecological Foundation** (☎034/433-9234, ⓦwww.negrosforests.org) is a rescue centre (Mon–Sat 9am–noon & 1–4pm; donation) where conservationists care for endangered animals endemic to Negros, including leopard cats, the Visayan spotted deer and the bleeding-heart pigeon.

Eating and drinking

Bacolod's dining scene has moved uptown and upscale of late, and there's a cosmopolitan range of choices along northern Lacson Street, while time-tested favourites still hold their own in the old city.

For **drinks**, food and billiards, Goldenfields Commercial Complex in Singcang is cited as the city's nightlife district, but in truth the majority of places here are girlie bars catering to an exclusively male crowd. This said, there are few regular bars and clubs including *MO2*, which has nightly live music in the punkah-cooled outdoors area, with a disco inside. Next door, *Annex* has pool tables and is equally salubrious.

6

THE VISAYAS | Negros

300

21 21st & Lacson St ☎034/433-4096, ⓦwww.21restaurant.com. A Bacolod institution dishing out amazing *batchoy* (noodle soup with crispy pork) and excellent seafood from barbecued squid to "crispy crablets". White tablecloths and attentive service complete the picture. Daily 11am–11pm.

Bistro Negrense 10th & Lacson St ☎034/433-4623. A welcome addition to Bacolod's restaurant scene, as you might guess, *Bistro Negrense* specializes in dishes from Negros. The *lechon kawali* (P139), *kare kare* (P159) and crispy pork leg (P349) are all recommended. Daily 10am–2pm & 5pm–midnight.

Café Uma 15th & Lacson St, next to *L'Fisher* ☎034/709-9966. Like *Trattoria Uma* just around the corner on Lacson St, this super-trendy little café is owned by the Gaston family. The café serves delicious but expensive drinks, snacks and meals including Eggs Benedict (P450), fish and chips (P400), and lemon-herb-roasted chicken (P400). There's free wi-fi for customers. Daily 9am–9.30pm.

Chicken House Araneta St ☎034/842-3096. An oldie but a goodie, *Chicken House* has been serving up sumptuous roast chicken (P65) for two decades and continues to draw in the local crowds with its distinctive flavours and low prices. Daily noon–10pm.

Sweet Greens 9th & Lacson St ☎034/709-0950. Lovely home-style restaurant with a nightly a la carte buffet prepared using super-fresh ingredients, and they also sell organic produce. Daily 11am–10pm.

Trattoria Uma 15th & Lacson St ☎034/709-1808. Owned by the Gaston family, *Trattoria* serves top-notch Italian specialities such as penne funghi con pancetta (P480), and minestrone soup (P200) at international prices. Daily 10.30am–2pm & 5.30–10pm.

Listings

Airlines Philippine Airlines has offices at the airport (☎034/435-2011), as do Airphil Express (☎034/435-2073), and Cebu Pacific (☎034/435-2156), who also have an office in Victoria Arcade in Rizal St (☎034/434-2052).

Banks There are plenty of banks with ATMs in Bacolod, many of which can be found on Araneta St, including BDO, BNP and BPI. There's also a BDO ATM out at Goldenfields.

Cinemas There's a Cineplex at Robinson's Place on the northern section of Lacson St.

Ferries Ticket offices for major ferry companies operating out of Bacolod are at Palanca port, on reclaimed land 500m west of the town plaza. Negros Navigation's ticket office (☎034/441-0645) is at the old Banago wharf 8km north of Bacolod, although there are outlets in the city itself.

Hospitals Bacolod Doctors' Hospital is on B.S. Aquino Drive northeast of the centre.

Internet access The trendy *Le Cafénet* on Lacson at 12th St is the most comfortable place to get online in Bacolod, but other places include *Sidestreet Internet* on San Juan St, in the malls, or on Hilado St around the West Negros College northeast of the centre.

Post The post office is on Gatuslao St, near the junction with Burgos St.

Police Police headquarters is at Magsaysay Ave in Singcang.

Shopping For a real taste of Sugarlandia, Bongbong's on Araneta St sells everything from banana-honey chips to *piyaya* (a hardened pancake with sugar melted inside) and delicious *bay ibayi* (sugar and coconut bar). Not far away on Yulo St, *Tia Dami Sugarlandia Delicacies*, has more of the same. For handicrafts, the extensive Negros Showroom (daily 9.30am–7pm) on Lacson by 9th St has top-quality products from all over the island. Finally for everyday needs plus clothes stores and fast-food outlets head for Robinson's Place on the northern section of Lacson St.

Around Bacolod: The Ruins

In Talisay on the edge of town, **The Ruins** (daily 10am–8pm; P50; ☎034/476-4334) makes a great short excursion from the city. Officially the "Don Mariano

Ledesma Lacson Mansion", The Ruins are the Philippines' answer to the Taj Mahal, hauntingly beautiful and complete with a sad story of love lost. The Lacsons were one of the island's pre-eminent sugar families in the nineteenth century. When Maria Lacson died during pregnancy with the couple's eleventh child, Don Mariano was inconsolable and set about building a memorial mansion. During the outbreak of World War II, the building was razed to prevent it being used as a headquarters by the Japanese. The fire left behind the building's complete superstructure, including the double-M motif used throughout. Mariano died in 1948, and the building was forgotten about, until his great-grandson, decided to open it to the public. There is also a **restaurant** (daily 10am–8pm) here which makes a wonderful spot for a special dinner. The easiest way to get here (and back) is to hire a taxi and get it to wait while you look around (P200–300 depending on how long you stay).

Silay

The elegant town of **SILAY**, about 20km north of Bacolod, is an atmospheric relic of a grander age, when Negros was rich from its cultivation of sugar cane. In the late eighteenth century it was talked about as the "Paris of Negros", with music performers from Europe arriving by steamship to take part in operettas and *zarzuelas*. This passion for music and the arts gave Silay – and the Philippines – its first international star, **Conchita Gaston**, a mezzo-soprano who performed in major opera houses in Europe in the postwar years. Japanese forces occupied the city in World War II, after which the sugar industry declined and Silay lost its lustre – many of its European residents departing for home. Today, Silay's major tourist draw is its **ancestral homes**, most of them built between 1880 and 1930 and some of the best open to the public.

The major annual festival here, the **Kansilay**, lasts one week and ends every November 13 with a re-enactment of a folk tale showing the bravery of a beautiful princess who offered her life for justice and freedom.

The Town

Two ancestral houses have been turned into lifestyle museums that give a glimpse of what life was like for the sugar barons. The **Balay Negrense Museum** on Cinco de Noviembre Street, five minutes' walk west of the plaza (Tues–Sun 10am–6pm; P40), was once the home of Don Victor Gaston, eldest son of Yves Germaine Leopold Gaston, a Frenchman who settled in Silay during the latter part of the nineteenth century. After World War II the house was left deserted and by 1980 was a sad ruin, known only by locals for the ghosts that were said to roam its corridors. Now restored by the Negros Foundation, the house is a glorious monument to Silay's golden age, with rooms of polished mahogany furnished with antiques donated by locals.

Hard to miss at the northernmost end of Rizal Street is the pink **Don Bernardino-Ysabel Jalandoni House Museum** (Tues–Sun 9am–5pm; P40; ☏034/495-5093), known throughout town as the Pink House. Built in 1908, it features displays of antique law books and Japanese occupation currency; in the garden is a huge metal vat that was used to make muscovado sugar.

A short walk from Balay Negrense, the **Manuel and Hilda Hofileña ancestral house** (open by appointment; enquire at the tourist office) is notable for housing works by contemporary Filipino painters and by masters such as Juan Luna and Amorsolo. It's also worth taking time to visit the **Church of San Diego**, on the north side of the public plaza. Built in 1925, it is a dramatic sight, with a great illuminated crucifix on top of the dome that is so bright at night it was once used by ships as a navigational aid. Behind the church are the ruins of the original sixteenth-century Spanish church, now converted into a grotto and prayer garden.

Silay is also known for **pottery** and in the barangay of **Guinhalaran** (about ten minutes by tricycle or jeepney from town) on the National Highway you can visit the potters and buy quality jars and vases at bargain prices.

Practicalities

Buses and jeepneys arrive at Rizal Street on the eastern side of the plaza, from where it's a short walk or tricycle ride to accommodation. The Silay **tourist office** (Mon–Fri 8am–5pm; ☎034/495-5553) in Plaridel Street, opposite the **police station**, has helpful staff who can arrange informal guided tours of some ancestral houses that aren't usually open to the public. For long-distance calls there's a **PLDT office** in Rizal Street; the *Silay Internet Cafe* is next door.

The best **accommodation** is the atmospheric former ancestral home *Baldevia Pension House* on busy Rizal Street (☎034/495-0272; ❷), close to its junction with Burgos Street (head 200m north from the Church of San Diego and it's the big white building on your left). *Baldevia* is low on modern amenities, but high on faded old-world charm. For **food** try *Café 1925* (☎034/714-7414) at 4 J. Ledesma St, an pretty little place dishing up Italian classics and excellent coffee. Also, don't miss the *El Ideal Bakery & Refreshment*. Established in 1920, it does a range of specialities that include coconut pie, cassava cake, meringue and *halo-halo*. Silay is also full of *manuglibod* (sweet-sellers), carrying their home-made goods in baskets on their heads. Milksweets – made with carabao milk – are delicious and cost P1.

Mount Kanlaon

At 2435m **Mount Kanlaon**, two hours south from Bacolod by jeepney, is the tallest peak in the central Philippines and offers a potentially dangerous challenge. One of the thirteen most active volcanoes in the country, there's the real possibility of violent eruptions and climbers have died scaling it. The rim of the crater is a forbidding knife-edge overhanging an apparently bottomless chasm. The dense surrounding forest contains all manner of wonderful fauna, including pythons and tube-nosed bats and locals believe the mountain is home to many spirits. It also features in Philippine history being where President Manuel Quezon hid from invading Japanese forces during World War II.

There are three main routes up the volcano itself. The Guintubdan trail is the easiest and most comon ascent, but even this should not be underestimated. The usual start point is Guintubdan, where there is basic accommodation at *The Pavilion* (❶) and *Rafael Salas Nature Camp* (❶). From here, although it's only 8km to the top, the trail is best broken with an overnight stop. The 14km-long Mananawin trail works best over three days and offers the chance to really get to know the region, while the short, steep Wesey trail is very exposed and only for experienced tropical mountaineers.

Whichever way you choose to ascend, a permit (P300) and guide (P500/day) are mandatory, and a porter (P300–500) might come in handy. The easiest way to make all of these arrangments is through Billy Torres at Next Stop Negros Tours (see p.298). Contact Billy as far in advance as possible (ideally a month), and he can arrange everything from permits, guides and porters to tents and meals (climbs around P4500/person excluding transport). Coming from further afield you can also arrange to climb Kanlaon through Dumaguete Outdoors in Dumaguete (see p.307).

The north coast

North of Silay along the rugged coast, the first significant settlement is **VICTORIAS**, where the **Victorias Milling Company**, the largest integrated mill and sugar refinery in Asia, is open to the public (Tues–Fri 9am–4pm; dress code of no sandals, shorts or short skirts). The mill, a ten-minute tricycle ride east from Victorias Plaza, has some fine examples of the old locomotives that were used for hauling sugar cane from the fields, including American Baldwins and German Henschells. Inside the mill compound stands one of the country's religious curiosities, the **Church of St Joseph the Worker**, built between 1948 and 1950. The church is home to a controversial modern mural called **The Angry Christ**, which depicts a square-jawed Jesus sitting in front of the hands of God, straddling a serpent-spewing skull. Other murals depict Mary and Joseph as Filipinos in native attire. To arrange a guided tour, it's best to phone ahead (☎034/398-5580), or alternatively you could pay a visit to the small public relations office just inside the mill gates. It's an informal arrangement so there's no guarantee you'll get in, but if you do the usual price of a tour is P20 per person.

Cadiz

A rough-and-ready port and fishing town 30km east of Victorias and 50km north of San Carlos, **CADIZ** is where much of Negros's sugar is stacked on cargo boats for shipment to Manila and beyond. For tourists it's little more than a possible exit point for Bantayan (see p.276) – there is one daily boat for the 3- to 4-hour ride. Cadiz's uninspiring **hotel** options include the *Cadiz Hotel* (☎034/493-1785; ❷) on the city plaza, with air-conditioned rooms and a tennis court and *RL Apartelle* (☎034/493-0253; ❶) near the Ceres bus depot on the main road.

Sagay Marine Reserve

SAGAY is a hectic industrial and fishing city 15km east along the coast from Cadiz, at the mouth of the Bulanon River. The city is the jumping-off point for one of the Philippines' least-visited natural wonders, the beautiful **Sagay Marine Reserve**. The sanctuary, which you can visit for a day (free admission) on a half-hour bangka ride from Sagay wharf, boasts some marvellous beaches and its reefs are a picture of health; with a mask and snorkel you can see giant clams, pufferfish, immense brain corals and the occasional inquisitive batfish.

There's one other thing to do in Sagay: head for the city plaza and take a look at the **Legendary Siete**, or Train Number Seven, an iron dinosaur that once hauled lumber for the Insular Lumber Company and now stands in the middle of the plaza, restored and sparkling in all her 75-tonne liveried glory.

San Carlos

SAN CARLOS on the northeast coast is the closest major urban centre to the Negros Occidental/Oriental border, from where the road continues south to Dumaguete, about three hours away, via Bais (more commonly visited from Dumaguete; see p.307), where there are opportunities for whale- and dolphin-spotting. Regular ferries run every day from San Carlos to Toledo on the west coast of Cebu.

Dumaguete and around

DUMAGUETE ("dum-a-get-eh"), known in the Philippines as the City of Gentle People, is capital of Negros Oriental and lies on the southeast coast of Negros, within sight of the southerly tip of Cebu Island. The city is becoming more of a mainstream tourist destination these days and it's easy to understand why: it has attractive architecture, a laidback university town ambience, and a lovely **seafront promenade** shaded by acacia trees and coconut palms and lined with lively bars and restaurants.

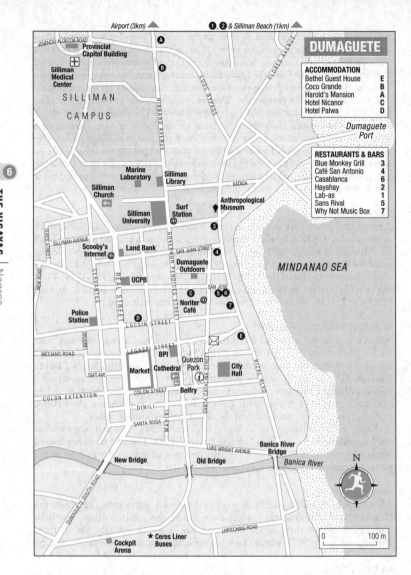

Day-trips from Dumaguete include the **Twin Lakes** of Balinsasayao and Danao. For dolphin- and whale-watching head to **Bais**, while for affordable resort accommodation the closest choices are to be found around **Dauin**, where you can also arrange scuba diving, and day-trips to **Malatapay Market** and **Tambobo Beach**.

Arrival and information

The small **airport** is a few kilometres north of the city centre on the far bank of the Bona River. Tricycles make the trip to the city for about P50; there are also jeepneys waiting for city-bound passengers outside the airport perimeter fence, or you can haggle with one of the private car drivers who greet incoming flights. The **ferry pier** is near the northern end of Rizal Boulevard, within easy walking distance of the centre. Ceres Liner **buses** arrive and depart at the **Ceres terminal** in Governor Perdices Street, on the southern side of the Banica River. A jeepney into the city costs P10, but if you haven't got much luggage you can walk it almost as fast. In town, there's a **tourism office kiosk** in Quezon Park (Mon–Fri 8am–4pm; ℡035/225-2500).

Accommodation

Dumaguete has plenty of inexpensive accommodation in the city centre or within walking distance of it, but rooms can get booked up fast in high season. Another option is to base yourself in Dauin (see p.307) and see Dumaguete on a day-trip – there are plenty of jeepneys and buses going back and forth between the two most hours of the day and night.

Bethel Guest House Rizal Blvd ℡035/225-2000, ⓦwww.bethelguesthouse.com. In an excellent location on the seafront, this modern four-storey building has clean studio rooms and doubles, some with a sea view (for which you'll pay extra). Rooms at the front are big and bright, with picture windows. Efficient and friendly staff, and a reasonable restaurant. Free in-room wi-fi. ❸

Coco Grande Hibbard Ave, a short walk north from Silliman University ℡035/422-0746. Under the same ownership as *Coco Grove* on Siquijor and *Apo Island Resort* on Apo, this is easily the most stylish place in town. The spacious rooms are attractively styled and come with a/c, cable TV and fridge, but are in need of some TLC. Free wi-fi in the lobby. ❸

Harold's Mansion 205 Hibbard Ave, a short walk north from Silliman University ℡035/225-8000, ⓦwww.haroldsmansion.com. Owned by affable adventurer Harold Biglete, this rambling hostel offers a relaxed atmosphere and some great-value rooms. A/c rooms (❸) have cable TV, private shower with hot and cold water, free wi-fi and included breakfast. Fan rooms are cheaper, but may be preferable as the a/c units can be noisy. A rooftop café and chill-out area should be completed in 2011. Harold is a great source of travel information and can make arrangements to visit the Twin Lakes, climb Mt Talinis, dive Apo Island or pretty much anything else you can think of. Dorm beds (P250), rooms ❶

Hotel Nicanor San José St ℡035/226-3330, ⓦwww.hotelnicanor.com. The newest addition to Dumaguete's hotel line-up has modern, comfortable rooms with a/c, cable TV, hot showers and free wi-fi. Standard rooms are windowless making it worth the extra P200 to upgrade to a bigger superior room. ❷

Hotel Palwa Locsin St ℡035/422-8995, ⓦwww.hotelpalwa.com. Excellent budget option with small but nicely styled a/c rooms with flat-screen TV. There's a pleasant café with free wi-fi in the lobby. ❷

Moving on from Dumaguete

By plane
There are daily flights to Manila with Philippine Airlines (2 daily). Cebu Pacific has one Manila and one Cebu flight each day.

By ferry
Oceanjet has daily fast ferries to Cebu, Siquijor, Tagbilaran and Dapitan on Mindanao. Delta Fast Ferries also operate fast craft to Siquijor. George & Peter Lines and Cokaliong both operate less frequent slow boats to Cebu and Dapitan.

By bus
Ceres Liner (℡035/225-9030) operates buses all over Negros, and also to Cebu via Oslob. For bus departures to the north of the island, it's worth making sure you get on an express bus, shaving a few hours from journey times.

The City

Dumaguete isn't a city of major sights, just a pleasant place to relax for a day or two. Dominated by the respected **Silliman University**, the oldest Protestant university in the Philippines, the city has a casual campus feel. Much of Silliman's reputation has been built on the work of its marine laboratory which has spearheaded efforts to protect the island's mangroves and stop illegal fishing. The university also has an interesting **anthropological museum** (Mon–Fri 9am–4pm; free) housing some Song and Ming dynasty porcelain and relics from minority tribes in the Philippines. The museum is in the Assembly Hall (go through the university gate on Hibbard Avenue and past the fountain). On the other side of campus, near the Silliman Medical Centre, **Centrop** (daily 9am–5pm; P10) offers a glimpse of Negros wildlife, including a reticulated python, long-tailed macaques and warty pigs.

Away from the university and seaside promenade, Dumaguete is centred on the grand **St Catherine of Alexandria Cathedral** which dominates Quezon Park. The cathedral was originally built in 1754, although the current version dates from 1957. Standing next to the cathedral, the **belfry** was completed in 1867, and its statue of the Lady of Lourdes is a popular site of worship in its own right.

Back on the seafront, a walk south along Rizal Boulevard and across the Banica River bridge brings you past the Ceres Liner bus terminal to the **Dumaguete Cockpit Arena**, where fights are held at weekends, usually on Sundays after church, and sometimes on weekday evenings. Just south of here the new Robinson's Mall is packed with the usual array of clothing outlets, fast-food joints, ATMs and internet cafés.

Eating and drinking

Dumaguete has an expanding food scene which features everything from fresh seafood stalls to fine European cuisine. **Nightlife** is mostly focused on Rizal Boulevard, particularly *Why Not Music Box* (Wed, Fri & Sat night cover charge), although, like many bars in Dumaguete, the scene gets a little sleazy here as the night wears on. Other seafront places for a drink include *Bogart's*, *Coco Amigos*, *Blue Monkey Grill* and *Hayahay*.

Café San Antonio San Juan St. Atmospheric place for a decent cup of coffee spread over two buildings, one of which has a traditional wooden facade. Daily 8am–8pm.

Casablanca Rizal Blvd ☏035/422-4080. Austrian-owned restaurant which offers fine European cuisine to a mainly expat clientele. Maybe not a place for the environmentally conscious as all of the meat is imported, however, the signature (Brazilian) Steak Casablanca with wasabi mash (P485) is excellent. The movie-themed restaurant also has its own bakery, a decent wine list, and a changing daily menu. Daily 8am–midnight.

Hayahay 201 Flores Ave, a few hundred metres north of the ferry port ☏035/225-1651. Lively pizza restaurant next to *Lab-as* (see below) which has nightly live music and stays open late. The extensive menu features some interesting options including fruit pizza (banana, mango and mozzarella; P235). Daily 10am–10pm.

Lab-as 201 Flores Ave. A few hundred metres north of the ferry port ☏035/225-1651. Deservedly Dumaguete's most popular seafood restaurant, *Lab-as* serves super-fresh fish, shrimps, squid and crab which can either be enjoyed in the cosy wooden interior, or outside looking over the road to the ocean. Daily 10am–10pm.

Sans Rival 1 San José St ☏035/225-4440. Lovely little teahouse which serves tea, coffee, shakes, sandwiches and cakes. Daily 9am–7.30pm.

Listings

Airlines Philippine Airlines has offices at the airport, as does Cebu Pacific who also have an office on Governor Perdices St, just south of Quezon Park.

Banks There are a number of banks with ATMs, including BPI on Governor Perdices St opposite Quezon Park and UCPB (United Coconut Planters Bank), Union Bank and Land Bank, all on the western edge of the city centre in Real St. Around the corner there's an Allied Bank and a Metrobank opposite one another on Locsin St.

Car rental Dumaguete Cars (☎035/424-8268) rents out cars with or without driver from P1900/day.

Ferries Ticket offices for Cokaliong, Delta, George & Peter Lines and Oceanjet are all at the port.

Hospitals Dumaguete's best hospital is the Silliman Medical Centre (☎035/420-2000) on Venencio Aldecoa Rd.

Immigration The office for visa extensions is in the Lu Dega Building, 38 Dr V. Locsin St (☎035/225-4401).

Internet access As you'd expect of a university town, there's no shortage of net cafés. One of the nicest places to get online is *Noriter Café* on Santa Catalina St, but there are also plenty of places around the university, including *Scooby's*

Internet on Real St, and *World Beat Net* on the airport road.

Post The post office on Santa Catalina St offers poste restante.

Police The main police station is at the west end of Locsin St near the Central Bank.

Travel agents To arrange trips to nearby attractions such as the Twin Lakes, or dolphin- and whale-spotting tours from Bais, there are a number of decent travel agencies and tour operators in town. *Harold's Mansion* runs good budget trips, while for more adventurous trips Dumaguete Outdoors (☎035/226-2110, ⓦwww .dumagueteoutdoors.com) on Noblefranca St is recommended and can also arrange Mount Kanlaon ascents.

Bais and Twin Lakes

The town of **BAIS**, about 40km to the north of Dumaguete, is a good place to see dolphins and whales in Bais Bay as they migrate through the Tanon Strait separating Negros from Cebu; March to September is the most promising time of year. The best accommodation here is at *La Planta Hotel* in Mabini Street (☎035/752-0307; ❺), a quaint and cosy place in a whitewashed old building that used to be the city's power plant.

A walk to the **Twin Lakes**, Balinsasayao and Danao, makes an excellent but strenuous day-trip; most hotels in Dumaguete and many of the resorts in Bais will help find a guide and arrange transport to the start of the trek. The lakes lie nestled in a jungled crater a 15km hike west from the main coastal road. The little town of **San José**, nearly midway between Dumaguete and Bais, is where you actually start heading inland for the lakes, taking you past a couple of waterfalls where you can swim and through settlements of the indigenous Bukidnon people who inhabit the area.

Dauin and around

South of Dumaguete is beach-and-dive-resort country, with a decent range of accommodation. However, beaches are brown sand and the sea can be choppy from November to May, which makes the nearby island of Siquijor a more appealing prospect for pure beach enthusiasts. This said, divers will find the quality of nearby dive sites is more than adequate compensation. **DAUIN** is a popular port of call twenty minutes from Dumaguete. The beach has a dramatic backdrop of palm trees and ruined watchtowers built in the nineteenth century as protection against raiding Moro pirates. Buses and jeepneys leave Dumaguete for Dauin from either the Ceres terminal or the area around the market.

About fifteen minutes southwest of Dauin by road – 20km from Dumaguete – one of the most unusual **markets** in the Philippines is held every Wednesday in the seaside barrio of **Malatapay**. Buyers and sellers at Malatapay market, also known as Zamboanguita market, still use the traditional native barter system, with farmers from the surrounding villages and Bukidnon tribespeople from the interior meeting with fishermen and housewives to swap everything for anything – livestock, fish, exotic fruit, strange vegetables and household items. Most of the resorts in Dauin arrange trips to the market, but you'll have to be up bright and early: the bartering begins at first light and is usually over well before noon.

If you want to make a day of it, combine a trip to the market with a visit to **Tambobo Beach**, a little further along the coast near **Siaton**. Tambobo is a

Apo Island and other dive sites

Tiny, volcanic **Apo Island**, 7km off the south coast of Negros, has become a prime destination for divers, most of whom head out for the day from Dumaguete, Dauin or Siquijor. Site of one of the Philippines' first and most successful marine reserves, Apo has a series of reefs teeming with marine life, from the smallest nudibranch to the largest deepwater fish. Snorkelling in the sanctuary costs P150 per person, while diving costs P300. The sanctuary area is on the island's southeast coast, while much of the flat land to the north is occupied by the only village, home to four hundred fisherfolk and farmers. Non-divers needn't be bored; Apo has some fantastic snorkelling and it's a great little island to explore on foot.

Most tourists visiting Apo take an organized trip from Dumaguete or Bais, though you can travel independently on one of the regular bangkas from Silliman Beach in Dumaguete and from Malatapay (see p.307). The trip takes about 45 minutes and the price should be P1500 for 5–6 people. There are only two places to **stay** on the island: *Liberty's Resort* (⑨) has a dive shop, dorms and rooms with private or shared bathrooms overlooking the ocean, while *Apo Island Beach Resort* (☏035/225-5490, ⓦwww.apoislandresort.com; ⑤) has lovely cottage rooms right on the beach, plus dorm beds (P700) and diving (P1300–1400 per dive).

Among other dive sites, **Calong-Calong Point** off the southern tip of Negros is known for its dazzling number of smaller reef fish. Nearby is **Tacot**, a tricky deep dive where sharks are common. From the coastal towns to the south of Dumaguete you can take a bangka to Siquijor (see p.292), where sites such as **Sandugan Point** and **San Juan** go as deep as 65m, and where you can expect to see tuna, barracuda and sharks plus, from March to August, manta rays. You can arrange trips to these sites through the dive operators in Dauin (see below) or Dumaguete.

beautiful palm-fringed crescent of glistening sand, a great place to spend a lazy afternoon swimming and snorkelling. Again, you can organize trips at most of the resorts, or you can hop on any jeepney from Dumaguete or Dauin going south along the coast. Ask to get off at Siaton, where you can either walk or take a tricycle to the beach itself.

Accommodation

Atlantis Beach Resort Dauin ☏035/425-2327, ⓦwww.atlantishotel.com. A/c cottages with TV, mini-bar and private bathrooms set amid lovely gardens, and for a little more, you can get sea views. *Atlantis* is primarily a dive resort, though it offers non-divers a large pool, loungers on the sand and day-trips to Dumaguete, Bais (for dolphin- and whale-watching) and Apo Island. ⑦

Atmosphere South of Dauin ☏035/425-2048, ⓦwww.atmosphereresorts.com. British-owned *Atmosphere* is easily the most upmarket place in this part of the world. Beautiful cottages with state-of-the-art facilities and wonderful outdoor bathrooms are spread through well-manicured

gardens. There's also a brand-new dive shop, a good restaurant and an infinity pool. ⑨

El Dorado Beach Resort Dauin ☏035/425-2274, ⓦwww.eldoradobeachresort.com. Large resort with family rooms, apartments and romantic premium rooms with four-poster beds and jacuzzis. There's a swimming pool, dive centre and a native-style restaurant. ⑤

Pura Vida Next to *El Dorado*, Dauin ☏035/425-2274, ⓦwww.pura-vida.ph. Stylish option with a range of tasteful native huts, a lovely beachside pool and free wi-fi in reception and at the restaurant. ⑥

Sipalay and around

Nearly 200km south of Bacolod, on the heel of Negros, **SIPALAY** is the access point for the lovely resorts of **Sugar Beach**, a few kilometres north of town, and

Punto Ballo to the south, the latter of which offers great snorkelling and diving from the shoreline.

Sipalay's historical focal point is the plaza and the church, but these days most activity centres around its pier and the main drag, Alvarez Street, where there are numerous canteens, bakeries and convenience stores. There's a small **tourist office** at the beach end of Alvarez Street where you can enquire about transport and accommodation. Ceres **buses** for Bacolod and Bayawan (for Dumaguete) stop outside of the *Sipalay Suites* hotel (T034/473-0350; ❷–❹) on Mercedes Boulevard. Given the proximity of the beaches there's really no need to stay here, but if you arrive very late at night, it offers the best (albeit overpriced) accommodation in town. The best **dining** in town is to be found at *Driftwood City* on the town beach, and at *Pat's Cantina* on Alvarez Street. For snacks Jamont Supermarket under *Sipalay Suites* has surprisingly well-stocked shelves. **Internet** can be found at *Lance's* on G.P. Avarez Street, which branches off Alvarez Street opposite *Pat's Cantina*.

Punta Ballo

Punto Ballo can be reached by tricycle from Sipalay (P150 direct with a driver, or P300 through a resort), and has a decent selection of resorts, the best of which are *Artistic Diving Beach Resort* (T034/453-2710, Wwww.artisticdiving.com; ❸–❻), which has beachfront accommodation in fan or air-conditioned rooms; and *Easy Diving* (T917/300-0381, Wwww.sipalay.com; ❸–❼), which offers simple fan rooms and pleasant air-conditioned stone cottages in attractive hillside gardens looking down to the white sand beach. Both are dive resorts (set up by Swiss Germans) and offer PADI courses and trips to a range of nearby dive sites including wrecks. *Easy Diving* has the best **restaurant** in Punta Ballo.

Further south, **Campomanes Bay**, also known as Maricalum Bay, is a natural harbour that's said to be deep enough to hide a submarine. Shaped like a horseshoe and 2km wide, it's backed by steep cliffs and accessible by tricycle from Sipalay and then on foot. It's a fantastic day-trip with some good snorkelling and scuba diving, though there's no accommodation here.

Sugar Beach

Beautiful **Sugar Beach** may not have the white sand and azure waters of Boracay, but it offers a remote tranquillity, a relaxed vibe and a good selection of small resorts ranging from ultra-budget to mid-range. All of the resorts can arrange bangka collection from Sipalay though getting here independently can make for an adventure: you can either take a chartered bangka from Sipalay (P150–300 depending on your bargaining skills and the time of day) or hop off the bus at Montilla and hire a tricycle to take you as far as Nauhang (P50), from where you'll

---

Moving on from Sipalay

There are hourly **buses** for Bacolod, but only one direct bus to Dumaguete which leaves at 4am. Presuming you don't want to miss a night's sleep, your best bet for Dumaguete is to take the first Hinoba-an- (40min; P32) or Bayawan- (2hr; P107) bound bus and change. The road is now almost entirely paved, with just a few bumpy sections between Hinoba-an and Bayawan, and the whole journey from Sipalay to Dumaguete should take less than five hours. An alternative, but equally attractive route is to take a bus north to Kabankalan, and change buses to head across the mountains. The journey should take around the same duration and many travellers who visit Sipalay from Dumaguete choose to do a loop, taking the mountain road there and the coastal route back.

need to rent a paddle boat (should be P5 but expect to pay up to P20 if you arrive after dark) for the five-minute trip across the river and then walk the last few hundred metres to the resorts.

Accommodation and eating

Except for *Fiesta Cove*, all of the below resorts have their own restaurants, and these are the only places to eat.

Bermuda Next to *Takutuka* ☎0920/529-2582, ⓦwww.bermuda-beach-resort.com. *Bermuda* offers spacious and tastefully decorated fan-cooled beachfront bungalows and smaller a/c rooms at the rear of the property. The restaurant serves Italian and Thai cuisine, but the Filipino dishes are recommended. Wi-fi costs P100/hr. ❷

Driftwood Village Halfway along the beach ☎0920/900-3663, ⓦwww.driftwood-village.com. A backpacker favourite, Swiss-owned *Driftwood* has a wide range of budget huts set in palms behind the beach. There's also a basic dorm (P300) and a café. ❷

Fiesta Cove At the far northern end of the beach. ☎0927/581-4999. One of the few locally owned places on Sugar Beach, *Fiesta* has modern, clean and comfortable second-floor rooms. Each of the four rooms has a/c, TV and hot water, plus a balcony with beach views, but there's no restaurant. ❹

Sulu Sunset Beach Resort Towards the northern end of the beach ☎0919/716-7182,

ⓦwww.sulusunset.com. German-owned *Sulu* has simple but attractive fan-cooled cottages which look straight out onto the beach. The restaurant serves Filipino food, a few European dishes including schnitzel, and cold beer! Free transfer from Sipalay if you stay three nights or more. ❷

Takutuka Lodge The furthest south of the resorts ☎0920/230-9174, ⓦwww.takutuka-lodge.com. This wonderfully wacky *Takutuka* is the result of the unhinged creativity of its Swiss-German owners. Each room features one-of-a-kind furnishings, from the pink Cadillac bed in the Superstar room, to the microphone light fittings in Rockadelic. All rooms have verandas, and given the quality and originality, rates are very reasonable. For a/c or hot showers you simply add P200–300/night. The restaurant serves the best food on the beach and the *salamizza* (salami rosti) is particularly recommended. Wi-fi costs P50/half-hour. *Takutuka* also has the only dive centre on Sugar Beach. ❸

Danjugan Island and Punta Bulata

Lying 3km off the southwest coast of Negros and accessible through the small town of **Bulata** about 10km north of Sipalay, **Danjugan** (pronounced "Danhoogan") **Island** is a little gem. Managed as a nature reserve by the Philippine Reef and Rainforest Foundation NGO, it's fringed completely by vibrant coral reefs and so well forested that it's home to such rarities as the white-bellied sea eagle and the barebacked fruit bat. There are also a number of small islets, including Manta Island and Manta Rock, and three offshore reefs that are home to about 270 species of fish.

Most people visit Danjugan as a **day-trip** (P1500 including transfers, forest treks and kayaking) from the mainland but **staying overnight** (P2500) is a magical experience. Accommodation is available in five "eco-cabanas", made of mud brick. Facilities are basic (no running water and solar-powered electricity) but perfectly comfortable and you'll be lulled to sleep by the sound of lapping waves on the beach. Meals and drinks as well as scuba diving can be arranged in advance – visit ⓦwww.prrcf.org for more information and bookings.

The departure point for the island is the pleasant *Punta Bulata White Beach Resort* (☎034/433-5160, ⓦwww.puntabulata.com; ❻), accessed along a 2km dirt road from Bulata town. The resort has a good range of comfortable huts, rooms, and family cabins for six, all air-conditioned. There's also a pleasant bar and a hillside native-style restaurant with ocean views.

Guimaras

Separated from the Panay mainland by the narrowest slither of ocean, the small island of **GUIMARAS** is best known for producing the tastiest mangoes in the Philippines. Yet for all its provincial simplicity Guimaras is much more than a day-trip destination. There are some good, affordable **resorts**, exceptional **beaches** – especially around **Nueva Valencia** on the southwest coast – and a few enticing **islands** offshore. The undulating **interior** and its numerous trails have also made the island a popular destination for mountain bikers. There's also a smattering of history, with defiant old Spanish churches and the country's only Trappist monastery. During the Filipino–American War, General Douglas MacArthur, then a first lieutenant, built the wharf at **Buenavista**, which is still being used today by ferries.

Guimaras was badly affected by an **oil spill** from the the tanker, *Solar 1*, which sank off the northern coast of the island in August 2006. Although today there is little evidence of the spill to the casual observer, and beaches look back to their pristine best, it will take decades for the island's mangrove ecosystems (and fish stocks) to fully recover.

Arrival, information and transport

Frequent bangkas (P13) leave **from Ortiz Wharf in Iloilo City** on Panay and take just 20 minutes to reach Hoskyn Port on the west coast of Guimaras. Some resorts can send a bangka to collect you at Iloilo, which usually adds about P1500 to your accommodation bill. Coming from Negros there is a daily bangka (P70) **from Valladolid** south of Bacolod, to **Cabalagnan** on Guimaras' south coast, and more frequent services from **Pulupandan to Suclaran** (P50) on the east coast.

On arrival there's a small **tourist office** at Hoskyn Port (daily 7.30am–4.30pm; ☎033/238-1500). The Philippine National **Police** station is in the barangay of Alaguisoc in Jordan. Medical care is better than you might expect, with a provincial **hospital** in San Miguel, Jordan, and others at Buenavista and Nueva Valencia. Outside of the resorts, the easiest place to make phone calls and use the internet is the island's small capital, **San Miguel**, where you'll find *Gaitan Internet Café*. San Miguel also has the island's only **ATM**, at the Land Bank.

Local **transport** comprises the usual three suspects: tricycle, jeepney and bangka. Some resorts also have motorbikes and bicycles for hire, and given how quiet the roads are, this is a good way to get around, although it's quite easy to get lost. An easier way to see Guimaras by bicycle is to take a **mountain bike tour** through Panay Adventure Travel & Tours, who are based in Iloilo (see p.320). Tours cost US$55 per person and include round-trip transfers, bike hire, guide and lunch.

Accommodation

Guimaras is a small enough island that it doesn't matter too much where you base yourself. Even if you choose the solitude of a resort on one of the smaller islands nearby, it's easy to hop on a bangka back to Guimaras itself if you want to explore.

Mainland

Baras Beach Resort 10km from San Miguel on a sheltered inlet on the island's west coast ☎0917/241-1422, ⊛baras.willig-web.com. A pretty little hideaway with fan double cottages on stilts, overlooking the bay and just a few steps away from the ocean. The food, almost all of it grown or caught by the staff, is good; there's not much of an à la carte menu, but there are ample buffet lunches and dinners for around P200. To get there either call

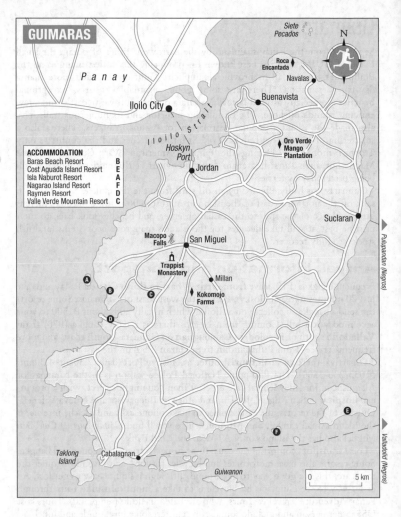

ACCOMMODATION

Baras Beach Resort	B
Cost Aguada Island Resort	E
Isla Naburot Resort	A
Nagarao Island Resort	F
Raymen Resort	D
Valle Verde Mountain Resort	C

ahead to arrange a pick-up or take a bangka (about P300) from Puyo wharf in Nueva Valencia. ❷

Raymen Resort Alubihod, Nueva Valencia ☎033/396-0383. On the island's southwest coast, the *Raymen Resort* has clean a/c rooms with TV (❺) and hot showers in a building set back from the beach, as well as cheaper fan rooms. For meals there's a simple canteen at the resort which serves set meals for P85. The resort is 40min by road south from Jordan (P400 by tricycle), or P3000 if you charter a bangka from Iloilo. Avoid weekends if you don't like karaoke. ❷

Valle Verde Mountain Resort Off the San Miguel to Nueva Valencia road ☎0918/730-3446. If you

can bear to be away from the beach, friendly *Valle Verde* offers simple rooms set in a lush valley looking down towards pretty Lawi Bay. There are only seven rooms and they range from very basic fan huts to (slightly) more comfortable a/c cottages (❹). As well as a natural spring at the bottom of the hill, there's also a large and inviting spring-water pool in the middle of the resort (P50 for non-residents). There's also motorbike hire (P600/day). ❷

Offshore

Costa Aguada Island Resort Around 20min off the east coast of Guimaras by boat, on the island of

Inampulugan ☎034/434-4541, ⓦwww.costa aguadaislandresort.com. Swish complex with spacious duplex as well as detached bamboo cottages, each with bathroom, telephone and balcony, plus a swimming pool, a beachside bamboo restaurant, a poolside bar, riding stables and tennis courts. ❹

Isla Naburot Resort On an island called Naburot off the west coast of Guimaras ☎0918/909-8500, ⓦislanaburot.multiply.com. Beautiful and romantic, *Isla Naburot* has six private cottages that were built partly from flotsam and jetsam, with driftwood for window frames and shells for walls. There's no electricity; after dark you'll have to read by paraffin lamp and eat by candlelight. All the food is caught or grown locally and prepared over primitive charcoal stoves. Activities include fishing, swimming, island-hopping, snorkelling and scuba diving. ❽

Nagarao Island Resort Nagarao Island off the southeast coast of Guimaras ☎033/329-0078, ⓦwww.nagaraoresort.com. Accessible only by bangka, so either call ahead for pick-up (P2300/ boat) or head for the barangay of St Isidro on Guimaras and take a ten-minute bangka ride. All rooms in the native-style hillside or beachfront bungalows have fan and private bathroom with shower, and there's a restaurant with room service. There are plenty of sports facilities – freshwater pool, tennis court, jogging paths, plus sailing and other activities on offer. ❼

Around the island

Tourists only visit **Jordan**, in the north of the island, because most bangkas from Iloilo arrive at Hoskyn Port 2km to the west. Nearby **San Miguel**, the capital, is rarely visited at all but is the handiest place hereabouts if you need cash or to make a phone call. There's no accommodation in either town and not much in the way of food – numerous no-nonsense **carinderias** offer little more than *adobo* and rice. If you do need some sustenance, try *Gladys' Refreshment House* and *Sailor's*, at the wharf in Jordan while in San Miguel you can select from *Victor's*, *Edna's*, *Vangie's* and *Gonzaga's*. There's also a small police outpost at Jordan wharf.

Guimaras has some marvellous waterfalls in its hinterland, the best of which is **Macopo Falls**, fifteen minutes to the south of Jordan and ten minutes northwest of San Miguel by tricycle, where you can pay P5 to swim in a beautifully chilly mountain pool formed by water gushing through a rocky gorge from high above. The path to the falls was being renovated at the time of writing but should reopen soon.

Another place well worth a visit is **Our Lady of the Philippines Trappist Monastery**, which lies on the main road southwest from San Miguel and twenty minutes by jeepney from Macopo Falls; you can easily see the falls and the monastery in a day-trip. Founded in 1972 by Americans, it's the only Trappist monastery in the Philippines. The monks seem to do very nicely, with orchards that grow assorted tropical fruit and an interesting souvenir shop where banana fries (P22), cashews (P30), guava jelly (P64), mango jam (P70) and even Holy Water (P25) are sold under the Trappist Monastic Products brand name.

Navalas and the north

The barangay of **NAVALAS** on the island's northern coast has two interesting sights, one religious, the other an imperious temple to Mammon. The seventeenth-century **Navalas Church**, an atmospherically decrepit relic of the Spanish regime, is a good starting point for exploring this coast. A short walk away on a promontory overlooking Iloilo Strait stands a villa known as **Roca Encantada** (Enchanted Rock) or, more sneeringly, Lopezville, vacation house of the wealthy Lopez clan who hail from Iloilo. Opposite the promontory is a pictur-esque group of coral islets called **Siete Pecados** (Isles of the Seven Sins) that can be reached in thirty minutes from Navalas or the neighbouring north coast barangays of Bacjao and San Miguel (not to be confused with the island's capital). The largest of the islets has an impressive house perched on top, but the others are bare. There are no beaches but it's worth the trip for the snorkelling.

The mango plantations

You could hardly leave Guimaras without a visit to one of the **mango plantations**. All have just the right soil, elevation and exposure to the elements to produce succulent fruit ready for the main harvest season in April and May. The most visitor-friendly plantation on the island is **Kokomojo Farms** near **Millan** (T033/337-7620 or 02/759-2302), roughly in the centre of Guimaras, where the owners will show you around personally if you call ahead. If your interest in mangoes runs deep, you can also visit the **National Mango Research and Development Centre** (T033/237-0912) just west of San Miguel on the road to Lawi.

Offshore islands

Another good day-trip is exploring the **beautiful islands** and islets in the south of Guimaras; all you need to do is rent a bangka which can be arranged at the port or through any of the resorts for around P300 per hour. Off the southeast coast there's Sereray Island and Nao-wai Island, both with tiny sandy coves where you can picnic and swim. Off the southwest coast is Taklong Island, a marine reserve whose mangroves and beds of sea grass are breeding grounds for hundreds of marine species.

Panay

The substantial, vaguely triangular island of **Panay** has been largely bypassed by tourism, perhaps because everyone seems to get sucked towards **Boracay** off its northern tip instead. There's room enough on Panay, though, for plenty of discovery and adventure: the island has a huge coastline and a mountainous, jungled interior that has yet to be fully mapped.

Panay comprises four provinces, **Antique** ("ant-ee-kay") on the west coast, **Aklan** in the north, **Capiz** in the northeast and **Iloilo** ("ee-lo-ee-lo") running along the east coast to the capital of province, **Iloilo City** in the south. The province that interests most tourists is Aklan, whose capital **Kalibo** is the site of the big and brash **Ati-Atihan festival**, held in the second week of January (see box below). This doesn't mean you should give the rest of Panay the brushoff. The northeast coast from **Concepcion** to **Batad** offers bangka access to a number of unspoilt islands while on the west side you'll find **Antique**, a raw, bucolic province of picturesque beaches and scrubby mountains.

Getting to Panay

There are four major **airports** on Panay, all served by daily flights from Manila. Panay's principal airport is in Iloilo on the south coast and has flights from Manila, Cebu and Davao. On the north coast there are airports at Roxas, Kalibo and Caticlan. Roxas only has a few flights per day, while Kalibo and particularly Caticlan are mainly used by visitors on their way to Boracay. Caticlan is a tiny airport but its proximity to Boracay has made it very popular and it receives upwards of thirty flights per day, the bulk of which are from Manila, although there are also services from Cebu.

Passenger **ferries** operated by Cokaliong and Trans Asia Shipping leave from Cebu for Iloilo, whilst Oceanjet, Supercat and Weesam run fast boats for the short trip between Bacolod and Iloilo. In the north Caticlan is served by boats from Roxas on Mindoro Oriental, part of the popular bus-ferry-bus-ferry route from Manila to Boracay. Coming from Romblon there are bangkas to Caticlan and Boracay from Looc on Tablas Island, or you can take a bangka to Carabao Island, north of Boracay, and from there to Boracay itself.

Ati-Atihan: keep on going, no tiring

Ati-Atihan is a quasi-religious mardi gras held every January in Kalibo. The culmination of the two-week event is a procession through the streets on the third Sunday of January, a sustained three-day, three-night frenzy of carousing and dancing. Transvestites bring out their best frocks and schoolgirls with hats made of coconuts join aborigines, celebrities and priests in a fancy-dress. Throw in the unending beat of massed drums and the average Filipino's predisposition for a good party, and the result is a flamboyant alfresco rave that claims to be the biggest and most prolonged in the country. The Ati-Atihan mantra *Hala Bira, Puera Pasma* translates as "Keep on going, no tiring."

The festival's **origins** can be traced to 1210, when refugees from Borneo fled north to Panay. Panay's Negrito natives, known as Atis, sold them land and both parties celebrated the deal with a feast, which was then repeated year on year. The fancy-dress element derives from the lighter-skinned Borneans blacking up their faces in affectionate imitation of the Atis. Later, Spanish friars co-opted the festival in honour of the **Santo Niño**, spreading the word among islanders that the baby Jesus had appeared to help drive off a pirate attack. It was a move calculated to hasten the propagation of Catholicism throughout the Philippines, and it worked. Ati-Atihan has since become so popular that similar festivals have cropped up all over the Visayas. Historians generally agree, however, that the Kalibo Ati-Atihan is the real thing.

Iloilo City and around

ILOILO CITY is a useful transit point for Guimaras Island (see p.311) and has good ferry connections to many other Visayan islands, but there's nothing to keep you here for more than a day or two. The city's handful of sights include a couple of reasonably interesting heritage-style museums. If you're visiting in January, the **Dinagyang** festival, loosely based on Kalibo's Ati-Atihan, adds some extra frenzy to the city during the fourth weekend. Three kilometres out of town, the old areas of **Molo** and **Jaro** both make pleasant distractions. The former has a church made of coral and the latter an impressive Spanish-era cathedral. In Jaro you can also wander among the old colonial homes of sugar barons and mooch through a number of dusty old antique shops, where prices are lower than in Manila.

There are also more adventurous pursuits to be enjoyed around Iloilo, including trekking and caving in Bulabog Puti-an National Park, and trips to local Ati villages. Day-trips can be most easily arranged through Panay Adventures Travel & Tours (see Listings, p.320).

Arrival and orientation

Iloilo's new **airport** is at Cabutuan, 15km from the city. A taxi from the airport to the city centre costs about P200, or you can take a share-van for P50 per person. Slow **ferries** from Cebu, Manila and Mindanao arrive at the wharf on the eastern edge of the city, a fifteen-minute walk or short jeepney/tricycle ride from General Luna Street. Fast ferries for Bacolod arrive beyond the post office on Muelle Loney Street. Finally Ortiz wharf, used by ferries from Jordan on Guimaras, is at the southern end of Ortiz Street near the market. Most buses now arrive at the new Tagbac **bus terminal** on the outskirts of town, from where it's a 20-minute ride into town by taxi or tricycle.

Iloilo has little to distinguish it from any other urban area in the country, with most of its central streets a claustrophobic jungle of fast-food restaurants, malls and overhead telephone cables. The city centre occupies a thin strip of land on the southern bank of the Iloilo River, with views across to Guimaras, but it's worth

ILOILO

◄ A Airport, Tagbac Bus Terminal & SM City

◄ B & Jaro

ACCOMMODATION

Amigo Terrace Hotel	G
Century 21	F
Chito's Hotel	H
Highway 21 Pension House	A
Hotel del Rio	D
Iloilo Business Hotel	C
Iloilo City Inn	B
Sarabia Charter Pension House	E
Sarabia Manor Hotel	E

RESTAURANTS & BARS

Afrique's	1
Al Dente	E
Butot Balat	3
Crave Burger	C
Freska	C
Green Mango	5
Jaq's Bar	C
Marina	2
Rooftop Brewery	C
Ted's Old Timer Lapaz Batchoy	4

Slow Ferry Port

Parola Wharf

Ortiz Wharf

RIZAL STREET

FORT SAN PEDRO DRIVE

MUELLE LONEY STREET

ZAMORA STREET

DE LA RAMA STREET

Bacolod Fast Ferry Terminals

San José Church

Landbank

City Hall

Plaza Libertad

Central Market

University

J.M. BASA STREET

ORTIZ STREET

Metrobank

IZNART STREET

Marymart Mall

YULO STREET

SOLIS STREET

Atrium Mall

Museo Iloilo

Forbes Bridge

Provincial Capitol Building

BONIFACIO DRIVE

Gaisano City Mall

Iloilo River

St Paul's Hospital

PNB

BPI

SM Mall

VALERIA STREET

Mercury Drug Store

Shark Byte Café

Jeepney Terminal

QUEZON STREET

City Police

GENERAL LUNA STREET

MABINI STREET

DELGADO STREET

IZNART STREET

Mercury Drug Store

Robinson's Place Shopping Mall

DE LEON STREET

RIZAL STREET

Iloilo Strait

Tavern Cyber Café

SAN AGUSTIN STREET

University of the Philippines

YBIERNAS AVENUE

TIMAWA AVENUE

TANZA STREET

All Seasons Travel & Tours

WEST AVENUE

Iloilo Doctors' Hospital

DIVERSION ROAD

M.H. DEL PILAR STREET

Ceres Liner Terminal

Smallville Commercial Complex

Molo Church

Iloilo Strait

N

◄ C Smallville Commercial Complex

▼ Molo (1km)

0   500 m

heading across the river for the dining and nightlife to be found at the Smallville Commercial Complex.

Information and transport

The city's helpful **tourist office** (Mon–Fri 8am–noon & 1–5pm; ℡033/335-0245) is in the grounds of the Capitol Building on Bonifacio Drive one block north of J.M. Basa Street next to the Museo Iloilo. There are plenty of taxis in Iloilo, but the city centre is compact enough to cover on foot. To get to the outlying areas of Molo and Jaro, there's a **jeepney terminal** on Ledesma Street.

Accommodation

Finding reasonably priced accommodation in Iloilo City isn't a problem, with much of it right in the city centre close to shops and transport.

Century 21 Quezon St ℡033/335-8821. Mid-sized glass-fronted building offering basic, affordable rooms with a/c and cable TV. Singles are among the cheapest in town for this sort of quality. Family rooms for four are good value at P1650. Free wi-fi in the lobby. ❷

Highway 21 Pension House General Luna St ℡033/335-1839 or 1840. Excellent budget choice close to the *Sarabia Manor Hotel* with modern rooms and staff who are on the ball. All rooms have a/c, cable TV and hot water, but some are windowless. Good location with lots of restaurants on the doorstep. Wi-fi costs P100 for 24hr. ❸

Hotel del Rio M.H. Del Pilar St, Molo ℡033/335-1171, ⓦwww.hoteldelrio.net. Stylish and very professional hotel in a pleasant location on the river. Standard rooms have a/c, fridge, cable TV, king-size bed and river views. Superior and deluxe rooms are newer and more tastefully styled (❼), but don't overlook the river. There's also a popular coffee shop and a good pool. ❺

Iloilo Business Hotel Benigno Aquino Ave, Smallville Commercial Complex ℡033/320-7972, ⓦwww.iloilobusinesshotel.com. This new hotel offers very modern and comfortable rooms in the heart of the city's newest restaurant and nightlife zone. All rooms are a/c and have safety deposit boxes, fridges and flat-screen TVs. Wi-fi is free in the lobby or costs P150 for 24hr in the room. ❺

Iloilo City Inn 113 Seminario St, Jaro ℡033/320-2186, ⓦwww.nagaraoresort.com. Owned by the same German-Filipina couple as *Nagarao Resort* on Guimaras, this friendly place enjoys a quiet location close to the sights in Jaro and has clean, comfortable a/c rooms at affordable prices. Downstairs, *Bavaria* serves good German food and beer and has wi-fi. The roof deck has views of the nearby cathedral. ❷

Sarabia Charter Pension House General Luna St ℡033/508-1853. Arguably the best budget option in town, the *Sarabia Charter* is in the same quiet complex as the *Sarabia Manor Hotel*. The small, simple rooms are set around a small garden, and guests are entitled to use the swimming pool at *Sarabia Manor*. ❷

Sarabia Manor Hotel General Luna St ℡033/335-1021, ⓦwww.sarabiamanorhotel .com. Iloilo's biggest hotel has seen better days, but is still worth considering for its vast array of rooms, pool and other facilities. All rooms come with a/c and have cable TV. Budget rooms (❸) are small and very dated, but the "economy" and travellers' rooms (❹) are good value. The Corporate rooms (❼–❽) are a considerable upgrade and also include breakfast. Promo rates are often available in all room categories. There's free wi-fi in the lobby or you can pay to use it in the room.

The City

The old residential and commercial buildings that survive in Iloilo City date back to Spanish and American colonial periods; they are mostly in J.M. Basa Street, which runs from Ledesma Street to the port area. In the southeastern quadrant of the city is **Plaza Libertad**, where the first flag of the Philippine Republic was raised in triumph after Spain surrendered the city on December 25, 1898. There's little to remind you of the history though – the square today is a concrete affair with fast-food restaurants and busy roads on all sides.

The only notable museum is the **Museo Iloilo** on Bonifacio Drive (Mon–Sat 8–11am & 2–5pm; P25). An engaging and clearly presented repository of Iloilo's cultural heritage, it has a diverse range of exhibits including fossils, shells and rocks

By plane

Cebu Pacific and Philippine Airlines each have 4 daily **flights** to Manila, whilst Airphil Express has three Manila flights and two for Cebu.

By ferry

Iloilo is a busy port city with good **ferry** connections. The most popular route is Iloilo–Bacolod, and Oceanjet, Supercat and Weesam each run 7–8 fast boats per day from wharfs on Muelle Loney Street. There are also less frequent and slower services to destinations further afield from the dock on Fort San Pedro Drive. Ferries for Cebu are operated by Cokaliong (3 weekly) and Trans Asia Shipping (daily) boats, while Superferry have boats for General Santos on Mindanao (1 weekly) and Manila (2 weekly). For **Guimaras**, there are big public bangkas (P13) leaving Ortiz wharf every thirty minutes for the short crossing to Jordan, starting at 5am.

By bus and taxi

Buses from the new Tagbac terminal connect Iloilo City to other towns on Panay. The most comfortable and reliable bus company is Ceres Liner (☎033/329-1223), which has frequent air-conditoned and ordinary services to Estancia (every 20min; 3hr 30min), Roxas (every 20min; 3hr), Kalibo (13 daily; 4hr) and Caticlan (13 daily; 5hr) in the north of Panay. For San José (every 30min; 2hr), capital of Antique in the west, and Libertad to the north, you'll need to head to the old Ceres Liner terminal on M.H. del Pilar Street in the west of town.

indicating the age of Panay Island, ornamental teeth, jewellery excavated from pre-Spanish burial sites, pottery from China and Siam, coffins, war relics and some modern art.

Molo

On the western edge of the city, the district of **Molo** makes for an interesting wander; it can be reached on foot from the city centre in twenty minutes (half that by tricycle or jeepney). In the sixteenth and seventeenth centuries Molo was a Chinese quarter like Parian in Manila. The main sight is **Molo Church** (St Anne's), a splendid nineteenth-century Gothic Renaissance example made of coral, with rows of female saints lining both sides of the aisle. Next door is the renowned **Asilo de Molo**, an orphanage (visits possible daily 10am–noon & 1–4pm; donation expected) where vestments are hand-embroidered by orphan girls under the tutelage of nuns.

Jaro

Another historical enclave worth exploring is **Jaro**, 3km north across the Forbes Bridge. You can get there on any jeepney marked Jaro or Tiko. Jaro's **plaza** is an inspiring little piece of old Asia, dominated by a dignified but crumbling old belfry that was partially destroyed by an earthquake in 1984. Opposite is the **Jaro Metro-politan Cathedral**, seat of the Catholic diocese in the Western Visayas, with its ivory-white stone facade, crooked bell tower of red brick and steps either side of the main doors leading up to a platform and the Shrine to the Divine Infant and Nuestra Señora de la Candelaria.

To the south of Jaro's plaza, the grandiose **Nelly Garden mansion**, stands back from Luna Street down a picturesque driveway lined with eucalyptus. The mansion, which has murals on the walls and a U-shaped dining room with a fountain in the middle, can only be visited by arrangement with the Iloilo tourist office. Nearby, Lourdes Dellota's on East Lopez Street (⊕033/337-4095) sells religious artefacts such as **santos**, and jewellery.

Eating and drinking

Iloilo City is one of the best places in the country to try seafood prepared the Filipino way. It's also known for a number of unique regional delicacies, including **pancit Molo soup**, a garlicky noodle soup containing pork dumplings, which is named after the Molo area of the city and is sold at numerous street stalls. **Batchoy**, an artery-hardening combination of liver, pork and beef with thin noodles, is also widely available.

For **nightlife** the Smallville Commercial Complex has everything from live bands at *Jaq's Bar*, to imported beers at the *Rooftop Brewery*. If you get peckish *Freska* has a range of *pulutan* (drinking snacks), or for something more substantial the burgers at *Crave Burger* are a lot tastier than you're average fast-food offering.

Afrique's Right behind the cathedral in Jaro. Atmospheric European restaurant in a lovely old colonial house. The menu is largely Italian and includes a huge range of pizzas along with specialities such as osso bucco pasta (P215). Daily 10am–10pm.

Al Dente In the *Sarabia Manor Hotel* ⊕033/336-7183. Stylish Italian restaurant serving tasty herb-roasted chicken (P145) and a range of delicious pasta dishes, all at very reasonable prices. Daily 11am–midnight.

Butot Balat Solis St ⊕033/509-6770. A haven of tropical tranquillity and greenery in the midst of the downtown mayhem, this popular restaurant offers candlelit dining under thatched *cabanas* surrounding a small pond. Dishes to try include chilli shrimps (P225), pork Bicol Express (P145), beef *kare-kare* (P285), or there's fish by weight. Daily noon–midnight.

Freska Smallville Commercial Complex, Benigno Aquino Drive ⊕033/321-3885. Bright, lively and fun restaurant serving traditional Ilonggo cuisine, including crispy fried *managat* (fish) with Guimaras

mango salad (P110/100g). *Freska* also serves "feast meals", which are good for 4 people, from P795, and the *pulutan* (drinking snacks) menu features oysters and *chicharon*. Daily 11am–3pm & 5.30pm–midnight.

Green Mango Plaza Libertad. Trendy Ilonggo fast-food chain with seven branches around the city, including one in Jaro Plaza and another in SM City Mall. The extensive menu covers everything from chicken or *bangus* barbecue (P69) to noodles (P60), *pandesal* (P39) and *halo-halo* (P55–75). Daily 8am–8pm.

Marina Benigno Aquino Ave, north of the river. The menu here includes oysters, lapu-lapu, all sorts of grilled meat and fish and some non-Visayan Filipino specials such as *kare-kare* (P118). Two can eat and have a few drinks for around P500, and there's live music every night. Daily 8am–1am.

Ted's Old Timer Lapaz Batchoy Valeria St. *Ted's* is *the* place to get an authentic helping of Ilonggo *batchoy* (P68). There's another branch on the ground floor of SM City Mall. Daily 10am–8pm.

Listings

Airlines Airphil Express (⊕033/508-5513), Cebu Pacific (⊕033/320-6582) and Philippine Airlines (⊕033/321-1333) all have ticket offices at the airport. Air tickets can also be obtained at travel agents or any of the city's Western Union offices.

Banks There are a countless banks with ATMs. BPI and PNB both have branches on Plaza Libertad and General Luna St, there's a Metrobank on Iznart St and there are also ATMs in the malls.

Ferries The main ticket offices are at the relevant docks (see Moving on opposite).

Hospital St Paul's Hospital is at the eastern end of General Luna St (⊕033/337-2741) close to the junction with Bonifacio Dr. Iloilo Doctors' Hospital is

a 5min drive to the west of the city centre in Timawa Ave (⊕033/337-7702).

Immigration The Bureau of Immigration is at the Old Customs House on Aduana St.

Internet access All of the big malls have internet cafés, including *Netopia* on the second floor of SM City, or you could try *Tavern Cyber Café* at the *Riverside Inn* on General Luna St, or *Shark Byte Café* on Yulo St.

Pharmacies There are pharmacies in every mall. There's also a large branch of Mercury Drug opposite St Paul's Hospital on General Luna St.

Post Iloilo's main post office is in Muelle Loney St, close to the junction with Guanco St, opposite the pier where boats leave for Jordan on Guimaras.

The south coast

Heading southwest from Iloilo City along the coastal road – the only road – takes you through the atmospheric Spanish-era towns of **Oton**, **Tigbauan**, **Guimbal**, **Miag-ao** and **San Joaquin**. Each one has an historic **church**, including the Baroque Tigbauan Church in Tigbauan (22km from Iloilo City) and Guimbal Roman Catholic Church in Guimbal (35km from Iloilo City), the latter of which stands close to a number of ruined seventeenth-century watchtowers. Pride of place, however, goes to **Miag-ao Church** (also known as the Church of Santo Tomas de Villanueva), built by the Augustinians between 1786 and 1797 as a fortress against Moro invasions. Declared a national landmark and a UNESCO World Heritage Site, the church is built of a local yellow-orange sandstone in Baroque-Romanesque style, a unique example of Filipino Rococo.

To visit the church towns of the southwest the easiest way is to hire a vehicle and driver in Iloilo for a day-trip, but if you have time on your hands then it's also simple enough to travel between the towns by public transport. All buses from Iloilo City bound for San Joaquin pass through Miag-ao (an hour's journey), and plenty of jeepneys also ply the west coast route.

There are a few options if you want to **stay** in the area. Closest to Iloilo, in Oton, is the upscale *Anhawan Beach Resort* (☎033/335-8949; ❼) which has a nice pool, spa, jet-skiing and horseriding. Further west in Tigbauan, *Coco Grove* (☎033/511-7909; ❷) has cheaper, passable air-conditioned and fan rooms, and in Guimbal, *Bantayan Beach Resort* (☎033/315-5009; ❷) has ordinary air-conditioned cottages and a Spanish-era watchtower on the property.

The west coast

Most of the west coast of Panay, made up largely of the province of **Antique**, is untouched by tourism. This is one of the poorest areas of the Philippines, with a solitary coastal road connecting a series of isolated villages and towns. It's an attractive coastline with a savage backdrop of jungled mountains which separate the province from the rest of Panay, and which are only just beginning to be explored and climbed. The journey along the province's coast, from **San José** in the south to **Libertad** in the north, provides an excellent opportunity to experience a simple provincial life, shielded from the rest of the Philippines by mountains on one side and sea on the other.

San José

SAN JOSÉ is a busy little port town whose major claim to fame – apart from being capital of Antique – seems to be that its cathedral has the tallest bell tower in Panay. There are no tourist sights here, just a chaotic wharf, a cracked plaza and a main street, the National Highway, lined with pawnshops, canteens and rice dealers. The town's annual **Binirayan Festival**, held from April 30 to May 2, commemorates the thirteenth-century landing of ten Malay chieftains who established the first Malayan settlement in the Philippines.

The **bus station** is in Isabel Street, 1km west of the centre and the **pier** is on the western edge of the town. There are daily ferries from here to Manila, as well as less frequent services to the Cuyo Islands in Palawan. *Centillion House* (☎036/540-9403; ❸) has clean, well-maintained rooms with air-conditioning and cable TV, and also serves the best meals in town.

Tibiao

About halfway along Panay's west coast, **TIBIAO** is at the head of the Tibiao River and in the shadow of Panay's highest peak, Mount Madjas-as (2090m). The town is trying to sell itself as a base for whitewater **rafting** and **trekking**; for information, call Tribal Adventures (☎036/288-3449, ⓦwww.tribaladventures .com), which runs adventure tours from its base at *Sandcastles Resort* on White Beach in Boracay. Tribal Adventures has a small lodge called *Kayak Inn* in the foothills outside Tibiao which organizes kayaking trips, climbing expeditions and outings to nearby waterfalls. North of here the coast road continues to Libertad and Caticlan.

The east coast

Panay's **east coast** – from Iloilo City north to **Estancia**, a route served by Ceres Liner buses – is an undeveloped area of wilderness and sun-drenched barrios rarely seen by tourists. There are some wonderfully pristine islands off the coast, many of them unfamiliar even to locals, but to explore them you'll need time on your hands, patience and a willingness to spend nights camped on beaches.

Both of the fishing towns of **CONCEPCION** and **SAN DIONISIO** make good jumping-off points for the islands and islets off Panay's northeast coast, the biggest of which is **Pan de Azucar** (Sugar Loaf) **Island**, which can be reached in about 45 minutes. Few of the Iloilo–Estancia buses pass through Concepcion or Dionisio, but you can hop off in nearby **Sara** and take a jeepney or tricycle. Concepcion is probably the better base of the two because you can stay at the *SBS Iyang Beach Resort* (❷) on the seafront, where the owners can help you arrange a bangka for island-hopping. Mount Manaphag on Pan de Azucar is a remarkable sight as you approach from the sea: it's not high (about 1000m) but its sides are steep, giving the impression of a blunted triangle. The mountain can be climbed from the friendly barangay of **Ponting** on the island's east coast, though it's a real wilderness trek, for experienced climbers only.

The unassuming seaside town of **ESTANCIA** offers more opportunities to explore beautiful islands off the coast, among them **Sicogon**, which has wide, sandy beaches, and **Gigantes** (Giant) where a rock formation does look undeniably like the inert profile of a man. In Estancia you can stay at *Pa-on Beach Resort* (☎033/397-0444; ❶), but there's no accommodation on any of the islands apart from homestays with friendly locals.

The north coast

The section of Panay's north coast from **Roxas** in the east to **Caticlan** in the west (transport gateway to Boracay; see p.325) is mostly industrial and has no notable beaches. Its biggest – in fact its only – attraction is the town of **Kalibo**, a drab place that every year transforms itself into the country's party capital by staging the **Ati-Atihan** festival.

Kalibo

KALIBO, the capital of Aklan province, lies on the well-trodden path to Boracay and for most visitors is simply the place they get off the plane and onto the bus. It's an uninteresting town, full of tricycles and fast-food outlets, but every second

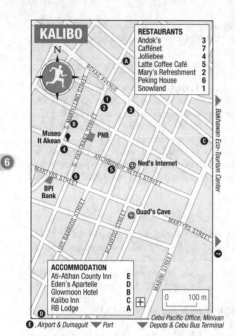

KALIBO

N

RESTAURANTS
Andok's	3
Caffénet	7
Jolliebee	4
Latte Coffee Café	5
Mary's Refreshment	2
Peking House	6
Snowland	1

ROXAS AVENUE

Museo It Akean · PNB

Ned's Internet

MARTYRS STREET

BPI Bank

Quad's Cave

MARTYRS STREET

ACCOMMODATION
Ati-Atihan County Inn	E
Eden's Apartelle	D
Glowmoon Hotel	B
Kalibo Inn	C
RB Lodge	A

0   100 m

Bakhawan Eco-Tourism Center

Cebu Pacific Office, Minivan Depots & Cebu Bus Terminal

E, Airport & Dumaguit ▼ Port

week of January it hosts what is probably the biggest street party in the country, the **Ati-Atihan** (see box, p.315), an exuberant festival that celebrates the original inhabitants of the area and the later arrival of Catholicism.

Arrival and information

Kalibo has sprawled beyond its original compact boundaries in recent years, but most of the essential places – banks, shops and accommodation – are within walking distance of one another. The major thoroughfare is **Roxas Avenue**, which runs into town from the **airport** in the southeast, with most streets leading off it to the southwest. The ten-minute tricycle ride into town from the airport, a distance of about 6km, costs around P100 for a "special ride". The **Ceres bus terminal** is 1km south of the town centre on Osmena Street, and vans for Roxas and Caticlan leave from just next door. **Ferries** arrive in **Dumaguit**, a fifteen-minute jeepney ride outside Kalibo.

There are a number of **banks with ATMs**, including a BPI on Martyr's Street and a PNB on G. Pastrana Street. The **post office** is in the Provincial Capitol Building in Mabini Street, off Roxas Avenue. There are many small **internet cafés**, including *Quad's Cave* on Acevedo Street but to surf in comfort you can't beat *Caffenet* (see opposite). For **telephone calls** there's a PLDT office in Burgos Street a short walk east of the market, but there are also call centres in Gaisano Mall. The Kalibo provincial **hospital**, an immense, modern, rose-pink building, is on Mabini Street.

Accommodation

Good accommodation can be hard to find during the Ati-Atihan, when rates double or triple, so if you're visiting during the festival, make sure you've booked a room (and, if you want to fly in, your plane ticket) in advance.

Ati-Atihan County Inn D. Maagma St ☎036/268-6116. Government-owned place offering good-value rooms with a/c, cable TV and hot showers set around a communal living area with wi-fi. Dorm beds cost P150. ❷
Eden's Apartelle C. Quimpo St ☎036/268-1966. New apartment-style hotel in a quiet location on the outskirts of town. Economy rooms have a shared living area with kitchenette, cable TV and wi-fi. ❷
Glowmoon Hotel S. Martelino St ☎036/262-2373. Brightly painted clean fan and a/c rooms, the latter of which have en-suite bathrooms. ❶

Kalibo Inn 467 N. Roldan St ☎036/268-4765. Well-furnished, airy, a/c rooms in a good location on the eastern edge of Kalibo, within walking distance of Gaisano Mall and other shops. Staff are efficient and helpful, and can arrange plane and ferry tickets, plus there's wi-fi. ❸
RB Lodge G. Pastrana St ☎036/262-4155. A variety of rooms right in the heart of town. The cheapest fan rooms are small and dark, but better a/c rooms on the second floor are surprisingly quiet, nicely furnished and look over banana palms in the neighbouring backyard. ❶

By plane

There are several flights to Manila daily. Philippine Airlines (℡036/262 3260), Airphil Express (℡036/288-7536) and Cebu Pacific (℡036/262-5407) all have ticket offices at the airport; Cebu Pacific also has an office on Toting Reyes Street, near the junction with Quezon Avenue.

By ferry

From Dumaguit port, there are twice-weekly services to Manila with Moreta Shipping Lines (℡036/262-3003), who have a ticket office on Regalado Street, near the junction with Acavedo Street. Most other services run from Caticlan, with buses shuttling passengers from Kalibo's bus terminal to the port.

By bus and van

Regular buses leave from the Ceres Liner terminal on Osmena Avenue for Iloilo (4hr; P184) and San José (4hr; P190). For Roxas (2hr) and Caticlan (2hr) you'll need to take a minivan from one of the private stands next to the bus terminal (or from the airport). RORO services also run from Kalibo bus terminal to Manila (via Caticlan, ferry to Roxas on Mindoro, bus to Calapan, ferry to Batangas, and bus to Manila) costing P1100 for the 12-hour journey.

The Town

Kalibo is home to one of Panay's best museums, the **Museo It Akean** in San Martelino Street at the junction with Burgos Street (Mon–Fri 8am–noon & 1–5pm; P10). Though modest, it's the only museum to document the cultural heritage of the Aklañons (Aklan people), and contains exhibits of the area's old **piña** textiles, pottery, religious relics, literature and Spanish-era artefacts, many on loan from affluent local families. Among the most interesting exhibits are rare costumes that were worn by Aklan tribespeople during festivals. Despite serious earthquake damage in the 1980s, the museum retains some of the original structure which, since its construction by the Spanish in 1882, has also been used as a school, a courtroom and a garrison.

The only other worthwhile attraction within easy reach is the **Bakhawan Eco-tourism Centre and Mangrove Park** (8am–5pm; P15) a short tricycle ride from town. The park is the site of a mangrove re-planting project and visitors can walk along a kilometre-long boardwalk to the beach.

Eating

There's not much in the way of gourmet dining in Kalibo, and choices are largely between fast-food outfits such as *Chowking*, *Jollibee* and (delicious) chicken from *Andok's*, but there are a few **restaurants** worth seeking out including *Peking House* on Luis Barrios Street, a popular place for inexpensive Chinese food (P130) and *Mary's* on G. Pastrana Street, a canteen-style place serving noodles, sandwiches and desserts. Good coffee can be found at *Latte Coffee Café* on Archbishop Reyes Street, and also at *Caffenet* on Bayanihan Road (off Toting Reyes St), which has internet access (P35/hr) and wi-fi, plus a music lounge on the fourth floor.

Boracay

Some 350km south of Manila, and just off the northeastern tip of Panay, the island of **Boracay** is famed for picture-perfect 4km **White Beach**, a wild nightlife scene and activities from scuba diving to kitesurfing, Boracay has something for everyone. It may be only 7km long and 1km wide at its narrowest point, but there are over thirty beaches and coves, and the sunsets are worth the journey in their own right. A short walk along the beach takes you past restaurants serving a veritable United Nations of cuisines, including Greek, Indian, Caribbean, French, Thai and more. The beach is also dotted with interesting little bars and bistros, some of them no more than a few chairs and tables on the beach, others where you can now sit in air-conditioned luxury eating Chateaubriand and smoking Cuban cigars.

Of course, unchecked **development** has had its downsides and it can be hard to relax with the constant blare of music on the beach and the hum of tricycles on the island's main road. The authorities are finally waking up to this and a new bypass will mean that Main Road should soon be one-way. A beach **smoking ban** has also been enforced, and threats to demolish resorts that have been built without permission may (eventually) come into effect. Many resort owners are aware of how fragile Boracay is and organize beach clean-ups and recycling seminars. Unlike the rest of the country, **topless sunbathing** is common at Boracay but the authorities are keen to keep the island as a family destination – in 2011 a "sex on the beach" ban was mooted after some Western couples were filmed being over amorous on New Year's Eve.

When to visit

The two distinct **climatic seasons** in the Philippines have

BORACAY

ACCOMMODATION
Balinghai	B
Boracay Beach Houses	F
Discovery Shores	E
Fridays	D
Mandala Spa	G
Nami	C
Shangri-La	A

Banyugan Beach
Puka Beach
Bat Cave
Punta-Bunga Beach
Punta Bunga
MAIN ROAD
Yapak
Punta-Ina
Hagdan
Ilig-Iligan
Shell Museum
Balinghai Beach
Ilig-Iligan Beach
Diniwid Beach
Diniwid
Fairways & Bluewater (Hotel & Golf Club)
Lapuz-Lapuz Beach
Horse Riding Stables
Lapuz-Lapuz
See 'White Beach' map for details
N
Balabag
Bolabog
White Beach
Bolabog Beach

RESTAURANTS & BARS
Prana	3
Red Pirate's Pub	2
Sirena	A
Tesebel's	1

Boracay Rock
SULU SEA
Ambulon
SIBUYAN SEA
Tulubhan
Mandala Spa
MAIN ROAD
Malabunot
Tambisaan
Manoc-Manoc
Crocodile Island
Cagban Beach
Cagban Ferry Pier
Manoc-Manoc Beach
Tabon Strait
Boats to Boracay
0   1 km
Panay
Caticlan Airport

Getting to and from Boracay

Travelling to and from Boracay has never been easier and ferries have largely been superseded by the countless **flights** which connect Caticlan (and further afield Kalibo) with **Manila** every day, while a handful head to and from **Cebu**. Cebu Pacific, Airphil Express, Philippine Airlines and Zest Air each have upwards of eight flights per day from Manila. Cebu is served by Cebu Pacific and Philippine Airlines. Kalibo is another airport within easy driving distance of Caticlan (2hr), and is also well served by flights from Manila by the same airlines. There is a **ferry-bus-ferry-bus** route to Manila via Roxas on Mindoro and Batangas, but given that it takes 12 hours and will only save you a few hundred pesos, this is only for the truly parsimonious. From **Mindoro** there are regular Montenegro, Starlite and Supershuttle ferries from Roxas to Caticlan which take around four hours and cost from P300. For **Romblon** there are bangkas from Caticlan to Looc and Santa Fe on Tablas or you can negotiate with a boat captain on White Beach to take you to Carabao, and then travel onwards to the main island group by bangka or pumpboat.

Kalibo aside, it's a long haul from Caticlan to almost anywhere on **Panay by road**. Travelling **by bus** it takes four hours to Roxas, and five hours to Iloilo.

---

a marked effect on Boracay. Because of the island's north–south orientation, White Beach takes the brunt of onshore winds during the wet season (June–Oct), so don't expect it to look at its well-barbered best at that time. The waves can be big, washing up old coconuts, seaweed and dead branches. Many beachfront resorts and restaurants are forced to erect unsightly tarpaulins to keep out the wind and sand and some even close during July and August, the wettest months. The onshore wind makes for some thrilling windsurfing and kiteboarding, but all other ocean activities move to calmer waters on the island's east side.

Arrival and transport

There are two main gateways to Boracay: **Caticlan** and **Kalibo** (from where you can get transport to Caticlan; see box above). Coming from elsewhere in Panay, many **buses** drop you on the main road through Caticlan, about 1km from the pier and airport, from where there are tricycles to take you the rest of the way. Other buses continue all the way to the pier.

Caticlan airstrip is a three-minute tricycle ride (P25/person) from the **ferry terminal**, where you buy tickets for the twenty-minute journey to Cagban pier in the south of Boracay (P25 during the day and P30 at night, plus P75 environmental fee and P50 boat terminal fee). From here it's just a short tricycle journey to White Beach (P50–100). If you're flying in and have booked to stay at a resort, you'll be met at the airstrip by their representative.

Tricycle fares should be no more than P150 for a trip along the length of the island's main road – make sure you agree to a fare before you climb on board as some drivers have a habit of adding "extras" at the end of the journey.

Information

The Department of Tourism has a small, ineffectual **tourist office** in D'Mall, on the right-hand side as you enter. A few minutes' walk to the south, the **Boracay Tourist Center** (daily 9am–10pm; ☏036/288-3704) is far more useful and as well as sending mail, exchanging cash and selling maps, it also holds a branch of **Filipino Travel Center** (daily 9am–6pm; ⓦ www.filipinotravel.com.ph), perhaps the best travel agent on the island; there's a useful notice board here advertising new boat services, adventure tours, activities, nightlife and accommodation.

Another good source of information is Ⓦ www.boracayisland.org, run by the Boracay Foundation and updated regularly with listings, accommodation news and events. Finally, the *Boracay Sun*, and *expat* newspapers are both distributed free and have the latest details of what's new and happening in Boracay.

Accommodation

There are about three hundred **resorts** on Boracay which means that except at peak times (Christmas and Easter, when prices rise sharply) you should be able to find a place to stay simply by taking a stroll down White Beach. Prices have risen sharply in recent years, with the best rooms in high-end places going for upwards of US$500 a night but there are still cheapies out there. Broadly speaking the beach is divided into **three sections**: Boat Station 1 and north is high end, Boat Station 2 and around is generally mid-range, while south of Boat Station 3 the lanes behind the beach hold a selection of budget backpacker options.

It's always worth negotiating for a discount, especially if you plan to stay a while. The prices used below are for peak season (excluding Christmas, Easter and Chinese New Year, when they can rise by as much as fifty percent).

Boat Station 1 and points north

Discovery Shores At the northern end of White Beach, beyond Boat Station 1 ☎ 036/288-4500, Ⓦ www.discoveryshoresboracay.com. The latest luxury offering to grace White Beach, *Discovery Shores* features bright, spacious and ultramodern rooms spanning back up the hill behind the beach. As you'd expect there's a pool and a decent restaurant, and all rooms are comfortable and contain an impressive array of amenities including iPod dock, flat-screen TV, DVD player and free wi-fi. The premier rooms have an expansive outdoor living area with a large jacuzzi and views down to the sea. ❾

Fridays Almost the last resort on White Beach, right at the northern end beyond Boat Station 1 ☎ 036/288-6200, Ⓦ www.fridaysboracay.com. One of Boracay's first resorts, and still one of the best, *Fridays* occupies a prime spot at the northern end of the beach and offers comfortable deluxe and premier rooms, and top-notch premier suites which enjoy great ocean views. Although it's only a three-star property the service and amenities run close to five-star and include a decent pool and wi-fi throughout. ❾

Seabird Resort Bar & Restaurant Set back from the beach a short walk north of D'Mall ☎ 036/288-3047, Ⓦ www.seabirdinternationalresort.com. An oldie but a goodie, *Seabird* continues to renovate to keep up with the new crowd and offers a range of rooms set in pleasant and quiet gardens just a minute's walk back from the beach. Good coffee, pancakes, breakfasts and fish in the restaurant. Free wi-fi. ❼

Boat Station 2

Bamboo Bungalows Just north of D'Mall. ☎ 036/288-6324, Ⓦ www.bbboracay.com. Great rooms and bungalows in the heart of the action, a stone's throw from D'Mall. There's a choice of cottages and apartments set around the lush garden, or some rooms at the front of the main building with beach views. ❼

Fat Jimmy's 100m inland, next to D'Mall ☎ 036/288-5562, Ⓦ www.fatjimmysresort.com. One of a number of budget resorts along a path next to D'Mall. Relaxed, quiet and friendly, *Fat Jimmy's* has 16 simple but charming fan-cooled or a/c rooms, five of which have their own small patio garden (❼). Family rooms sleep four with a bunk bed for the kids and rates include a choice of Filipino or American breakfast. Free wi-fi and all-round good value. ❹

Frendz 100m off Main Rd, near Elementary School ☎ 036/288-3803, Ⓔ frendzresort@hotmail .com. Tucked halfway between the beach and Main Road, the simple cottages at *Frendz* present no-frills laidback beach living. The native huts have double beds, hot and cold showers, and nice verandas. There are also separate male and female dorms (P600) and a café with wi-fi internet access. ❹

Mango-Ray On the beach 50m north of Boat Station 2 ☎ 036/288-6129, Ⓦ www.mango-ray .com. Nine tastefully furnished a/c rooms with fridge, cable TV, telephone and spacious porch, plus one suite at the front of the property looking out over the ocean. Floors are tiled, the whitewashed walls are decorated with tasteful Filipino art and the surrounding gardens are lush and peaceful. Breakfast and wi-fi included. ❽

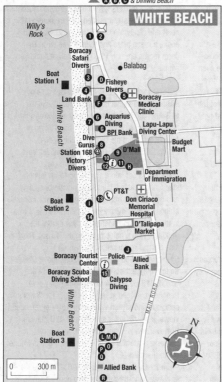

WHITE BEACH

▲ **A**, **B**, **C** & Diniwid Beach

Willy's Rock

Boracay Safari Divers

Boat Station 1

● Balabag

Fisheye Divers

Land Bank

Boracay Medical Clinic

Aquarius Diving

Lapu-Lapu Diving Center

BPI Bank

Dive Gurus

Station 168

Victory Divers

D'Mall

Budget Mart

Department of Immigration

PT&T

Don Ciriaco Memorial Hospital

Boat Station 2

D'Talipapa Market

Boracay Tourist Center

Police

Allied Bank

Boracay Scuba Diving School

Calypso Diving

White Beach

White Beach

MAIN ROAD

Boat Station 3

Allied Bank

0   300 m

N

ACCOMMODATION	
Angol Point Beach Resort	P
Bamboo Bungalows	F
Blue Mango	Q
Casa Pilar	K
Dave's Straw Hat Inn	O
Discovery Shores	A
Fat Jimmy's	H
Frendz	D
Fridays	B
Mango-Ray	G
Marzon Beach Resort	L
Moreno's Cottages	M
Nami	C
Nigi Nigi Nu Noos 'e'Nu Nu Noos	I
Orchids Resort	N
Pinjalo	J
Seabird Resort Bar & Restaurant	E
Treehouse Beach Resort	R

RESTAURANTS, BARS & CLUBS	
Aria	10
Bazura	8
Beachcomber	1
Bom Bom bar	6
Charlh's Bar	14
Cyma	11
English Bakery and Tea Rooms	5
Floremar Pizzeria de Mario	R
Lemon i Café	9
Manana	4
Shooters Bar	2
Steakhouse Boracay	3
Summer Place	12
The Wreck Bar	15
True Food Restaurant	7
Wave	13

Nigi Nigi Nu Noos 'e' Nu Nu Noos A 5min walk north of the Boracay Tourist Centre ☏036/288-3101, ⊛ www.niginigi.com. Long-standing and enduringly popular resident of White Beach featuring Indonesian-style cottages set in tranquil tropical gardens. All of the spacious cottages have thatched pagoda roofs and shady verandas. Free wi-fi and a decent restaurant and bar. **7**

Pinjalo Down the footpath beside the Tourist Centre, on the left ☏036/288-3206, ⊛ www .calypso-boracay.com. Owned and operated by Calypso Diving, this place is worth the effort to find if you're looking for good-value, comfortable accommodation close to the beach but away from the noise of the bars and clubs. Standard rooms are on the small side making it worth paying the extra for the deluxe options. All rooms are tastefully furnished and look onto peaceful gardens, and there's poolside wi-fi. Calypso Diving also have some ultra-chic rooms and suites next to their diveshop. **8**

Boat Station 3 and points south

Angol Point Beach Resort At the south end of the beach ☏036/288-3107. It's a little more pricey than many resorts of its ilk because the conservationist owner, Francis, has built only one cottage where most developers would have put three or four – which means you get expansive rooms, huge verandas and the benefit of acres of space in the peaceful coconut grove where the resort stands. It's a short walk from bars and restaurants and very quiet. Good choice for families. **6**

Blue Mango Southern end of the beach ☏036/288-5107, ⊛ www.bluemangoinn .com. This is a great-value choice with a wide range of rooms, either facing the beach, or set around the wonderfully jungly garden. All rooms are attractively decorated and have a/c, cable TV, fridge and hot and cold shower. There's also a decent café with wi-fi on site and sunbeds on the beach for the use of guests. **3**

Dave's Straw Hat Inn Down the path next to *Angol Point Beach Resort* ☏036/288-5465, ⓦwww.davesstrawhatinn.com. *Dave's* is a charming, homey little resort with comfortable a/c and fan rooms and good food. Fan-cooled rooms are one of the best deals on the island, while even deluxe doubles (**⑥**) have extra roll-out beds so a family of four can fit in at no extra charge. **④**

Marzon Beach Resort At the southern end of the beach ☏036/268-2188. One of the cheapest right-on-the-beach options, *Marzon* has dated standard rooms and plusher deluxe rooms, set around a sandy courtyard, with the glistening blue of the ocean just beyond. All rooms have a/c and cable TV, plus there's free wi-fi. **⑥**

Moreno's Cottages At the southern end of the beach opposite *Dave's Straw Hat Inn* ☏0939/118-9616. This friendly, local option has small and simple fan and a/c rooms set around a pleasant garden, just a two-minute walk from a lovely section of White Beach. **③**

Orchids Resort A short walk inland from *Moreno's Cottages* ☏036/288-3313, ⓦwww.orchidsboracay.com. Owned by an affable American, *Orchids* offers great-value rooms and nipa huts a few minutes' walk from White Beach. Standard fan rooms are clean and have hot and cold showers, while the fan cottages offer more space and have cozy verandas with hammocks. A/c rooms also have cable TV, and there's wi-fi connection (P50/day) throughout. A few minutes' walk up the hillside, *Orchids* has newer concrete villas with thatch roofs (**⑤**) which have two beds in the a/c downstairs and a living room with cable TV, kitchen and balcony upstairs. **②**

Tree House Beach Resort At the southern end of the beach behind *Floremar Pizza de Mario* ☏036/288-3601, ⓦwww.boracaytreehouse.com. Rooms may be slightly dated, but are comfortable, quiet and nicely furnished. The owner Mario also cooks a mean pizza and there's free wi-fi. The dorm rooms are only P200, but cramped and very simple. **④**

Elsewhere on Boracay

Balinghai Balinghai Beach ☏036/288-3646, Ⓔ Balinghai@hotmail.com. If you are looking for desert-island solitude and don't mind being a tricycle ride from the buzz of White Beach, *Balinghai* fits the bill. On a small, secluded cove surrounded by cliffs on the northern part of Boracay, it's set into a steep slope with lots of steps, and boasts a handful of private bungalows and houses built from local materials, with consideration for the environment. One house has a tree in the kitchen and another is carved from the rockface, with a balcony facing the sunset. There is also a small restaurant with wi-fi. **⑥**

Nami Nestled on the cliffside 20m above Diniwid Beach, the next cove along from White Beach ☏032/818-6237, ⓦwww.namiboracay.com. Reached by steep steps or a rickety lift, *Nami's* spacious and stylish villas offer 180-degree ocean views, jacuzzi, butler service and DVD players. However, while *Nami* bills itself as a very upmarket establishment, the service doesn't quite make the mark. **⑨**

Shangri-La Barangay Vapak ☏032/288-4988, ⓦwww.shangrila.com. Perched above its own private beach, the *Shangri-La* presents a range of attractively styled rooms and villas which blend comfortably into the lush hills. Service is top-notch and all of the usual *Shangri-La* facilities are on offer, along with nature trails and a dive centre. **⑨**

The beaches

Most visitors fall in love with **White Beach**, but don't miss **Puka Beach** on the north coast, which is famous for shiny white seashells called *puka*. A pleasant way to get there is to hire a bangka on White Beach (P500 one-way), and then take a tricycle back (P150). To the north of White Beach sits the little village of **Diniwid** with its two-hundred-metre beach, accessible from White Beach on a path carved out of the cliffs. At the end of a steep path over the next hill is the tiny **Balinghai Beach**, enclosed by walls of rock.

On the northeast side of the island **Ilig-Iligan Beach** has coves and caves, as well as jungle full of fruit bats. From the beach here a path leads a short way up the hill through the scrub to **Bat Cave**, which you can climb into and explore. It's fantastic to be here at dusk when the bats leave the cave in immense flocks.

Activities

Boracay has the biggest range of **activities** to be found anywhere in the Philippines. You'll find **touts** offering all the following activities along the beach,

Diving around Boracay

Boracay's diving isn't as varied or extreme as diving in Palawan or Puerto Galera, but there's still enough to keep everyone happy. The **dive sites** around the island, all easily accessible by bangka, include gentle drift dives, coral gardens and some deeper dives with a good chance of encounters with sharks. At **Crocodile Island**, fifteen minutes southeast of Boracay, there's a shallow reef that drops off to 25m and a number of small canyons where sea snakes gather. **Big and Small Laurel** are neighbouring islets with some of the best soft coral in the Visayas and shoals of snappers, sweetlips, eels, sea snakes, morays, puffers and boxfish. Probably the star attraction for divers here is **Yapak**, where you freefall into the big blue, eventually finding at 30m the top of a marine wall where there are batfish, wahoo, tuna, barracuda and cruising grey reef sharks. On Boracay's northern shore are the **Bat Caves**, where after a swim through a cave you'll emerge into an immense cavern inhabited by thousands of fruit bats. The smell is unforgettable. **Lapu Wall** is a day-trip from Boracay to the northern coast of Panay, but the diving is some of the most challenging in the area, with overhangs and caverns. Another good day-trip is north to Carabao Island (see p.337), in the province of Romblon, where there are splendid reefs, some peaceful, powdery beaches and one resort if you want to stay overnight.

Dive operators and PADI courses

There are dozens of licensed **dive operators** along White Beach. A Discover Scuba introductory session with a dive master costs around P3000, while a full PADI Open Water Course (3–4 days) costs around P20,000. you can even try **helmet diving** (P3000/30min), whereby air is supplied underwater through a helmet. Of the countless dive operators on the island, the following are some of the best established and are all PADI 5-star rated: Calypso Diving Resort ☏036/288-3206, ⓦwww.calypso.ph; Dive Gurus Boracay ☏036/288-5486, ⓦwww.divegurus.com; Sea World Dive Center ☏036/288-3033, ⓦwww.seaworldboracay.com.

but the best place to arrange them is through Allan B Fun Tour (☏036/288-5577) near Boat Station 2, or alternatively the Boracay Tourist Center.

Apart from scuba diving (see box above) and snorkelling, **watersports** on offer include jet-skiing (P2000/30min), waterskiing (P2500), banana boat rides (P250), sailboat (P2500/hr) and speedboat (P3500/hr) hire, ocean kayaking (P500/hr), parasailing (P2500). For a true adrenaline experience you could try **cliff diving** at Ariel's Point, a short boat ride away. Contact *Boracay Beach Club* at Boat Station 1 for details.

There's also been a boom in **kiteboarding**, with boarders gathering on Bulabog Beach to take advantage of the constant wind during the peak season, while in the off-season the focus shifts to White Beach. There are a number of schools offering lessons, including equipment rental. Two hours of "discover kiteboarding" costs P3100 and the International Kiteboarding Organisation (IKO) beginners' course takes 12 hours over three or four days and costs P19000. The best school is Hanging Kite Centre (☏036/288-1805, ⓦwww.kiteboardingboracay.com) at the Neilpride Test Centre besides Laguna de Boracay on White Beach.

On **land** the choices are equally extensive and you can take your pick from **mountain biking** (P150/hr), quad bikes (P2500/hr), **golf** at Fairways and Bluewater (from P2000), **horseriding** (P645/hr), zip-lining (P700) and zorbing (P580). Finally up in the air you can get great views from even a ten-minute **helicopter ride** (P3500/person).

Eating

Boracay has a more diverse dining scene than most cities in the Philippines and even in a two-week stay you need never eat in the same **restaurant** twice (although some are so good that you'll want to). Many restaurants are listed in the local info booklet *My Boracay*, which also has meal discount vouchers. As well as the listings below there are also plenty of local vendors who set up barbecues on the beach at sundown to cook everything from fresh lapu-lapu and squid to tasty local bananas sprinkled with muscovado sugar. The only cautionary note is to be wary of the big seafood buffet places on the seafront, as sometimes the fish isn't quite as fresh as you might think and can be a fast track to stomach problems.

Cafés

English Bakery and Tea Rooms Halfway between White Beach and Bulabog ☏036/288-3158. The only remaining branch of the *English Bakery* in Boracay serves up great breakfasts (P130–175), yoghurts (P75), meals, cakes and shakes (P95). Shaded tables looking out over a small lagoon make a great spot to escape the heat and partake in a cup of Lyons English tea and some banana bread. Daily 6am–6pm.

Lemon i Café In D'Mall ☏036/288-6781. Terrific bright and airy little café. Breakfast items include Eggs Benedict (P260), and delicious coconut pancakes. For lunch or dinner there's outstanding pan-fried mahi-mahi with warm potato salad and lemon butter garlic sauce (P390), lemon and thyme roast chicken with sauteed potatoes (P390), and a range of lemon desserts. Drinks range from refreshing *kalamansi* juice, or a lemonijito (P130) if you feel like something stronger. Daily 8am–11pm.

Restaurants

Aria Beach Entrance to D'Mall ☏036/288-5573. This popular Italian place offers attractive alfresco dining under the palms. Pizzas (P380–560) and pastas (P310–425) are reliably good, and coffee and desserts are available from neighbouring *Café del Sol*. Daily 11am–11pm.

Cyma In D'Mall ☏036/-288-42833. The owners may not be Greek, but *Cyma* serves the best tzaziki (P150) in Boracay in a tiny but boldly decorated restaurant. Delicious *horiatiki* (Greek salad; P220), souvlaki (P300–440) and baklava (P200) are also on the menu, and it's worth checking the specials board. Daily 11am–11pm.

Floremar Pizzeria de Mario Inside *Treehouse Resort*, at the southern end of White Beach. Thin-crust pizza, pasta and risotto, all cooked to perfection by the Italian owner and served in simple surrounds with gorgeous views over the beach. Daily 8am–11pm.

Manana Next to *Starbucks* between Boat Stations 1 and 2 ☏036/288-3608. This lively Mexican restaurant serves tasty fajitas (P363), enchiladas and chimichangas (P352–418) which can be enjoyed in the brightly decorated interior or on tables out on the beach to the backbeat of Latino tunes. A giant frozen mango daiquiri (P143) rounds the meal off perfectly. Daily 7am–11pm.

Prana Inside Mandala Spa, at the southern end of the main road. This classy vegetarian restaurant at the upmarket Mandala Spa offers super-healthy dining in a wooden dining room looking out to dense tropical foliage. The menu, created by a Swedish chef especially for the restaurant, includes interesting starters such as wasabi salad (P170), main courses like penne pasta with roasted vegetables (P260) and pan-fried tofu with asparagus, Baguio beans and peanut sauce (P260). Daily 7am–10pm.

Sirena *Shangri-La*, Barangay Vapak ☏032/288-4988, ⊛www.shangrila.com. Sophisticated seafood dining from a lofty perch overlooking two bays, this is the place to come for a splurge. Arrive for sunset drinks and see if you can snag one of the wonderful outdoor cliff perches before indulging in succulent wahoo, crispy fried prawns and *ube* crème brûlée, along with good wines. Expect to pay upwards of P2000 per person for a three-course meal. Daily 11am–2pm & 5–9pm.

Steakhouse Boracay A few steps from Boat Station 1 ☏036/288-6102. Excellent steak and salad restaurant which enjoys a great location looking out over the beach. Imported steaks (P495–510) are the mainstay, but the raclette is also worth a try. Daily 10am–11pm.

True Food Restaurant Next door to *Mango-Ray*, a short walk north of Boat Station 2 ☏036/288-3142. Tastefully styled restaurant where delicious Indian meals can be enjoyed sitting on cushions around a low table. There are dishes from all over the subcontinent including aloo jeera, biriani, pakora (P230) and masala dosa (P295), and the menu also extends to North Africa with its couscous offerings. Meals are nicely rounded off with a good old-fashioned cup of Indian chai. Daily noon–10.30pm.

Tesebel's On the Main Rd just off Puka Beach. This long-standing restaurant is nothing fancy to look at, but people go back for the delicious fresh seafood, which includes garlic prawns with buttered honey (P175) and tangy *sinigang* awith catch of the day. Head here for a lazy lunch if you're in the Puka Beach area. Daily 6am–11pm.

Drinking and nightlife

Nightlife in Boracay starts with drinks at sunset and continues all night. Hardcore partiers don't even warm up until midnight, with many dancing and drinking until sunrise. As well as the listings below there are countless other options which range from upscale resort bars to beach shacks.

Beach bars

Beachcomber At the far north of White Beach. Simple bamboo bar on the sand, ideal for a few casual drinks before you move on to something more lively.

Bom Bom Bar Right on the beach a few metres north of D'Mall. Another atmospheric little chilled-out beach hut, with cushions on the sand where you can stretch out while listening to local musicians come together for jam sessions on native instruments.

Red Pirates Pub South end of White Beach beyond Boat Station 3. Bare feet and sarongs are the order of the evening at this chilled-out little beach club far from the madding crowd. The music ranges from reggae to chill-out to tribal, ethnic and acoustic sounds. The owner, Captain Joey, has a sailing boat and offers sunset cruises, adventure tours and snorkelling trips around the island.

Sand Bar Boat Station 1 at the northern end of White Beach. Trendy (but pricey) bar with sofas on the sand under a huge canopy. The nightly fire *poi* dancers are the best on the island and flavoured hookahs are also available while you watch the show.

Summer Place A few hundred metres south of D'Mall. U-shaped bamboo bar facing the beach, with a dancefloor and music until the sun comes up, or until the last customer leaves.

The Wreck Bar Calypso Diving Centre, just south of the Boracay Tourist Centre. Casual native-style bar where divers gather for après-scuba tall stories. Friendly atmosphere and good food; the eclectic menu includes seafood provençale, Hawaiian chicken and chicken *adobo*.

Clubs

Bazura One hundred metres north of Boat Station 2. Lively and long-established disco with an outdoor dancefloor, cheap drinks and a thumping sound system. Rarely gets going much before midnight.

Shooters Bar Near *Jony's Beach Resort* at the northern end of White Beach. (In)famous for drinking games involving potent cocktails. Raucous until the wee hours.

Wave *Boracay Regency Beach Resort*, near Boat Station 2. A subterranean a/c cavern with live bands, DJs and karaoke rooms.

Listings

Airlines Inside the Boracay Tourist Centre is a branch of Filipino Travel Centre where you can book tickets for Philippine Airlines, Airphil Express, Cebu Pacific and Zest Air.

Banks and exchange There are several banks with ATMs on Boracay, but during peak season they often run out of cash by the afternoon, so it's best to go in the mornings, and before the weekend. There's an Allied Bank on the beach path at Boat Station 3, and another on the main road next to Boracay Tropics; a BPI next to Budget Mart at the road entrance to D'Mall; and a Metrobank on the main road a few hundred metres north of D'Mall. All banks change cash and traveller's cheques, as does the Boracay Tourist Centre.

Hospitals and clinics The main hospital is the 24hr Don Ciriaco Senares Tirol Senior Memorial Hospital (☏036/288-3041) off Main Rd by the *Aloja Delicatessen*. The Metropolitan Doctors Medical Clinic on Main Rd (☏036/288-6357) by the market can also provide first aid or deal with emergencies and will send a doctor to your hotel.

Immigration Visa extensions are available at the small Department of Immigration office (☏036/254-374) in the *Nirvana Beach Resort* on the Main Rd. The office is open Mondays and Tuesdays from 7.30am to 5.30pm and to extend your visa you'll need to take along a photocopy of your passport (front cover and arrival stamp), and fill in an application form.

Internet access Getting online in Boracay is a little more expensive than many parts of the country; reckon on anything between P60 and P150 an hour. The internet café at the Boracay Tourist Centre is convenient and has fast connection for P70/hour. Other options are the business centre at *Nigi Nigi Nu's* (P70/hr), *Station 168* (P70/hr) at the entrance to D'Mall and the *Sheridan Internet Café* (P60/hr) at Boat Station 3.

Laundry The place you're staying will probably arrange laundry for you, but for a cheaper service there are several launderettes on the island which charge around P40/kg: Laundry Wascherei Is a little south of Boat Station 3, Lavandera Ko is next to *Cocomangas*, and Speedwash is on the main road inland from Boat Station 3.

Pharmacies There are pharmacies selling most necessities in D'Mall, Boracay Tourist Centre and D'Talipapa.

Phones Most resorts will let you make telephone calls, but the rates can be high. For cheaper rates head to the Boracay Tourist Centre.

Police The police station (☎036/288-3035) is a short walk inland between Boat Stations 2 and 3, immediately behind the Boracay Tourist Centre. If you have lost something you can ask the friendly staff at the local radio station, YESFM 91.1, to broadcast an appeal for help. They claim to have a good record of finding lost property, from wallets and passports to labrador puppies. The station office (☎036/288-6107) is on Main Rd close to Boat Station 1.

Post The post office in Balabag, the small community halfway along White Beach, is open Mon–Fri 9am–5pm. The Boracay Tourist Centre on White Beach has poste restante costing P5 per letter.

Shopping Essentials are not hard to come by on Boracay. There's a minimart selling snacks, drinks and toiletries at the Boracay Tourist Centre, or for a better selection head to Budget Mart or the department store at the Main Rd end of D'Mall. D'Mall is packed with other stores selling everything from books to souvenirs, but for the best and cheapest selection of beachwear try D'Talipapa.

Romblon

Off the northern coast of Panay, between Mindoro and Bicol, the province of **Romblon** consists of three main islands – Tablas, Romblon and Sibuyan, and a dozen or so more smaller islands. The province is largely overlooked by visitors because it's difficult to reach, and once you're here, to put it simply, there's not that much to do. There are few resorts and the most sophisticated Romblon's nightlife gets is the occasional wooden shack with a karaoke machine. There are, however, some beautiful and rarely visited **beaches** and coral reefs, making it an excellent off-the-beaten-track destination for scuba diving, snorkelling or just exploring and getting a sense of provincial life in the archipelago.

Romblon Town itself is a pretty place, with Spanish forts, a cathedral built in 1726 and breathtaking views across the Romblon Strait from Sabang lighthouse. On **Sibuyan** you can explore **Mount Guiting Guiting Natural Park** and climb the mountain itself, an extinct volcano. To the south of Tablas Island is beautiful little **Carabao Island** (usually visited via Boracay) where there's some terrific diving.

Arrival

There's a small **airport** at Tugdan on Tablas Island, which is served by regular flights from Manila by both Seair (Mon, Wed & Fri) and Zest Air (Tues, Thurs & Sat). Coming **from Manila** the only ferry is the MBRS Lines (☎02/426-1612 in Manila, 042/243-5886 in Romblon) M/V *Mary the Queen* which sails to Romblon Town (12hr), and on to Cajidiocan (Sibuyan). There are far more ferry services **from Batangas** to Odiongan, including: Montenegro Shipping Lines which has a service at 5pm (8hr) every day except Tuesdays; and Supershuttle which has three services a week (Mon, Wed and Fri) at 3pm. Coming **from Boracay**, MBRS Lines has one weekly ferry (Sun) from Caticlan to Odiongan, and there are also daily big bangkas from **Caticlan** to Santa Fe and Looc on

Tablas Island. Alternatively you can also charter bangkas in Boracay itself for Carabao Island, the furthest south of the Romblon group. Finally, **from Mindoro**, there's a Montenegro Shipping Lines ferry three times a week from Roxas to Odiongan, while Cajidiocan on Sibuyan's east coast is linked by bangka with Mandaon on **Masbate**.

Tablas Island

Tablas, the largest and best connected of the Romblon group, is a narrow island with a sealed coastal road. Chartering a jeepney for a tour around the island is worth considering. The road that cuts across the island from Concepcion to Odiongan is a real thrill, winding along a ridge with, on a clear day, views as far as Sibuyan in the east and Boracay in the south.

If you arrive by air, it's typical to head first to **Odiongan**, a pleasant little town with a few simple places to stay. The best place for a short stay is *Odiongan Plaza Lodge* (☎042/567-5760; ❶) which is in a central location opposite the town hall on the plaza and has acceptable, well-kept air-conditioned rooms with tiled floors and hot showers. There's also a small **internet café** right next door, and a PNB **bank** with ATM on Formilleza Street. From Odiongan it's easy to explore the beautiful northwest coast up to **San Andres**, a neat and tidy little place with paved roads and low-rise wooden houses. There's no accommodation here, but there are a number of houses at the rear of the beach where residents will be willing to put you up. San Andres has a beautiful sweeping bay of fine sand on

Getting around Romblon

Below is a list of the major bangka links between the three main islands:

From Tablas Island: There are local bangkas from San Agustin to Romblon Town (1hr) on Romblon, and San Fernando on Sibuyan. There are also bangkas from Santa Fe to Carabao.

From Romblon Island: There are daily bangkas from Romblon Town to San Agustin (1hr) on Tablas, and Magdawing, Cajidiocan and San Fernando on Sibuyan (2hr).

From Sibuyan: There are daily bangkas from San Fernando to San Agustin on Tablas Island and Romblon Town on Romblon Island. There are also bangkas from Magdawing and San Fernando for Romblon Town (2hr).

one side and on the other dazzling paddy fields that stretch to the foothills of Mount Kang-Ayong (Table Mountain), which can be climbed with a guide – ask at the town hall in the plaza.

The next town north of San Andres is **Calatrava**, from where you can charter a bangka for the short hop to the **Enchanted Hidden Sea**, an incredibly beautiful forty-metre-wide pool of water barely 10m from the sea through a gap in the rocks. To most local folks the pool is an enchanted place, home to supernatural beings though you're more likely to see white-breasted eagles, monkeys, butterflies, sharks and turtles.

If you want to head to Romblon or Sibuyan, take a jeepney to **San Agustin** on the northeast coast of Tablas, where you can cross by local bangka to Romblon Town or San Fernando. There's an adequate little lodging house in San Agustin, the *August Inn* (℡0919/592-2495; ❷) in the town plaza, with air-conditioned rooms (the doubles have private showers too) and food on request. Another option, right next door, is *Kamella Lodge* (℡0919/610-7104; ❷), which has small, ordinary air-conditioned rooms that are okay for a short stay.

Looc

The main town on Tablas is **LOOC**, a scenic place huddled among palm trees against a curtain of jungled hills, and facing a wide natural harbour. There's a **tourist office** (8am–noon & 1–5pm) in the Capitol Building on the town plaza, and nearby, the *Brainstorm Internet Café* has reasonably fast web access. Looc's pier is at the southern edge of town near the *Morales Lodging Inn*. There are daily bangkas from here to Boracay and Caticlan (P180). One boat leaves at 7.30am, but depending on demand there may be others at 9.30am and noon. Ferries leave Looc on Mondays, Thursdays and Saturdays for Roxas on Mindoro.

It's worth hiring a bangka to explore the pretty bay and coves around Looc. Of principal interest is the **Looc Bay Marine Refuge and Sanctuary**, an area of the bay guarded 24 hours a day to allow corals damaged by dynamite fishing to regenerate. The guards, all volunteers, are stationed on a bamboo platform and are happy to welcome tourists aboard and let them snorkel in the area. Donations in the form of soft drinks and snacks are appreciated.

Accommodation and eating

If you're spending a night in Looc while waiting for a ferry, head for the *Marduke Hotel* (℡042/509-4078; ❶), on Grimares Street near the town plaza. The eight rooms all have air conditioning and private bathrooms, and there's a simple restaurant. The *Morales Lodging Inn* (❶) at the pier is a little run-down but reasonably comfortable. The owner is friendly and something of an oracle on ferry schedules. If you want to stay away from the noise of the town centre, the best option is

Roda I and II Beach Resort (❷) 3km south in the barangay of **Kamandag**. Easily reached from Looc by tricycle, *Roda* is right on a pleasant beach and has a choice of family cottages and air-conditioned twin or double rooms.For an altogether different experience, you can rent out an entire island for the night for only P5000 through *Morel's Private Island Resort* (☏02/986-6775, ⓦwww.morelisland .com; ❹), a short hop to the south from Santa Fe.

The best **place to eat** in Looc is the *Pacific Garden Restaurant*, a Chinese place serving noodle soup, piping-hot fried rice and deliciously peppery *adobo* that comes with a lump of freshly steamed rice. For fresh fruit, there's a good daily market near the plaza.

Romblon Island

Romblon Island has been extensively quarried for decades to get at the beautiful Romblon marble, a favourite with the rich and famous in Manila. It's a picturesque island, with a pretty harbourside capital, an interior buzzing with wildlife and a coastal road, partly cemented, that you can whip around in half a day, past some enticing beaches with a number of simple resorts.

Romblon Town

One of the most attractive towns in the Philippines, low-rise **ROMBLON TOWN**, the provincial capital, sits on a sweeping deep port with red-roofed houses lining the water's edge and thickly jungled hills behind. Happily dozing in the balm of a more sedentary age, the town feels a few centuries behind the rest of the Philippines. In the mornings all you can hear is cockerels and in the afternoons almost everything stops for a siesta, stirring again at 3pm when the worst of the heat has gone from the sun and children can play along the shore.

The town has a few sights, all reachable on foot. Slap in the middle overlooking the quaint little Spanish plaza is **St Joseph's Cathedral**, a richly atmospheric seventeenth-century church where almost everyone in town turns out for Mass on Sunday at 8am and on weekdays in the early evening. On the seafront are the remains of **Fort San Andres** and **Fort San Pedro**, reminders of the risk Romblon Town once faced from pirates.

There's a helpful **tourist office** (Mon–Fri 8am–noon & 1–4pm; ☏042/507-2202) in the Provincial Capitol Building, a short tricycle ride from the pier. MBRS Lines has a ferry for Manila (12hr) every Wednesday. For Sibuyan, bangkas run daily to Magdiwang, Cajidiocan and San Fernando.

The main **hotel** in town is the *Romblon Plaza* (☏042/507-2269; ❷), one block away from the pier and, with four storeys, the tallest building in Romblon. There are six types of room, from en-suite doubles with fan to air-conditioned superior suites, also with private bathroom. The hotel has its own very pleasant rooftop restaurant with daily specials, including some delicious fresh seafood. *Jak's Restaurant & Bar* on the plaza has some surprisingly good Western favourites including spaghetti, plus curry and grilled fish.

Beaches and resorts

There are good beaches with very simple hut accommodation at **Lonos**, 3km south from Romblon. One of the best is **Bonbon Beach**, about 500m long and with a gently sloping ocean floor that makes it safe for swimming. Also here is **Tiamban Beach**, a short stretch of white sand flanked by palm trees and wooden shacks.

A number of **resorts** have sprung up along this stretch of coast. The first one you reach if you head south from town is *Tiamban Beach Resort* (☏02/723-6710; ❹), a well-run place with native-style cottages right on the beach, many with shady verandas and sunset views. Prices include transfers from the pier and all meals and the resort can also organize island-hopping, mountain biking and diving. Next door are the bamboo cottages of the less grand but equally friendly *Palm Beach Garden Resort* (❷), which has a restaurant in a shady garden. Seven kilometres further south is Ginablan, where you'll find *Marble Beach Resort* (☎0919/643-7497; ❸), which has bamboo cottages with shady verandas right on a pretty beach. A few minutes south of Ginablan in the barangay of **San Pedro** is *San Pedro Beach Resort* (☎0928/273-0515; ❷), a charming, relaxing hideaway with cottages nestled along a hillside overlooking sandy Talipasak Beach. There's home cooking in the restaurant and staff can arrange island-hopping and trekking.

❻ Sibuyan Island

Dominated by the ragged saw-like bulk of Mount Guiting Guiting, verdant **Sibuyan Island** in the easternmost of the Romblon group has everything an adventure traveller could dream of: a sparkling coastline, a thickly forested interior and a couple of daunting mountain peaks. Dubbed "The Galapagos of Asia", Sibuyan boasts an extraordinarily rich range of **wildlife** including 700 plant species and 131 species of bird. Five mammal species (one fruit bat and four rodents) are unique to the island. Much of the Sibuyan was declared a nature reserve in 1996. However, this has not prevented the island from being targeted as a potential mineral mining site, and much to the dismay of environmentalists and local communities, a Canadian mining company was granted exploratory mining rights in 2009.

Sibuyan's 47,000 residents, mostly subsistence farmers and hunters who rely on the forest and the ocean to supplement their meagre incomes, rarely see tourists but know every cove, trail and cave on the island and are happy to act as guides. Most of them live in three towns, **San Fernando**, **Cajidiocan** and **Magdiwang**.

Arrival and accommodation

Bangkas leave Romblon Town every day for Magdiwang, Cajidiocan and San Fernando. There are also irregular boats from to Sibuyan from Mandaon on Masbate (see p.228). Ask around and you'll be pointed in the direction of one of the island's **homestays**. In Magdiwang, the Feliciano family has a pretty wooden house close to the pier with clean rooms and a shared cold shower; P100 a night is the usual rate, plus a little extra if you want Mrs Feliciano to cook. In San Fernando, *Vicky's Place* on M.H. Del Pilar Street is a family home featuring some bright, airy upstairs guest rooms, with a shared bathroom. Any tricycle driver at the pier can take you there.

Mount Guiting Guiting

Rising directly from the coastal plain to a height of 2050m, **Mount Guiting Guiting** is an unforgettable sight. This is not a climb to be undertaken lightly and if you plan on doing any serious trekking or climbing, you'll have to bring all your equipment with you. The trail to the top of the mountain (affectionately known as G2 by climbers) starts from the Mount Guiting Guiting Natural Park headquarters, a short tricycle ride to the east of Magdiwang where most ferries dock. Here you can organize permits, a guide and porters (both P300/day). The trail starts gently enough, winding through pleasant lowlands, but soon becomes very steep and culminates in a precarious traverse across "the knife edge" to the summit. Even experienced mountaineers regularly fail to summit, and you'll need to allow three or four days for the round trip including ten hours for the ascent. Next to Guiting Guiting is **Mayo's Peak** (1530m), a secondary summit that, like its neighbour, is cloaked in mossy forests, ferns and rare orchids. The trek to the top is more straightforward, requiring only 24 hours.

Diving in the Philippines

The Philippines is blessed by a dazzling richness and diversity of marine life. Under the waves lies an underwater wonderland of stupefying coral gardens teeming with brilliantly coloured reef fish, turtles, giant clams and starfish, while deep down there are giant rays and prowling sharks. Indeed, this vast tropical archipelago is at the heart of Southeast Asia's "coral triangle" the most biologically diverse marine ecosystem on earth, with over 300 types of coral and 350 fish species. Diving here is affordable and thanks to warm waters, is possible year-round.

Angelfish ▲

Clownfish ▼

Unmissable marine life

The beauty of diving in the Philippines is that you don't have to dive deep to see some incredible marine life. Pottering about in warm coral waters at just a few metres, where sunlight is brightest, you'll come across a multitude of species. Among the commonest are the exotic and brightly coloured **angelfish**, **damselfish** and eye-catching **humbugs**, striped black and white like the sweet. In shallow coral gardens you'll see inquisitive **clownfish** defending their coral nests either singly or in pairs, perhaps with minuscule juveniles at their sides. Also unmissable are the frenetic shoals of **dragonets** and **dottybacks**, with their psychedelic colouring. **Moray eels** take shelter in crevices in the reef and it's not unusual to see one even in the shallows. Even **turtles** can be seen at this depth.

Where the coral plunges away steeply into an inky darkness, at depths of five or six metres, you'll see bright green **parrot fish** and mesmerizing **batfish**, who patrol the reef edge in family shoals. These slopes and fore reefs are also home to **snappers**, **goatfish** and **wrasses**, the largest of which – the Napoleon wrasse – can dwarf a person. Deeper still, but usually in the more isolated dive sites such as Tubbataha and Pescador, it's possible to see sharks, including **whitetip reef sharks** and **grey reef sharks**, while if you're lucky an immense but gentle **manta ray** or **whale shark** might drift lazily past.

Poisonous species include the beautifully hypnotic **lionfish** (also called the flamefish), which hunts at night and has spines along its back that can deliver a nasty dose of venom, while shoals of **jellyfish** are common at certain times of the year.

Green turtle ▼

Saving the reefs

Coral reefs are home to 25 percent of all marine life and form the nurseries for about a quarter of the oceans' fish. Sadly, they are increasingly under threat. Eighty percent of the Philippines' reef system is at risk of being lost as a result of coastal development, cyanide fishing, pollution, global warming and reckless tourism. One illustration of the global-warming threat is a marked increase in the number of spiny, toxic coral-destroying **crown-of-thorns starfish** appearing around the archipelago, outbreaks of which often occur when ocean temperatures and nutrient levels increase. To make matters worse, some of the starfish's major predators, such as lumphead wrasse and giant triton, have declined in recent years as a result of overfishing, meaning that these voracious creatures can wipe out large areas of coral; an individual can consume up to six square metres of living reef per year.

▲ Crown-of-thorns starfish

▼ Spear fishing

All aboard

If you're serious about your diving, booking a trip on a liveaboard can be a memorable experience, giving you the opportunity to get away from the more popular dive resorts and explore the wilderness. In turn, this means you'll have an almost guaranteed chance of some real thrills, including encounters with immense manta rays, whale sharks, dolphins, reef sharks and hammerheads. You'll be able to do as many as five dives a day, including deep, drift, wreck and night dives. And at the end of a hard day underwater you'll return to a good dinner prepared by the ship's cook. Everything is usually included in the rate – except the beer. For a list of liveaboards see p.38.

▼ Diver, Cabilao Island

Scuba diving, Apo Island ▲

Anthias, Puerto Galera ▼

Shark, Panglao Island ▼

Top 10 dive sites

▶▶ **Anilao** Closest dive site to Manila and justly celebrated for Cathedral Rock, a marine sanctuary just offshore swarming with fish. See p.121.

▶▶ **Apo Island** Not to be confused with the reef (see below), this island off Negros is a fabulous place to go diving, with hordes of fish and forests of coral. See p.308.

▶▶ **Apo Reef** One of the best sites in the Philippines with few divers and lots of big fish, two hours off the coast of Mindoro (day-trips or liveaboards possible). See p.254.

▶▶ **Coron** The best wreck diving in the country, possibly in the world. There are 24 chartered wrecks, Japanese ships sunk in one massive attack by US aircraft in 1944. See p.382.

▶▶ **Puerto Galera** Unrivalled all-round destination with something for everyone, from novices to old hands. The most celebrated site is known as the Sabang Wrecks (one steel yacht and two decaying wood boats), smothered in batfish, scorpion fish, giant moray eels, lionfish and crabs. See p.237.

▶▶ **Padre Burgos** Out of the way in undeveloped southern Leyte and a prime spot for discovering new dive sites. See p.353.

▶▶ **Panglao Island** The dive sites close to the congenial Alona Beach resorts offer an exceptional range of marine life, from Napoleon wrasse to barracuda and whitetip sharks. See p.285.

▶▶ **Samal Island** This sleepy island just off the coast of Davao, Mindanao, harbours numerous dive sites, including the pink corals of Pinnacle Point. See p.415.

▶▶ **Subic Bay** The former US Navy base is an exceptional location for wreck dives, with the USS *New York* one of the highlights. See p.129.

▶▶ **Tubbataha Reef** You'll need to book a liveaboard trip, but it's worth it, with guaranteed sightings of sharks, and a good chance of mantas and whale sharks. See p.364.

Carabao Island

Less than an hour south of Santa Fe on Tablas Island by bangka, beautiful little **Carabao Island** is also easy to reach from Boracay (see box, p.329). All the Boracay dive operators and resorts run trips to the island, or you can rent your own bangka for around P2000 for the round trip. Only 6km wide from the capital of **San José** on the east coast to **Lanas** on the west, Carabao Island is an idyllic place where fishing is the main industry and tourism has only just begun to have an impact. Divers arrive on day-trips to explore the dozen well-known dive sites in the reefs around the island, or, if you want to stay longer there are a few decent resorts. It's easy to hire a motorbike in San José to get around; an enjoyable ride takes you to Tagaytay Point, the highest point on the island from where there are magnificent views across to Boracay and beyond.

Bangkas **arrive** at **Port Said**, a couple of minutes' walk from the island's best beach, **Inobahan Beach**, a 1km stretch of powdery white sand. Here you can **stay** at the friendly and comfortable *Ivy's Vine Beach Resort* (☎0929/715-7881, ⓦwww .asianbeachresort.com; ❸), which has good beach cottages and a dive centre. Another option is the *Republic of Inobahan Beach Resort* (❸), which has four thatched cottages, each spacious enough for three. It also has a small restaurant – intriguingly named the *Sir Polyon Lounge* – serving breakfast, soup, hamburgers and grilled meat and fish. A matter of metres away is the *Ging Grill and Restaurant*, where the food is straightforward and cheap, including hot dog sandwiches, noodles and burgers for a bargain basement P20.

Samar

The island of **Samar**, between Bicol and Leyte and 320km from top to toe, has yet to take off as a major tourist destination, which is both a shame and a blessing as large parts of the island remain unspoilt, wild and beautiful. One reason not to miss it is the marvellous **Sohoton Natural Bridge National Park**, a prehistoric wilderness in Western Samar province, full of caves, waterfalls and underground rivers, while further north around the towns of Calbayog and Catbalogan lie some of Southeast Asia's biggest cave systems. There are also dozens of relatively untouched islands off the north coast. In **Eastern Samar**, Borongan, and further south, Guiuan and the beautiful island of Calicoan are deservedly popular stops on the surfing circuit. On a historical note, **Homonhon Island** in Eastern Samar is where Ferdinand Magellan is reputed to have set foot for the first time on Philippine soil in 1521.

Samar has a different **climate** from the rest of the country, with a dry period in May and June only. Apart from that, rainfall is possible throughout the year. Most of the rain falls from the beginning of November until February when there can also be fierce typhoons. The best time to visit is from May to September, although the growing number of surfers who come here to take advantage of the swells that rip in from the Pacific might argue that the typhoon season is best.

Getting to Samar

There are **airports** at Calbayog and Catarman, both served by Cebu Pacific, Airphil Express and Zest Air. **Ferries** from Matnog on the southernmost tip of Bicol make the one-hour trip to the Balwharteco Terminal in Allen, northwestern Samar, several times each morning. Tacloban on neighbouring Leyte is linked to Samar by regular **buses** and **minivans**, crossing the 2km San Juanico Bridge, which spans the San Juanico Strait. From Manila, Eagle Star buses cross on the

Matnog–Allen ferry and run down the coastal road to Calbayog, taking about twelve hours.

Northern Samar

Arriving from Luzon by bus or ferry, your first taste of Samar is the small port town of **ALLEN**. From here there are dozens of buses and jeepneys a day that run east to Catarman and beyond, and south to Calbayog and Catbalogan, where you can catch an onward bus to the southern half of the island. Buses heading south and east from Allen all pick up passengers at the port itself where you can also catch a jeepney into town, 5km to the south.

There are limited **accommodation** options in Allen and the only reason you'd stay the night is if you couldn't move on. If you find yourself stuck here, *Wayang Wayang Resort* (℡0920/614-7536; ❷) is a quiet, simple complex of cottages 5km south of town overlooking the sea, easily accessible by tricycle.

The Balicuatro Islands

The remote **Balicuatro Islands** off Samar's northwest coast afford the chance to find your own slice of paradise for the day, although currently only the largest island, Dalupiri has anywhere to stay. From **San Isidro**, on the coast road south of Allen, there are bangkas to Dalupiri (every 20min; 30min) and other islands in the group. The capital of Dalupiri, where bangkas arrive, is **SAN ANTONIO**, a sleepy barrio with a post office, a small hospital and dozens of little bangkas that can take you on day-trips to the other islands. You can stay 3km west of here at the eccentric *Flying Dog Resort* (℡02/521-5085; ❷), featuring eye-catching pyramid-style huts and an alfresco bamboo restaurant where simple food such as grilled fish and chicken is served. This is a really tranquil "escape to nowhere" place, with electricity for only a few hours every evening, and though the huts are a little tatty, the setting is marvellous, with a white sand beach and a coral reef offshore. The other option on Dalupiri is the *Octopussy Bungalow Resort* (℡916/399-4297, ⓦwww.octopussy.ch; ❸) which has pretty concrete-and-thatch cottages in quiet gardens close to some marvellous beaches. There aren't many places to eat in the area, but the resort offers half- and full board for a little extra.

The rest of the islands, also largely unexplored by tourists, are mostly home to farmers and fishermen. **Capul**, for example, is a picturesque little island about one hour from San Isidro, with a majestic seventeenth-century fortified stone church built by the Spanish, and an almost derelict coastal road that takes you past some incredible coves and beaches.

Catarman and around

The ramshackle north coast port city of **CATARMAN** is served by daily flights from Manila and – though it has never been a tourist destination – makes a good point of entry to Northern Samar if you want to save yourself a long bus or ferry journey. Tricycles (P50 or P10/person if you share) wait at the **airport** to take arriving passengers the 5km into town. All three airlines have offices at the airport, and also on J.P. Rizal Street in town. To move on from Catarman, **buses** from the terminal behind the market leave for Allen (1hr), Calbayog (90min), Catbalogan (3hr) and Tacloban (7hr). There are also Silver Star services for Manila via Allen and Matnog (12hr; P600/1100 for ordinary/a/c). A quicker way for destinations south is to take a Grand Tours, or D'Turbanada van, which leave hourly.

There are a few **banks** with ATMs in Catarman, including a Metrobank on Garcia Street and a PNB on Jacinto Street. To get **online**, try *Asphire Computer Works* on Jacinta Street.

There's surprisingly good **accommodation** to be found in Catarman, the best of which is *Sasa Pension House* (☎055/251-8515; ❶) on Jacinto Street, which has clean, comfortable rooms with wi-fi and is often fully booked. Just across the road on Roxas Street, *Pink City Pension House* (☎055/251-8695; ❷) has bright pink rooms with air conditioniong, cable TV and hot water, plus there's free wi-fi in the lobby. At the eastern end of town on Marcos Street, *GV Hotel* (☎055/500-6373; ❶) has clean rooms with air conditioning, cable TV and cold showers.

For meals, as well as the usual offerings of *Jollibee* and *Chooks to Go*, there are also a few reasonable **restaurants**, including *The Nest* on Garcia Street, which has pizza (P200–300) and pasta dishes and serves as a bar in the evenings with live music on Wednesdays, Thursdays and Fridays. Other options include *Michz*, at the western end of Jacinta Street, a popular café serving sandwiches (P35–70), budget meals and drinks. For a decent cup of coffee head to *Gilda's Coffee Shop* on Annunciacion Street, which also has free wi-fi and a small selection of local handicrafts for sale, the profits of which go to help local children and the elderly.

From **San José** (all bus services stop here) thirty minutes east of Allen by road and 45 minutes west of Catarman, you can charter a bangka (expect to pay at least P1500 for a day-trip, and to have to provide food for the boatman) to explore the tantalizingly undeveloped cluster of islands called **Biri-Las Rosas**. Somewhere among this group of idyllic outcrops, many with fine beaches, you can find one to call your own for the day. Most are only inhabited by poor fisherfolk and infrastructure is nonexistent, so staying the night is difficult unless you're willing to rough it.

Western Samar

Western Samar is dominated by its limestone topography, and has **caves**, gorges and waterfalls galore. Aside from the famous Sohoton Natural Bridge National Park, most natural attractions are still relatively undiscovered, and there is little tourist infrastructure. The provincial towns of **Calbayog** and **Catbalogan** are the best bases for exploring the region. Of the two, Calbayog is the more attractive and has better hotels and restaurants, but to really get up close and personal with the caves, a stop at Trexplore in Catbalogan (see p.340) is recommended.

Calbayog

Sitting pretty with the Calbayog River on one side and the Samar Sea on the other, **CALBAYOG** on the west coast makes a pleasant enough place for a stop on your way through Samar. Pretty **Bangon and Tarangban Falls** are within easy reach of the city, as is Guinogo-an Cave. To get to the falls take a jeepney to Tinaplacan, and then walk (45min), or take a *habal-habal* direct. Once there you can swim in the plunge pool or hike up to Tarangban Falls. For **Guinogo-an Cave** you need to take a jeepney to Lungsod, from where you can hire a boat (P300 return) and then you'll have to walk the last 15 minutes to the cave. It's best to take a guide with you, which can be organized through the tourist office. The vast Calbiga cave system is also accessible from Calbayog, but it is best to organize trips here through Trexplore in Catbalogan (see p.340).

Arrival

The **airport** is 8km out of town and a tricycle into the centre costs P100. **Buses** and jeepneys arrive at the **Capoocan transport terminal** north of the river, ten minutes by tricycle from the town centre. Arriving from Cebu by ferry, the **port** lies on reclaimed land 2km from town. Calbayog's friendly **tourist office** (Mon–Fri 8am–noon & 1–5pm; ☎055/209-4041) has a few brochures about local attractions and can offer transport advice as well as helping to arrange guides.

By plane

Airphil Express and Zest Air each have three weekly flights from Manila.

By ferry

Calbayog has three weekly ferries for Cebu (12hr; P595–960), operated by Cokaliong and Palacio Shipping Lines, both of which have ticket offices at the port.

By bus and van

There are buses every 30 minutes for Catbalogan (2hr; P80) and Tacloban (4hr; P180). For Catarman there are four services a day (2hr; P100), while Allen (2hr; P80) is served by jeepneys which also leave from the bus station. A quicker alternative to the buses is to take a Grand Tours or Van-Vans van. Both companies have hourly services for Catarman, Catbalogan and Tacloban, which leave from their private terminals. Grand Tours is on Bugalion Street, and Van-Vans is at the bus station. Finally, there are also Eagle Star bus-ferry-bus services for Manila.

Opposite the Legislative Hall there's a park and a **post office**, and there's a daily **market** in Orquin Street, on the northern edge of town near the river. To replenish cash, there are several **banks** with ATMs, including a UCPB on Gomez Street, and a Metrobank on Rosales Boulevard. There are a number of small **internet cafés** around town, such as *Chatwave* on Nijaga Street.

Accommodation and eating

In town the best accommodation option is *Almira Garden Hotel* (☎055/209-3240; ❷), on Gelera Street, which has clean and nicely painted rooms with comfy beds, hot and cold water, refrigerators, cable TV and free wi-fi, although most rooms are windowless. South of town on the National Highway, the newly opened *Ciriaco Hotel* (☎055/209-6521; ❼), is by far Calbayog's best hotel, and has excellent rooms with all mod cons, the more expensive of which look straight out to sea. There's also a trendy lobby café, with free wi-fi, and a pool was under construction at the time of writing.

Along with the obligatory *Jollibee* and *Chooks to Go*, Calbayog's dining options span to *Carlos n' Carmelos* on Nijaga Street, which has fast-food favourites including burgers (P37) and fries, as well as more interesting choices such as fried mozzarella (P69). Next door, *SO Coffee* has cakes, smoothies (P60) and free wi-fi, and just along the street *Isla Coffee* has more of the same, plus sandwiches.

Catbalogan

Two hours south of Calbayog, the bustling port town of **CATBALOGAN** is the ramshackle capital of Western Samar. It is, however, of increasing interest to travellers as a base from which to explore the wilds of Western Samar, particularly the huge **cave systems** to be found within a couple of hours of the city. Of the many caves in the region, **Jiabong**, just 12km from Catbalogan, is the most easily visitable. A little further away, **Langun Gobingob**, in Calbiga, is the largest cave system in Southeast Asia. The best way to get underground is to arrange a **guided trip** through Joni Bonifacio at the Trexplore outdoor shop (☎055/251-2301, ⓦwww.trexplore.blogspot.com) on Allen Avenue. Joni can arrange day (P3000) or overnight (P7000) trips to the caves (P3000) including meals, permits, equipment and transport.

Practically speaking, Catbalogan has most things a traveller should need: there's an RCBC, a BDO and an Allied Bank, all with **ATMs** on Del Rosario Street, and there are plenty of **internet** cafés scattered around the city – try *Movies n' Magic* or *Cyber Surf*, both of which are on San Roque Street.

Accommodation

Casa Cristina San Roque St ☏0921/660-6665. A cheap-and-cheerful option with clean, brightly painted rooms with cold showers, but no windows. ❶

Maqueda Bay Hotel Del Rosario St ☏055/251-2386. On the edge of town, the *Maqueda Bay* looks straight out to sea and has newly painted deluxe rooms with a/c, cable TV and hot showers. ❷

Rolet Hotel Mabini Ave ☏055/251-5512. The best option in town, with a/c rooms, cable TV and good bathrooms. The friendly proprietors, Odie and Lolit Letaba, can answer most travel-related questions for the area, and there's wi-fi in the canteen. ❷

Rose Scent Pensionne House Curry Ave ☏055/251-5785. Hard to resist the name, and once inside, the pension has clean and functional rooms with powerful cold showers. ❶

Eating

As well as the hotels, *Jollibee* and *Chooks to Go*, other dining choices include:

Pizza Factory San Roque St ☏055/251-5512. Turns out half-decent pizzas (P135–160) in a modern café-restaurant. Daily 9am–10pm.

Tony's Kitchen Next to Pizza Factory on San Roque St. Tony's does a good line in fried dishes – the whole chicken (P260) is particularly tasty. Daily 8am–8pm.

Sohoton Natural Bridge National Park

Best known for a natural rock formation that forms a bridge across a gorge, the **Sohoton Natural Bridge National Park** includes some remarkable limestone caves and gorges and lowland rainforest where you can see, even around the park's picnic areas, monitor lizards, macaques and wild boar. Much of the area can be toured by boat, although to reach the natural bridge itself you'll have to get out and walk; and as there are few marked trails, you'll need to hire a **guide** to find your way around. The boat trip into the park is spectacular, heading up the Cadacan River's estuary which is lined by mangroves and nipa palms. As you approach the park the river begins to twist and is then funnelled into a gorge of limestone cliffs and caves. The most accessible of the park's many impressive caves is **Panhuughan I**, which has extensive stalactite and stalagmite formations in every passage and chamber, many that sparkle when the light from your flashlight falls on them. If you're lucky you might come across a number of specialized

---

Moving on from Catbalogan

By ferry
Catbalogan has one ferry per week for Cebu (Fri 8pm) which leaves from the pier at the end of Allen Avenue.

By bus, jeepney and van
There are buses every 30 minutes for Calbayog (2hr; P80) and Tacloban (3hr; P100), and less frequent services for Catarman (4hr; P180) and Borongan (5hr; P140). A quicker alternative to the buses is to take a Duptours, Grand Tours or Van-Vans van. All three companies have regular services for Calbayog, Catarman and Tacloban, which leave from their private terminals. Grand Tours and Van-Vans are on San Bartoleme Street, and the Duptours terminal is just around the corner on Allen Avenue. Finally, there are also two Eagle Star bus-ferry-bus services for the 18-hour journey to Manila: the first ordinary service (P1090) is at 9am, and the second air-conditioned bus is at 10.30am.

spiders and millipedes that live their lives here in total darkness. There have been many significant archeological finds in the caves, including burial jars, decorated human teeth and Chinese ceramics. During World War II Filipino guerrillas used the caves as hideouts in their campaign against the occupying Japanese forces.

Park practicalities

The park is in the southern part of Samar, the only approach being through **Basey**, on Samar's southwest coast 10km from the barangay of Sohoton and the entrance to the park. The quickest way to get there is via **Tacloban** on Leyte, from where you can catch an early minivan or jeepney to Basey (45min), then a tricycle to the Department of Environment and Natural Resources (☎055/276-1025) near Basey's plaza, where you pay the P150 entrance fee, and can arrange a **guide** (P300), head flashlight (P300) and a bangka (P1200 for a 7-seater) to take you to and from the park. You can also get information about visiting the park at the tourist office in Tacloban (see p.347). There's no **accommodation** in the park, but there are a couple of lodging houses in Basey. The best is *Distrajo's Place* (☎053/276-1191; ❷), which has singles and doubles with fan, but local homestays can also be arranged through the tourist office in Tacloban.

Marabut Islands

Two hours south of Catbalogan, Marabut is the jumping-off point for exploring the **Marabut Islands**, a striking collection of toothy limestone outcrops rising out of the sea only a few hundred metres offshore. In Marabut you can hire a bangka and there are also places in town where you can hire a kayak for the day. There's no **accommodation** on any of the islands, but in Marabut itself there's the wonderful **Marabut** *Marine Park Beach Resort* (☎053/520-0414; ❸), which has several simple but perfectly comfortable wooden cottages and a restaurant serving fresh seafood. A short jeepney ride east along the coast from Marabut is **Lawaan**, a rustic and friendly coastal community where you can stay at *Jasmine House* (☎0170/9630-543; ❸), a private holiday home set in peaceful gardens with a number of well-kept rooms and studio for rent. More luxurious accommodation is available at the upmarket *Caluwayan Palm Island Resort* (☎055/276-5206, Ⓦ www.caluwayanresort.com; ❺), 17km northwest along the coast from Marabut, which has lovely native-style cottages on a pretty stretch of beach.

Eastern Samar

This part of Samar is surf country, particularly around **Borongan**, and further south on beautiful, peaceful **Calicoan Island**, accessed from the small and sleepy town of **Guian**. Calicoan has terrific beaches, caves and lagoons which are only just starting to see tourism development. You can reach this part of the island by bus from Catbalogan or Tacloban.

Borongan

The bus trip from Catbalogan across to the east coast is one of the great little road journeys in the Philippines, taking you up through the rugged, jungle-clad interior past isolated barrios and along terrifying cliff roads. The bus emerges from the wilderness at **Taft** after about four hours and turns south to **BORONGAN**, where you can find good surf most times of the year. If the surf's not up, you could always hire a bangka at the wharf in Borongan and take a trip along the coast or out to the pretty island of **Divinubo**, which doesn't have any accommodation but is an idyllic day-trip destination for exploring and snorkelling; make sure you take something to eat and drink.

Arrival and information

There is a small **tourist office** (Mon–Sat 8am–4pm; ☎055/330-1139) in the Provincial Capitol Building facing Borongan plaza. To get cash, there's a Metrobank opposite the church, and a PNB across from the Uptown Mall by *Hotel Dona Vicenta*, both of which have **ATMs**. For **internet** head for *Jah's Internet Games* near the *Domsowir Hotel* on Real Street.

Moving on from Borongan there are a few **buses** that ply the mountain route across to Catbalogan (5hr; P140), as well as jeepneys and vans for Guiuan. The Duptours terminal is on Real Street and Van-Vans is on E. Cinco Street. If you like long road trips, Eagle Star has one daily bus for Manila at 5.30am which takes 21 hours to reach Pasay.

Accommodation and eating

There are a few **places to stay** in and around Borongan, many of which cater to surf dudes. The *Pirate's Cove Beach & Surf Resort* (☎0919/880-9157; ❹) in the barangay of Bato is an eclectic place right on the ocean, run by amiable surfer Pete and his wife. As well as having interesting rooms that range from a treehouse to family cottages, all of which have kitchens, the resort also has a pool, jacuzzi, wi-fi, and one of the most impressive Scalextric setups you'll ever see. In town the best accommodation is at the grand-looking *Hotel Dona Vicenta* (☎055/261-3585; ❷) on Real Street, which has comfortable air-conditioned rooms with cable TV, although many suffer from being too close to the noisy bar that stays open until 2am. A little further along Real Street, *GV Pension* (☎055/261-2580; ❷) has clean, simple rooms with air conditioning and cable TV. **Dining** options are limited, but include *Kandaga Resto Grill* on Real Street, which serves burger meals (P80), pizzas (P100–120), and Filipino dishes including *lumpia* with rice (P69).

Guiuan

At the tip of a peninsula which juts from Sothern Samar into the Pacific, **GUIUAN** is the access point for the wonderfully wild island of Calicoan, but the town itself has a beautiful old church and a unique history. By a strange twist of fate, Guiuan was once one of the country's boom towns, a small economic miracle that began when it was chosen to take in six thousand Byelorussian refugees fleeing communism in China. They came in waves from 1945 to 1951, and businesses prospered as local entrepreneurs sold them everything from food to clothes and lumber so they could build houses. A number of their descendants still live in the region.

Arrival and information

Buses pull into the bus station by the port, while minivans stop along Guiuan's one main road, Lugay Street. There's a small, helpful **tourist information** and *pasalubong* centre in front of the church on Lugay Street, and a BNP **bank** with ATM next to the *Guiuan Pension Extension* on San Nicolas Street. For **internet** access try *Surf Na Internet Café* on San Francisco Street. Heading on to Borongan (3hr) there are jeepneys (P130) or Duptours vans at 5.30am and 5.30pm, while Tacloban can be reached by **bus** (5hr; P120) or hourly Duptours and Van-Vans vans.

Accommodation and eating

Accommodation options in town are limited. The rooms at *Khaishra* (☎055/271-2376; ❷) on Lugay Street are clean but are overpriced given that bathrooms are shared and beds are very soft. A few minutes' walk along Lugay Street, *Guiuan Pension* (☎0926/509-4317; ❶) is the cheapest place to stay in town, but their extension, just around the corner on San Nicolas Street (☎0935/949-7668; ❷), has nicer rooms. By far the best choice is to head out to *Tanghay View Lodge* (❶) on the waterfront about 1km to the north of Guiuan, which has quiet, clean motel-style rooms and a **restaurant** that serves excellent cheap seafood and has wi-fi. The owner, an avid photographer, is a great source of local information and advice. **Dining** options are equally thin on the ground, and aside from the *Tanghay*, the best bet is probably *Chooks to Go* next to Mercury Drug on Lugay Street.

The Town

At the heart of Guiuan, a tidy and friendly provincial town, is the strikingly white **Church of the Immaculate Conception** (daily 6am–9pm), whose construction was overseen by Augustinian friars who arrived during the second expedition to the Philippines from Spain. Completed in 1595 after twenty years of hard labour by the locals, the building is one of the most beautiful in the eastern Visayas. Designed to double as a fortress, the church once had a bulwark at each corner (only two remain) on which six pieces of artillery were once mounted. Inside the spacious interior an exuberant altar bears images of saints carved from ivory, as well as a frescoed ceiling based on the Sistine Chapel.

For great views of the east coast and the Pacific, head to the weather station at the top of **Tingtingon Hill**. You'll need to climb up from the former **US Air Force air base** (you can get a tricycle there from the centre), where the remains of its immense runway are now once again preparing for action pending proposed flights from Manila and Cebu.

Calicoan Island

From Guiuan it's a short hop by jeepney across a causeway to **Calicoan**, which has been getting a lot of attention in recent years as the country's most exciting new destination, not only for the wild surf which crashes into the island's east coast, but also for its untouched natural beauty – don't be surprised to see the occasional monkey cross the road or find yourself sharing a beach with huge monitor lizards. There's plenty to do here, too, with walking trails, caves, lagoons, surfing, diving, kayaking and so on. To make the most of your time, take a guide.

Accommodation options are still few and far between, but on a beach known as ABCD, the island's prime surfing area, the upmarket *Calicoan Surf Camp* (☎0917/628-6615, ⊛www.calicoansurfcamp.com; ❽) has eight luxurious air-conditioned cottages set in beautiful gardens with a pool overlooking the Pacific. Just north of here, *Calicoan Villas* (☎0927/871-0588) is an English-owned hotel right on the rugged Pacific and has a choice of rooms, from simple cottages (❸) to stylish rooms in the main building (❼). On the calmer western side of the island there are a few more simple resorts including the newly opened *La Luna* ☎0915/833-1884), an Italian–Filipino venture with tasteful fan (❹) and air-conditioned (❻) rooms, the more expensive of which look out to the ocean.

On the northern tip of the island a ridge of Palawan-style limestone cliffs are attracting rock climbers, while south of here there's thick jungle perfect for trekking. Ask first in Guian about hiring a guide as even on a small island like this it's easy to get lost. The island's middle section has fantastic almost virginal beaches on either side. On the east coast is **Ngolos Beach**, which is very reminiscent of Boracay before tourism arrived, and on the west coast is **White Sand Beach** – eight kilometres of wild tropical beauty. There are ten other beaches dotted around the island; many of the small coves can only be reached on foot.

Homonhon Island

Two hours off the coast of Guiuan, or an hour by bangka from the southern tip of Calicoan, lies **Homonhon Island**, where Magellan first set foot on Philippine soil on

March 16, 1521. Magellan extended a message of goodwill from the king of Spain and a feast was held and gifts were exchanged. On March 25 he sailed on to Limasawa (see p.354), where it is thought the first Mass in the Philippines was held. There's not much here that commemorates Magellan, just a faded old marker at the landing site and an annual **pageant** on or around March 17 that re-enacts the landing. You can get a public bangka here from Guiuan, but the sea is fickle in this area so boats don't always run and if they do they might not be able to return right away. There's no formal **accommodation**, though as ever you can pay to be put up by local people.

Leyte

The east Visayan island of **Leyte** ("LAY-tay"), separated from Samar to the north by a mere slither of ocean, the San Juanico Strait, is another sizeable chunk of the Philippines that has a great deal to offer visitors but is often overlooked. You could spend months on this island and still only scratch the surface: the coastline is immense, the interior rugged and there are lakes and mountains that are well off the tourist map, known only to farmers who have tilled their shores and foothills for generations.

In the sixteenth century, Magellan passed through Leyte on his way to Cebu, making a blood compact with the local chieftain as he did so. But to many Filipinos and war historians, Leyte will always be associated with **World War II**, when its jungled hinterlands became the base for a formidable force of guerrillas who fought a number of bloody encounters with the Japanese. It was because of this loyalty among the inhabitants that General Douglas MacArthur landed at Leyte on October 20, 1944, fulfilling the famous promise he had made to Filipinos, "I shall return."

Around the provincial capital of **Tacloban**, the usual arrival point, there are a number of sights associated with the war, notably the Leyte Landing Memorial, marking the spot where MacArthur waded ashore to liberate the archipelago. To the north of Tacloban is the beautiful island of **Biliran** and, a short bangka ride away from Biliran, the islands of **Maripipi** and **Higatangan**, which both have terrific beaches, rock formations and caves. To the south of Ormoc the coastal road takes you through **Baybay** and **Maasin**, both ferry ports, before reaching **Padre Burgos**, renowned for its scuba diving. Off the southern tip of Leyte is **Limasawa Island**, an isolated outcrop where some believe Magellan conducted the first Catholic Mass in the Philippines.

Getting to Leyte

Leyte's only major airport is at Tacloban, served by **flights** from Manila with Cebu Pacific, Philippine Airlines and Zest Air. Fast **ferry** connections link the port of **Ormoc** with Cebu, and there are also slower boats from Cebu and Tagbilaran to Maasin on Leyte's west coast. There are also sailings between Cebu City and Naval on the island of Biliran.

Buses to Leyte operate from Manila (a long haul through Bicol and Samar) and there are also regular daily services to Tacloban from Biliran Island off Leyte's north coast, and from Samar via the San Juanico Bridge.

Tacloban and around

On the northeast coast, **TACLOBAN** is associated by most Filipinos with that tireless collector of shoes, Imelda Marcos, who was born a little south of here in the small coastal town of Tolosa, to the prominent Romualdez family. Numerous streets and buildings bear the Romualdez name, including the airport. In her youth, Imelda was a local beauty queen, and referred to herself in later life as "the rose of Tacloban". The famed San Juanico Bridge, presented by Ferdinand to Imelda as testimony to his love, is another legacy of the Marcos connection.

Tacloban is a busy, dirty city, with most activity centred around the port and the market. There are few tourist attractions, though if you are here for a day or two you'll find the city has everything you need: some good accommodation, numerous ticket outlets for onward journeys, and banks and restaurants huddled in the compact centre to the south of Magsaysay Boulevard. The city's major fiesta is the **Tacloban Festival** in the last week of June, kicking off with the Subiran Regatta, a boat race held at the eastern entrance of the San Juanico Strait. Tacloban

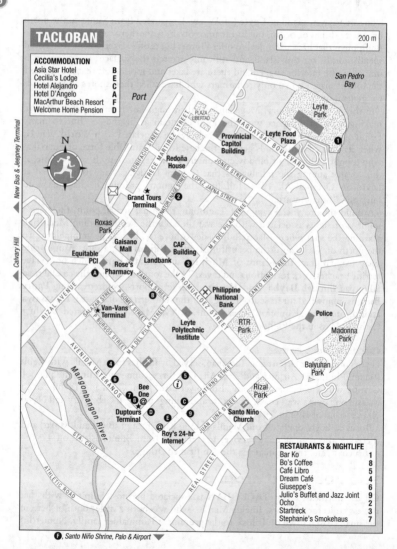

is also a good starting point for the **Sohoton National Park** in neighbouring Samar (see p.341).

Arrival, transport and information

Tacloban's **Daniel Z. Romualdez Airport** is south of the city along Real Street. A jeepney into town costs P12, a taxi around P150. All of the airlines have ticket offices at the airport, and Philippine Airlines has an office on Senator Enage Street (℡053/321-7771), near to the joint Cebu Pacific (℡053/321-9410) and Zest Air office (℡053/321-9378). **Buses** and **jeepneys** from all points arrive at a new terminal 2km northwest of the city. Cebu Pacific, Zest Air, Cebu Ferries and Supercat all have ticket kiosks at the bus terminal.

Staff at the **tourist office**, on Santo Nino Street (Mon–Fri 8am–5pm; ℡053/321-2048), are organized and helpful and their *Do-it-Yourself Tour of Tacloban & Environs* brochure outlines a number of interesting sights that you can cover on foot.

There's a **post office** near the harbour on Bonifacio Street, while *Roy's 24-hr Internet* on P. Paterno Street, and *Bee One*, opposite *Welcome Home Pension* on Santo Nino Street, are just a couple of the countless small **internet** places. Most **banks** in Tacloban have ATMs and give cash advances against credit cards. Metrobank is on P. Burgos, Street, and there's a BPI on Rizal Street close to *McDonald's*. The grandly monikered Dona Remedios T. Romualdez Memorial Hospital and Puericulture Centre (named after Imelda's mum) is on J. Romualdez Street. Local **police** headquarters are located on the P. Paterno Extension near the RTR Park.

Accommodation

Accommodation ranges from simple budget accommodation to affordable mid-range hotels. There are also a couple of plush hotels to consider, one of them a little way out of town at Palo but easy to reach by jeepney.

Asia Star Hotel Zamora St ℡053/321-5388. Quiet doubles with fan or a/c and all with private shower. Some rooms have cable TV and a fridge. Unattractive from the outside, but the rooms are fine, the staff friendly and the location central. Free in-room wi-fi. ❸

Cecilia's Lodge 178 P. Paterno St ℡053/523-1759. This modest but comfortable little pension house is the one many backpackers head to. It offers simple, clean singles, doubles and family rooms, most with a private shower and toilet. There's also a women-only building and staff are friendly and helpful. ❶

Hotel Alejandro P. Paterno St ℡053/321-7033. Attractive and well-managed hotel in an attractive 1930s building that was used as a refuge for WWII evacuee families. Rooms are tastefully styled and have a/c, cable TV and fridges, although not all have external windows. There's a fascinating display of historic photographs on the second and third floors, and

downstairs the restaurant and coffee shop has free wi-fi. ❸

Hotel D' Angelo Rizal Ave ℡053/325-2341. Well-located and clean mid-sized establishment with simple, modern rooms with tiled floors and good bathrooms. The rooms on the upper floors have pleasant views across the city and of the sea. Free wi-fi in the lobby. ❸

MacArthur Beach Resort Palo, 5km south of Tacloban ℡053/323-3015. In a terrific location close to the Leyte Landing Memorial (see p.348), this formerly government-run establishment recently purchased by a Singaporean investor and was being renovated at the time of writing, but is due to reopen in 2011. ❼

Welcome Home Pension South end of Santo Niño St opposite the Caltex petrol station ℡053/321-2739. Mid-sized establishment with good-value rooms, and often fully booked as a result. Choice of a/c rooms with (❷) or without en-suite bathroom. ❶

The city and around

One of your earliest stops on any tour of Tacloban must be to gawp at the **Santo Niño Shrine & Heritage Museum** (Mon–Sat 8–11.30am & 1–4.30pm; P200 for

By plane

Tacloban is connected by air to Manila with Cebu Pacific (2 daily), Philippine Airlines (3 daily) and Zest Air (2 daily).

By bus and van

There are regular buses from Tacloban's new terminal for Catbalogan (every 30min; P100), Calbayog, Catarman, Guiuan (hourly; 4hr; P130) and Borongan (hourly; 5hr; P180), all on Samar, as well as Ormoc (3hr; P90) on Leyte, and Naval on Biliran. Many of these routes are also operated by quicker Duptours, Grand Tours and Van-Vans minivans, each of which leaves from their designated terminal. Duptours is opposite the *Welcome Home Pension*, on Santo Nino Street, Grand Tours leave from Trece Martinez Street, near the post office, and Van-Vans terminal is on P. Burgos Street. Finally, there are also three Eagle Star bus-ferry-bus services for Manila (24hr) every morning.

obligatory guide), a fifteen-minute walk south from the junction of Real Street and Avenida Veteranos, on the west side of the road opposite a Petron petrol station. A grand folly of a house that Imelda Marcos ordered built but never slept in, it was sequestered by the government after the Marcos regime was overthrown. Inside there is evidence aplenty that nothing was too opulent or tasteless for La Imelda. Her personal chapel has sparkling diamond chandeliers, gold-framed mirrors and an expensive replica of the miraculous Santo Niño de Leyte (the original resides in the Santo Niño Church opposite Santo Niño Park in Real Street). There is also a dazzling collection of gifts that she acquired on her many overseas shopping trips.

It's worth the sweat of taking a walk to the top of **Calvary Hill** on the western edge of Tacloban along Avenida Veteranos. This is a place of pilgrimage during Holy Week (before Easter) and the ascent is marked by the fourteen Stations of the Cross, with a five-metre statue of the Sacred Heart of Jesus at the summit. A good time to start the climb is late afternoon so you reach the top in time to watch the sun set. The views across Tacloban and San Pedro Bay are especially pretty after dark when the lights come on.

One of Tacloban's most remarkable legacies of World War II is the extraordinarily flamboyant **CAP Building** on J. Romualdez Avenue. Formerly known as Price Mansion, this became General Douglas MacArthur's HQ after he landed in Leyte to set in motion the liberation of the Philippines; memorabilia of his stay are on display here in the MacArthur Room (Mon–Fri 9am–5.30pm, Sat 8.30am–noon; P25). A five-minute walk north, in Senator Enage Street, is another war curiosity, **Redoña House** (no admission), the residence of President Sergio Osmeña and his staff during the liberation.

Palo

About 5km south of Tacloban is the small town of **PALO**, known for its associations with General Douglas MacArthur and the liberation of the Philippines towards the end of World War II. It was at Palo's **Red Beach**, about 1km from the town centre, that MacArthur waded ashore on October 20, 1944, fulfilling his famous vow to return. The spot is marked by the dramatic **Leyte Landing Memorial**, an oversized sculpture of the general and his associates, among them Sergio Osmeña, the first President of the Commonwealth, walking purposefully through the shallows to the beach. Just outside Palo, on **Hill 522**, there's an old Spanish church that was turned into a hospital during the war, and the remnants of a number of Japanese foxholes and bunkers. It's worth chartering a tricycle for the day when you reach Palo to take you from sight to sight.

Eating, drinking and nightlife

These days Tacloban has a pretty sophisticated **restaurant scene**, and in between meals, there are plenty of local specialties to snack on – *binagul*, a hot sticky concoction made of coconut and nuts, and chocolate *meron* can be bought freshly made every morning from hawkers along Rizal Avenue. There are also a number of places to get a decent cup of coffee including *Bo's Coffee* on Avenida Veteranos, *Startreck* on M.H. Del Pilar Street, and *Café Libro* on P. Gomez, the latter of which is a quirky little café with good cakes and a book exchange.

Restaurants

Dream Café 222 M.H. Del Pilar St. Clean and friendly Australian–Filipino-owned little diner serving sandwiches (P70–120), soups (P95–275) and tasty carrot cake (P98) around the clock. Free wi-fi.

Giuseppe's 173 Avenida Veteranos. Genuine Italian food in sophisticated surroundings. The stone-baked pizzas (P320–475) are as good as you'll find in this part of the world, and there's also ravioli ragu (P220), spaghetti marinara (P220), tiramisu, good coffee and free wi-fi.

Ocho Senator Enage St. Stylish restaurant where you choose from super-fresh salads, fish, fruit and desserts laid out at the back of the restaurant, and then have your main course cooked to your taste. Two can dine for around P500.

Stephanie's Smokehaus Avenida Veteranos. Popular and good-value buffet restaurant where P200 buys an all-you-can-eat spread.

Bars

Bar Ko On the seafront in the *Leyte Park Hotel* complex. A great place for a sunset beer looking out to the ocean.

Julio's Buffet & Jazz Joint P. Paterno St. Cosy venue for live acoustic music from 9pm Wednesdays to Saturdays.

Biliran and around

The beautiful and largely undiscovered island of **Biliran** lies off the north coast of Leyte, connected by a bridge. Biliran, an autonomous province, is the Philippines in microcosm: there's a lengthy coastline of coves and beaches, a jungled, mountainous interior with some wonderful waterfalls and even its own small version of Banaue's **rice terraces** at Iyusan in the island's western interior. Among the many natural wonders are nearly a dozen thundering waterfalls, most with deep, clear pools that are perfect for swimming: **Kasabanga Falls** is in the barangay of **Balaquid** on the south coast; **Casiawan Falls** a little further along the coast near **Casiawan** village; **Tinago Waterfall** near Cabibihan in the island's southeast; and last but not least **Bagongbong** near Iyusan.

Two of the best beaches on Biliran are on opposite sides of the island, but even on a day-trip you'll have time to see them both. On the east coast near Culaba is the beautifully deserted **Looc White Beach**, while the **Shifting Sand Bar**, 45 minutes by bangka towards Higatangan from the west coast capital of **NAVAL**, is a curving spit of sand surrounded by shallow water ideal for swimming, though note that there's no shade.

If you get to Biliran make sure you allow enough time to take a bangka to some of the surrounding islands. **Maripipi** is a picturesque place of friendly people dominated by a stunning nine-hundred-metre volcano, while Higatangan Rocks on **Higatangan Island**, one hour west of Naval by bangka, should also be on your itinerary. The beach here is beautiful and the rocks have been curved into extraordinary formations by time and tide. Ask your guide (see below) to take you to Cavintan Cave, said in local legend to extend all the way to Masbate and to contain deadly legions of venomous snakes – neither story appears true. Both islands have places to stay (see p.350).

Arrival and information

There are **buses** and Duptours minivans to Naval from Tacloban and Ormoc. Roble Shipping and Supershuttle Ferry operate **daily ferries** from Cebu City to Naval (9hr), but if you want to save time it's far quicker to take a fast ferry to Ormoc, and then a minivan from there (free if you travel with Supercat). There's a small provincial **tourist office** (℡053/500-9627; Mon–Fri 8am–5pm) and museum in the capitol building in Naval. For **internet**, *Roderick's Internet Café* is next to *Chooks to Go* by the State University on Naval Street. There are Metrobank and PNB **banks**, both with ATM, on Sabenorio Street.

To explore the more remote areas of the islands and to find the waterfalls, it's best to employ the services of a **local guide** (P300/day) which you can enquire about at the tourist office. From Naval there are jeepneys north to Almeria (P20), Kawayan (P25) and east to Caibiran and Culaba (P60), but no further in either direction. For Maripipi there are two **boats** daily (10am and 10.30am; P60) which take one hour and return at 5am the following day. There are three daily boats for Higantangan (10am, 10.30am and 11am; P40) which take 40 minutes to reach the island.

Accommodation and eating

There are a number of simple lodgings in Naval though better accommodation can be found out of town and on the offshore islands of Maripipi and Higatangan.

Naval

Brigida Inn Castin St ℡053/500-9379; Simple but quiet place close to the sea, with basic fan (**1**) and a/c rooms. **2**

Marvin's Seaside Inn 2km north of town ℡053/500-9171. A far better bet than staying in town, *Marvin's* has a choice of seaside rooms with cable TV and hot showers (but without sea views) in the main bright yellow block, and bigger, nicer rooms with the same facilities set around the pool in a building across the road. The restaurant has a decent range of Western and Filipino dishes, plus free wi-fi. **3**

Elsewhere on Biliran

Estrella's Sunset View Barangay Masagongsong, Kawayan ℡0921/542-2003. Quiet little resort with a/c and cable TV in the rooms, and a nice spring pool. **2**

VRC Resort On the coast north of Almeria ℡0916/466-5809. Small, clean, friendly and family-run resort with well-maintained rooms and a pool. **2**

Higantangan & Maripipi

Higantangan Island Resort Higatangan Island ℡927/697-9804, ⓦwww.higataganislandresort .com. A good range of rooms and cottages (**5**) spread through manicured gardens on the seashore. The resort can also arrange local hikes, bike and kayak rental, and provides a free shuttle to a nearby sand bar, a romantic spot at full moon. **2**

Napo Beach Resort Maripipi Island ℡0921/347-6620. Maripipi's only place to stay is an attractive resort with brightly painted fan (**2**) and a/c huts set at the base of mountains and looking straight out to sea. The resort has its own jetty, and two small pools. **4**

Ormoc

The small and relatively neat town of **ORMOC** on Leyte's west coast faces Ormoc Bay at the mouth of the Isla Verde River. A clean, attractive place, Ormoc has been largely rebuilt after floods in 1992 caused untold damage and resulted in the loss of eight thousand lives. It now has a lovely bayside park and drive from where the sunsets are marvellous. There's little else to see in town but **Lake Danao**, 19km away, can be reached by jeepney (P30). Once there you can hike to a number of different waterfalls including Inawasan Falls (30min), Tigbawan Falls (2hr) Maga-aso Falls (3–4hr), or just relax on a floating cottage on the lake (P150/hour).

Arrival and information

Ferries arrive at the port which is within walking distance of the town centre and many of the hotels. The main **bus terminal** and **jeepney terminal** are next to each other on Ebony Street, near the pier. No airlines fly to Ormoc, but **Philippine Airlines** does have an office (℡053/225-2081) in the Superdome, and Cebu Pacific has an office in Gaisano Mall.

There are plenty of **banks** with ATMs in Ormoc, including a BPI on Lopez Jaena Street, and a PNB on Bonifacio Street. **Western Union** has an office in the PPL Building. For **internet access** there are a number of cybercafés dotted around town including *Huey's Internet Café* on Malacadios street, and *Movies n' Magic* on the corner of Aviles and Bonifacio streets. Ormoc's **police** station is on the corner of J. Navarro and Aviles Streets. The ciy's best **hospital** is OSPA (Ormoc Sugar Planter's Association), east of town in Carlota Hills.

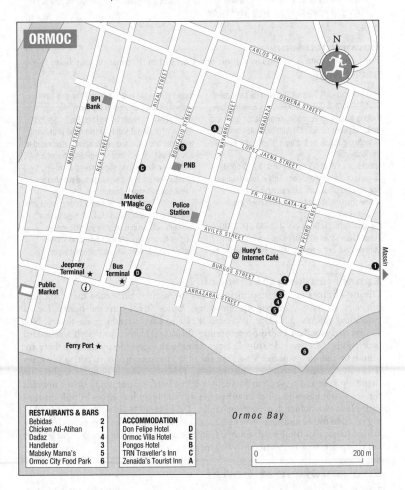

ORMOC

N

CARLOS TAN

RIZAL STREET

BPI Bank

MABINI STREET

REAL STREET

BONIFACIO STREET

J. NAVARRO STREET

ARRADAZA

OSMEÑA STREET

Ⓐ

Ⓑ

Ⓒ

PNB

LOPEZ JAENA STREET

Movies N'Magic @

Police Station

FR. ISMAEL CATA-AG

AVILES STREET

SAN PEDRO STREET

Huey's @ Internet Café

Jeepney Terminal ★

Bus Terminal ★ Ⓓ

BURGOS STREET

❶

Massin ▶

Public Market ⓘ

LARRAZABAL STREET

❷

Ⓔ

❸

❹

❺

Ferry Port ★

❻

RESTAURANTS & BARS	
Bebidas	2
Chicken Ati-Atihan	1
Dadaz	4
Handlebar	3
Mabsky Mama's	5
Ormoc City Food Park	6

ACCOMMODATION	
Don Felipe Hotel	D
Ormoc Villa Hotel	E
Pongos Hotel	B
TRN Traveller's Inn	C
Zenaida's Tourist Inn	A

Ormoc Bay

0   200 m

Moving on from Ormoc

By ferry

Supercat has three fast ferries per day between Cebu City and Ormoc (2hr 35min; P600–800) and Weesam has two fast boats daily. Cebu Ferries, Lite Shipping, Roble Shipping and Supershuttle all have slower services for Cebu (5–6hr). There are ticket offices for all ferries at the port, which is within walking distance of the town centre.

By bus and van

Regular buses run from Ormoc to Baybay (1hr; P60), Maasin (3hr; P130), Tacloban (3hr; P96) and Naval on Biliran (3hr; P96). Jeepneys also operate some of these routes but are far slower. The quickest way to move on is by Duptours van, which cost slightly more than the buses, and leave from the ferry pier. Note that if you arrive in Ormoc by Supercat ferry, Duptours vans to Maasin, Naval and Tacloban are free – you just need to show your ferry ticket.

Accommodation

For a small town, Ormoc has a good selection of hotels, most of which are in the heart of town.

Don Felipe Hotel Opposite the port on Larrazabal Blvd ☎053/255-2460. *Don Felipe* is an imposing-looking place with economy rooms at the back and better superior rooms (④) with balconies looking straight out to sea on the front. There's free wi-fi in the lobby. ❸

Ormoc Villa Hotel Obrero St ☎053/255-5006, ⓦwww.ormocvillahotel.com. This is an attractive and upscale place with forty smart a/c rooms, coffee shop, restaurant, swimming pool, spa and free wi-fi. ❺

Pongos Hotel On Bonifacio St ☎053/255-2540. *Pongos* has a vast array of rooms, ranging from tatty doubles in the main building (①) to better a/c rooms (❸) in the new building. They also have a restaurant and free wi-fi in the lobby. ❷

TRN Traveller's Inn Rizal St ☎053/255-7700. Great-value budget hotel with small but clean and quiet rooms attractively decorated in a white and beige colour scheme. All rooms are a/c and have cable TV and some have free wi-fi access. There's also a small gym, a roof terrace, snack bar and music lounge. ❸

Zenaida's Tourist Inn Corner of Lopez Jaena and J. Navarro sts ☎053/255-2517. A friendly establishment with simple, brightly painted rooms. Singles have a fan and their own cold shower, while many doubles have a/c and hot water. ❷

Eating, drinking and nightlife

Dining choices in Ormoc principally revolve around barbecued meat and fish, but sure are tasty. *Chicken Ati-Atihan* on Aviles Street can't be beaten for its barbecued chicken with rice (P68) and they also have refreshing *ube* shakes. Not too far away on San Pedro Street trendy *Bebidas* welcomes you with a billboard proclaiming "Coffee – do stupid things faster with more energy". Inside there are murals on the walls and free wi-fi, and the menu includes spaghetti and sandwiches (P15–60), coffees, brownies and desserts. *Bebidas* is also a popular night-time **drinking** spot and serves San Miguel for P35 a bottle. Continuing down towards the sea you'll pass a number of other trendy bars including neon-lit hole-in-the-wall *Handlebar*, which has outdoor tables, *Dadaz*, and *Mabsky Mama's* which has nightly live music and also serves pizza. At the bottom of the street, on the other side of Larrazabal Boulevard, Ormoc City Food Park is a night market where stalls sell cheap meals of barbecued fish and meat.

The southwest coast

Two hours south of Ormoc by road is the frenetic port of **BAYBAY**, which is connected by small, slow ferries to Cebu. Baybay is a functional town with a very busy wharf area and a main street lined with carinderias, convenience stores, pawnshops and a few banks. The best place to stay is the *Uptown Plaza Hotel* in Magsaysay Avenue (℡053/563-8075; ❷), which has some rooms with air conditioning (❹) and private bathroom, with occasional hot water.

About halfway between Baybay and Maasin, **HILONGOS** is a clean, easy-going town with ferry connections to Cebu City. From the bus and jeepney terminal on the main road opposite the pier, numerous vehicles head south to Padre Burgos, or north to Baybay and Ormoc. There are a number of canteens huddled around a simple pier, but nowhere to stay. A little south of Hilongos, the port town of **Bato** has daily Kinswell (℡032/255-7572 in Cebu) ferries to and from Cebu City. This is another useful jump-off point for Padre Burgos.

Maasin

At the mouth of the Maasin River in southern Leyte, the otherwise dull, industrial port of **MAASIN** makes a good starting point if you're heading for the far south of Leyte, an area that is opening up for scuba diving and whale shark-watching. You can get up-to-date information on these activities from the Provincial Planning Development Office in Maasin's Provincial Capitol Building (℡053/570-9017).

Cokaliong and Trans-Asia Shipping Lines both run **ferries** between Cebu City and Maasin (6hr; P365). The boats are sometimes full, so make sure you book in advance; both these firms have offices at Maasin pier. If you're arriving **by air** in Tacloban you can catch an air-conditioned minivan direct to Maasin (4hr; P180). Otherwise buses from Tacloban take up to six hours, an unpredictable and frustrating trip.

Most travellers only pass through Maasin on the way to Padre Burgos, but if you do want to **stay**, take a tricycle for the short trip to *Maasin Country Lodge* (℡053/570-8858; ❷), which is a little inland on the banks of the Canturing River and has comfortable air-conditioned rooms that are spacious and well maintained, some with a TV, and there's also free wi-fi. In town there are a number of basic, cheap places, including *Ampil Pensionne* (℡053/570-8084; ❶) in Tomas Upos Street and *National Pensionne House* in Kangleon Street (℡053/570-8424; ❶).

Padre Burgos

The area around **PADRE BURGOS** on Leyte's southern tip is making a name for itself as an exciting scuba-diving destination, with more than twenty sites which have been documented by local divers. Whale sharks, dolphins and manta rays can be seen in **Sogod Bay** immediately to the east.

The closest major port to Padre Burgos is **Maasin**, which is served by ferries from Cebu City, although it's quicker to take a fast ferry to Ormoc, then a minivan.

Accommodation

Peter's Dive Resort Padre Burgos ℡053/573-0015, ⓦwww.whaleofadive.com. Affordable accommodation in standard rooms or duplex cottages for two and breathtaking views of Sogod Bay. The main building's lower terrace has a games room, where you can enjoy a round or two of pool, or play ping pong. There's also a pool and an excellent little restaurant where the owners serve home-cooked food. The resort provides a pick-up service from Maasin and Hilongos (P1800). ❹

Southern Leyte Divers San Roque, Macrohon ℡053/572-4011, ⓦwww.leyte-divers.com. Fifteen minutes northwest of Padre Burgos by jeepney, is a small German-owned lodge with charming native-style cottages in an idyllic beachside location. The restaurant serves German food, fish dishes and curry; the owners can, of course, arrange diving trips. ❸

Sogod Bay Scuba Resort Lungsodaan ℡053/573-0131, ⓦwww.sogodbayscubaresort.com.

Lovely Spanish-style concrete rooms on the beach, diving facilities and internet. The restaurant has some appetizing fare, including Ron's Beef and Beer Meat Pies; Alisha's steamed fish in banana leaves; and the "world famous" Dopey Burger. The owners can help you arrange everything from diving and trekking to motorbike hire and caving trips. ❸

Limasawa Island

It was atop a prominent hill on tiny **Limasawa Island**, that Magellan is said to have conducted the first Catholic Mass in the Philippines on March 31, 1521. After an often choppy hour's boat ride from Padre Burgos, visitors can walk up concrete steps to a monument at the top of the hill, from where there are commanding views over the whole island. Limasawa also has some marvellous beaches and coves for snorkelling.

Bangkas leave Padre Burgos two or three times early in the morning for the barangay of Magallanes on Limasawa (45min; P60). If you miss the boat back you shouldn't have much trouble finding a home to stay in for the night, though do the polite thing and enquire first with the mayor.

Palawan

CHAPTER 7 # Highlights

✳ **Dining out in Puerto Princesa** The best place to eat in Palawan boasts authentic Vietnamese noodles, tasty mangrove worms and top-notch seafood. See p.361

✳ **The Underground River** Take a boat trip under limestone cliffs and through sepulchral chambers, along a subterranean river that's said to be the longest in the world. See p.367

✳ **Port Barton** Laidback and convivial beach town with simple accommodation, rustic nightlife and a pristine bay of reefs and untouched islands. See p.368

✳ **Long Beach** Enjoy one of the nation's most alluring stretches of bone-white sand, before the developers arrive. See p.370

✳ **The Bacuit archipelago** Explore majestic limestone islands, beaches and lagoons that stud the bays around El Nido. See p.374

✳ **Scuba diving around Coron** Some of the wildest diving in Asia, on sunken Japanese World War II wrecks. See p.379

✳ **Kayangan Lake** Arrive by bangka at a hidden blue lagoon off Coron Island, from where you scramble uphill to this dazzling volcanic lake. See p.383

▲ The Underground River

Palawan

Palawan is the Philippines' last frontier, a largely unexplored and unexploited province of wonderful scenery and idyllic tropical beauty. Beyond the centres of Coron, El Nido and Puerto Princesa, tourism has yet to penetrate much of this long, sword-shaped island to the southwest of Luzon, and travellers who make it here will find a marvellous Jurassic landscape of coves, beaches, lagoons and razor-sharp limestone cliffs that rise from crystal-clear water. Offshore, despite some damage from dynamite fishing and coral bleaching, there always seems an untouched reef to discover.

The capital of Palawan, **Puerto Princesa**, is the main entry point and is close to the mangrove islands of **Honda Bay** and the immense flooded cave systems that make up the mind-boggling **Underground River**. Further north you'll find the pretty beach resort town of **Port Barton**, the old fortress town of **Taytay** and the incredibly beautiful islands and lagoons of **El Nido** and the **Bacuit archipelago**. Many areas are still relatively unaffected by tourism, such as the friendly little fishing village of **San Vicente** and nearby **Long Beach**, one of the finest stretches of sand anywhere. Undeveloped **Southern Palawan** contains some of the least visited areas in the whole country, from the remains of a Neolithic community in the **Tabon Caves** and the turtle and cockatoo sanctuaries at **Narra**, to **Brooke's Point**, the access point for **Mount Matalingajan**.

The **Calamian group** of islands, scattered off the northern tip of the main island of Palawan, has a deserved reputation for some of the best **scuba diving** in Asia, mostly on sunken World War II wrecks. Even if you're not a diver, there's plenty to do here. The little town of **Coron** on Busuanga is the jumping-off point for trips to mesmerizing **Coron Island**, with its hidden lagoons and volcanic lake and, to the south, the former leper colony of **Culion**.

It's best to **bring cash** to cover your stay in Palawan: outside Puerto Princesa credit cards are only accepted by some of the more established resorts (and will cost you between 6 and 10 percent commission), banks are few and ATMs almost nonexistent.

Puerto Princesa and around

The provincial capital **PUERTO PRINCESA** is the only major urban sprawl in Palawan, with just over 250,000 residents, a third of the total population. There are a few sights around Puerto Princesa, but hardly any in the city itself (it was founded by the Spanish only in 1872), which is why most visitors treat it as a one-night stop on the way to or from Palawan's beaches and islands.

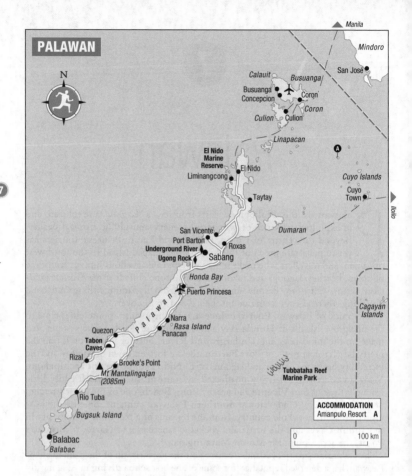

PALAWAN

N

Manila

Mindoro

San José

Calauit
Busuanga
Busuanga
Concepcion
Coron
Coron
Culion
Culion

Linapacan

El Nido
Marine
Reserve
El Nido
Liminangcong

Taytay

Cuyo Islands

Cuyo
Town

Dumaran

San Vicente
Port Barton
Underground River
Ugong Rock
Roxas
Sabang

Honda Bay

Puerto Princesa

Narra
Rasa Island
Quezon
Panacan
Tabon
Caves
Rizal
Brooke's Point
Mt Mantalingajan
(2085m)

Rio Tuba

Bugsuk Island

Balabac
Balabac

Iloilo

Cagayan
Islands

Tubbataha Reef
Marine Park

ACCOMMODATION
Amanpulo Resort **A**

0   100 km

There are several attractions around Puerto Princesa that you can easily visit in
a day or less, including **Honda Bay** (p.363) and the **Underground River** (see
p.367). All the hotels in the area sell essentially the same tours taking in the
nearest sights for around P600 per person in a minivan, or P500–700 per tricycle
(Honda Bay and the Underground River are more expensive). You can also try
to negotiate with tricycle drivers in the street, but you are unlikely to get much
of a discount.

Arrival and information

Flights arrive at tiny **Puerto Princesa Airport** at the eastern edge of the city on
Rizal Avenue, the main drag. A small tourist office (☎048/433-2983) opens to
meet flights. Most hotels will arrange to pick you up for free; tricycles cost around
P40 to the city. Rizal Avenue runs west from the airport 3km through the centre
of the city to the **ferry port**; along the way you'll find all the banks, internet cafés
and, closer to the airport, the best places to eat and drink (see p.361).

Buses and jeepneys pull into the bus terminal at San José (also known as "New
Market"), 7km north of Puerto Princesa, also known as or "New Market". From here

you'll need to switch to a tricycle to get into the city (P50–100, depending on how many people).

There are no taxis in Puerto Princesa, but it's not difficult finding a **tricycle.** The standard fare per person within the city – including the airport and port – is P8 (P10 or more after 9pm), while hiring a tricycle privately will cost P50.

The **tourist office** (Mon–Sat 9am–5pm; ☏048/433-2968) is in the Provincial Capitol Building on Rizal Avenue, 1km west of the airport at the busy junction with the National Highway, and has maps of the city for P50, but they're not as useful as the map in this guide or the *EZ Map* of Puerto Princesa and Palawan, which many of the city's hotels sell.

Accommodation

There are more than fifty places to **stay** dotted around Puerto Princesa, with the best of them at the quieter and greener airport end of Rizal Avenue.

Casa Linda Inn Trinidad Rd, behind *Badjao Inn*, off Rizal Ave ☏048/433-2606. Simple, friendly and convenient, with the bonus of good European and Asian food in the breezy café. The rooms (10 a/c, 3 with fan) are large and arranged around a spacious courtyard garden. All rooms are native-style, with wooden floors and walls made of dried grass, and the place is always clean and orderly. Wi-fi is P30/hr. ❷

Deep Forest Garden Inn Abueg Rd, Bancao-Bancao ☏048/434-1702, ☏www.deepforestinn .com. One of the new generation of *Princesa* hotels, around 1.5km from the airport (free pick-up), with smart modern rooms (with flat-screen TVs, wi-fi and a/c) arranged around a garden, pool and jacuzzi. Dorm beds are P650/person, but there needs to be a minimum of eight – call to check. ❹

Dolce Vita Hotel 4 Victoria Romasanta St, San Pedro ☏048/434-5357, ☏www .hotels-palawan.com. This German-owned hotel is a real gem, with romantic canopy beds set in two-storey pavilions (cable TV, wi-fi, breakfast and a/c included). There's a decent pool and bar. Short tricycle ride from the centre of town. ❺

Hibiscus Garden Inn Manolo Extension, close to the airport ☏048/434-1273, ☏www.puertoprincesahotel.com. Great staff and friendly service, huge rooms with spotless tiled floors, a/c, cable TV and hot showers, a leafy garden courtyard with hammocks and outdoor tables where breakfast is served (P120). Free airport pick-up and wi-fi. ❹

Legend Hotel Northeastern end of Malvar St, not far from the centre ☏048/434-4270, ☏www .legendpalawan.com.ph. The poshest option in the city, luxurious a/c rooms and big, tiled bathrooms. The rate includes a buffet breakfast. ❼

Lotus Garden Suites 371 Rizal Ave ☏048/434-1132, ☏thelotusgardenphils.com. This native-style restaurant also runs the four Japanese-inspired *Jordan's Jacuzzi Suites*, with fabulous decor (canopy beds, jacuzzi tubs) and complimentary breakfast. ❺

Manny's Guest House 2B Mendoza St, on the corner of Cuito St (aka Reynoso St), at the port end of Rizal Ave ☏048/723-3615 or 0912/872-1294, ☏www.intothespace.com/manny. Best-value backpacker or homestay accommodation in town, with three simple but clean and spacious fan rooms in an old Spanish-style wooden house (the smallest room is just P400), and lovely views over the bay and rooftops. Shared bathroom and kitchen; wi-fi is P25/day. ❷

Pads by Legend Hotel Malvar St ☏02/702-2700 or 0917/702-2700, ☏www.pads.com.ph. Stylish budget accommodation from the *Legend* chain, with a choice of en-suite singles (❸) or twin rooms (two single beds) decked out in minimalist Ikea-like decor, all with a/c and cable TV. ❹

Puerto Pension 35 Malvar St, close to the ferry port ☏048/433-2969. Cool, clean and quiet, with an alfresco top-floor restaurant that has views across the bay. Fan or a/c rooms, all with private bathrooms (with hot water) and cable TV; worth the bit extra for deluxe rooms. ❸

The City

Puerto Princesa is a useful service centre for travellers heading further into Palawan (and has some excellent places to eat; see p.361), though there are few attractions in the city itself. The **Immaculate Conception Cathedral** (daily 6am–7pm) at the west end of Rizal Avenue in Plaza Cuartel is a pretty white and blue Neo-Romanesque structure with twin towers, though the interior is fairly

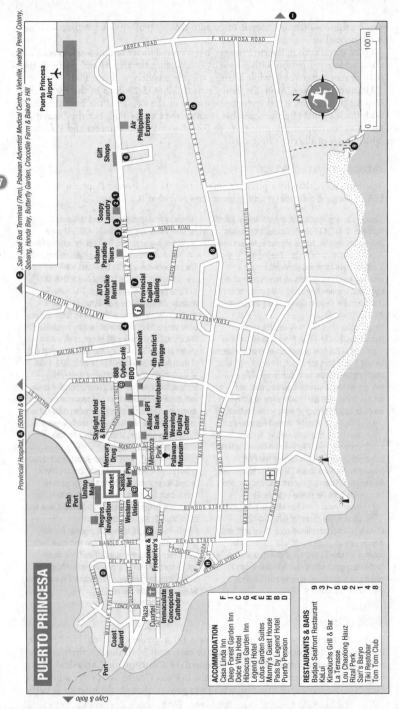

PUERTO PRINCESA

◀ *Cuyo & Iloilo*

▲ *Iloilo*

◀ *Provincial Hospital, ⓐ (500m) & ⓑ*

◀ *ⓖ San José Bus Terminal (7km), Palawan Adventist Medical Centre, Vietville, Iwahig Penal Colony,*
Sabang, Honda Bay, Butterfly Garden, Crocodile Farm & Baker's Hill

ⓘ

ABREA ROAD

F. VILLAROSA ROAD

Puerto Princesa
Airport

N

100 m

0

ⓢ 5

Air
Philippines
Express

Gift
Shops
ⓢ 6

Soapy
Laundry
ⓢ 2 1
ⓔ
ⓢ 3

A. RENGEL ROAD

Island
Paradise
Tours
ⓕ

ⓢ 8

ATO
Motorbike
Rental

RIZAL AVENUE

MANALO EXTENSION

ABAD SANTOS EXTENSION

RIZAL ROAD

ⓢ 7
Provincial
Capitol
Building

ⓘ

LAGEN STREET

NATIONAL HIGHWAY

FERNANDEZ STREET

ⓢ 4

BALTAN STREET

Landbank

888
Cyber café
BDO

4th District
Tiangge

LACAO STREET

Skylight Hotel
& Restaurant

CARANDANG STREET

Allied BPI
Bank

Metrobank

MANALO STREET

Handloom
Weaving
Display
Center

ABAD SANTOS STREET

Mercury
Drug

MANDOZA ST.

Mendoza
Park

Palawan
Museum

VALENCIA ST.

SaisIa
Net PNB

⊕

Market
Western
Union

Negros
Navigation

BUNGAN STREET

BURGOS STREET

MALIN STREET

ARIEL ROAD

Fish
Port

Unitop
Mall

MANOLO STREET

MANGA ST.

DEL PILAR STREET

ROXAS STREET

Iconex &
Frederico's

B. MENDOZA ST.

RETIROSO STREET

ⓗ

Coast
Guard

QUEZON STREET

SANDOVAL STREET

Plaza
Cuartel

⊕

Immaculate
Concepcion
Cathedral

LA PAREL ST.

CONCEPCION

MALVAR STREET

GOMEZ STREET

ⓓ

Port

ACCOMMODATION

Casa Linda Inn	F
Deep Forest Garden Inn	I
Dolce Vita Hotel	C
Hibiscus Garden Inn	G
Legend Hotel	A
Lotus Garden Suites	E
Manny's Guest House	H
Pads by Legend Hotel	B
Puerto Pension	D

RESTAURANTS & BARS

Badjao Seafront Restaurant	9
KaLui	3
Kinabuchs Grill & Bar	7
La Terrasse	5
Lou Chaolong Hauz	6
Rizal Perk	2
Sari's Baryo	1
Tiki Restobar	4
Tom Tom Club	8

ordinary. The plaza is dedicated to the 143 American soldiers who were burnt alive here by the retreating Japanese Army in 1944. The **Palawan Museum**, in Mendoza Park on Rizal Avenue (Mon, Tues, Thurs & Fri 8.30am–noon & 2–5pm; P20), offers an overview of the history, art and culture of Palawan, but is only worth the effort if you're really at a loose end. Most of the exhibits are fossils and old tools.

Eating and drinking

There are plenty of enticing **restaurants** in Puerto Princesa, and several **bars**, most of them clustered between the airport and the city centre. For cheap eats and beers check out the **4th District Tiangge** (Mon–Sat 10am–2am, Sun 5pm–2am; ☎048/725-5527) on Rizal Street, a small cluster of stalls in the centre of town. In the 1970s and 1980s the city was also home to a large community of Vietnamese refugees, and though most have left, a few 24hr Vietnamese **noodle shops**, known locally as *chaolaongan*, remain. The main refugee settlement was **Vietville**, 15km north of town and inhabited by just five families today – their noodles and French-style baguettes are better than the places in the city, but unless you are a real aficionado it's a bit of a drag to get here.

Badjao Seafront Restaurant Abueg Rd, Bagong Sikat ☎048/433-3501. Open-air native-style restaurant with terrific views of the sea. It's reached on foot from Abueg Rd, at the end of Bonifacio St across a dainty bamboo bridge. Expect to pay about P500 a head for a meal of fresh, tasty grilled seafood like salt and pepper squid and butter garlic shrimp. If you're here in the evening, getting transport back to the centre can be tricky, so you might want to pay a tricycle driver P150 to wait for the return trip. Daily 10am–10pm.

KaLui 369 Rizal Ave ☎048/433-2580, ⊛www .kaluirestaurant.com. Everyone who comes to Princesa seems to end up at this pretty bamboo restaurant. It's a bit overrated, but the beautifully crafted daily set meals (P395) are built around either seafood or meat, and most come with a salad and a small portion of fresh, raw seaweed. There's also an à la carte menu featuring items such as stingray in coco cream (P150), blue marlin (P200) and grilled prawns (P195). Reservations essential for dinner (ask your hotel). Mon–Sat 11am–2pm & 6–11pm.

Kinabuchs Grill & Bar Rizal Ave ☎048/434-5194. The enticing bar and garden at this Filipino restaurant is often just as packed as *KaLui* across the street. The main attraction is the *tamilok* or "mangrove worms" (P115), believed to be an aphrodisiac rich in protein (actually a mollusc that tastes a bit like squid tentacle). The classic Filipino food is also excellent; try the sizzling seafood *sisig* (P185) or *sinigang na baboy* (P145). Daily 5pm–3am.

La Terrasse Rizal Ave ☎048/434-1787, ⊛www .laterrassepalawan.com. Upscale but reasonably priced restaurant specializing in a fusion of Filipino

and European cuisines – the interior is elegant and the food a real delight, with dishes such as "adobo overload" (chicken and pork *adobo* fried twice and served with *adobo* fried rice) for P210, goat curry (P165) and the "Palawan flavours" plate (roasted cashews, sweet & spicy *dilis*, a sardine-like fish, roasted peanuts and crispy squid; P120). Daily 10am–11pm.

Lou Chaolong Hauz Rizal Ave. One of the remaining Vietnamese diners, close to the airport and still justly popular for its noodles (the beef stew is the most flavourful; P50) and French bread sandwiches (from P35), despite now being owned by Filipinos. The hand-pulled noodles, however, are sourced from a local Vietnamese supplier. Daily 11am–10pm.

Sari's Baryo 375 Rizal Ave ☎048/433-4899. Try this Filipino restaurant for the best *kare-kare* (peanut-based stew) in Palawan, as well as plenty of other tasty local dishes – reckon on around P500 for a meal. Mon–Sat 11am–11pm.

Tiki Restobar Junction 1, Rizal Ave ☎048/434-1797. The bar is little more than a two-level shack on the main junction in town but it's a great place to watch the city going about its business. Getting to be a major venue for live bands (there's a regular reggae band) and events (when there's a P100 cover) such as the Kabilugan ng Buwan Fire Dancing Competition (Nov).

Tom Tom Club Manalo Extension ☎048/433-3111. This Swiss-owned bar/restaurant is an expat favourite, with a decent selection of steaks (pepper steak is the specialty), paella and a good sound system to accompany late-night drinks. Fri–Wed 4pm–late.

Moving on from Puerto Princesa

Puerto Princesa Airport handles up to eight flights a day to Manila, via Airphil Express, Cebu Pacific, Philippine Airlines and Zest Airways (some Airphil flights go via **Coron** and Cebu Pacific also flies to **Cebu**). Most passengers book tickets online (where rates can be very cheap), but hotels will also book them (for a fee). Philippine Airlines has an office at the airport (daily 8am–4.30pm; ☎048/433-4565), while Cebu Pacific (☎048/433-554) and the other airlines tend to open for flights only.

At the time of writing both SuperFerry and Negros Navigation had cancelled all **ferry** services to and from Puerto Princesa, in part due to the abundance of cheap flights. Check the respective websites (p.23) for the latest.

Buses, **minivans** and **jeepneys** to all major destinations in Palawan depart various terminals clustered together 7km north of Princesa in San José, known as the San José Terminal or just "New Market" after the public market next door. Tricycles will charge P80–100 from the city centre to San José, but you can also catch multicabs (minivan version of a jeepney) and jeepneys from the corner of Rizal and the National Highway (junction 1).

In San José jeepneys leave from one dedicated terminal: jeepneys for **Sabang** (see p.367 for more details) leave at 7am and 9am, and for **Port Barton** at 9am (see p.368 for more details). Other buses depart various company garages nearby; it's fairly easy to work out destinations served, and plenty of locals will point you in the right direction if required. Try to get here early, as departures trail off in the afternoons. Some examples include the RBL (Royalista) Terminal, closest to the main road (behind the Petron station), with departures to **Taytay** at 5am, 7am, 9am and 11am (5–6hr). Further along is Charing Bus Lines minibus terminal, with hourly departures to **Quezon** (3hr) and **Narra** (2hr) every thirty minutes. Centro Transport runs to **Brooke's Point** (5hr).

For **El Nido** you can take the public bus, which is cheap but uncomfortable and takes about 8 hours, or a Fort Wally (☎0917/276-2875) air-conditioned **minivan** from San José via Roxas, which is much more expensive but takes 5 hour 30 minute (most departures 7–11am). Hiring a private van will cost around P7500. Rather than go straight to El Nido from Puerto Princesa many visitors prefer to travel via Sabang or Port Barton and then take a boat (see p.376).

Listings

Banks and exchange There are plenty of banks in the centre, with Allied Bank, Metrobank, BDO and BPI on the same strip of Rizal Ave (all with ATMs), in between Mendoza Park and the National Hwy. Make sure you get enough cash for the rest of your trip (there are no more ATMs till Coron Town).

Emergencies ☎117.

Hospitals and clinics There are two good hospitals, the Palawan Adventist Medical Center (☎048/433-2244, ⓦwww.palawanadventist hospital.org) on the National Hwy, 4km north of the city centre, and the Provincial Hospital, 1km north of the city centre on Malvar St.

Internet access *Iconex*, *Frederico's*, *Saisla Net* and *888 CyberCafé* all charge P15–20/hr (P10/30min) and open daily from around 9am–midnight. Most hotels and resorts also have internet access.

Laundry Soapy Laundry Shop, Rizal Ave (Mon–Sat 8am–noon & 1–8pm, Sun 1.30–8.30pm).

Motorbike rental There are numerous motorbike rental shops near the airport on Rizal Ave, all charging around P600/day or P3850/week (P800–1000/day for the bigger Honda trail bikes). ATO Motorbike Rentals (☎0920/491-3069) is a reputable operator.

Pharmacies Mercury Drug (6am–midnight; ☎048/433-3875) on Rizal Ave, opposite Mendoza Park. The branch at the Alicon Building, Malvar St (☎048/434-8618) is open 24hr.

Post The main post office is on Burgos St at its junction with Rizal Ave.

Travel agents Tours El Mundo (☎0921/7566-762): P600 city tour, P1100 Honda Bay, P1500 Underground River; P2500 Dos Palmas, P1400 Estrella Falls, including entrance and lunch. Topstar, Rizal Ave (☎048/433-8247), also does the Tabon Caves for P1600/person.

Around Puerto Princesa

There are several attractions around Puerto Princesa that you can easily visit in a day or less, including **Honda Bay** and the **Underground River**. All the hotels in the area sell essentially the same tours taking in the nearest sights for around P600 per person in a minivan, or P500–700 per tricycle (Honda Bay and the Underground River are more expensive). Most tours take in **Butterfly Garden** (daily 7am–5pm; P50), a small but blossom-filled tropical garden laced with hundreds of brightly hued butterflies, and **Baker's Hill**, a manicured park and snack stop with a couple of aviaries thrown in. The **Crocodile Farm & Nature Park** (Mon–Sat 9am–noon & 1–4pm, Sun 2–4pm; P50) breeds endangered crocodiles, while the **Iwahig Prison & Penal Farm** (daily 8am–7pm; free) is an odd though intriguing "Prison Without Bars" established in 1904. Tourists are welcome to wander around the village and take snaps of the surrounding paddies and flocks of egrets, though the main focus is the shop selling handicrafts made by the inmates.

Honda Bay

Picturesque **Honda Bay**, 10km north of Puerto Princesa, is a shallow, lagoon-like expanse of water, backed by the spectacular range of mountains on the main island. The bay contains seven low-lying islands, most little more than sand bars fringed by mangrove swamp and small beds of coral, but is perfect for a day of island-hopping, lounging, snorkelling or a longer stay at *Dos Palmas* resort – if you have the money.

Arrival, information and accommodation

Outrigger bangkas tour Honda Bay from the San Lourdes pier, 11km north of Princesa; the departure point is signposted around 1km off the National Highway. To get to the pier, hotels will arrange minivans (P1500) or tricycles (P400–500), but though this comes with the added convenience of a return trip, it's cheaper to grab a tricycle on the street – you should get to the pier for P100–150 one-way, though you might have to wait a while to get one heading back.

Hotels in Princesa offer **Honda Bay tours** for P1500 per person, including transport to the pier, stops at three islands (usually Starfish, Snake and Pandan) and a picnic lunch. While this is convenient, you can save money (especially in a group) by arranging tours independently. The **Honda Bay Boat Owners Association** (daily 7am–5pm; ☏0929/864-9255 or 0908/635-3326) organizes boats at the San Lourdes pier; **rental** of the whole bangka is P1300–1500 depending on the size of the vessel, and there's a P21 per person **terminal fee**. Boats are hired by the day, and it's usual to make just three stops, plus Pambato Reef, but you can specify which islands you want to visit. You can rent masks, fins and booties (reef shoes) for P100 each.

Accommodation in Honda Bay is limited to the *Dos Palmas Island Resort & Spa* (☏048/434-3118, ⓦwww.dospalmas.com.ph; ◐) a luxurious place on a private island with chic accommodation in huts either on stilts above the ocean or set around a lush garden, and with restaurants, bars, watersports and a spa.

Touring the islands

The most popular stop in Honda Bay is **Snake Island** (free), named after the curving sand bar that forms its main body. The central beach area here can be a bit of a carnival, with bangkas lined up offshore, large groups snorkelling, a row of trinket stalls, a bar and even some cooked food available. Walk a while and you'll have the fine white sand to yourself, though the snorkelling opposite the stalls is best; there's an incredibly steep drop-off just beyond the beach, with great schools of tropical fish (in part encouraged by the dubious practice of feeding them).

Located in the middle of the Sulu Sea, 181km southeast of Puerto Princesa, **Tubbataha Reef Natural Park** (℡048/434-5759, ⓦwww.tubbatahareef.org) has become a magnet for scuba divers, who reach it on liveaboard boats – most departing from Puerto Princesa between March and June. The reef is one of the finest in the world, with sightings of sharks, manta rays and turtles a daily occurrence, as well as huge shoals of other marine life and a dazzling array of smaller reef fish.

Dive operators in Manila, Puerto Princesa and Coron Town can arrange **packages** for around US$1200–1600 for a one-week trip, including domestic flights, food, the Conservation Fee of P3000 and unlimited diving. A typical liveaboard schedule entails sailing overnight from Puerto Princesa to Tubbataha (12hr), followed by a number of days of diving at locations such as Jessie Beazley Reef, Black Rock and Bird Island. For details of liveaboards, some of which visit the reef, see ⓦexpedition fleet.com, ⓦwww.moonshadow.ch or visit the park office at 41 Abad Santos St, Puerto Princesa.

To snorkel at the lush **Pambato Reef** (P50), the best place in Honda Bay for coral and giant clams, boats moor at a floating pier. **Starfish Island** (P50) is a sand bar backed by mangroves named after the abundant horned sea star (starfish) that carpet much of the inner shallows around the island. The island also has some fine snorkelling towards the northern end, with delicate soft corals, butterfly fish and even moray eels further out. **Pandan Island** (P50) comes much closer to a stereotypical desert island, with palm trees and a white sand beach perfect for swimming – the snorkelling here is not so great. There are plenty of huts and shelters for picnics. The least visited islands are **Luli Island** (P50), only accessible at low tide, and tranquil **Cowrie Island** (P25). It's also possible to visit *Dos Palmas Resort* (see p.363) for an extra P500; this will add an extra 20–30 minutes, but you can use the resort facilities (Princesa hotels charge P2500 for this trip).

Southern Palawan

A journey through southern Palawan represents one of the last great travel challenges in the Philippines. Much of the area is sparsely populated, with limited accommodation and nothing in the way of dependable transport, communications or electricity. The major attraction is **Tabon Caves**, a little south of the town of **Quezon**, one of the country's most significant archeological sites. On the east coast, around **Brooke's Point**, travelling becomes a little tricky as there are hardly any buses and few jeepneys, but if you do make it here you'll find unspoilt countryside, quiet barrios and deserted, palm-fringed beaches backed by craggy mountains.

Narra

The small town of **NARRA**, about two hours by bus and 92km south of Puerto Princesa, makes a good introduction to the south, with several empty beaches in the area and **Rasa Island**, 3km offshore, the only place in the wild you can see the endangered Philippine cockatoo (there are around 70 birds here). The island is a thirty-minute boat trip from the village of Panacan, a short tricycle ride from Narra. Further offshore, the **Isla Arena Marine Turtle Sanctuary** is a major nesting site for green turtles, where the tiny hatchlings are protected before being released into the wild.

Inland, the most rewarding excursion is to the **Estrella Waterfalls**, around 15km from Narra on the road back to Puerto Princesa. The water is wonderfully fresh and pure (you can swim here), and the falls are surrounded by lush jungle inhabited by monkeys.

If you have plenty of cash, you can base yourself at the *Crystal Paradise Resort* (☎048/723-0952, ⊛www.crystalparadiseresort.com; ❾), on Sea Road in Antipuluan (on the edge of Narra), which has luxurious rooms, a pool and a spa, and can arrange trips to all the above attractions.

Tabon Caves

It was inside the **Tabon Caves** in 1962 that archeologists discovered a fragment of the skull dubbed "**Tabon Man**", dating to 22,000 years ago, making it the oldest known human relic from the archipelago at the time. Crude tools and evidence of cooking fires going back some 50,000 years have been unearthed in the caves, along with fossils and a large quantity of Chinese pottery dating back to the fifth century BC. Most of these items have been transferred to the National Museum in Manila for preservation, though some artefacts are on display in the caves. It's still intriguing to wander through the damp caverns and tunnels, which may have been a kind of Neolithic workshop for making stone tools; researchers are still working here and are happy to show visitors the latest finds.

A number of hotels and travel agents in Puerto Princesa organize day-trips to the **Tabon Caves** for around P1200 per person, which is definitely the easiest option if you are short of time. Alternatively, you can catch a bus to **Quezon**, a fishing village consisting mainly of wooden houses on stilts, around 150km from Puerto Princesa. At Quezon's wharf, bangkas can be chartered for P1000 for the thirty-minute ride to the caves and back. Stop first at the **National Museum** (Mon–Fri 9am–4pm; free) near the wharf in Quezon for orientation and information. There are actually more than 200 caves in the area, but only 29 have been fully explored and of those only three are open to the public (same hours as museum). The best **place to stay** close to the caves is the *Tabon Village Resort* (☎0910/239-8381; ❶) in the village of **Tabon**, which has simple cottage-style accommodation with fans and private bathrooms right on the water, plus a good restaurant.

Brooke's Point and Mount Mantalingajan

Deep in the southern half of Palawan, 192km from Puerto Princesa, the town of **BROOKE'S POINT** is flanked by the sea on one side and formidable mountains on the other. The town was named after the eccentric nineteenth-century British adventurer James Brooke, who became the Rajah of Sarawak (now Malaysia), after helping a local chieftain suppress a revolt. From Borneo he travelled north to Palawan, landing at what is now Brooke's Point and building an imposing **watchtower** there, the remains of which stand next to a newer **lighthouse**. Accommodation in Brooke's Point includes the functional *Silayan Lodge* (☎0928/347-0075; ❶) in the plaza opposite the town hall. There's not much to do in town, though if you're looking for adventure you can hire a guide at the town hall to climb nearby **Mount Mantalingajan**, at 2086m the highest peak in Palawan. This is a tough climb that can take up to five days, so make sure you come well prepared; there's no equipment for hire locally. The usual route actually starts on the west coast from the barangay of Ransang near **Rizal** (6hr from Princesa by Charing Bus Lines). In Rizal you can stay at the *Castelar Lodge* (☎0921/504-4108; ❶).

Northern Palawan

Northern Palawan is where most visitors focus their time, a wild mountainous land that crumbles into the mesmerizing islands of the Calamian chain. A short boat ride north of Princesa, the **Underground River** is the sight most visitors want to see. It meanders past a bewildering array of stalactites, stalagmites, caverns, chambers and pools, the formations made eerier on your ride through by the shadows cast by the boatman's torch. From here, **Port Barton** makes for a soothing stopover on the journey north to El Nido, with plenty of cheap accommodation and enticing snorkelling spots in the bay. **El Nido** itself is a wonderfully scenic resort town that remains relatively low-key, a gateway to the clear waters and jungle-smothered limestone islands of the **Bacuit archipelago**. If you have time, extend your trip to the islands around Coron Town, laced with crystal-clear lagoons, isolated beaches and dive sites enhanced with World War II shipwrecks.

Sabang

The jumping-off point for the Underground River is **SABANG**, a small village and laidback beach resort some 78km and two hours north of Puerto Princesa by road. Sabang's main appeal is its lovely white sand **beach** facing St Paul's Bay, fringed with palm trees and sprinkled with massage tents (P350/30min) and simple places to eat and spend the night – for now.

Accommodation

Dab Dab ☏0908/452-2215 (no advance reservations). This budget option is a 10min walk west from the wharf, facing a rocky shoreline. The seven spotless cottages (all en suite) are scattered around a lush garden; there are some cheaper huts for just P400 with shared bath. There's a gorgeous wooden restaurant, too. ❷

Daluyon Beach Resort ☏048/723-0889, ⓦwww.daluyonresort.com. Tucked away at the far eastern end of the beach, these attractive two-storey cottages have thatched roofs and luxurious rooms that open out to the sea. ❼

Green Verde ☏0910/978-4539. Prime beachfront fan rooms with bathrooms and access to laundry and massage services – this is also the best local restaurant on the strip (see below). Offers Underground River packages for just P175/person (minimum 8 people). ❸

Mary's Beach Resort ☏0919/757-7582. Cheapest accommodation in Sabang; no-frills, slightly shabby cottages right on the sand a 10min walk east of the pier at the far end of Sabang Beach. Shared bath ❶; with bath ❷

Robert's Restaurant & Cottages ☏0927/312-3621. Great location right in the middle of the beach, next to the *Sheridan* (see below), offering a series of simple but well-maintained nipa huts with bathrooms. Standard ❷; family room ❹

Sheridan Beach Resort & Spa ☏02/514-2126, ⓦwww.sheridanbeachresort.com. Ultra-posh (and expensive) hotel opened right in the middle of the beach. To be fair the buildings have been well designed, with stylish, modern rooms, a huge pool and a host of extras. The hotel charges P3000 for pick-ups from Princesa. ❾

Eating and drinking

Coco Grove ☏0905/255-9729. Small place at the wharf end of the beach, near the bus stop, serving decent food (mains P120–150) and selling boat and bus tickets. It's a good place to catch up with other travellers. Daily 7am–midnight.

Green Verde ☏0910/978-4539. This wooden beach house restaurant is the best place to eat in Sabang, with a garden of individual *cabañas* facing the beach and very attentive staff; expect fresh lapu-lapu, tuna

and tasty barbecue pork for around P110; the crab curry (P130–150) or steamed crab in Sprite (P130–150) is definitely worth a try. Daily 7am–9pm.

Pawikan Restaurant and Coco Beach Bar Daluyon Beach Resort ☏048/723-0889, ⓦwww .daluyonresort.com. This refined resort restaurant makes for a quieter evening, with frozen margaritas, pizza and pasta and excellent Filipino dishes on offer. The bar is open daily 6–10pm.

Moving on from Sabang, you can take bangkas to **Port Barton** (P1200/person) or **El Nido** (P1800/person); these usually depart 7am and 1pm, depending on demand: ask at the *Coco Grove* restaurant (see opposite; or call Miguel ☏0999/665-7289). You can rent whole bangkas but this is pricey: P5000–6000 to Port Barton (one-way). By land you'll have to take a jeepney to Roxas, and change there for Port Barton or El Nido.

The Underground River

Justly one of Palawan's top attractions, **Puerto Princesa Subterranean River National Park** (aka Underground River; Ⓦwww.puerto-undergroundriver .com), protects a unique underwater river system that cuts through the limestone hills for 8.2km before emptying out into the South China Sea. The caves are completely natural and unlit, ranging from fairly low-lying passages to vast, stadium-like caverns. It's also a refreshingly well-managed and untouched slice of Palawan, with visitor numbers restricted by a daily quota.

From Sabang, you'll take a twenty-minute bangka to the next bay along, followed by a short 150m walk through the forest to the river – languid **monitor lizards** often congregate near the rangers' hut, while macaque monkeys hang out in the trees, looking to grab any loose snacks – don't feed them (or the lizards). If you are arranging independently you'll need to show your permit before getting into the special pump boats that paddle into the caves. Your boatman acts as a guide, pointing out the various rock formations and wildlife inside (there are over 400,000 bats). Memorable features include "**the Cathedral**", a vast chamber containing stalactites that resemble Mary, Jesus and friends, and a second 62-metre-high cavern that soars into the darkness. Visitors get to see just 1.5km of the cave (45min); you can travel up to 4.3km into the system, but you'll need to arrange a special permit three days in advance from the park office in Puerto Princesa (11 National Hwy, just north of Rizal Ave ☏048/434-2509).

You can also **hike** to the caves via the Jungle Trail (5.3km) or Monkey Trail (5.2km) from Sabang, though this is steep and sometimes slippery, especially after rain.

Access to the national park is by **guided boat tour** only, and numbers are currently restricted to 600 people per day (a quota that is often filled). **Day-tours** from Princesa are P1500 per person, departing at around 7.30am, and including all fees, a basic lunch buffet on Sabang beach and a short time for swimming. If you want to stay on in Sabang they'll drop you off after the tour. Renting a whole van for a day-trip to the Underground River will be at least P3500.

While taking a tour is the most convenient option, it's much cheaper to arrange a visit independently, especially if you have a group. You'll need to take a minivan or jeepney (2–3hr) to Sabang Wharf from the San José Terminal in Puerto Princesa (see p.362); at the wharf's Tourist Assistance Information Center you can buy the **permit** (P200/person) required to visit the national park, and arrange a **bangka** (P700/boat, return trip) to take you to the entrance. Because of the quota, you'll need to get here early. Your permit includes the cost of a guide and the second boat into the actual cave. To save the bangka fare you can also walk to the cave from Sabang (see opposite).

Ugong Rock

Some twenty minutes south of Sabang in the village of **Tagabinet**, on the road to Princesa, is the trailhead for **Ugong Rock**, a jagged limestone outcrop riddled with passageways and caves. The rock is just 300m from the road; it takes around one hour to clamber through the narrow ladders and walkways of the honeycomb interior with a local guide (P100/person). At the top a platform provides fine views of the outcrops and paddies below. Ugong is set to become a major Palawan attraction with the opening of a **zip line** in 2011.

Port Barton

On the northwest coast of Palawan, roughly halfway between Puerto Princesa and El Nido, **PORT BARTON** is far less developed than either of its busier rivals. The streets are all dirt tracks, there are no day-trippers and the rhythms of Filipino life go on largely undisturbed by the small groups of travellers lounging in the handful of budget beach hotels. These face crescent-shaped **Pagdanan Bay**, with magical sunset views – Port Barton beach itself is a gorgeous strip of sugary sand and fine for a quick swim, but the water is often cloudy (especially after rain). Minutes away are fourteen pristine white sand islands, a number of top-notch dive and snorkelling sites and even a couple of waterfalls. Note that **electricity** is usually available between 6pm and midnight only in Port Barton and there are no banks.

Accommodation

Arriving by bus or by boat in Port Barton you are likely to be met by staff from any number of **hotels**, but if you don't have a reservation you are better off ignoring them; dump your gear at *Jambalaya* (see opposite) first before making a choice. High season runs mid-November to May – you'll get much cheaper deals outside this period.

Deep Gold Resort ☎0999/383-2901, ⓦdeepgoldresorts.com. Right on the beach a short walk from Rizal St, sporting big A-frame cottages that resemble Swiss chalets, all with balconies and private bathrooms right on the sand. Also offers internet access. ❸

Getting to Port Barton

From Puerto Princesa you can hire a minivan to Port Barton for around P4500 (2hr 30min) or take the once daily jeepney (9am; 3hr 30min) from Puerto Princesa's San José Terminal (see p.362). This arrives on Rizal Street, very close to the beach and the town centre. The highway is open year-round, with only small stretches of dirt road. **From El Nido** to Port Barton you'll need to charter a minivan or take a cheap Princesa-bound bus or jeepney as far as Roxas; from here one daily jeepney runs to Port Barton (1hr) at around 10.30–11am. In the other direction jeepneys leave Port Barton for Roxas at around 8am; from Roxas you can pick up services to El Nido, but be prepared to wait.

By far the most appealing way to reach Port Barton is by boat. From **Sabang**, bangkas charge P1200 per person (minimum eight people), or P6000 per boat (2hr 30min); it's cheaper to call Dave Gooding at *Greenviews* (see opposite) in Port Barton, who can arrange a boat to pick you up for just P3500 (deposit required). *Greenviews* also runs an on-demand boat service from **El Nido** (5hr 30min) to Port Barton for P1200 per person (minimum six people; ask about fewer people). Regular bangkas from El Nido charge P1500 per person or P6000 per boat (P8000 for larger boats).

Local bangkas to and from **San Vicente** (45min–1hr) cost around P1000 (P1200 for a return trip). Once San Vicente Airport opens in 2011, the road to Port Barton (just 25km away) is also expected to be rebuilt.

El Busero Inn ☎0906/745-2463. Best budget option, with basic rooms above the restaurant for P250–300. Discounts are available for extended stays. There are also two cottages for P1000; the beachfront cottage is OK, but the back cottage is not good value. Extra beds are P150. ❶

Elsa's Beach Resort (Next to *Deep Gold*, see opposite) ☎0919/424-6975. Great location right on a pleasant stretch of beach, towards the southern end of the strip, with an excellent restaurant and comfy cottages (some facing the garden). ❷

🏃 Greenviews Resort At the far northern end of the beach ☎0929/268-5333, Ⓦwww.palawandg.clara.net. Spotless nipa huts equipped with fan and bathrooms (cold showers only) set within a lush garden that attracts giant

birdwing butterflies, sunbirds and the odd monitor lizard. Managed by affable owners Dave and Tina Gooding, who also own the *Greenviews Resort* in El Nido and can arrange onward transport and trips to the Underground River for P4000. Laundry service and wi-fi is also offered. Cottages ❷; family rooms (for 3–4). ❹

Summer Homes ☎0921/401-6906, Ⓦwww .portbarton.info/summerhomes. One of the few places built of concrete and bricks rather than wood, but good value nevertheless. Rooms are simple but adequate (some have hot showers), they take credit cards and have wi-fi (free); non-guests can use it provided they spend a minimum P150 in the restaurant (11am–3pm & 6–10pm). Also rent kayaks (P400/day) and motorbikes (P700/day). ❸

Eating and drinking

Most of the **eating** in Port Barton is at the resorts themselves; *Elsa's* has a good restaurant offering Filipino and European food for P200 or less per person, while *Greenviews* offers exceptionally high-quality meals. **Nightlife** is not part of Port Barton's appeal– there are a couple of local karaoke bars if you are desperate, and the quiet *Owl's Nest Sunset Bar* next to *Greenviews*, but most people drink where they eat. Everything tends to shut down by 10pm.

🏃 Jambalaya Cajun Café A great place to eat, sip coffee and get the latest information, right on the beach next to the main pier, Caltex station and jeepney terminal. They serve excellent jambalaya and play real Cajun music. You can leave luggage here too (free), and there's free internet. Daily 7am–8pm.

Judy's ☎0921/683-4592. Tiny *Judy's* serves cheap international food (decent pizzas), plenty of veggie options and Filipino dishes. It's the best place for a beer or two. Daily 7am–midnight.

Pagdanan Bay

From Port Baron, it costs P1000–1500 to rent a bangka for a day of island-hopping in **Pagdanan Bay**, aka Port Barton Marine Park. Popular targets include the spectacular coral reefs at **Twin Rocks** and **Aquarium Reef** (both a few minutes' ride from Port Barton); the former in particular offers vast banks of hard coral, including plenty of spiny staghorn, and hordes of tropical fish. The bay islands themselves are traditional desert island types, where you can swim or just chill out. Most trips take in the beach at **Exotic Island**, which you'll usually have to yourself. The island is being developed as a cashew nut farm, but the beach is open to the public, and you can wade across the narrow sand bar to **Albaguen Island**. You can stay here at the 🏃 *Blue Cove Island Resort* (☎0908/562-0879, Ⓦwww.bluecoveresort.com; ❸), an extremely tranquil collection of nipa huts (some with hot showers) overlooking the bay. **Diving** trips can be arranged by Palawan Easy Dive (starting at around P2000; Ⓦpalawaneasydive.com) at the far southern end of the beach.

San Vicente

About 15km north of Port Barton is the sleepy fishing village of **San Vicente**, accessible by bangka or bone-shaking jeepney ride from Princesa. It has a small market, a petrol station and a couple of snacks stalls but little else; it does offer an alternative to taking longer bangka rides between Port Barton and El Nido however, as it has road links to the north coast and Taytay.

From the pier bangkas can be chartered for Port Barton, but unless you arrive early enough to catch the Princesa jeepney (P300), onward travel is best by chartered minivan (tricycles are not recommended until the road is surfaced). Locals should be able to rustle up a driver; count on P1700–2000 to Taytay depending on your negotiating skills. It's a rough, bumpy 2 hour 30 minute ride, with only the main highway between Roxas and Taytay surfaced. This may change once **San Vicente Airport** opens in 2011.

The only reason to linger around here is **Long Beach**, a so-far undeveloped 14km stretch of sand south of town that ranks as one of the most extraordinary beaches in the country – you can see both ends only on a brilliantly clear day. Enjoy it while you can, as the new airport has already prompted the construction of large resorts and it is only a matter of time before the beach is "discovered" by package tours. For now the best place to stay in San Vicente is the simple but friendly *Picardal Lodge* (☎0920/476-4854; ❷), which has wi-fi, a short walk from the pier. To get to Long Beach you'll need to catch a lift on a motorcycle from San Vicente's market, near the pier, for around P50.

Taytay

On the northeast coast of Palawan, about 140km north of Port Barton by road and 50km south of El Nido, the quaint and friendly town of **TAYTAY** ("tie-tie") was capital of Palawan from the earliest days of Spanish conquest in the seventeenth century until Princesa assumed the role in 1903. Today little remains to show off this history save the half-ruined **Puerto de Santa Isabel** (free), the smallish, squat stone fortress built by the Spanish between 1667 and 1738. As with many places in Palawan, the main attractions lie offshore – you can tour the wonderfully untouched islands in the bay by chartering a bangka for the day from the harbour (P1000–1500). **Elephant Island** is best known for its hidden lagoon, with a natural skylight in the roof that makes it a wonderful place to swim.

Arrival and information

Buses and jeepneys from Puerto Princesa and El Nido will drop you at the bus terminal on the edge of town; tricycles should shuttle you to the harbour (for tours of the bay) for P50. There are a couple of banks in Taytay but neither have ATMs – you may be able to get a cash advance with your credit card in an emergency. Electricity is available from 5.30pm until 5.30am.

Accommodation

Accommodation in Taytay itself is limited to a handful of simple lodgings, while the plush resorts in the bay offer a huge step up in style and comfort.

Taytay town

Casa Rosa ☎0920/895-0092. Pleasant little resort on a low hill behind the town hall. The cottages are good value, with views of the ocean, while the café has delicious home-cooked spaghetti, pizza, fish and grilled chicken. ❶

Pem's Pension House and Restaurant Rizal St (near the fort) ☎0916/461-0334 or 048/723-0463. Offers single rooms with a shared bathroom, plus smallish cottages with private bathrooms (❷) and a choice of fan or a/c. ❶

Taytay Bay

Apulit Island Resort Apulit Island ☎02/894-5644, ⓦwww.elnidoresorts.com. This swish resort is the closest to Taytay and offers accommodation in luxury cottages built on stilts over the water; you can spot baby sharks from your balcony. The resort has various bars and restaurants, including a lovely little bar high on a rocky cliff at the back of the beach, reached by 109 steps. ❾

Flower Island Resort Flower Island ☎02/893-6455 in Manila ☎0918/924-8895, ⓦwww.flowerisland-resort.com. This idyllic resort features 24 simple but romantic and attractively furnished nipa huts scattered along the shore, equipped with bathrooms (cold showers only), fans (some have a/c) and verandas with

hammocks. The restaurant serves buffet meals (it's all-inclusive). The *Art Café* (p.373) in El Nido offers US$98 per person packages (plus transfer from Batakalan). ⑨

El Nido

The small but booming resort town of **EL NIDO** in the far northwest of Palawan is the departure point for trips to the mesmerizing **Bacuit archipelago** (see p.374). With its scruffy beach, narrow, tricycle-choked streets and unplanned rows of concrete hotels, El Nido makes a poor first impression, but the surroundings are truly inspirational – the town is hemmed in between spectacular cliffs of jagged karst and an iridescent bay littered with jungle smothered outcrops of limestone.

The archipelago itself is the largest marine sanctuary in the Philippines, though the area's striking beauty has not gone unnoticed by developers, who have established a number of **exclusive resorts** on some of the islands. If over US$200 a night (per person) for a taste of paradise is too much for you, stay in El Nido itself – where **electricity** runs 2pm to 6am only – and island-hop by day. Note that mandatory "**Eco Development Fee**" tickets (P200/person) are sold at the tourist office and most hotels, and are valid for ten days – this won't be included in any tours or hotel rates.

Arrival and information

From tiny **El Nido Airport** it's 7km and a twenty-minute tricycle ride into town (P100/person). **Buses** and jeepneys arrive at the northern end of Calle Hama ("calle" means "street" in Tagalog, from the Spanish), a stone's throw from the beach. The **ferry and bangka pier** is at the southern end of the beach, a short walk from accommodation. **Tricycles** should only charge P7–8 for rides along the main strip in town, and P10 to Corong-Corong.

The **tourist office** is on Calle Real (daily 8am–8pm; ℡0926/993-8803, Ⓦwww .elnidotourism.com), inside the DENR building near the town hall, one block

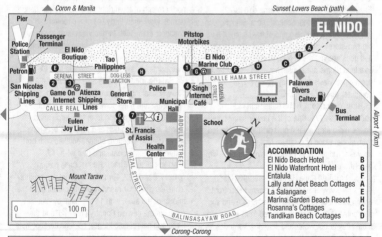

Dive El Nido

The waters off El Nido are popular targets for divers, especially those looking to do a PADI course. Snorkelling is good, though much of the reef system has been killed off over the years, thanks to crown of thorns starfish, bleaching and dynamite fishing.

There are three reliable **dive operators** in El Nido; Palawan Divers (dives from P1800; PADI from P20,900; ☎0908/330-6778, ⓦwww.palawan-divers.org) on Calle Hama; El Nido Marine Club (☎0916/668-2748, ⓦelnidomarineclub.com), right in the middle of the beach; and Sea Dog Divers (☎0916/777-6917, ⓦwww.seadogdiving palawan.com), which offers similar rates and services. These companies can also advise about trips to the Tubbataha Reef (p.364) and Apo Reef (p.254).

inland from the beach. Another good source of up-to-date local information is the **El Nido Boutique and Art Café** on Serena Street (travel centre daily 7am–9pm; ☎0920/906-6317, ⓦwww.elnidoboutiqueandartcafe.com). You can book tours here, change money, use the internet (P90/hr) or make international calls (P30/min).

Bizarrely, there are no banks or ATMs in El Nido: you can **change money** at many of the resorts or use your credit card to withdraw cash from the Petron petrol station (daily 7am–7pm) at the southern end of the beach near the pier (they charge 7 percent commission, while the *Art Café* takes 8 percent).

There are numerous **internet** cafés in town: on Calle Hama try *Singh Internet Café* or *Shift e-add Internet Café* opposite; on Serena Street there's *Game On Internet Café*. Most of these places open 2pm–1am and charge P50 per hour or P25 per 30minutes.

Accommodation

It's easy to walk from the bus and jeepney terminal to all El Nido's **accommodation**, of which there's no shortage; the quieter lodgings at the little barangay of **Corong-Corong**, south of El Nido, are a P10 tricycle ride away. Reservations long in advance are crucial for travel at Christmas, Easter or Chinese New Year.

El Nido

El Nido Beach Hotel Calle Hama ☎048/723-0887, ⓦwww.elnidobeachhotel.com. Slick Korean-run hotel at the southern end of the beach; it's a big two-storey modern building that some might feel goes against the El Nido budget vibe, but the spacious rooms are stylish, have hot water, a/c and sensational views of the bay. Free wi-fi or computer use for P60/hr. **❼**

El Nido Waterfront Hotel Calle Hama ☎0918/663-2771. One of the newer small hotels on the main strip, with rooms artfully constructed from stone, wood and rattan, replete with hot showers, fridge, cable TV and private terrace. **❹**; beachfront **❻**

🏃 **Entalula** Calle Hama ☎0920/906-6550, ⓦwww.entalula.com. Elegant beachfront option with four fan-cooled *cabañas* (**❹**) and six a/c rooms (**❺**), beautifully crafted from wood and nipa, all with hot water and sea-view verandas. Laundry is P70/kilo. Nov–April (high season) only walk-in guests are accepted (no reservations).

Lally and Abet Beach Cottages ☎0920/905-6822 or 048/723-0498, ⓦwww.lallyandabet.com.

Long-established and well-run resort at the northern end of town right on the shore (off Calle Hama). More than thirty fan or a/c rooms and cottages, many with terrific views across the bay and with balconies where you can sit and watch the world go by; some of the rooms are a bit past their prime so check before checking in. **❺**

La Salangane 33 Serena St ☎0916/648-6994, ⓦwww.lasalangane.com. Enticing French restaurant and hotel combo with a choice of accommodation ranging from four large apartments with kitchen (**❻**) and romantic beachfront suites (**❼**), to excellent budget doubles with hot water in the bathrooms and free wi-fi (**❹**).

Marina Garden Beach Resort Calle Hama ☎0917/624-7722, ⓦmarinagardenelnido.multiply .com. Very popular resort (booking essential) in the middle of the strip, with 14 a/c "shabby-chic" rooms in the newish Country Villa (**❹**), and the three original rustic cottages, no-frills bamboo huts on stilts facing the beach (**❷**).

🏃 **Rosanna's Cottages** Calle Hama ☎0920/605-4631, ⓦrosannas.multiply .com. Top budget choice, with four spacious doubles in a large building on the beach, and two cottages in a neighbouring small garden. The eponymous Rosanna and her husband are friendly and helpful hosts. Reservations are essential here. ❷

Tandikan Beach Cottages Calle Hama ☎0920/318-4882. Rustic resort in a fine location with sea and mountain views. The nine cottages are simple, but the service is friendly; you'll wake in the morning to find a flask of hot water on your balcony for coffee. ❷

Corong-Corong

Dolarog Beach Resort ☎0927/420-7083, Ⓦwww.dolarog.com. Peaceful beachside accommodation in the quiet and rather isolated little barangay of Corong-Corong, south of El Nido. The thatched cottages and rooms stand in a grassy coconut grove on a private beach. The resort is well run, serves excellent meals and is easy enough to reach from town by tricycle (P10 per person) or bankga (about P200 for the boat). You can also make arrangements for resort staff to meet you at the airport. ❼

Greenviews Corong Corong ☎0921/586-1442, Ⓦwww.palawandg.clara.net. Popular resort 3km south of town (P10 via tricycle or 25min walk) with free wi-fi and gorgeous sunset views all year (El Nido gets them May/June only). Owners Dave and Tina Gooding lay on handy free buses back from town 9pm–midnight – a nice touch. Kayaks are P700/day or P350/half-day. ❹

The Town

For now, **EL NIDO** remains refreshingly low-key, provincial and relatively cheap, with plenty of sari-sari stores selling San Miguel and snacks along the two main streets, Calle Hama and Calle Real. Don't miss the climb to the top of the marble cliffs of **Mount Taraw** (the ridge that backs El Nido); it's a strenuous haul, but the views are magnificent. Guided hikes take around three hours and cost P500 per person (ask at the *Art Café*).

The bayfront has ravishing views, but the **beach** itself is only average and not especially attractive for swimming because of the number of bangkas coming and going. **Sunset Lovers Beach** is much better and only a short walk along the coastal path heading north. An even better option is **Napsan Beach,** a vast swathe of usually empty white sand 35–40 minutes tricycle ride north of El Nido; take insect repellent because the sandflies can be voracious. **Mountain bikes** are P500 per day from *Art Café* if you want to explore the area at leisure.

Eating and drinking

Dining and nightlife in El Nido are very relaxed affairs, with a handful of laidback **beach bars** offering simple food and cold beer, while cheap local places line Calle Real and Rizal behind the beach.

Art Café Serena St ☎0920/902-6317, Ⓦwww.elnidoboutiqueandartcafe.com. The heart of El Nido's traveller scene thanks to its excellent travel centre, the café itself offers friendly service, superb breakfasts, home-made bread, yoghurts and brewed coffee. Lunch and dinner features well-prepared seafood, pizza and pasta. The bar often hosts local bands. Daily 6.30am–11pm.

Balay Tubay Calle Real ☎0916/730-7266. Historic wooden house and restaurant that has regular jam sessions on native instruments, reggae and other live bands, as well as well-prepared Filipino food; choose fresh fish or squid and they'll grill it outside (mains 100–150). There's a smaller branch on Calle Hama. Daily 5pm–midnight.

Bhing's Bizz Curry House Calle Real (near the church) ☎0915/624-4590. Just off the main drag, this is one of El Nido's best-kept secrets, at least for those craving Indian food. It's a great place to eat or just chill out with a book when it rains; it doubles as a spa and handicraft store. Daily 8am–9pm.

Habibi Restaurant & Shisha Café Serena St ☎0905/484-1764, Ⓦhabibicafe.npage.de. This German-owned place is justly lauded for its delicious food, an eclectic mix of fresh fish, some of the best coffee in town and that retro backpacker staple, banana pancakes. Shisha pipes are on offer, too – try the mint or Red Bull flavours (P250). Open breakfast to dinner.

La Salangane 33 Serena St ☎09166/486-994, Ⓦwww.lasalangane.com. Stylish place overlooking the beach, with a cool bar and great Filipino/French cuisine. The best deals are for fresh fish (from P90), but it's worth shelling out for the steak tartare (P295) and amazing apple tart with calvados (P170). Daily 7am–11pm.

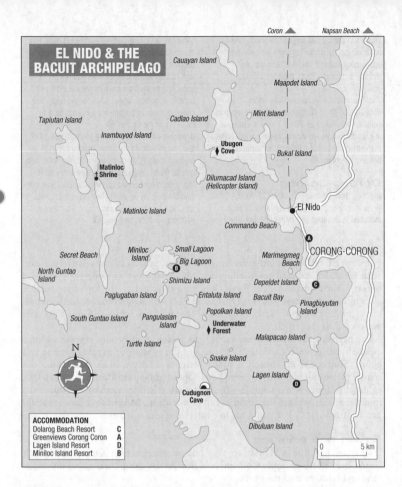

EL NIDO & THE BACUIT ARCHIPELAGO

Cauayan Island

Maapdet Island

Mint Island

Tapiutan Island

Cadlao Island

Inambuyod Island

Ubugon Cove

Bukal Island

Matinloc Shrine

Dilumacad Island (Helicopter Island)

Matinloc Island

El Nido ●

Commando Beach

CORONG-CORONG Ⓐ

Secret Beach

Miniloc Island

Small Lagoon

Big Lagoon ⒷB

Marimegmeg Beach

North Guntao Island

Shimizu Island

Depeldet Island

Ⓒ

Paglugaban Island

Entaluta Island

Bacuit Bay

Pinagbuyutan Island

Popolkan Island

South Guntao Island

Pangulasian Island

Underwater Forest

Malapacao Island

Turtle Island

N

Snake Island

Lagen Island

Ⓓ

Cudugnon Cave

Dibuluan Island

0   5 km

ACCOMMODATION
Dolarog Beach Resort	C
Greenviews Corong Coron	A
Lagen Island Resort	D
Miniloc Island Resort	B

Midtown Bakery Rizal St. Best local bakery in town, with the usual buttery buns, white bread, *pandesal* (bread rolls) and tempting array of cakes like the sumptuous pan de coco and chocolate cookies, all for a few pesos – plenty of travellers on a budget load up here. Mon–Sat 7am–7pm.

Sea Slugs Calle Hama (on the beach). El Nido's favourite beach bar, open till around 11.30pm most days, with tiki torches lighting the deck overlooking the beach. Comfort food such as pasta and pizza available.

Skyline Grill Rizal St ☎0927/203-7937. Cheapest diner in town, with tasty meals for under P150. The burgers are pretty good (P100) and the foot-long sandwiches are a bargain at P65. Upstairs becomes a popular karaoke bar most nights. Daily 7am–11pm.

Squidos Calle Hama ☎0919/227-5537. It's not on the beach, but this is one of the most popular backpacker hangouts in town, with cosy tables, free wi-fi and decent seafood (P150–200). Daily 7am–11pm.

The Bacuit archipelago

The main reason most people visit El Nido is to go **island-hopping** around the enchanting **Bacuit archipelago**, 45 limestone outcrops riddled with karst cliffs, sinkholes and idyllic lagoons. **Tours** (generally 9am–4pm) of the islands have been standardized into packages, and prices only differ very slightly between agents and operators (prices are per person; including a packed lunch): tour A (P500–600) takes in the attractions of Miniloc and Shimizu islands; B (P650–700) goes to Snake Island, Cathedral Cave and points south; C and D (P600–700) usually take in Mantinloc and Tapiutan islands. The highlights are, naturally enough, scattered throughout each itinerary, designed to encourage several days of touring. If time is short you can **charter your own boat** taking in all the best locations listed below; reckon on P4000–5000 per bangka. Another option is **kayak tours**: Cadlao Island tours are around P1100; tours to other islands around P1350. If you simply want to stay put on a **beach** for a few hours and do some snorkelling, you can charter a boat for P1200 to 7 Commando Beach (which has a small bar behind a lovely strip of sand), P1300 to Helicopter Island or P1600 to Shimizu Island.

Accommodation

The most luxurious (and exorbitantly priced) places to stay near El Nido are the *Miniloc Island Resort* and *Lagen Island Resort* (both ☎02/894-5644, ⓦ www .elnidoresorts.com; ⑨), located on private islands with superb beaches and diving, and offering similarly stylish tropical accommodation in fan-cooled or air-conditioned cottages. Both also have package rates including meals and watersports such as kayaking and scuba diving.

Cadlao Island and Helicopter Island

The dramatic tower of rock just off El Nido is **Cadlao Island** (640m). The star here is **Ubugon Cove** at the back of the island, hemmed in by jagged rock, where you can snorkel, but this is also one of the few islands you can also explore on land. One-hour trekking tours (P2300 for three people) take in the unusual saltwater Makaamo Lagoon. Nearby Dilumacad Island (aka **Helicopter Island**), which does look a bit like a blade-less helicopter, has a gorgeous 300-metre-long beach smothered in rare blue coral and lots of multicoloured shells.

Miniloc Island and Shimizu Island

Miniloc Island, forty-five minutes by boat from El Nido, boasts one of the area's greatest treasures, the **Big Lagoon**, surrounded by towering limestone cliffs that look like a cathedral rising from the water. The lagoon is spectacular at any time, but even more so during a full moon, when light pours in from the top, illuminating the water. Bangkas take a spin around the lagoon, but usually don't stop. Nearby, the similarly awe-inspiring **Small Lagoon** is only accessible by swimming (or sometimes kayaking) through a small gap in the rocks.

Nearby **Shimizu Island** (named after a couple of Japanese divers that died in the island's underwater caverns) would be unremarkable but for the dubious practice of fish feeding that takes place here; you can see great clouds of tropical fish as a result.

Mantiloc Island

One of the largest islands in the group, **Mantiloc Island** takes a bit longer to reach (around 1hr from El Nido), but is well worth the journey, with several intriguing targets tucked away along its jagged shore. **Hidden Beach** lies around a tight bend in the rocks, a gorgeous cove hidden from view. On the other side of the island is the **Mantiloc Shrine**, completed in 1993 – this Catholic shrine is usually quiet and windswept other than on May 31, when it's mobbed by believers for the Feast of the Lady of Mantiloc.

Mantiloc's main draw is **Secret Beach**, reached by a tiny gap you can swim through; on the other side is a spell-binding cove facing a white sand beach surrounded by steep rock walls. Legend has it that this inspired Alex Garland's novel *The Beach* (which was mostly written while the author was in El Nido).

Tours also usually stop in the Tapitan Strait off Mantiloc for the chance to see **turtles** lolling around, but it depends on weather conditions.

Southern islands

The main attractions in the southern archipelago include **Snake Island**, a serpentine sand bar lapped by crystal-clear waters, making it a great spot for sunbathing and a dip at low tide, and **Pangalusian Island** with its long, palm-fringed, white sand beach, perfect for swimming and snorkelling at any time.

Moving on from El Nido

The **El Nido Boutique & Art Café Travel Center** on Serena Street (daily 7am–8pm; ☎0920/902-6317, Ⓦwww.elnidoboutiqueandcafe.com) is a one-stop shop for transport and tour bookings (they charge 6 percent extra for credit card purchases). **Island Transvoyager** (☎02/851-5664, Ⓦwww.islandtransvoyager.com), a small charter operator, is the only year-round provider of flights between El Nido and Manila; fares are expensive (P6750), there are no toilets on board and there's a strictly enforced 5kg baggage limit (US$1/kilo for excess) on the 19-seat Dornier aircraft. Flights usually depart at 9.30am, 1pm and 5pm, but tickets can only be purchased five days or less in advance.

By ferry

Ferries from El Nido to **Coron Town** run every day at 8am (the 7.30am listed time is to make sure you turn up early) and take 7–8hr (P2200). The *Jessabel* (Tues, Fri & Sun) is slightly bigger than the *Welia* and *Overcomer II* (Mon, Wed, Thurs & Sat), but otherwise they are all essentially big bangkas with enclosed seating areas and a small toilet on board – bring food and drink with you. There's a terminal fee of P20 per person payable before departure from the passenger terminal. An adventurous if pricey alternative is to join an El Nido to Coron boat trip organized by **Tao Philippines** (5day/4night for P17,500/person; Ⓦwww.taophilippines.com), stopping at remote islands and villages along the way.

For other destinations you generally have to charter your own bangka: it's P8500 to **Port Barton** (4hr 30min) and P12,500 to **Sabang** (7hr). A cheaper alternative is the boat operated by *Greenviews Corong-Corong* (see p.373), which runs an on-demand boat service to and from Port Barton (5hr 30min) for P1200 per person (minimum six people). For **Manila**, San Nicolas Lines (☎02/245-2830) runs the M/V *Asuncion IV* from El Nido every Tuesday and Saturday (30hr; P1100 including food). Atienza Shipping Line (☎02/243-8845 or 0918/566-6786) also runs a less reliable service to Manila (P1100) via Coron (10hr; P900) on cargo ship *Josélle 2*, but check times in advance.

By road

The highway between Puerto Princesa and El Nido is much improved. Fort Wally (☎0917/276-2875) and Savior (☎0929/622-5974) run air-conditioned **minivans** (5hr) between El Nido and Princesa's San José Terminal via Taytay, but departures are usually early mornings only. Both companies will often pick up at your hotel. For **Port Barton**, you'll need to get off the Princesa bus at Roxas, but there is usually only one connecting jeepney at 10.30am or 11am, so leave El Nido early. For **Sabang** you must get off the Princesa bus at the Salvacion junction and pick up a Sabang-bound jeepney. These stop running after noon, so again, take the earliest departure from El Nido. Hiring your own minivan to Puerto Princesa is P7500, and P8500 to Sabang. Eulen Joy Liner (☎0919/716-2210), whose little office is on Calle Real, runs cheaper **buses** from El Nido to Puerto Princesa, **Roxas** and **Taytay**. Buses depart at 5am, 7am and 9am, but can take up to 8hr to Princesa. Minivans to Taytay should be P200, and P450 to Roxas.

The Calamian Islands

The island-hopping, kayaking, diving and trekking in the **Calamian Islands**, to the north of mainland Palawan, in many ways trumps the parent island, especially when it comes to its world-famous **wreck diving**. From the main settlement of Coron Town on the largest island, Busuanga, you can explore the awe-inspiring islands and reefs of Coron Bay, beginning with the lagoons and coves hidden among the staggering limestone cliffs of **Coron Island**. Here you can climb up to volcanic **Kayangan Lake**, not only a bewitching place to swim but also one of the Philippines' most unusual dive sites. Further south is **Culion Island**, the intriguing former home of a leper colony, while off the northern tip of Busuanga, **Calauit** is the home of a bizarre African **wildlife sanctuary**. The waters around the Calamians are also feeding grounds for the endangered **dugong** – the best tours are arranged by *Club Paradise* (see p.379).

Busuanga Island and Coron Town

Busuanga is the largest island in the group, but is mostly wild and undeveloped, with little to see beyond the lively fishing community of **CORON TOWN** on the south coast, the main base for exploring the shipwrecks in adjacent **Coron Bay**.

Non-divers will find the pristine snorkelling, swimming and hiking trails nearby just as enticing, and the phenomenal views across the bay from the town to Coron Island never get old; these are best appreciated from the top of **Mount Tapyas**, a steep 30 to 45-minute hike along the trail at the end of San Agustin Street.

With narrow streets shaded by trees, a thriving waterside market and a ramshackle wharf, Coron Town itself retains an old-fashioned provincial charm – for now. The town is a major resort-in-the-making, with frequent flights from Manila helping to ramp up development, ambitious reclamation projects, ever growing numbers of tricycles in the streets and even posh condos in the works.

Arrival and information

Flights arrive at **Busuanga (Coron) Airport**, with its small terminal building and handful of sari-sari stores. There's a tourist information counter next to the baggage claim (℡0918/725-4665), but no ATM. The airport is half an hour north of Coron Town on a paved road by **minivan**; these meet all flights (P150/person). Buses tend to serve the airport from town at 8.30am–9am only, but if you have a later flight and want to avoid hiring your own van (P1500), go to the bus terminal area next to the *Gateway Hotel* in the morning and talk to one of the drivers directly to set something up (they should still charge just P150 each with a minimum of three people).

Large ferries arrive at **Coron Port** east of the town itself, from where it's a short tricycle ride (P10) into the centre; Atienza Shipping Line (℡02/243-8845 or ℡0918/566-6786) operates an unreliable service to Manila and El Nido on cargo ship *Josélle 2*, but it is crucial to check times in advance. The Super Ferry service from Manila was suspended at the time of writing; check ⓦwww.superferry .com.ph for the latest. Bangkas from El Nido pull up right in the centre of town, and usually disembark at the Sea Dive Resort.

The centre of activity in Coron Town is around the reclaimed waterfront section (where bangkas can be chartered) and the market; buses, jeepneys and tricycles use the empty field opposite the *Gateway Hotel* as a terminal. The **Tourist Centre** faces the market square (Mon–Fri 9am–noon & 1–5pm; ⓦcorontourism.info).

Internet cafés are easy to find; try *Globe Telecom & Internet Café*, a short walk east of town along Don Pedro Street; the PAL office on Don Pedro Street; or *Interspeed*

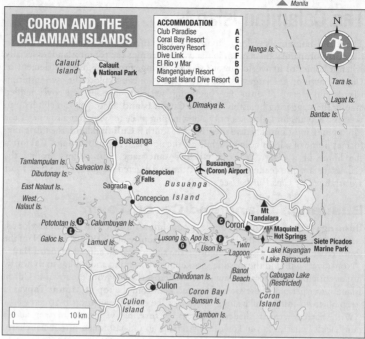

CORON AND THE CALAMIAN ISLANDS

▲ Manila

N

ACCOMMODATION

Club Paradise	A
Coral Bay Resort	E
Discovery Resort	C
Dive Link	F
El Rio y Mar	B
Mangenguey Resort	D
Sangat Island Dive Resort	G

Nanga Is.

Tara Is.

Calauit Island

Calauit National Park

Lagat Is.

Bantac Is.

A Dimakya Is.

B

Busuanga

Busuanga (Coron) Airport

Tamlampulan Is.

Salvacion Is.

Concepcion Falls

Busuanga Island

Dibutonay Is.

Sagrada

Concepcion

East Nalaut Is.

Concepcion Island

West Nalaut Is.

Mt Tandalara

Potototan Is. D Calumbuyan Is.

C Coron

Maquinit Hot Springs

Siete Picados Marine Park

Galoc Is.

Lamud Is.

Lusong Is. Apo Is.

F

G

Uson Is.

Twin Lagoon

Lake Kayangan

Lake Barracuda

Banol Beach

Cabugao Lake (Restricted)

Chindonan Is.

Coron Culion

Coron Bay

Bunsun Is.

Coron Island

Culion Island

Tambon Is.

0 ————— 10 km

Banana Island ▼▼   ▼▼ Malcapuya Island & El Nido

Internet on the National Highway at San Augustin Street (all open around 11am–10pm; P30/hr). There are several **banks** in town, and most of these have ATMs that accept foreign cards. BPI is the best, up on the National Highway (Cirrus, Plus, Visa, Electron and Mastercard accepted; P200 fee); Allied Savings Bank on Don Pedro takes Visa. Western Union (Mon–Sat 8am–6pm, Sun 8am–5pm) is on Real Street and also sells air tickets.

Accommodation

There are plenty of budget **places to stay** in Coron Town, as well as a growing number of mid-range options. While convenient, note that hotels around the market and harbour can be noisy. Some of the most luxurious and serene resorts in the Calamian chain lie off the north coast of Busuanga, a bus ride and boat ride from the airport and a 1hr drive from Coron Town. (See p.381 for resorts in Coron Bay).

Coron Town

Coron Gateway Hotel Don Pedro St, at Coron Public Market ☎02/887-7107, ⓦwww .corongateway.com. This plush hotel is right on the reclaimed waterfront next to the market, which is a plus or minus for some. Rooms are huge and stylishly decorated, with bathrooms with giant tubs, Japanese-style raised bed areas, cable TV and shared balconies, but the restaurant is mediocre, the wi-fi is not dependable and the staff are a bit disorganized (book tours elsewhere). ❽

Coron Village Lodge 134 National Hwy ☎02/805-5965 or 0908/108-9772, ⓦwww .coronvillagelodge.com. Ex-family home and lush garden now a friendly hotel with 25 rooms and a five-room apartment (with kitchen). Rooms are bare-bones but spotless and come with a/c, bathroom and TV. It also has some of the best tour packages in town, which is handy. ❹

Darayonan Lodge 132 National Hwy ☎0915/297-6426, ⓦwww.darayonan.com. This rambling bamboo hotel can be a good deal if you get a

It's the World War II **Japanese shipwrecks** in the Coron area that most divers come for. There are 24 wrecks in all, boats sunk in one massive attack by US aircraft on September 24, 1944.

Irako The best of the wrecks and still almost intact; it's home to turtles and enormous groupers, who hang in mid-water and eyeball you as you float past. A swim through the engine room reveals a network of pipes and valves inhabited by moray eels and lionfish, which look like liquid flame and have spines that deliver a hefty dose of poison.

Akitsushima A big ship lying on her side with a crane once used for hoisting a seaplane. Between Culion and Busuanga islands, near Manglet Island, the wreck attracts huge schools of giant batfish and barracuda.

Kogyo Maru Japanese freighter lying on her starboard side in 34m of water. In the large cargo holds you can see loaded construction materials, a cement mixer and a small bulldozer, while there are anti-aircraft weapons on deck.

Morazan Maru Japanese freighter sitting upright at 28m. Large shoals of banana fish, giant batfish and pufferfish the size of footballs can be seen, especially around the mast, bow and stern. It's easy to get into the cargo holds, making this a good wreck dive for beginners.

Taiei Maru Japanese tanker covered with beautiful corals and a large variety of marine life. The deck is relatively shallow at between 10m and 16m deep, and is well suited to wreck-dive beginners.

Dive operators

There are a dozen or so dive operators in Coron Town: Dive Right (ⓦ www.diveright -coron.com) is near *L&M Pe Lodge*; Discovery Divers (ⓦ www.ddivers.com) is a short walk out of town towards the airport; and *Sea Dive Resort* (see below) has a well-equipped dive operation and is popular with beginners and advanced divers.

---

deluxe room in the newer wing; the older rooms are a bit shabby. The pool is a nice extra, and the free wi-fi (in common areas) is pretty reliable. They have an alfresco restaurant, *Raphaella's*, serving breakfast, lunch and dinner. ❸

Ralph's Pension House 172 National Hwy, Barangay 3 ☎ 0921/631-5449, ⓦ www.ralphs pensionhouse.webs.com. Cosy little guesthouse with ten bright, modern a/c rooms with bathroom, flat-screen TVs and verandas; you also get wi-fi, roof-deck bar, free coffee and mineral water. ❸

Sea Dive Resort ☎ 0918/400-0448, ⓦ www.seadiveresort.com. Popular divers' resort offering a variety of simple but comfortable en-suite fan rooms (P800) and a/c rooms (P900), built around a pier close to the market. There's a decent restaurant, bar and internet access, and the dive facilities are first-rate. Visa and Mastercard accepted plus 5 percent. ❶

Northern Busuanga

Club Paradise Dimakya Island ☎ 02/838-4956 or 4960, ⓦ www.clubparadisepalawan.com. Slick, German-owned place with cosy, modern a/c cottages a stone's throw from the beach and a fabulous house reef – turtles and dugongs have been sighted here. The rate includes the cost of collecting you at the airport. Full board ❾

El Rio y Mar Port Caltom, San José ☎ 02/838-4964, front desk ☎ 02/668-3929, ⓦ www.elrioymar.com, ⓦ dugongdivecenter.com. Set on a 500m-stretch of beach facing a lagoon (it's on a promontory, not an island), with infinity pool, 24 spotless and beautifully maintained native *cabañas* or cedar *cabañas* (that have TV and video); all have hot water and there's basic wi-fi at the restaurant. Lots of activities, diving and tours on offer, but these are extra; kayaks are P750/day, north coast island tour is P2500/person and Coron Island is P3900. ❽

Eating, drinking and nightlife

Eating options in Coron Town have improved dramatically in recent years, with plenty of restaurants ranging from backpacker standards to a variety of places serving Filipino cuisine; dishes tend to be simple, however, with fresh fish often in

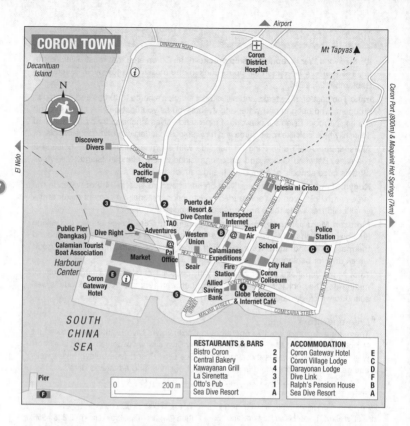

CORON TOWN

Airport
Mt Tapyas
Decanituan Island
Coron District Hospital
N
DINAGPAN ROAD
Coron Port (800m) & Maquinit Hot Springs (7km)
El Nido
Discovery Divers
COASTAL ROAD
Cebu Pacific Office ❶
NUEVA STREET
Iglesia ni Cristo
ROSARIO STREET
SAN AUGUSTIN STREET
BUHANG STREET
REAL STREET
Puerto del Resort & Dive Center
Interspeed Internet
Zest Air ❷ ⓑ
BPI
Police Station
TAO Adventures Ⓐ
NATIONAL HWY
Public Pier (bangkas)
Dive Right
@ Western Union
Calamianes Expeditions
School
ⓒ ⓓ
Calamian Tourist Boat Association
Pal Office
REAL STREET
Seair
Fire Station
City Hall
Coron Coliseum
Harbour Center
Market
DON PEDRO STREET
Coron Gateway Hotel
Ⓔ ⓘ
Allied Saving Bank
Globe Telecom & Internet Café
MONTEFORO STREET
❺
❹
SOUTH CHINA SEA
MALVAR STREET
COMESARIA STREET
Pier
Ⓕ
0   200 m

RESTAURANTS & BARS		ACCOMMODATION	
Bistro Coron	2	Coron Gateway Hotel	E
Central Bakery	5	Coron Village Lodge	C
Kawayanan Grill	4	Darayonan Lodge	D
La Sirenetta	3	Dive Link	F
Otto's Pub	1	Ralph's Pension House	B
Sea Dive Resort	A	Sea Dive Resort	A

short supply. The **Coron Public Market** (most stalls daily 6am–7pm) by the piers in the centre of town contains cheap snack stalls and open-air grills. **Nightlife** is limited to a handful of Western-oriented bars, though Coron does have a seemingly inexhaustible appetite for videoke.

Bistro Coron National Hwy, at Don Pedro St ☎0918/305-0750. Convenient and solid choice, serving mostly continental/European cuisine; dishes like chicken cordon bleu, coq au vin, pizzas, pastas and the odd Filipino choice; grilled fish usually has to be ordered in advance (mains P150–P250). Breakfasts are great value (P250). Daily 8am–10pm.
Central Bakery Don Pedro St. This is the most convenient place to stock up on fresh buns, cakes, *hopia* (sweet bean-filled pastries) and *pandesal* (bread rolls) from P30 – usually open early mornings till early evening.

Kawayanan Grill Don Pedro St ☎0905/320-2376. Rustic Filipino restaurant with thatched candlelit *cabañas* and a lush garden, handicraft store and videoke. Great place for drinks, with so-so live bands and decent food; the *kare-kare* (P250) is an excellent peanut-packed

delight, but the *adobo* (P175) really isn't very authentic. The fresh coconut (P75), *halo halo* (P120) and barbecue meats (P100) are safer bets. Daily 11am–11pm.
La Sirenetta Reef pier (accessible via the alleyway beside Coron Divers and *Coron Reef Pension House*) ☎0918/903-7063. Best location in town, if not the best food, stuck out on a pier opposite *Sea Dive Resort* with romantic views across the bay and tasty margaritas. The seafood isn't bad; mangrove crabs, mahi-mahi, Culion tiger prawns and local lobster usually grace the menu (mains around P250). Daily 11am–10pm.
Otto's Pub National Hwy (towards the airport). Popular foreign hangout owned by local celebrity and Austrian expat Otto Putz, serving cold beers with Austro-German food (think bratwurst, beef gonlash and meat loaf). Open till late most days.

Sea Dive Resort ☏0918/400-0448, ⓦwww
.seadiveresort.com. This popular resort (see p.379)
is traveller central, offering a good range of breakfasts (P140), pancakes (P90), burritos (P160),
pizzas (P240), sandwiches and burgers (P150),
pastas (P130–240), basic veggie dishes like
pinakbet (P160) and lots of fresh seafood. Wi-fi is
free and there's one terminal in the corner. The
Helldivers Bar next door is the place to grab a beer.
Daily 7am–11pm.

Around Busuanga

Most travellers to Coron Town come for the idyllic islands of **Coron Bay** (see
below), but there are a few worthy attractions in the areas of **Busuanga Island**
close to town. Hikers can tackle the fairly easy five-hour round trip to **Mount
Tandalara** (936m), the highest point in northern Palawan, though the trail is not
marked and it's best to hire a guide (P300) – *Sea Dive* can help. Facing Coron Bay
just 7km east of town, the **Maquinit Hot Springs** (daily 7am–10pm; P100)
comprise a series of enticing open pools of spring water that feed each other before
cascading into the sea; because the water temperature often tops 40°C, the springs
are best visited during rain or after 6pm, when things cool down. Tricycles should
charge P300 return from Coron Town for up to four people (they usually wait for
two hours). Private minivan hire is P1200–1500, and some boat tours of Coron
Bay include the springs.

Calauit

In 1977 President Marcos created a game reserve on **Calauit** (park manager
☏0921/215-5482), an island separated from the north coast of Busuanga by a narrow
mangrove channel. All the original giraffes, zebras, elands, impalas and gazelles from
Kenya have since died, but their offspring have multiplied to number over five
hundred. Also doing well are more than one thousand native **Calamian deer**. Other
rare indigenous species here include the Palawan peacock, mouse deer, bearcats,
pythons and porcupines. The draw for most visitors is the chance to **feed** the giraffes
by hand, though this merely emphasizes how tame the animals have become.

    Admission to the island costs P350, but with an area of 282 square kilometres,
you really need to arrange an additional motorized **tour** to see the animals (2hr;
P1000 for a group of six). Day-trips will usually not include these costs in the price,
which will only cover transport to Calauit; you'll pay less from the north Busuanga
resorts (see p.379), but from Coron expect a bangka all the way to be P7500–9000
for up to eight people (4hr one-way). You can take a faster minivan overland (2hr
30min; P6500 for up to six people), but you'll also need to hire a bangka (10min;
P500) to cross over to Calauit. If you are alone you can save money by joining an
organized tour (P2600/person with Calamianes Expeditions). Determined budget
travellers can take a jeepney to the village of Macalachao and take a bangka from
there (10min), but this requires a very early start and lots of patience – ask at the
visitor centre in Coron Town for departure times.

Coron Bay islands

The primary reason to stay in Coron Town is to explore the spell-binding islands
and coves scattered around **Coron Bay** (see p.379 for diving). Bangka trips are easy
to arrange, but it's worth comparing the various packages on offer (see box, p.382).
Coron Island is the most popular destination, but try to spend time on the smaller,
less visited islands.

Accommodation

The self-contained resorts of the Coron Bay islands offer far more solitude than
places in Coron Town, and while these are generally more expensive, some offer
good deals online.

Coron tours

Most hotels can arrange various tours of the islands and attractions near Coron Town, but it's worth shopping around as itineraries and prices do vary. The best place to start is **Sea Dive** (which also runs dive trips see p.379), There's also the **Calamian Tourist Boat Association** at the town pier (behind the market), which has its own fixed prices for island-hopping. An excellent budget choice is **Calamianes Expeditions & Ecotours** at 11 San Agustin St (☏0919-3054363, ⓦwww.corongaleri.com .ph). They need a minimum of five people to run tours, but they will pair you with other groups to make up the numbers. Coron Island tours start at just P650 per person including all admission charges and lunch.

Coral Bay Resort Pototatan Island, at the western edge of the group ☏0919/888-1910, ⓦcoralbay.ph. Comfy, rustic accommodation in fan-cooled wooden huts on a 900m white sand beach about 1hr 30min from Coron Town by bangka. This is a peaceful place to chill out, and you can trek around the island or snorkel just offshore on a beautiful reef teeming with tropical fish. Owned by the same people as *Dive Link* (see below), so you can arrange a "twin resort" package. Full board. ❽

Discovery Resort Decanituan Island, a 10min bangka ride from Coron Town ☏0920/901-2414, ⓦwww.ddivers.com. Popular dive-oriented resort with a 24hr shuttle service back and forth to Coron Town. The bungalows all have private bathrooms and terraces with fine views of the bay. Staff are friendly and reasonably efficient, and there's a good restaurant. The beach here is nothing special, but horseriding and kayaking are available. ❼

Dive Link Uson Island, 10min west of Coron Town by bangka ☏02/413-6007 or 0918/926-1546, ⓦwww.divelink.com.ph. Twin, double and family cottages with a/c and private bathrooms (and hot water). Wi-fi and a/c are available daily 5pm–9am. There's only a small patch of brown beach amid the mangroves, but there's compensation in the terrific views from the cottages, and there's a large pool. Full board ❼

Mangenguey Resort Mangenguey Island ☏0908/896-8488, ⓦwww.mangenguey .com. Top choice for splendid isolation, this luxury resort is a 1hr 30min boat ride from Coron Town – the island is private (with plenty of snorkelling and trekking), the suites are beautifully designed and furnished with art, and there's wi-fi, a/c and cable TV. Verandas provide views of the ocean and the food is exquisite. ❾

Sangat Island Dive Resort Sangat Island, 30min from Coron Town ☏0919/617-5187, ⓦwww.sangat.com.ph. Established by a British expat in 1994 on a gorgeous island with a giddy interior of cliffs and jungle, and a shore of coves and coral reefs. Accommodation is in 13 native-style beachfront and hillside cottages (with fans), and the resort specializes in dive courses. Free wi-fi or P100/hr for internet. Full board. ❼

Coron Island

Most hotels and tour operators in Coron Town offer day-trips to **Coron Island**, an enchanting cluster of jagged limestone cliffs and peaks just fifteen minutes across the bay. The island offers truly spectacular landscapes and some rich snorkelling sites, though visitors are confined to the northern coast; Coron is the traditional home of the **Tagbanua** people and the rest of the island is strictly off-limits to outsiders. The Tagbanua now make most of their living from admission fees on the island, income that supplements their otherwise meagre living from fishing in the two main east coast communities of Banuangdaan (Old Coron Town) and Acabugao.

Tours involve plenty of snorkelling and swimming, and run for around P1500 for a bangka of up to four people (at *Sea Dive*, see p.379; the boat association charges P2000), not including admission fees. Lunch is usually an extra P250 per person. In between Coron Island and Coron Town you'll typically stop at the **Siete Picados Marine Park** (P100), offering a relatively rich spread of coral and marine life (sea snakes, sea fans, clownfish and whale sharks are sometimes spotted on the deeper side of the reef).

To visit volcanic **Kayangan Lake** (daily 8am–4pm; P200) boats dock at a gorgeous lagoon rimmed with coral and turquoise waters – here the Tagbanua have a small hut with basic information about the island and the tribe, with staff on hand to answer any questions. The lake itself is reached by climbing up a steep flight of steps – at the top turn left along a narrow path to tiny **Kayangan Cave** for awe-inspiring views of the lagoon below. The main path continues down to the lake, where you can snorkel in the warm waters and spy schools of odd-looking needlefish.

Nearby **Barracuda Lake** (daily 8am–4pm; P100) offers similar scenery, but is only worth the additional entrance fee if you are on a **dive trip**; on the surface the water is the usual temperature, but 18 metres down it heats up so much that you can drift along on hot thermals. To the west are the **Twin Lagoons** (P100), hemmed in by jagged pillars of limestone towering over the water like abstract sculptures. Boats dock at the end of the first lagoon, where you can swim through a low-lying water tunnel into the second one, a tranquil and very deep inlet (the other end opens to the sea). Odd coral formations cling to the sides of the lagoon, looking like a sunken city under the surface. A little further along the coast is **Skeleton Wreck** (P100), a sunken Japanese fishing vessel easily viewed by snorkellers, and a series of narrow **beaches** backed by sheer cliffs. Tours usually have lunch on one of these (Banol Beach is the most popular), but each one charges a P100 fee.

Culion

Few travellers make it to the curious island of **Culion**, around two hours south of Coron Town by boat, once the world's largest **leper colony** and a place that inspired fear and often, revulsion. Today the leper colony has all but been erased, but some haunting monuments of the island's past remain, as well as some totally untouched beaches you'll have to yourself. Like Busuanga, the island is actually quite large and undeveloped, but the main attractions lie in the pretty little capital, **Culion Town**.

Some history

In 1904 the Americans decided to create an isolated but self-sufficient **leper colony** here, and the inhabitants were relocated to Concepcion on Busuanga. The US regime rounded up all the lepers they could find in the Philippines and forcibly removed them to Culion. Given the concern about leprosy at the time, this was considered neither cruel nor unusual, simply a way of bringing the sick together in one place so a cure could be found and transmission limited. The colony opened in 1906, receiving around eight hundred lepers in its first year. A 1920s travelogue described Culion as "practically an independent nation" – it even had its own currency. Cost-cutting in the 1930s and World War II meant a dramatic scaling down of the colony; by 1980 there were only 637 patients. A permanent cure for leprosy was discovered in 1987, and the disease was considered eliminated from the island by 2000. Today the old hospital serves as the Culion Sanatorium and General Hospital for the whole island.

Arrival, information and accommodation

Culion can only be reached by bangka from Coron Town; the M/V *Santa Barbara* (P200) leaves at around noon daily from Coron Port (1hr 30min). Every day it overnights in Culion – returning at 9am – so you'll have to stay unless you hire a private bangka from the boat association for a return trip (2hr one-way; P2500–3500 depending on boat size), or join the Calamianes Expeditions tour (P1150/person). On arrival you can get information from the small tourist office inside the Municipal Hall (Mon–Fri 9am–5pm; ☎0917/552-2277).

Culion's best **hotel** is *Hotel Maya* (℡0939/254-2744, Ⓦwww.islaculionhotel maya.com; ❸) next to the church, actually a teaching hotel operated by the Jesuit-run Loyola College of Culion. Another comfy option is the modern *Tabing Dagat Lodging House* (℡0921/653-1470; ❷; credit cards accepted), five minutes' walk from the port opposite the local government offices. It also operates a decent Filipino **restaurant**.

Note that **electricity** only runs noon to midnight in Culion, which can make for a hot night when there's no breeze. There are no banks or ATMs and credit cards are rarely accepted, so bring plenty of cash.

The Town

The approach to Culion Town is dominated by the striking coral-walled **La Inmaculada Concepcion Church**. The church was substantially rebuilt in 1933 on the site of an older fortified Spanish chapel, completed in 1740. Beside the church is the old lighthouse, with tremendous views north to Coron Town. The **Culion Museum** inside the hospital compound (Mon–Fri 9am–noon & 1–4pm; P50), housed in the former leprosy research lab built in 1930, details the history of the colony and contains medical relics and photographs from the turn of the last century. The museum is one of the most intriguing in the Philippines, with a vast archive of original photographs and patient records that you can browse. The rooms where doctors worked have been maintained as they were and contain equipment the doctors actually used, much of it looking like instruments of torture.

The southern islands

One hour south of Coron Town lies the enticing trio of **Malcapuya Island**, **Banana Island** (entry P100) and **Bolog Island** (entry P100), classical desert islands where the main activity is lounging on the beach. Malcapuya has monkeys inland while Bolog features alluring **Malaroyroy Beach**, a curving sand bar of silky white sand. The boat association (p.382) runs tours for P3500 per boat, while Calamianes Expeditions charges just P950 per person.

Sangat Island

Trips to **Sangat Island**, west of Coron Town (1hr 30min by boat), allow non-divers to snorkel over low-lying wrecks at low tide, as well as plenty of coral gardens laced with tropical fish. *Sea Dive* charges P3500 per boat, while the boat association rate is P2500; Calamianes Expeditions charges just P750 per person, but this doesn't include the *Lusong* gunboat wreck.

Mindanao

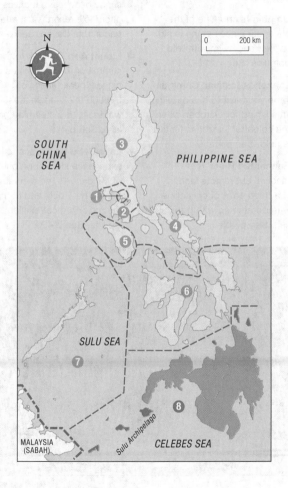

CHAPTER 8

Highlights

* **Whitewater rafting on the Cagayan de Oro River** Ride the fourteen frothing rapids near Cagayan de Oro, with the full 15km course offering four hours of thrills. See p.394

* **Dolphin Island** One of the cheapest places in the world to feed and swim with wild dolphins. See p.398

* **Lanzones festival, Camiguin** Time your visit to this dazzling little island for October, when the colourful Lanzones festival is held. See p.400

* **Enchanted River** This magical but remote lagoon is a deep cove of crystalline water crammed with tropical fish. See p.403

* **Siargao Island** Tranquil resorts, powdery beaches, top-notch surfing and some laidback nightlife. See p.405

* **Samal Island** Take a few days to explore this rustic island of sandy beaches, bat caves and affordable resorts, just a few hours from Davao. See p.415

* **Mount Apo** The trek to the summit of the Philippines' highest peak takes you through thick jungle, past waterfalls to a steaming blue lake. See p.418

* **Lake Sebu** Best place to experience life among one of Mindanao's most creative tribes, the T'boli, and home to the nation's most exhilarating zip line. See p.420

▲ *Pearl Farm Resort*, Samal

8

Mindanao

M indanao, the massive island at the foot of the Philippine archipelago, is in many ways the **cultural heart** of the country, a place where indigenous tribes still farm their ancient homelands and Christians live alongside Muslims who first settled here in the fourteenth century. Spanish rule came late to much of the island, and was tenuous at best throughout the nineteenth century; when the Americans occupied the islands, it was here that they met their most bitter resistance. Contrary to popular perception, most of the island today is **peaceful**, friendly and stunningly beautiful. Yet it is true that Mindanao is one of the most impoverished areas in the Philippines and some parts are considered **unsafe** for tourists (see box, p.389).

North Mindanao, from the lively gateway city of **Cagayan de Oro** in the centre to the surf magnet of **Siargao Island** in the east, is the area most tourists are interested in and is completely safe. In between lies **Camiguin**, a ravishing volcanic island off Mindanao's northern coast, the untouched **Agusan Marsh Wildlife Sanctuary**, inhabited by the Manobo tribe, and the hypnotic azure waters of the **Enchanted River**. Also worth exploring are the western cities of **Iligan** and **Dapitan** (where national hero José Rizal was sent into exile), and **Mount Malindang National Park**, a little-known area of dense rainforest near Ozamiz.

Davao in the south, the island's de facto capital, is a friendly provincial metropolis with excellent restaurants, nightlife and endless heaps of durian, the stinky fruit that tastes like gourmet custard. Nearby are the beaches of **Samal Island** and majestic **Mount Apo**. West of the frenetic city of **General Santos**, around the shores of **Lake Sebu**, the friendly and artistic **T'boli** people still live in traditional wooden houses and wear hand-woven tribal garments and adornments. Much of western Mindanao is part of the **Autonomous Region in Muslim Mindanao**, or ARMM, an area of huge tourism potential but with the security situation in a state of flux. Highlights include the traditional Muslim city of **Marawi**, which stands on the northern shore of serene **Lake Lanao**, and the hundreds of islands that make up the spectacular **Sulu archipelago**, especially Tawi-Tawi. You'll need to check the current security situation before visiting.

The north coast

Some of the most accessible (and safest) parts of Mindanao lie along the **north coast**, starting with the inviting city of **Cagayan de Oro**. The northwest coast stretching from **Iligan** to **Dipolog** is mostly rural and undeveloped, but peppered with alluring port towns and national parks, while the pint-sized island of

MINDANAO

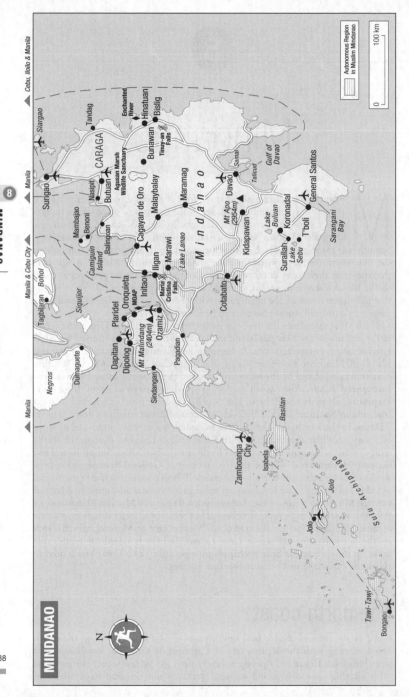

N

Negros

Dumaguete

◄ Manila

Tagbilaran

Siquijor

Bohol

◄ Manila & Cebu City

Camiguin
Island

Mambajao
Benoni

Balingoan

Dapitan
Dipolog
Plaridel
Oroquieta
MOAP
Ozamiz
Mt Malindang
(2404m)
Sindangan

Pagadian

Zamboanga
City

Isabela

Basilan

Jolo

Sulu Archipelago

Jolo

Tawi-Tawi

Bongao

◄ Manila & Cebu City

Surigao

Nasipit
Butuan

Cagayan de Oro

Iligan
Marawi
Maria
Cristina
Falls

Cotabato

CARAGA

Agusan Marsh
Wildlife Sanctuary

Malaybalay

Lake Lanao

Maramag

Tandag

Bunawan

Tinuy-an
Falls

Enchanted
River
Hinatuan
Bislig

Siargao

◄ Manila

◄ Cebu, Iloilo & Manila

Mindanao

Mt Apo
(2954m)

Kidapawan

Surallah
Lake
Sebu

Koronadal

T'boli

Samal

Davao

Talicud

Gulf of
Davao

General Santos

Lake
Buluan

Sarangani
Bay

Autonomous Region
in Muslim Mindanao

0   100 km

Despite its volatile political situation and advice from Western governments to avoid travelling to *all* of Mindanao, much of the island is safe for foreign travellers. However, you should always check the **current situation** before travelling and read our advice on trouble spots (see p.420). Politically the situation is fluid and confusing, with a number of factions and splinter groups calling for varying degrees of autonomy from Manila.

The thorniest issue involves Mindanao's Muslims (also known as Moros), who are seeking self-determination. The **Moro National Liberation Front** (MNLF) started a war for independence in the 1970s that dragged on until 1987, when it signed an agreement accepting the government's offer of autonomy. As a result, the **Autonomous Region in Muslim Mindanao**, or ARMM, was created in 1990, covering the provinces of Basilan, Lanao del Sur, Maguindanao, Sulu and Tawi-Tawi, plus Marawi City. The more radical **Moro Islamic Liberation Front** (MILF) splintered from the MNLF in 1981 and refused to accept the 1987 accord. It has since continued fighting and making uneasy truces, broken many times. In 2008 MILF broke the latest ceasefire after the Supreme Court ruled that a government deal offering them large areas of the south went against the constitution. At the height of the fighting, more than 750,000 people were displaced, and about 400 people killed. At the time of writing things appeared to have calmed; President Benigno Aquino had reopened negotiations with the MILF, proposing a wider Muslim ancestral homeland in Mindanao.

Mindanao's problems don't end with the MILF, however. One disaffected group of fighters formed **Abu Sayyaf**, whose centre of operations is largely **Basilan Island**, off Mindanao's south coast. Abu Sayyaf, whose name means "Bearer of the Sword", is said to have ties to a number of Islamic fundamentalist organizations including al-Qaeda. The group finances its operations mainly through robbery, piracy and **kidnappings**. They are believed to have been responsible for the bombing of *Superferry 14* in February 2004, which sank off the coast of Manila with the loss of 116 lives. In 2006 the group's leader, Khadaffy Janjalani, was shot dead in an encounter with government troops. However, kidnapping remains a threat.

And then there's the **communist rebels** (aka New People's Army), who have also been fighting since 1969 for the establishment of a communist state in Mindanao; they remain active in remote parts of the island.

Finally, much of the ARMM remains dangerous territory thanks to private armies aligned to corrupt local politicians. In 2009, 57 men and women (including 34 journalists) were tortured and brutally murdered in what was dubbed the **Maguindanao Massacre**, apparently for attempting to register a rival candidate for the upcoming elections; the perpetrators were a private militia controlled by the powerful Ampatuan clan (who were arrested and tried in 2010).

Camiguin to the northeast is one of the country's most appealing tourist spots. Northeastern Mindanao is known as **Caraga** (aka Region XIII), an area generally overlooked by foreign tourists though rich in eco-tourism potential. Highlights include the ancient wooden boat discovered at **Butuan**, the spell-binding **Enchanted River** and the surfing hotspot of **Surigao**.

Cagayan de Oro

Sprawled along the north coast of Mindanao, the city of **CAGAYAN DE ORO** makes an ideal introduction to the island, with a smattering of sights and fine restaurants in the city, and a handful of enticing attractions in the mountains beyond, including **whitewater rafting** on the Cagayan de Oro River.

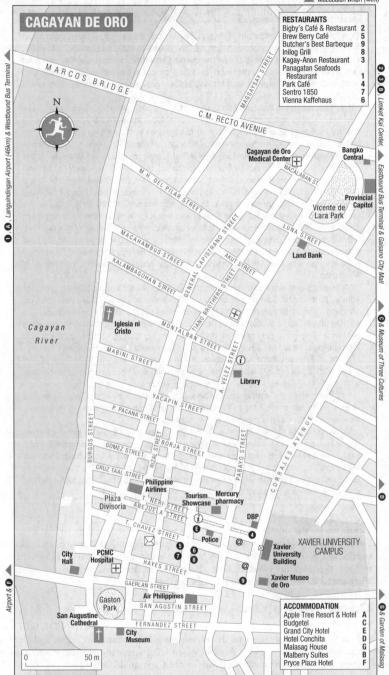

CAGAYAN DE ORO

Macabalan Wharf (4km)

MARCOS BRIDGE

C.M. RECTO AVENUE

MAGSAYSAY STREET

Cagayan de Oro
Medical Center

NACALABAN ST

Bangko
Central

Provincial
Capitol

Vicente de
Lara Park

LUNA STREET

Land Bank

M.H. DEL PILAR STREET

GENERAL CAPISTRANO STREET

AKUT STREET

TIANO BROTHERS STREET

MACAHAMBUS STREET

KALAMBAGOHAN STREET

Iglesia ni
Cristo

MONTALBAN STREET

A. VELEZ STREET

MABINI STREET

Library

Cagayan
River

YACAPIN STREET

P. PACANA STREET

BURGOS STREET

RIZAL STREET

BORJA STREET

PABAYO STREET

CORRALES AVENUE

GOMEZ STREET

CRUZ TAAL STREET

Philippine
Airlines

T. NERI STREET

Plaza
Divisoria

ABEJUELA STREET

Tourism
Showcase

Mercury
pharmacy

DBP

T. CHAVEZ STREET

E

Police

4

5

6

8

@

Xavier
University
Building

XAVIER UNIVERSITY
CAMPUS

City
Hall

PCMC
Hospital

HAYES STREET

@

GAERLAN STREET

9

Xavier Museo
de Oro

Air Philippines

SAN AGUSTIN STREET

Gaston
Park

San Augustine
Cathedral

FERNANDEZ STREET

City
Museum

RESTAURANTS
Bigby's Café & Restaurant	2
Brew Berry Café	5
Butcher's Best Barbeque	9
Inilog Grill	8
Kagay-Anon Restaurant	3
Panagatan Seafoods Restaurant	1
Park Café	4
Sentro 1850	7
Vienna Kaffehaus	6

ACCOMMODATION
Apple Tree Resort & Hotel	A
Budgetel	C
Grand City Hotel	E
Hotel Conchita	D
Malasag House	G
Malberry Suites	B
Pryce Plaza Hotel	F

Languindingan Airport (46km) & Westbound Bus Terminal

Limket Kai Center, Eastbound Bus Terminal & Gaisano City Mall

Museum of Three Cultures

Airport & F

G & Garden of Malasag

0   50 m

Arrival and information

Laguindingan International Airport, 46km west of the city, should be open by early 2012; taxis will charge around P500 into the city, while shuttle buses should cost P150–200. Until it opens flights will arrive at the old Lumbia **airport**, 10km south of the city – a taxi ride into Cagayan will set you back at least P110. **Ferries** arrive at Macabalan, 4km north of the centre; a taxi from here into the city costs about P60. Buses arrive at either the **westbound** or **eastbound bus terminals** (see p.393), from where it's an easy jeepney ride into town.

To **get around** most locals use **tricycles** that charge P6 for trips within the city (6am–10pm; at night the fare rises to P10). **Jeepneys** charge P6.50 per sector; maximum fares are P25. The regional **tourist office** (Mon–Sat 8am–noon & 1–5pm; ☎088/227-27275) is on A. Velez Street, a short walk north of the city centre, and has maps, details of guided tours and lists of accommodation. There's also the **Tourism Showcase** (Mon–Thurs 9am–5pm, Fri & Sat 9am–11pm) in the middle of Plaza Divisoria, stocked with basic information. Note that Cagayan de Oro has two area codes: 08822 (Misortel) and 088 (Philcom).

Accommodation

The area between T. Neri Street and Gaston Park is the location of most of the town's budget **accommodation**. Some of it is of poor quality, so look at your room before committing yourself. Cagayan also has some excellent mid-range hotels.

Apple Tree Resort & Hotel Taboc Beach, Opol ☎8822/754-525, ⓦwww.appletreeresortcdo.ph. Ten minutes from the city by taxi, this is the best seaside option near Cagayan. The beach often gets swamped with locals at the weekends and it can be a struggle to keep it clean, but the location, with views of Camiguin Island, is fabulous; the whole property will be renovated through 2011 (and will stay open). Rooms overlook the large pool and smaller jacuzzi pools, while suites (❼) have views of the ocean. Free pick-up from the airport or bus station. ❹

🏃 **Budgetel** Corrales Extension, north of Recto ☎088/856-4200, ⓦwww.budgetel.ph. Out of the centre but handy for the bus terminal for Camiguin, this bargain hotel offers 34 en-suite a/c singles and doubles with free wi-fi and breakfast, and dorm beds (from P250) with shared bathroom and laundry. ❷

Grand City Hotel A. Velez St at Abejuela St ☎088/857-1900, ⓦwww.grandnatures.com. Acceptable mid-range establishment with an unbeatable location in the centre of the city. Rooms are a little worn, but they're very clean and all have a/c and spacious bathrooms. Free wi-fi. ❷

Hotel Conchita Guillermo and Yacapin Ext sts ☎088/856-3856, ⓦwww.hotelconchita.com.

Comfortable business hotel in the centre of town, midway between the central plaza and Limketkai. The cheaper standard rooms are perfectly adequate and come with a/c, cable TV and free wi-fi. ❸

🏃 **Malasag House** Gardens of Malasag Eco-Tourism Village, Cugman ☎0917/596-1453, ⓦwww.themalasaghouse.com. For a real treat stay in this lovely curio-filled B&B high above the city with scintillating views and a 1950s retro feel. The spacious rooms occupy a two-storey wooden lodge, with wonderful hosts and food making it tempting to simply hang out and read on the veranda – make sure you catch the sunset. This is a place to escape the city – it's a long taxi ride from the centre. ❹

Malberry Suites Robinsons Mall, Limketkai Center ☎088/854-9999, ⓦwww.malberrysuites.com. Top business-class hotel in the city centre, handy for Limketkai shops and restaurants. Rates are reasonable, with smart, modern rooms with wi-fi and breakfast included. ❺

Pryce Plaza Hotel Carmen Hill ☎088/858-4536, ⓦwww.pryceplaza.ph. Cagayan's swankiest hotel, with five-star rooms and service, set in pleasant grounds on a hill to the west of the city, across the river. The location isn't ideal, but if you've got the budget, it's better than anything else on offer. ❼

The City

Cagayan de Oro sits on the eastern bank of the wide Cagayan de Oro River and stretches from **Vicente de Lara Park** in the north, with its age-old mahogany trees, to circular **Gaston Park** in the south, once the site of city executions, bull-fights and parades. You'll find the **San Augustine Cathedral**, a dour off-white stone edifice rebuilt in the 1950s just south of Gaston Park, with a gold-plated altar and immense stained-glass windows. The **City Museum** (Mon–Fri 8am–5pm; free) nearby occupies a water tower built in 1922 and contains a few old photos, ceramics and bits and pieces chronicling the history of Cagayan.

There's another park, a narrow strip of open space called **Plaza Divisoria**, running east–west between Neri Street and Abejuela Street, a good area for convenience stores and fast food. You'll find a tourist office, the weekend night market and the *Park Café* (opposite) located here. Plaza Divisoria ends at Corrales Avenue and the city's premier education establishment, Xavier University, which contains the somewhat faded **Museo de Oro** (Tues–Fri 9am–5pm, Sat 9am–noon; P20) and its earnest overview of local history and culture. The first room is dedicated to traditional belief in Mindanao and contains an eclectic group of exhibits including prehistoric artefacts from the Huluga Caves (8km south of the city), wooden coffins from Butuan, Chinese ceramics and a 150-year-old altar saved from a church in Camiguin. Other rooms are dedicated to José Rizal's exile in Mindanao (with a rare menu taken from the formal independence dinner in 1898), tribal costume and crafts, and local art exhibitions.

Museum of Three Cultures

For more history jump in a tricycle and head north along Corrales to Capitol University, where a similar collection to the Museo de Oro has been transformed into the far more polished **Museum of Three Cultures** (Mon–Fri 9am–noon & 1.30–5.30pm, Sat 9am–noon, Sun 10am–noon & 3–5pm; P100; ☎08822/723-349). The three cultures in question are the Christian, Muslim and the seven indigenous traditions (or "Lumad") of northern Mindanao: the first gallery is dedicated to history, with exhibits on the Huluga Caves, early trade with China and the Butuan boats (see p.402). The second hall is dedicated to the M'ranao of Marawi, and is the most intriguing section for those unable to visit Marawi themselves; exhibits cover Islamic brass work, giant ceremonial swords owned by the sultans and traditional *torogan*-style houses.

Eating and drinking

Cagayan de Oro is the best place to eat in northern Mindanao, with a range of afford-able **restaurants** and watering holes. The **Limketkai Center** and the adjacent Rosario Strip form the hip, modern heart of the city, crammed with Western-style restaurants and coffee shops, while the old centre contains plenty of cheaper Filipino joints. One experience not to miss is the **Divisoria Night Café and Market**, when tempting snack stalls set up on Friday and Saturday nights along Plaza Divisoria.

Restaurants

Bigby's Café & Restaurant Rosario Arcade, Limketkai Center ☎088/857-5511, ⓦwww .bigbyscafe.net. Local chain offering a fusion of Western and Filipino dishes; from "Rack a Bye Baby" (P399) and katsu dinner chops (P159) to sandwiches from P175. Don't miss the Midnight Dream Cake (P99/slice), the best sweet treat in the city.

Brew Berry Café A. Velez and Chavez sts. ☎08822/725-291. Good coffee anytime, but worth a visit for the excellent-value buffets; breakfast (mix of Western and Filipino dishes) is P139, while dinner (manly Filipino dishes) is P199 and includes some of the best pork *adobo* in the country. Daily 6.30am–10pm.

Butcher's Best Barbeque (Xavier branch) Corrales and Hayes sts ☎08822/710-142. Justly popular budget barbecue restaurant estab-lished by college students in 1998, with a/c and open terrace areas. Chargrilled sticks of pork, chicken and fish run P12–15, but the Kenny Rogers Ribs (P75) and sizzling *sisig* (P75) are real treats. There's a second branch at 87 Hayes St and Pabayo St. Mon–Sat 11am–2pm & 5–11pm, Sun 11am–2pm & 5–10pm.

Inilog Grill A. Velez St (second branch on Tiano St). Local favourite serving some interesting dishes: sizzling ostrich (P220) and goat *adobo* from P170. San Miguel is P40, and there's usually live music at night. The Velez restaurant is more like a dimly lit bar (with a/c) while the Tiano branch is open-air. Unlimited rice. Daily 5pm–2am.

Kagay-Anon Restaurant Rosario Arcade, Limketkai Center ☎08822/729-003. Best Filipino restaurant in the city, but also famous for local ostrich meat, raised down here since the early 1990s; the ostrich *salpicao* (P430) is delicious. Other dishes to try include steamed *lapu* (P280–370), chicken pork *adobo* (P180), *pinakbet* (vegetable stew) and tuna *kinilaw*. Daily 10am–2pm & 5–10pm.

Maxi A. Velez and Fernandez sts. This 24hr open-air café is popular with students and locals alike, for its comfort food and breakfast *tapsilog* (P70), beef jerky, rice and egg, as much as the cheap beer (P40) and live music. Look out for the "poker house" at the back, hosting plenty of serious card games every night.

Park Café Plaza Divisoria and Corrales Ave ☎088/856-4444. Classic open-air bar and café in the heart of the city; sip San Miguel, coffee (from P40), fruit shakes (P45), munch sandwiches (P110) or take breakfast (from P70) as the city flows past. Open 24hr.

Sentro 1850 50 A. Velez St ☎08822/731-850. Modern Filipino and Asian cuisine from the same folks behind *Butcher's Best*. Try the Emperor's Super Bowl (P140), a mix of rice, fish, tofu and mushrooms, Ima's Kawahi (P200), deep-fried pork belly and liver sauce, or the kamikaze burger (P140), a chargrilled burger with wasabi mayo. Apple or peach cobbler are the best desserts (P90). Unlimited soft drinks.

Vienna Kaffehaus 54 A. Velez St at Chavez St (in front of *Grand City Hotel*) ☎08822/712-700. Great coffee, snacks and a great story; the rival store in Limketkai Center with the same name was established by the former girlfriend of the owner, after an acrimonious split. Western breakfast and mains from P200.

Listings

Banks and exchange All the major Philippine banks have branches in Cagayan de Oro and most have ATMs. Land Bank is on the south side of Vicente de Lara Park while Citibank (☎088/856-2547) has a branch in Limketkai Center.

Emergencies ☎117.

Hospitals and clinics Cagayan de Oro Medical Center, Nacalaban and Tiano Brothers sts ☎08822/722-256.

Internet access There are numerous places for internet access near Xavier University in the centre of town: *Cyberium* and *Domain* on Plaza Divisoria, and *Cyber Club* on Corrales – you shouldn't pay more than P20/hour. There is free wi-fi at the SM Mall, south of the city.

Laundry Labanderos, 135 Hayes St at Pabayo St (Mon–Sat 8am–8pm, Sun 8am–5pm; P23/kilo; ☎0918/309-4333).

Pharmacies Mercury Drug has a 24hr store on T. Neri St (☎08822/722-770).

Post The post office is on T. Chavez St, between Tiano Brothers and Rizal.

Moving on from Cagayan de Oro

Philippine Airlines and Cebu Pacific have daily **flights** from Cagayan de Oro to Manila (1hr 30min) and Cebu City (1hr), while Airphil Express just serves Manila and Davao (2 weekly; 50min). Philippine Airlines has ticket offices at the airport (Mon–Fri 8.15am–4.30pm; ☎088/858-8864) and at 21 Tirso Neri St (same hours; ☎088/851-2295). Airphil Express has offices at the airport (☎08822/729-963) and in the Santiago Building (☎08822/721-478), on Gaerlan Street close to Gaston Park. Cebu Pacific (☎088/858-3936) is at the airport.

Superferry and Negros Navigation both run **ferries** from Cagayan de Oro to Iloilo (1 weekly; 24hr), Cebu City (6 weekly; 10hr) and Manila (1 daily; 35hr). The main Superferry ticket office is at the pier at Macabalan, but a number of more convenient agents are located in town.

The **Eastbound Integrated Bus Terminal** near the Limketkai Center, 3km east of the centre (off Recto Ave), handles bus services to and from Butuan (hourly; 4hr; P300), Camp Philips (P50), Surigao (2 daily; 6hr; P500), Davao (7hr 30min; P460) and Balingoan (hourly; 1hr; P140; for the ferry going to **Camiguin**). The **Westbound Integrated Bus and Jeepney Station**, 6km west of the centre on the Illigan road, handles buses to and from Iligan (hourly; 1hr 30min; P80–100), Marawi (2hr; P250), Ozamiz (4hr; P150), Dipolog (2 daily; 6–7hr; P200) and Zamboanga (12hr; P750).

Around Cagayan de Oro

The lush, mountainous terrain around Cagayan de Oro contains several worthy attractions, not least the **whitewater rafting** on the Cagayan de Oro River (see box below). Closest to the city is the **Gardens of Malasag Eco-Tourism Village** (open 24hr; P30 day entry, P50 night entry; swimming pool additional P50; ☎088/855-6183), located in a reforested area in hills south of Cagayan de Oro. The "village" contains faithful replicas of various tribal houses in the region, hosts tribal singing concerts (daily 4.30pm) and has panoramic views of Macajalar Bay. Taxis from the centre should charge P250.

Camp Philips

Some 40km southeast of Cagayan on the highway to Davao, the small settlement of Camp Philips makes for an intriguing day-trip. The former US base is now at the centre of the massive Del Monte Philippines pineapple plantation, the largest in Southeast Asia, and stumpy, prickly pineapple plants smother the landscape in every direction. Today the camp houses Del Monte staff in pretty wooden houses that blend US and Filipino styles, but there's not much to do other than admire the fruit. The main attraction is just outside town in the form of thrilling **ultralight flights** operated by Carlito Freias (☎0916/593-7034); you'll soar high above the surrounding plantations, crisscross a couple of lush canyons and see a magnificent waterfall, with hazy mountains in the distance. Rides are P1000 per 15 minutes, but you must book in advance (he's prepared to fly any day).

The swish **Del Monte Golf Club** is the best place to eat: the *Cawayanon* restaurant (☎088/855-5976) inside the clubhouse offers a fine menu of steaks (from P425), sandwiches (from P100) and unlimited **pineapple juice** to members of the public. Minivans to Camp Philips are P50 from Cagayan de Oro's eastbound bus terminal (p.393).

Dahilayan Adventure Park

Some 15km south of Camp Philips on a dirt road, the **Dahilayan Adventure Park** (☎0922/880-1319, ⓦwww.dahilayanadventurepark.com) makes for another entertaining day out, primarily for its 840m **zip line** and refreshingly cool alpine location – the park nestles in the hills some 1370 metres above sea level. The main attraction, the **Dahilayan Zip Zone** (daily 8am–5pm), comprises three zip lines: an exhilarating 320m section and a tamer 150m segment (P250 for both); and the 840m finale, where you are chained into a full body harness before hurtling down the mountain at 90km/ph (P500). It's P600 for all three rides, but the best value are

---

Rafting the Cagayan de Oro River

Whitewater rafting along the fourteen major rapids of the Cagayan de Oro River gained popularity after former President Gloria Macapagal-Arroyo took a ride here in 2002. The jump-off point is at Barangay Mambuaya, a 30- to 40-minute ride from the city proper. The wet months of September and October are best for intermediate and professional levels (when the rapids range from class 3 to 4), while the rest of the year is OK for beginners.

Reliable operators include Great White Water Tours (☎088/310-5495, ⓦwww .riverraftingcdo.com) which offers half-day tours (3–4hr) or full days (6–7hr), inclusive of snacks and meals, from P1200. It also offers a P1999 package with Dahilayan Zip Zone (see above), with pick-up from your hotel. Otherwise the normal prices include transportation from *P. Joe's Diner* at the Limketkai Center. Bugsay River Rafting (☎088/309-1991, ⓦbugsayrafting.com) tailors trips from beginners (12km, 3hr; P700) to extreme thrill seekers (15km, 4hr; P2000).

the P1999 packages that include whitewater rafting; these include minibus transport to both locations from Cagayan de Oro, a meal and snacks.

You can **get here** on public transport; take a van to Camp Philips and look for the passenger-taking motorbikes (*habal-habal*) next door to the final bus station; these charge P150 for the bone-shaking ride to the park. Alternatively, renting a van and driver in Cagayan should cost around P2500 to P3000 for the day.

Iligan

Some 90km west of Cagayan de Oro, the port city of **ILIGAN** has been working hard to shed its drab industrial image in recent years, rebranding itself as the "city of waterfalls". Little more than a village in the early 1900s, Iligan boomed as an industrial centre after the creation of a hydroelectric power scheme in the 1950s. With a population of around 300,000 it's a friendly, laidback place these days, with a peaceful mix of Christian locals and M'ranao Muslims visiting from nearby Marawi, though the biggest draw for visitors lies outside the city proper in the form of those justly famed cascades. For **Marawi** and **Lake Lanao**, see p.421.

Arrival and information

Iligan is served by regular **ferries** from Manila and Cebu, making it an alternative gateway to Mindanao if you're travelling on a budget. Ferries from Manila (3 weekly; 34hr) dock on the edge of the downtown area; walk towards the first traffic circle and you'll find plenty of taxis and jeepneys. The closest **airport** is Cagayan de Oro.

The northbound **bus terminal**, off Bonifacio Avenue 3km north of the centre, serves Cagayan de Oro (hourly; 2hr; first class P80–100). The southbound terminal off Roxas Avenue just south of the centre, serves Dapitan (several daily; 4hr) and Ozamiz (hourly; 2hr) to the west, and Marawi (hourly; 2hr) and Zamboanga (2 daily; 7–8hr) to the south. Jeepneys and taxis are usually easy to find near both terminals. Most **jeepney** rides around town cost P6.50; air-conditioned **taxis** shouldn't charge more than P60 for most destinations (the non-a/c "PU" taxis run fixed routes for a set rate of P30). Taxis should charge around P100 per hour for tours of the waterfalls.

The **tourist office** (Mon–Fri 8am–5pm; ☎063/221-3426, ⊛iligancitytourism .yolasite.com) is at Bahay Salakot on leafy Buhanginan Hill, next to City Hall at the far eastern end of Quezon Avenue; take a taxi or jeepney up here from downtown. The enthusiastic staff have maps and can help with transport and guides – ask here also about trips to Lake Lanao and Marawi (p.421).

Accommodation

The best **place to stay** in Iligan is the *Cheradel Suites* (☎063/223-8118; ❸) off Raymund Jeffrey Road (north of Quezon Extension), a pleasant whitewashed property set around a small pool, with comfy en-suite rooms (includes cable TV and a/c; breakfast from P240). Down a notch in price is *Elena Tower Inn* (☎063/221-5995; ❷) on Bonifacio Avenue near Mindanao State University, with good-value air-conditioned twins and doubles, all with bathroom, free wi-fi and cable TV. Budget choices include the basic but clean *Celadon Pension House*, Ubaldo Laya Avenue Circle (☎063/221-0711; ❶), just north of Quezon Extension.

The waterfalls

Iligan's biggest draws are the **waterfalls** that puncture the surrounding countryside, as there's little to see inside the city itself; most of Iligan was rebuilt after a devastating fire in 1957. The best cluster lies on the west side on the highway towards Ozamiz and Zamboanga; take any jeepney (P6–12) towards **Buru-un** and tell them where you want to get off.

The most impressive cascade is the **Maria Cristina Falls**, 8.5km to the southwest of Iligan, which also serves as the main source of power for much of Mindanao. One hundred metres high, the twin falls (named after two heartbroken girls that are supposed to have jumped from the top), plunge into the torrential Agus River, but are at their best Saturday and Sunday at 11am, when the Agus VI Hydroelectric Plant upstream releases the most water. The falls are located with the **NPC Nature Park** (daily 9am–4pm; P30; ☎063/221-9032), which also contains some shabby animal exhibits and a three-stage zip line across the river (closed Tues; P200). From the jeepney stop on the highway it's around 150m to the park entrance; walking on to the falls from the entrance takes around 20min (800m), or there's a park shuttle for P10. The falls can only be viewed from a deck inside the power station building – you can't get up close.

Another 1km along the highway are the ice-cold, crystal-clear and non-chlorinated **Timoga Springs** that flow freely to around seventeen privately owned swimming pools and resorts. Most resorts charge P50 for use of the pools (daily 9am–6pm) and can get very crowded in the summer.

Next door to the springs, right on the highway, is the **Macaraeg-Macapagal House** (Mon–Fri 8am–noon & 1–5pm, Sat & Sun 9am–noon & 1–4pm; free), former summer home of ex-President Gloria Macapagal-Arroyo. Built in 1950 by her maternal grandfather, the young Gloria spent many happy days here in her childhood, and the handsome property has been well maintained, rooms and bedrooms preserved as they would have looked in the 1950s. There's not much inside other than numerous family portraits, including a sultry study of the ex-president from 1983, and a statue of her as a child outside, playing on a swing.

Further along the Zamboanga highway is the turning for the **Tinago Falls** (P10), a beautiful ribbon of water that cascades 73 metres into a deep-blue pool. Jeepneys will drop you off on the highway where you can hike or take a *habal-habal* (motorbike ride) to the falls (P20 for two or P40 one person; arrange a return pick-up). The falls are located in a dramatic ravine, 365 steps down – don't go if it's raining.

Eating and drinking

Iligan is home to plenty of decent **restaurants** and several celebrated food products. Try the spicy coconut vinegar known as *pinakurat*, produced by *Suka Pinakurat* at 5 Sparrow Rd, near the end of Quezon Extension, or grab a bag of addictive toasted peanuts at *Cheding's Peanuts*, Sabayale Street, downtown near the port (P42 for a quarter kilo).

Gloria's Ihaw-Ihaw Zamboanga Highway, opposite Timoga Springs and Macapagal House. Handy for touring the waterfalls, you can buy *lechon* (P350/kilo) or whole roast chicken (P190) from the stalls outside this no-frills waterside restaurant and eat in the garden overlooking the sea. It's also known for stewed fish-jaw (tuna). Named after ex-president Macapagal's cousin (also Gloria). Open lunch only (usually 11am–3pm).

Iliganon Restobar Quezon Ave Extension at Seminary Drive ☎063/225-4577. Serves decent coffee and excellent pizzas, morphing into a popular bar at night when local bands supply live music. Free wi-fi. Daily 10am–midnight.

Sunburst Fried Chicken House Tino Badelles St at Lumboy St ☎063/221-3401. Home of the now nationally famous fried chicken chain, though aficionados claim that the taste at this store is different (and much better). It's not health food, but the fried chicken skin (P90) is certainly a mouth-watering treat. Daily 10am–10pm.

The Strip Quezon Ave Extension at Ubaldo Laya Ave. Small complex containing several Western-oriented restaurants and nightspots, including *Calda Pizza* (home of the enormous 36-inch pizza; P1000), the grill at *Crisven* and stylish *Silvestro's Bistro*. Usually noon–midnight.

Zoey Café Aguinaldo St at Echiverri St ☎063/221-2876. Free wi-fi, roasted coffee and a selection of delectable treats (try the carrot walnut cake) make this the best coffee shop in town. Mon–Thurs 9am–8.30pm, Fri & Sat 9am–9pm.

Ozamiz

Heading west from Iligan, buses save a huge detour by taking the frequent car ferries (passengers P25; you get off the bus to pay) across Panguil Bay from Mukas to the sprawling and somewhat tumbledown port city of **OZAMIZ** (also spelled Ozamis). Buses continue from the port (in the centre of town), to the main bus terminal on the outskirts and on to Dapitan (hourly; 2hr) and Zamboanga (2 daily; 6hr), but there are plenty of tricycles near the wharf to whisk you around the city should you wish to stay: there's not much to see, but it's a decent base for Dolphin Island (see p.398) and Mount Malindang (below).

Ozamiz was renamed in honour of World War II hero Senator José Ozamiz in 1948 (it was originally Misamis), but the only real sight is old **Fort Santiago**, or "Cotta" (daily 8am–6pm; P5) on the seafront, built by the Spanish in 1756. It was badly damaged by an earthquake in 1955, but from its crumbling walls there are panoramic views across Panguil Bay. Part of the outer walls house a venerated image of Mary (said to be miraculously growing), centrepiece of the open-air **Shrine of Nuestra Señora del Triunfo de la Cruz** (or *Birhen sa Cotta*).

Practicalities

Tiny **Ozamiz Airport** has flights from Cebu City (2 daily; 50min) and Manila (1 daily; 1hr 25min); take a taxi into town (P60). Tricycles should be just P6 per person within the city. Ozamiz boasts some adequate budget **accommodation** such as *Sky Lodge* (☎088/521-1425; ❶) on the main street, Rizal Avenue, a homely, spick-and-span option with pleasant air-conditioned rooms, all with clean showers and toilet. A little west of the city on the Bañadero Highway and easy to reach by tricycle, is a gem of a place, *Naomi's Botanical Garden and Tourist Inn* (☎088/521-2441; ❸), where pretty air-conditioned rooms look out onto a beautiful garden. The best hotel in Ozamiz is the *Bethany Gardens Resort* (☎088/521-5240, ⓦwww.bethanygardensresort.com; ❹) near the airport, with elegant, spacious rooms and a huge pool.

Ozamiz is celebrated for its **crabs**, with plenty sold cheap by vendors all over the city, though it can be frustratingly hard to get anyone to cook them. Decent eating options include the *New Central Restaurant* (☎088/521-0013) on Don Mariano Avenue, and *Dewberry Coffee* near City Hall, along Don Anselmo Bernad Avenue (next door is *M Bar*, a live music venue and club).

Mount Malindang National Park

Little known and little explored, **Mount Malindang National Park** is a densely forested region that offers some tough trekking and the opportunity to see rare species such as the tarsier and flying lemur.

There are actually four main peaks in Mount Malindang National Park: North Peak, South Peak, Mount Ampiro and Mount Malindang itself, which is the tallest at 2404m. The area was extensively logged before being declared a national park in 1971, so most of the forest growth today is relatively new. There's a long-established tribal group living in the park, the **Subanon**, whom you may well encounter at their Lake Duminagat settlement. They consider Mount Malindang their tribal homeland and source of strength. The best time to visit the park is during the months of January to April when the trails are dry.

You need a **permit** (P200) to enter the park, which is available from the Protected Area Office (Mon–Fri 8am–4pm; ☎088/531-2184) at the back of the Provincial Capitol Building in **Orquieta**, a one-hour bus ride north from Ozamiz. A guide is essential and can be arranged here for P1500 a day.

Misamis Occidental Aquamarine Park (MOAP) and Dolphin Island

Just thirty minutes drive north along the coast from Ozamiz in the village of Sinacaban, the **Misamis Occidental Aquamarine Park** (MOAP; P10) is an ambitious eco-tourism project that combines dolphins, fish ponds, mangrove restoration and chalet-style accommodation via the *Dolphin Island Resort* (T088/586-0292). Rooms range from deluxe suites (⑥) to smaller cottages (④), all on stilts overlooking the shallow bay with hot showers and TV. There are also dorm beds from P250.

The real attraction here is **Dolphin Island**, a series of man-made stilt huts over a sand bar 2km offshore. It's principally a dolphin rescue centre, with fenced-in seawater pens providing a safe haven for animals trapped or injured by fishermen – after rehabilitation they are released into nearby dolphin communities. At the time of writing the island was home to five spotted dolphins and one green turtle. You can swim with the dolphins here for just P250 – an incredible deal. There's a basic restaurant on the island that serves fried chicken, pork and rice, and another restaurant onshore at the resort. The fifteen-minute boat ride to the island costs P30 round-trip (every hour, daily 8am–4pm; last boat back 5.30pm), and you can rent snorkelling gear (P50/hr), kayaks (P100/hr) or organize dive trips (from P2300). Tricycles to MOAP from the Ozamiz ferry charge around P200.

Dapitan

The scenic north coast city of **DAPITAN**, with its red-roofed houses and sweeping ocean bay, is best known for its connection to national hero **José Rizal** (see box below), who was exiled here in the 1890s. The main drag in Dapitan is Sunset Boulevard, a romantic seafront promenade where you'll find banks, shops and a number of hotels. The **Rizal Shrine** (Tues–Sun 9am–4pm; free) on the northern edge of the city is a pleasant parkland area encompassing the grounds where Rizal spent his exile. The park contains faithful reproductions of the simple cottage he lived in (Casa Cuadrada), the octagonal schoolroom where he taught (Casa Redonda), his chicken house (Casa Redonda Pequeña) and two clinics (Casitas de Salud) where he worked. The **Rizal Museum** (same hours; free) is also here, and contains memorabilia such as his books, notebooks and medical equipment. To get here either take a tricycle from the city centre or walk – it's only ten minutes via Bagting Bridge with Dapitan Bay on your left. Rizal also designed a huge grass **Relief Map of Mindanao** that still exists today in F. Saguin Street.

José Rizal in Dapitan

The decision to exile **José Rizal** to Dapitan was taken so he could contemplate his sins against Spain and, "publicly retract his errors concerning religion, and make statements that were clearly pro-Spanish and against revolution". He arrived in 1892 and left shortly before his execution in 1896. During his four-year exile Rizal was famously productive: he practised medicine and pursued scientific studies, continued his artistic and literary works, widened his knowledge of languages and established a school for boys. It was also in Dapitan that he first set eyes on Josephine Bracken, the smouldering Irish beauty whom he married in a private ceremony in his cell two hours before his execution. Tragically the son she bore Rizal was stillborn and is buried in an unmarked grave somewhere in Dapitan. Bracken married again in Hong Kong, but died of tuberculosis at the age of 26.

Practicalities

Dipolog **airport** is only 12km away, with regular buses and minivans making the journey to Dapitan. Superferry **ferries** arrive at Palauan wharf, halfway between Dapitan and Dipolog. Getting into Dapitan from the wharf is no problem: jeepneys cost P10 and minibuses P20. **Buses** from Cagayan de Oro (2 daily; 6–7hr), Dipolog (hourly; 45min) and Ozamiz (hourly; 2hr) arrive at a terminal on the National Highway in the south of the city. There's no tourist information office in Dapitan and no major banks.

Top choice in Dapitan for **accommodation** is the *Dapitan City Resort Hotel* (℡065/213-6413; ❹) on Sunset Boulevard. Rooms are plain but comfortable and have air conditioning, hot showers, TVs and fridges. The hotel has a **restaurant** where the speciality is very reasonably priced seafood. Fast-food restaurants line Sunset Boulevard, and in the city plaza you'll find the venerable old bistro *Corazan de Dapitan*, (℡065/213-6639) where Filipino dishes range fromP50–200.

Camiguin Island

Lying around 20km off the north coast of mainland Mindanao, the pint-sized island of **Camiguin** ("cam-ee-*gin*") is one of the country's most appealing tourist spots, offering ivory beaches, iridescent lagoons and jagged mountain scenery. There's no shortage of adventure here either, with reasonable scuba diving and some tremendous trekking and climbing in the rugged interior, especially on

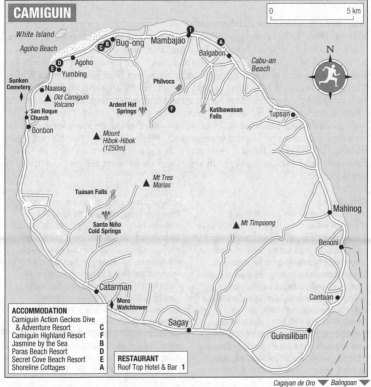

CAMIGUIN

0   5 km

White Island
Agoho Beach
ⓒ Ⓑ Bug-ong   Mambajao   ❶
Ⓐ
Balgabon
Cabu-an Beach
Ⓓ Agoho
Ⓔ Yumbing
Sunken Cemetery
Naasag
Philvocs
Old Camiguin Volcano
Ardent Hot Springs
Ⓕ
Katibawasan Falls
San Roque Church
Tupsan
Bonbon
Mount Hibok-Hibok (1250m)
Mt Tres Marias
Tuasan Falls
Santo Niño Cold Springs
Mt Timpoong
Mahinog
Benoni
Catarman
Moro Watchtower
Cantaan
Sagay
Guinsiliban

N

ACCOMMODATION
Camiguin Action Geckos Dive & Adventure Resort   C
Camiguin Highland Resort   F
Jasmine by the Sea   B
Paras Beach Resort   D
Secret Cove Beach Resort   E
Shoreline Cottages   A

RESTAURANT
Roof Top Hotel & Bar   1

Cagayan de Oro ▼ Balingoan ▼

With the airport closed indefinitely, the easiest way to get to **Camiguin** is via Cagayan de Oro. The most convenient option is the Parras Sea Cat (call the *Paras Beach Resort* for the latest; ☎088/387-9008), which sails direct from Cagayan de Oro port to **Benoni** on Camiguin's southeast coast (2hr; P500), though the service is often cancelled for prolonged periods, so call first to make sure it's running. The safest option is to take any bus from Cagayan's eastbound bus terminal to **Balingoan** (45min to 1hr; P140), about 88km northeast of Cagayan, then a ferry from Balingoan to Benoni. Ferries run hourly throughout the day (5.15am–5.40pm; P135) and the trip takes 30 to 45 minutes (the last boat back is 6pm). From Benoni several jeepneys run every day to Mambajao on the north coast. You can take a tricycle straight to your resort; in many cases the resort will send a vehicle to meet you.

volcanic **Mount Hibok-Hibok**. Another major tourist draw is the annual **Lanzones festival**, held in the fourth week of October. Revellers dressed only in *lanzones* leaves stomp and dance in the streets as a tribute to the humble fruit, one of the island's major sources of income.

The beauty of Camiguin is that it doesn't really matter where you stay because you can visit all the sights easily from anywhere. The **coastal road** is almost 70km long, making it feasible to circle the island in a day. If you don't want to depend on public transport, consider hiring your own private jeepney or tricycle for the trip. Many resorts also offer motorcycle rental.

Accommodation and eating

Most of the seaside **accommodation** in Camiguin is west of Mambajao on the beaches between the small towns of **Bug-ong** and **Naasag**. The resorts in this area have lots of information about diving and trekking; resorts near the town of Agoho, a little west of Bug-ong, are popular because of their good access to White Island. To the east of Mambajao around the village of **Balgabon** you'll find more resorts, although the beach here isn't as good as Agoho, Yumbing and Naasag.

Eating on Camiguin is mostly limited to your resort or one of a few nipa-style restaurants dotting the beaches. In Mumbajao itself there are some local eateries clustered around the Capitol Compound, while ☀ *Roof Top Hotel & Bar* (☎088/387-0511) in Rizal Street bakes its own sumptuous chocolate cake, cheesecake and knocks out light international meals from burgers and fries to Greek classics.

Resorts

Camiguin Action Geckos Dive & Adventure Resort Agoho ☎088/387-9146, ⓦwww.camiguin.ph. What makes this friendly resort stand out is the budget "traveler" rooms for P700 (shared bathroom), while the standard a/c en-suite cottages right on the beach are also great value; lovely wood cottages with verandas, hammocks and rocking chairs. Dives from P1250 and PADI courses from P13,000. ❹

Camiguin Highland Resort Lakas, Soro-soro ☎088/387-0515, ⓦwww.camiguinhighlandresort .com. Unusually, this tranquil resort is nowhere near the beach; instead you get awe-inspiring views of the coast, beautiful mountains and a top-notch restaurant, service and luxurious accommodation. There's also a soothing pool and jacuzzi. ❺

Jasmine by the Sea Bug-ong ☎088/387-9015, ⓦwww.silent-gardens.com. One of the closest resorts to Mambajao, *Jasmine* is excellent value, with spacious fan cottages on the shore and a restaurant that serves some organic dishes. ❷

Paras Beach Resort 4km beyond Bug-ong in Yumbing ☎088/387-9008, ⓦwww.paras beachresort.com. This was a private beach house belonging to the Paras family until they decided to add compact a/c rooms (with hot showers and cable TV) and open it to the public. It's in a spectacular position on the shore, and the staff are efficient organizers of tours. ❹

Secret Cove Beach Resort Yumbing
☎088/387-9084, ⓦwww.secretcove
camiguin.net. The Canadian–Filipino owned resort
is a hidden gem with seven spacious and clean a/c
rooms, restaurant, bar and internet access. On-site
Johnny's Dive & Fun organizes dive trips. ❸

Shoreline Cottages Balgabon, east of
Mambajao ☎088/387-9033. Typical of the budget
accommodation on this stretch of beach, with
ordinary single, twin and double huts and cold
showers. ❶

Mambajao and around

There's no reason to hang around in **MAMBAJAO** ("mah-bow-ha") the island's
capital, other than to sort out the practicalities of your stay. The **tourist office**
(Mon–Fri 8am–5pm; ☎088/387-1097) in the Capitol Compound has information about accommodation and climbing Hibok-Hibok. There are several **banks**
in town with ATMs, and internet cafés on Rizal Street. **Cabu-An Beach** to the
east of Mambajao, near the barangay of Balbagon, is marginally the closest and has
some nice coral close to the shore, as well as half a dozen decent resorts. **Agoho
Beach**, 7km west of Mambajao, is wider and sandier than Cabu-An, with many
resorts and is an ideal place to base yourself for all sorts of activities, including
scuba diving, bangka-hopping and walks into the island's interior.

From Balbagon you can trek inland along a marked trail to **Katibawasan Falls**
(P30), a clear stream plunging 70 metres over a rocky cliff into a deep pool that
makes for a heavenly swim after the walk: getting to the falls on foot takes about
two hours, or you can hire a tricycle or minivan (P300–400).

At **Philvocs** (Mon–Fri 9am–4pm), an easy trip inland from Mambajao by
tricycle, vulcanologists who monitor Mount Hibok-Hibok will be only too happy
to give you a few personal insights into their work, as well as showing spectacular
photographs of past eruptions. Three kilometres inland from the barangay of
Tagdo, **Ardent Hot Springs** (daily 9am–10pm; P30) can be reached in about an
hour on foot from Mambajao or Agoho Beach. Hot here means very hot: the
water in these pools, which lie in a verdant valley surrounded by jungle, is warmed
by the volcanic interior of Mount Hibok-Hibok and reaches 40°C. The best time
to visit is from the late afternoon, when the sun is less fierce, or consider an after-
dark visit, when you can sit in one of the pools with a cold drink and gaze at the
stars. There's a good little restaurant, a coffee shop and accommodation in a
number of simple cottages.

The only active volcano on Camiguin, **Mount Hibok-Hibok** had its last major
eruption in 1951, with tremors and landslides that killed 500 people. At a
relatively modest 1250m it can be climbed in a day, but the strenuous trail crosses
some very steep slopes and treacherous rocks and shouldn't be attempted alone.
Many resorts have lists of local **guides** who can be hired for around P1500. Along
the way you'll see steam vents and hot pools, while at the top there's a crater lake.
Views from the summit are unforgettable, with the coast of Mindanao to the south
and the islands of the Visayas to the north.

About halfway between Mambajao and Bonbon off the island's northwest coast
is one of Camiguin's most popular attractions, **White Island**, a dazzling serpentine ribbon of sand only visible at low tide and easily reached in a short bangka hop
from nearby resorts. The views and the water are gorgeous, but there's no shade,
so make sure you take a wide-brimmed hat and lots of sunblock. Return trips are
usually around P500.

The west coast

The small fishing town of **BONBON** on Camiguin's west coast has an attractive
little plaza and a pretty, whitewashed church; it also lies a few kilometres south
of the slopes of the **Old Camiguin Volcano**, which you can climb easily in an

hour. The path to the summit, from where the views are stunning, is marked by life-size alabaster statues representing the **Stations of the Cross**, beginning with Christ being sentenced and ending with his shrouded body being lowered into the sepulchre.

A little south of the old volcano you'll see the striking sight of an enormous **white cross** floating on a pontoon in the bay. This marks the site of the **Sunken Cemetery**, which slipped into the sea during a volcanic eruption in 1871 – if you so desire you can observe reef fishes massing around the decaying tombs on a diving or snorkelling trip. The same eruption destroyed the seventeenth-century Spanish **San Roque Church** in Gui-ob on the northern fringes of modern Bonbon; its brooding ruins still stand, with a memorial altar inside.

There are some quiet stretches of sandy beach further south near the ramshackle little town of **CATARMAN**, 24km south of Mambajao, but there's no accommodation in the area. Six kilometres north of Catarman are the **Tuasan Falls** and nearby **Santo Niño Cold Springs** (P20) which can both be reached either on foot from the coastal road or by tricycle along a rather rough track. Both have deep pools that are good for swimming and the surroundings are pleasant, with rich vegetation and a few simple huts (P100 a day) where you can change and take a nap. On the southern coast near Guinsiliban, fifteen minutes east by jeepney from Catarman, is a 300-year-old **Moro Watchtower**; climb to the top for panoramic views across to mainland Mindanao.

Butuan

The bustling capital of Agusan del Norte province, **BUTUAN**, lies around 200km east of Cagayan de Oro. Butuan is thought to have been the first coastal trading settlement in the Philippines; in 1976 a carefully crafted and ornate oceangoing outrigger (*balangay*) was unearthed on the banks of the Agusan River and carbon-dated, astonishingly, to 320 AD. Of nine boats since discovered in the mud, two more have been excavated, dating from 1215 and 1250 respectively and adding to the growing wealth of evidence that the Philippines was actively trading with Asia long before the Spanish arrived. The original "Butuan boat" is now in the small **Balangay Shrine** (Mon–Fri 9am–4pm; free) around 5km west of the city, along with the remains of a number of other ancient boats and various archeological and ethnological treasures such as ceramics and coffins.

The **Butuan National Museum** (Mon–Sat 9am–noon & 1–4.30pm; P20) a kilometre north of the city centre in the City Hall compound is home to a small but intriguing collection including cooking implements and jewellery from pre-Hispanic Butuan. The museum has two galleries: the Archaeological Hall which exhibits specimens of stone crafts, metal objects, pots, gold and burial coffins; and the Ethnological Hall, which focuses on the culture of the Manobo, Mamanua, Higaonon and lowland Butuanons.

Practicalities

The provincial **Department of Tourism** office is at the Grateful Realty Corp Building, on Pili Drive (Mon–Fri 8am–5pm; ☎085/341-8413). The **airport**, served by Philippine Airlines from Manila (4 daily; 1hr 40min) and Cebu Pacific from Cebu City (1 daily; 45min), is 10km west of the city. Superferry (to Manila; 42hr) and Cebu Ferries (Bohol and Cebu) dock at the port town of **Nasipit**, 24km west of Butuan, from where it's a thirty-minute jeepney ride into the city. Frequent **buses** connect with Cagayan de Oro (hourly; 4hr; P300), Davao (5–6 hr; P486) and Surigao (hourly; 2hr; P180). The bus terminal is on the northern outskirts of Butuan off Montilla Boulevard; there are plenty of tricycles to take you into the centre.

The best place to **stay** in Butuan is the mid-range *Almont City Hotel* (☎085/342-05263; ❹), San José Street, Rizal Park, which has spacious and airy rooms, all with air conditioning, private bathrooms and cable TV. Rooms at the front have pleasant city views and the coffee shop with tinkling indoor waterfalls offers light meals and pastries. *Hotel Karaga* (☎085/225-3888, ⓦhotelkaraga.com; ❷) is well located on Montilla Boulevard and has bargain air-conditioned rooms with cable TV and free internet.

The top **restaurant** in Butuan is *Rosario's* (daily 10am–2pm & 5–10pm) on JC Aquino Street, best known for its tasty Chinese dishes; there's a fine dining section and cheaper fast-food area. The cakes and pastries at *Red Apple Restaurant*, AD Curato St (daily 7am–10pm), are hard to resist, but this cafeteria-style place is also good for Filipino food and breakfasts. *Margie's Kitchen* (daily 10am–1am) on JC Aquino Street is the best place for a coffee, burger or snack, while your best bet for nightlife is open-air *Caraga Square* on JC Aquino Avenue in the centre of town, which features local live bands most nights.

Agusan Marsh Wildlife Sanctuary

About 70km south of Butuan on the road to Davao, the **Agusan Marsh Wildlife Sanctuary** is a giant maze of interconnecting rivers, channels and lakes, with dramatic areas of **swamp forest** consisting largely of sago trees and inhabited by parrots, purple herons, serpent eagles and a good number of saltwater and Philippine **crocodiles**.

The marsh is around 2 hours 30 minutes from Butuan and 3 hour from Davao; whichever direction you're coming from, you need to get off the bus in the town of **Bunawan** (only slow non-a/c buses stop here), and then take a tricycle west to the **town hall** (☎910/984-0285) to register. From here you can hire a boat and guide for the three-hour ride along the river to the marsh area itself – be prepared for a full day out and take lots of water and sunblock. Hotels in Butuan can help arrange trips, but a locally arranged day **tour** in Bunawan costs around P1500 for the boat plus P1000 for the guide. Despite its isolation, the marsh is inhabited by about 2600 people, mainly the Manobo, an animist group that live across much of eastern Mindanao. Their houses are floating wooden structures with thatched roofs and rest on a platform lashed to enormous logs. Whole communities exist like this, their houses tethered to one another in one place, but moveable at any time. There is some very basic accommodation in Bunawan if you get stuck, and some of the floating Manobo villages also offer lodgings – ask at the town hall.

The Enchanted River

Swimming in the **Enchanted River** (daily; P10) is one of the highlights of Mindanao. The accessible part of the river is more like a narrow saltwater lagoon that ends at an underwater cave and ravine crammed with all sorts of tropical fish that get fed every day at noon. The colours are mesmerizing; the water glows like liquid sapphire, surrounded by dense jungle and karst outcrops.

The site is managed by the local authorities as a small park (you can wander to a small beach from here), but it's well off the beaten path and very few foreign tourists make it this far. The park lies at the end of a 12km dirt road, just beyond the fishing village of **Talisay** – the village is almost as enchanting as the lagoon, with neat, nipa and wood cottages, some with stilts over the water, and plenty of blossomy gardens.

The turning to the river and Talisay is signposted 2km north of **Hinatuan** on the main coast road, 150km south of Butuan; the main road is served by frequent buses plying between Butuan and Mangagoy; without your own transport it's a very long walk or *habal-habal* ride from Hinatuan.

Tinuy-An Falls

Around 10km south of the turning to the Enchanted River, near the port town of **Bislig**, another turning along a dirt road leads some 15km to the astounding **Tinuy-An Falls** (daily: P10), a thunderous, multi-tiered 95-metre cascade that almost justifies the moniker "Philippines' Niagara". Get here early and it's a magical place, with lush jungle, durian trees and giant ferns drooping over the river – you can lounge on the bank and enjoy the views or clamber up to the higher levels and paddle or swim in the pools, where a bamboo raft takes you closer in to get thoroughly soaked.

Most people hire a minivan and driver in Butuan (from P3000), but you can take a bus to Bislig or Mangagoy, stay at the modern and spotless *Paper Country Inn*, Osmena Street, Tabon, Bislig (⊕086/853-3079; ❷), and then take local transport (*habal-habal* or minivan) to the falls.

Lake Mainit

The Philippines' fourth largest stretch of fresh water, serene **Lake Mainit** is located halfway between Surigao and Butuan, a relaxing place to break the journey. The *Almont Lake Resort* (⊕086/826-2424, ⓦwww.almont.com.ph) lies just off the main highway; one spacious deluxe room (❸) overlooks the lake with a balcony while standard rooms underneath the excellent **restaurant** also have views and small terraces (❷). Breakfast is included, while the lunch and dinner menu features fresh tilapia and eel from the lake (figure on P200/head). There's not much to do here other than enjoy views and cool breezes, but you can rent kayaks for P200 per day.

Surigao

The ramshackle capital of the province of Surigao del Norte, **SURIGAO** is some 120km north of Butuan and essentially just a place to pass through to reach Siargao Island. The **airport**, just outside the city on the road to Butuan, is served by flights from Cebu City (2 daily; 45min) and Manila (2 daily; 1hr 50min); tricycles charge P150 into the centre. **Buses** from Butuan (hourly; 2hr), Cagayan de Oro (2 daily; 6hr) and Davao (1 daily; 9hr) arrive at the terminal 4km west of the city centre; tricycles should take you anywhere for around P8 per person (P30 for the whole thing). Cokaliong Shipping Lines (6 weekly), Superferry (1 weekly) and Cebu Ferries (3 weekly) also serve Surigao (tickets from Cebu range P688–885), arriving at **Eva M. Macapagal Passenger Terminal** on the harbourfront; you can walk or take a tricycle from here to the city centre. The terminal fee is P20 for all departures.

At the southern end of Rizal Street near the grandstand, you'll find the helpful **Department of Tourism** (⊕086/231-9271), where you can get information about accommodation and ferries to Siargao and Dinagat islands. The best place to look for **internet** cafés is around the central plaza and Magallanes Street.

The best **accommodation** in town is the *Tavern Hotel* (⊕086/231-7300; ⓦwww.tavernhotel.com; ❸) on Borromeo Street, not far from the ferries, with smart modern rooms in the newer wing and slightly cheaper rooms in the older building. Breakfast and free pick-up service included. A couple of blocks further north along Borromeo Street, the *Leomondee Hotel* (⊕086/826-0634; ❷) is a basic but clean budget option. Rooms are ordinary but all have air conditioning and bathrooms. For a bit more luxury make for the *Almont Beach Resort* in Lipata (⊕086/826-7544), a fifteen-minute tricycle ride from the port. There's a decent pool, rooms come with sensational views of the bay and cable TV and on-site *Café Maharlika* is open daily 6am to 10pm (free wi-fi).

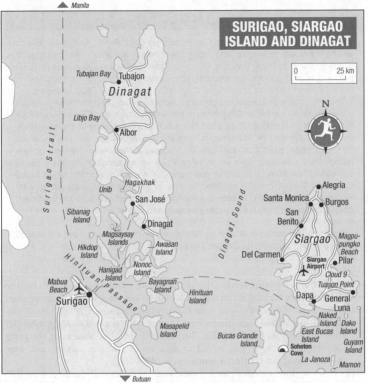

There's no shortage of fast **food** in Surigao, but for something more substantial the *City Garden Restaurant* (daily 6am–10pm) at the *Tavern Hotel* is probably your best bet. *Dominic's Sports Bar* (daily 5pm–1am) is also at the *Tavern* with large TVs for sports events and live bands at the weekends. A decent standby is *4As Barbecue* (daily 9.30am–11.30pm; ☎086/231-8898) at Navarro and Borromeo streets near the ferries, a no-frills canteen offering tasty barbecue chicken and pork.

Siargao Island

Off the northeastern tip of Mindanao lies the teardrop-shaped island of **SIARGAO**, a largely undeveloped backwater with languid beaches, dramatic coves and lagoons battered by the Pacific Ocean and a verdant hinterland of rustic little barrios and coconut groves. Some of the first tourists here were **surfers**, who discovered a break at Tuason Point that was so good they called it Cloud Nine, and though it's still off the tourist trail, word of mouth is bringing an increasing number of surfers from around the world.

Arrival and getting around

Most visitors arrive by ferry at **Dapa**, 16km from the modest but comfortable resorts around the island's friendly little capital of **General Luna**, known as GL, on the east coast. There are no banks and credit cards aren't accepted in most places, so bring **cash**.

Getting to Siargao

You can **fly** to Siargao from Cebu City (50min) via Cebu Pacific, but at the time of writing flights ran on Monday and Friday only. The tiny airport is in the barangay of Sayak on the west coast; minivans will run to General Luna and Cloud Nine for P300 per person or P1500 for the whole vehicle – check with your accommodation in advance about pick-ups. *Habal-habal* (motorbike) riders charge P500 for the trip.

The only other way to reach Siargao is by **ferry** from **Surigao**. From here you have a choice of slow car ferries (3hr 30min) or fast ferries (2hr), though the latter are little more than high-speed outriggers and can make for a bumpy ride in rough weather. Car ferries operated by Montenegro Lines (@montenegrolines.com.ph), depart at 6am and noon daily from the Eva M. Macapagal Passenger Terminal on the harbourfront; one-way fares are P144 or P173 for air conditioning (the latter is sometimes not offered). Note that you must also pay a P20 terminal fee to board the boats. There's an ATM outside the terminal and plenty of snack stalls. Fast ferries depart twice a day at 6am and noon from the wharf along Surilao Boulevard around the corner from the main ferry terminal and charge around P200 – check all times in advance.

Surigao is connected to Butuan (p.402) by regular buses, where there are onward connections to Cagayan de Oro and Davao.

Your choices for getting around the island are fairly limited. Most locals use the **habal-habal** (motorcycle) drivers, good for up to two people and light luggage. Rates are fixed: Dapa to Cloud 9 is P200, while Dapa to GL is P150. Rides between GL and Cloud 9 should be P15. Drivers will take you to Magpupungko for P300 or the Tak-Tak Falls near Burgos for P1000; in both cases the price includes the trip back. If you intend to do a lot of roaming around, ask your accommodation about **renting a motorcycle** (P500/day).

The other options are **tricycles** and **minivans**: tricycles will charge at least P30 per person (P150/vehicle) between Dapa and GL, but sometimes ask for a lot more (it depends on how much commission they are expecting from your hotel). Minivans charge P300 per person or P1500 per trip to the airport – other trips will be charged according to time and distance. For **bangka** trips see opposite.

Accommodation

Accommodation in Siargao covers the whole range, from modest lodges aimed at backpackers and low-budget surfers, to upmarket tropical resorts. Most accommodation is a short distance from GL, and can help arrange motorbike rentals, bangka trips and other forms of transportation.

Cherinicole Beach Resort ☎0928/609-8963 or 0918/244-4407, @cherinicolebeachresort.com. A short tricycle ride from GL or a 15min walk. Mid-range, well-run place with 17 spacious and substantial wooden a/c cottages on the beach or in a pleasant garden. Family cottages with two double beds are good value. There's a swimming pool, café and beach bar. Standard rooms (**④**); ocean view (**⑥**)

Island Dream @www.islanddreamsiargao.com. Opened in 2010 halfway between GL and Cloud 9, with plush, new cottages near the seafront and small pool in the garden; all have a/c, spacious bathrooms, hot water but no TVs. **⑤**

Kanilaw Resort @www.kalinawresort.com. Most luxurious (and expensive) option, next door to *Island Dream* facing a pristine beach. The immaculate wooden villas have gorgeous minimalist interiors, free wi-fi, balconies and satellite TV. There's also a top-notch French restaurant on site. **⑨**

Ocean 101 Cloud 9 ☎0910/848-0893, @www .ocean101cloud9.com. Popular with surfers and offering a range of accommodation from spartan singles with shared bathroom at the back of the resort to a/c doubles with enough space for an extra bed. There's also a cosy restaurant and bar, free internet and credit cards are accepted. **①**

Patrick's on the Beach Resort ☎0920/402-4356, ⓦwww.patrickonthebeach.com. Basic local-style beach hut accommodation, with spacious beachfront cottages, garden cottages and a number of economy cottages – check before paying as some are better than others. Helpful staff can arrange everything from boats, air tickets and babysitting to laundry, massage and manicure. They have kayaks and wi-fi, and you can rents tents for just P400. Walking distance from GL. ❸

Sagana Resort Cloud 9 ☎0919/809-5769, ⓦwww.cloud9surf.com. The best choice at Cloud 9, *Sagana* has six Laotian-inspired cottages – two a/c and four with fan – in a landscaped garden with coconut trees and large, leafy plants. Rates here (P3300/person) are inclusive of three meals, and the restaurant is one of the island's best, with daily seafood such as tuna, marlin, and Spanish mackerel, as well as mud crabs and prawns from local fish farms. Free wi-fi. ❻

Exploring the island

Resorts line the coast north of GL, and though there isn't really a beach here it's a lush laidback strip, with swathes of coconut palms linked by a sand road. The whole area is generally referred to as **Cloud 9**, though the world-renowned break is actually at Tuason Point, 2km north of GL, towards the end of the hotel strip. The peak surf season is September and October, while things tend to slow down at the end of the year; beginners will find the weaker surf in June and July more manageable. Even if you don't surf, wander out to the viewpoint at the end of the Cloud 9 **boardwalk**, a rickety wooden pier that cuts across the lagoon to the edge of the biggest waves.

Some 35km north of GL via mostly dirt road is **PILAR**, a village of traditional wooden stilt houses on the edge of the mangroves. It's best known for **Magpupungko Beach**, 2km further north and the site of regular beach parties every Friday night (P20). The sandy beach is one of the island's best, but the highlight is the giant natural swimming pool (basically a huge rockpool) that forms to the far left of the beach at low tide. The water is beautifully clear and inviting, assuming the weather cooperates. There's a nominal charge of P50 per person, but this isn't always enforced. Minivan drivers should take you for P2000–2500 (1hr). It's a long and bumpy ride by motorcycle.

Siargao island-hopping

The seas around Siargao are littered with unspoiled and rarely visited **islands**, but you'd need your own boat and lots of time to explore them all. The easiest to visit are the three islands just off the coast of GL (around 30min by bangka): day-trips to all three cost P1500 or P2500 depending on the size of the boat. Most resorts can fix you up with local bangka operators.

Naked Island is little more than a giant sand bar and perfect for lounging in the sun. **Dako Island** is the largest of the three, smothered in coconut palms and home to a small fishing community. The villagers will happily serve you fresh coconut (P20) or even barbecue chicken (P150) if required. Tiny **Guyam Island** comes closest to the stereotype of a classic desert island, a circular clump of sand and palm trees ideal for picnics, swimming or sunbathing. The island caretaker usually charges a fee of P10 per person. **Snorkelling** isn't much good off any of these islands – the best reefs lie in between them, so ask your boat to make an extra stop.

Another appealing day-trip from Siargao is to **La Janoza** and **Mamon**, the easternmost islands in the archipelago – the bangka ride takes around one hour and costs around P3500 per boat. There's a powdery white sand beach and a quaint fishing village on La Janoza and between the two islands is a pellucid lagoon that's wonderful for swimming and snorkelling; both islands are also **surfing** hotspots.

Eating and drinking

Most people **eat** at their hotels on Siargao, but on the main road in GL you can get cheap beer and home-cooked Filipino food at 🍴*Maridyl's* (daily 7am–9pm), where dishes knocked out by the amiable Maridyl range from local squid and *adobo* to grilled tuna and, (a rarity in these parts) fresh vegetables (P50–75/dish).

Nightlife is fairly subdued, but there is a handful of bars in the resort area starting with *Bones Sports Pub*, a surfer favourite right on the seafront at Cloud 9, run by an Australian expat and serving curries and ice-cold beer (P35 during happy hour, daily 5–6pm). The Swedish-owned *Nine Bar* outside GL on the beach road (just beyond *Patricks* and *Cherincole*) cooks up huge burritos. *Jungle Disco Bar* aka *Tattoo* in the centre of GL is the only thing resembling a club on Siargao – it's usually open Thursday to Saturday from early evening till 4 or 5am (cover P10).

Bucas Grande and Sohoton Cove

The enticing island of **Bucas Grande** lies between Siargao and Mindanao proper, with mushroom-shaped limestone rocks sprouting from its shimmering waters. **Sohoton Cove**, an entrancing inland lagoon on the east side of the island, is the top excursion from Siargao, a two-hour journey by bangka from GL – you'll need the best part of a day to do it justice. Most boats will charge around P5000 for the trip, but it really depends on your group size and negotiation skills. The best time to visit is March to July, when the weather and waves are calmer.

Once at the cove you'll have to sign in and pay P150 per person for a local guide and a short briefing about the site; you'll also transfer into another boat that will cost around P1000. This will take you through the cave entrance into the lagoon, a cavernous space hemmed in by soaring vine-smothered cliffs and home to giant jellyfish (the non-stinging kind). It's a phenomenal sight and just about worth the expense, assuming the weather is good. There are several other caves here that your *banquero* should be able to guide you to with no extra charge: if you can hold your breath for long enough (unless it's low tide when there is a small gap), you can swim through a short tunnel into **Hagukan Cave** where there are bats, strange fishes, stalactites, rock oysters and wild orchids.

Dinagat Island

Wild and undeveloped **Dinagat Island**, around 60km from tip to toe, is an adventure paradise-in-waiting, with only a handful of travellers making it this far. It's only a short bangka hop from Surigao and its rugged coastline has some tantalizing **islets**, beautiful sugary sand **beaches** and sheer cliffs that are attracting an increasing number of **rock climbers**. The main drawback is the lack of **accommodation**: there are some basic beach huts on the southwest coast around the town of Dinagat, but not much else. The best way to get an overview of what Dinagat has to offer is to hire a bangka when you get to the island; you can do this for about P1000 for half a day in San José, where ferries arrive from Surigao. On the west coast islet of **Unib** you'll find unspoiled Bitaug beach and several immense, largely unexplored caves. The waters of this area are fringed by good coral and deep sea walls, but there's no equipment for rent so whatever you need you'll have to bring, including snorkelling gear. In the same area, the uninhabited islet of **Hagakhak** is another beauty, with scintillating above-water and under-water rock formations.

At least getting to Dinagat is straightforward. There's a daily **ferry** (P100) from Surigao to San José at 5pm (and sometimes 1pm) via Superferry shuttle (T0922/880-2520); it returns at 1pm. From San José bangkas can take you virtually anywhere along the coast of Dinagat.

Davao and the southeast

The **southeast** is home to Mindanao's largest city, **Davao**, a diverse and friendly place best known for its fresh fruit. Davao itself is not a city of legendary sights, but the nearby countryside and coast harbour plenty of attractions, from idyllic **Samal Island** to crocodile parks, zip lines and the **Philippine Eagle Center**. Davao is also the gateway to **Mount Apo**, the nation's highest peak and a magnet for trekkers and climbers. Further south, the tuna port of **General Santos** is the closest city to enigmatic **Lake Sebu**.

Davao

Known as the **durian** capital of the Philippines, **DAVAO** is a relaxed city that also has a justly deserved reputation for delicious seafood. Though there's little to see, Davao makes a good base for the surrounding area, and its formidable line-up of **annual festivals** are certainly worth attending, especially the mardi-gras-style **Kadayawan**, a harvest festival held during the third week of August. One of the festival's major components is horse fighting, which pits untrained stallions against each other.

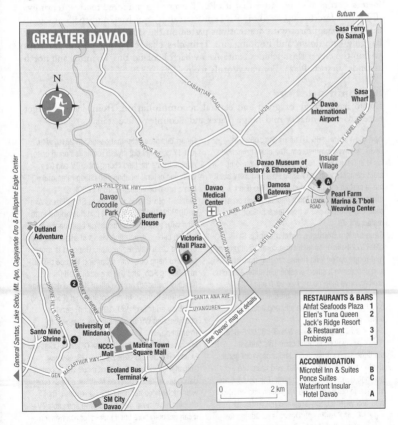

GREATER DAVAO

Butuan

Sasa Ferry
(to Samal)

Sasa
Wharf

CABANTIAN ROAD

AH26

Davao
International
Airport

J. P. LAUREL AVENUE

MANDUG ROAD

PAN-PHILIPPINE HWY

Davao Museum of
History & Ethnography

Insular
Village

Damosa
Gateway

Davao
Medical
Center

C. LIZADA
ROAD

Pearl Farm
Marina & T'boli
Weaving Center

Davao
Crocodile
Park

Butterfly
House

J.P. LAUREL AVENUE

DACUDAO AVENUE

CABAGUIO AVENUE

R. CASTILLO STREET

Outland
Adventure

Victoria
Mall Plaza

DON JUAN RODRIGUEZ SR. AVENUE

SANTA ANA AVE

UYANGUREN

SHRINE HILLS ROAD

Santo Niño
Shrine

University of
Mindanao

NCCC
Mall

Matina Town
Square Mall

See 'Davao' map for details

GEN. MACARTHUR HWY

Ecoland Bus
Terminal

SM City
Davao

0   2 km

General Santas, Lake Sebu, Mt. Apo, Cagayande Oro & Philippine Eagle Center

RESTAURANTS & BARS
Ahfat Seafoods Plaza   1
Ellen's Tuna Queen   2
Jack's Ridge Resort
 & Restaurant   3
Probinsya   1

ACCOMMODATION
Microtel Inn & Suites   B
Ponce Suites   C
Waterfront Insular
 Hotel Davao   A

Arrival and information

The modern and spacious **Davao International Airport** lies 11km north of the city centre; taxis should use the meter into the city, with fares around P100 to P130 depending on how far you go. **Ferries** dock 7km to the east at **Sasa Wharf**, from where there are frequent jeepneys and tricycles to the city. **Buses** arrive at the Ecoland Bus Terminal on Quimpo Boulevard, across the Davao River on the southwestern outskirts of the city, a short taxi or jeepney ride into the city centre.

The **tourist information office** (Mon–Fri 8am–noon & 1–5pm; ☎082/222-1956, ⓦ www.davaotourism.com) is inside Magsaysay Park (on the south side), with basic maps and leaflets, though you'll probably get as much information from your hotel. There's also the **Regional Department of Tourism** on the fifth floor of the Landco Pacific Building on J.P. Laurel Ave, near Victoria Plaza (Mon–Fri 8am–5pm; ☎082/221-6955, ⓦ www.discoverdavao.com), which can help with trips outside the city, including hikes up Mount Apo. For internet cafés, banks, post office and hospitals see "Listings", p.415. Note that smoking in public places is banned in Davao.

City transport

It's cheap and easy to get around Davao by **taxi**; you can hail them in the street, meters start at P30 and after that it's P2.50 every few hundred metres. **Jeepneys** (P7 initial fare for up to 4km; P1/1km thereafter) run back and forth along all major thoroughfares with destinations pasted on the side – it's just a question of flagging one down and hopping on. **Tricycles** charge P6 per person for trips within the city – this includes Santa Ana wharf, Ecoland Bus Terminal and north as far as Victoria Plaza. For **car rentals** see p.415.

Accommodation

Davao has a range of good and central **accommodation**, from decent budget hotels to some quality mid-range places and a couple of five-stars.

Apo View Hotel 150 J. Camus St ☎082/221-6430, ⓦ www.apoview.com. The older upmarket hotel in Davao, with big, comfortable a/c rooms – it can't compete with the *Marco Polo* for luxury but it has a certain old-fashioned charm. You don't always get a view of Mount Apo, although on a clear day you can see it from the top-floor restaurant. ❽

Casa Leticia Boutique Hotel J. Camus St ☎082/224-0501, ⓦ casaleticia.com. An attractive mid-range option with rooms ranging from studios and doubles to a smart presidential suite. All rooms are a/c, have bathrooms, free wi-fi and LCD TVs. Boasts a reasonable restaurant and a lively music bar, *Toto's*, with jazz, Latin and pop acts every night. ❺

C5 Dormitel Roxas Ave ☎082/228-6186, ⓦ www.c5dormitel.com. This budget boutique sports artsy decor and a cool roof garden; single rates are cheap (P800), and there are two-bed dorms for P4500/month. The doubles are mid-range price-wise and very clean and comfy, with a/c, wi-fi, laundry area and hot water. ❸

First Pacific Inn Davao 498 Quirino Ave ☎082/305-6183, ⓦ www.hotelindavao.com.

Smart business hotel that opened in 2010, with just 17 compact but stylish rooms featuring crisp, minimalist decor, tiled floors, cable TV and free wi-fi; the central location and cheap rates make this a great deal (singles from P880). ❸

Marco Polo Davao C.M. Recto St, at Roxas Ave ☎082/221-0888. The most luxurious hotel in the city, with spacious rooms, large bathrooms, flat-screen cable TV, and fine views of either the sea or, on a clear day, Mount Apo. The pool is a great place to hang out, with a bar and terrace restaurant facing Apo, and the breakfast buffets (usually included) are excellent. On the downside you normally have to pay for internet (P500/day) and they add "tax", VAT, 10 percent service charges, and VAT on the service charges, to everything. ❼

Microtel Inn & Suites Damosa Gateway Complex, Mamay Rd, Lanang ☎082/233-2333, ⓦ www.microtel-davao.com. Excellent motel-like accommodation opposite the Damosa Mall; the suites come with kitchen counter and microwave, while the doubles have clean tiled floors, wi-fi and cable TV – it can get busy here but it makes for a convenient base (and the breakfast is pretty good). ❺

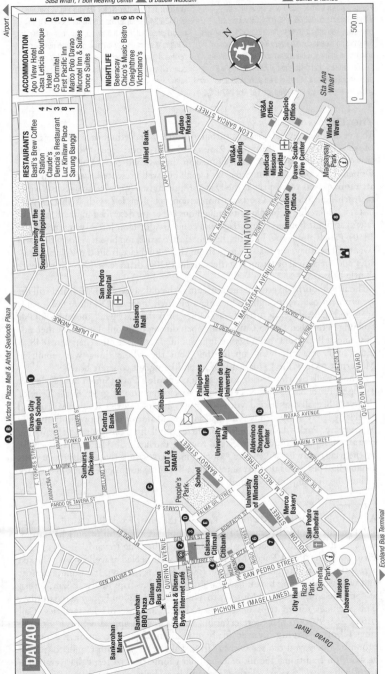

DAVAO

Airport ◄

Sasa Wharf, T'Boli Weaving Center ▲ & Dabaw Museum   ▲ Samal & Talikud

University of the
Southern Philippines

J.P. LAUREL AVENUE

◄ A, B Victoria Plaza Mall & Ahfat Seafoods Plaza ▲

Allied Bank

Agdao Market

WG&A
Office

Sulpicio
Office

WG&A
Building

LEON GARCIA STREET

Sta Ana
Wharf

Medical
Mission
Hospital

Davao Scuba
Dive Center

Magsaysay
Park

Wind &
Wave

San Pedro
Hospital

STA ANA AVENUE

MONTEVERDE STREET

Immigration
Office

CHINATOWN

R. MAGSAYSAY AVENUE

SALES ST

ILINO ST

8

Gaisano
Mall

LAPU-LAPU STREET

GUERRERO ST

CHAVEZ ST

S. SUAZO ST

D. SUAZO STREET

PONCE STREET

Davao City
High School

HSBC

Central
Bank

Citibank

Philippines
Airlines

Ateneo de Davao
University

E. JACINTO STREET

AURORA QUEZON ST

QUEZON BOULEVARD

F. TORRES STREET

ARAULLO ST

A. MABINI ST

A. MABINI S

TIONKO AVENUE

AVANCEÑA ST

ABELLANO S

PARDO DE TAVERA ST

Sunburst
Chicken

G

PLDT &
SMART

People's
Park

School

J. CAMUS S

C. BANGOY STREET

University
Mall

F

Aldevinco
Shopping
Center

G

ROXAS AVENUE

MABINI STREET

C. M. RECTO STREET

University of
Mindanao

S. DE JESUS STREET

METHARA ST

University of Mindanao
MA APO ST

GEN MALVAR ST

Bankerohan Market

Bankerohan
BBQ Plaza

Calinan
Bus Station

E. QUIRINO AVENUE

Chikachat & Disney
Bytes Internet café

GEN. LUNA ST

V. ILUSTRE S

PALMA GIL STREET

D

E

Gaisano
Citimall

PELAYO ST

C. LITTERIE ST

RIZAL ST

4

3

②

Citibank

5

PELAYO RIZAL STREET

HIZO STREET

BONIFACIO STREET

Merco
Bakery

6

7

San Pedro
Cathedral

BOLTON S

SAN PEDRO STREET

Jack's Ridge ▲

PICHON ST (MAGELLANES)

City Hall

Rizal
Park

i

San Pedro
Cathedral

Osmeña
Park

Museo
Dabawenyo

Davao River

◄ Ecoland Bus Terminal

N

0   500 m

1

0

Ponce Suites Corner Rds 3 & 4, Doña Vicenta Village, Bajada ⊤082/227-9070, ⓦwww.ponce suites.net. You are unlikely to have stayed in a budget hotel like this before, with every inch of wall space smothered in the exuberant artwork of Kublai Millan (his sculptures also decorate the city). Rooms are more modest affairs but all are en suite with basic cable TV and free wi-fi; singles start at just P470. ❷

Waterfront Insular Hotel Davao km 7, Lanang ⊤082/234-3050, ⓦwaterfronthotels.net. Plush resort-style hotel on the shore, 5km out of town in Lanang district. Pretty a/c rooms, large outdoor pool and a small beach area. It's the pick of the bunch if you've got the budget and are looking for relaxation and fresh sea breezes. ❽

The City

To get an overview of Davao's turbulent history and ethnic make-up, visit the **Museo Dabawenyo** (Mon–Sat 9am–noon & 1–6pm; free; ⊤082/222-6011, ⓦwww.museodabawenyo.com), housed in the restored court building opposite Osmeña Park on A. Pichon Street. It's small but well presented, and though there are more objects on display at the Davao Museum (see opposite), this one is easier to reach (and it's free). The main impression you'll be left with is that Davao's history is incredibly complex; its indigenous tribes are described in detail, as is the fateful struggle between Datu Bago and conquistador Don José Uyanguren in the 1840s. Panels also throw light on the American occupation boom years in the early twentieth century, the massive migrations that took place from the Visayas thereafter and the arrival of Japanese settlers in the 1930s – hard to believe this was once "Little Tokyo".

The neighbourhood around the museum is the oldest part of Davao and still the government centre, though it's looking a bit tired these days as more fashionable areas and malls develop further out. Other than the City Hall the only notable building is the **San Pedro Cathedral** (open during mass only), on the other side of Osmeña Park from the museum; it began life as a simple nipa chapel in 1848. A more solid structure went up in 1886, but the whole thing was rebuilt in Modernist style in the 1970s – it looks a bit like a giant concrete bowl.

A short walk or tricycle ride to the north, **People's Park** (Sun–Thurs 5–8am & 1–10pm, Fri & Sat 5–8am & 1–11pm) is a welcome slice of green in the heart of the city, liberally sprinkled with sculptures by local artist Kublai Millan and especially lively at weekends. The eastern seaward side of downtown is framed by **Magsaysay Park** (daily 5am–9pm) where you'll find the tourist information centre, a couple of outdoor cafés and rows of **durian** stalls just outside operated by the Magsaysay Fruit Vendors Association; this luscious (but smelly) treat costs around P50 per kilo, but most hotel won't allow durians inside – snack in the park or buy the durian jams or candy instead.

Lanang

Around 6km north of Magsaysay Park via the coast road (R. Castillo St then J.P. Laurel Ave), the barangay of **Lanang** contains a handful of enticing attractions, easily reached via jeepney (anything that is heading towards "Sasa") or taxi. First up is the **Pearl Farm Marina**, where well-heeled travellers are whisked across the bay to the *Pearl Farm Resort* (see p.416 for review). It's a unique resort and well worth seeing if you have cash to spare – day-trips (daily at 8am; return at 4pm) are a pricey P1550 Monday to Thursday and P2000 Friday and Saturday. This includes return trips on the boat, lunch, and use of the facilities. Call ⊤082/221-9970 to make a reservation. If that doesn't appeal, you can visit the tiny **T'boli Weaving Center** (daily 8am–5pm; free) just inside the marina grounds, where you can see weavers from Lake Sebu in South Cotabato (p.420) at work on traditional looms, crafting bold geometrical patterns that symbolize tribal beliefs on "tinalak" cloth. Colourful bags, belts, shoes, wallets, floor rugs and floor hangings are on sale. The marina is at the end of C. Lizada Road, which juts off J.P. Laurel Avenue just north of the junction with Castillo; look for the signs to the "Pearl Farm Resort" on the right. From J.P. Laurel (where jeepneys will drop you) you can walk there in ten to fifteen minutes, or take a pedal-cab (taxis will take you all the way).

Back on J.P Laurel Avenue, a short walk north takes you to the gated community of Insular Village 1 (sign in at the gate). Tucked away at the back (turn right at the entrance), a five-minute walk or so, is the small but enlightening **Davao Museum of History & Ethnography** (Mon–Sat 9am–noon & 1–5pm; P100). On the ground floor a detailed timeline describes the city's key events, with temporary exhibits such as rare *santos* sculptures on display. Upstairs there's a decent introduction to Davao's fifteen indigenous tribes such as the Bagobos, with displays of ancient weaponry, betel nut boxes, jewellery (including a wildcat tooth necklace) and fancy brass work.

Ma-a

The western suburb of **Ma-a** contains several activity-based attractions, which can be a lot of fun, especially for kids. The flagship attraction is the **Davao Crocodile Park** (daily 8am–7pm; P200 ☎082/286-8883, ⓦwww.psdgroupph.com) at the Riverfront, Corporate City, Diversion Highway, with huge crocodiles and touristy shows every Friday, Saturday and Sunday at 4.45pm, where the crocs are fed at a distance (the babies are fed close up). There's also a popular **Butterfly House** (same hours), and the **Davao Wildwater Adventure** (☎082/221-7823, ⓦwaterrafting.psdgroupph.com), which offers whitewater rafting on the Davao River for P2000 per person (daily trips from 8.30am to 4.30pm; minimum of five people) including transportation from the Crocodile Park and lunch.

Nearby you can ride one of the fastest and tallest **zip lines** in Asia at **Outland Adventure** (Mon–Sat 8am–5pm, Sun 1–5pm; P300; ☎082/224-5855; ⓦwww .outlandadventure.org), also on the Diversion Highway across from the GAP Farm. The zip is accessed after a short hike and raft ride across a lake, while the zip itself takes you soaring over the river and forest at high speed.

Getting here requires a taxi ride or multiple jeepney rides via the NCCC Mall, west of the centre on the MacArthur Highway; from here jeepneys chug up to Ma-a and Diversion road, where *habal-habal* motorcycles can take you to a specific attraction.

Eating

Eating is a real pleasure in Davao, with seafood (especially tuna) and fresh fruits such as **durian** taking centre stage (see p.30). You can buy freshly chopped durian

Diving and dugongs in Davao

Most of Davao's **dive shops** are clustered at the end of Monteverde Street next to Magsaysay Park and the Santa Ana Wharf; their favoured destination is usually the sparkling waters around Samal and especially Talicud (just 45min by boat), where there are some decent coral reefs and plenty of fish.

A good choice is the Davao Scuba Dive Center (☎082/226-2588, ⓦwww.davao scubadive.com), which offers two-tank dives from P1800 and PADI courses (3–4 days) from P18,000 by Danish expat Frank Rasmussen. He can also help locate the area's dwindling **dugong** population (less than 20 by some accounts); you can snorkel near these gentle creatures, but not dive.

Nearby Wind & Wave Davao (☎082/300-7914, ⓦwww.windandwavedavao.com) offers days dives and PADI courses at similar rates.

and all sorts of derivative products at the Magsaysay Fruit Vendors Association (see p.412).

Davao's best **restaurants** are scattered all over the city, but the safest bet for a cheap meal are the food courts located in or around shopping malls. The fare is hygienic, variety is reasonable and most dishes cost less than P70; the large car parking area outside Victoria Plaza Mall is good for Chinese and Korean restaurants; the Bankerohan BBQ Plaza offers cheap lechon and barbecue meats from P17 per plate; and Market Basket (daily 9am–8pm) at Damosa Gateway is a great food court, with plenty of choices.

Ahfat Seafoods Plaza Victoria Plaza Mall, J.P. Laurel Ave (facing the car park behind the mall) ☎082/226-2688. Cheap Chinese food in three separate buildings, but all excellent quality; the original place is more like a canteen (daily 10am–11pm), while *Ahfat III* nearby is also open for dim sum from 7am to 4.30pm (closes 11pm). Try the steamed shrimp, spicy spare ribs and crab (dishes average P160–200).

Basti's Brew Coffee Station Victoria Plaza, also R.J. Holmes Building, Legaspi St. *Basti's* is a local chain leading the coffee revolution in Davao, with excellent "mild" or "strong" roast coffee. Enhance the experience with local snacks like durian cheesecake. Free wi-fi. Daily 9.30am–8pm.

Claude's 29 Rizal St ☎082/222-4287. Superb French and Mediterranean restaurant, owned and operated by a French native Claude Le Neindre who has been living in Davao for over twenty years. The steaks, seafood and jambalaya gumbo are especially good here. Was set to move into fabulous new premises across the road at the time of writing, the elegant 1920s Oboza Family Heritage House.

Dencia's Restaurant General Luna St at Ilustre St ☎082/227-6777. Classic Davao-Chinese cuisine served in an elegant, old-fashioned dining room packed out at lunchtime. Best orders are *tokwa't baboy*, congee, fresh *lumpia* and pancit *canton*.

Jack's Ridge Resort & Restaurant Shrine Hills, Matina ☎082/297-8831, ⊛www .jacksridgedavao.com. Just across from the Santo Niño Shrine this complex is all about the views and cool breezes, but the Filipino food in the main *Taklobo Restaurant* is delicious: the *sinigang*, *lechon*, grilled tuna and barbecue chicken are all superb. Often has live bands at night and is also a great place for a beer or coffee. You might see the odd monkey up here. Take a taxi (P100). Daily 11.30am–1.30pm & 4.30pm–midnight.

Luz Kinilaw Place Quezon Ave, short walk from Magsaysay Park ☎082/226-4612. Classic, no-frills Davao local favourite, with tuna, chicken and assorted seafood flame-grilled on the street just outside. Walk upstairs and enjoy sumptuous plates of squid and tuna. Have a gut-busting breakfast or get there early for lunch or dinner to avoid a wait. Daily 6am–10pm.

Sarung Banggi F. Torres St ☎082/221-5615. Fun native-style dining, with waiting staff decked out in various tribal-style outfits. The menu is imaginative and offers much more choice than most of the local grill restaurants. Notable dishes include seafood soup with sour mango and rice, and Bicol Express with pork ribs and chilli, and simple grilled tuna or swordfish served with lime. Daily 11am–2pm & 5–10pm, 11pm Fri & Sat.

Nightlife

It may not be as avant-garde as Manila, but there's some entertaining **nightlife** on offer in Davao, with cosy live music venues, karaoke bars and discos. Apart from the odd spot downtown, most places tend to be clustered around newish malls or specially built compounds such as the large car parking area outside Victoria Plaza Mall, Damosa Gateway and in various places along **Torres Street**, the busiest of the lot. A good bet for a lively evening is **Rizal Promenade**, on Guerrero Street, home to several restaurants and bars; the best are *Beeracay* and *Oneighthree* (183), which have free wi-fi and P40 beers. Elsewhere, *Victoriano's* at Illustre and General Luna streets features an upstairs, open-air bar (P30 cover), while *Chico's Music Bistro* (☎082/255-5675) at 29 Rizal St is a rare old wooden house and a fun place to eat or drink, with decent live acts every night and happy hour 7 to 9pm.

Daily **flights** connect Davao to Manila (8 daily; 1hr 45min) and Cebu City (2 daily; 1hr), while Airphil Express and Cebu Pacific also operate handy routes to Cagayan de Oro (2 weekly; 50min) and Zamboanga (2 daily; 1hr 15min). The only international destination is Singapore (2hr 15min), served by Silk Air. For all flights, you'll have to pay a P200 terminal fee before departure. **Superferry** sails from Sasa Wharf in northern Davao to Manila, but the journey takes over two and half days.

All **buses** depart the **Ecoland Bus Terminal** on Quimpo Boulevard, across the Davao River from the centre of the city. Bachelor Express (☏082/244-0654) runs buses to Butuan (daily 1am–5pm; 6hr; P486) every 20 minutes, a direct bus to Surigao at 8am only (9hr; P680) and buses to Mangagoy at 2.30am and 2.30pm (5hr; P340). Rural Trans (☏082/244-0637) runs to Cagayan de Oro (daily 4am–10.30pm; 7hr 30min; P460) every 30 minutes. Buses (24hr) also depart to Korondal (for Lake Sebu; 4hr 30min; P306) via General Santos (3hr 15min; P218) every 25 minutes or so and to Cotabato (6hr; P294) via Kidapawan (for Mt Abo; 2hr 30min; P140) from 4.30am to 1.30pm, every 25 minutes (Weena Express ☏082/244-0033). All the above information refers to express a/c buses; non-a/c buses are usually more frequent, cheaper and slower. For the surrounding area, see the relevant sections.

Listings

Airlines Philippine Airlines (☏082/221-5513) has a ticket office at the Ateneo de Davao University Building in C.M. Recto St, opposite the *Marco Polo Hotel*; Cebu Pacific is at Summit World, 2/F Victoria Plaza Mall at the northern end of J.P. Laurel Ave (☏082/224-0960); Silk Air is at Suite 056, 5/F, Pryce Tower, J.P. Laurel Ave (Mon–Fri 8.30am–12.30pm & 1.30–5.30pm; ☏082/227-5301); Cathay Pacific is at RRS Worldwide Destinations Inc, M Floor, *Royal Mandaya Hotel*, J. Palma Gil St (☏082/222-8901).

Banks and exchange There are plenty of banks in Davao; for reliable ATMs head to Victoria Plaza or Gaisano mall. Citibank has a couple of branches with ATMs; G/F Philamlife Building, J.P. Rizal St and Candelaria Building, 547 J.P. Laurel Ave, while HSBC is on Jacinto Extension.

Car rental Avis (daily 6am–7pm; ☏082/225-3337) is inside the *Apo View Hotel;* Europcar (🖳www .europcar.com.ph) will deliver to your hotel and has desks at the airport (☏082/304-2438) and in the lobbies of the *Marco Polo Davao* (☏082/221-0888)

and *Pearl Farm* (Mindanao side; ☏082/304-4958). Rates start at around P3000/day including insurance.

Hospitals The city's major hospital is the Davao Doctors' Hospital (☏082/224-0616), E. Quirino Ave, southwest of the city centre. San Pedro Hospital (☏082/224 0616) is on Guerrero St in the city centre.

Internet access There are dozens of internet cafés on the main road outside Victoria Plaza; in the centre there's *Chickachat* and *Disney Bytes* on Illustre St near Rizal St (both daily 9am–2am; P15/hr). *BoyzTrek* is a reliable chain with branches at Jacinto and Juan Luna sts.

Post The main post office is on Roxas Ave, close to the junction with C.M. Recto Ave and Magsaysay Ave.

Shopping For souvenirs and handicrafts, go to the Aldevinco Shopping Center opposite the *Marco Polo Hotel* between C.M. Recto Ave and Roxas Ave. It's a maze of small shops selling tribal artefacts and cheap batik clothes. With a little hard bargaining, you can grab a sarong for P100 or statues and masks from P400.

Samal Island

Just across the narrow Pakiputan Strait from Davao, **Samal Island** is graced with lovely coves, beaches, excellent scuba diving and huge bat caves – there are also plenty of resorts to choose from. You can arrange **diving** trips at many resorts on Samal and also in Davao (see box, p.413).

Most tourists visit Samal on organized tours but it's also easy to arrange a trip independently (see box, p.416). You can choose to spend time at one of the resorts (most of which allow day guests for a fee), or jump on a *habal-habal* and tour the island by motorbike.

Getting to Samal

Getting to Samal is relatively straightforward. Most resorts have private boats that zip guests across the Pakiputan Strait direct to the hotel grounds, and some of these – notably *Pearl Farm Resort* – also take day-trippers, for a fee (see below). Most hotels in Davao will also arrange day tours to the island for around P1000. If you want to explore on your own you have three main ferry choices. Closest to the city are the outrigger motorboats that ply between Santa Ana Wharf near Magsaysay Park and **Kaputian** at the southern end of Samal (45min; P60). Boats leave from the second pier, left of the entrance, but some go straight to Talicud, so check before jumping on board.

Around 8km north along J.P. Laurel Avenue in Sasa, a car ferry (daily 4am–10pm; 15min; P10/person) runs to **Kinawitnon Wharf** in Barangay Caliclic, Babak District; you must board the Island City Express bus to cross here (or catch the bus at its terminal at Magsaysay Park; P35 including ferry), as walk-on passengers are not allowed.

A short walk north of the car ferry are the public bangkas (daily 6am–10pm; P13) that sail every 15min or so from Sasa to **Babak** at the northern end of Samal; you must walk through the market to reach the pier (the entrance on J.P. Laurel Ave, km 11, is next to a footbridge). Jeepneys marked "Sasa" will take you from Davao city centre to within spitting distance of the departure point; taxis should cost around P100.

Accommodation

Most reasonably priced **resorts** on Samal are on the northwest coast, south of the village of Caliclic. From the wharf at Babak you can walk to many of these resorts, or hop on a tricycle. All the major resorts have private boats for guests – these depart from piers off R. Castillo Street north of the city (some allow day guests to use them for a fee; see below).

Bali Bali Beach Resort Catagman ☎0922/838-7214, ⊛www.balibaliresort.com. Luxury resort with just six plush villas, all with elegant, spacious interiors, facing an enticing infinity pool and the sea beyond. ❾

Bluewaters Beach Resort Caliclic ☎084/301-4075, ⊛www.ebluwaters.com. Fairly simple garden houses and bigger cottages, just a 4min boat ride from Davao; it's not luxury but good value, and day guests can use the pool, water-sports (rentals extra) and the resort beach for P100/day (P10 for the boat; 7am–5pm). Fan (❸); a/c (❹)

Paradise Island Park & Beach Resort Caliclic ☎082/233-0251, ⊛www.paradiseislanddavao.com.

This huge (75 rooms) and popular resort can get busy at weekends with day-trippers escaping the city, but has attractive fan and a/c cottages under shady trees in landscaped gardens, a convivial native-style restaurant and scuba diving. Day guests P100. ❺

Pearl Farm Resort ☎082/221-9970, ⊛www.pearlfarmresort.com. South along the west coast is the island's classiest and most expensive resort, which has more than seventy native-style cottages either on a hillside overlooking the bay or perched on stilts in the sea. There are also seven luxurious and secluded villas on beautiful little Malipano island, a short hop from the main resort. ❾

Touring the island

Samal is bigger than it seems, with an area of over 300 square kilometres and around 90,000 permanent inhabitants. Most of the resorts lie close to the Babak/Caliclic ferries; *Pearl Farm* is closer to Kaputian. No matter which port you arrive at, if you want to get beyond the resorts plenty of *habal-habal* riders will be there to offer personalized tours; it's a good idea to hire one for the whole day rather than try and get separate lifts. Rates vary, but expect to pay around P300 for a half-day; riders will suggest visiting all sorts of wondrous attractions, but the most popular are covered below. Tricycles and minivans are also available, but unless you have a group, these are much more expensive.

Don't miss the **Monfort Bat Cave** (P20; P40 after 5pm) in the northern part of the island, a vast cavern jam-packed with around 1.8 million fruit bats – it's a bit like staring at a giant black carpet. The bats usually hang in the cave during the day, but come sundown they flood out like a dark cloud – it's a chilling experience.

Of Samal's many beaches, it's worth the bumpy, hour-long ride across the island to **Canibad Beach Cove**, a pristine, untouched swathe of sand with little more than a sari-sari store selling soft drinks. In the far south lies the chalky white sands of **Kaputian Beach Park Resort** (P10; overnight fee P75) near *Pearl Farm Resort*; look out for the stuffed sealion. You can stay the night here in basic beachfront cottages (P400).

Elsewhere on Samal you can visit bubbling waterfalls (modest but pretty **Hagimit Falls** is P30), numerous caves or even make the relatively quick hike up Samal's highest point, **Mount Puting Bato** (410m), for fine views of Davao and Mount Apo.

Talicud

Talicud Island lies off the southwest coast of Samal and is even more torpid than its big brother, making it a perfect place to escape Davao's crowds for a day or two. On the west coast there's good, easy diving and snorkelling in an area known as Coral Gardens, while there are a couple of more demanding drop-off dives off the north coast. On the east coast, five minutes' walk from the pier at Santa Cruz, the *Isla Reta Beach Resort* (❷; day tour P75; ☎0917/622-3610), has simple wooden cottages for overnight stays. Outrigger **ferries** regularly chug between Santa Aña Wharf near Magsaysay Park in Davao and **Santa Cruz** on Talicud (1hr to 1hr 30min; P60). Boats leave from the second pier, left of the wharf entrance, from 6am to 6pm, at least once an hour; just jump on and pay. You can also hire a bangka from Kaputian on Samal Island (P300).

Calinan

The small but lively town of **CALINAN**, 45km northwest of Davao on the main highway to Cagayan de Oro, became a major Japanese farming community in the 1930s. This curious and largely forgotten history is explored by the **Philippine Japanese Museum** (Mon–Sat 8am–5.30pm; P20) on De Lara Street in the Durian Village section of Calinan (get a *habal-habal* – it's hard to find). Though the exhibits are rather sparse (mostly old photos), the images of Japanese life, written information and testimonies of some of the former Japanese settlers are fascinating; many married local Filipinos and the "Nikkei Jin Kai" of Davao have since been thoroughly researched by Japanese volunteers. You'll also see pictures of the many Japanese memorials to those killed during World War II in the area.

The Philippine Eagle Center

The **Philippine Eagle Center** (daily 8am–5pm; P50; ☎082/224-3021, ⓦwww .philippineeagle.org), a few kilometres west of Calinan in Malagos, is known for its excellent work breeding the Philippine eagle, a majestic creature with a fearsome beak, distinctive frilly head feathers and two-metre wingspan. Sadly, the eagle is now officially on the endangered species list, with only a maximum of four hundred believed to be living in the wilds of Mindanao, Samar and Leyte. The centre's captive breeding programme focuses on developing a viable gene pool, the goal being to reintroduce the birds into their natural habitat. The centre is now home to around eighteen Philippine eagles.

To get to the centre you first walk through the Malagos Garden Park (P5), before reaching the entrance proper and a pleasant café overlooking a lily pond. Apart from the large aviaries containing the big eagles, there are plenty of other birds of prey on display, from grass owls and kites to screeching fish eagles, and there are compounds for the Philippine brown deer, warty pig, long-tailed macaques and even a giant crocodile. In truth the centre is a bit like an old-fashioned zoo – some of the birdcages are very small. Note also it can be uncomfortably busy at weekends, so try to schedule your visit for a weekday when staff will sometimes let you handle and feed the birds. Overall it's certainly educational and the eagles are awe-inspiring – just remember that eventually they will be released.

Practicalities

Many hotels and travel agents in Davao offer **day-trips** to the eagle centre, but travelling independently is easy and cheap. Take one of the frequent air-conditioned **jeepneys** (P40) to Calinan (45min) from the Annil transport terminal on San Pedro, just north of Quirino Avenue near the Bankerohan Market; small buses also make the same trip from here if you want more breathing space. Once in Calinan flag down the first tricycle or *habal-habal* (motorbike) you see. Locals pay just P10 to any of the sights mentioned above, and P20 between the eagle centre and the Japanese Museum, though you'll be lucky to get those rates. Tricycle operators will ask a lot more for trips to the eagle centre (P50 plus), while *habal-habal* riders should take you for P20–30.

Mount Apo National Park

Looming over all Davao, **Mount Apo** (2954m) is the highest mountain in the country: the name Apo means "grandfather of all mountains". Apo is actually a volcano, but is certified inactive and has no recorded eruptions. What it does have is enough flora and fauna to make your head spin – thundering waterfalls, rapids, lakes, geysers, sulphur pillars, primeval trees, endangered plant and animal species and a steaming blue lake. Then there are exotic ferns, carnivorous pitcher plants and the queen of Philippine orchids, the *waling-waling*. The local tribes, the Bagobos, believe the gods Apo and Mandaragan inhabit Apo's upper slopes; they revere it as a sacred mountain, calling it Sandawa or "Mountain of Sulphur".

Climbing Mount Apo

Climbing Mount Apo is not as hard as it sounds. The summit can be approached via two main routes: the **Kidapawan Trail** on the Cotabato side features hot springs, river crossings and a steep forested trail that leads to the peak via swampy Lake Venado, while the **Kapatagan Trail** on the Davao side is tougher but cuts through more stereotypically volcanic terrain, culminating in a boulder-strewn slope up to the crater.

In both cases you'll need to buy a **permit** and to hire a **guide** from one of the local tourist offices in charge of each route. They'll also do a required equipment check and arrange an orientation laying out all the usual rules (no rubbish, no swimming, stick to the trail, no picking anything etc). These offices will recommend a three- to four-day expedition, but experienced climbers could tackle the hike in two days with early starts. Climbing is generally permitted November through May only (dry season), but even so, you'll need rainproof clothes and a small tent as rain is possible anytime and it gets cold at night. It's a tough trek, but well worth it: the trail is lined with flowers and the views are mesmerizing, with the whole of Mindanao spread out before you.

Kidapawan Trail

The **Kidapawan Trail** starts from Agko Springs near **Kidapawan**, 106km and two hours by bus from Davao. Your first stop should be the **Kidapawan Tourist**

Center (☎064/278-3344) next to City Hall to get a permit (P750), organize a guide (from P500/day) and porters if required. The trailhead is around 20km from Kidapawan: jeepneys will take you there in about 45 minutes. To get an early start stay the night in Kidapawan at the *Old Barracks Suites* (☎064/288-1299; ❷), which has clean rooms, wi-fi and a good restaurant, or at the *Lake Agko Mountain Resort* (☎0905/603-0607; ❷), right next to the trailhead.

From Lake Agko you'll cross the Marbel River several times before reaching the first campsite at **Mainit Hot Springs**, where you can take a refreshing dip in a small pool. Around five hours from here (via a couple of rope and ladder-assisted scrambles) is dramatic **Lake Venado**, which looks like a scene from the Jurassic age, with giant trees, vines and a fine fog floating above the lake itself. From here allow three hours for the summit itself – most climbers plan to arrive for sunrise, which means camping near the lake.

Kapatagan Trail

To tackle the Kapatagan Trail contact the tourist office in Santa Cruz (Camilla Infiesto ☎0920/3136-792 or Julius Paner ☎0920/856-7991). To get to the trailhead you'll need to take a bus from Davao to Digos and then a local jeepney to Kapatagan where you can register and arrange guides (same prices as above). From here climbers usually take a *habal-habal* to the Mainit trailhead, taking two days to reach the summit via the spectacular "boulder trail".

General Santos

Around 140km southwest of Davao on Sarangani Bay, **GENERAL SANTOS** – or "Jen-san" – is the Philippines' southernmost city, a dense, noisy metropolis of over half a million that isn't a significant tourist destination; it's something of a frontier town, founded by General Paulino Santos and 62 pioneers from Luzon in 1939, and best known as the centre of the tuna industry. It's also the gateway to **Lake Sebu**.

Arrival

General Santos International Airport is about twenty minutes and 12km west of the city, an easy trip by taxi (P300–350), or *habal-habal* (P100) if you don't have much luggage. Despite the name there are only domestic flights connecting the city with Cebu (2 daily; 1hr 5min) and Manila (2 daily; 1hr 45min). **Ferries** arrive at Makar wharf, ten minutes and 2km west of the centre on P. Acharon Boulevard. **Buses** from Cotabato (several daily; 5hr), Davao (hourly; 3hr 15min) and Koronodal (hourly; 3hr) arrive at the City Terminal near Bulaong Avenue on the western edge of the centre, near the river. Once in the city, tricycles are the best way to get around.

Accommodation

The two main areas for **accomodation** are along the National Highway northeast of Freedom Park, and on and around Pioneer Avenue, south of City Hall. Of the two, the City Hall area is marginally better because it's quieter and closer to amenities such as banks and malls.

On the National Highway is the ritziest hotel in town, the *East Asia Royale* (☎083/553-4119, ⓦwww.eastasiaroyalehotel.com; ❺), with large air-conditioned rooms, a coffee shop and two restaurants. Also on the National Highway, the *Tierra Montana Hotel* (☎083/554-7733, ⓦwww.tierramontanahotel.com; ❹) is a modern, stylish alternative and much cheaper. At the long-standing *Dolores Hotel* (☎083/552-2921; ❷) on Santiago Boulevard – a few minutes' walk to the east of City Hall – there's a choice of double or twin rooms either with air conditioning or fan, but all with private bathrooms.

Eating and drinking

There are lots of functional but **cheap restaurants** in General Santos serving grilled fish – tuna (and *opah*, or sunfish) figures prominently on all the menus. *Ranchero's Grill* (☎083/563-9298) on the National Highway serves sumptuous grilled seafood, steak, ribs, steamed tuna belly and grilled tuna jaw. For cheaper Filipino home-style cooking try *Marasa Grill* at 41 Kadulasan St (☎083/552-4628). *Babes Bar* inside the *East Asia Royale* (p.419) is a popular club and live music venue, while the *JMIX Bar*, JMP Building 2, Aparente St (☎083/554-2368) is owned by boxing legend **Manny Pacquiao** (who grew up in Gensan and still lives here).

T'boli and Lake Sebu

To the west of General Santos, the small town of **T'BOLI** sits on the shores of enchanting **Lake Sebu**, in a natural bowl surrounded by wooded hills and rolling plantations. This is the ancestral homeland of the T'boli tribe, whose members often wear traditional woven clothes and eye-catching handmade jewellery. It's a great place to see T'Boli culture at first hand; you can also rent a boat and take a **trip on the lake** itself and shop in the weekly **Saturday market** for brassware, beads and fabric. The main sights around the lake are the **Seven Falls**, a series of plunging cascades you hike up to or fly over on what is probably the most thrilling **zip line** in the Philippines (P250). The annual Lem-Lunay T'boli **festival** is held here every year on the second Friday of November and concludes with traditional horse fights.

Practicalities

To reach T'boli, take a **bus** from General Santos or Davao to **Koronadal** (1hr), from where jeepneys and air-conditioned minivans head south to Surallah (45min). From Surallah it's another thirty minutes or so to T'boli and the lake by minivan or *habal-habal*. On arrival make for the Lake Sebu Tourism Office (☎0906/389-0328) which can help with accommodation and tours. Alternatively contact a travel agent like Go Sarangani Travel (☎083/304-4398, ⓦwww.gosarangani .com), which can arrange the whole trip from General Santos.

Motorcycles (*habal-habal*) are the main form of transport in T'boli; short trips cost P10 but it's best to hire a rider for half a day to travel around the lake (P250). **Boat tours** of Lake Sebu are usually around P400 and take 45 minutes.

There is some reasonably good **accommodation** around Lake Sebu. The best is *Punta Isla Lake Resort* (☎083/826-0962; ❷), a short ride out of town along the lakeshore, which has rudimentary but adequate cottages and a breezy restaurant that serves catch of the day from the lake, usually tilapia.

Autonomous Region in Muslim Mindanao

Potentially one of the most beguiling areas of the Philippines, the **Autonomous Region in Muslim Mindanao (ARMM)** is a patchwork of several predominantly Muslim provinces in the western part of the island. Created in 1989, the regional government (based in Cotabato), has the power to levy taxes and apply Shariah law to Muslims. Despite this autonomy, the region remains extremely poor and the epicentre for anti-government protest – Philippine Tourism authorities, most Filipinos (and the US, UK and Australian governments) usually advise foreigners to avoid the region.

The situation on the ground is less clear-cut. Actual incidents are rare, but those that do occur often end in tragedy. Kidnapping is still a lucrative business on the island of **Basilan**, the northernmost island in the Sulu chain, and if any unequivocal recommendation can be given it is that you shouldn't go there.

It's best to seek the advice of the local tourism office before visiting any of the following locations, and where possible, to arrange a local guide when travelling. Avoid travelling at night altogether.

Marawi and Lake Lanao

Nestled on the shores of Lake Lanao just 25km south of Iligan (p.395), **MARAWI** is the centre of the Islamic religion in the Philippines: 92 percent of the population is Muslim. During the Marcos years, the area around Marawi was where kidnappers were said to hide their victims, but these days the city is generally peaceful, with incidents related to the fight for Muslim autonomy exceedingly rare; visiting with a driver and a guide is still recommended, however (contact Iligan tourist office, p.395).

Marawi's greatest natural attraction is placid **Lake Lanao**, which sits in a green bowl circled by distant mountains. It's the second largest lake in the Philippines and easy to explore via a circumferential road; there are said to be some 350 mosques ringing the lake and it's the best place to see striking *torogans*, the traditional wooden homes of Marawi's upper class.

Marawi has no **tourist office**, but the staff at the *Marawi Resort Hotel* (T 063/520-981; ❷), on the **Mindanao State University** campus (which has the best views of the lake), have good local knowledge. It's also the best place to stay in the area, a quiet establishment surrounded by greenery with a good choice of well-maintained rooms. Also on the campus is the **Aga Kahn Museum** (Mon–Fri 9–11.30am & 2–4.30pm; free), which has an interesting collection of Moro art from Mindanao, Sulu and Palawan. The **palitan** is a two-storey market in the heart of the city where you can find virtually any type of clothing, from jeans to traditional tribal garments, colourful raw cloth and batik products, gold jewellery, exquisite wooden chests and **brassware**, manufactured in the nearby barangay of Tugaya. The city's annual festival is the **Kalilang** (April 10–15), which is dominated by Koran-reading competitions and traditional singing and dancing.

Zamboanga City

Right on the southernmost tip of the Zamboanga peninsula, **ZAMBOANGA CITY** is closer to both Malaysia and Indonesia than it is to the capital of the Philippines: it feels like another country, where different dialects are spoken (the native language of Zamboanga City is **Chavacano**, a Spanish Creole), and Manila is well off the radar. There's no doubt Zamboanga has a reputation as a no-go area for tourists (a suicide bomber killed himself and a bystander at the airport in 2010), but locals claim this is only because it has been unfairly tarred by its proximity to the Sulu archipelago, stronghold of Abu Sayyaf. Indeed the local economy has grown considerably in the last ten years and the city itself is actually fairly safe.

The city's major attraction is **Fort Pilar**, ruined fortress, outdoor Catholic shrine and a branch of the **National Museum** (daily 8.30am–noon & 1.30–5pm; free), a ten-minute taxi ride east of the city centre along Valderosa Street. The squat stone structure was built by the Spanish in 1635 and is today dedicated to Nuestra Señora del Pilar, patroness of Zamboanga. The museum highlights local marine life and the history and culture of three tribes: the Sama Dilaut of Tawi-Tawi; the Subanon of Zamboanga del Sur and Zamboanga del Norte; and the Yakan of Basilan. A short walk east of Fort Pilar is **Rio Hondo**, a Muslim village on stilts. The dome of its mosque is clearly visible from some way off, but if you want to penetrate the village, which is a maze of bamboo walkways and open-fronted homes, it's advisable to take a local guide who can smooth the way: enquire at the tourist office.

Practicalities

Flights link Zamboanga with Cebu City (3 weekly; 1hr), Davao (2 daily; 1hr 15min), Jolo (3 weekly; 40min), Manila (4 daily; 1hr 40min) and Tawi-Tawi (1 daily; 1hr). From the **airport** on the northern outskirts of the city it takes about twenty minutes to get to the city centre by taxi; you can take a tricycle for P40 or a jeepney marked for "Canelar" for P7. Taxis charge P150–200.

The **ferry** wharf is at the southern end of Lorenzo Street and easy to reach by taxi, jeepney and tricycle. **Buses** from **Dipolog** (2 daily; 7hr), **Iligan** (2 daily; 7–8hr), **Ozamis** (2 daily; 6hr) arrive at one of two terminals – they're right next to each other – at the northern end of Veterans' Avenue.

The best **tourist office** (Mon–Sat 8am–noon & 1–5pm; ☎062/991-0218) is the DoT's regional office in the *Lantaka Hotel*, on the waterfront in Valderosa Street. There's a **travel agent** in the *Lantaka* and there are a number of **banks** with ATMs and **internet cafés** in the centre of town. The best **accommodation** is supplied by the ageing *Lantaka Hotel* (☎062/991-2033; ❹), a concrete establishment with old-fashioned but spacious rooms, a pool and free wi-fi in the lobby. A newer alternative is the *Marcian Business Hotel* at Mayor Cesar C. Climaco Avenue (☎062/991-0005, Ⓦmarcianhotels.com; ❷), with air conditioning, cable TV, internet and restaurant. One of the best **restaurants** is *Alavar Seafood House* (☎062/981-2483), ten minutes northeast of the city by tricycle (P40) in barangay of Tetuan, best known for its delicious crab dishes (from P200). *Mano Mano Na Greenfield Restaurant* (☎062/992-4717), Governor Ramos Street, Barangay Santa Maria, is a cheaper alternative (P80) with native-style food served on bamboo trays.

The Sulu archipelago

Despite boasting some of the most unspoiled beaches in Asia, the volcanic **Sulu archipelago** is undiscovered country in tourist terms, and even Filipino tourists rarely come here. Much of the island chain has a well-deserved reputation for lawlessness and violence, so you need to coordinate very carefully with the tourist office in Zamboanga before heading south. At the time of writing only Tawi-Tawi was considered safe to visit. The archipelago actually comprises around 870 islands off southwest Mindanao, covering an area of 2700 square kilometres from Basilan in the north to Borneo in the south, and is home to a surprisingly large population of around twelve million. Access is either by **ferry** from Zamboanga (to Jolo; 1 daily; 12hr) or on an Airphil Express **flight** from Zamboanga to Jolo (3 times weekly; 40min) and Tawi-Tawi (1 daily; 1hr).

Tawi-Tawi and around

At the southern end of the peninsula lies the island of **Tawi-Tawi**, whose busy little capital **BONGAO** is a commercial fishing centre. From **Sanga-Sanga Airport** just outside Bongao there are jeepneys into town for P10. There are several cheap hotels in Bongao, one of the better ones being the *Beachside Inn* (☎068/268-1446; ❷), on the outskirts near the beach, which has singles, doubles (with a/c and TV) and a decent restaurant.

Bongao Peak is a ten-minute walk inland from the town and a fairly easy climb. The peak holds mystical powers for the locals, and villagers take sick people to the top to offer prayers. Don't forget to buy some bananas at the market to take on your hike up the mountain – **macaques** guard the trail and bananas are your currency with them. From the top, 300m above sea level, you can see all of Bongao and the surrounding islands. It's also fun to poke around the **market** near the pier, known as the Chinese market, where you can buy herbs, baskets, traditional hats, prayer mats, scarves and batik clothes. Local delicacies on sale here include turtles' eggs and *tarrang bulan*, pancakes sprinkled with peanuts.

Contexts

Contexts

History

Philippine history is frequently dismissed as "beginning with the Spanish and ending with the Americans", yet the modern country is a result of many diverse influences – Malay, Chinese, Spanish and American – that have collided in the archipelago down the centuries. While the influence of Spain and the US is significant, recent scholarship has thrown light on the native and Islamic civilizations that flourished here before Magellan's arrival in 1521, and – thanks to new archeological discoveries – their highly developed trade links with the rest of Asia. Today one issue looms over all others; in 1960 the population of the Philippines was just 27 million, yet by 2015 it is expected to top 100 million. Such explosive growth has meant that real economic gains made in the last fifty years have had a negligible effect on poverty and it remains, along with corruption, one of the country's biggest problems.

Prehistory

Human fossil remains found in Palawan suggest that humans first migrated to the Philippines across land bridges from Borneo during the Ice Age, some 50,000 years ago. Carbon dating of fossilized human remains discovered at Tabon Cave in Palawan showed so-called "Tabon Man" was living in the cave about 22,000 years ago. Deeper excavations of the cave indicated humans were in the area from 45,000 to 50,000 years ago.

The Aeta or **Negritos**, the country's indigenous people, are said to be descended from these first migrants. Successive migrations populated the islands through the centuries. Malays from Indonesia and the Malay peninsula streamed into the islands more than 2000 years ago, sailing through the Sulu Sea and settling first in the Visayas and southwestern Luzon. Their outrigger boats, equipped with lateen sails, each carried a family or clans led by a chief. Once ashore, they remained together in villages – or barangays, as their boats were called. The bulk of Filipinos today, at least in the Visayas and Mindanao, are descended from these Malay settlers.

Hindu kingdoms and Islamic sultanates

The early Malay communities gradually developed into a complex patchwork of kingdoms such as the Rajahnates of Butuan and Cebu, influenced by the powerful **Hindu empires** in Java and Sumatra. Several archeological finds hint at the sophistication and wealth of these early civilizations: the *Laguna Copperplate*, the earliest written document found in the Philippines, dates from around 900 AD and concerns a debt of gold in the Hindu-Malay state of Tondo around today's Manila Bay. Equally enlightening is the Surigao Treasure, a trove of sensational gold objects dug up by accident in Mindanao in 1981 and dating from the tenth to thirteenth centuries. Also decorated with gold, the *Boxer Codex*, created in around 1595, includes fifteen drawings of Filipino natives of the sixteenth century. Finally, recently excavated Chinese shipwrecks loaded with porcelain prove that trade ties with China and the rest of Asia were extensive by the tenth century.

Contact with Arab traders, which reached its peak in the twelfth century, drew Sufis and missionaries who began the propagation of Islam in the Philippines. In 1380, the Arab scholar Karim ul' Makdum arrived in Jolo and established the Sultanate of Sulu. In 1475 Shariff Mohammed Kabungsuwan of Johor (Malaysia), married a native princess and established the Sultanate of Maguindanao, ruling large parts of Mindanao. During the reign of Sultan Bolkiah (1485–1521), the Sultanate of Brunei absorbed Tondo; by the time the Spanish arrived, **Islam** was established as far north as Luzon, where a great Muslim chief, Rajah Sulaiman II, ruled Manila.

Spanish rule

The country's turbulent relationship with Spain began on April 24, 1521 when **Ferdinand Magellan** arrived in Cebu after sailing for four months across the vast ocean he named the Pacific. Magellan planted a wooden cross to claim the islands for **Spain**, baptizing a local king, Raja Humabon. **Lapu-Lapu** (1491–1542), a chief on the nearby island of Mactan, and Humabon's traditional enemy, resisted; in a subsequent skirmish known as the Battle of Mactan (see p.274), Magellan was killed and Spain's conquest of the Philippines was put on hold. Lapu-Lapu is now regarded as a Filipino hero.

Spanish conquistador Ruy López de Villalobos tried once again to claim the islands for Spain in 1543, but was driven out by the natives a year later after naming the Philippines in honour of the future King Philip II. In 1564 **Miguel López de Legazpi**, (1502–72), a minor Basque aristocrat, was chosen to lead a hazardous expedition to establish a permanent base in the Philippines, which the Spanish hoped would act as a wedge between Portugal and China. Legazpi sailed to the Philippines on board the *Capitana*, establishing a colony in Bohol in 1565 and then moving on to Cebu where he erected the first Spanish fort in the Philippines. But a series of misunderstandings – one involving the gift of a concubine that Legazpi piously refused – made the situation in Cebu perilous, and Legazpi looked for a more solid base.

In 1570 a Spanish expedition defeated Rajah Sulaiman III, and a year later Legazpi occupied his former base; a new Spanish capital – **Manila** – was established on the site of Sulaiman's old Islamic kingdom. Spanish conquistadors and friars zealously set about propagating **Catholicism**, building churches and bringing rural folk *debajo de las compañas* (under the bells), into organized Spanish *pueblos*, establishing many of the country's towns and cities. They imposed a **feudal system**, concentrating populations under their control into new towns and estates, and resulting in numerous small revolts. Most of the Philippines, however, remained beyond the pale of the colonial authorities.

The Friarocracy

The islands were administered from the Spanish colony of **Mexico**, and its Spanish residents, especially those in Manila, grew prosperous and corrupt on the strength of the galleon trade, a venture that involved re-exporting goods from China through Manila to Mexico. The Catholic Church, dreading change, did nothing to improve the subsistence economy, while in the capital, according to an early diarist, "the rich spend ten months of the year with nothing to do".

In theory, the Philippines was ruled by civil and military representatives of the King of Spain, but in practice it was the Catholic **friars** who ran the show. They derived their power from the enormous influence of the monastic orders – Augustinian, Dominican and Franciscan – which spanned the world like global corporations. Secular officials came and went, but the clergy stayed. Many friars ignored their vows of celibacy and sired children with local women. They exercised their power through a number of administrative functions, including setting budgets, conducting the parish census, screening recruits for the military and presiding over the police. There were cosmetic local administrations, but they could not act without the friars' consent.

It wasn't until the late eighteenth century that the ossification brought about by the colonial regime began to ease, the result of a series of external shocks. Attempts by the Dutch, Portuguese and Chinese to establish a presence in the archipelago were repelled. But the **British** managed to occupy Manila in 1762, raiding it in a sideshow to the Seven Years' War. They handed it back to Spain under the conditions of the Treaty of Paris, signed in 1763, but their easy victory served notice that the Philippines was vulnerable. In 1821 Mexico became independent, and the Philippines were administered directly from Madrid thereafter, ushering in a period of relatively enlightened colonial rule and prosperity.

The independence movement

The Spanish began to establish a free public school system in the Philippines in 1863, increasing the number of educated and Spanish-speaking Filipinos. The opening of the Suez Canal in 1869 (combined with the increasing use of steam power) cut travel times between Spain and the Philippines to weeks rather than months, and many of this new generation were able to continue their studies in Europe – they frequently returned with liberal ideas and talk of freedom.

A small **revolt** in Cavite in 1872 was quickly put down, but the anger and frustration Filipinos felt about colonial rule would not go away. Intellectuals such as Marcelo H. Del Pilar and Juan Luna were the spiritual founders of the independence movement, but it was the writings of a diminutive young doctor from Laguna province, **José Rizal** (1861–96), that provided the spark for the flame. His novel *Noli Me Tangere* was written while he was studying in Spain in the 1880s, and portrayed colonial rule as a cancer and the Spanish friars as fat, pompous fools. It was promptly banned by the Spanish, but distributed underground along with other inflammatory essays by Rizal and, later, his second novel, *El Filibusterismo*.

In 1892, Rizal returned to Manila and founded the reform movement Liga Filipina, which never espoused revolution, only moderate reform. Its members swore oaths and took part in blood rites, and, innocuous as the movement was, the friars smelled sedition. Rizal was arrested and exiled to Dapitan on Mindanao. **Andrés Bonifacio** (1863–97) took over the reins by establishing the secret society known as the Katipunan or KKK. Its full name was Kataastaasan, Kagalanggalang na Katipunan nang mga Anak ng Bayan, which means "Honorable, respectable sons and daughters of the nation". In August 1896, the armed struggle for independence broke out, and Rizal was accused of masterminding it. Rizal had, in fact, called the revolution "absurd and savage" and had earlier turned down an invitation from Bonifacio to participate in it. His trial lasted a day, one of the seven military judges concluding that Rizal's being a native must be considered "an aggravating factor". Rizal's Spanish military lawyer did little for him so he finally rose to defend himself. "I have sought political liberty," he said, "but never the freedom to rebel." He was duly found guilty and executed by firing squad in Manila in what is now known as Rizal Park on December 30, 1896. The night before he died he wrote *Mi Ultimo Adios*, a farewell poem to the country he loved.

The Philippine Revolution

News of Rizal's martyrdom inflamed the uprising ignited by Bonifacio. Spanish officials deluded themselves, blaming it on a few troublemakers, but by now Bonifacio had decided violence was the only option and, with the young firebrand general, **Emilio Aguinaldo** (1869–1964) he called openly for a government "like that of the United States". In 1897, when it became clear they were facing all-out insurrection, the Spanish negotiated a truce with Aguinaldo, who had by now declared himself generalissimo, and had fallen out with his former partner; he had a kangaroo court condemn Bonifacio to death. The Spanish would pay the rebels 800,000 pesos, half immediately, a quarter when they laid down their arms and the rest after a Te Deum to mark the armistice was chanted in Manila Cathedral. In exchange Aguinaldo agreed to go abroad. A cheque in his pocket, he sailed for Hong Kong, disavowing his rebellion and declaring his loyalty to Spain.

In 1898, as a result of a dispute over Cuba, war broke out between the **United States** and Spain, and as an extension of it the US decided to expel Spain from the Philippines. The Spanish fleet was soundly beaten in Manila Bay by ships under the command of George Dewey, who on the morning of April 30, 1898, gave the famous order to his captain, "You may fire when you are ready, Gridley." The Filipinos fought on the side of the US, and when the battle was over General Aguinaldo, now back from Hong Kong having disavowed his disavowal of the rebellion, declared the Philippines independent; the First Philippine Republic was formally established by the Malolos Constitution in January 1899, with Aguinaldo as first president. The US, however, had other ideas and paid Spain US$20 million for its former possession. Having got rid of one colonizing power, Filipinos were now answerable to another.

American rule

After the Spanish left the country, the Filipinos continued to fight for independence in what's known as the **Philippine–American War**, a savage conflict that is virtually forgotten in the US today. The war began outside Manila in 1899 and lasted for three years, although skirmishes continued for another seven years, especially in Mindanao. It resulted in the death of at least 600,000 Filipinos and 4,234 Americans (exact records were not kept of Filipino casualties). US troops used tactics they would later employ in Vietnam, such as strategic hamleting and scorched-earth, to pacify locals, and by March 1899, Manila was ablaze as American troops fanned out across the city. But crushing the Filipinos was not easy. The US forces, for all their superior firepower, were nagged by relentless heat, torrential rain and pervasive disease. Aguinaldo still commanded Filipino forces, though the intensity of the Manila assault had shocked him. Malolos, to the north of Manila, the seat of his revolutionary government, was overrun, but by June 1899 the Americans had become bogged down and controlled territory no more than 40km from Manila. The war degenerated into a **manhunt** for Aguinaldo, and when he was finally captured in March 1902 in Palanan on Luzon's east coast, the war ended officially three months later. After a brief internment, the wily general took an oath of allegiance to the US, was granted a pension from the US government and retired from public life until 1935 (see below).

From the beginning, Washington was divided over how much independence its erstwhile charge should be given, what measures would be in place to ensure the protection of US interests there and who would be president.

Benevolent assimilation

When the Philippine–American War ended, American teachers fanned out across the country to begin President McKinley's policy of "**benevolent assimilation**", and soon became known as Thomasites, after the ship on which they had arrived. The spread of schools has been applauded by historians as America's single greatest achievement in the Philippines. The Thomasites took to their task with apostolic fervour and Filipinos quickly achieved the highest literacy rate in Southeast Asia.

The American administration in the Philippines, guided by Washington, sought to inculcate Filipinos with American ethics, to turn the Philippines into a stable, prosperous, self-confident model of democracy in a developing country. Filipinos learned to behave, dress and eat like Americans, sing American songs and speak Americanized English. American educators decided that teaching Filipinos in their many own languages would require too many textbooks, so American English became the lingua franca of the Philippines. Meanwhile, the debate was still raging over what form of government the Philippines would have. It wasn't until 1935 that a bill was passed in Washington allowing President Roosevelt to recognize a new Philippine constitution and the ten-year transition status of "Commonwealth of the Philippines" – autonomous but not completely independent. Presidential elections were held in September of that year and won by **Manuel Quezon** (1878–1944), leading light among a new breed of postwar politicians, who soundly beat Aguinaldo, who had come out of retirement. Aguinaldo was to cooperate with the Japanese in World War II, but after briefly being jailed by the Americans a second time, lived to see Philippine independence.

World War II

One of the questions about the new Commonwealth was a military one: could it defend itself? Quezon realized how vulnerable the archipelago was and invited the US commander of the country, **General Douglas MacArthur**, to become military adviser to the autonomous regime. MacArthur accepted, demanding US$33,000 a year and an air-conditioned suite in the *Manila Hotel*.

Hostilities broke out in the Philippines within minutes of the attack on **Pearl Harbor**, as waves of Japanese Mitsubishi bombers targeted military bases in Cavite and at Clark. MacArthur appealed for help from Washington, but it never came. He declared Manila an open city to save its population and prepared for a tactical retreat to Corregidor, the island citadel at the mouth of Manila Bay, from where he would supervise the defence of the strategic Bataan peninsula. Quezon, now increasingly frail from tuberculosis, went with him.

The Philippines, especially Manila, underwent heavy **bombardment** during World War II and casualties were high. Japanese troops landed on Luzon and occupied Manila on January 2, 1942. MacArthur and Quezon abandoned Corregidor when it became clear the situation was hopeless, but after arriving in Darwin, Australia, MacArthur promised Filipinos, "I have come through and I shall return."

When he fled, MacArthur left behind soldiers engaged in a protracted and bloody struggle for **Bataan**. When the peninsula inevitably fell to Japanese forces, Corregidor was next. The Japanese launched an all-out assault on May 5, 1942, and the island, defended by starving and demoralized troops huddled in damp tunnels, capitulated within days. During the notorious Bataan Death March that followed, as many as 10,000 Americans and Filipinos died from disease, malnutrition and wanton brutality. The exact figure is unknown even today.

Two years of **Japanese military rule** followed. Frustrated in their efforts to quell an elusive population and a nascent guerrilla movement, the Japanese turned increasingly to brutality, beheading innocent victims and displaying their bodies as an example. The guerrillas multiplied, however, until their various movements comprised 200,000 men. The strongest force was the People's Anti-Japanese Army, in Tagalog the Hukbalahap or the **Huks** for short, most of them poor sharecroppers and farm workers looking for any opportunity to improve their abysmal lot. MacArthur, meanwhile, kept his promise to return. On October 19, 1944, with Quezon at his side, he waded ashore at Leyte, forcing a showdown with the Japanese and driving across the island to the port of Ormoc. The Huks later helped the US **liberate Luzon**, acting as guides in the push towards Manila and freeing Americans from Japanese prison camps. No guerrilla exploited his wartime adventures more than an ambitious young lawyer from Ilocos who now had his sights set on entering the political arena in Manila: Ferdinand Marcos.

The Marcos years

The Philippines received full **independence** from the US on July 4, 1946, when Manuel Roxas, an experienced politician from Panay, was sworn in as the first President of the Republic. His government marred by corruption and conflict with the now outlawed Huks, Roxas died of a heart attack in 1948 and was replaced by his Ilocano vice-president Elpidio Quirino. The 1950s were something of a golden age for the Philippines, with the presidency of Ramón Magsaysay (1953–57) considered a high point. In the early 1960s, however, the Liberal government of Diosdado Macapagal was crippled by Nacionalista Party opposition in Congress. It was in these years that **Ferdinand Marcos** came to power, promoting himself as a force for unification and reform.

Marcos (1917–89) was born in Sarrat, Ilocos Norte. A brilliant young lawyer who had successfully defended himself against a murder charge, he was elected to the Philippine House of Representatives in 1949, to the Senate in 1959 and became president in 1965 on the Nacionalista Party ticket, defeating incumbent Macapagal. Marcos's first term as president was innovative and inspirational. He invigorated both populace and bureaucracy, embarking on a huge **infrastructure** programme and unifying scattered islands with a network of roads, bridges, railways and ports. During these early years of the Marcos presidency, before the madness of martial law, First Lady Imelda (see box opposite) busied herself with social welfare and cultural projects that complemented Marcos's work in economics and foreign affairs.

Martial law

In 1969 Marcos became the first Filipino president to be re-elected for a **second term.** The country's problems, however, were grave. Poverty, social inequality and rural stagnation were rife. Marcos was trapped between the entrenched oligarchy, which controlled Congress, and a rising communist insurgency that traced its roots back to the Huks (see above), fuelled mostly by landless, frustrated peasants led by the articulate and patriarchal José Marie Sison (who lives today in exile in the Netherlands). The country was roiled by student, labour and peasant unrest, much of it stoked by communists and their fledgling military wing, the

New People's Army. Marcos used the protests, and the spurious excuse of several attempts to liquidate him, to perpetuate his hold on power. On September 21, 1972, he declared **martial law**, arresting **Benigno "Ninoy" Aquino** and other opposition leaders. A curfew was imposed and Congress was suspended. Marcos announced he was pioneering a Third World approach to democracy through his "New Society" and his new political party the New Society Movement. His regime became a byword for profligacy, corruption and repression.

The **Mindanao** problem also festered. After the Jabidah Massacre in 1968, when Filipino troops executed 28 Muslim recruits who refused to take part in a hopelessly misconceived invasion of Sabah, Muslims took up arms against the government, forming the Mindanao Independence Movement (see box, p.389).

The Iron Butterfly

Imelda Remedios Visitacion was born on July 2, 1929, in the little town of Tolosa in Leyte. Her youth was troubled, her parents always quarrelling, separating and reconciling, her feckless father unable to hold down a job. Aged 23 she left Leyte for Manila with just five pesos in her purse, seeking her fortune. Her break came in 1953, when a magazine editor featured her face on his cover; she then entered a beauty contest and won the title of Miss Manila. Ferdinand Marcos later recounted that he saw the magazine picture and told friends, "I'm getting married." He arranged an introduction and, after an eleven-day courtship, proposed.

Following his 1965 election victory, Marcos said of Imelda, "She was worth a million votes." In fact, Imelda had cleverly inveigled tycoon Fernando Lopez into standing as Marcos's vice president, bringing with him his family's immeasurable fortune. Once the election was won, Imelda announced she would be "more than a mere decorative figure" and in 1966 made her international debut when she sang to Lyndon Johnson at a White House dinner. "A blessing not only to her country, but also to the world", gushed a US newspaper columnist.

Imelda believed that nothing succeeds like excess and laid on lavish fiestas for every visiting dignitary. She also posed as a patron of the arts flying in international stars such as Margot Fonteyn. Her husband later made her **governor of Manila** with a brief to turn the city into a showpiece. She set about the task with gusto, spending US$31 million on the Coconut Palace (see p.81) and US$21 million on the Manila Film Center (see p.81). As well as a patron of the arts, the First Lady also appointed herself the country's roving envoy, relentlessly roaming the world on jumbo jets "borrowed" from Philippine Airlines to meet the likes of Fidel Castro, Emperor Hirohito and Chairman Mao. A prodigious social climber, she pursued Rockefellers and Fords, and dreamed of betrothing her daughter Imee to Prince Charles.

Throughout much of the 1980s she went on notoriously profligate **shopping binges** to New York and Los Angeles, spending million of dollars on grotesque art, jewellery and the occasional apartment. In Geneva, another favourite haunt, she spent US$12 million in jewellery in a single day. After her husband's downfall in 1986, Imelda became deeply upset at reports that three thousand pairs of **shoes** had been found inside the Malacañang Palace, claiming she had only accumulated them to promote the Philippine shoe industry in her trips abroad. The shoes became the most potent symbol of her mad spending.

Imelda returned to Manila in 1991, and in a shocking confirmation of her continued popularity in some quarters, she was elected Congresswoman of Leyte (her home province), four years later; in 2010 she was elected to represent the second district of Ilocos Norte, replacing her son Ferdinand Marcos, Jr (who was elected to the Senate). Various corruption cases against Imelda have dragged on painfully through the courts over the years, but her nickname – the Iron Butterfly, for her thick-skinned bravura – is surely well deserved.

Marcos made few real efforts to quell the insurgency in the south, knowing it would give him another unassailable excuse for martial law. The US became worried that the longer Marcos's excesses continued the faster the communist insurgency would spread, threatening their military bases in the islands, which had long been of mutual benefit to both the US and the Philippines.

The People Power Revolution (EDSA)

By the 1980s it looked as if Marcos would never relinquish power or martial law – with his American allies seemingly unwilling or unable to influence the dictator, it took a real ground-roots movement to oust him.

The revolution was sparked by the martyrdom of **Ninoy Aquino**, who by the spring of 1980 had been languishing in jail for seven years. Aquino was released from jail on condition he went into exile in the US. In 1983 he decided to return and when he emerged from his plane at Manila airport on August 21, 1983, he was assassinated. The country was outraged. In a snap election called in panic by Marcos on February 7, 1986, the opposition united behind Aquino's widow, **Corazón Aquino** (1933–2009), and her running mate Salvador Laurel. On February 25, both Marcos and Aquino claimed victory and were sworn in at separate ceremonies. Aquino, known by the people as Cory became a rallying point for change and was backed by the Catholic Church in the form of Archbishop Cardinal Jaime Sin, who urged people to take to the streets; the **People Power Revolution** (also known as the EDSA Revolution) had begun.

When Marcos's key allies saw which way the wind was blowing and deserted him, the game was up. Defence Minister Juan Ponce Enrile and Deputy Chief of Staff of the Armed Forces, General **Fidel Ramos**, later to become president, announced a coup d'état. The US prevaricated, but eventually told Marcos to "cut and cut cleanly". Ferdinand and Imelda fled from the Malacañang Palace to Clark in helicopters provided by the CIA, and from there into exile in Hawaii, where Ferdinand died in 1989. Conservative estimates of their plunder put the figure at US\$10 billion, US\$600 million of it spirited into Swiss bank accounts – rumours persist that Marcos had also appropriated a hoard of Japanese war loot dubbed "Yamashita's Gold", though this has never been proven conclusively. Back in Manila, the people stormed through the gates of the Malacañang Palace.

The return of democracy

Having ousted Marcos, hopes were high for the presidency of **Cory Aquino**, but she never managed to bring the powerful feudal families or the armed forces under her control. **Land reform** was eagerly awaited by the country's landless masses, but when Aquino realized reform would also involve her own family's haciendas in Tarlac, she quietly shelved the idea: most of the country's farmers remain beholden to landlords today. Aquino survived seven coup attempts and made little headway in improving life for the majority of Filipinos who were – and still are – living below the poverty line. The communist New People's Army (NPA) emerged once again as a threat, and human rights abuses continued.

Aquino also had to deal with another thorny issue: the presence of **US military bases** in the country; Clark Air Base and Subic Naval Base. Public opinion had been turning against the bases for some time, with many seeing them as a colonial imposition. In 1987 Congress voted not to renew the bases treaty and the US withdrawal, set for 1991, was hastened by the portentous eruption of **Mount Pinatubo**, which scattered ash over both Clark and Subic, causing millions of dollars of damage to US aircraft and ships. The pullout made jobless 600,000 Filipinos who had depended on the bases for employment either directly or indirectly.

Ultimately, Aquino's only legacy was that she maintained some semblance of a democracy, which was something for her successor, **Fidel Ramos** (b.1928) to build on. President Ramos took office on July 1, 1992 and announced plans to create jobs, revitalize the economy and reduce the burdensome foreign debt of US$32 billion. But the first thing he had to do was establish a reliable electricity supply. The country was being paralysed for hours every day by **power cuts**, and no multinational companies wanted to invest their hard-earned money under such difficult conditions. Ramos's success in breathing new life into the ailing energy sector – at least in Manila and many cities – laid the foundations for a moderate influx of foreign investment, for industrial parks and new manufacturing facilities. The economy picked up, but foreign debt was crippling and tax collection was so lax that the government had nothing in the coffers to fall back on. Infrastructure improved marginally and new roads and transit systems began to take shape. Ramos also liberalized the banking sector and travelled extensively to promote the Philippines abroad. Most Filipinos view his years in office as a success, although when he stepped down at the end of his six-year term in 1998, poverty and crime were still rife.

Erap: scandal and EDSA II

Ramos's successor, former vice president **Joseph Estrada** (b.1937) was a former tough-guy film actor with pomaded hair and a cowboy swagger who is known universally in the islands as **Erap**, a play on the slang word *pare*, which means friend or buddy. Estrada had a folksy, macho charm that appealed to the masses and was elected to the presidency in 1998 against politicians of greater stature on a **pro-poor** platform. His rallying cry was *Erap para sa mahirap*, or "Erap for the poor". He promised food security, jobs, mass housing, education and health for all, but got off to a troubled start in the Malacañang Palace, plagued by a series of tawdry scandals that he swept aside. More seriously, accusations surfaced in the media of a lack of direction and a return to the **cronyism** of the Marcos years. Erap bumbled his way from one mismanaged disaster to the next. The **economy** was floundering and every day there was some new allegation, always denied by Erap with a combative flourish, of mismanagement, favours for friends or plain incompetence.

The Philippine Center for Investigative Journalism (PCIJ) began its research into Estrada's wealth in the first quarter of 2000. Its report listed seventeen pieces of **real estate** worth P2 billion that had been acquired by Estrada and his various family members since 1998. Some, it was alleged, were for his favourite mistress, former actress Laarni Enriquez. Later in 2000 Luis Singson, governor of Ilocos Sur, alleged that Estrada had received P500 million in **gambling payoffs** from an illegal numbers game known as *jueteng* (pronounced "wet-eng"). On November 13, 2000 Joseph Estrada became the first president of the Philippines to be **impeached**, setting the stage for a trial in the Senate that would hold the nation in its grip for weeks.

The trial came to a climax when the prosecution claimed it had new evidence, sealed in an envelope, that would prove Estrada's guilt beyond doubt. Estrada's allies in the Senate insisted on a vote to decide whether the new evidence was admissible. The Senate was comprised of eleven pro-Erap senators and ten anti-Erap senators. Not surprisingly, the vote went according to loyalties, and it looked as though Erap had survived.

Filipinos felt robbed of a real chance for truth and justice, and people soon began gathering on the streets to demand the president's resignation. The church and its leader, Cardinal Jaime Sin again became involved and urged Estrada to step down. Half a million people gathered at the EDSA shrine in Ortigas in scenes reminiscent of those before the downfall of Marcos – the four-day demonstrations were later dubbed EDSA II. Fifty thousand militants massed near Malacañang Palace, preparing to kick out the president by force if necessary. On the evening of Friday January 19, 2001, cabinet members saw the cause was lost and began to defect.

The decisive blow came when the **military** announced it had withdrawn its support for Estrada. The next morning he was ushered ignominiously from the Malacañang Palace and vice president Gloria Macapagal-Arroyo was promptly sworn in as the fourteenth President of the Republic of the Philippines. Anti-Erap forces hailed what they deemed a noble moral victory. But a nagging question remained. Estrada had been voted into office by a landslide of 10.7 million people and removed by a predominantly middle-class movement of 500,000 who took to the streets. His impeachment trial had been aborted and he had been found guilty of nothing.

Macapagal-Arroyo: the politics of the elite

The presidency of **Gloria Macapagal–Arroyo** (b.1947) proved slightly less dramatic than her predecessors, but just as divisive. During her two terms in office Macapagal-Arroyo made great play of her economic prowess and the fact that she was an assiduous administrator, not a flamboyant but empty figurehead. The first years of her presidency were solid if unspectacular, her main priority simply to survive and bring some level of stability. The House of Representatives and Senate were bitterly divided along pro- and anti-Estrada lines, with the two main parties unable to agree on anything; in 2007 Estrada was finally found guilty of plunder, but was promptly pardoned by the president.

The Greatest and the Pacman

Boxing has been a Filipino passion for over one hundred years. Ferdinand Marcos capitalized on the nation's love of the sport by using government money to finance the **"Thrilla in Manila"** in 1975, a notoriously brutal encounter between Muhammad Ali and Joe Frazier often ranked as one of the greatest fights of twentieth-century boxing. Fought at the Araneta Coliseum in Quezon City, Ali won in the 15th and final round. The beneficent Marcos even stumped up the cash for the fight's multimillion-dollar purse. Filipinos have never made it in the high-profile heavyweight game, but in the lighter divisions they've excelled. In recent years, one name stands out in particular: **Manny "the Pacman" Pacquiao**, the poor boy from Mindanao who became world super featherweight champion, made a movie, made millions and was the first boxer in history to win ten world titles in eight different weight divisions (he's current super welterweight champ). In probably his most famous bout, he defeated Oscar De La Hoya in Las Vegas in 2008, in what was dubbed the "Dream Match". In 2010 Pacquiao was elected to the House of Representatives, representing the province of Sarangani, fuelling rumours about his political ambition; it's conceivable he could stand for higher office once he retires from boxing.

After winning her second term in 2004, things started to unravel for Macapagal-Arroyo; she was accused of vote-rigging, though two attempts to impeach her failed. In 2006 an army plot led to a state of emergency being implemented across the country. On the economy – her strong suit – the president could claim some success, with GDP growth rates over five percent a year the strongest in decades. Critics claimed the figures were inaccurate, and in any case, had failed to improve the lives of poorer citizens.

Macapagal-Arroyo's term finished in 2010, marred by claims of cronyism, extrajudicial killings, torture and illegal arrests; corruption still ran unchecked, and the gap between the impoverished and a thin layer of super-wealthy grew ever wider, with the dirt-poor growing in numbers and wretchedness, accounting probably for sixty percent of the population of near 100 million. After standing down as president, Macapagal-Arroyo defied convention and remained in politics, currently serving as a member of the House of Representatives for the 2nd District of Pampanga.

The return of the Aquinos

The presidential election of 2010 was typically dramatic. In 2009, Cory Aquino died from colon cancer, aged 76, sending the country into a five-day period of deep mourning – the former president was genuinely loved. As a direct consequence, Liberal Party candidate for the presidency Manuel Roxas withdrew to be replaced by fellow senator **Benigno Aquino III** (b.1960) Cory's son, until then not expected to run. His main rival in the election was none other than Joseph Estrada, the convicted and now-pardoned ex-president that seemed as feisty as ever. After a keenly fought campaign Aquino became president after winning 42.08 percent of the vote; Estrada came second with 26.25 percent.

Benigno Aquino – "Noynoy Aquino" or just "PNoy" – is a fascinating character, respected for his family connections, obsessed over in the tabloids for his love life (the president is the first to be a bachelor), a teetotaller, and self-styled fighter of corruption; one of his first acts was to establish a truth commission to investigate corruption allegations against Macapagal-Arroyo. More controversially, Aquino tacitly supports the promotion of contraceptive use enshrined in the proposed Reproductive Health Bill, which in various forms has been stalled in Congress for years and is unlikely to pass anytime soon. In a sign of what he's up against, the head of the Catholic Bishops' Conference of the Philippines has said that Aquino might face excommunication from the Catholic Church for supporting the bill – this despite a huge body of research linking a fast-growing population and poverty.

Beliefs and culture

n *El Filibusterismo*, José Rizal worried that Filipinos would become "a people without a soul". It's a theme that has been much developed by travel writers ever since, from Pico Iyer's description of "lush sentimentality" and Filipina obsession with high-school romance and pageants, to Michael Palin observing that American interest in the country is "unashamedly obvious". Yet there is a lot more to Philippine culture than cover bands, girlie bars and endless beauty pageants. Religious belief – among Muslims as well as Christians – is genuine and deeply held, while Filipino writers, rappers, film-makers and artists have developed distinctive styles that incorporate elements of all the nation's disparate cultural elements.

Religious belief

The Philippines is one of only two **predominantly Catholic** nations in Asia (the other being East Timor) – more than eighty percent of the population is Catholic, with around 10 percent Protestant. In addition to the Christian majority, there is a Muslim minority of between five and ten percent, concentrated on the southern islands of Mindanao and Sulu.

Yet to describe the Philippines as a Roman Catholic country is an over-simplification. Elements of tribal belief absorbed into Catholicism have resulted in a form of "folk Catholicism" that manifests itself in various homespun observances – a folk healer might use Catholic liturgy mixed with native rituals, or suited entrepreneurs might be seen scattering rice around their premises to ensure their ventures are profitable. And the infamous re-enactments of the Crucifixion held near San Fernando, Pampanga, every year are frowned upon by the official church. Even the Chinese minority has been influential in colouring Filipino Catholicism with the beliefs and practices of Buddhism, Confucianism and Taoism; many Catholic Filipinos believe in the balance of *yin* and *yang*, and that time is cyclical in nature.

The new Catholic movements

Today, the supremacy of the Catholic Church in the Philippines is being challenged by a variety of Christian sects. The largest of these is **El Shaddai**, established by lay preacher Mike Velarde on his weekly Bible-quoting radio show in the 1980s. Known to his followers as Brother Mike, Velarde has captured the imagination of poor Catholics, many of whom feel isolated from the mainstream Church. Velarde started preaching in colloquial and heavily accented Tagalog at huge open-air gatherings every weekend on Roxas Boulevard – the movement moved into a purpose-built P1 billion "House of Prayer" in Paranaque, Metro Manila, in 2009. Velarde tends to wears screamingly loud made-to-measure suits and outrageous bow ties, but his message is straightforward: give to the Lord and He will return it to you tenfold. He now has over eight million followers, most of whom suffer from *sakit sa bulsa*, or "ailment of the pocket", but are nevertheless happy to pay ten percent of their income to become card-carrying members of the flock. Brother Mike's relationship with the mainstream Catholic Church is uneasy. His relationship with politicians is not. With so many followers hanging on his every word, Brother Mike is a potent political ally and few candidates for high office are willing to upset him. In the 1998 elections, Brother Mike backed Joseph Estrada, which was a significant factor in the former movie actor's initial success. The Neocatechumenal Way, a Catholic movement that started in Spain in the 1960s, also has a very large and expanding presence in the Philippines.

Protestant sects

Some of the fastest growing religious movements in the Philippines are actually Protestant. One of the candidates in the 2004 elections (he came last), Eddie Villanueva established the charismatic **Jesus is Lord Church** in 1978, which he claims has some six million members with branches in Asia, Europe and North America.

You'll see the distinctive fairy-tale spires of Iglesia ni Cristo churches throughout the Philippines, an independent, purely Filipino movement founded by Felix Manalo in 1914 (his grandson currently runs the movement). Iglesia ni Cristo is explicitly anti-Catholic in its beliefs (the doctrine of the Trinity is rejected, for example) and is very influential during elections. Membership is estimated to be over three million. One of the churches most successful at expanding overseas is the Pentecostal Missionary Church of Christ, founded in 1973 and based in Marikina City. The United Methodist Church in the Philippines is an umbrella group for around one million Methodists in the country, while there about twenty different Baptist groups in the Philippines, at least half a million Mormons and half a million Seventh-Day Adventists.

Another well-known loose affiliation of groups, the **Rizalistas**, have only a tenuous connection with standard Christian doctrine. All regard José Rizal (see p.427) as the second son of God and a reincarnation of Christ, and some hold Mount Banahaw (see p.197) in Quezon province to be sacred, regularly attending pilgrimages to the mountain.

Islam in the Philippines

Islam spread north to the Philippines from Indonesia and Malaysia in the fourteenth century, and by the time the Spanish arrived it was firmly established on Mindanao and Sulu, with outposts on Cebu and Luzon.

Islam remains a very dominant influence in the southern Philippines (25 percent of Mindanao's population is Muslim), and Muslims have added cultural character to the nation, with Filipino Christians expressing admiration over their warlike defiance of colonization. However, many Muslims feel they have become strangers in their own country, ignored by the Manila-centric government and marginalized by people resettled in Mindanao from Luzon; the Autonomous Region in Muslim Mindanao was established in 1990, the only region that has its own government (for more on the Mindanao problem, see box, p.389).

While all Filipino Muslims follow the basic tenets of Islam, their religion has absorbed a number of indigenous elements, such as making offerings to spirits which are known as **diwatas**. A spirit known as **Bal-Bal** is believed in among many Muslim tribes; with the body of a man and the wings of a bird, Bal-Bal is credited with the habit of eating out the livers of unburied bodies. In Jolo and Tawi-Tawi Muslims use mediums to contact the dead, while many Muslim groups trade amulets, wearing them as necklaces to ward off ill fortune.

Muslim **women** are freer in the Philippines than in many Islamic countries, and have traditionally played a prominent role in everything from war to ceremonies. "The women of Jolo," wrote a Spanish infantryman in the eighteenth century, "prepare for combat in the same manner as their husbands and brothers and are more desperate and determined than the men. With her child suspended to her

The aswang who came to dinner

Heard the one about the pretty young housewife in a remote Visayan village who was possessed by the spirit of a jealous witch? Or the poor woman from a Manila shanty-town who had taken to flying through the barrio, terrorizing her neighbours? These are stories from the pages of Manila's daily tabloid newspapers, reported as if they actually happened. Foreign visitors greet news of the latest barrio haunting with healthy cynicism, but when you are lying in your creaking nipa hut in the pitch dark of a moonless evening it's not hard to see why so many Filipinos grow up embracing strange stories about creatures that inhabit the night. Even urbane professionals, when returning to the barrio of their childhood on holiday, can be heard muttering the incantation *tabi tabi lang-po* as they walk through paddy field or forest. Meaning "please let us pass safely", it's a request to the spirits and dwarves that might be lying in wait.

Most Filipino spirits are not the abstract souls of Western folklore who live in a netherworld; they are corporeal entities who live in trees or hang around the jeepney station, waiting to inflict unspeakable horrors on those who offend them. The most feared and widely talked about creature of Philippine folklore is the **aswang**; hundreds of cheesy films have been made about the havoc they wreak and hundreds of *aswang* sightings have been carried by the tabloid press. By day the *aswang* is a beautiful woman. The only way to identify her is by looking into her eyes at night, when they turn red. The *aswang* kills her victims as they sleep; threading her long tongue through the gaps in the floor or walls and inserting it into one of the body's orifices to suck out the internal organs.

Other creatures on the bogeyman list include the arboreal *tikbalang*, which has the head of a nag and the body of a man, and specializes in the abduction of virgins. Then there's the *duwende*, an elderly, grizzled dwarf who lurks in the forest and can predict the future, and the *engkanto*, who hides in trees and throws dust in the faces of passers-by, giving them permanently twisted lips.

breast or slung across her back, the Moro woman enters the fight with the ferocity of a panther."

Fine arts

Classical painting in the Philippines goes back to the Spanish period, but there are two acknowledged Filipino masters: **Juan Luna** (1859–99) and **Félix Hidalgo** (1855–1913). The artists helped shine attention on the Philippines after submitting paintings to the 1884 Exposicion General de Bellas Artes in Madrid. Luna's huge and drama-laced *Spolarium* (1884) is perhaps the most famous painting in the Philippines (on display at the National Gallery, p.77), while his equally admired *The Blood Compact* graces the Malacañang Palace. Luna spent most of his career in Europe and died in Hong Kong, and he's best known today for painting literary and historical scenes. Hidalgo also spent much of his career in Europe and died in Spain, creating haunting works such as *Las Virgenes Cristianas Expuestas al Populacho* ("The Christian Virgins Exposed to the Populace") and *Laguna Estigia* ("The Styx").

With the end of Spanish rule and a growing sense of **independence** in the twentieth century, Filipino painters were more content to develop their craft at home. **Fernando Amorsolo** (1892–1972) studied at the University of the Philippines' School of Fine Arts and gained prominence during the 1920s and 1930s for popularizing images of Philippine landscapes and demure rural Filipinas; his *Rice Planting* (1922) became one of the most popular images of the American period, and he became the first "National Artist" in 1972. Meanwhile, **Victorio**

Edades (1895–1985) introduced Modernism to the Philippines with *The Builders* of 1928, a style he'd developed in the US in direct contrast to Amorsolo. He went on to establish the UST College of Fine Arts in the 1930s, a bastion of avant-garde art.

World War II changed the way artists saw the world: Amorsolo's pastoral scenes gave way to **Vicente Manansala**'s grimmer, urban images portrayed in work like *Jeepneys* (1951). Other notable late twentieth-century painters include **José T. Joya** (1931–95), the Filipino abstract artist, and **Fernando Zóbel de Ayala y Montojo** (1924–84), the Modernist painter that also developed his craft in the US. In 2008, Zobel's *Noche Clara* fetched P6 million at auction, making it the most expensive Philippine painting ever sold.

The **contemporary art scene** in the Philippines is dynamic and eclectic, fed in part by exceptionally good art schools in the capital, with everything from installation art and video, to realism and street art on offer. Pilipinas Street Plan (Ⓦ pilipinasstreetplan.blogspot.com) and the Juju Bag (Ⓦ thejujubag.wordpress .com) are art communities that showcase street art, graffiti, posters, stickers and installations, while Rocking Society through Alternative Education (Rock Ed; Ⓦ www.rockedphilippines.org) has produced some cutting-edge art through its work with schools and prisons. One of the hottest visual artists today is Maya Muñoz, whose work is often displayed in Manila's galleries.

Film

Film-making has a distinguished history in the Philippines, but though locally made movies (and their stars) remain popular, they remain a long way behind their Hollywood counterparts in terms of audience and income.

Early movies arrived in the Philippines in the late 1890s, but the first genuinely Filipino film is credited to **Jose Nepumuceno**, the "Father of Philippine Movies", who made a version of a popular play *Dalagang Bukid* (Country Maiden) in 1919. The domestic film industry didn't really get going until the 1950s, when four big studios (Sampaguita, LVN, Premiere and Lebran) churned out hundreds of movies such as Gerardo de Leon's *Ifugao* (1954) and Manuel Conde's *Genghis Khan* (1952). Despite Gerardo de Leon's lauded adaptations of the Rizal novels *Noli Me Tangere* (1961) and *El Filibusterismo* (1962), the following decade was much poorer creatively and all four studios eventually closed.

Despite censorship during the Marcos years, **avant-garde** movie-making flourished in the 1970s, with Lino Brocka's *The Claws of Light* (1975) considered by many critics to be the greatest Philippine film ever made, and Kidlat Tahimik's *Mababangong Bangungot* ("Perfumed Nightmare") winning the International Critic's Prize at the Berlin Film Festival of 1977. Brocka's *This Is My Country*, which tackles the issue of labour union control under Marcos, was entered into the 1984 Cannes Film Festival.

The late 1980s and 1990s is regarded as a weaker period, but since the turn of the century **independent Filipino movies** have been undergoing something of a renaissance, in part thanks to digital technology. In 2003 Mark Meily scored a big hit with the comedy *Crying Ladies*, about three Filipinas working as professional mourners in Manila's Chinatown, while *Ang Pagdadalaga ni Maximo Oliveros* (2005) by Auraeus Solito and *Kubrador* (2006) by Jeffrey Jeturian were internationally acclaimed. Filipinos have also excelled in other formats: Carlo Ledesma won best short film at the Cannes Film Festival in 2007 for *The Haircut*.

In 2008, Brillante Mendoza's *Serbis* ("Service") became the first full-length Filipino film to compete at Cannes since 1984; the account of a day in the life of a family running a porno film theatre in Angeles City is bawdy and brutally realistic. Mendoza's *Kinatay* ("Butchered") competed at Cannes the following year. The Metro Manila Film Festival showcases the latest Filipino films over the Christmas period every year; it's not all arthouse material, with the 2009 winner *Ang Panday* ("The Blacksmith") an adaptation of a local fantasy comic series.

Music

Any Friday night in Manila and all over Asia, countless Filipino **showbands** can be seen in countless hotel lobbies performing accomplished cover versions of Western classics. While there's no doubt that when Filipinos mimic they do it exceedingly well, **indigenous music** does survive. Tagalog pop, rap and to a lesser extent rock have all been making a comeback in recent years, part of a slow but discernible trend away from the adulation of all things American.

Traditional tribal

Folk songs and stories, handed down orally, are still sung at tribal gatherings and ceremonies among indigenous peoples. Among the ethnic and tribal groups of Mindanao and the Sulu archipelago there's a sophisticated musical genre called **kulintang**, in which the main instruments are bossed gongs similar to those used in Indonesia. *Kulintang* is commonly performed by small ensembles playing instruments that include the kulintang itself (a series of small gongs for the melody), the *agung* (large gongs for the lower tones) and the *gandingan* (four large vertical gongs used as a secondary melodic instrument). *Kulintang* music serves as a means of entertainment and a demonstration of hospitality; it's used at weddings, festivals, coronations, to entertain visiting dignitaries and to honour those heading off on or coming back from a pilgrimage. It is also used to accompany healing ceremonies and, up to the beginning of the twentieth century, was a form of communication, using goatskin drums to beat messages across the valleys.

The Manila Sound

The "**Manila Sound**" was the sound of the 1970s in the Philippines. Against a backdrop of student riots and martial law, some audiences found comfort with bell-bottom-wearing bands, like the Hotdogs and the Boyfriends, who set romantic novelty lyrics to catchy melodic hooks. Some sneered at the frivolity of it all, but the Manila Sound was as big as disco. Today the Manila Sound is effectively extinct and hardly any survives on CD, but it gave rise to a number of major stars who evolved and are still going strong. The most well known is indefatigable diva Sharon Cuneta, who is known throughout the country by the modest moniker "The Megastar". She first appeared in the Philippine pop charts at the age of 12 singing the disco tune "Mr. D.J" and has since released 38 albums including one of duets with other apparently ageless Filipina singers such as Pops Fernandez and Sunshine Cruz.

The folkies

In the 1970s the only truly original artists performing in Manila were folksy beatniks such as singer-songwriters **Joey Ayala** and **Freddie Aguilar**. In the 1980s Aguilar wrote a popular ballad called "**Anak**" and found himself a fan in First Lady Imelda Marcos who, ever eager to bathe herself in the reflected glory of Manila's celebs, invited him to Malacañang Palace so they could sing the song together at banquets. Aguilar was appalled by the excesses he saw inside the palace and never went back.

As the anti-Marcos movement grew, so did the popularity of "Anak". Aguilar, by now something of a talisman for left-wing groups opposing martial law, took the opportunity to become even more political, recording a heartfelt version of "Bayan Ko" ("My Country"), a patriotic anthem that now took on extraordinary political significance.

One of the most well-known groups of the new generation was Apo Hiking Society, a foursome from Ateneo University whose anthem "Handog ng Pilipino sa Mundo" ("A New And Better Way") has been covered by fifteen Filipino artists. Its lyrics are carved on the wall of Manila's Our Lady of Edsa Shrine, traditionally a focal point of protests and revolutions.

Tribal-pop and OPM (Original Pilipino Music)

In the 1990s – largely as a reaction to the decline of the protest movement and the creeping Americanization of Filipino music – a roots movement emerged that took the traditional rhythms and chants of tribal music such as *kulintang* and merged them with contemporary instruments and production techniques. One of the chief exponents of so-called tribal-pop (the term **Original Pilipino Music** or Original Pinoy Music was coined in the late 1980s) was Grace Nono. She never quite cracked the big time, but cleared the path for others, including Pinikpikan, the most successful tribal-pop band in the country (the band reformed as Kalayo World Music Group in 2007). Over the last few years the term OPM has become diluted, and now encompasses the **young stars** of the twenty-first century, most of whom have modelled themselves on Celine Dion and Michael Bublé, not the revolutionary Manila singers of the Marcos years. This new generation includes Kyla, Erik Santos, Sarah Geronimo and Christian Bautista.

The mainstream

Any consideration of mainstream popular music in the Philippines won't get off the ground without reference to the irreverent **Eraserheads**. After more than a decade at the top they disbanded in 2003, but remain the most popular Filipino band ever. Many current popular groups have been inspired by their infectious blend of irony and irresistibly melodic pop, including Rivermaya, still producing platinum-selling albums at a rate of knots, and Parokya ni Edgar, one of the few bands that have come close to equalling the Eraserheads; their 1996 debut album, "Khangkhung-kherrnitz", features a tribute to the nation's favourite food: instant noodles. Today Filipino pop, rock and alternative music is flourishing, with bands such as 6CycleMind, Kamikazee, Chicosci, Sandwich and Bamboo leading the scene.

But despite the proliferation of progressive acts, the popular Philippine music scene has become dominated in recent years by comely solo performers singing plaintive ballads in the style of Whitney Houston or Mariah Carey. In the hierarchy of balladeers, Regine Velasquez and Martin Nievera are at the top. **Regine Velasquez**'s story is the quintessential Tagalog movie script: a beautiful girl from the sticks – she grew up in Leyte in the 1970s – wins a singing contest in 1989 (with a performance of "You'll Never Walk Alone", in Hong Kong) and heads off to Manila. Her repertoire is typical of the Filipina diva canon, comprising misty-eyed love songs such as "Could It Be?", "What You Are to Me" and "Long For Him". Named most popular Philippine artist in the MTV Asia awards for 2003, Velasquez follows in the tradition of Sharon Cuneta, Pops Fernandez and Kuh Ledesma, who at one time or another have all been dubbed the country's "concert queen" by the media. **Martin Nievera** puts his success – he's been recording since 1982 – down to the fact that Filipinos love a good drama. His songs are indeed melodramatic, his album *Forever, Forever* being an open book about his high-profile marital breakup with singer-actress Pops Fernandez.

Filipino hip-hop

Filipino hip-hop or **Pinoy rap** emerged in the late 1980s, with tracks by Dyords Javier and Vincent Dafalong. The genre developed slowly, but hit the mainstream with Francis Magalona's debut album, *Yo!* in 1990, which included the nationalistic hit "Mga Kababayan" ("My Countrymen"), a call to political arms that bore the hallmarks of Freddie Aguilar. In 1994, Death Threat released the first Filipino gangsta rap album *Gusto Kong Bumaet* ("I Want to be Good"). Since 2004 the Philippine Hip-Hop Music Awards has been held annually in Metro Manila and the genre remains incredibly popular throughout the country; current stars include Gloc-9 (former member of Death Threat), DiCE and k9 aka Mobbstarr and Pikaso. The most successful Filipino-American rapper is the Black Eyed Peas's apl.de.ap, who was born in Angeles City in 1974 and moved to L A at the age of fourteen.

Discography

A useful website for general information about Filipino music is Ⓦ www .philmusic.com.

Folk

Freddie Aguilar *Collection* (Ivory). A mixture of studio and live recordings featuring most of the folk hero's greatest songs, including "Trabaho" and a cover version of Joey Ayala's "Mindanao". "Pinoy" is a dark, but melodic exposition of the average Filipino's lot, while the lyrical "Magdalena" was based on conversations Aguilar had with Manila prostitutes, all of whom desperately wanted to escape the life. There's no "Anak", but there are plenty of other Freddie Aguilar collections that feature it.

Tribal-pop

Barbie's Cradle *Music from the Buffet Table* (Warner Music Philippines). Their semi-acoustic sound dominated by the frail but evocative voice of Barbie Almalbis, Barbie's Cradle injected a new note of realism into OPM songwriting, with lyrics – in both English and Tagalog – that spoke not of love and happiness, but of vulnerability and dysfunction. Highlights include "Money for Food", a musical poem about poverty, and "It's Dark and I Am Lonely", a personal and frank assessment of modern life for young people.

Cynthia Alexander *Insomnia and Other Lullabyes* (Dypro). Introspective but affecting collection of progressive/ tribal ballads from Joey Ayala's talented little sister. The navel-gazing becomes wearisome at times, but there are also some memorable moments, including "No Umbrella", a pleading love song with sonorous strings and plaintive fretless bass.

Grace Nono *Isang Buhay* (Tao Music). Quintessential Nono, this is an album of sometimes strident but hypnotic tribal rhythms and original tribal songs blended with additional lyrics drawing attention to the plight of the tribes, the environment and the avarice of the country's rulers.

Joey Ayala *Hubad* (Jeepney Dash). Eleven tracks chosen by Ayala himself for this "Best Of" collection, which is a fine introduction to his unique tribal-influenced folk and rock. Two of the tracks – "1896", about the revolt against Spain, and "Maglakad" ("Walk"), were recorded live in Japan. The best-known song on the album is "Mindanao", at once a paean to Ayala's birthplace and a haunting appeal for the Manila government to sit up and take notice of the island's problems. *Isang Buhay* means one house; the title track is Nono's plea for unity.

Pinikpikan *Kaamulan* (Tropical). Psychedelia meets tribal tradition on this, Pinikpikan's third album, released in 2003. The band's influences are eclectic and worn on the sleeve, from the Hindu overtones on "Child" to the flute solos – inspired by the wooden-flute music of the Manobo tribe of Mindanao – on "Butanding", a haunting stream-of-consciousness piece about the endangered whale shark.

Mainstream rock and pop

Bamboo *Tomorrow Becomes Yesterday* (EMI Philippines). Bamboo's fourth and best album; intelligent and thoughtful indie rock in Tagalog and English, with everything from acoustic ballads to hard rock anthems.

Eraserheads *Ultraelectromagneticpop* (BMG Pilipinas). Thoroughly enjoyable debut album featuring spirited Beatles-inspired pop, novelty pieces that poke fun at everyone and everything, and the brilliant "Pare Ko" (My Friend), which had the establishment in a spin because it contained a couple of swear words and gay references. The band matured after this and even got better – their second album, *Circus*, includes the track "Butterscotch" which takes a not so gentle dig at the Catholic Church ("Father Markus said to me/Just confess and you'll be free/Sit yer down upon me lap/And tell me all yer sins") – but *Ultraelectromagneticpop* will always be special because it blazed a trail.

Gloc-9 *Matrikula* (Sony). The fourth album from current godfather of Tagalog rap sees speed-rapper Gloc-9 in more chilled-out mode; the hit single *Upuan* features bluesy singer Jeazell Grutas and an R&B vibe.

Kitchie Nadal *Kitchie Nadal* (Warner Music). The debut album of the soulful Filipino singer-songwriter Nadal, featuring the award-winning "Wag na Wag Mong Sasabihin", an indie anthem worthy of Coldplay.

Martin Nievera *Live with the Philippine Philharmonic Orchestra* (MCA). Two-disc set recorded in Manila that captures some of the energy of Nievera live, when he's a much greater force than on many of his overly sentimental studio recordings. A master of patter and performance, Nievera sings in English, in Tagalog, on his own and with guests including the popular Filipina singing sisters Dessa and Cris Villonco, and his dad, Bert. The highlight is a mammoth montage of Broadway hits from *Carousel*, *West Side Story* and *Evita*, the nadir a self-indulgent spoken preamble to one of his signature songs, "Before You Say Goodbye".

Regine Velasquez *Unsolo* (Polycosmic). This was the album that marked the beginning of Velasquez's attempts to become an international star, or at least a pan-Asian one, raising her profile with duets featuring the likes of David Hasselhoff – for a syrupy rendition of "More Than Words Can Say" – and Jacky Cheung. There's only one song in Tagalog.

Rivermaya *It's Not Easy Being Green* (BMG Pilipinas). Rivermaya's audience is unashamedly middle of the road and so is their music, an amiable blend of guitar-driven pop and laidback love songs for 20-somethings. This album is typical, suffused with British influences ranging from the Beatles to Belle and Sebastian. The highpoint, however, is pure pinoy, the ironic ballad "Grounded ang Girlfriend Ko" ("My Girlfriend's Grounded Me"), which owes more to the Eraserheads than Britpop.

Books

The Philippines hasn't been as well documented in fiction or non-fiction as many of its Asian neighbours. There are, however, a number of good investigative accounts of two subjects – American involvement in the Philippines and the excesses of the Marcoses.

Some of the books reviewed below are published in the Philippines, and are unlikely to be on sale in bookstores outside the country; you should have more luck online.

History and politics

Alan Berlow *Dead Season: A Story of Murder and Revenge*. This brilliantly atmospheric work is the story of three murders that took place in the 1970s on Negros, against the backdrop of communist guerrilla activity and appeals for land reform. It's impossible to read without feeling intense despair for a country where humble, peaceful people have often become pawns in a game of power and money played out around them. Cory Aquino comes out of it badly – the Church asked her to investigate the murders but she refused, fearful that this might entail treading on too many toes.

Raymond Bonner *Waltzing with a Dictator*. Former *New York Times* correspondent Bonner reports on the complex twenty-year US relationship with the Marcos regime and how Washington kept Marcos in power long after his sell-by date: US bases in the country needed a patron and Marcos was the right man. Marcos cleverly played up the threat of a communist insurgency in the Philippines, making it seem to Washington that he was their only hope of stability.

Luis Francia *History of the Philippines: From Indios Bravos to Filipinos*. A welcome new history of the archipelago offering the perfect introduction to the country and plenty of new insights about the Spanish and American periods in particular.

James Hamilton-Paterson *America's Boy: The Rise and Fall of Ferdinand Marcos and Other Misadventures of US Colonialism in the Philippines*. A controversial narrative history of the US-supported dictatorship that came to define the Philippines. The author makes the very plausible claim that the Marcoses were merely the latest in a long line of corrupt Filipino leaders in a country which had historically been ruled by oligarchies, and gathers firsthand information from senators, cronies, rivals and Marcos family members, including Imelda.

James D. Hornfischer *The Last Stand of the Tin Can Sailors*. Gripping and in parts harrowing narrative of the battle between the Americans and Japanese off Samar in October 1944, and the larger battle of Leyte Gulf that followed, the beginning of the American liberation of the Philippines. Hornfischer also intelligently provides a Japanese perspective to the battle. Well written and easy to read.

Stanley Karnow *In Our Image: America's Empire in the Philippines*. This Pulitzer Prize-winning effort is really a book about America, not about the Philippines. The Philippines is the landscape, but the story is of America going abroad for the first time in its history at the turn of the last century. The book examines how America sought to remake the Philippines as a clone of itself, an experiment marked from the outset by blundering, ignorance and mutual misunderstanding.

Eric Morris *Corregidor*. Intimate account of the defence of the island fortress, based on interviews with more than forty Filipinos and Americans who battled hunger, dysentery and malaria in the run-up to the critical battle with Japanese forces. As the book explains, the poorly equipped Allied troops, abandoned by General MacArthur and almost forgotten by military strategists in Washington, had little chance of winning, though against all the odds Corregidor held out for six months.

Ambeth Ocampo *Rizal without the Overcoat* (Anvil). This collection of essays and musings (originally a column in the *Philippine Daily Globe*) offer entertaining and easily digested insights into the great Filipino hero – it's become almost as common in schools as Rizal's *Noli*.

Beth Day Romulo *Inside the Palace: The Rise and Fall of Ferdinand and Imelda Marcos*. Beth Day Romulo, wife of Ferdinand Marcos's foreign minister Carlos Romulo, was among those who enjoyed the privileges of being a Malacañang insider, something she feels the need to excuse and justify on almost every page. Her book borders

on being a Marcos hagiography – she clearly didn't want to upset her old friend Imelda too much – and is gossipy more than investigative, but does nevertheless offer some insight into Imelda's lavish and frivolous lifestyle, and the disintegration of the regime.

William Henry Scott *Barangay: Sixteenth Century Philippine Culture and Society* (Ateneo de Manila University Press). This lucid account of life in the Philippines during the century the Spanish arrived is the best there is of the period. The author's love for the Philippines and his deep knowledge of its customs are reflected in this scholarly but accessible investigation into Hispanic-era society, the country's elite, its tribes and their rituals – everything from that most quotidian of rituals, taking a bath, to the once common practice of penis piercing.

Hampton Sides *Ghost Soldiers: The Epic Account of World War II's Greatest Rescue Mission*. Recounts the astonishing and mostly forgotten story of the combined US Ranger and Filipino guerrilla force that managed to free hundreds of POWs from behind Japanese lines in 1944.

Culture and society

Sheila Coronel (ed) *Pork and Other Perks* (Philippine Center for Investigative Journalism). Comprising nine case studies by some of the country's foremost investigative journalists, this pioneering work uncovers the many forms corruption takes in the Philippines and points fingers at those responsible. The book is concerned mainly with what happens to "pork", the budget allocated annually to every senator and congressman. It's thought that much of the money goes towards hiring corrupt contractors who use below-par materials on infrastructure projects, with the politicians themselves benefiting from the

discrepancy between the official and actual cost of the projects concerned.

James Hamilton-Paterson *Playing With Water: Passion and Solitude on a Philippine Island*. "No money, no honey," says one of the characters in Hamilton-Paterson's lyrical account of several seasons spent among the impoverished fishermen of Marinduque. This is a rich and original book, which by turns warms you and disturbs you. The author's love of the Philippine landscape and the people – many of whom think he must be related to US actor George Hamilton – is stunningly rendered. The diving accounts will stay with you forever, as will the episode in which H-P discovers he has worms.

🏃 **F. Sionil José** *We Filipinos: Our Moral Malaise, Our Heroic Heritage* (Solidaridad). By turns deeply cynical and incredibly patriotic in equal measure, this collection of essays from the nation's pre-eminent writer is required reading for anyone wanting to get under the skin of Philippine culture.

🏃 **Manny Pacquiao** *Pacman: My Story of Hope, Resilience, and Never-Say-Never Determination.* Ghost-written – certainly; full of corny sentiment – perhaps. But Pacquiao's story is so remarkable it's hard to put this "autobiography" down, charting the tenacious fighter's rise from the

backstreets of Mindanao to boxing champion of the world and multi-millionaire. Inspirational stuff.

Earl K. Wilkinson *The Philippines: Damaged Culture?* (Book of Dreams). Written by a longtime expat, this book explores the underlying reasons for the many maladies affecting the country. *Damaged Culture* is never pontificating or presumptuous, but it is sometimes shocking in its revelations of corruption in high places, highlighting a number of travesties of justice which the author campaigned to put right. He also offers solutions, arguing that the nation's entrenched elite could start the recovery ball rolling by abandoning its traditional antipathy towards free-market competition.

Architecture

Pedro Galende *San Agustin* (Bookmark). An evocative tribute to the first Spanish stone church to be built in the Philippines, San Agustin in Intramuros. The first part of the book is a detailed account of the church's history, while the second is a walking tour, illustrated with photographs, through the church and the neighbouring monastery.

Pedro Galende & Rene Javelana *Great Churches of the Philippines* (Bookmark).

Coffee-table book full of beautiful colour photographs of most of the country's notable Spanish-era churches. The accompanying text explains the evolution of the unique "earthquake Baroque" style developed to protect stone structures against earthquakes and which typifies Philippine churches and provides a reminder that many of these stunning buildings are in a perilous state, with little money available to guarantee their upkeep and survival.

The environment

Robin Broad et al. *Plundering Paradise: the Struggle for the Environment in the Philippines.* Disturbing but often inspiring account of how livelihoods and habitats are disappearing throughout the Philippines as big business harvests everything from fish to trees, turned into packaging for multi-national companies and chopsticks for restaurants. The authors travelled through the Philippines, recording the experiences of people who are fighting back by working alongside NGOs and

environmental groups to police the environment and report illegal logging, poaching and fishing, much of which is allowed to take place through the bribing of local officials.

Nigel Hicks *The National Parks and Other Wild Places of the Philippines.* Illuminating celebration of the Philippines' natural heritage, with terrific photographs. The book describes all the major protected areas in the country, as well as a number of other wild areas that even Filipinos are largely unaware of. Some of the practical information is a little out of date, but there's great coverage of scenery, wildlife, tribes and conservation projects.

Gutsy Tuason and Eduardo Cu *Anilao* (Bookmark). Winner of the Palme d'Or at the World Festival of Underwater Images in Antibes, France, this hard-to-get but stunning coffee-table collection of colour photographs were all taken around Anilao, Batangas, one of the country's most popular diving areas. What's remarkable about the book is the way it makes you take notice of the small marine life many divers ignore; the images of bobbit worms, ghost pipefish and sea fans are terrific.

Food

Reynaldo Alejandro et al. *The Food of the Philippines*. Proof that there's so much more to Filipino cuisine than *adobo* and rice. The recipes range from classics such as chilli crab simmered in coconut milk to a fail-safe method for that trickiest of desserts, leche flan. Every recipe details how to find the right ingredients and what to use as a substitute if you can't. There's also a revealing history of Filipino food.

Glenda Rosales-Barretto *Flavors of the Philippines* (Bookmark). Rosales-Barretto is chief executive officer of the popular *Via Mare* restaurant chain in Manila, and what she doesn't know about Filipino food isn't worth knowing. This lavishly illustrated hardback highlights recipes region by region. There's a classic Bicol Express, with lots of spices and fish paste, but many of the recipes here are far from standard – instead, modern variations feature, such as fresh vegetarian pancake rolls with peanut sauce and roast chicken with passionfruit.

Fiction

Cecilia Manguerra Brainard *When the Rainbow Goddess Wept*. The moving story of Yvonne Macaraig, a young Filipina during the Japanese invasion of the Philippines in World War II; the myths and legends of Philippine folklore sustain her despite the carnage all around. Though some of Brainard's character development and language is uneven, it's this connection with the rural, pre-Hispanic Philippines that makes the book so memorable. Brainard was born in Cebu but emigrated to the US in 1968.

F. Sionil José *Dusk*. This is the fifth book in the author's acclaimed saga of the landowning Rosales family at the end of the nineteenth century. It wouldn't be a quintessential Filipino novel if it didn't touch on the themes of poverty, corruption, tyranny and love; all are on display here, presented through the tale of one man, a common peasant, and his search for contentment. *Dusk* has been published in the US in paperback, though you can always buy it from José's bookshop, Solidaridad at 531 Padre Faura St, Ermita, Manila.

F. Sionil José *Ermita* (Solidaridad). Eminently readable novella that atmospherically evokes the Philippines from World War II until the 1960s and stands as a potent allegory of the nation's ills. The Ermita of the title, apart from being the *mise en scène*, is also a girl, the unwanted child of a rich Filipina raped in her own home by a drunken Japanese soldier. The story follows young Ermita, abandoned in an orphanage, as she tries to trace her mother and then sets about exacting revenge on those she feels have wronged her.

José Rizal *Noli Me Tangere*. Published in 1886 (and banned by the Spanish), this is a passionate exposure of the evils of the friars' rule. It tells the story of Crisostomo Ibarra's love for the beautiful Maria Clara, infusing it with tragedy and significance of almost Shakespearean proportions, documenting the double standards and the rank injustice of colonial rule; it's still required reading for every Filipino schoolchild. Rizal's second novel *El Filibusterismo* takes up Ibarra's story thirteen years later, but the conclusion is just as bitter.

Miguel Syjuco *Ilustrado* (FSG). Winner of the 2008 Man Asian Literary Prize, this gripping saga takes over 150 years of Philippine history, as well as offering a scathing indictment of corruption and inequity among the Filipino ruling classes. Syjuco is a Filipino writer now based in Montreal.

The Philippines in foreign literature

William Boyd *The Blue Afternoon*. Boyd has never been to the Philippines, but spent hours researching the country from England. Remarkably, he seems to get Manila at the start of the twentieth century just right. In flashbacks, the novel moves from 1930s Hollywood to the exotic, violent world of the Philippines in 1902, recounting a tale of medicine, the murder of American soldiers and the creation of a magical flying machine.

Alex Garland *The Tesseract*. Alex Garland loves the Philippines, so it's hardly surprising that the follow-up to *The Beach* is set there. Garland may get most of his Tagalog wrong (it's *tsismis*, not chismis and *konti* not conte), but his prose captures perfectly the marginal existence of his characters. The story involves a foreigner abroad, a villainous tycoon called Don Pepe, some urchins and a beautiful girl. The characters may be straight from Cliché Street, but Garland's plot is so intriguing that it's impossible not to be swept along by the baleful atmosphere the book creates.

Jessica Hagedorn *Dogeaters*. Filipino-American Jessica Hagedorn assembles a cast of diverse and dubious characters that comes as close to encapsulating the mania of life in Manila as any writer has ever come. Urchins, pimps, seedy tycoons and corpulent politicos are brought together in a brutal but beautiful narrative that pulls no punches and serves as a jolting reminder of all the country's frailties and woes. Hagedorn also wrote the equally emotive *The Gangster of Love*, about a Filipino immigrant family in America.

James Hamilton-Paterson *Ghosts of Manila*. Hamilton-Paterson's excoriating novel is haunting, powerful and for the most part alarmingly accurate. Much of it is taken from real life: the extra-judicial "salvagings" (a local word for liquidation) of suspected criminals, the corruption and the abhorrent saga of Imelda Marcos's infamous film centre. From the despair and detritus, the author conjures up a lucid story that is thriller, morality play and documentary in one. Pretty it's not, but if you want Manila dissected, look no further.

Timothy Mo *Brownout on Breadfruit Boulevard*. Mo wrote this blunt satire of cultural and imperial domination in 1995 when he'd fallen out with his publisher (the book is still self-published), and his career subsequently fell off a cliff; the novel starts with a now infamous sex scene involving excrement. This story is much better than its sales (and the first page) suggested, though, set in the fictional town of Gobernador de Leon and following a motley bunch of locals and foreigners attending a conference.

Language

Language

Language

nglish is widely spoken in the Philippines, a legacy of the country's time under US rule. Most everyday transactions – checking into a hotel, ordering a meal, buying a ferry ticket – can be carried out in English, and most people working in tourism speak it reasonably well. Even off the beaten track, many Filipinos understand enough to help with basics such as accommodation and directions. However, it's worth learning a few words of **Tagalog**, the official language of the islands. You will be a source of amusement if you try even though the response will most likely come in English. Tagalog has assimilated many **Spanish** words, such as *mesa* (table) and *cuarto* (bedroom, written *kuwarto* in Tagalog) though few Filipinos can speak Spanish today. **Cebuano** (or "Visayan") spoken in the south of the archipelago uses even more Spanish – including all the numbers. This section focuses on Tagalog; for more on Cebuano see p.261.

Tagalog

Tagalog, also known as Filipino or Pilipino, is spoken as a first language by seventeen million people mostly on Luzon and was made the official language in 1947. The structure of Tagalog is simple, though the **word order** is different from English; as an example, take "*kumain ng mangga ang bata*", which literally translates as "ate a mango the child". Another key difference between the two languages is the lack of the verb "to be" in Tagalog, which means a simple sentence such as "the woman is kind" is rendered *mabait ang babae*, literally "kind the woman". For **plurals**, the word *mga* is used – hence *bahay/mga bahay* for house/houses – although in many cases Filipinos simply state the actual number of objects or use *marami* (several) before the noun.

Tagalog sounds staccato to the foreign ear, with clipped vowels and consonants. The **p**, **t** and **k** sounds are never aspirated and sound a little gentler than in English. The **g** is always hard, as in g**e**t. The letter **c** seldom crops up in Tagalog and where it does – in names such as Boracay and Bulacan, for example – it's pronounced like *k*. The hardest sound to master for most beginners is the **ng** sound as in the English word "si**nging**" (with the *g* gently nazalized, not hard); in Tagalog this sound can occur at the beginning of a word, eg in **ng**ayon (now). The *mg* combination in the word *mga* above looks tricky but is in fact straightforward to pronounce, as *mang*. As for vowels and diphthongs (vowel combinations):

a is pronounced as in **a**pple

e as in m**e**ss

i as in d**i**tto, though a little more elongated than in English

o as in b**o**re

u as in p**u**t

ay as in b**uy**

aw in m**ou**nt

iw is a sound that simply doesn't exist in English; it's close to the ieu sound in lieu, but with greater separation between the vowels (almost as in lee-you)

oy as in n**oi**se

uw as in q**uar**ter

uy produced making the sound oo and continuing it to the i sound in *ditto*.

Vowels that fall consecutively in a word are always pronounced individually, as is every syllable, adding to the choppy nature of the language; for example, *tao* meaning person or people is pronounced ta-o, while *oo* for yes is pronounced o-o (with each vowel closer to the *o* in *show* than in *bore*).

Most words are spoken as they are written, though working out which syllable to **stress** is tricky. In words of two syllables the first syllable tends to be stressed, while in words of three or more syllables the stress is almost always on the final or penultimate syllable. In the vocabulary lists that follow, stressed syllables are indicated in **bold** text except where the term in question is obviously an English loan word. Note that English loan words may be rendered a little differently in Tagalog, in line with the rules mentioned above; thus "bus" for instance has the vowel sound of the English word "put".

Formal language: the use of "po"

Tagalog has formal and informal **forms of address**, the formal usually reserved for people who are significantly older. The "po" suffix indicates respect and can be added to almost any word or phrase: *o-po* is a respectful "yes" and it's common to hear Filipinos say *sorry-po* for "sorry". Even the lowliest beggar is given esteem by language: the standard reply to beggars is *patawarin-po*, literally, "forgive me, sir". First names are fine for people of your own generation; for your elders, use Mr or Mrs (if you know a woman is married) before the surname. It's common to use *manong/manang* (uncle/aunt) and *kuya* (brother/sister) to address superiors informally, even if they are not blood relatives (eg *manong* Jun, *kuya* Beth).

Phrasebooks and dictionaries

The number of Tagalog **phrasebooks**, **dictionaries** and **coursebooks** outside the Philippines is limited, although with a little effort you should be able to track down any of the titles listed here. *Basic Tagalog for Foreigners and Non-Tagalogs* by Paraluman Aspillera (Tuttle Publishing) is a straightforward coursebook. *Pilipino–English/English–Pilipino Phrasebook and Dictionary* by Jesusa Salvador and Raymond Barrager (Hippocrene Books) is compact enough to carry around and concentrates on useful words and phrases. The *Pocket Filipino Dictionary* (Periplus Editions/Berkeley Books) and the *Concise English–Tagalog Dictionary* (Tuttle) by José Panganiban are both handy references.

Taglish: Filipino English

Educated Filipinos move seamlessly between English and Tagalog, often in the space of the same sentence, and many English words have been adopted by Filipinos, giving rise to a small canon of patois known affectionately as **Taglish**. Many of these peculiarities stem from the habit of translating something literally from Tagalog, resulting in Filipinos "closing" or "opening" the light, or "getting down" from a taxi. Among those who don't speak English so well, an inability to pronounce the f-sound is common, simply because it doesn't exist in any Philippine tongue. Filipinos are well aware of this trait and often make self-deprecating jokes about it, referring to forks as porks and vice versa. Other ear-catching Taglish phrases include "I'll be the one to" – as in "I'll be the one to buy lunch" instead of "I'll buy lunch" – and "for a while", meaning "wait a moment" or "hang on".

Greetings and common terms

hello/how are you?	ka**mus**ta
Fine, thanks	ma**bu**ti, sa**la**mat (*formal*) okay lang (*informal*)
goodbye	bye
good morning	magan**dang** u**ma**ga
good afternoon	magan**dang ha**pon
good evening/ good night	magan**dang** ga**bi**
please ... (before a request)	**pa**ki ...
thank you	sa**la**mat
excuse me (to say sorry)	ipagpau**man**hin mo **ak**
excuse me (to get past)	makikira**an** lang **po**/ pa**sen**siya ka na
sorry	sorry
what's your name?	a**nong** pa**nga**lan mo?
my name is ...	ang pa**nga**lan ko ay ...
do you speak English?	ma**ru**nong ka bang mag-**Ing**les?
I (don't) understand	(hin**di**) ko naiintindi**han**
could you repeat that?	**pa**ki-u**lit**
where are you from?	**ta**ga **sa**an ka?
I am from ... (most countries are rendered as in English)	**ta**ga ... **a**ko
I don't know (used to avoid confrontation)	**ew**an

okay?/is that okay?	**puwe**de?/**puwe**de ba?
Filipino/Filipina	**pi**noy/**pi**nay (*slang*)
mate, buddy	**pa**re (*see opposite for formal terms*)

Common terms

yes	**oo**
no	hin**di**
maybe	si**gu**ro
good/bad	ma**ga**ling/ma**sa**ma
big/small	mala**ki**/mali**it**
easy/difficult	ma**da**li/ma**hi**rap
open/closed	**bu**kas/sa**ra**do
hot/cold	ma**i**nit/mala**mig**
cheap/expensive	**mu**ra/ma**hal**
a lot/a little	ma**da**mi/**kon**ti
one more/another...	**i**sa pa ...
beautiful	magan**da**
hungry	**gu**tom
thirsty	na**uu**haw
very ... (followed by adjective)	**tu**nay ...
with/without ...	**me**ron/wa**la** ...
watch out!	**in**gat!
who?	**si**no?
what?	a**no**?
why?	**ba**kit?
when?	**kai**lan?
how?	pa**a**no?

Getting around

airport	airport
bus/train station	is**ta**syon ng bus/tren
pier	pier
aeroplane	ero**pla**no
ferry	bar**co** (*for large vessels – "ferry" will also do*) **bang**ka (*outrigger boat*)
taxi	taxi
bicycle	bisi**kle**ta
car	**kot**se
where do I/we catch the ...to ... ?	sa**an puwe**deng ku**mu**ha ng ... pa**pun**tang ...?

when does the ... for ... leave?	**kai**lan a**a**lis ang ... pa**pun**tang ...?
when does the next ... leave?	a**nong o**ras **ho** a**a**lis ang ...?
ticket	**ti**ket
can I/we book a seat	**puwe**deng bu**mi**li ka**a**gad ng ticket **pa**ra i-reser**ba** ang upu**an**
I'd/we'd like to go to the ... please	**gus**to **na**ming pu**mun**ta sa ...
[I'd like to] pay	**ba**yad po (*to pay your fare to a jeepney or tricycle driver*)

how long does it take?	gaano katagal?
how many kilometres is it to …?	ilang kilometro papunta sa …?
please stop here	paki-tigil ditto or para
I'm in a hurry	nagmamadali ako

Directions

where is the …?	saan ang …?
bank	banko
beach	beach
church	simbahan
cinema	sinehan
filling station	gasolinahan
hotel	hotel
market	palengke

moneychanger	taga-palit ng pera (or just "money-changer")
pharmacy	botika
post office	koreo or post office
restaurant	restoran (see also p.31)
town hall	town hall
left	kaliwa
right	kanan
straight on	derecho/diretso
opposite	katapat ng
in front of	sa harap ng
behind	sa likod ng
near/far	malapit/malayo
north	hilaga
south	timog
east	silangan
west	kanluran

Accommodation

do you have any rooms?	meron pa kayong kuwarto?
could I have the bill please?	puwedeng kunin ang check
bathroom	CR (comfort room) or banyo
room with a private bathroom	kuwarto na may sariling banyo
single room	kuwarto para sa isa
double room	kuwarto para sa dalawang tao

clean/dirty	malinis/marumi
air-conditioner	aircon
fan	elektrik fan
key	susi
telephone	telepono
cellphone/mobile phone	cellphone or cell
laundry	labahan
passport	pasaporte

Shopping

do you have …?	meron kang …?
[we have] none	wala
money	pera
how much?	magkano?
it's too expensive	masyadong mahal or sobra (too much)

I'll take this one	kukunin ko ito
cigarettes	sigarilyo
matches	posporo
soap	sabon
toilet paper	tisyu

Emergencies

fire!	sunog!
help!	saklolo!
there's been an accident	may aksidente

please call a doctor	paki-tawag ng duktor
ill	may sakit
hospital	ospital
police station	istasyon ng pulis

Numbers

Filipinos often resort to Spanish numbers, spelt as they are pronounced, especially when telling the time.

	Tagalog	Filipino Spanish
0	zero	sero
1	isa	uno
2	dalawa	dos
3	tatlo	tres
4	apat	kuwatro
5	lima	singko
6	anim	seis
7	pito	siyete
8	walo	otso
9	siyam	nuwebe
10	sampu	dyis
11	labing isa	onse
12	labing dalawa	dose
13	labing tatlo	trese
20	dalawampu	bente
21	dalawampu't isa	benteuno
22	dalawampu't dalawa	bentedos
30	tatlumpu	trenta
40	apatnapu	kwarenta
50	limampu	singkwenta
60	animnapu	sesenta
70	pitumpu	setenta
80	walampu	otsenta
90	siyamnapu	nobenta
100	sandaan	syen
1000	isang libo	mil
1,000,000	isang milyun	un miyon
a half	kalahati	medio/a

Dates and times

Days of the week and months of the year are mostly derived from Spanish:

what's the time?	anong oras na?
midnight	hating-gabi
morning	umaga
noon	tanghali
afternoon	hapon
evening/night	gabi
minute	minuto
hour	oras
day	araw
week	linggo
month	buwan
year	taon
today/now	ngayon
tomorrow	bukas
yesterday	kahapon
9 o'clock	alas nuwebe
10.30	alas diyes y media

Monday	Lunes
Tuesday	Martes
Wednesday	Miyerkoles
Thursday	Huwebes
Friday	Biyernes
Saturday	Sabado
Sunday	Linggo
January	Enero
February	Pebrero
March	Marso
April	Abril
May	Mayo
June	Hunyo
July	Hulyo
August	Agosto
September	Setyembre
October	Oktubre
November	Nobyembre
December	Disyembre

Food and drink terms

Most menus in the Philippines are in English, although in places that specialize in Filipino cuisine you'll see Tagalog on the menu, usually with an explanation in English below. For foods that arrived in the Philippines comparatively recently there often isn't an equivalent Filipino word, so to have cake, for example, you ask for cake. Even in the provinces waiters and waitresses tend to speak enough English to understand what you're after.

General terms

restaurant	restoran (*see p.31 for other terms*)	I'm vegetarian	vegetarian ako or gulay lang ang kinakain ko (literally "I only eat vegetables")
can I see the menu?	patingin ng menu?		
I would like …	gusto ko …		
delicious	sarap	breakfast	almusal
hot (spicy)	maanghang	lunch	tanghalian
can I have the bill please?	puwede kunin ang check	dinner	hapunan (rare) or dinner
		fork	tinidor
to go Dutch	KKB (from kanya-kanyang bayad, literally "each his own pays")	glass	baso
		knife	kutsilyo
		plate	plato
		spoon	kutsara

Common ingredients

bread	tinapay	noodles	pancit
bread rolls	pan de sal	onion	sibuyas
butter	mantikilya	pepper	paminta
cheese	keso	rice	bigas (the uncooked grain) or kanin (cooked rice)
chillies	sili		
coconut milk	gata		
egg	itlog	salt	asin
fermented fish/ shrimp paste	bagoong	soy sauce	toyo
		sugar	asukal
fish sauce	patis	tomato	kamatis
garlic	bawang	vegetables	gulay
ginger	luya		

Meat (*karne*) and poultry

baboy	pork
baka	beef
kambing	goat
kordero/karnero	lamb
lengua	tongue
manok	chicken
pata	pig's knuckle (trotters)
pato	duck
pugo	quail
tenga ng baboy	pig's ears

Common meat dishes

adobo	chicken and/or pork simmered in soy sauce and vinegar with pepper and garlic
beef tapa	beef marinated in vinegar, sugar and garlic, then dried in the sun and fried
Bicol Express	fiery dish of pork ribs cooked in coconut milk, soy sauce, vinegar, *bagoong* and hot chillies

bistek tagalog	beef tenderloin with lime and onion
bulalo	beef shank in onion broth
dinuguan	pork cubes simmered in pig's blood with garlic, onion and laurel leaves
ginisang monggo	any combination of pork, vegetables or shrimp sautéed with mung beans
kaldereta	spicy mutton stew
kare-kare	rich oxtail stew with egg plant, peanut and *puso ng saging* (banana hearts)
lechon (de leche)	roast whole (suckling) pig, dipped in a liver paste sauce

longganisa/ longganiza	small beef or pork sausages, with a lot of garlic
longsilog	longganisa with garlic rice and fried egg
mechado	braised beef
pochero	boiled beef and vegetables
sisig	fried chopped pork, liver and onions
tapsilog	beef tapa with garlic rice and fried egg
tinola	tangy soup with chicken, papaya and ginger
tocino	marinated fried pork
tosilog	marinated fried pork with garlic rice and fried egg

Fish (*isda*) and seafood

alimango	crab
bangus	milkfish
hipon	shrimps
hito	catfish
lapu-lapu	grouper
panga ng tuna	tuna jaw
pusit	squid
sugpo	prawns
tahong	mussels
talaba	oysters
tanguingue	popular and affordable sea fish, not unlike tuna in flavour

Common seafood dishes

daing na bangus	*bangus* marinated in vinegar and spices, then fried
gambas	shrimps sautéed in chilli and garlic sauce
pinaksiw na lapu-lapu	lapu-lapu marinated in vinegar and spices, served cold
rellenong bangus	stuffed *bangus*

Snacks (*merienda*) and street food

adidas	chicken's feet served on a stick with a choice of sauces for dipping
arroz caldo	rice porridge with chicken
balut	raw, half-formed duck embryo
camote	sweet potato fried with brown sugar, or boiled and served with a pat of butter
chicharon	fried pork skin, served with a vinegar dip

dilis	dried anchovies, eaten whole and dipped in vinegar as a bar snack or added to vegetable stews
ensaimada	sweet cheese rolls
fishballs, squidballs	mashed fish or squid blended with wheat flour and deep fried; served on a stick with a sweet sauce

goto	rice porridge often containing pork and garlic
isaw	grilled chicken or pig's intestines served with a cup of vinegar for dipping
lugaw	plain rice porridge
mami	noodle soup
mais	steamed corn-on-the-cob

pugo	hard-boiled quail's eggs, sold in packets of fifteen to twenty
puto	rice muffins
siopao	Chinese buns filled with spicy pork
sorbetes	ice cream
sumsumon	pig's ear

Fruit (*fruitas*)

atis	custard apple
balimbing	starfruit (aka carambola)
bayabas	guava
buko	coconut
calamansi	lime
chico	sapodilla (roughly the size of an egg with brown skin and sticky, soft flesh)
guayabano	soursop (large, oval fruit with knobbly spines outside and fragrant flesh inside)
kaimito	star apple (plum-coloured and round, about the size of a tennis ball, with leathery skin and soft white pulp inside)

langka	jackfruit
lanzones	outside the size and colour of a small potato; inside there's sweet, translucent flesh with a bitter seed
mangga	mango (available in sweet and sour varieties)
mangosteen	round, with a shiny dark purple skin and soft white flesh inside
pakwan	watermelon
papaya	papaya
piña	pineapple
saging	banana (there are dozens of varieties, from the cooking banana *sabo* to finger-like *senoritas* and red-skinned *morado*)

Desserts

bibingka	cake made of ground rice, sugar and coconut milk, baked in a clay stove and served hot with fresh, salted duck's eggs on top
bilo-bilo	glutinous rice and small pieces of tapioca in coconut milk
brazos	meringues, often with cashew-nut filling
cassava cake	sticky, dark cake with a fudge-like consistency
champorado	chocolate rice pudding
guinatan	chocolate pudding served with lashings of coconut cream

halo-halo	sweet concoction made from ice cream, shaved ice, jelly, beans and tinned milk; the name literally means "mix-mix"
kutsinta	brown rice cake with coconut shavings
leche flan	caramel custard
maja blanca	blancmange of corn and coconut cream
polvoron	sweets made from butter, sugar and toasted flour, pale in colour with a crumbly texture
puto bumbong	glutinous rice steamed in a bamboo tube, infusing it with a delicate, woody taste

sago at nata de coco	blend of sago and coconut served cold in a glass	suman	sweet and sticky rice cake served inside a banana leaf

Drinks (*inumin*)

merong/walang yelo/asukal	with/without ice/sugar	juice	juice
		kape	coffee
alak	wine (in practice, everyone just says "wine")	lambanog	alcoholic drink made from fermented fruit and available in a range of flavours
beer	beer		
buko juice	coconut water	mineral	mineral water
calamansi juice/soda	*calamansi* juice made into a cold drink by adding soda or a hot one by adding boiled water and a touch of honey	rum	rum (the popular Tanduay brand has become almost synonymous with rum)
		tapuy	rice wine
chocolate-eh	thick hot chocolate	tsa	tea
gatas	milk	tubig	water
ginebra	gin	tubo juice	sugar-cane juice

Glossary

amihan the northwest monsoon from November to April (dry season)

bahay house

bahay kubo wooden house

bahay na bato house built of stone

bangka boat carved from wood, with stabilizing outriggers made from bamboo; the so-called "big bangkas" are used as ferries and often feature cabins

barangay the smallest political voting unit, whose residents elect "barangay captains" to represent their views to the mayor; barangays take different forms, ranging from part of a village through a whole village to a district of a town or city

barong or **barong tagalog** formal shirt worn by men, woven from fine fabric such as *piña* and worn hanging outside the pants

barrio village

bulol rice god carved from wood, used by many northern hill tribes in religious rituals

buri type of palm used to make mats and rugs

butanding whale shark

calesas/kalesas horse-drawn carriages, still seen in some areas including Chinatown in Manila and Vigan

capiz a white seashell that's almost translucent when flattened and is used to make windows and screens

carabao water buffalo

carinderia canteen where food is presented in pots on a counter-top

chinito a Filipino/Filipina who looks Chinese

chinoy slang for Filipino/Filipina Chinese

cogon/kogon wild grass that is often used as thatch on provincial homes and beach cottages

CR toilet (= "comfort room")

DoT Department of Tourism

earthquake Baroque style of church architecture typical of Spanish churches in the Philippines, which were built with thick buttresses to protect them from earthquakes and a separate bell tower that wouldn't hit the main church if the tower collapsed

GRO guest relations officer; waitress or hostess in a bar who receives a cut of the payment for the drinks a customer buys her; often a euphemism for sex worker

habagat southwest monsoon from May to October (wet season)

ilustrado the wealthy elite

isla island

kalye street

kuweba cave

mabuhay lit. "long live". Used most often used at toasts, at rallies, or to welcome guests (and in tourism campaigns).

malong tube-like woven garment worn by many Muslims in Mindanao, similar to a sarong

Moro Muslim

narra the national tree, whose wood is considered best for furniture

nipa short, sturdy palm that is dried and used for building houses

nito native vine woven into hats, mats and decorative items such as lampshades

Pilipino Filipino; also means Tagalog

pinay/pinoy slang for Filipina/Filipino

piña fibre taken from the outside of the pineapple and woven into fine, shiny cloth

poblacion town centre

sabong cockfighting

sala living room

santo saint; also small statues of the saints found in churches and sold in antique shops

Santo Niño the Christ Child; patron of many communities, revered by Christian Filipinos

sari-sari store small store, often no more than a hut, selling essentials such as matches, snacks, shampoo and toothpaste

sikat native grass woven into various items, especially rugs

sitio small village or outpost, often consisting of no more than a few houses

tamaraw dwarf water buffalo, an endangered species found only on Mindoro

terno classic Filipino formal gown popularized by Imelda Marcos, with high butterfly sleeves and low, square-cut neckline

tinikling folk dance in which participants hop adeptly between heavy bamboo poles as they are struck together at shin-height, at increasing speed

tsinoy slang for Filipino/Filipina Chinese

zarzuela style of light opera introduced to the Philippines from Spain at the end of the nineteenth century

Travel store

So now we've told you about the things not to miss, the best places to stay, the top restaurants, the liveliest bars and the most spectacular sights, it only seems fair to tell you about the best travel insurance around

WorldNomads.com

keep travelling safely

Recommended by Rough Guides

NOTES

Small print and
Index

A Rough Guide to Rough Guides

Published in 1982, the first Rough Guide – to Greece – was a student scheme that became a publishing phenomenon. Mark Ellingham, a recent graduate in English from Bristol University, had been travelling in Greece the previous summer and couldn't find the right guidebook. With a small group of friends he wrote his own guide, combining a highly contemporary, journalistic style with a thoroughly practical approach to travellers' needs.

The immediate success of the book spawned a series that rapidly covered dozens of destinations. And, in addition to impecunious backpackers, Rough Guides soon acquired a much broader and older readership that relished the guides' wit and inquisitiveness as much as their enthusiastic, critical approach and value-for-money ethos.

These days, Rough Guides include recommendations from shoestring to luxury and cover more than 200 destinations around the globe, including almost every country in the Americas and Europe, more than half of Africa and most of Asia and Australasia. Our ever-growing team of authors and photographers is spread all over the world, particularly in Europe, the US and Australia.

In the early 1990s, Rough Guides branched out of travel, with the publication of Rough Guides to World Music, Classical Music and the Internet. All three have become benchmark titles in their fields, spearheading the publication of a wide range of books under the Rough Guide name.

Including the travel series, Rough Guides now number more than 350 titles, covering: phrasebooks, waterproof maps, music guides from Opera to Heavy Metal, reference works as diverse as Conspiracy Theories and Shakespeare, and popular culture books from iPods to Poker. Rough Guides also produce a series of more than 120 World Music CDs in partnership with World Music Network.

Visit www.roughguides.com to see our latest publications.

SMALL PRINT

Rough Guide credits

Text editors: Andy Turner, Lucy White
Layout: Jessica Subramanian
Cartography: Deshpal Dabas
Picture editor: Mark Thomas
Production: Erika Pepe
Proofreader: Karen Parker
Cover design: Nicole Newman, Dan May
Editorial: **London** Keith Drew, Edward Aves,
Alice Park, Jo Kirby, James Smart, Natasha
Foges, James Rice, Emma Beatson, Emma
Gibbs, Kathryn Lane, Monica Woods, Mani
Ramaswamy, Harry Wilson, Alison Roberts, Lara
Kavanagh, Eleanor Aldridge, Ian Blenkinsop,
Charlotte Melville, Joe Staines, Matthew Milton,
Tracy Hopkins; **Delhi** Madhavi Singh, Jalpreen
Kaur Chhatwal, Dipika Dasgupta
Design & Pictures: **London** Scott Stickland,
Dan May, Diana Jarvis, Nicole Newman,

Rhiannon Furbear; **Delhi** Umesh Aggarwal, Ajay
Verma, Ankur Guha, Pradeep Thapliyal, Sachin
Tanwar, Anita Singh, Nikhil Agarwal, Sachin Gupta
Production: Rebecca Short, Liz Cherry, Louise
Minihane
Cartography: **London** Ed Wright, Katie Lloyd-
Jones; **Delhi** Rajesh Chhibber, Ashutosh Bharti,
Rajesh Mishra, Animesh Pathak, Jasbir Sandhu,
Swati Handoo, Lokamata Sahu
Marketing, Publicity & roughguides.com:
Liz Statham
Digital Travel Publisher: Peter Buckley
Reference Director: Andrew Lockett
Operations Coordinator: Becky Doyle
Operations Assistant: Johanna Wurm
Publishing Director (Travel): Clare Currie
Commercial Manager: Gino Magnotta
Managing Director: John Duhigg

Publishing information

This third edition published October 2011 by
Rough Guides Ltd,
80 Strand, London WC2R 0RL
11, Community Centre, Panchsheel Park,
New Delhi 110017, India
Distributed by the Penguin Group
Penguin Books Ltd,
80 Strand, London WC2R 0RL
Penguin Group (USA)
375 Hudson Street, NY 10014, USA
Penguin Group (Australia)
250 Camberwell Road, Camberwell,
Victoria 3124, Australia
Penguin Group (NZ)
67 Apollo Drive, Mairangi Bay, Auckland 1310,
New Zealand
Rough Guides is represented in Canada by
Tourmaline Editions Inc. 662 King Street West,
Suite 304, Toronto, Ontario M5V 1M7
Cover concept by Peter Dyer.
Typeset in Bembo and Helvetica to an original
design by Henry Iles.

Printed in Singapore
© David Dalton and Stephen Keeling
Maps © Rough Guides

480pp includes index
A catalogue record for this book is available from
the British Library
ISBN: 978-1-40538-113-0

The publishers and authors have done their
best to ensure the accuracy and currency of
all the information in **The Rough Guide to
The Philippines**, however, they can accept
no responsibility for any loss, injury, or
inconvenience sustained by any traveller as a
result of information or advice contained in the
guide.

11 12 13 14 8   7   6   5   4   3   2   1

MIX
Paper from
responsible sources
FSC FSC™ C018179
www.fsc.org

SMALL PRINT

Help us update

We've gone to a lot of effort to ensure that
the third edition of **The Rough Guide to The
Philippines** is accurate and up-to-date. However,
things change – places get "discovered", opening
hours are notoriously fickle, restaurants and
rooms raise prices or lower standards. If you
feel we've got it wrong or left something out,
we'd like to know, and if you can remember the
address, the price, the hours, the phone number,
so much the better.

Please send your comments with the subject
line "**Rough Guide The Philippines Update**"
to ©mail@uk.roughguides.com. We'll credit all
contributions and send a copy of the next edition
(or any other Rough Guide if you prefer) for the
very best emails.
   Find more travel information, connect with
fellow travellers and book your trip on ®www
.roughguides.com

Acknowledgements

Stephen Keeling: Thanks to Emilio and Aning Go for their kindness, advice and hospitality in Manila, Connie Wu and Helen Tan for being such fearless travel companions, Daisy and Agustin Tiu for their incredible generosity and help in Mindanao, Basilio and Mary Ngo for the day-trips and dinners, Manuel Gaw for all his help in Subic Bay and Taal, Milo Dahilan for all his expert guidance in Mindanao, Dave and Tina Gooding in Port Barton, Mayor Lawrence Cruz and his team in Iligan, Pat Noel and Jabbar Elli Abdhala Malicsi in Subic Bay; thanks also to my fellow authors John Oates and Simon Foster; editors Andy Turner and Lucy White, who did a great job in London, Róisín Cameron for getting things started, and as always, Tiffany Wu, without whose love and support none of this would have been possible.

Simon Foster: In the Philippines thanks go to Marti in Sabang, Jimmy in Cebu, Jochen & Jinky in Panagsama, Sonja in Panglao, Imelda Tinsay, Billy Torres and Angelo Bibar in Bacolod, Lynn in Boracay, Harold Biglete in Dumaguete and Pete in Borongan. Also, thanks to Christine, Tot, Andrew & Jadranka.

John Oates: Thanks are due first and foremost to Chit Afuang, Chicoy Enerio and Tess Ballester from the Department of Tourism, without whose advice and assistance my research would have taken twice as long and been half as successful. In Manila, thanks also to Carlos Celdran for his warm welcome and to Mike Litton for his friendship and his help in tracking down elusive facts and figures. On the road in the Cordillera, I could not have asked for better guides and companions than Jaime Munar and Mang Ben Polon. I would also like to thank: Gillian Abadilla, Angie Agnes, Mena Aguila, Camilo Alumit, Jos Baleno, Damian Ball, Elias Bulut, Carmel Bonifacio-Garcia, Theofrenz Cayambas, Kray Cielo, Edwin De Lara, Richard De Villa, Johnny Dickpus, Dan Esdicul, Debbie Francisco, Ivan Henares, Lito Mendoza, Rio Dale Humiwat, Gerry Jamilla, Maika Labaupa, Reynaldo Livara, Jayrick Mendiola, Dely Millan, Chona Pacis, Lorelyn Rillo, Bing Rivera, Steve Rogers, Roger Sacyaten, PJ Sadiwa, Harold Sadornas, Berry Sangao, Mean Santos, Ned Sickles, Graham Taylor, Martin Valera, Jovi Villareal, and the DoT Region 2 office in Tuguegarao. Finally, I'm grateful to Sheryll Sulit for introducing me to her country of birth.

Readers' letters

Thanks to everyone who took the trouble to write in with amendments and additions. Apologies for any misspellings or omissions:

Julien Anseau, Brian Bate, Solange Berchemin, Sarah Derengowski Nicole Kisslig, Jeroen van Marle, Steve Roney.

SMALL PRINT

Photo credits

All photos © Rough Guides except the following:

Introduction
Casororo Waterfall, near Dumaguete © Stuart Westmorland/Getty Images
Boracay Beach © Laurie Noble/Getty Images
Eye of Parrotfish © Jurgan Freund/Axiom
Jeepney © Thomas Cockrem/Alamy
Taytay Bay, Palawan © Michael Melford/Getty Images
Dinagyang festival, Iloilo © Peter Adams/Getty Images
Cordilera Mountains © John Warburton Lee Photography/Alamy

Things not to miss
01 White Beach, Boracay © Asia Images/Getty Images
02 Ati-Atihan festival © Peter Adams/Getty Images
03 El Nido © JS Callahan/Tropicalpix/Alamy
04 Rice terraces, Banaue © Laurie Noble/Getty Images
05 *Halo-halo* © Thomas Cockrem/Alamy
06 Vigan © Laurie Noble/Getty Images
07 Whale sharks © Martin Stmiska/Alamy
08 Coran Island © Laurie Noble/Getty Images
09 Chocolate Hills, Bohol © Philippe Body/Hemis/Corbis
10 San Agustin Church, Manila © Catherine Kranow/Corbis
11 Surfing, Siargau © LOOK/Alamy
12 Apo Reef © Specialist Stock/Corbis
13 Massage treatment, Puerto Galera © Danita Delimont/Alamy
14 Underground River, Palawan © Franck Guiziou/Hemis/Corbis
15 Mount Mayon © Bill Freeman/Alamy
16 Tarsier © Bruno Morandi/Getty Images
17 Mount Pinatubo © Imagebroker/Alamy
18 Corregidor © LOOK/Alamy

Diving in the Philippines colour section
Snorkeller © Chris Simpson/Getty Images
Angelfish © Stephen Frink
Clownfish © Linda Pitkin/Getty Images
Green turtle © Science Faction/Getty Images
Crown-of-thorns starfish © Margo Steley/Alamy
Spear fishing © Aurora Photos/Alamy
Diving off Cabilao Island © Waterframe/Alamy
Diving off Apo Island © Waterfrom/Alamy
Anthias, Puerto Galera © ArteSub/Alamy
Shark © Chip Yates/Getty Images

Filipino Food colour section
Boy with watermelons © Stuart Dee/Getty Images
Rice paddies © Peter Adams/Alamy
Grilled seafood © Andrew Watson/Photolibrary
Shrimp *sinigang* © Practical Pictures/Photolibrary
Lechon © Jochen Tack/Corbis
Pastries © Thomas Cockrem/Alamy
Ice-cream seller © Painet/Alamy
Beef *adobo* © David A Goldfarb/Alamy
Fruit stand © Stuart Dee/Getty Images
Barbecued chicken © Jay Directo/Getty Images

Black and whites
p.58 Makati district, Manila © Gabriel M Covian/Getty Images
p.108 Tagaytay view © Luca Tettoni/Getty Images
p.132 St Paul's Cathedral, Vigan © Andrea Pistolesi
p.192 Caramoan Peninsula © Robert Harding/Alamy
p.256 Chocolate Hills, Bohol © Tony Waltham/Getty Images

SMALL PRINT

Index

Map entries are in colour.

INDEX

477

Map symbols

I

━ ━ ━	International boundary		⊞	Hospital
━ ━ ‥	Province boundary		ⓘ	Tourist office
━ ━ ━	Chapter division boundary		⊠	Post office
═══	Major road		ℂ	Phone office
═══	Minor road		🄿	Parking
▬▬▬	Motorway		🄴	Embassy/consulate
ⅢⅢⅢ	Steps		♠	Museum
───	Unpaved road		⊙	Statue/memorial
‒ ‒ ‒	Path		⛳	Golf course
━╸━	Railway		@	Internet access
─ ─	Ferry route		★	Bus stop
─Ⓜ─	Metro line & station		⛽	Fuel station
───	River		∴	Ruins
━━━	Wall		⚓	Shipwreck
⊠	Gate		≍	Dive site
≍	Bridge		✝	Church (regional maps)
⑃	Spring/spa		🛆	Monastery
▲	Mountain peak		🕌	Mosque
⌃⌃	Mountain range		🏯	Chinese pagoda
🕉	Waterfall		✛	Church (town maps)
⸱⸱⸱	Reef		▮	Building
⌂⌂	Cliff		▢	Market
◆	Point of interest		◯	Stadium
⚘	Viewpoint		▦	Park
⋎	Lighthouse		⊞	Cemetery
◠	Cave		▦	Beach
✈	Airport		⸺	Swamp
◉	Accommodation			